The Financial Desk Book

The Financial Desk Book

Consolidated Capital Communications Group, Inc.

Published by Consolidated Capital Communications Group, Inc.,
2000 Powell Street, Emeryville, California 94608

Designed by Fifth Street Design

Cover design by Larry Westdal

Manufactured in the United States of America

10 9 8 7 6 5 4 3 2 1

Library of Congress Cataloging in Publication Data
Main entry under title:

The Financial Desk Book

Includes index.
1. Finance, Personal—United States.
2. Investments—United States.
3. Taxation—United States.
4. Estate planning—United States.
I. Consolidated Capital Communications Group, Inc.
HG179.F46   1985   332.024   85-71636
ISBN 0-930032-10-1

FOREWORD

The *Financial Desk Book* represents the culmination of a unique collaboration between publishing professionals and expert financial consultants committed to a single formidable goal: to create the most comprehensive and most useful one-volume reference book for financial professionals and serious investors.

The concept of the *Financial Desk Book* originated in a casual conversation at a conference of financial advisers. A colleague expressed to me her dismay at not being able to find a convenient reference book that provided information and data she needed to augment her ability to make comprehensive financial and investment recommendations. I assured her that such a book—although I couldn't name it—must exist: a compilation of data on a broad variety of investments and economic indicators, with summaries of relevant tax laws, and information on insurance, estate planning, retirement, and other topics pertinent to personal financial decision making.

But when I discussed the matter with financial professionals across the country, I discovered two things: that no one knew of such a book and that everyone wanted one. As publisher of Consolidated Capital Communications Group, I saw the solution as a simple one. Certainly, we had the editorial capacity, financial knowledge, and production resources to create the book that everyone in the financial services industry and, in particular, comprehensive financial planners, needed. Since we knew exactly who wanted the book, we would ask them exactly what they wanted us to put in it.

So our in-house editors and experts on taxation, investments, and financial marketing set out to compile a master list of topics for the book. This list was then reviewed by dozens of financial professionals—financial planners, insurance specialists, brokers, CPAs, and attorneys—and outside consultants from all sectors of the financial services industry. Next, Linda Lazare and Wendy Nurock began to collect the data and develop the analyses for each topic. They sorted through an ocean of periodicals and government publications to find the most reliable and up-to-date information. At this point, editors Frances Bowles and Amy Einsohn were assigned to organize the material and provide introductions and explanatory text. John Munz of the San Francisco office of Arthur Young & Company carefully reviewed and revised the sections on taxation and estate planning; Samuel Weiner reviewed and updated the charts and tables. Finally, after almost two years of research and developmental editing, we had assembled our typewritten manuscript—an eighteen-inch monument of facts and statistics. The transformation of that manuscript into a bound volume was accomplished by production manager Deborah Merkle and her assistants Chris Mole, Rita Robillard, and Susan Dennler; the staff of George Litho; Jerry Meek and Nancy Austin of Fifth Street Design; word processor Nanette Mentz; proofreaders from editcetera, in Berkeley; indexer, Eleanor Lindheimer; Michael Beaucage of Aurora Productions (chart production); and my copublishers at Consolidated Capital, Jim Miller, Vicki Lateano, and Joe Leadem.

Of course, although accuracy and thoroughness were our bywords in canvassing professionals, researching sources, and synthesizing data, in a work of this scope omissions and errors are almost inevitable. For that reason, we have bound in a reader response card at the end of this volume. We sincerely hope that you will take the time to send us your suggestions for improving the book. While we trust you will agree with us that the *Financial Desk Book* is an invaluable aid in financial decision making, we are already envisioning an expanded, updated, and revised second edition, and your comments will help us continue our collaborative effort.

Richard G. Wollack
Publisher
Consolidated Capital Communications Group

HOW TO USE THIS BOOK

This unique financial reference book is the first specifically designed to meet all the many needs of investors as well as financial professionals. It provides basic background information necessary to make good decisions about finances, taxation, insurance, and investing.

Desk Book Reference Tools

We have tried to make it easy for you to look up any subject:

- The **main table of contents** (pp. viii–ix) gives you an overview of general areas at a glance. However, only principal topics are listed here, so you will also frequently refer to the *index* and the more detailed individual *chapter tables of contents*.

- The **chapter tables of contents** (at the beginning of each chapter) provide a detailed listing of all topics covered in a chapter.

- The **index** at the end of the book (pp. 10.3–10.27) provides the quickest route to a specific subject. Detailed and comprehensive, it is an excellent tool for locating any topic, and it includes cross-references to other relevant entries.

- **Pagination** is arranged by chapters: The chapter number comes before the decimal point, with the page number following it. Thus, "3.116" refers to page 116 of Chapter 3.

- The 36 **charts** are listed on p. x as well as in the individual chapter tables of contents. The page numbers of the numerous statistical and historical **tables** are italicized in both the index and the individual chapter tables of contents.

How to Look Something Up

If you are looking for a *specific term* or *type of data,* the detailed index at the end of the book will help you locate it easily.

If you are looking for *general information* in a subject area, turn first to the main table of contents to find the chapter in which the information is located; then turn to the chapter table of contents to locate the sections you want to review.

With these reference techniques you will find *The Financial Desk Book* easy to use.

CONTENTS

CHARTS

CHAPTER 1

Personal Financial Planning

CONTENTS

Tables are indicated by page numbers in italics; accompanying charts by a dagger: †

1.04 Insurance   1.35

1.05 Estate Planning   1.51

1.10 Social Security and Medicare (continued)

Personal financial planning involves the analysis of all aspects of an individual's financial situation, the specification of short- and long-term financial objectives, the devising and implementation of coordinated strategies to meet those objectives, and the ongoing review of the individual's progress toward them.

A financial plan is thus a highly personal statement. Yet regardless of the individual's situation and objectives, five considerations are of primary importance to any comprehensive financial plan:

- *Investment planning* to accumulate wealth

- *Insurance planning* to protect assets and provide for emergencies

- *Retirement planning* to maintain standard of living after retirement

- *Estate planning* to distribute assets after death

- *Tax planning* to minimize the effect of taxes on wealth

Information and data relevant to the first four of these topics are presented in this chapter; taxation is the subject of Chapter 2.

1.01 **Basic Personal Finances**

TIMETABLE FOR FINANCIAL PLANNING

Ages Twenty-Five to Thirty-Five

- Establish credit by making credit payments promptly
- Develop a budget that includes allocations for savings, investments, and expected expenses
- Create an emergency fund
- Obtain adequate insurance—i.e., disability, health, homeowners or tenant-homeowners including liability, and automobile insurance
- Develop an investment program, possibly including savings, money market funds, blue chip stocks, certificates of deposit
- Begin retirement planning, taking advantage of Keoghs, IRAs, and investments in moderate-risk mutual funds
- Draw up a will and any appropriate trusts, including considerations for parents or other older dependents

WITH CHILDREN

- Adjust insurance coverage to include children
- Begin saving for children's education, using long-term investment programs
- Include guardianship and trust provisions in will

Ages Thirty-Six to Forty-Five

- Monitor insurance coverage and maintain an inventory of possessions; this list should be kept in a safety deposit box
- To protect increasing income and assets from taxes, consider tax-exempt and tax-deferred investments, as well as long-term capital gains
- Continue retirement savings, contributing maximum amounts to IRAs and Keogh plans, as well as any other pension plans
- Update will to reflect changing assets and family situation

WITH CHILDREN

- Increase savings for children's education, take advantage of tax-free gifts to children, and establish trust agreements
- Consult an estate planning attorney to determine how best to manage assets to avoid taxes

Ages Forty-Six to Fifty-Five

- Continue saving for retirement

- Protect income from taxes by increasing tax-sheltered holdings and investing in long-term capital gains assets

- Keep insurance current by updating home inventory and making sure insurance reflects current values

WITH CHILDREN

- Revise wills and trusts to reflect current educational planning and other long-term considerations

- Continue providing funds for children's education (consider giving income-producing assets to children)

Ages Fifty-Six to Sixty-Four

- Plan retirement, estimating income needed to live comfortably and buy retirement home if that is a consideration

- Consolidate investments; develop a more liquid portfolio and explore such vehicles as tax-deferred annuities

- Keep will and insurance updated

Retirement

- Provide for stable monthly income from investments, switching to low-risk, fixed income vehicles

- Plan for future cash needs, retaining some growth investments as hedges against inflation

- Maintain adequate insurance coverage; review and revise will

- Complete all details of estate planning

FINANCIAL PLANNING INVENTORY CHECKLIST

In order to assess an individual's current financial situation, a financial planner or advisor generally needs the following documents and information:

Tax returns

Personal and/or business
Partnerships, trusts, etc.

Legal documents

Wills
Trust agreements
Business agreements
Domestic separation (decrees, dissolution, child support, etc.)

Employment benefits

Descriptive booklets
Account records, annual reports, etc.

Income and expense

Salary and bonus totals
Living expenses

Insurance policies

Life insurance
Disability insurance
Medical insurance
Home and automobile insurance
Other insurance

Savings and investments

Savings account and certificate of deposit records
Securities (stocks, bonds, etc.) account records
Real estate investment records
Other

Other property

Home
Personal property
Checking accounts
Other (antiques, art, etc.)
Precious metals, gems, etc.

List of debts

Mortgages
Notes
Installment department store accounts, loan accounts, credit cards, etc.

Children's assets

Other

Source: Loren Dunton, *Your Book of Financial Planning*, 1983. Reprinted with permission of Reston Publishing Company, a Prentice-Hall Company, 11480 Sunset Hills Road, Reston, Va. 22090.

BALANCE SHEET

A balance sheet provides a snapshot of an individual's current financial situation: total liabilities are subtracted from total assets to show current net worth.

Assets

Fixed-Dollar Assets

Checking accounts	$_____
Savings accounts	_____
Bonds	_____
Life insurance cash values	_____
Life insurance — term or other	_____
Profit-sharing account	_____
Keogh plan	_____
Individual Retirement Account	_____
Receivables	_____
_____	_____

Equity Dollar Assets

Stocks	$_____
Mutual funds	_____
Real estate	_____
Business value	_____
Professional practice values	_____
Profit-sharing account	_____
Pension account	_____
Keogh plan	_____
Individual Retirement Account	_____
_____	_____
_____	_____

Non–Income-Producing Assets

Home and lot	$_____
Personal property	_____
Collectibles	_____
_____	_____
Total Assets	$_____

Liabilities

Charge accounts	$_____
Notes	_____
Mortgage on home	_____
_____	_____
Total Liabilities	$_____

Net Worth

$_____

Source: Loren Dunton, *Your Book of Financial Planning*, 1983. Reprinted with permission of Reston Publishing Company, a Prentice-Hall Company, 11480 Sunset Hills Road, Reston, Va. 22090.

CASH FLOW STATEMENT

A cash flow statement shows income and expenses over a specified period of time, usually one calendar or tax year. Total expenses are subtracted from total income to show net (or discretionary) income.

Income

Salary and/or other earned
   income $_____
Bonuses   _____
Business or practice income   _____
Interest   _____
Dividends   _____
Rents   _____
Partnership income   _____

_____   _____
_____   _____

       Total Income $_____

Expenses

Housing:
   Mortgage/rent $_____
   Utilities   _____
   Telephone   _____
   Maintenance & repair   _____
   Yard maintenance   _____
   Domestic help   _____
   Homeowner property insurance   _____
   Property taxes   _____
   New household purchases   _____
   Other (pool, etc.)   _____

   _____   _____

Food:
   Meals at home $_____
   Meals out   _____
   Coffee breaks & snacks   _____

   _____   _____

Clothing:
   Essential $_____
   Nonessential   _____
   Laundry/dry cleaning   _____

   _____   _____

Transportation:
   Car payments $_____
   Gas, oil & tires   _____
   Public transportation   _____
   Maintenance & repair   _____
   Licenses & insurance   _____

   _____   _____

Pets:
 Food $_____
 Veterinary & medicine   _____
 _____   _____

Recreation:
 Entertainment $_____
 Vacations   _____
 Club dues   _____
 Other (horses, boats, etc.)   _____
 _____   _____
 _____   _____

Medical:
 Doctors $_____
 Dentists   _____
 Medicines   _____
 Hospitals   _____
 Insurance   _____
 _____   _____

Alimony and/or child support:
 _____ $_____

Personal:
 Grooming $_____
 Education   _____
 Lessons   _____
 Subscriptions   _____
 Allowances   _____
 _____   _____

Investment Expenses:
 Property upkeep $_____
 _____   _____

Gifts & Contributions:
 _____ $_____

Other:
 Unreimbursed business
  expenses, etc. $_____
 Cigarettes etc.   _____
 Liquor, beer, soft drinks   _____

Total income $_____

Total expenses $_____

Net income $_____

Source: Loren Dunton, *Your Book of Financial Planning*, 1983. Reprinted with permission of Reston Publishing Company, a Prentice-Hall Company, 11480 Sunset Hills Road, Reston, Va 22090.

FINANCIAL GOALS STATEMENT

EMERGENCY RESERVE

Reserve needed (six months'
   living expenses) $_____
Less: Cash and equivalents $_____
Reserve deficit (surplus) $_____

Monthly investment earning
_____% needed to eliminate deficit $_____

DISABILITY RESERVE

Monthly disability income needed $_____
   (at least 60% of present income)   _____
Less: Social Security benefits   _____
Less: Employee benefits   _____
Less: Personal disability income policies   _____
Less: Earnings from capital   _____
Monthly disability income still needed $_____

Present amount $_____   vs. Needed amount $_____
Present outlay $_____   vs. Needed outlay $_____

CHILDREN'S EDUCATION*

Child	Amount Needed	Monthly Investment to Meet Need
_____	$_____	$_____
_____	_____	_____
_____	_____	_____
_____	$_____	$_____

For a method to estimate college costs and calculate monthly investment needed, see page 1.25.

RETIREMENT*

Monthly retirement income needed at age _____ $_____
Less: Expected retirement plan benefits   _____
Less: Expected Social Security benefits   _____
Less: Expected earnings from capital at work   _____
Monthly income still needed $_____

Investment earning _____% required to
provide income needed $_____

*For calculations to estimate retirement income needed to maintain preretirement standard of living, see page 1.16.
For calculations to estimate Social Security benefits, see page 1.99.*

OTHER FINANCIAL GOALS

Goal: _____
Cash needed: $_____
Cash on hand toward goal: $_____
Difference: $_____

Source: Loren Dunton, *Your Book of Financial Planning*, 1983. Reprinted with permission of Reston Publishing
Company, a Prentice-Hall Company, 11480 Sunset Hills Road, Reston, Va. 22090.

MAINTAINING A COMFORTABLE LIFESTYLE AFTER RETIREMENT

During their working years, most people establish a comfortable standard of living, and they hope to continue that lifestyle when they retire. A long-term financial plan should include an estimate of how much annual income an individual will need to maintain his or her current standard of living after retirement. By comparing this estimate to expected sources of retirement income (Social Security, pensions, investment income, etc.), an individual can begin to budget savings toward retirement.

Most retirees find that they can maintain their standard of living on much less income—provided that income keeps up with inflation—because they no longer need budget for work-related expenses and income taxes, savings and investments, living and educational expenses for their children, and other costs usually associated with a specific income bracket.

The table shown here, which does not take inflation into consideration, provides estimates for the level of post-retirement income needed to maintain one's pre-retirement lifestyle.

Pre-retirement Income	− Pre-retirement Taxes	+ Work-related Expenses	+ Savings & Investment	= Retirement Standard	+ Post-Retirement Taxes	= Required Post-Retirement Income
$ 20,000	$ 3,850	$1,000	$ 1,300	$13,900	$ 0	$13,900
40,000	11,100	1,700	3,500	23,700	500	24,100
60,000	18,900	2,500	6,600	32,100	2,300	34,400
80,000	27,800	3,100	10,400	38,600	5,900	44,500
100,000	37,100	3,800	15,100	44,000	11,300	55,300

POVERTY LEVELS AMONG THE ELDERLY

Persons 65 and Over	Percentage Living in Poverty		
	1959	1970	1980
All persons 65 years and over	35.2	24.6	15.7
In families	26.9	14.8	8.5
Head	29.1	16.5	9.1
Male	29.1	15.9	8.2
Female	28.8	20.1	15.2
Other family members	24.6	13.0	7.8*
Unrelated individuals	61.9	47.2	30.6
Male	59.0	38.9	24.4
Female	63.3	49.8	32.3
White	33.1	22.6	13.6
Black	62.5	47.7	38.1
Hispanic	n/av.	n/av.	30.8

* *Other family members in families with married couples only; the 1980 figure for other family members in families without married couples was 6.7%.*

Source: U.S. Bureau of the Census.

1.02 **Common Personal Financial Issues**

OPTIONS FOR SAVINGS

Option	Minimum Deposit	Maturity	Comments
Passbook Savings	None	None	Low interest rate; money may be withdrawn at any time
NOW Accounts	Varies	None	Checks may be written; minimum balance may be required
Super NOW Accounts	$2,500	None	High rate paid on readily available cash; no limit on checking
7-to-31-Day Time Deposits	$2,500	7–31 days	Savings earn market yields; checking privileges; penalty for early withdrawal
Money Market Deposit Accounts	$2,500	None	Money market rate paid on savings; six automatic monthly transfers allowed, of which three may be checks
91-Day Certificates	$2,500	91 days	Market yields; no checking privileges; penalty for early withdrawal
6-Month Money Market Time Deposits	$2,500	6 months	Savings earn market yields; penalty for early withdrawal; no compounding of interest
18-Month Small-Savers Certificates	Varies	18 months	High yields for small deposits
Long-Term Certificates	Varies	2½ years +	Savings locked up for long time; savers may shop around for best yields. Interest compounded
Individual Retirement Account Certificates	Varies	Varies	Federal income taxes on both deposits and interest income are deferred until money is withdrawn; may be opened with brokerage firms, banks, savings and loans, insurance companies or mutual funds; $2,000 maximum annual contribution
Money Market Mutual Funds	$100–$1,000	None	Market yields paid on funds that may be withdrawn at any time; checks may be written; no federal deposit insurance
Bond Funds	Varies	None	Shares may easily be resold but lose value if interest rates rise
Stock Funds	Varies	None	Small investors may diversify their holdings; shares lose value if stock prices fall
Tax-Exempt Bond Funds	Varies	None	Interest income is exempt from federal taxes and generally not taxed in the state where issued; shares lose value if interest rates rise
Treasury Bills	$10,000	6 months	Market yields and safety; easily sold; not subject to state and local income taxes
U.S. Savings Bonds	$25	10 years	Safe; long term
Corporate Bonds	$1,000	10–30 years	Market yields and liquidity; investment will lose value if interest rates rise
Common Stocks	None	None	Potential for dividends, long-term capital gains; risk of capital loss
Zero-Coupon Bonds	$1,000 (usually)	6 months to 10 years +	Yields fixed for term of investment; backed by U.S. securities and sold at a deep discount; no interest is received until notes mature and are redeemed at face value

Source: *The World Almanac & Book of Facts,* 1984 edition, copyright © Newspaper Enterprise Association, Inc., 1984, New York, NY 10166.

ANNUITIES

An annuity is an investment contract, usually purchased from an insurance company, that will provide the purchaser (*annuitant*) with future payments at regular intervals or with a lump-sum payout. A *straight life annuity* will continue to pay periodic benefits for the duration of the annuitant's life; a *nonlife, periodic, annuity* will pay benefits for only a specified number of years—if the annuitant dies during the payout period, the remaining benefits are paid to his named beneficiary. Various combinations of life and period annuities are available.

In a *fixed annuity,* the insurance company invests the annuitant's principal in fixed-income instruments (bonds, mortgages, etc.) and guarantees the principal and a minimum payout. If the investments outperform expectations, the payout will be raised. In a *variable annuity,* the insurance company invests the annuitant's principal in equities (common stock, for example) and neither principal nor payout is guaranteed. Some contracts allow the annuitant to split the principal between fixed and variable components or to switch from a fixed plan to a variable one before the payout period begins.

Funds placed in an annuity accumulate and compound tax-free until they are withdrawn. At withdrawal, part of the payout is considered return of principal and is therefore exempt from income tax; only the income portion of the payout is taxable. Early withdrawals are subject to a surrender charge and are fully taxable. "Bail out" clauses permit the annuitant to move his funds elsewhere without penalty if the annuity's rate of return falls below a specified standard.

Annuities may be purchased by a single payment (usually a minimum of $5,000 to $10,000) or through periodic (monthly or annual) installments; each insurance company has its own schedules. No-load annuities charge no commissions; for loaded annuities the commission may reach 5% of the principal.

Bests's Insurance Reports, published by Best's Rating Service, provides extensive information on the financial soundness of annuity sponsors, and Lipper Analytical Service tracks performance data on sponsors' rates of return.

CREDIT AND BORROWING

Establishing credit is one of the first priorities for young adults. In order to establish a credit history, one has to borrow, but before borrowing one must determine how much debt is affordable. As a rule of thumb, installment debt should not exceed 10% of take-home pay, not including mortgage payments. Taking on more than 20% almost guarantees later trouble in meeting obligations.

To determine the advisability of taking out a new personal loan, make the following calculations:

- Determine annual take-home income and divide by 12 to get monthly take-home income.

- Total annual expenses, including gasoline and car costs, other transportation, heating, utilities, food, rent or mortgage, insurance, real estate taxes, educational expenses, amounts budgeted for clothes and savings and any current loan payments. Divide this total by 12 to get monthly expenses.

- Subtract the monthly expense total from monthly take-home income. The balance is the monthly optional spending amount. Individuals are urged to refrain from taking out any loan requiring monthly payments that exceed this amount.

There are specific signs that suggest that a person is financially overextended:

- A checkbook balance that is declining lower each month
- Inability to pay the minimum due on charge accounts each month
- Erosion of savings
- Need to write overdrafts to cover financial commitments
- Borrowing against life insurance and inability to repay it
- Dependence on unreliable secondary income sources to cover expenses
- Consistently in arrears on one or more installment payments
- Need to utilize credit cards to cover daily living expenses (often using company credit cards for this purpose)
- Reaching and staying at the limit on one or more credit cards
- Using cash advances to pay off unrelated debts
- Receiving calls and notices about overdue payments
- Need to ask for extension on due dates
- Increase in family disputes relating to tight money
- Having to borrow to pay off periodic financial commitments, such as real estate taxes, income taxes
- Realization that current income is insufficient to reduce debt, and can just cover interest expense on loans

For those in serious financial trouble, a few options are available—drastically cut optional spending, turn some assets into cash if possible, and perhaps even contact creditors and candidly explain the situation. If the problem has gone beyond such measures, an individual might seek credit counseling from a local consumer credit counseling office or consumer affairs department, consumer finance companies, credit unions, or his employer's personnel department. Referrals may also be obtained from:

The Family Service Association of America
    44 East 23rd Street
    New York, NY 10010

or

The National Foundation for Consumer Credit
    1819 H Street N.W.
    Washington, D.C. 20006

Credit Bureaus

There are approximately 2,000 credit bureaus nationwide, which issue over 150 million consumer credit reports annually. An individual's record with such bureaus starts when he or she first applies for a credit card. Information on such reports includes employment, income, and all credit purchases. Lenders such as banks supply information about their account holders.

Anyone is entitled to see his or her credit file, particularly if a credit denial has been based on its contents. It is advisable to contact the credit bureau within 30 days after the application has been denied. The bureau must report the contents of the file, without charge. After the 30-day period, the fee is generally around $5.

Applying For Credit

Commercial banks use rating charts when determining the creditworthiness of a potential borrower. This chart scores the applicant in eleven main categories:

Preferred Situation

Age	Between 16 and 64
Marital status	Married
Dependents	One to three dependents
Living facilities	Own with or without mortgage
Years at present address	Over 6 years
Years at previous address	Over 6 years
Total Monthly Income	Over $800/month
Years with present employer	Over 4 years
Occupation	Skilled or professional, full-time
Bonus points	Awarded for such things as having a phone in your name, having a loan, checking or savings account with the bank to which you are applying, and having a loan history with that bank.

The maximum number of points a potential borrower can score is about 46, and the number required might be about 26 points. The minimum would be in a range of about 19 points to qualify for loan consideration.

It is generally recommended that credit applicants not list a finance company as a credit reference. Computers used by most large lenders will subtract points if a finance company appears on a credit history. However, any loan still outstanding at time of application must be listed. False or incomplete applications are often the stated reason for denying discharge of a debt in bankruptcy.

Two people who cohabitate may insist that their incomes be combined to determine their creditworthiness for a joint-mortgage application. This right was established through the Equal Credit Opportunity Act, which bars discrimination on the basis of marital status.

Credit Card Responsibility

Should a credit card be lost or stolen, the cardholder is liable for the first $50 in unauthorized use even if the loss is reported before the card is used. The cardholder's responsibility may be as high as $500 if the loss of a debit card is not reported promptly and someone has used the account for a teller-machine withdrawal. Thus, the potential loss is ten times greater in the case of debit cards.

Cardholders should never disclose the account number of a check-cashing ID or electronic funds transfer card, even when reporting it lost or stolen. The authorities should know the number, and revealing such information to the wrong party can subject the cardholder to unauthorized use of the card.

It is recommended that credit card statements be reviewed carefully. Store clerks have been known to run off several slips when processing a card for a legitimate use. When using a credit card, it is advisable to take the carbons as well as the receipt for each transaction, to prevent tracing of the signature.

Shopping for Credit

Under federal law, all institutions that extend or arrange for the extension of consumer credit must give the borrower meaningful information about the cost of each loan. The cost must be expressed as the dollar amount of the interest or finance charge, and as the annual percentage rate computed on the amount financed.

To be sure the loan or credit agreement you are considering suits both your budget and your individual needs, shop around. And ask questions to compare and evaluate a lender's rate and services. For instance:

1. What is the annual percentage rate?

2. What is the total cost of the loan in dollars?

3. How long do you have to pay off the loan?

4. What are the number, amounts, and due dates of payments?

5. What is the cost of deferring or extending the time period of the loan?

6. What is the cost of late charges for overdue payments?

7. If you pay the loan off early, are there any prepayment penalties?

8. Does the loan have to be secured? If so, what collateral is required?

9. What is the cost of credit life or other insurance that is being offered or may be required?

10. Are there any other charges you may have to pay?

Source: *The World Almanac & Book of Facts,* 1985 edition, copyright © Newspaper Enterprise Association, Inc., 1984, New York, NY 10166.

Fair Credit

Federal legislation has made it easier for you to be treated fairly in credit-related areas:

BILLING

Don't let the anonymous computer get you down. The Fair Credit Billing Act states that, if you find an error in the amount of $50 or more in your credit card statement or department store revolving charge statement and you write to the company about it (on a separate sheet of paper, not the bill), the company must acknowledge your letter within 30 days and must resolve the dispute within 90 days.

EQUAL CREDIT

The Equal Credit Opportunity Act (ECOA) bans any discrimination according to sex or marital status in the granting of credit. Discrimination is also prohibited on the basis of age, race, color, religion, national origin, or receipt of public assistance payments.

However, the creditor may ask questions relating to these areas if they have a bearing on your creditworthiness. The creditor does have the right to determine whether you are willing and able to repay your debts. For instance, the creditor can ask you if you are "married," "unmarried," or "separated" if, and only if, you are applying jointly with your spouse; your spouse will be an authorized user of the account; you live in a community property state or you list assets located in a community property state. Similarly, a creditor may ask about alimony, child support, and separate maintenance if, and only if, you are depending on these as sources to establish your ability to repay your debts. In this case, the creditor may ask whether there is a court order that requires the payments or may inquire about the length of time and regularity of the payments, as well as your ex-spouse's credit history.

The ECOA also requires that, if you are turned down for credit, the creditor must tell you the reason you were turned down.

MAIL-ORDER MERCHANDISE

By law, you have the right to receive merchandise ordered through the mail within 30 days, unless another deadline has been specified. Promises such as "one week" or "4 to 6 weeks" must be met. If either the seller's or the FTC's deadline is missed, you have the right to cancel and have all your money returned. If you run into a problem with late or nondelivery, contact the Federal Trade Commission for help.

Source: *The World Almanac & Book of Facts,* 1985 edition, copyright © Newspaper Enterprise Association, Inc., 1984, New York, NY 10166.

INTEREST LAWS AND CONSUMER FINANCE LOAN RATES

Most states have laws regulating interest rates. These laws fix a legal or conventional rate which applies when there is no contract for interest. They also fix a general maximum contract rate, but in many states there are so many exceptions that the general contract maximum actually applies only to exceptional cases. Also, federal law has preempted state limits on first home mortgages, subject to each state's right to reinstate its own law and given depository institutions parity with other state lenders.

Legal rate of interest. The legal or conventional rate of interest applies to money obligations when no interest rate is contracted for and also to judgments. The rate is usually somewhat below the general interest rate.

General maximum contract rates. General interest laws in most states set the maximum rate between 8% and 16% per year. The general maximum is fixed by the state constitution at 5% over the Federal Reserve discount rate in Arkansas. Loans to corporations are frequently exempted or subject to a higher maximum. In recent years, it has also been common to provide special rates for home mortgage loans and variable usury rates that are indexed to federal rates.

Specific enabling acts. In many states special statutes permit industrial loan companies, second mortgage lenders, and banks to charge 1.5% a month or more. Laws regulating revolving loans, charge accounts and credit cards generally limit charges between 1.5% and 2% per month plus annual fees for credit cards. Rates for installment sales contracts in most states are somewhat higher. Credit unions may generally charge 1% to 1½% a month. Pawnbrokers' rates vary widely. Savings and loan associations, and loans insured by federal agencies, are also specially regulated. A number of states allow regulated lenders to charge any rate agreed upon with the customer.

Consumer finance loan statutes. Most consumer finance loan statutes are based on early models drafted by the Russell Sage Foundation (1916 – 42) to provide small loans to wage earners under license and other protective regulations. Since 1969 the model has frequently been the Uniform Consumer Credit Code which applies to credit sales and loans for consumer purposes. In general, licensed lenders may charge 3% a month for loans of smaller amounts and reduced rates for additional amounts. A few states permit add-on rates of 17% to 20% to $300 and lower rates for additional amounts. An add-on of 17% ($17 per $100) per year yields about 2.5% per month if paid in equal monthly installments. Discount rates produce higher yields than add-on rates of the same amount. In the table below unless otherwise stated, monthly and annual rates are based on reducing principal balances, annual add-on rates are based on the original principal for the full term, and two or more rates apply to different portions of balance or original principal.

STATE CONSUMER FINANCE LOAN LAWS
Rates of Charge as of October 1, 1984

Alabama	Annual add-on: 15% to $750, 10% to $2,000, 8% over $2,000 (min. 1.5% on unpaid balances), plus 2% fee (max. $20). Higher rates for loans up to $749. Over $2,000, any agreed rate.
Alaska	3% to $850, 2% to $10,000, flat rate to $25,000. Over $10,000, any agreed rate.
Arizona	To $1,000: 3%. Over $1,000: 3% to $500, 2% to $10,000. Over $10,000, any agreed rate.
California	2.5% to $225, 2% to $900, 1.5% to $1,650, 1% to $5,000 (1.6% min.). Over $5,000, any agreed rate. 5% fee (max. $50) to $2,500.
Colorado	36% per year to $630, 21% to $2,100, 15% to $25,000 (21% min.).
Connecticut	Annual add-on: 17% to $600, 11% to $5,000; 11% over $1,800 to $5,000 for certain secured loans.
Delaware	Any agreed rate.
Florida	30% per year to $500, 24% to $1,000, 18% to $2,500; 18% per year on any amount over $2,500 to $25,000.
Georgia	10% per year discount to 18 months, add-on to 36½ months; 8% fee to $600, 4% on excess plus $2 per month; max. $3,000. Over $3,000, any agreed rate.
Hawaii	3.5% to $100, 2.5% to $300; 2% on entire balance over $300.
Idaho	Any agreed rate.
Illinois	Any agreed rate.
Indiana	36% per year to $720, 21% to $2,400, 15% to $60,000 (21% min.).
Iowa	3% to $500, 2% to $1,200, 1.5% to $2,000; or equivalent flat rate. Over $2,000, 10% per year discount.
Kansas	36% per year to $570, 21% to $1,900, 14.45% to $25,000 (21% min.).
Kentucky	3% to $1,000, 2% to $3,000. Over $3,000, 2%.
Louisiana	36% per year to $1,400, 27% to $4,000, 24% to $7,000, 21% over $7,000, plus $25 fee.
Maine	30% per year to $690, 21% to $1,900, 15% to $55,000 (18% min.).
Maryland	2.75% to $500, 2% to $2,000. Over $2,000, 2%.
Massachusetts	23% per year plus $20 fee to $6,000.
Michigan	31% per year to $500, 13% to $3,000 (18% min.).
Minnesota	33% per year to $385, 19% to $38,500 (21.75% min.).
Mississippi	36% per year to $800, 33% to $1,800, 24% to $4,500, 12% over $4,500.
Missouri	2.218% to $800, 1.25% to $2,500, 10% per year over $2,500, plus 5% fee (max. $15).
Montana	Annual add-on; 20% to $550, 16% to $1,100, 12% to $8,750. 2% per mo. over $7,500 to $25,000.
Nebraska	24% per year to $1,000. 21% over, plus fee of 7% to $2,000 and 5% over (max. $500).
Nevada	Any agreed rate.
New Hampshire	2% to $600, 1.5% to $1,500; any agreed rate to $10,000.
New Jersey	30% per year to $5,000.
New Mexico	Any agreed rate.
New York	Any agreed rate.

(Continued)

State Consumer Finance Loan Laws

North Carolina	3% to $600, 1.25% to $3,000.
North Dakota	2.5% to $250, 2% to $500, 1.75% to $750, 1.5% to $1,000; any agreed rate on entire amount over $1,000 to $15,000.
Ohio	28% per year to $1,000, 22% to $3,000; 25% on entire amount over $3,000.
Oklahoma	30% per annum to $630, 21% to $2,100, 15% to $47,500. (21% min.). Special rates to $100.
Oregon	Any agreed rate.
Pennsylvania	9.5% per year discount to 36 months, 6% for remaining time plus 2% fee (min. 2%) to $5,000.
Puerto Rico	27% per year.
Rhode Island	3% to $300, 2.5% for loans between $300 and $800; 2% for larger loans to $2,500.
South Carolina	Any agreed rate.
South Dakota	Any agreed rate.
Tennessee	Over $100, 24% per year plus fees.
Texas	Annual add-on: 18% to $870, 8% to $7,200 or formula rate (max. 24% per year on unpaid balances.)
Utah	36% per year to $840, 21% to $2,800, 15% to $55,000 (18% min.) or, by rule, 19.6%.
Vermont	2% to $1,000, 1% to $3,000 (min. 1.5%).
Virginia	3% to $600, 2.25% to $1,800, 1.5% to $2,800; or annual add-on of 21% to $600, 17% to $1,800, 13% to $2,800; 2% fee.
Washington	2.5% to $500, 1.5% to $1,000, 1% to $2,500.
West Virginia	36% per year to $500, 24% to $1,500, 18% to $2,000.
Wisconsin	23% per year to $3,000; 21% on entire balance over $3,000; any agreed rate, 11/1/84 to 10/31/87.
Wyoming	36% per year to $1,000, 21% to $25,000 (21% min.).

Note: *Maximum monthly rates are computed on unpaid balances, unless otherwise stated.*

Source: *The World Almanac & Book of Facts*, 1985 edition, copyright © Newspaper Enterprise Association, Inc., 1985, New York, NY 10166

Consumer Installment Credit
Estimates of Amounts Outstanding in Millions of Dollars, Not Seasonally Adjusted

End of year or month	Total	By holder					By type			
		Commercial banks	Finance companies	Credit unions	Retailers	Savings— loans and other	Automobile	Mobile homes	Revolving	All others
1976	193,525	93,728	38,918	31,169	19,260	10,450	67,707	14,573	17,189	94,056
1977	230,564	112,373	44,868	37,605	23,490	12,228	82,911	14,945	39,274	93,434
1978	273,645	136,016	54,298	44,334	25,987	13,010	101,647	15,235	48,309	108,454
1979	312,024	154,177	68,318	46,517	28,119	14,893	116,362	16,838	56,937	121,887
1980	313,472	147,013	76,756	44,041	28,448	17,214	116,838	17,322	58,352	120,960
1981	331,697	147,622	89,818	45,954	29,551	18,752	125,331	18,373	62,819	125,174
1982	344,798	152,069	94,322	47,253	30,202	20,952	130,227	18,988	67,184	128,399
1983	396,082	171,978	102,862	53,471	35,911	31,860	142,449	23,680	80,823	149,130
1984 June	360,605	191,519	104,460	59,893	34,206	37,487	155,937	24,427	84,598	162,603

Source: Federal Reserve System.

ESTIMATING COLLEGE COSTS

For most people, a child's college education is the second costliest purchase (after that of a home) they will ever make. Estimating the cost of a college education for a child who is now a toddler is difficult, but the following method provides an educated guess.

1. Determine the year in which the child will enter college.

2. Choose an inflation forecast; the table shown here provides estimates for forecasts of 5%, 7.5%, and 10%.

3. Use the following table to estimate the cost of a four-year education, based on the year the child will enter college, the inflation forecast, and the choice of a public or private institution.

Annual Cost

Inflation Forecast	Public Universities			Private Universities		
	5%	7.5%	10%	5%	7.5%	10%
1986–87	4,136	4,545	4,982	10,376	11,401	12,499
1987–88	4,343	4,885	5,481	10,896	12,256	13,749
1988–89	4,560	5,252	6,029	11,440	13,175	15,124
1989–90	4,788	5,646	6,631	12,012	14,163	16,636
1990–91	5,028	6,069	7,295	12,613	15,226	18,300
1991–92	5,279	6,524	8,024	13,244	16,367	20,130
1992–93	5,543	7,014	8,827	13,906	17,595	22,143
1993–94	5,820	7,540	9,709	14,601	18,915	24,357
1994–95	6,111	8,105	10,680	15,331	20,333	26,793
1995–96	6,417	8,713	11,748	16,098	21,858	29,473
1996–97	6,738	9,367	12,923	16,903	23,498	32,419
1997–98	7,075	10,069	14,215	17,748	25,260	35,661
1998–1999	7,428	10,824	15,637	18,635	27,154	30,227
1999–2000	7,800	11,636	17,200	19,567	29,191	43,150
2000–01	8,190	12,509	18,920	20,545	31,380	47,465
2001–02	8,599	13,447	20,812	21,573	33,734	52,212
2002–03	9,029	14,455	22,894	22,651	36,264	57,433
2003–04	9,479	15,537	25,188	23,785	38,985	63,176
2004–05	9,953	16,702	27,707	24,974	41,909	69,494
2005–06	10,451	17,537	29,092	26,223	45,052	76,443

4. To calculate how much money must be invested annually to provide for each child's education:

   a. Select a reasonable after-tax rate of return on the monies to be invested for education; the table shown on page 1.26 provides the data for after-tax returns of 5%, 7.5%, and 10%.

   b. Based on the after-tax rate of return and the number of years until the child is to begin college, select from the table below the appropriate value.

   c. Divide the total four-year cost for the child by the value selected in step b. The result is the annual amount the parents must invest to provide for the child's education.

   d. Repeat this process for each child, and total the annual investments needed to provide for all the children.

Source: David R. Berson, "How to Figure the Cost of Higher Education," *Digest of Financial Planning Ideas*, April 1984; © Consolidated Capital Communications Group, Inc.

Value of $1 per Annum Compounded Annually
After-Tax Rate of Return

End of Year	5%	7.5%	10%
1	1.0500	1.0750	1.1000
2	2.1525	2.2325	2.3100
3	3.3101	3.4616	3.6410
4	4.5256	4.6987	5.1051
5	5.8019	6.2588	6.7156
6	7.1420	7.8120	8.4871
7	8.5491	9.4891	10.4359
8	10.0266	11.3066	12.5795
9	11.5779	12.9877	14.3974
10	13.2068	15.3696	17.5312
11	14.9171	17.6507	20.3843
12	16.7130	20.1179	23.5227
13	18.5986	22.7868	26.9750
14	20.5786	25.6756	30.7725
15	22.6575	28.8036	34.9497
16	24.8404	32.1924	39.5447
17	27.1324	35.8658	44.5992
18	29.5390	39.8491	50.1591
19	32.0660	44.1705	56.2750
20	34.7193	48.1416	63.0025

TUITION AND FEES AT SELECTED COLLEGES AND UNIVERSITIES

Tuition and fees vary considerably among institutions, depending on their type (university, college), control (public or private), quality, and location. Figures presented here are for the 1984–85 school year. For more detailed information, as well as estimates of the costs for room and board, books and supplies, and living expenses, see *The College Handbook* or *The College Cost Book,* both published by the College Entrance Examination Board and revised annually.

Public Colleges and Universities

	In-state residents	Out-of-state residents
Univ. Arizona, Tucson	$ 950	$3700
Auburn Univ.	1080	2490
Univ. California, Berkeley	1247	4912
City Univ. New York, Queens	1375	2175
Clemson Univ.	1652	3580
Univ. Connecticut	1657*	4593
Univ. Delaware	1671	4281
Univ. Florida	801	2031
Univ. Texas, Houston	490	1570
Idaho State Univ.	1011	2911
Univ. Illinois, Urbana	1722	4218
Indiana Univ., Bloomington	1532	4292

Public Colleges and Universities (Continued)

	In-state residents	Out-of-state residents
Univ. Iowa	1242	3450
Univ. Maryland	1410	3805
Univ. Massachusetts, Amherst	1846	4786
Univ. Michigan	2218	6346
Univ. Minnesota, Twin Cities	1834	4601
Univ. North Carolina, Chapel Hill	766	3128
Ohio State Univ.	1557	3984
Pennsylvania State Univ.	2312	4644
Purdue Univ.	1532	4556
Univ. Pittsburgh	2758	5408
Rutgers, Douglass College	1840	3330
State Univ. New York, Stony Brook	1455	3305
Univ. Texas, Austin	420	1506
Univ. Virginia	1846	4356
Univ. Washington	1302	3618
Univ. Wisconsin, Madison	1278	4190

* *Additional $250 for out-of-district state residents.*

Private Colleges and Universities

American Univ.	$7670
Baylor Univ.	3366
Bucknell Univ.	9115
California Inst. Technology	9384
Univ. Chicago	8952
Colorado Coll.	7500
Connecticut Coll.	9500
Univ. Denver	3139
Duke Univ.	7681
Emory Univ.	7630
Fisk Univ.	4200
Grinnell Coll.	7805
Harvard Univ.	9800
Howard Univ.	3045
Lewis & Clark Coll.	7569
New York Univ.	7850
Univ. Pennsylvania	9600
Rice Univ.	4100
St. Louis Univ.	5340
Univ. of the South	7785
Southern Methodist Univ.	6880
Stanford Univ.	9705
Tulane Univ.	8050
Vassar Coll.	9050
Yale Univ.	9750

REFINANCING A HIGH-INTEREST MORTGAGE

Many bankers use a simple—but inadequate—rule of thumb: It pays to refinance when the borrower can get a rate at least 2% lower than the rate on the mortgage he or she now holds. Bankers also often use a simple—but equally inadequate—formula to show a borrower how soon he can recapture the closing costs on a refinanced loan: Divide the total closing costs by the monthly difference in payments.

$$\frac{\text{Closing costs}}{\text{Saving on monthly payment}} = \frac{\text{Number of months}}{\text{to recapture closing costs}}$$

According to this formula, if the closing costs are $4,000 and the new mortgage is $200 a month less than the old one, the new loan will pay for itself in 20 months. But this simple formula ignores three important factors:

- The borrower's tax bracket,

- The tax value of interest write-offs, and

- The investment potential of the money used for the closing costs.

The following method provides a realistic estimate of the break-even point for refinancing; it requires a programmable financial calculator or a basic calculator and standard amortization tables. (Amortization tables are given on pages 4.42–83 of this volume.)

The example worked out here is for a 30-year $100,000 mortgage at 16% that the borrower could refinance at 14%; the borrower is in the 38% tax bracket.

1. Determine the monthly after-tax savings of the new loan (steps 1 through 4)

   Mortgage payment tables show that the monthly payment on a 30-year $100,000 mortgage at 16% is about $1,345. At 14% the payment drops to $1,185. The difference: $160 a month before taxes. However, in the 38% bracket the borrower is also losing $61 a month in deductions by reducing payment. So the actual after-tax saving is only $99 a month.

2. Determine the after-tax closing costs (steps 5 through 7)

   Estimate how much the borrower will have to pay for points, attorney's fees, recording costs, title search, etc., and subtract from that total the tax saving on deductible expenses. In most, but not all, cases points charged on a loan for a principal residence are deductible in the year paid. Other costs, however, are usually added to the basis of the property.

3. Calculate the provisional break-even point (step 8)

   Divide the after-tax closing costs (line 7) by the after-tax difference in monthly payments (line 4). The answer represents the number of months it will take merely to recoup the cost of refinancing, but does not take into consideration what the borrower *would have earned* on the after-tax closing costs had the money been invested. In itself, this provisional break-even point means little because, if the borrower does not refinance, he will be able to invest the $3,360 he would otherwise spend out-of-pocket on closing costs.

4. Calculate the value of the after-tax closing costs (steps 9 through 12)

   To calculate the value of the after-tax closing costs over the provisional break-even period, use a standard compound interest rate table or calculator to figure the total return for the number of months shown in step 8. Our example uses a 6% after-tax return.

Since the borrower would give up more than $600 in potential earnings by committing $3,360 to after-tax closing costs, the true break-even point will not be reached for at least 6 more months (step 10). Meanwhile, the alternative investment of $3,360—grown to $3,981 by the 34th month—would continue to earn income at approximately $20 a month. Thus the true break-even point will not come for another 7.5 months—or during the 42nd month (steps 11 through 13).

Steps	Example
1. Current monthly payments	$1,345
2. Less: Proposed monthly payments	1,185
3. Monthly pretax saving	$ 160
4. Multiply line 3 x (1.0 − client's tax bracket) for monthly after-tax savings (160 x .62)	$ 99
5. Total closing costs	$4,500
6. Less: Deductible closing costs x client's tax bracket ($3,000 x .38)	1,140
7. After-tax closing costs	$3,360
8. Divide line 7 by line 4 for provisional break-even point	34 months
9. Figure potential after-tax earnings of line 7 over months indicated in line 8 ($3,360 × 6%)	$ 621
10. Divide line 9 by line 4 for additional months until break-even	6.2 months
11. Figure additional earnings on line 7 + line 9 over number of months indicated on line 10 ($3,981 at 6% for 6.2 months)	$ 125
12. Divide line 11 by line 4 for additional months until break-even	1.3 months
13. Add line 8, line 10 and line 12 for total number of months until true break-even	41.5 months

Source: Steven Enright, "Should I Refinance My High-Interest Mortgage?" *Digest of Financial Planning Ideas,* June 1984.

BANKRUPTCY

Passage of the Federal Bankruptcy Act of 1978 significantly liberalized the procedures for filing for personal bankruptcy. Chapter 7 of the Act discusses liquidation, formerly referred to colloquially as straight bankruptcy. It involves the trustee's collection and distribution to creditors of all the bankrupt's nonexempt property, in the manner required by the Act. Chapter 7 makes no reference to the debtor's income, and exempt property includes up to $7,500 equity in the debtor's home ($15,000 if both spouses file), $1,200 in automobile equity, $4,000 in accrued dividends, $500 in jewelry, and $200 per category of household items (books, clothing, etc.). For tax purposes, the individual taxpayer and what is called the *estate,* which is created on commencement of bankruptcy, are treated as separate taxable entities, and it is the estate that winds up the bankruptcy proceeding.

Both Chapters 11 and 13 differ from straight bankruptcy in that the debtor seeks to rehabilitate and reorganize, rather than liquidate, and the creditor, in order to satisfy claims, looks to future earnings of the bankrupt, rather than to property held by the bankrupt. Chapter 13 requires that debtors show only a regular income to handle a reasonable three-year pay-back plan. A court definition of *reasonable* might be as little as 1% to 10% of the total debts, even if it is believed that 50% or more could realistically be handled. The law no longer specifically requires a bankrupt to show financial hardship. The debtor simply claims bankruptcy, eliminates most outstanding debt, and keeps most tangible assets. The filing of bankruptcy under Chapter 13 creates no separate taxable entity.

In 1982, the U.S. Supreme Court found portions of the Bankruptcy Act of 1978 pertaining to the power and tenure of bankruptcy judges to be unconstitutional. Congress is, therefore, rewriting the Code. This revison will probably extend beyond the areas relating to tenure and the power of judges. Currently, U.S. District Courts are presiding over all bankruptcy cases.

1.03 Investment Planning

Despite the proliferation of investment vehicles and products, personal investment planning remains a four-step process:

1. **Self-assessment.** Before looking at any investment opportunities, the investor needs to evaluate his or her current financial situation and to assess economic objectives (e.g., current income, capital appreciation, tax shelter), liquidity needs, and short- and long-term financial goals. This self-assessment should also include questions of temperament: How much risk can the investor afford financially and emotionally? How much time is the investor willing to devote to managing investments? How disciplined is he or she about regularly setting aside money for an investment portfolio?

2. **Research.** During the research phase, the investor seeks first to become more familiar with various types of investment vehicles and then with specific products. Although no one can accurately forecast the future of the economy, many investors try to broaden their understanding of the national and global economic systems.

3. **Selection.** In selecting investments, the investor will need to synthesize the information obtained from the self-assessment and product research and consider the twin strategies of diversification and hedging.

4. **Ongoing review.** Since an investor's financial situation and objectives will change over time, investors should plan to review periodically their holdings and the recent performance of individual investments and to make appropriate adjustments.

Selected materials relevant to investment planning are provided in this section; detailed performance data for a variety of investments and economic indicators are presented in Chapters 3 and 5.

RISK AND REWARD: THE INVESTMENT PYRAMID

The investment pyramid illustrates the relationship between potential risk and potential reward for a wide array of investment vehicles. The most conservative instruments are at the bottom, the riskiest at the top. As the arrows on each side indicate, every investment is a compromise of sorts: there are no certain rewards and no absolutely risk-free investments. For example, while the investor who places funds in a federally insured savings account knows that the principal and interest are guaranteed, he or she runs the risk that the yield will not keep up with inflation.

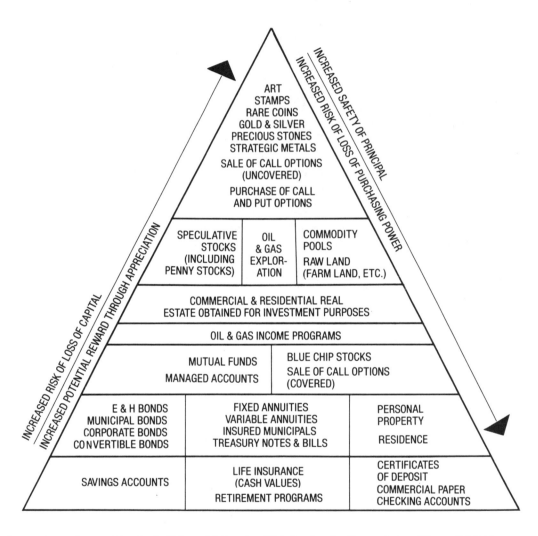

Source: Loren Dunton, *Your Book of Financial Planning,* 1983. Reprinted with permission of Reston Publishing Company, a Prentice-Hall Company, 11480 Sunset Hills Road, Reston, Va. 22090.

INVESTMENT OBJECTIVES RATING MODEL

The Investment Objectives Rating model was designed to help clarify the risk-reward ratios of a variety of investment opportunities. The model is predicated on three basic assumptions:

1. Investments have the potential of producing four economic benefits:

   - Tax shelter

   - Cash flow (current yield)

   - Capital growth (appreciation)

   - Safety of principal

2. Any given investment represents a trade-off among these four basic benefits: potential strengths in some categories are offset by potential weaknesses in others.

3. All investments can be expected to provide the same total amount of benefits, though in different proportions.

Although no model can predict the actual performance of investments, by using the Investment Objectives Ratings model, investors can appraise the realistic trade-offs among the benefits to be expected from a given investment and can match those trade-offs with their personal investment objectives.

Using the Model

1. Rate an investment on a 4-point scale for each objective (tax shelter, cash flow, capital growth, and safety) according to the following system:

   4 points = Excellent (among the top 20% of all investments in providing this benefit)

   3 points = Very good (better than 60% to 80% of all other investments in providing this benefit)

   2 points = Good (better than 40% to 60% of all other investments in providing this benefit)

   1 point = Fair (better than 20% to 40% of all other investments in providing this benefit)

   0 points = Poor (among the bottom 20% of all investments in providing this benefit).

2. Adjust the ratings until the total assigned to any investment is 8 points. One may use half points, but any finer gradations exceed the model's precision.

3. Allocate 8 points among the four benefits to represent the investor's objectives.

4. Use the ratings to compare the probable performance of selected investments and match them to the investor's objectives.

Examples

HIGH-QUALITY MUNICIPAL BOND.

A plausible rating for a high-quality municipal bond is:

- Tax shelter — 2 points. While municipal bonds produce tax-exempt income, their tax advantages are not as high as those produced by high-quality real estate, oil drilling, or equipment leasing partnerships.

- Cash flow (current yield) — 2 points. Again, municipal bonds provide good, but not outstanding, benefits.

- Capital growth (appreciation) — 0 points. Municipal bonds do not appreciate, and their value prior to maturity may even erode in periods of rising interest rates.

- Safety of principal — 4 points. A high-quality municipal bond is among the very safest of investments.

COMPARISON OF REAL ESTATE INVESTMENTS.

The same type of reasoning would produce the following ratings for four types of real estate investments:

	Tax Shelter	Cash Flow	Capital Growth	Safety
Leveraged income	2.0	1.0	3.0	2.0
New construction	2.5	0.5	3.5	1.5
Low-leverage income (apartments, office buildings)	0.5	2.0	2.5	3.0
Subsidized housing	4.0	1.0	1.0	2.0

COMPARISON OF OIL AND GAS PARTNERSHIPS.

Similarly, one can compare various oil and gas limited partnerships:

	Tax Shelter	Cash Flow	Capital Growth	Safety
Exploratory	3.0	0	3.5	1.5
Development	2.0	1.5	2.0	2.5
Income	1.0	2.5	1.0	3.5

Source: Alan Parisse and Richard Wollack, *Tax-Advantaged Investments,* Consolidated Capital Communications Group, Inc., © 1983.

1.04 Insurance

In order to protect personal assets properly, individuals should maintain a good working relationship with an insurance agent. Many different types of coverage are available and limits can be increased for certain items or coverage may be broadened. Through knowledge of the insured's individual situation and particular assets, a professional can provide valuable advice and can tailor coverage to meet the insured's specific needs.

PERSONAL PROPERTY AND CASUALTY INSURANCE

Property and casualty insurance for personal assets is available from an independent agent who represents many companies or one who only represents a single company. It is important to choose a knowledgeable and trustworthy agent and to review and update insurance annually or in conjunction with a major purchase.

Homeowner's Insurance

In most cases, the recommended homeowner's policy is the HO-3, which provides broad coverage on the home's structure and a more limited coverage on contents. The policy specifies limits on the home, the contents (50% of home value), appurtenant structures (10%), and additional living expense (20%). Additional living expense will generally pay for rental of substitute housing and related extraordinary costs if a fire or other insured disaster makes the home uninhabitable. For example, insurance coverage (excluding liability), for a home valued at $100,000 would include:

Home	$100,000
Contents	50,000
Appurtenant structures	
(e.g., shed, unattached garage)	10,000
Additional living expense	20,000
Total	$180,000

The home itself is covered on a replacement cost basis, i.e., no deduction is made for depreciation as long as adequate limits are purchased. Many companies now offer an additional rider that provides full replacement cost, even exceeding the stated amount, in the event that extreme inflation should raise the home value substantially above the stated amount. For a minimum premium, usually between $25 and $50 annually, most companies offer a replacement cost rider for contents. Most agents strongly recommend this coverage.

Floaters

Most policies have specific limits on valuable items. These limits may vary from company to company, but usually apply to money, silver, jewelry, coin and stamp collections, furs, and guns. Floater coverage supersedes the dollar limits on valuables and provides much broader protection. Antiques and fine art items should be considered for floater coverage. To do this, the agent will specify a rate per $100 of coverage and will usually require an appraisal of the valuables.

Homeowner's Liability Insurance

A homeowner's policy will include liability protection for bodily injury and property damage. Liability insurance is a third-party coverage that pays for defense expenses and any judgments for property damage or bodily injury suffered by someone else as a result of the insured's negligence.

In most cases, a rider can be added to cover residential rental properties the insured owns. Recommended limits depend on the individual situation, but a minimum of $100,000 liability should be carried, and $300,000 or more is advisable. On the HO-3 policy, some companies will provide $1,000,000 and up in coverage, or an umbrella policy may be obtained. An umbrella can provide increased liability protection to cover not only the home, but also cars, boats, and recreational vehicles.

Disaster Coverage

A homeowner's policy will not automatically cover damage from an earthquake, flood, mudslide, etc. Depending on the property location, a rider or separate policy may be available for this type of extended coverage. A professional agent can provide information about specific coverage in terms of limits, deductibles, and cost.

Deductibles

Deductibles only apply to physical damage to the insured's property and, thus, do not apply to third-party (i.e., liability) claims. If concern is primarily for substantial losses, premiums may be reduced by increasing the insured's deductible. Savings in premiums can outweigh the increased deductible, especially if losses are infrequent. Homeowner's deductibles are often $100 and may typically be increased to $250, $500, or $1,000.

Renter's and Condominium Owner's Policies

A renter's policy, HO-4, covers the renter's possessions and provides liability protection. The coverage is basically the same as an HO-3, except the structure is not insured. As with the HO-3, the renter must add replacement cost coverage for his possessions, or depreciation will be deducted in the event of a loss. The same restrictions apply to valuable items as on the HO-3, so floaters are recommended.

A condominium or townhouse owner will typically have coverage for the structure itself on a master policy covering the whole complex. It is crucial that this master policy be updated annually, and the individual owner should check into the specific coverage provided. The owner will also need an HO-6 to cover his possessions, liability, and any additions or alterations made to the unit. Once again, replacement cost riders and floater coverage are available. The master policy may cover only the basic structure, and additions and alterations coverage will usually be needed for improvements of any kind. Other coverages, such as that for loss assessment, are also available to owners of condominiums.

AUTOMOBILE INSURANCE

Automobile insurance varies considerably, depending on each particular state's laws. To assure proper coverage, it is important to consult a local agent. The following table lists the states in which no-fault laws apply and some of the provisions of those laws.

NO-FAULT MOTOR VEHICLE INSURANCE LAWS

State or Other Jurisdiction	Purchase of First-Party Benefits	Minimum Tort Liability Threshold[1]	Maximum First-Party (No-Fault) Benefits					Survivors'/ Funeral Benefits
			Overall	Medical	Income Loss	Replacement Services		
Arkansas	Optional	None		$5,000 if incurred within 2 years of accident.	70% of lost income up to $140/week beginning 8 days after accident, for up to 52 weeks	Up to $70/week beginning 8 days after accident, for up to 52 weeks		$5,000
Colorado	Mandatory	$500		$25,000 if incurred within 3 years (additional $25,000 for rehabilitation expenses incurred within 5 years of accident)	Up to $125/week for up to 52 weeks	Up to $15/day for up to 52 weeks		$1,000
Connecticut	Mandatory	$400	$5,000	Limited only by total benefits limit	85% of lost income up to $200/wk	85% of replacement services up to $200/wk		85% of actual loss for income & replacement services up to $200/week. Funeral benefit: $2,000
Delaware	Mandatory	None; but amt. of no-fault benefits received cannot be used as evidence in suits for general damage	$10,000 per person $20,000 per accident	Limited only by total benefits limit, but must be incurred within 2 years of accident	Limited only by total benefits limit, but must be incurred within 2 years of accident	Limited only by total benefits limit, but must be incurred within 2 years of accident		Funeral benefit: $2,000 (must be incurred within 2 years of accident)

(Continued)

No-Fault Motor Vehicle Insurance Laws

State or Other Jurisdiction	Purchase of First-Party Benefits	Minimum Tort Liability Threshold[1]	Maximum First-Party (No-Fault) Benefits				
			Overall	Medical	Income Loss	Replacement Services	Survivors' / Funeral Benefits
Florida	Mandatory	No dollar threshold[2]	$10,000	80% of all costs	60% of lost income	Limited only by total benefits limit	Funeral benefit: $1,750
Georgia	Mandatory	$500	$5,000	$2,500	85% of lost income up to $200/week	$20/day	Maximum wage loss & replacement services amounts. Funeral benefit: $1,500
Hawaii	Mandatory	Floating threshold set annually by insurance commissioner	$15,000	Limited only by total benefits limit	Up to $800/month for income loss and replacement services		Up to $800/month. Funeral benefit: $1,500
Kansas	Mandatory	$500		$2,000 (additional $2,000 for rehabilitation)	85% of lost income up to $650/month for 1 year	$12/day for 365 days	Up to $650/month for lost income & $12/day for replacement services for up to 1 year, less disability payments received before death. Funeral benefit: $1,000
Kentucky	See note 3	$1,000	$10,000	Limited only by total benefits limit	85% of lost income (more if tax advantage is less than 15%) up to $200/week	Up to $200/week	Up to $200/week each for survivors' economic loss & replacement services loss. Funeral benefits: $1,000

(Continued)

No-Fault Motor Vehicle Insurance Laws

State or Other Jurisdiction	Purchase of First-Party Benefits	Minimum Tort Liability Threshold[1]	Maximum First-Party (No-Fault) Benefits					Survivors'/ Funeral Benefits
			Overall	Medical	Income Loss	Replacement Services		
Maryland	Mandatory	None	$2,500	Limited only by total benefits limit	Limited only by total benefits limit.	Limited only by total benefits limit; payable only to nonwage-earners		Funeral benefit: limited only by total benefits limit
Massachusetts	Mandatory	$500	$2,000	Limited only by total benefits limit, if incurred within 2 years	Up to 75% of lost income	Limited only by total benefits limit; payment made to nonfamily members for services that would have been performed by victim		Funeral benefit: limited only by total benefits limit
Michigan[4]	Mandatory	No dollar threshold[5]		Unlimited	85% of lost income up to $1,475/30-day period for up to 3 years; max. amt. adjusted annually for cost of living	$20/day for 3 years		Up to $1,475/30-day period for lost income for up to 3 years & $20/day for replacement services. Funeral benefit: $1,000
Minnesota	Mandatory	$4,000	$10,000	$20,000	85% of lost income up to $200/week	$15/day, beginning 8 days after accident		Up to $200/week for income loss & replacement services. Funeral benefit: $1,250

(Continued)

No-Fault Motor Vehicle Insurance Laws

| State or Other Jurisdiction | Purchase of First-Party Benefits | Minimum Tort Liability Threshold[1] | Maximum First-Party (No-Fault) Benefits | | | | | |
			Overall	Medical	Income Loss	Replacement Services	Survivors'/ Funeral Benefits
New Jersey	Mandatory	$200		Unlimited	Up to $100/wk. to maximum of $5,200/person	Up to $12/day to a maximum of $4,380/person	Maximum amount of benefits victim would have received. Funeral benefit: $1,000
New York	Mandatory	No dollar threshold[6]	$50,000	Limited only by total benefits limit	80% of lost income up to $1,000/month for 3 years	$25/day for 1 year	$2,000 in addition to other benefits
North Dakota	Mandatory	$1,000	$15,000	Limited only by total benefits limit	85% of lost income up to $150/week	$15/day	Up to $150/week for survivors income & $15/day for replacement services. Funeral benefit: $1,000
Oregon	Mandatory	None		$5,000 if incurred within 1 year of accident	70% of lost income up to $750/month for up to 52 weeks, if victim is disabled for at least 14 days	Up to $18/day for up to 52 weeks, if victim is disabled for at least 14 days	Funeral benefit: $1,000
Pennsylvania	Mandatory	$750		Unlimited	Up to $15,000[7]	Up to $25/day for 1 year	Up to $5,000 for survivors' income loss and lost benefits victim would have received. Funeral benefit: $1,500

(Continued)

No-Fault Motor Vehicle Insurance Laws

State or Other Jurisdiction	Purchase of First-Party Benefits	Minimum Tort Liability Threshold[1]	Maximum First-Party (No-Fault) Benefits				
			Overall	Medical	Income Loss	Replacement Services	Survivors'/ Funeral Benefits
South Carolina	Optional	None	$1,000	Limited only by total benefits limit if incurred within 3 years of accident	Limited only by total benefits limit	Limited only by total benefits limit	Funeral benefit: limited only by total benefits limit
South Dakota	Optional	None		$2,000 if incurred within 2 years of accident	$60/week for up to 52 weeks for disability extending beyond 14 days of date of accident	None	$10,000 if death occurs within 90 days of accident
Texas	Optional	None	$2,500	Limited only by total benefits limit if incurred within 3 years of accident	Limited only by total benefits limit if incurred within 3 years of accident	Limited only by total benefits limit if incurred within 3 years of accident. Payable only to nonwage-earners	Limited only by total benefits limit if incurred within 3 years of accident
Utah	Mandatory	$500		$2,000	85% of lost income up to $150/week for up to 52 weeks subject to 3-day waiting period, which does not apply if disability lasts longer than 14 days	$12/day for up to 365 days subject to 3-day waiting period, which does not apply if disability lasts longer than 14 days	$2,000 survivors' benefit. Funeral benefit: $1,000

(Continued)

No-Fault Motor Vehicle Insurance Laws

State or Other Jurisdiction	Purchase of First-Party Benefits	Minimum Tort Liability Threshold[1]	Maximum First-Party (No-Fault) Benefits				
			Overall	Medical	Income Loss	Replacement Services	Survivors'/Funeral Benefits
Virginia	Optional	None		$2,000 if incurred within 1 year of accident	100% of lost income up to $100/week for up to 52 weeks	None	Funeral benefit included in medical benefit
District of Columbia	Mandatory	$5,000 (to be adjusted annually to reflect cost-of-living changes)		$100,000 (medical and rehabilitation)	80% of lost income up to $2,000/month (maximum of $24,000)	Up to $50/day up to 3 years (maximum of $24,000)	Funeral benefit: $2,000

1 Refers to minimum amount of medical expenses necessary before victim can sue for general damages ("pain and suffering"). Lawsuits are allowed in all states for injuries resulting in death and permanent disability. Some states allow lawsuits for one or more of the following: serious and permanent disfigurement, certain temporary disabilities, loss of body member, loss of certain bodily functions, certain fractures, or economic losses (other than medical) that exceed stated limits.

2 Victim cannot sue for general damages unless injury results in significant and permanent loss of important body function, permanent injury, significant and permanent scarring or disfigurement, or death.

3 Accident victim is not bound by tort restriction if he has rejected the tort limitation in writing or is injured by a driver who has rejected the tort limitation in writing. Rejection bars recovery of first-party benefits.

4 Liability for property damage for all states with no-fault insurance is under the state tort system. Michigan has no tort liability for vehicle damage.

5 Victim cannot sue for general damages unless injuries result in death, serious impairment of bodily function, or serious permanent disfigurement.

6 Victim cannot recover general damages unless injury results in inability to perform usual daily activities for at least 90 days during the 180 days following the accident; dismemberment; significant disfigurement; fracture; permanent loss of use of a body organ, member, function, or system; permanent consequential limitation of use of a body organ or member; significant limitation of use of a body function or system; or death.

7 Maximum monthly income loss benefit of $1,000 multiplied by the percentage that the state's per capita income bears to the nation's per capita income. Up to 20% may be subtracted to offset income tax savings.

Source: *Book of the States, 1984–85*, Council of State Governments.

LIFE INSURANCE

There are any number of reasons for considering the different types of life insurance available. As a method of estate building, life insurance is an investment that will provide funds to one's beneficiaries, often funds that would otherwise not be there. It can thus avert much of the financial loss caused by the death of an individual.

As a funding device, life insurance may be used to provide money for business purposes. For example, a partnership might require or allow for a surviving partner to buy out the interest of the deceased partner. Such agreements are commonly called *buy-out agreements* and they come in many forms. Each partner might take out insurance on the other's life equal in value to a half-interest in the corporation, so that funds would be provided to buy out the deceased partner's interest.

Life insurance provides liquidity to pay taxes and other expenses arising because of a person's death. Since it becomes immediately available upon death, other less liquid assets within the estate can be passed on whole, undiluted by the losses that usually accompany a forced liquidation.

As an investment vehicle, life insurance creates a secure, almost automatic vehicle for savings. Reasonably small scheduled payments make it possible for even a weak-willed individual to maintain a policy for his or her family.

Term Insurance

Term insurance is temporary insurance that covers a specified period of time, whether it be one, five, or ten years. If the insured survives that period, the policy expires and protection ends, although usually the policyholder may elect to extend the period by paying an additional premium. Guaranteed renewable policies specify the age to which they can be renewed even to a very advanced age, at which time the insured receives the face value.

Term insurance is, at least initially, the least expensive form of insurance. However, being age-based, it becomes more expensive with every renewal and, if continued long enough, will ultimately exceed the comparative cost of permanent insurance. In addition, some term policies cannot be renewed after age 65 or 70, at which point it is usually too late to obtain other, permanent insurance.

The best uses for term insurance are in conjunction with a permanent insurance on a convertible basis for a young income earner who cannot afford the higher premiums on fully permanent insurance; as a form of mortgage insurance so that a premature death would not result in loss of a home; or in a business situation, to insure someone key to the development of a special product or service so that his or her untimely death would not result in an investment loss.

ANNUAL RENEWABLE TERM

Annual contract provides set amount of coverage for the present year and guarantees the policyholder the right to renew the policy for the following year at a specified rate.

LEVEL TERM

Policy extends for a fixed period of years (e.g., five to thirty years, or until insured reaches age 65) and total premiums for the entire period of coverage are divided into equal annual (or semiannual) installments.

DECREASING TERM (DECLINING BALANCE TERM)

Annual premiums remain constant over the period of coverage, but the amount of coverage decreases annually; may include a guaranteed fixed monthly income to the beneficiaries if the insured dies during the covered period.

MODIFIED TERM

After a specified period of coverage, the policy is automatically converted to a whole-life policy.

Whole Life Insurance

The major difference between term and whole life insurance is that the premiums are fixed at the age of policy origination with whole life, but increase with age with term insurance. Whole life is permanent insurance and will pay off whenever the insured dies. It takes two forms—ordinary life and limited payment life—which differ primarily in the length of time premium payments are required.

ORDINARY LIFE

With this type of insurance, premium payments are scheduled for the entire life of the insured and are divided into two parts: risk protection and investment. The risk portion represents term insurance, while the investment part acts as a savings account within the policy, providing the cash value of the policy. With time, the portion of the premium attributed to risk decreases, and the value portion increases, providing a gradual buildup in the cash value of the policy. This provides a liquid asset, always available for borrowing.

The cash value of the policy is usually free of income taxes because of *tax-sheltered treatment.* When the policy is surrendered for its cash value, the policyholder pays income taxes only on the amount that exceeds the total amount of premiums paid less dividends received.

LIMITED LIFE

With limited payment life, the period of premium payments is limited to a specified number of years, such as 10 or 20 years, or perhaps to a certain age. At this point, the policy is paid up to its full face amount. The payments are understandably higher than those for an equal face amount of ordinary life, but the cash value increases at a much greater rate.

This type of insurance might be favored by individuals with good income who wish to complete policy payments well before reaching retirement age, or for those who anticipate having lower income in later years—e.g., athletes, models, entertainers, etc.

SINGLE PREMIUM LIFE

This form of permanent insurance is similar to limited payment life, though here the entire premium is paid in one lump sum. An ordinary or limited payment life policy can be converted to a paid-up policy, with a reduced face amount tied to the cash value in the existing policy. This value serves as a single premium, taking into account the age of the insured when the policy is converted.

Universal Life

Beyond offering death protection and cash value accumulations, universal life offers several special features not found in traditional permanent life insurance.

- Cash values of universal life earn interest at current Treasury bill rates, those of other government securities, or other money market funds, with the money continually rolling over into these instruments so that the cash value earnings reflect current economic conditions. The earnings accumulations are not currently taxed to the policyholder.

- Provided enough is paid to cover the cost of the protection portion, the timing and amount of premium payments are generally up to the policyowner.

- The policyowner can adjust the amount of the death benefit. He can maintain a level death benefit, which includes both cash values and pure insurance protection, or keep the insurance protection portion constant in addition to the growing cash values. As his long-term plans evolve, he can switch back and forth between these two options.

- The policyowner has access to cash values. Within certain limits, he can draw funds or borrow against the cash values without an interest charge, as one might do with a traditional policy, as long as he maintains sufficient cash value to pay the cost of protection.

Until the passage of the Tax Reduction Act of 1984, universal life insurance had been treated by the IRS as an investment. The new tax act redefined life insurance in such a way that universal life now falls within the guidelines for life insurance, a provision that benefits policyholders.

Variable Life Insurance

Like permanent life insurance, a variable life policy stipulates fixed premiums and guaranteed minimum death benefits. But the cash-value accumulation and death benefits can rise or decline (though the death benefit can never decline below the guaranteed minimum) based on the performance of the underlying investment vehicle (stocks, bonds, money market or equity funds) selected by the policyholder. The policyholder is permitted to switch the cash-value accumulation from one vehicle to another, depending on his needs and perceptions of the market, and can borrow against the cash value.

Universal/Variable Life Insurance

A hybrid policy that combines universal life's flexibility in premium payments and amount of coverage with variable life's investment flexibility.

Endowment Insurance

Endowment insurance provides a means of building a retirement fund, financing a child's education, or obtaining a given sum of money at some future date. It covers a fixed period of time, paying out the face amount either at the end of this time or on the death of the insured, if death occurs before this period ends. It is similar to limited payment life, but the endowment feature requires that the face amount of the policy be accumulated and is thus an enforced savings plan. Since a larger portion of the endowment premiums is allocated to savings, the premium is considerably higher than for other forms of insurance.

Should the insured survive to the endowment time, the endowment amount paid always exceeds that paid in as premiums and, consequently, there is an income tax on the excess received over the amount paid into the policy.

Retirement Annuity

With this type of insurance, the life insurance company pays the insured an annuity if and when he lives beyond his life expectancy, paying a fixed sum for the balance of his life. This annuity payment is a combination of previous payments on the investment, plus the interest earned on it.

Retirement annuity is important in that it provides for the possibility that an insured may live well past his life expectancy. The annuity is designed such that he can never outlive its payments of principal and interest, a feature no other type of investment provides. With life spans gradually increasing, it is practical to assume that a person could live to 80, 90, or older—well past retirement age. If there is a potential problem in finding sufficient income to live on for these 20 to 30 years, retirement annuity insurance would provide for this period.

INSURANCE RIDERS

Many standard policies carry a variety of riders to include additional provisions for which the insured pays additional premiums. The following briefly describes some of the more commonly added riders.

Double Indemnity

With a double indemnity rider, beneficiaries receive double the face value of the policy in the case of accidental death, and sometimes triple this amount if the accident occurs while the insured is a passenger on a common carrier, such as a bus or plane.

Disability Waiver

This rider provides for a waiver of premiums should the insured become disabled before the age of 60 or 65, depending on the policy. Should the insured become permanently disabled, the company pays the premium, and all of the provisions of the insurance contract can thus remain in effect. Usually this waiver covers only disabilities that last more than six months and is retroactive to the onset of the disability.

This not only provides protection against a loss of security, but at the same time can act as a money-making device. While it operates, the cash value grows and may be borrowed against if emergency funds are needed, or withdrawn if the insured later decides to terminate the policy.

Mortgage Redemption

Because it is used to pay off a reducing mortgage, the face value of a mortgage redemption rider gradually diminishes. It is usually less expensive to attach such a rider to an existing policy than to write a separate policy offering the same coverage.

Family Income

With this type of rider, if the insured dies within a given period, the insurance company will pay his or her family a certain monthly income for a specified period of time, then pay out the face amount of the basic ordinary life policy. This payment may be in one lump sum or over a series of installments.

Insurability Protection

This rider allows the insured to buy additional insurance of specified amounts at certain ages—generally up to the age of 40—without having to have a new physical exam. This is an excellent provision for a young family man or woman, in that the additional premiums are low and insurability is guaranteed, regardless of health problems that might develop later.

DETERMINING LIFE INSURANCE NEEDS

Despite the numerous formulas available for determining personal insurance needs, the only realistic approach is to assess the insured's family's needs, basing the calculations on future income and life expectancy. The following suggestions offer a step-by-step approach to making such an estimate.

Step 1. Estimate the Future Needs of Beneficiaries

Keep in mind that income needs will vary. Expenses for a family with young children might initially be quite high, then ebb for a period, and peak again when the children reach college age. During the middle period, a surviving spouse might be able to work to augment the family income. In later years, that spouse might have higher medical expenses and be unable to work, thus requiring more supplemental income.

Step 2. Determine Cash Flow from Other Sources

Determine whether there is enough income-producing property in the insured's estate to provide for the expected income needs of beneficiaries.

Step 3. Assess Liquidity Needs

Determine immediate needs by estimating federal estate taxes, state inheritance taxes, and any probate costs that might be incurred. If the insured is married, determine these same expenses for his or her spouse, given the assumption that the spouse is the first to die.

The amount and type of insurance should be adequate to make up any deficiency between the income expected and the income needed.

Life Insurance Adequacy Test

Cash needed
    Education $_____
    Mortgages or rent   _____
    Burial and related expenses   _____
    Emergency fund   _____
    Estate costs   _____

Assets needed to meet
    income requirement
    Current income need,
        per month $_____
    Less: Estimated Social Security
        income, per month $_____
        (see factor below)
    Total capital (assets) needed $_____

Less:
    Capital at work $_____
    + Face amount of insurance $_____
    − Cash value of insurance $_____ $_____

Life insurance needed (surplus) $_____

Present amount $_____   vs.   Needed amount $_____
Present outlay $_____   vs.   Needed outlay $_____

Factors for Various Capital Earning Rates

Capital Earning Rate Available	Factor
6%	200
8%	150
10%	120
12%	100

The factor number is determined by the following equation:

$$\frac{\text{(Monthly income needed} \times \text{12 months)}}{\text{Interest rate available}} = \text{Capital needed for investment}$$

LIFE EXPECTANCY
Expectation of Life at Birth (in Years)

Year	Total			White			Black and Other		
	Total	Male	Female	Total	Male	Female	Total	Male	Female
1920	54.1	53.6	54.6	54.9	54.4	55.6	45.3	45.5	45.2
1930	59.7	58.1	61.6	61.4	59.7	63.5	48.1	47.3	49.2
1940	62.9	60.8	65.2	64.2	62.1	66.6	53.1	51.5	54.9
1950	68.2	65.6	71.1	69.1	66.5	72.2	60.8	59.1	62.9
1955	69.6	66.7	72.8	70.5	67.4	73.7	63.7	61.4	66.1
1960	69.7	66.6	73.1	70.6	67.4	74.1	63.6	61.1	66.3
1965	70.2	66.8	73.7	71.0	67.6	74.7	64.1	61.1	67.4
1970	70.9	67.1	74.8	71.7	68.0	75.6	65.3	61.3	69.4
1971	71.1	67.4	75.0	72.0	68.3	75.8	65.6	61.6	69.7
1972	71.1	67.4	75.1	72.0	68.3	75.9	65.6	61.5	69.9
1973	71.3	67.6	75.3	72.2	68.4	76.1	65.9	61.9	70.1
1974	71.9	68.1	75.8	72.7	68.9	76.6	67.0	62.9	71.3
1975	72.5	68.7	76.5	73.2	69.4	77.2	67.9	63.6	72.3
1976	72.8	69.0	76.7	73.5	69.7	77.3	68.3	64.1	72.6
1977	73.2	69.3	77.1	73.8	70.0	77.7	68.8	64.6	73.1
1978	73.3	69.5	77.2	74.0	70.2	77.8	69.2	65.0	73.6
1979	73.9	70.0	77.8	74.6	70.8	78.4	69.8	65.4	74.1
1980	73.7	70.0	77.5	74.4	70.7	78.1	69.5	65.3	73.6
1981	74.2	70.4	77.9	74.7	71.1	78.5	70.3	66.1	74.5
1982	74.5	70.9	78.2	75.1	71.4	78.7	70.9	66.5	75.2
1983	74.7	71.0	78.3	75.2	71.6	78.8	71.3	67.1	75.3

Note: *Prior to 1960, excludes Alaska and Hawaii. Data prior to 1940 for death-registration states only. Beginning 1970, excludes deaths of nonresidents of the United States. Data for 1982 and 1983 are preliminary.*

Source: *Statistical Abstract of the United States, 1984.*

SELECTED LIFE TABLE VALUES

Age and Sex	White					Black and Other					Black	
	1949–1951	1959–1961	1969–1971	1975	1980	1949–1951	1959–1961	1969–1971	1975	1980	1975	1980
Average Expectation of Life in Years												
At birth:												
male	66.3	67.6	67.9	69.4	70.7	58.9	61.5	61.0	63.7	65.3	62.4	63.7
female	72.0	74.2	75.5	77.2	78.1	62.7	66.5	69.1	72.4	73.6	71.3	72.3
Age 20:												
male	49.5	50.3	50.2	51.4	52.4	43.7	45.8	44.4	46.4	47.5	45.2	46.0
female	54.6	56.3	57.2	58.6	59.4	46.8	50.1	51.9	54.7	55.5	53.7	54.3
Age 40:												
male	31.2	31.7	31.9	33.0	34.0	27.3	28.7	28.3	29.8	30.3	28.8	29.1
female	35.6	37.1	38.1	39.4	40.1	29.8	32.2	33.9	36.3	36.8	35.3	35.7
Age 50:												
male	22.8	23.2	23.3	24.3	25.2	20.3	21.3	21.2	21.4	22.6	21.6	21.6
female	26.8	28.1	29.1	30.3	30.9	22.7	24.3	26.0	28.0	28.3	27.2	27.3
Age 65:												
male	12.8	13.0	13.0	13.7	14.2	12.8	12.8	12.9	13.6	13.5	13.1	12.9
female	15.0	15.9	16.9	18.1	18.5	14.5	15.1	16.0	17.9	17.3	16.7	16.5
Annual Deaths Expected per 1,000 Alive at Specified Age												
At birth:												
male	30.7	25.9	20.1	15.9	12.3	50.9	47.0	34.1	26.3	20.9	28.4	23.4
female	23.6	19.6	15.3	12.3	9.7	40.9	38.3	27.7	22.2	17.6	24.1	19.5
Age 20:												
male	1.6	1.6	1.9	1.8	1.8	3.1	2.4	3.6	2.7	2.3	2.8	2.4
female	.7	.6	.6	.6	.6	2.3	1.2	1.2	.9	.7	1.0	.7
Age 40:												
male	3.9	3.3	3.4	2.9	2.6	8.8	7.5	9.0	7.2	6.0	8.0	7.0
female	2.4	1.9	1.9	1.7	1.4	7.7	5.6	5.1	3.6	3.0	4.0	3.3
Age 50:												
male	10.1	9.6	8.9	8.0	7.1	19.1	15.7	16.8	14.9	13.4	16.2	15.1
female	5.6	4.7	4.7	4.2	3.8	16.0	11.7	10.1	7.9	7.0	8.5	7.8
Age 65:												
male	34.5	33.9	33.9	30.0	27.5	45.8	43.7	41.7	36.2	36.2	38.1	39.3
female	20.6	17.4	15.6	13.7	13.7	37.0	30.7	27.4	20.3	20.4	20.9	21.9
Number Surviving to Specified Age per 1,000 Born Live												
Age 20:												
male	951	959	964	970	975	919	931	943	956	964	954	961
female	965	971	976	980	983	935	947	959	968	974	966	972
Age 40:												
male	912	924	925	935	939	828	857	844	870	894	863	883
female	941	953	957	964	969	861	897	912	933	943	929	941
Age 50:												
male	856	874	877	890	901	729	772	747	787	819	772	798
female	907	925	929	939	947	770	830	850	883	903	876	893
Age 65:												
male	635	658	652	695	723	452	514	496	543	580	521	545
female	768	807	809	834	847	524	608	661	715	750	704	728

Note: *Prior to 1960, excludes Alaska and Hawaii. Beginning 1970, excludes deaths of nonresidents of the United States.*

Source: *Statistical Abstract of the United States, 1984.*

1.05 Estate Planning

WILLS

Any adult who has assets or personal property should consider drawing up a will. For those who have minor children, a current, valid will is a necessity. Among the compelling advantages of having a will are:

- One can choose one's beneficiaries, provide for their specific needs, and determine how and when they will receive their inheritances.

- One can establish trusts to oversee how older minors will receive assets and property, and thereby possibly eliminate the need to appoint a guardian or conservator.

- One can nominate the legal guardians for one's young minor children.

Intestacy

When a person dies without leaving a will, state law directs the way in which property in the estate will be distributed. While the laws governing intestacy are as fair and equitable as possible, they are an attempt to apply general principles to a variety of situations. Consequently, they are unlikely to conform to what the objectives of the deceased might have been.

The law applied is that of the state in which the deceased lived and owned real property. Though intestacy laws vary from state to state, there are common patterns.

SPOUSE

Depending on state of residence, a surviving spouse is entitled to from one-third to one-half of the estate. In some states, the spouse's share is equal to a child's share, and that share depends upon the number of children—if there were five children, the spouse would get one-sixth. In such a case, the spouse may become dependent on the children.

Under the intestate distribution laws of many states, a surviving spouse shares the estate with the deceased spouse's parents or siblings, or even nieces and nephews. Thus, a childless couple cannot assume that the surviving spouse will automatically inherit the entire estate.

CHILDREN

Except for what goes to the surviving spouse, the children are treated alike. If there is no surviving husband or wife, the children share the entire estate to the exclusion of all other relatives. Children of a deceased child usually inherit the share their parent would have taken.

MINORS

In the case of intestacy, the surviving children usually receive an outright inheritance, which makes it necessary to appoint a guardian, conservator, or trustee. This involves the complications of a bond, periodic accountings, and judicial proceedings for authorization for any action taken.

EXPENSES

When there is no will, the cost of administering the estate may be greater. In most states the administrator must furnish a bond to protect the beneficiaries and creditors of the estate. This premium cost must be paid either out of the estate or out of the administrator's fees. Also, in order for the administrator to sell property, distribute the estate, or settle claims, he must obtain judicial authorization. The cost of each proceeding or approval is paid out of the estate.

ADMINISTRATOR

The law selects the administrator of an intestate estate. Usually this means that the surviving spouse has the first right to be appointed. If the surviving spouse does not want to be the administrator or if there is no surviving spouse, the general rule is that the *children have an equal right* to be appointed—sometimes jointly.

TAXES

Intestacy may cost the estate unnecessary taxes, since the deceased will not have taken advantage of current regulations that might lessen the tax burden on the estate and, consequently, on the heirs.

Types of Wills

NUNCUPATIVE WILL

A nuncuptive will is an oral will, very restricted in its use. Most states limit it to situations where a lucid person is close to death and has no other will. It is applicable only to personal property and then to a very minimal amount, such as $1,000.

HOLOGRAPHIC WILL

A holographic will is a signed and dated will written entirely in the testator's own handwriting. In those states that permit them—about half—a holographic will is an acceptable legal document. Authenticity is sometimes a problem. Also, since the testator is not trained to write for those who will ultimately translate and implement the will, the document may not convey his or her intent, and misinterpretation may cause additional expense to the estate.

FORMAL, WITNESSED WILL

A formal, witnessed will must meet all legal formalities, with the format dependent on the state in which it pertains. The will must be subscribed at the end by the testator, or by someone acting in his or her behalf, in the testator's presence. The subscription must be done in the presence of the witnesses, who must see it done. The testator must declare that it is his or her will and request witnesses to witness the signature, though they are not required to read the will. Most states require two witnesses, but some require three. Each of the witnesses must sign at the end of the document at the testator's request and in the presence of both the testator and all other witnesses.

Spouses may state their mutual agreement as to the disposition of their joint estate upon the death of either. This is done by writing a joint and mutual will. Because of the potential for disastrous tax consequences related to the marital deduction and later disputes, joint and mutual wills are normally not recommended.

In most states a gift in a will to any of the witnesses is void. The possible exception would be situations in which the witness would have benefited as much had the testator died intestate, when such a witness would inherit at least the intestate share. To avoid possible complications, anyone benefitting from the will should not be chosen as a witness.

Capacity

The testator, to execute a valid will, must not only adhere to all the legal formalities but also possess the ability, or capacity, to make a will. One element of capacity is age. The minimum age to execute a will is usually eighteen or twenty-one, depending on the state. Another element is mental capacity, i.e., "being of sound mind." This need only exist as of the time the will is made, regardless of whether the testator was previously, or might in the future be, of unsound mind. Generally, it is required that the testator can remember and comprehend his relatives and property, as well as understand the nature of the act of making a will.

Codocils and Revocation

A will may be revised as often as the testator wishes by an amendment called a *codocil.* A codocil must meet the same formalities as those required of the original will. Should the will be amended several times, it would be wise to rewrite the entire will, to avoid the possibility of confusion.

The execution of a new will automatically revokes all prior, conflicting wills. Revoking a will also revokes its codicils. However, revoking a codicil does not revoke the will and may reinstate the prior amended provisions.

PROBATE

Probate is a process of law undertaken to prove the genuineness of a will. In the U.S., this validity is established in a civil court, which will, if necessary, also undertake to administer the will.

Survey of State Probate Fees

The following is a survey of the commissions or compensation allowed by the various states for administrators and executors. Some of the statutes provide for "reasonable compensation" of the representative. In those instances it should be determined what the customary practice is in the state or the local jurisdiction.

This information has been abstracted from the 1984 *Martindale-Hubbell Law Digest,* Volume VII. Please note that the statutes can be amended periodically by the states. (The information in parentheses is a reference to the specific code sections.)

ALABAMA

Administrators and executors are given such commissions on receipts and disbursements as the court may deem just and fair, but not in excess of 2½% upon receipts and 2½% upon disbursements. Court may also allow their actual expenses, including premiums on their bonds, and just compensation for extraordinary services. For selling lands for division they are allowed 2½% but not more than $100 unless lands are sold under terms of will (§ 433–680, 681).

ALASKA

A personal representative is entitled to reasonable compensation for his services. If a will provides for compensation of the personal representative and there is no contract with the decedent regarding compensation, he may renounce the provision before qualifying and be entitled to reasonable compensation. A personal representative also may renounce his right to all or any part of the compensation. A written renunciation of fee may be filed with the court.

ARIZONA

Representative is entitled to reasonable compensation for services. He may renounce compensation set forth in will and be entitled to reasonable compensation unless compensation is set by contract with decedent (§ 14–3719).

ARKANSAS

Compensation is allowable when and as earned but not to exceed 10% of first $1,000, 5% of next $4,000, and 3% of balance of value of personal property (§ 62.2208), but when personal representative has performed substantial duties with respect to real property, court may allow additional compensation to be borne as provided in will or by distributees benefited by such service (§ 62.2208).

Compensation for legal services, unless otherwise contracted with personal representative or heirs, is allowable on basis of total market value of real and personal property as follows: 5% of first $5,000; 4% of next $20,000; 3% of next $75,000; 2¾% of next $300,000; 2½% of next $600,000; and 2% of balance of value of all other property and may be increased if necessary to provide adequate compensation (§ 62.2208).

CALIFORNIA

Commissions of executors or administrators and fees for attorneys of either are each computed at rate of 4% on first $15,000; 3% on next $85,000; 2% on next $900,000; and 1% on all over $1,000,000 (Prob. C. 901, 910). Contract with heirs, devisees or legatees for higher compensation is void (Prob. C. 903), but provision in will fixing compensation of representatives will be enforced (Prob. C. 900). Court may allow additional commissions for extraordinary services (Prob. C. 902).

COLORADO

Same as Arizona (§ 15–12–719).

CONNECTICUT

Compensation to executor or administrator is allowed on his final account at such amount as is claimed by him if found by probate court to be reasonable, there being no statutory rate of compensation (98 Conn. 374, 119 Atl. 341). In practice, executors and administrators, particularly corporations, often compute their level of compensation on the basis of a fixed percentage of the gross estate administered.

DELAWARE

See Rule 132 of the Court of Chancery (§ 12–2305).

DISTRICT OF COLUMBIA

Reasonable compensation for work performed by personal representative, special administrator or attorney with respect to administration of estate, or additional compensation if will provides stated compensation for personal representative, may be paid upon approval by court of written request, to be accompanied by verified documentation of following: (1) reasonable relationship of proposed compensation to work, (2) statement by attorney that as soon as feasible he gave estimate of costs and any change in costs, (3) reasonableness of time spent, including hours and usual hourly compensation, (4) results achieved, (5) statement by personal representative that all time limitations have been met, or, if not met, dates of compliance and reasons for delay. Copy of request must be sent by certified or registered mail to all interested persons, who have 20 days to file exception (§ 20–751).

FLORIDA

Personal representatives, attorneys and others are entitled to reasonable compensation. Testamentary provision for compensation of personal representative may be renounced by the representative entitling him to reasonable compensation unless there is a contract with the decedent regarding compensation.

GEORGIA

Executors and administrators allowed commissions of 2½% on money received and 2½% on money paid out. Whenever any portion of dividends, interest or rents payable to an administrator or executor are required by law of the United States or other governmental unit to be withheld by person paying same for income tax purposes, amounts so withheld are deemed to have been collected by administrator or executor (§ 53–6–140). No commission on money paid to himself (§ 53–6–144). On property delivered in kind, probate judge may allow reasonable fee not exceeding 3% of value (§ 53–6–143). Reasonable expenses allowed, and extra compensation allowed for extraordinary service only so long as not compensated by corporation or other business enterprise (§ 53–6–148–151).

Testator and executor may agree by contract in writing on executor's compensation which shall be binding upon estate and executor, which fee must not exceed legal rate unless executor has regularly published fee schedule, in which case fee must not exceed schedule (§ 53–6–1).

HAWAII

Representatives are allowed fees and expenses as follows: On moneys received in nature of revenue or income, 7% on first $5,000 and 5% for all over $5,000, allowance being made on each accounting, but not oftener than once a year. On principal of estate, 5% on first $1,000, 4% on next $9,000, 3% on next $10,000, 2% for all over $20,000. Principal of estate is taken to be appraised value as of date of decedent's death, but no fees are allowed on real estate sold under foreclosure during administration, nor real estate subject to agreement of sale, save as to balance due from vendee. Court may make further allowance for special services, but contract for higher compensation is void (§ 607–18).

IDAHO

Same as Alaska.

ILLINOIS

Representatives and their attorneys are allowed reasonable compensation (§ 110.5–28–2).

INDIANA

In the absence of a provision for compensation in the will, a personal representative is entitled to just and reasonable compensation. Executors may renounce all claims for compensation provided for by the will before qualification and have their compensation determined by the court (IC 29–1–10–13).

IOWA

Executors and administrators are allowed reasonable fees, as determined by the court, not in excess of the following percentages upon gross assets listed for Iowa inheritance tax purposes: 6% on the first $1,000; 4% on the excess up to $5,000; 2% on the excess over $5,000. Fees of the attorney for the representative are determined in the same manner and subject to the same limitations. Further allowances may, however, be made by the court to executors or administrators and their attorneys for actual, necessary and extraordinary services or expenses (§ 633,197–199).

KANSAS

Executor or administrator is allowed his necessary expenses and reasonable compensation for his services and those of his attorneys (§ 59–1717). If will makes provision for executor's compensation, this must be taken as full compensation unless executor files waiver of will's provisions. Heir or beneficiary who prosecutes or defends action for benefit of estate may receive expenses (§ 59–1504). If executor or administrator fails or refuses to perform any duty imposed on him by law, he may be removed and his compensation reduced or forfeited in discretion of court (§ 59–1711).

KENTUCKY

Compensation of representatives may not exceed 5% of the value of the personal estate plus 5% of income collected, except that the court may allow additional compensation for services that are unusual and extraordinary and for services in connection with real estate or with estate or inheritance taxes (KRS 395.150, construed in 292 Ky. 701, 168 S.W.2d 24).

LOUISIANA

Executor allowed reasonable amount as is provided in testament in which he is appointed; administrator allowed such reasonable amount as is provided by agreement between administrator and surviving spouse, and all competent heirs or legatees of deceased. In absence of specified testamentary amount or agreement with survivors, executor or administrator is entitled to fee of 2½% on value of estate, as appraised in inventory (C.C.P. 3351, as amended Act 281 of 1982).

MAINE

Same as Alaska.

MARYLAND

Unless larger measure is provided by will, court may allow such commissions as it deems appropriate, but not to exceed 10% on first $20,000 and 4% on balance over $20,000 (§ 7–601(b)). Real estate (but not income thereon for estates of decedents dying on or after July 1, 1974 only) is excluded from estate in computation of commissions, but court may allow commissions not to exceed 10% on real estate sold by personal representative. (§ 7–601(d)). Fees paid to broker are expense of administration and not deducted from commissions. (§ 7–601(b), (d)). If will provides stated compensation, additional compensation shall be allowed if provision is deemed insufficient by court (§ 7601(a)). Personal representative must give notice to all unpaid creditors and interested persons of commissions and counsel fees, including expenses of litigation, requested and basis for same and of right to hearing; any request for hearing must be filed within 20 days; other court approval is final. (§ 7–502, 7–602, 7–603).

MASSACHUSETTS

Administrators and executors are entitled to compensation for services as court may allow (c. 206, § 16). No statutory rate, but compensation at rate of 6% or 7% of income and, on principal, 5% on first $100,000, 4% on next $200,000, and diminishing percentages on balance is customarily considered not unreasonable. In certain instances, larger compensation may be approved.

MICHIGAN

Fiduciaries shall be allowed reasonable compensaton for expenses and services as approved by the court. (MCLA § 700.541; MSA § 27–5541).

MINNESOTA

Same as Alaska.

MISSISSIPPI

The court fixes in its own discretion the compensation of an executor or administrator, but such compensation may not exceed 7% of the entire estate (§ 91-7-299). Executor or administrator credited for attorney's fees where attorney's services proper (§ 91-7-281).

MISSOURI

Compensation of representative is a commission on personal property and proceeds of sale of realty. Scale is specified in § 473.153.

NEBRASKA

Same as Alaska.

NEVADA

Compensation of administrator and of executor, unless specific compensation is provided by the will, is at following rates on personal estate accounted for: 6% on first $1,000; 4% on next $4,000; 2% on excess over $5,000. If there are two or more executors or administrators, compensation is apportioned (§ 150.020). Further allowances for extraordinary services such as management, sales, litigation and services concerning realty may be made by court (§ 150.030). Contracts for compensation higher than that allowed by statute are void (§ 150.040).

Claim against executor is not affected by his being named as such in the will, but his commissions must be applied on his debt to the estate (§ 144.050).

Attorney for executor or administrator in charge of decedent's estate is entitled to reasonable compensation paid out of estate, in amount agreed to by attorney and executor or administrator or, in absence of agreement, set by court (§ 150.060).

NEW HAMPSHIRE

No statutory provisions. As a matter of practice, the executor or administrator presents a claim for compensation when he renders his account to the probate court, and the same, if deemed reasonable, is allowed to be paid out of the estate.

NEW JERSEY

Commission of 5% on first $100,000; and on excess, such percentage, not exceeding 5%, as court may determine. Additional commissions may be allowed by the court upon a showing of unusual or extraordinary services (Tit. 3B, c.18, § 1, 14-17; Rule 4:88-1).

NEW MEXICO

Same as Arizona (§ 45-3-719).

NEW YORK

Commission of 5% for receiving and paying out the first $100,000, 4% for the next $200,000, 3% for the next $700,000, 2½% for the next $4,000,000 and 2% for all sums over $5,000,000. Value of any property received or distributed, except in case of specific legacy or devise, is considered money in computing commissions (S.C.P.A. § 2307).

NORTH CAROLINA

Personal representatives, collectors or public administrators are entitled to commission in discretion of clerk, not exceeding 5% of receipts and expenditures that shall appear to be fairly made in course of administration; provided clerk may fix commission where estate is $2,000 or less (§ 28A–23–3).

NORTH DAKOTA

Same as Alaska.

OHIO

Compensation is 4% on first $100,000, 3% on next $300,000 and 2% on balance of estate, determined with reference to personal property and income received and accounted for, and proceeds of real estate sold under testamentary power. Further commission of 1% allowed on real estate not sold and property not subject to probate administration but includable for purpose of computing Ohio estate tax, except joint and survivor property (§ 2113.35). Compensation for extraordinary services governed by § 2113.36. Services in land sale proceedings are compensated as court deems fit (§ 2127.38). Attorneys' fees are set by court rule (§ 2113.36).

OKLAHOMA

If not provided for in the will or if renounced, commission, excluding property not ranked as assets, at the rate of 5% on the first $1,000, 4% on the next $4,000, 2½% on excess over $5,000. Further allowance not exceeding the above rates of commission may be made by district judge for extraordinary services (§ 58–525).

OREGON

Upon application to court, personal representative is entitled to receive compensation for services, as follows: (a) Upon property subject to jurisdiction of court, including income and realized gains: (1) 7% of any sum not exceeding $1,000, (2) 4% of all above $1,000 and not exceeding $10,000, (3) 3% of all above $10,000 and not exceeding $50,000, (4) 2% of all above $50,000; (b) 1% of property, exclusive of life insurance proceeds, not subject to jurisdiction of court, but reportable for Oregon inheritance tax or federal estate tax purposes. In all cases, such further compensation as is just and reasonable may be allowed by court. When decedent by his will has made special provision for compensation, personal representative is not entitled to any other compensaton for services unless prior to employment he signs and files with clerk of court written renunciation of compensation provided by will (§ 116.173).

PENNSYLVANIA

Compensation as is just and reasonable. Compensation may be calculated on a graduated percentage (§ 20–3537).

RHODE ISLAND

Compensation is at the discretion of the court (§ 33–14–8).

SOUTH CAROLINA

Commissions for administering: 2½% on appraised value of personal assets received and 2½% on appraised value of personal assets paid out; for lending money at interest, 10% on interest received; no commission on collection of debt of executor or administrator of estate (§ 21–15–1450). Additional compensation for extra services, not to exceed 5% more than amount already allowed, may be allowed by court of common pleas (upon verdict of jury) on action brought therefor (§ 21–15–1460).

SOUTH DAKOTA

Unless executor accepts such provision as is made for him by will, he must be allowed commissions upon amount of personal property accounted for by him, excluding all personal property not ranked as assets, as follows: On first $1,000 at rate of 5%; on all sums in excess of $1,000 and under $5,000, at rate of 4%; on all sums in excess of $5,000, at rate of 2½%. Upon all real property accounted for by him, executor is entitled to receive just compensation for services performed. All real estate sold as part of proceedings in probate must be considered as personal property. Administrators are allowed same commissions and compensation as executors for like services (§ 30–25–6 to 10).

TENNESSEE

Reasonable compensation for the representative (§ 30–736).

TEXAS

Executors and administrators may retain 5% on all sums received in cash and 5% on all sums paid in cash. This commission is not allowed for receiving cash on hand at decedent's death or for paying money to heirs or legatees, as such, but commission can never be more than 5% of gross fair market value of estate. Adjustments can be made for management of business (Prob. C. § 241).

VERMONT

Compensation of $4 per day while attending to duties of office. Further compensation may be allowed in cases of unusual difficulty or responsibility (§ 32–1143).

UTAH

Same as Alaska.

VIRGINIA

Reasonable compensation is allowed; usually 5%, but may vary depending on performance (213 Va. 165).

WASHINGTON

Compensation is what court deems just and reasonable unless fixed by will (§ 11.48.210).

WEST VIRGINIA

Reasonable compensation; usually 5% on receipts (c.44, art. 4, § 12).

WISCONSIN

Personal representative is allowed all necessary expenses and commissions at rate of 2% of inventory value of property for which personal representative is accountable, less mortgages or liens, plus net corpus gains. Court may allow further sums in cases of unusual difficulty or extraordinary services. If personal representative is derelict in duty, compensation may be reduced or denied. If personal representative or his law firm also serves as attorney for estate, court may allow either commissions or attorney's fees or may allow both if will authorizes payment (§ 857.05).

WYOMING

Statutory fees are as follows: on first $1,000, 10%; from $1,000 to $5,000, 5%; between $5,000 and $20,000, 3%; for amounts over $20,000, 2%. In case of extraordinary services, extra allowance may be made by court (§ 2–7–803). Contracts between beneficiaries and personal representatives for fees larger than those provided by statute are void (§ 2–7–805).

Source: *Martindale-Hubbell Law Digest*, Volume VII. © 1984. Reprinted with permission.

Probate Timetable

The following outline traces the course of an average probate. However, because state probate laws vary, this table cannot account for any particular process.

TASK	USUAL TIME PERIOD
File petition for probate of will, or for letters of administration in Intestacy	Up to 30 days after death
Publish or post notice to creditors	Immediately upon granting of petition for probate
Apply for family or widow's allowance, or probate homestead	Immediately upon granting of petition for probate
Gather assets and prepare formal inventory of estate; present to appraiser if required	Promptly after representative assumes his office
Period for notice to creditors elapses	Varies widely; normally from 2 to 6 months after first publication or posting
Sell estate property to raise cash for taxes or distribution	Any time after representative is appointed
Make preliminary distributions	Usually after notice to creditors period elapses
Prepare and file state inheritance tax papers	Usually from 6 to 9 months after appointment of representative
Alternate valuation date for federal estate tax purposes	6 months after date of death
Where no federal estate tax return required, make final accounting and distribution, and close estate	Approximately one month after notice to creditors period elapses and state taxes paid
File federal estate tax return and pay federal estate taxes	9 months after date of death, unless extensions applied for and granted
Where no wish to wait for audit of federal return, make final accounting and distribution, and close estate	Approximately 1 to 2 months after estate tax paid
Keep estate open until federal return is audited, or audit period elapses	3 years after estate tax return is filed
When audit period elapses, make final accounting and distribution, and close estate	1 to 3 months after audit period elapses
To keep securing income tax advantages of probate estate, keep it open	As long as possible
Gigantic or extraordinarily complex estates	May stay open for many years

Source: Peter E. Lippett, *Estate Planning After The Reagan Tax Cut,* 1982. Reprinted with permission of Reston Publishing Company, a Prentice-Hall Company, 11480 Sunset Hills Rd., Reston, Va. 22090.

PROPERTY AND TITLING

A single person holding title to property in his or her name alone need not be too concerned about estate planning problems, as that property would descend to heirs either by will or intestacy. However, in cases of co-ownership, in marriage or otherwise, the effects of titling on estate planning must be considered.

In community property states, until recently, any property in the husband's name alone was presumed to be community property. In contrast, property in a wife's name alone was considered to be her own separate property, unless an alternative was clearly expressed. This also applied to any property the wife held in common with persons other than her spouse. The presumption about the husband's holdings still remains. However, it is now generally understood that property in the wife's name, either alone or in common with others, is also presumed to be community property and no longer her own separate property.

Sole and Separate Property

If a spouse does have property that should be recognized as separate property, title should be in that spouse's name, with the addition of the wording: *"as his(her) Sole and Separate Property."*

Couples in community property states should clearly differentiate between that which is separate property and that which should be regarded as community property. The wording for the latter would be: *"John and Mary Jones, as Community Property."*

Tenancy in Common

There are few problems associated with tenancy in common, because each owner's undivided interest is treated as property owned by a single person; it will descend to the owner's heirs either by will or intestacy. However, tenants in common might create an agreement whereby the surviving co-tenants would have the right to buy out the decedent's heirs, thus avoiding co-ownership with these heirs. Thus, a relatively simple device would in effect become an estate planning document.

Joint Tenancy

The built-in right of survivorship that is inherent to joint tenancy ownership can be costly for wealthier married couples. In most instances, joint tenancy can, and probably will, result in unnecessary death taxes. There is widespread ignorance of this problem, even among real estate professionals, escrow officers, and accountants. Consequently, people are often erroneously counseled to take title to property in this way.

The critical factor is that joint tenancy limits the step-up basis (revaluation of basis using current market value) at death, confining the new basis to the portion included in the decedent's gross estate. Since joint tenancy goes automatically to the surviving spouse outright, no tax reducing or tax eliminating plans are possible with title held in this form. Because of changes in tax law, this problem will become a factor by 1987 if the total marital estate is worth more than $600,000.

Example:

Assume Mr. and Mrs. Jones have $1,500,000 worth of property held in joint tenancy in 1987. Mrs. Jones dies and the property in her estate is worth $750,000. Because of the right of survivorship, this passes automatically to Mr. Jones and qualifies for the unlimited marital deduction, with no tax owing at this time.

When Mr. Jones dies, all the property is subject to taxation; the tax would be $363,000. Had the property not been held in joint tenancy, the first spouse to die could have put the exempt amount in a by-pass trust, leaving the balance to the survivor in a way that would qualify for the marital deduction. In this way, there would be no tax at the first death and less tax upon the second. The use of another form of titling would have permitted other tax saving devices, resulting in a tax of $114,000—a savings of $249,000.

Community Ownership

Since stepped-up basis applies to the whole of community property, regardless of which spouse dies first, this form is most desirable for appreciated property. Otherwise, the increased basis only applies to the decedent's undivided interest in tenancy-in-common property, or to the half of joint tenancy property that is to be included in the decedent's gross estate.

Community property also offers continuing options for estate planning (e.g., taxes, trusts, etc.), as well as probate avoidance for property passing to the spouse (by joint tenancy) or flexibility of disposition, where that is more critical (by tenancy in common).

Transfer of Property

Under the Tax Reduction Act of 1984, property transfers between spouses — or incident to divorce, between former spouses — will not result in recognition of loss or gain. The transferee will hold the property at the transferrer's base. This applies to transfers after July 18, 1984 (other than transfers pursuant to agreements in effect on that date where the parties do not elect to have these provisions apply). Parties may elect to have the provisions apply to transfers after December 31, 1983.

Titling is a complex area of law, and most questions about how to take title to property can be resolved only in consultation with an attorney.

TRUST AND ESTATE PLANNING

The two major types of trust are *testamentary* and *living* (or *inter vivos*). Testamentary trusts are those created by will that only become effective upon death. The governing provisions are included in the trustor's will rather than in a separate trust document. When probate is concluded, property is distributed to the newly created trust, not to the individual heirs.

Living trusts are created by an agreement for application during one's lifetime, but may continue after death. The advantage of living over testamentary trusts is that the former are not subject to probate, since the trustee rather than the decedent is the legal owner of the property. Even if the decedent were also the trustee, there would be no probate, because this trusteeship would be considered an office that would outlive the current occupant. Should a trustee die, a successor trustee then assumes the office: the trusteeship continues uninterrupted.

State laws and the terms of the trust agreement dictate what the trust does and how it will operate. These laws vary from state to state, but generally apply various limitations on the powers of the trustee and on the length of time the property can be held in trust. No state will allow a trust to operate indefinitely (except in the cases of charitable or employee trusts).

Within the guidelines set up by the state in which the trust will be effective, the person who creates the trust, the trustor, can determine how the trust will operate. The trustor determines the purpose of the trust, the amount and type of property it will contain, the length of time it will last, the beneficiaries, how much they will receive, and when they will receive it. The trustor can also specify conditions that a beneficiary must meet in order to receive income or principal from the trust.

Changes in Trust Taxation

Before the Tax Reform Act of 1984, it was possible to reduce income taxes by creating more than one trust having the same grantor and beneficiaries. Because trusts are taxed as separate entities under separate, progressive tax rate schedules, overall tax savings could be realized by splitting assets and income among the trusts. The 1984 Tax Reform Act adopts a consolidation rule for multiple or mirror trusts for years beginning after March 1, 1984, if the trust has substantially the same grantor and beneficiary and the principal reason for the trust is tax avoidance. There is also a two-trust rule, which pre-dates the 1984 Act and continues after that Act, that limits the favorable treatment available for distributions of accumulated income.

Court Trusts and Non-Court Trusts

A court, or judicially supervised, trust is subject to the ongoing jurisdiction of the probate court. The trustee must make periodic accountings to the court of all income and all expenditures. When the accounting has been submitted and approved, a court judgment is issued that ratifies, confirms and approves all the acts and transactions of the trustee. This protects the trustee from liability for any acts or omissions covered by the accounting and approved by the court. The trustee may also seek instruction from the court in dealing with difficult or confusing issues. The court will then provide a court judgment, instructing him as to how he should proceed. This provides the trustee with protection against any future allegations of wrongdoing.

In most states, a living trust is not subject to the jurisdiction of any court and is thus a non-court, or non-judicially supervised, trust. This frees the trustee from having to go to court with periodic accountings, but it also removes the protection of a court judgment covering his actions. Some states, such as California, have modified traditional aspects of court and non-court trusts so that the trustee may voluntarily submit accountings and requests for instruction.

Revocable and Irrevocable Trusts

In some states, a living trust is assumed to be revocable unless otherwise specified, while in other states a living trust must expressly be declared as revocable.

A trustor can always change a revocable trust, either wholly or in part, during the remainder of his life. An irrevocable trust is a serious, irreversible step. Neither the trust nor any of its terms can be changed in any way or form—no matter what the reasons might be.

ADVANTAGES OF IRREVOCABLE TRUSTS

Irrevocable trusts, in general, offer two advantages over revocable trusts: income and estate tax savings. A person who sets up an irrevocable trust will not have to pay any income taxes on the trust fund's income, provided that:

- The trustor does not receive any of this income

- It is not used to support someone the trustor is already legally obligated to support

- It is not used to discharge the trustor's legal obligations

- It is not accumulated for the trustor or the trustor's spouse

- The income is not used to pay premiums on life insurance for the trustor or the trustor's spouse

- Certain powers are not returned or transferred to a non-adverse party (friend or family)

In this manner, the trust operates just as the lifetime gift does: taxes are avoided by diverting income to low-bracket taxpayers or by creating new taxpayers.

Property in an irrevocable living trust is not taxed in the trustor's gross estate. This means little, however, since the value of the transfer has already paid transfer taxes and is added back to the estate to compute the estate's tax bracket. The gift tax is based on the value of the property at the date of the gift, and thus all appreciation in the value of that property is not taxable in the gross estate.

ADVANTAGES OF REVOCABLE TRUSTS

The revocable trust offers its own advantages, the major one being an avoidance of probate. Because property transferred into the trust then belongs to the trustee rather than the trustor, it is not considered to be part of the estate. If a revocable trust is to be used in order to avoid probate, it must be funded. That is, property must be legally transferred into the ownership of the trustee. Revocable trusts have other advantages. Trustors can:

- Avoid publicity and interruption of income to family members as the trust continues operating the day following the trustor's death

- Provide for future incapacity of the grantor and thus eliminate the need for a court-controlled conservatorship

- In some states place property beyond the reach of creditors

- Develop or supervise an inexperienced trustee

Pour-Over Trusts

A pour-over trust is a living trust under which only a portion of the trustor's property is held in trust during his lifetime, and the remaining property is willed to the trust upon his death. This technique can effectively place the bulk of a trustor's estate outside court jurisdiction, since the property ''pours over'' into a non-court living trust. It has the additional advantage of keeping the property within the trustor's control during his or her lifetime. To set up the trust, a minimal amount of property, i.e., $100, must be placed within the trust during the trustor's lifetime.

An added advantage is that a non-court trust may easily be moved from state to state if an out-of-state trustee is used. This is not a method for avoiding probate, since the property must pass through probate as it moves into the trust.

Life Insurance Trusts

Living trusts in which the property is the ownership of a policy of life insurance or in which a trust would be the beneficiary of a life insurance policy are called life insurance trusts. Such trusts provide trustee management over the proceeds of the policy. They also capitalize on the tax advantages of trust ownership. If carefully written, the irrevocable life insurance trust can shelter the proceeds not only from the insured's gross estate, but also:

- From the probate estate of the beneficiary

- From the gross estate of the spouse or other contemporary or older-generation donee

- From the gross estates and partially from the generation-skipping transfers of children of the insured (to the extent of $250,000 each)

The trust, putting aside the proceeds outright, also permits income-tax planning for the future earnings of the insurance proceeds. In addition, it offers the advantages of property management and flexibility with respect to the benefits and eventual disposition of the property.

An irrevocable life insurance trust may be funded or unfunded. The income from funding assets will be taxable to the donor-insured to the extent that the income may be used to pay premiums. If unfunded, future premium payments by the donor will constitute additional gifts, and those payments made within three years of death are still subject to taxes.

The Crummey Doctrine

One method for obtaining annual exclusions for gifts upon the creation of a trust and upon the subsequent payment of premiums is through the use of immediate powers of withdrawal vested in one or more trust beneficiaries. Incorporating this option within a trust is referred to as "using Crummey powers." The Crummey doctrine may apply even though the policyholder is a minor for whom no guardian has been appointed, provided this does not conflict with local law. The power of withdrawal would be limited in duration so as to arise and expire in the year in which a particular transfer or addition to the trust takes place. The terms of the trust require:

- That the trustee promptly notify the donee in writing of any additions and of his or her withdrawal rights; and

- That withdrawable liquid funds be required to be kept on hand throughout the duration of those withdrawal rights.

The contribution for each beneficiary and the right of withdrawal of each will generally be limited to the sum of $10,000, as this is the likely dollar amount for disregarding what would otherwise be considered "lapses" of general powers of appointment. If not exercised, the power of withdrawal would enable the trust to qualify for the annual exclusion under the Crummey doctrine, and the power of withdrawal would then cease to exist. This can generally be structured so that the lapse is not treated as a taxable lapse for estate and gift tax purposes.

Because the Crummey doctrine, with respect to irrevocable life insurance trusts, is not altogether developed at this time, it is important to seek professional assistance in drawing up a trust in which these withdrawal powers are incorporated.

Clifford Trusts

A Clifford trust is an irrevocable trust lasting more than ten years after the date of transfer of property, after which the property reverts to the original creator of the trust. It is used primarily as an income tax-saving device, and may, in fact, make the trustor's estate or gift taxes more costly. If appreciated property is contributed to the trust and sold, the grantor in most cases is taxed currently on the income from the sale. With careful drafting, the trust income will be taxed to the beneficiary during the ten-year period. If the beneficiary is in a much lower income tax bracket than is the trustor, significant income taxes may be saved annually over the ten-year period.

The cost of establishing such a trust is that gift taxes apply to the transaction. These taxes are based on the present value of receiving the income from the property over the ten-year period. Generally, discount tables—based on a discount or income factor of 10%—are used to value the gift aspects of the transfer to the trust. Under these tables, the present value of the right to income from a ten-year trust is currently 61.4457%. This results in a transfer of $16,274 having a gift value of under $10,000, resulting in no gift tax (up to a maximum of $32,549 for joint gifts). Should the trustor die during the course of the trust, the then present value of the reversionary interest in the trust property will be taxed in the gross estate. If the trustor dies after the ten-year period, and the trust property has reverted back to him or her, the total value of the property will be included in the total estate.

Bypass Trusts

In order to avoid either the double death taxes or the second tax, it is possible to create a trust giving the surviving spouse or beneficiary a lifetime interest, and thus bypass estate taxes at the second death. Bypass trusts are not limited to married persons; they can be used by anyone wishing to leave a beneficial interest in property to any other person.

Marital Deduction Trusts

As a result of the Economic Recovery Tax Act of 1981, married persons may either give during their lifetime or leave at death an unlimited amount of their assets to the other spouse. The dollar limit and the percentage limitation on marital transfers have been entirely removed. In order to qualify for the marital deduction, property transferred to a spouse may be left either outright by specific bequests in a will, by having jointly held property pass automatically to the surviving spouse, or by leaving assets in a trust from which the surviving spouse receives all the income (paid at least annually) and has the unrestricted right to control the principal during lifetime or at death (or both if this power is desired).

It may not always be desirable to transfer all the estate of the first spouse to die to the other spouse. Among other things, it may be preferable to leave enough out of the marital deduction trust to take full advantage of the decedent's exemption equivalent amount ($275,000 in 1983 through 1986, and $600,000 in 1987 and thereafter). By using the marital deduction and then the exemption equivalent amount, estate plans may be structured so that the exemptive amount is set aside in a bypass trust and the remaining assets go into a marital trust or outright to the surviving spouse. This will ensure that assets held in the bypass trust will not be taxed at either the death of the first or surviving spouse.

Qualified Terminable Interest Property (Q-Tip) Trusts

The Q-Tip trust also qualifies for the marital deduction and offers a major advantage in not requiring the "power of appointment," which benefits a spouse who would otherwise forfeit the tax advantages of the marital deduction because of concerns about giving a surviving spouse the freedom to decide who, at his or her death, will inherit the property, e.g., children from a previous marriage. Trusts with a general power of appointment allow the surviving spouse to direct the property to whomever he or she wishes.

The nickname "Q-Tip" derived from tax laws which state that to qualify for the marital deduction, the property left to the survivor must not be a "terminable interest," and called this manner of marital deduction allowance "qualifying terminable interest property."

In a Q-Tip trust, it must be specified that the surviving spouse will receive all of the annual income and that during the surviving spouse's lifetime no one can appoint any part of the property to anyone other than the surviving spouse. An executor must make this election on the decedent spouse's estate tax return. To use this trust with the exempt amount plan, the exempt amount goes into a standard bypass trust so that it won't be taxed at the survivor's death, and the balance of the marital property goes into the Q-Tip trust.

In both the bypass and the Q-Tip trust, the decedent spouse can name the remainder beneficiaries upon the surviving spouse's death. The power of appointment trust would now be used primarily by a couple wanting the survivor to reassess the estate in the future in order to select the beneficiaries.

Charitable Remainder Trusts

A trustor may leave property in trust to a spouse or to some other person for life, with the balance eventually going to a charity. There currently are three trusts in which the remainder will qualify for a charitable deduction: pooled income fund, charitable remainder annuity trust, and charitable remainder unitrust. A pooled income fund is maintained by a charitable organization for the purpose of receiving contributions from a variety of donors, such that each life beneficiary receives a specified portion of the fund's annual income. This percentage is based upon a comparison of the value of what was contributed to the value of the fund at the time of the contribution. The principal cannot be used; upon the death of the life beneficiary, the charity becomes the outright owner of that contributed amount.

The charitable remainder annuity trust and charitable remainder unitrust are quite similar:

- The beneficiary annually receives a predetermined amount from the trust either throughout his life or for less than 20 years, though method of calculation differs.

- The beneficiary cannot normally deplete the principal, nor can anyone else, except where it might be necessary to augment deficiencies in the predetermined amount.

With the charitable remainder annuity trust, the beneficiary must receive a specified, identical amount each year—either an absolute dollar amount or a percentage of the fair market value of the trust. Usually, the guaranteed annual amount must be a minimum of 5% of the initial fair market value of the trust.

The only difference between the charitable remainder unitrust and the charitable remainder annuity relates to the guaranteed amount. Although the charitable remainder unitrust is subject to the 5% rule, it can be a fixed percentage of the fair market value of the trust assets as determined annually. The charitable remainder annuity trust fixes the guaranteed amount when the trust is created.

An interspousal transfer, either during life or upon death, may qualify for the marital deduction if the spouse is granted an annuity or unitrust interest in a qualified charitable remainder trust in which the other spouse (and the donor, in the case of an inter vivos transfer) is the only noncharitable beneficiary. Both the life interest and the charitable remainder are then deductible for income tax purposes.

Sprinkling Trusts

A sprinkling trust allows an independent trustee to "sprinkle" or "spray" income among a group of beneficiaries. This gives the trust flexibility and minimizes family tax costs.

As an example, a grandmother might create a trust with the income going to her children and grandchildren in such amounts as "the trustee may determine." At a later date, the trustor's oldest grandchild enters college for which the yearly expenses would be $6,000. If her father were in the 50% tax bracket and called on the trust for help, he would have to withdraw about $12,000 from the trust in order to pay this $6,000. However, because the trustee has sprinkling powers, he can, using the granddaughter's lower tax bracket, withdraw only $7,200 from the trust fund to produce the $6,000, which he would pay directly to the granddaughter.

Spendthrift Provisos

A trust with a spendthrift provision may be used to prevent a potentially irresponsible beneficiary from assigning or selling his or her interest in the trust by placing it beyond the reach of creditors. It is usually structured to provide that the beneficiary's interest will not be included in his estate if he goes bankrupt, and that the interest may not be touched by a creditor who may have obtained a judgment or claim against him.

The spendthrift provision may also allow the trustee to use his own discretion, handling money on the beneficiary's behalf as he sees fit, rather than making large distributions to the beneficiary. For example, the trustee might pay the beneficiary's rent and other specified necessities out of trust income, while attempting to conserve the bulk of the property within the trust.

Other Types of Trusts

A *support trust* is one in which the income is specifically directed to support one or more beneficiaries. *Accumulation trusts* accumulate income within the trust, hold the funds until a given date, and then distribute them as principal. A *discretionary trust* gives the trustee the power to allocate the income among the various beneficiaries as he or she sees fit, rather than providing for distributions at the will of the trustor (as is the case with a "sprinkling" trust).

Commonly Used Trusts

TYPE	MAJOR IDENTIFYING CHARACTERISTIC
Pour-over trust	A living trust designed to receive property to be "poured over" from the trustor's will via his probate estate
Life insurance trust	A living trust designed to receive the proceeds of life insurance and sometimes also to own life insurance
Clifford trust	A living trust, established for tax reasons, to last at least ten years
Bypass trust	A trust that gives a surviving spouse or beneficiary a lifetime interest, to avoid estate taxes on second death
Marital deduction trust	A trust that takes advantage of the ERTA marital deduction by placing assets in trust, so that the survivor has control of both income and principal
Q-Tip trust	A trust, also qualifying for the marital deduction, in which the spouse has rights to income from the trust until his or her death but has no control over the property within the trust
Charitable trust	A trust that has a charity as its beneficiary
Support trust	A trust designed to provide the funds necessary to support a beneficiary
Accumulation trust	A trust that retains, rather than distributing, all the income it earns
Discretionary trust **Sprinkling trust**	Both are trusts in which the trustee has the power to retain or pay out the income earned in whatever proportions he deems best
Spendthrift trust	A trust in which the principal is protected from a beneficiary's creditors

Source: Peter E. Lippett, *Estate Planning After the Reagan Tax Cut*, 1982. Reprinted with permission of Reston Publishing Company, a Prentice-Hall Company, 11480 Sunset Hills Road, Reston, Va. 22090.

1.06 Individual Retirement Accounts

Anyone who has earned income may establish an Individual Retirement Account (IRA). The advantages of an IRA are its flexibility and administrative simplicity. An IRA is easy to establish through the financial institutions that handle such accounts and usually have standardized forms, which have been approved by the IRS, to be executed when an IRA investment is made. An IRA is flexible in that the funds may be moved from one type of account to another; from, for example, certificates of deposit to common stock. Among the questions commonly asked about IRAs are the following.

How much money can be invested in an IRA each year?

A maximum of $2,000, or 100% of an individual's taxable compensation for the year, whichever is *less*. If both a husband and wife are wage earners, each may contribute up to this limit.

What is the rule if a spouse is not employed?

The working spouse can contribute to an account for the benefit of the nonworking spouse. This IRA belongs to the nonworking spouse. The total combined amount that may be contributed each year to the wage earner's and the nonworking spouse's accounts is $2,250 or 100% of the working spouse's compensation for the year, whichever is less. The contributions between the two accounts may be divided as the couple wishes, provided neither exceeds $2,000 per year.

What kind of compensation qualifies?

Compensation may be wages, salaries, tips, professional fees, bonuses, and other amounts earned for providing personal services. Commissions and net income obtained from self-employment also are considered compensation. An active partner's share of the partnership's earned income is compensation. Unearned income such as rental income, interest income, and dividend income is not considered compensation. For years after 1984 alimony that is includable in a divorced person's gross income is considered compensation that qualifies for contributions to an IRA.

Is there a minimum amount of time a person must work each year to qualify for an IRA?

No.

Is there a lower or upper income limit for IRA eligibility?

No.

Are part-time workers eligible?

Yes.

Is there a minimum amount that must be contributed to an IRA each year?

No.

May investments into an IRA be staggered over the year?

Yes, or the entire amount may be invested at one time.

What is the cutoff date for contributions to the IRA each year?

Under the Tax Reform Act of 1984 and effective December 31, 1984, contributions for the current tax year may be made through the due date for that year's income tax return, i.e., April 15 of the following year. Individuals filing for and obtaining filing extensions can no longer make late contributions.

Where may IRA money be invested?

IRA money may be invested in passbook savings accounts, certificates of deposit, annuities, mutual funds (including money market funds), individual stocks and bonds, certain kinds of real estate, such as real estate limited partnerships, government retirement bonds, and credit unions.

Are any investments excluded?

Yes. Assets used to acquire a collectible are treated as immediate distributions from the account and are taxed accordingly. They may also be subject to penalties for premature distribution. Collectibles include works of art, antiques, gems, rugs, metals, stamps, coins, and alcoholic beverages. Money invested in life insurance contracts generally does not qualify for an IRA contribution, but annuities do qualify.

Can a person have more than one IRA account in one year?

Yes. Provided the total contributions to all accounts do not exceed 100% of compensation or $2,000, whichever is less.

Is there a penalty for investing more than the deductible limit into an IRA in any one year?

Yes. An excise tax of 6% is levied on any amount contributed beyond the deductible amount—unless the excess and any earnings on the excess are taken out before the due date for income tax filing.

Can a person request distributions to be paid directly to him?

Yes. However, distributions from the IRA paid to the participant may be subject to federal withholding tax. Unless the participant files a written election with the custodian not to have income tax withheld from a distribution that is requested to be made directly to the participant, the custodian will withhold federal income tax from the distribution.

May IRA accounts be moved?

Yes. An individual may withdraw part or all of the assets in an IRA and invest them in another IRA, tax free. This is commonly called a *rollover.* The reinvestment must be completed within 60 days after the withdrawal, and individuals are limited to one rollover in any 12-month period. If the money does not pass through the individual's hands but is handled exclusively by the institutions involved, the transaction is not considered a rollover and the one-year waiting period does not apply.

Is there a minimum age requirement on opening an IRA account?

No. One may not, however, make payments to an IRA in or after the year in which one will reach 70½ years of age.

When can I begin withdrawing from my IRA?

Normally, you can start withdrawals at the age of 59½. Early withdrawals are permitted in the case of disability or death.

How is money in an IRA normally paid out?

The money can be paid out in a single payment between the age of 59½ and the end of the year during which you reach 70½. Or you may receive regular payments over a fixed period of time that is not greater than your life expectancy or the combined life expectancy of you and your spouse. You may also choose an annuity that would make regular payments for life or the combined lives of you and your spouse. Payments must begin by the end of the tax year during which you become 70½.

Must I withdraw money by a certain age?

You must begin receiving payments from your account before the end of the year in which you became 70½, whether you are retired or not. You may not invest any money after you reach 70½. There is a heavy penalty for failing to make proper distribution of the money.

What factors should I consider in determining when to begin receiving retirement income from my account?

Since everything you receive is taxed as ordinary income, your timing decision should take into account:

- Your financial needs and desires
- Taxation laws at the time
- Your other income
- Your estate planning needs

You might want to receive regular monthly amounts to replace the salary you give up upon retirement, or draw out the entire amount if you have an overriding need for a large amount of capital.

Is money placed into an IRA taxed each year?

No. You deduct your contribution from your gross income and thereby exclude it from your taxable income. Once you begin making withdrawals from your IRA, you pay taxes on the amounts withdrawn.

Is there a penalty for early withdrawals?

Early withdrawals are taxed as ordinary income, and you must pay an additional 10% tax, which is nondeductible. Neither tax applies to a rollover.

Upon my death, does my IRA account become part of my estate?

For decedents dying before December 31, 1984, the first $100,000 may be excluded if it is paid to your beneficiary for his or her lifetime or during a period of at least 36 months. For decedents dying after December 31, 1984, the entire amount is includable in the estate. However, only 50% will be includable in the estate in community property states.

What about gift taxes?

A distribution payable to a beneficiary will not be subject to federal gift taxes.

Is interest or other money earned by my IRA taxed each year?

With a few exceptions, money is not taxed as it accumulates in your account.

When is the IRA account taxed?

Money from your IRA is taxed as ordinary income upon withdrawal, unless you roll it over, tax-free. There is a tax penalty if you withdraw money before you are 59½ years old. A penalty-free withdrawal can be made upon disability or death.

Is it worthwhile for an older person to open an IRA account?

Yes. Even if you have only a short time to participate before retirement. In just five years your $10,000 in contributions could grow to $14,230 at a 12% compounded return. Further, without an IRA, the government would take a large tax bite out of the $10,000, leaving you with much less to either spend or save.

What can an IRA do for me?

The following shows the effects of investing an IRA, with the amount the government contributes depending on your top tax bracket:

Your Top Tax Bracket	Tax Savings on a $2,000 Contribution	Amount You Must Add
20%	$ 400	$1,600
30%	600	1,400
40%	800	1,200
50%	1,000	1,000

Besides this tax break, all earnings inside your IRA accumulate without being taxed.

What happens to the balance of my IRA account if I die before drawing out the full value?

Your heirs still benefit. There are a variety of ways in which they can recieve their shares—among them inclusion in their own IRA accounts. The nature of such distributions should be considered in your estate plan.

Are there any disadvantages in investing in an IRA?

Yes. For example, why should you make a tax-deductible contribution of money on which no tax is due? If you have little or no tax to pay in a particular year because of tax planning or other circumstances, it would not make sense to contribute to an IRA. However, if you are carrying a tax loss back to prior years or forward to future ones, it might make sense.

Banks

What IRA options are available through banks?

Banks are offering a variety of options for IRAs that are patterned after conventional certificates of deposit, but are far more flexible. Many banks offer more than one option. Conventional certificates of deposit require sizable payments, but an IRA account can be opened with a modest amount, perhaps $100.

Can I stagger my investments over the year?

Yes. After the initial investment you can deposit as much as you like, whenever you like, depending on the legal limit each year. You can even stop paying and your account will remain active.

What about maintenance charges?

Most banks do not charge maintenance costs.

What types of options are available?

Certificates vary in the rate of interest, frequency of compounding, and maturity date. Some IRAs have variable, or floating, interest rates. Others have fixed interest rates. Both rates are generally tied to the rates of U.S. government securities and other investments.

What happens when a time certificate matures?

Although IRA certificates have maturities of at least 18 months, some banks will renew IRAs with variable interest rates automatically if the customer wishes.

What if I wish to move my account when the certificate matures?

If you are dissatisfied with the new terms offered, you may move your account. But the banks may charge a penalty if you move the money before the certificate's maturity.

What about security?

Accounts in most commercial and mutual savings banks are federally insured up to $100,000. Others are not, but they may be insured by your home state.

Savings and Loan Associations

What are the characteristics of IRAs offered through savings and loan associations?

The options are almost identical to those relating to banks in general.

Insurance Companies

What do the insurance companies have to offer?

An IRA set up with an insurance company is an annuity, which guarantees you an income as long as you live. It is the only IRA that can provide this guarantee.

How do their interest rates compare to those of other possible IRA investments?

Insurance companies will set a fixed minimum rate of interest at the time you open the account. The advantage is that guaranteed interest is not subject to market fluctuations. For example, the guaranteed rate could be relatively high in the first or early years and then lower for succeeding years. The guaranteed rate from insurance companies, however, has been considerably lower in recent years than rates offered by other financial institutions. In reality, insurance companies have been paying interest that is higher than the guaranteed rate and is competitive with other institutions. The only *guaranteed* rate, however, is the one spelled out in the policy.

What restrictions apply to payment of premiums?

IRAs have flexible premiums. You can put as much as you like in your IRA at any time, as long as you do not exceed the maximum set by law each year. You can even stop paying and your policy still will be in force. Some companies will accept $50 or less as an opening account.

Are there any special expenses that apply?

Some companies are tailoring policies especially for IRAs by offering fixed-interest annuities that have no *front loads* (sales costs). But you can expect to pay sizable penalties if you withdraw your money prematurely, particularly in the early years of the policy. This is called *backload.*

What about maintenance fees?

Maintenance fees run to between $20 and $25 a year.

Do all insurance IRAs have guaranteed interest?

No, some insurance companies also offer IRAs that do not have guaranteed interest. The value of these variable annuities fluctuates, depending on market conditions.

What about security?

Money in your annuity will not be federally insured, but state agencies that regulate insurance companies emphasize safety and diversity in investments.

Credit Unions

Can I invest in an IRA through my credit union?

Yes. Almost all credit unions offer IRAs. They expect to pay interest that is competitive with other financial institutions.

What restrictions might I expect in setting up an IRA through my credit union?

Credit unions design IRAs keyed to their size and nature. Interest is set by the board of directors of the credit union. Some may offer savings certificates with a time limit and a penalty for premature withdrawal.

Are there any specific advantages to having an IRA in my credit union?

Convenience is one of the key advantages of a credit union, and many credit unions may maximize convenience by offering payroll deductions for their IRAs.

What about minimum deposits?

The initial deposit required generally is very low, such as $25 or less. For those not taking advantage of payroll deduction, additional deposits generally can be made at any time and in any amount, as long as they do not exceed the legal limit each year. For the most part, no maintenance fees are charged.

What about security?

Accounts in federal credit unions are federally insured for up to $100,000. Some state-chartered institutions also are federally insured. Others may be insured by the state for a comparable amount.

Mutual Funds

What is the nature of a mutual fund investment?

When you put your money in a mutual fund, you are buying shares in a pool of money that is invested in securities chosen by professional money managers. The most familiar type of mutual fund is the money market fund, where money is invested in short-term securities, and the rate of return varies daily. Other mutual funds invest in stocks and bonds.

What kind of return can I expect from a mutual fund?

Mutual funds do not guarantee a specific rate of return on the investment. Some funds have far outstripped increases in the consumer price index. However, it is also possible to lose money in a mutual fund investment.

Are there any additional expenses involved in a mutual fund investment?

Mutual funds are known as load and no-load funds. The *load,* or charge, is a sales commission paid to a broker or sales agent for advice and services. The sales charge usually is around 8.5% of the cost of every purchase of shares in the fund.

Is there a difference in the investments of no-load and load funds?

Virtually, no. You must be given a prospectus spelling out the objectives and terms of each fund.

Can an IRA investment in a mutual fund be moved?

Yes, you can move your IRA from one mutual fund to another as your own investment objectives change. Generally there is no charge when you sell fund shares.

Are there any special requirements for maintaining a mutual fund IRA?

Some funds may require that you invest at least a minimum amount — perhaps $100 — every time you buy shares. Others require no minimum.

Are there any other fees?

Each year, there will be a management fee that is usually around 1% of the value of your shares. Money market funds generally charge half this amount. Many funds also charge a maintenance fee for your IRA of about $10 a year.

How can I minimize risks relating to mutual fund investments?

Mutual funds seek to achieve investment growth, safety and stability by diversifying investments, but you should carefully check the sales prospectus to evaluate how much risk is involved. In a mutual fund, your money is not insured against loss due to normal market action.

Brokerage Firms

What do brokerage firms have to offer?

An investor may establish an IRA with a brokerage firm for investments in stocks, bonds, mutual funds, or limited partnerships. However, IRA investors are prohibited from trading on margin and therefore cannot invest in commodities, options, or leveraged real estate. Uninvested funds may be parked in a money market account.

Each brokerage firm sets its own minimum for opening an IRA (usually $250 or $500) and determines its own schedule of custodial fees. Any one-time fee for opening an account and all annual maintenance fees (usually $20 to $50 a year) may be paid by separate check and are tax-deductible expenses for taxpayers who itemize. Brokers' commissions, however, are paid from the IRA principal.

Source: U.S. Government Printing Office.

1.07 **Qualified Employee Benefit Plans**

The passage of the Employee Retirement Income Security Act (ERISA) in 1974 increased interest in retirement planning programs. Qualified employee benefit plans, including pension, profit-sharing, and stock bonus plans, offer exceptional tax benefits to both shareholder-employees and regular employees. Certain tax law requirements must be met for the plan to qualify, and it is advisable and customary to seek advance approval of the plan from the IRS. The following summary briefly describes qualified plans, non-qualified plans, and additional employee benefits. Changes covered in the Tax Equity and Fiscal Responsibility Act of 1982 (TEFRA) (see page 2.21), and more recently, the Tax Reform Act of 1984 (see page 2.25) are included.

TAX ADVANTAGES

A qualified employee benefit plan provides a number of tax advantages for both the employer and the employee. The principal advantages are:

1. The employer gets an immediate deduction for contributions under the plan.

2. The income earned by the funds while held under the plan is tax-exempt.

3. The employee is not taxed on his share of the funds until amounts are distributed.

4. Qualifying lump-sum distributions can be treated as long-term capital gain to the extent of the employee's pre-1974 active participation in the plan. The ordinary income portion of the distribution can qualify for favorable ten-year averaging.

5. Qualifying lump-sum distributions and plan termination payouts can be rolled over tax-free to another plan or an IRA.

6. Payments on the death of an employee can qualify for a $5,000 death benefit exemption from income tax.

7. If qualifying distributions are made in the form of stock of the employer corporation, tax on the appreciation in value of the stock is long-term capital gain and is deferred until the stock is sold.

QUALIFICATION REQUIREMENTS

A qualified employee benefit plan must meet the following requirements:

1. The plan must be a specific written program communicated to the employees.

2. The plan must be established by the employer for the *exclusive* benefit of the *employees or their beneficiaries*.

3. In a plan maintained by more than one employer, all plan participants are considered to be his employees in determining whether the plan of any one employer is for the exclusive benefit of his employees and their beneficiaries.

4. The plan must meet certain vesting requirements and must be funded.

5. A trust that forms part of the plan must generally be created or organized in the U.S. in order to be exempt from tax on its income.

6. The plan must meet tests intended to encourage broad coverage and eligibility of employees.

7. The plan must not discriminate in favor of officers, shareholders, or highly paid employees with respect to contributions or benefits.

8. A qualified plan subject to certain vesting rules must provide that the rights of all affected employees to accrued benefits (to the extent funded) or to amounts credited to their accounts at the date a plan terminates or partially terminates become nonforfeitable (vest) upon such termination or partial termination.

9. Under a pension plan, forfeitures must not be applied to increase the benefits of the employees.

10. The employer's commitment need not be in the nature of an enforceable obligation in order for the plan to qualify, but, according to the IRS, the statutory term *plan* implies that there must be a permanent, as distinguished from a merely a temporary, program. The IRS concedes that an employer may reserve the right to change a plan, to terminate it altogether, and to discontinue contributions, but the actual discontinuance, whether with or without advance warning, still requires justification to avoid disqualification of the plan.

11. The IRS states that if a plan provides for annuity benefits, married employees, unless they elect otherwise, must receive a joint and survivor annuity if the annuity payments begin in a plan year starting after 1975. There are exceptions intended to protect plans against excessive cost that would result from adverse selection. However, the tax court states that the plan may offer a joint and survivor annuity on an optional basis, rather than offering it as the normal form of payment.

12. In the event of a merger or consolidation with, or transfer of assets or liabilities to, any other plan, each participant must be entitled to benefits on a termination basis after the plan change takes place. These benefits must be at least equal to what the termination benefits were before the plan changed.

13. A plan must generally provide that benefits cannot be assigned, except for voluntary and revocable assignments that do not exceed 10% of any benefit payment.

14. Benefit payments generally must begin not later than 60 days after the plan year in which the employee reaches 65, completes 10 years of participation in the plan, or terminates service, whichever occurs last.

15. The plan cannot provide that, if an employee withdraws any benefits derived from his own contributions, he forfeits accrued benefits derived from employer contributions, if the employee is at least 50% vested in these benefits.

16. The plan may not provide for contributions or benefits that exceed specified overall limitations.

Requirements for Top-Heavy Plans

In addition to these general requirements, TEFRA established specific qualification rules for "top-heavy" plans for years beginning after 1983. Top-heaviness often applies in the case of small employers, but the rules apply equally to plans maintained by corporations, partnerships, or sole proprietorships. Briefly, a top-heavy defined benefit plan is one in which the present value of accrued benefits of key employees exceeds 60% of the present value of accrued benefits of all plan participants. A defined contribution plan is top heavy if more than 60% of the account balances have been accumulated on behalf of key employees. For both types of plan, key employees are considered officers with annual salaries of over $45,000, 5% owners, 1% owners earning more than $150,000, and employees owning the ten largest interests in the company.

The top-heavy requirements include accelerated vesting, a ceiling of $200,000 on compensation considered under the plan, a minimum level of benefits and/or contributions for non-key employees, and limits on additional benefits for key employees who participate in both a defined benefit and a defined contribution plan. Also, a 10% premature distribution penalty will be imposed on distributions to key employees before they reach the age of 59½, except in the case of disability or death. Distributions to key employees must begin no later than the tax year in which they reach age 70½.

Additional Requirements

Professional and service corporations are subject to a set of special rules intended to prevent discrimination in coverage and benefits in favor of the owners.

The Retirement Equity Act of 1984 now requires automatic survivor benefits in the form of a joint and survivor annuity for years after 1984. Other benefit forms may, however, be elected. Prior to this Act, the law required that a joint and survivor annuity be one of the offered forms of benefit payment.

LIMITATIONS ON CONTRIBUTIONS AND BENEFITS

Qualified plans can be either of two types: defined contribution or defined benefit. TEFRA reduced allowed benefit amounts for qualified defined benefit plans and allowed contribution amounts for defined contribution plans. The changes are as follows:

	Pre-TEFRA Maximum	**Current Maximum**
Defined Benefit Plan (annual benefit)	The *lesser* of 100% of average compensation (based on three high consecutive years) *or* $136,425	The *lesser* of 100% of average compensation (based on three high consecutive years) *or* $90,000
Defined Contribution Plan (annual contribution)	The *lesser* of 25% of compensation *or* $45,475	The *lesser* of 25% of compensation *or* $30,000

Note: *These limits became effective in 1983 for existing plans, or July 1, 1982, for new plans and may not be increased for any year after 1982 or before January 1, 1988.*

DISTRIBUTIONS FROM QUALIFIED PLANS

Retirement plan distributions are made in a lump sum or a series of annuity payments. Qualified plans may also allow employees to borrow against their accounts before retirement.

Lump-Sum Distributions

A lump-sum distribution is a distribution of the balance of a participant's account in a qualified plan within one taxable year after the participant reaches age 59½, separates from service, or dies. A lump-sum distribution is allocated between a capital gain and ordinary income portion, although capital gain treatment was limited by ERISA. Distributed benefits attributable to service after 1973 are not eligible for capital gain treatment and are taxed using a special ten-year averaging rule for lump-sum distributions.

The ten-year averaging tax is approximately ten times the theoretical tax computed as if the taxpayer received one-tenth of the full distribution as his or her only income. The ordinary income portion is added to the capital gain portion, and any relevant death benefit exclusion is deducted. The distribution must be on account of death, separation from service (except for self-employed individuals), attainment of age 59½, or disability (only for self-employed individuals). The recipient must have participated in the plan for ten years unless the distribution is on account of death.

An individual may continue to defer tax on lump-sum distributions from qualified plans if they are rolled over to an IRA or another qualified plan within 60 days of the distribution. This deferral applies to cash or property. A qualifying rollover distribution is: a distribution made on account of discontinuing a plan; any lump-sum distribution (it need not qualify for special lump-sum distribution treatment; or a distribution of accumulated deductible voluntary employee contributions treated as IRA contributions.

If property other than cash is received, it may not be possible to transfer it to another qualified plan. The property can be sold and, if the proceeds are placed in the new plan, the transaction will be treated as a rollover. When part of a lump-sum distribution is rolled over to an IRA or another qualified plan, only the part rolled over will be deferred from tax. Any portion not rolled over is treated as ordinary income, not capital gain, and it is not eligible for ten-year averaging.

Annuity Distributions

When a distribution is not a lump-sum distribution, it is taxed under the special rules for annuities. If the employee contributions are recoverable in three years from the annuity starting date, no part of the annuity is taxed until it is fully recovered. Under the annuity rules, an exclusion ratio is determined by the employee's age, life expectancy, and total of employee contributions to the plan. For example, consider an employee who is 65 years old, receives $500 a month, and whose employee contributions total $20,000. If life expectancy is 15 more years, the projected return is $90,000 (12 months x 500 x 15 years). The exclusion ratio will be $20,000 (employee contributions)/ $90,000 or 22%.

Unrealized Appreciation

The taxation of net unrealized appreciation on securities of the employer corporation is deferred until the securities are sold after a lump-sum distribution. If a distribution is not a lump-sum distribution, taxation of unrealized appreciation will be deferred only to the extent attributable to employee contributions.

Employee Loans

Qualified plans, particularly profit-sharing plans, often allow participants to borrow against their vested benefits. The employee can borrow the lesser of $50,000 or one-half of his account's current balance. If the balance is less than $20,000, the employee may still borrow up to $10,000. Employee loans must be adequately secured, be at a fair rate of interest, and be repaid under a definite repayment schedule, generally within five years. Also, plan loans must be made available to all plan participants or their beneficiaries on a reasonable basis.

DEFINED BENEFIT PLANS

Traditionally, large firms have provided defined benefit plans for their employees. Employees covered by a defined benefit plan are generally guaranteed a specified benefit after attaining a certain age. The defined benefit plan thus places the risk of market fluctuations and changes in plan assets on the employer. The employee's benefit is usually a percentage of pre-retirement salary. The employer must contribute an actuarially determined amount each year to provide the promised benefit. The employee's right to contributions made on his behalf by the employer accrues and vests based on the length of time he has participated in the plan. A defined benefit plan cannot allow an active employee to withdraw any part of the contributions made on his behalf; voluntary contributions made by the employee can be withdrawn. Distributions from defined benefit plans cannot be made before death, retirement, or separation from service of the employee.

DEFINED CONTRIBUTION PLANS

Defined contribution plans include a variety of programs such as profit-sharing plans, money purchase plans, employee stock ownership plans and others discussed below. The key difference between a pension plan and a defined contribution plan is that the latter permits the employer to transfer the market risk of plan investments to the employee.

In a defined contribution plan, individual accounts are maintained for each employee and an annual contribution is made to each account. The contributions may be based on a fixed or discretionary percentage of the employer's profits, a fixed percentage of the employee's salary, or a formula taking a combination of facts into account—e.g., salary and length of service. The amount distributed to the employee in any defined contribution plan will depend on the return of plan investment and can be more flexible than in a defined benefit plan.

Profit-Sharing Plans

Profit-sharing plans, one type of defined contribution plan, are distinguished from other kinds of plans by the requirement that contributions be made out of profits. Profits are defined broadly to include current and accumulated profits. The amount contributed each year may be determined at the employer's discretion. There is merely a requirement of "substantial and recurring" contributions. This requirement prevents profit-sharing plans from being created to shelter company profits from tax in any one year.

Profit-sharing plans can allow withdrawals of funds that have been in the plan for two years. A plan may allow a participant who has been in the plan for five years to withdraw all funds. Unlike a defined benefit plan, a profit-sharing plan allows accelerated distributions in the case of financial hardship or physical disability. Profit-sharing plans may provide loans to participants. The loans must be available to all participants on a nondiscriminatory basis. They must bear a reasonable rate of return and be repaid within a specified period of time.

Stock Bonus Plans

Subject to rules similar to profit-sharing plans, stock bonus benefits were historically distributable only in employer stock, but a recent change allows the employee to receive cash instead. If an employer establishes a stock bonus plan and distributes stock that is not traded on an established market, the employee must have the right to require the employer to purchase back the stock at a price determined by a fair valuation formula. Stock bonus plans are exempt from ERISA requirements concerning liquidity, diversification, and fair return on plan investments. The stock bonus plan can invest in any assets. It merely has to make distributions of employer securities.

Money Purchase Plans

A money purchase plan has characteristics of both a pension plan and a profit-sharing plan. An employee's benefits are based on the length of time he has been in the plan, but employers often contribute a small amount to past service. No benefit is guaranteed. Employers' contributions are not geared to profits in a money purchase plan, but are normally a flat percentage of compensation. Other formulas often run afoul of the technical anti-discrimination rules. A money purchase plan can be a thrift plan in which an employer's contribution matches the employee's contribution.

Employee Stock Ownership Plans (ESOPs)

A qualified plan designed to invest primarily in the employer's securities, an employee stock ownership plan (ESOP) gives employees an ownership interest in their employer. ESOPs are a type of stock bonus plan and are generally subject to the same qualification requirements. The ESOP may have a stated formula for determining contributions or the employer can decide how much to contribute each year. Unlike a profit-sharing plan, contributions do not have to be made out of profits. The ESOP is exempt from the general requirement that plan assets earn a fair return, allowing the ESOP to invest exclusively in employer stock. ESOP benefits must also be distributable in employer stock. In addition, ESOPs can be part of a money purchase plan/stock bonus plan combination that can increase deductible contributions to a nonleveraged ESOP from 15 to 25%.

TAX CREDIT EMPLOYEE STOCK OWNERSHIP PLAN (PAYSOPs)

An employer may establish a tax credit employee stock ownership plan— commonly called a PAYSOP — instead of an ESOP. A tax credit ESOP may be any type of defined contribution plan while an ESOP must be a stock bonus plan. However, the major difference between an ESOP and a PAYSOP is that a PAYSOP generates a tax credit instead of a tax deduction. The amount of the tax credit is the lesser of the value of the employer securities transferred by the corporation to the PAYSOP, or a credit of one-half of 1% of the compensation paid to employees who participate in the PAYSOP. The credit is applied against the full tax liability up to $25,000 but up to 90% of tax liability for amounts above $25,000. Unused credits may be used to offset prior or future years' tax liability. Any employer may contribute cash to a PAYSOP if the cash is used to purchase employer securities within 30 days. A PAYSOP limitation is that no more than one-third of the employer contributions be credited to officers, shareholders owning more than 10% of the employer, or highly compensated employees.

LEVERAGED EMPLOYEE STOCK OWNERSHIP PLAN (LESOPs)

The key characteristic of the third type of employee stock ownership plan, the leveraged ESOP (LESOP), is that it may borrow money to purchase qualifying employer securities. The loans will be guaranteed by the employer and the purchased securities will be collateral for the loan. Then the employer's annual cash contributions to the plan will be used to pay off the original loan. These contributions are deductible to the same extent as a direct contribution of employer securities, up to 25% of compensation. LESOPs can be used in place of conventional debt financing and are especially useful in mergers or spinoffs and shareholder buy-outs. Tax advisors have often used the LESOP to help transfer a closely held corporation from a founder to a group of key employees.

A shareholder who sells stock to an ESOP may defer any tax due on the capital gain by purchasing qualified replacement securities, generally the stock or securities of any domestic operating company. The taxpayer can only elect this deferral if the ESOP owns 30% of the total value of the employer securities after the sale and the qualified replacement is made within 15 months. The basis of the seller in replacement securities acquired during the qualified period is reduced by the amount of gain not recognized.

Cash or Deferred Plans (401(k) Plans)

An employee may elect to place a portion of salary into a tax-sheltered retirement plan, instead of receiving it currently in cash. This deferred portion is paid into the employee's profit-sharing account, along with the company's regular profit-sharing contribution for the employee. This allows employees with lower current cash needs — generally highly paid employees — to defer salary and increase their payments into the plan.

The 401(k) is a type of profit-sharing or stock bonus plan that can be integrated into the employer's existing pension and profit-sharing plan or can be the only retirement program provided. The plan is best for an employer who does not want to contribute to a qualified retirement plan but does want to allow employees to take advantages of the benefits of a retirement program. The employer's sole cost is that of administering the plan.

This type of plan offers a number of tax savings: Money set aside is not taxable to the employee and is deductible by the company; contributions and earnings grow tax-free until such time as they are withdrawn; and lump-sum distributions from the plan qualify for ten-year averaging treatment when paid out. Deferred salary can only be distributed upon retirement, separation from service, death, disability, the employee's reaching the age of 59½, or in case of hardship. The IRS may define financial hardship to include down payments on principal residences and college tuition.

A 401(k) plan must meet specific requirements. The plan must benefit all employees and comply with special nondiscrimination rules based on the percentage of income actually deferred by both the highly paid and lower-paid employees. (Under this provision, 70% or more of all employees must be eligible for cash-or-deferred plans.) The percentage of salary deferred by the highest paid one-third must not be more than 150% of the percentage of salary deferred by other employees, or 250% of the percentage of salary deferred by other employees, but only if that percentage is not more than 3% greater than the salary deferred by other employees. The Tax Reform Act of 1984 (effective with plan years beginning after December 31, 1984) requires that the actual deferral percentages test — *not* the general nondiscrimination rules for qualified plans — must be satisfied to have a qualified cash or deferred arrangement. Employee participation must be aggregated for purposes of determining whether the test is met. Failure to meet this test will not of itself disqualify the plan, but does mean that employees will be taxed currently on contributions made to the plan on their behalf.

While a 401(k) is similar to an IRA in many respects, it differs in that an employee can borrow from his 401(k) plan the lesser of $50,000 or one-half of his account balance. If the balance is less than $20,000, the employee may still borrow up to $10,000. The loan generally must be repaid within five years and a reasonable rate of interest must be charged.

Target Benefit Plans

Characteristics of the defined benefit, defined contribution, and money purchase plan are included in target benefit plans, which normally provide for a target of a specified percentage of salary at retirement. This target merely sets the annual contribution that will be made. Once the contribution level is actuarially determined, the target is ignored. In other respects, the plan has the same rules as a money purchase plan.

Tax-Sheltered Annuity Programs (403(b) Plans)

A public school system, an exempt educational, charitable, or religious organization, and the Uniformed Services University of the Health Services (with respect to civilian faculty and staff) may provide retirement benefits for their employees through the purchase of nonexempt annuities or by contributing to a custodial account invested in mutual funds. Whichever funding medium is used, the employee's rights must be nonforfeitable, except for failure to pay future premiums.

The exclusion allowance is generally equal to 20% of the employee's pay for the last 12-month period, multiplied by the number of years of the employee's past service, less any amounts contributed by the employer that were excluded in prior tax years and tax-free contributions to state and local deferred compensation plans. Contributions remain subject to the general limit of the lesser of $25,000 or 25% of an employee's compensation. For tax years beginning after 1981, church employees with an adjusted gross income of $17,000 or less have a minimum exclusion allowance equal to the *lesser* of $3,000 or 100% of their compensation.

Lump-sum distributions or transfers from plans of exempt organizations or public schools are eligible for tax-free rollovers, into IRAs, or other employer plans, the terms of which allow them to accept rollovers. In figuring service, full-time employment for a full year is considered to be one year of service. Part-time employees are credited with fractional years.

Payments to any employee under the annuity contract or from the custodial account are taxable to the employee when made, but any contributions by the employer that were excludable from the employee's income under the 20% rule are not treated as part of the employee's investment in the contract.

Distributions from the custodial account may be made because of:

- An employee's death

- Disability

- Separation from the employer's service

- Attainment of age 59½

- Financial hardship

The "up to $5,000" death benefit exclusion is available for as much of the distribution as is represented by the employer's contributions and as falls within the 20% exclusion.

EXAMPLE:

X University pays premiums of $10,000 in 1983 and $13,000 in 1984 for the purchase of an annuity for Beth White, who became a full-time employee on January 1, 1983.

Beth drew a salary of $40,000 in 1983 and $45,000 in 1984, reporting salary on the calendar year basis.

For 1983, she may exclude $8,000 (20% of $40,000) and include $2,000 ($10,000 contribution for 1983—$8,000 exclusion).

For 1984, she would exclude $9,000 (20% of $45,000) x 2 (years of service) = $18,000, minus $8,000 (the amount contributed by her employer that was excluded in 1983), or a total of $10,000. She will include $3,000 ($13,000 contribution −$10,000 exclusion).

Keogh Plans (HR-10)

The 1962 Self-Employed Individuals Tax Retirement Act introduced by Congressman Eugene J. Keogh gave self-employed individuals access to qualified plans. Also known as HR-10, this Act contained a variety of restrictions that made Keogh plans far less favorable than similar programs allowed for those employed by others. Subsequent tax legislation has gradually equalized treatment of Keogh and corporate-type plans, though gaps still remain. TEFRA specifically reduced many of the key restrictions, repealing contribution and deduction limits. Now, the overall limits on benefits and contributions are applicable to plans generally, including Keogh plans. The Keogh has been made into a defined contribution plan that is available to employees of partnerships and sole proprietorships. The new Keogh plan rules also apply to simplified employee pensions and to contributions by shareholder employees of Subchapter S corporations who hold more than 5% interest in the corporation.

The following commonly asked questions incorporate all of the recent law changes.

Who can establish a Keogh?

Any self-employed individual who operates a full-time or part-time unincorporated business and whose earned income comes from personal services.

When should an individual establish such a plan?

Before the end of the fiscal or calendar year.

What limits apply to contributions?

The limit is $30,000 for defined contribution plans. This may be increased to $90,000 by using a defined benefit Keogh plan, using actuarial assumptions and relatively low earnings estimates. Because of the complications and actuarial costs, few defined benefit Keogh plans are used.

Which employees should be included?

The plan must cover all employees who are full-time employees (one thousand hours a year or more), although they may be required to wait as long as three years after employment begins. A spouse can be included in the plan if he or she is a full-time employee. A plan must be 100% vested in the employee at all times.

Are voluntary contributions allowed?

Yes, but only if one participating member of the plan is not an owner-employee. Voluntary contributions are limited to 10% of earned income, the maximum being $2,500 a year.

When can a participant begin receiving distributions?

A participant may start taking distributions at the age of 59½ and must start taking distributions by age 70½. If a participant becomes disabled, he or she may make withdrawals without penalty. Upon a participant's death, his or her beneficiary may start drawing on the plan. All post-1974 contributions to a plan are taxed as ordinary income in the year of distribution.

In what form can distribution be taken?

Distributions may take the form of an annuity for one life or a joint and survivor annuity. Or a participant may arrange to make withdrawals over a period of time, not to exceed the normal life expectancy of the participant and spouse.

What happens when an employee participant leaves?

All proceeds from his or her account in the Keogh plan are paid out. These may be rolled over into an IRA plan to postpone paying the tax until retirement.

Can the owner or employee participate in other retirement plans?

Yes, both may also make contributions to an IRA plan.

A RETIREMENT FUND WITH A KEOGH PLAN
40% Tax Bracket

Year	Before-tax Income Set Aside	After-tax Amount Contributed	10% Interest	Taxes	Value
1	$5,000	$5,000	$ 500	0	$ 5,500
2	5,000	5,000	1,050	0	11,550
3	5,000	5,000	1,655	0	18,205
4	5,000	5,000	2,321	0	25,526
5	5,000	5,000	3,053	0	33,578
6	5,000	5,000	3,858	0	42,436
7	5,000	5,000	4,744	0	52,180
8	5,000	5,000	5,718	0	62,898
9	5,000	5,000	6,790	0	74,688
10	5,000	5,000	7,969	0	87,657

A RETIREMENT FUND WITHOUT A KEOGH PLAN
40% Tax Bracket

Year	Before-tax Income Set Aside	After-tax Amount Contributed	10% Interest	Taxes	Value
1	$5,000	$3,000	$ 300	$ 120	$ 3,180
2	5,000	3,000	618	247	6,551
3	5,000	3,000	955	382	10,124
4	5,000	3,000	1,312	525	13,911
5	5,000	3,000	1,691	676	17,926
6	5,000	3,000	2,093	837	22,182
7	5,000	3,000	2,518	1,007	26,693
8	5,000	3,000	2,969	1,188	31,474
9	5,000	3,000	3,447	1,379	36,542
10	5,000	3,000	3,954	1,582	41,914

What are acceptable investments?

Investments that qualify include:

- Corporate or government bonds
- Common stock
- Mutual funds
- Limited partnerships for real estate or oil
- Annuity trust
- Custodial account

Are there penalties for early withdrawals?

Benefits payments cannot begin until the age of 59½ unless one is permanently disabled. Premature distributions are subject to a 10% penalty tax and the owner-employee is prohibited from making contributions to the account in the following five years.

If an employer has a bad year with little or no profits, does he have to make a contribution for employees?

Not necessarily. Some plans have provisions that allow a minimum profit threshold, so that if profits of the business do not reach a certain level, no contribution is required for either the employer or employee.

Are there ways in which employer with a number of employees can reduce his cost of adopting a Keogh plan?

Yes. There are plans that can be integrated with Social Security limitations. However, such plans are complex and difficult to administer, and should only be considered if cost is a problem in the adoption of a Keogh plan.

If unhappy with the investment used for a Keogh plan, can the employer change it?

Yes, the employer may adopt a new plan and have the assets of the old plan transferred to it, but such a transaction must comply with various rules.

Simplified Employee Pensions (SEPs)

Simplified Employee Pension Plans (SEPs) provide a relatively simple method through which employers can provide retirement benefits, by using an increased deduction to make contributions to an employee's IRA. Employer contributions to the SEP are included in the employee's income, and the employer can claim a deduction for contributions made to a SEP. Likewise, the employee may claim a deduction on Form 1040 for the amount of the contribution made by the employer. The maximum deduction allowed the employee for employer contributions is the lesser of $30,000 or 15% of includable compensation, after 1983.

QUALIFICATION REQUIREMENTS

- There must be an IRA annuity for each covered employee.

- Employer contributions must be made for each employee who, during the calendar year, has reached age 25 and who has performed services for the employer in at least three of the preceding five calendar years.

- The rate of contribution must not discriminate in favor of employees who are officers, shareholders, self-employed, or highly compensated.

- Employee withdrawal of employee contributions must be permitted without penalty.

- Contributions must be made according to a definite written allocation formula.

There are a few exceptions to these requirements, pertaining to nonresident aliens and individuals who are members of a collective bargaining unit.

EMPLOYER'S DEDUCTIONS

- Contributions for a calendar year are deductible for the tax year with or within which the calendar year ends.

- Contributions for a calendar year must be made within three and a half months after the end of that calendar year.

- The deduction cannot exceed 15% of the employee's compensation for the calendar year, but any excess may be carried over and deducted (subject to the 15% limitation for the carryover year) in later years.

The deduction for contributions to a SEP lowers the allowable contributions to qualified profit-sharing and stock bonus plans, the 25% limitation on deductible contributions to a combination of plans, and the limitation on deductible contributions made on behalf of a self-employed person.

EXCESS CONTRIBUTIONS

Individuals must withdraw any excess contributions before the date for filing their tax returns or be liable for the 6% excise tax on the excess. Individuals may, however, withdraw excess employer contributions to a SEP free of the 10% penalty tax on early distributions to the extent that no deduction was allowed for the contributions. The withdrawal cannot exceed the amount of employer contributions or $30,000, whichever is less.

Although an employee cannot deduct contributions made to an IRA during a year in which he attains the age of 70½, this rule does not apply to a SEP.

An employee for whom an employer contributes under a SEP is allowed a deduction for his own IRA contribution, limited to the lesser of $2,000 or 10% of compensation, as well as a deduction for employer contributions to the SEP.

Example: In 1983, Mr. Potter has compensation of $20,000. His employer contributes $3,000 to Potter's IRA, which is part of a SEP. In addition, Mr. Potter contributes $2,000 of his own money to the IRA. He must include the $3,000 employer contribution to the SEP as part of gross income on his 1983 federal tax return, but he may claim a deduction from gross income of $5,000 ($3,000 plus $2,000) for IRA contributions.

Amounts distributed to an individual from an IRA, including a SEP, are usually taxed in full as ordinary income.

1.08 **Nonqualified (Excess Benefit) Plans**

Allowing an employer to provide to key employees benefits that are above the limitations for qualified plans, nonqualified plans need not be currently funded by the employer. While unfunded plans are exempt from all ERISA requirements, funded plans are subject to ERISA's reporting and disclosure requirements, its fiduciary rules, and its enforcement provisions.

Three key areas must be examined when deciding between a qualified and a nonqualified arrangement: the timing of the tax deduction; the tax exemption for earnings on plan assets; and the taxation of benefit distributions.

As benefits from unfunded, nonqualified deferred compensation arrangements are exempt from taxation until received, the employer will not be entitled to the deduction until the employee is taxed on the benefits. Benefits in funded excess benefit plans will be taxed when they are substantially vested.

ADVANTAGES

Nonqualified plans may be preferable to qualified plans for the following reasons:

- Recent changes have significantly reduced the ability to exclude large amounts of income from tax through the use of pension and profit-sharing plans.

- Additional rules, supplementing the traditional antidiscrimination requirements, further restrict plans that favor highly compensated and key employees.

- New rules require plan distributions to commence earlier and proceed more quickly than in the past.

- Reductions in basic tax rates have had a substantial impact on the need for qualified plans.

DISADVANTAGES

Although the distribution of excess plan benefits is usually integrated with distributions from the qualified plan, there are certain advantages to the employees' making contributions to the qualified portion of a contributory plan instead of the nonqualified portion: the employer would then be able to take the current deduction that is available for contributions to a qualified plan; and the employee may prefer to contribute to the qualified plan to avoid being an unsecured creditor, as there are no vesting rules for excess benefit plans. Employers can also include forfeiture for competition clauses in the nonqualified plan agreement.

TOP HAT PLANS

One type of nonqualified program, introduced and maintained by an employer primarily to provide deferred compensation for a select group of management or highly compensated employees, top hat plans are exempt from ERISA reporting requirements.

The plans allow employees to defer receipt of earnings above a specified amount to later years. Some accrual is often added to these deferrals based on an interest rate or company performance. For example, an employee can elect to defer all compensation earned in excess of a stated amount until the next year. The employer will not get a deduction and the employee will not recognize income until that time. To avoid the constructive receipt of income, the employee must make the deferred compensation election before the income is incurred. An additional caveat is that the employee becomes an unsecured, general creditor of the employer. Through the use of a grantor trust, this risk can generally be eliminated and taxation still avoided until benefits are received.

1.09 Miscellaneous Employee Benefit Plans

FRINGE BENEFITS

Taxation of fringe benefits has been a controversial area for many years, in that fringe benefits often represent income to the recipient. While taxation of fringe benefits can create administrative and valuation difficulties, the 1984 Tax Reform Act clarifies tax treatment by excluding certain benefits from gross income.

Nontaxable Benefits

There are five major nontaxable fringe benefits:

- *No additional-cost service.* Any service provided by an employer to employees that: is offered for sale to customers in the line of business of the employer in which the employee works, represents no substantial additional cost to the employer in providing the service to the employee and is provided on a nondiscriminatory basis to all employees.

- *Qualified employee discount.* This discount cannot exceed the gross profit percentage of the sales price to customers and in the cases of services, cannot exceed 20%. The discounts must be provided on a nondiscriminatory basis.

- *Working condition fringe benefits.* These include expenses that would be deductible or depreciable by the employer — e.g., use of a company car or plane, club memberships, and on-the-job training.

- *De minimis fringe benefits.* These benefits are defined as any property or service provided to the employee that is of so little value that it is unreasonable or administratively impractical to account for it. Such benefits include occasional dinner money or taxi fare associated with overtime work, coffee and doughnuts, and personal use of copying machines. Subsidized eating facilities are considered de minimis fringe benefits if they are operated to break even on direct operating costs and do not discriminate in favor of officers and highly paid employees.

- *On-premises athletic facilities.* Such facilities must be available for the use of all employees, and should therefore be provided for use by both men and women.

Other benefits will be taxed. Companies may want to review their entire fringe benefit program to ensure that they are all tax-free under the new law.

CAFETERIA PLANS

A cafeteria plan, or flexible benefit plan, allows each participant to select from a menu of benefits including group-term life insurance, disability and medical benefits, dependent care, and group legal services. Prior to the Tax Reform Act of 1984, a cafeteria plan could offer a choice of taxable or nontaxable benefits. Beginning in 1985, such a plan can offer benefits that are specifically excludable from gross income (group-term life insurance is treated as a statutory nontaxable benefit). A cafeteria plan may include former employees and beneficiaries of participants.

Requirements

- There must be a written plan

- All participants in the plan must be employees

- The participants in the plan may choose among cash and one or more statutory, nontaxable benefits

Discrimination

Cafeteria plan benefits cannot discriminate in favor of key employees. A key employee is defined as any participant in an employer plan who, at any time during the last five years, was an officer of the employer, one of the ten employees owning the largest interests in the employer, a 5% owner of the employer, or a highly compensated employee.

Benefits

Benefits to key employees cannot exceed 25% of the total nontaxable benefits provided by the plan. If a plan is discriminatory, all the benefits received by key employees will be taxed. A non-key employee will not have benefits applied to gross income even if the cafeteria plan is discriminatory.

Filing Requirements

The Tax Reform Act of 1984 requires every employer with a cafeteria plan to file a return showing the following:

- The number of employees

- The number of employees participating in the plan

- The total cost of the plan during the year

- The employer's name, address, and taxpayer identification number

- The type of business in which the employer is engaged

Cafeteria plans that do not meet the requirements of the Tax Reform Act include plans by which the employee is reimbursed for unused benefits at the end of each year or in which amounts are not specifically allocated to an account until an expense is incurred. The transitional rules protect flexible spending accounts that were in place on February 10, 1984; they remain qualified until January 1, 1985. There is an additional transitional rate for plans that reimburse employees for expenses that are not actually incurred.

VOLUNTARY EMPLOYEES' BENEFICIARY ASSOCIATIONS (VEBAs):

VEBAs are tax-exempt trusts that can accumulate tax-free income-producing reserves generally for the payment of life, medical, and disability benefits for their members. VEBAs initially achieved tax-exempt status as associations formed and funded by employees. Over the years, changes in the law have permitted such associations to be funded by employers as well. Consequently, VEBAs are now effective employee benefits vehicles for employers to provide increasing amounts and additional types of employee benefits.

Under IRS Code 501, an organization must meet four requirements to qualify as a VEBA:

- The organization must be an employees' association

- Membership in the association must be voluntary

- The organization must provide for the payment of life, sick, accident, or other benefits to its members, their dependents, or designated beneficiaries, and substantially all of its operations must be aimed at providing such benefits

- No part of the net earnings of the organization must inure (other than by payment of the benefits) to the benefit of any private shareholder or individual

Before the Tax Reform Act of 1984, an employer's contribution to a VEBA was deductible when paid or accrued rather than when the benefit was provided. TRA set limits on the amount of deductible contributions based on the VEBA's current cost of providing benefits.

New Code Section 505 prevents discrimination in favor of highly paid employees. VEBA benefits must be found to be nondiscriminatory by the Treasury Department. Employees who do not participate in the VEBA must be considered in testing for nondiscrimination. Certain employees (e.g., those who have completed less than three years of service) may be excluded from nondiscrimination testing.

Excise taxes will be imposed on advanced funding where certain funds are used by a key employee. Vacation benefits, in general, may no longer be provided through the use of a VEBA. Rules apply to plan years beginning after December 31, 1985. Certain rules apply to taxable years beginning after December 31, 1984.

Advantages

The two principal advantages of VEBAs are:

A VEBA can reduce the cost of benefits normally provided by an outside insurer. The employee trust does not have to provide the same level of reserves that insurance carriers must.

Employers who self-fund their plans tend to obtain more information about their employee benefit programs as they become more directly involved in administering and monitoring them. Consequently, they use their increased information more effectively to control costs. Employers frequently become shrewd purchasers of the array of services offered as employee benefits.

Disadvantages

The two principal disadvantages of VEBAs are:

- Costs in management time and effort, and

- The risk of excessive benefit costs (this is often covered by stop-loss insurance, e.g., a major medical policy).

Employers considering self-funding should accumulate and analyze the relevant data in order to evaluate the costs savings and risks involved, as well as the impact on employer relations and the cost of additional administrative burdens. For some employers the disadvantages outweigh the advantages, but for many, acting alone or through an industry association, self-funded employee benefit programs can be cost effective.

Insurance Rates

On December 1, 1983, the IRS issued final regulations revising the uniform premium table used to calculate the cost of group-term life insurance coverage provided to an employee by an employer. The New Table I rates are significantly lower than the previous ones, especially for the older age brackets. The new table will apply for group-term life insurance coverage provided after December 31, 1982.

RATES FOR GROUP-TERM LIFE INSURANCE

Ages	Previous Table I Rates (per $1,000 of coverage per month)	New Table I Rates (per $1,000 of coverage per month)
Under 30	$.08	$.08
30-34	.10	.09
35-39	.14	.11
40-44	.23	.17
45-49	.40	.29
50-54	.68	.48
55-59	1.10	.75
60-64	1.63	1.17

Source: North American Life and Casualty Company.

Beginning in 1984, if an employer has a "discriminatory" plan of group life insurance (which basically results from not offering similar benefits to all classes of employees), the key employees are not entitled to the exclusion of the first $50,000 of group life protection. The full cost paid by the employer for the taxable year is included in the income of the employee. Under the Tax Reform Act of 1984, the cost may not be determined using the Table I rates but will be the *actual* cost of the life insurance provided. In addition, the same rules that apply to active employees will apply to retired employees, except for retired disabled employees to whom employer-paid premiums for group term are 100% tax free.

STOCK OPTIONS

Incentive Stock Option (ISO)

The incentive stock option plan (ISO) allows employers to provide an incentive to employees and employees to turn compensation for services into capital gain. The cost to the employer corporation is the loss of a tax deduction. If the ISO fails to meet the technical requirements or if the employee makes a disqualifying disposition of the stock, the transaction will be treated as a nonqualified or nonstatutory option:

- An incentive stock option plan must describe the employees eligible to participate and state the maximum number of shares subject to the plan.

- The aggregate fair market value of stock for which an employee is granted options during the calendar year must not exceed $100,000 plus any partial carryovers of unused limits from prior years.

- The option cannot be exercisable after ten years from the date of grant.

- ISOs must be exercised by the employee and cannot be transferred.

- Options must be exercised in the order which they were granted.

- Employees who own more than 10 % of the employing company must be granted options at a price that is at least 110 % of the fair market value at the time of the grant; other employees will normally be granted options at the fair market value of the stock.

To get capital gains treatment on the sale of the stock, the employee must not dispose of any stock transferred to him pursuant to the option within two years from the date of grant of the option and must hold the stock for at least six months. The sequential exercise rule prohibits employees from exercising options that were granted at a lower price before exercising previously granted higher-priced options. Thus, an employee with options with an exercise price of $10 granted in 1981 and options with an exercise price of $8 granted in 1983, must exercise all 1981 options before the 1983 options or wait until the 1981 options expire. To increase employees' flexibility regarding the sequential exercise rule, the employer may reduce the option period below the statutory ten years.

An employee may consider exercising an ISO in installments in order to reduce the alternative minimum tax exposure. In computing the alternative minimum tax, the difference between the option price and the fair market value on the date of exercise and 60% of the capital gain on disposition of the stock will be a tax preference item.

Stock Appreciation Right (SAR)

An employer may combine an ISO with a stock appreciation right (SAR) at the time of the grant. An SAR gives the employee the right to receive the value of the appreciation in stock from the date of the grant to the date of the exercise.

Tandem ISO-SAR

- The SAR must expire no later than the expiration of the underlying ISO.

- The cash payable under the SAR cannot be greater than the difference between the market price and exercise price of the stock subject to the ISO when the SAR is exercised.

- The SAR is subject to the same restrictions on transferability.

- The SAR is exercisable only when the ISO is exercisable.

- The SAR may be exercised only when the market price of the stock subject to the option exceeds the exercise price.

Nonstatutory Stock Options

A nonstatutory option is any stock option that does not meet the above requirements. It is taxed on its value at ordinary income rates, not capital gains rates. The recipient of a nonstatutory option will be taxed at either the time of granting the option or when the option is exercised. The employee may make a statutory election to have the option taxed at the time it is granted but only if the option has a readily ascertainable fair market value. If the nonstatutory option is taxed when granted the appreciation on the property underlying the option receives capital gain treatment on any further appreciation, and the employer will receive his compensation deduction at that time. If the option is taxed when exercised, the employer deducts the value then and takes a larger deduction.

1.10 Social Security and Medicare

U nder the aegis of the Social Security Administration are programs that provide re- tirement benefits, disability benefits, survivors' benefits, and health insurance for qualified workers and their dependents. These insurance programs—often called OASDHI, for Old-Age, Survivors, Disability, and Hospital Insurance—are financed by a tax on the earnings of individuals in the current workforce.

In 1985 employees and their employers are each required to contribute 7.05% of the first $39,600 of the employee's annual wages (maximum contribution, $2791.80). The tax rate is scheduled to rise every two years for the rest of the decade, as follows:

1986	7.15%
1988	7.51%
1990	7.65%

Self-employed persons whose net annual earnings exceed $400 are required to pay the tax on their net self-employment income. In 1985 the effective rate is 11.8% of the first $39,600 (maximum contribution, $4,672.80) and the effective rates are scheduled to rise as follows:

1986	12.30%
1988	13.02%
1990	13.30%

RETIREMENT BENEFITS

Eligibility

To receive retirement benefits, a worker must be at least 62 years of age (65 to receive full benefits) and have worked a specified number of quarters in employment or self- employment covered by Social Security:

Year of birth	Quarters required
1917	28
1918	29
1919	30
1920	31
1921–1924	32
1925–1928	36
1929 and after	40

On January 1, 1984, Social Security coverage was extended to all employees of non- profit organizations. Mandatorily covered employees who were age 55 or older on that date may be eligible for benefits even if they do not have the mandatory quarters of cov- ered credits.

Special benefits ($130 a month in 1984) are available for persons aged 72 and over who do not meet the work-credit requirements and are not receiving public assistance.

Primary Insurance Amount (PIA)

An individual's primary insurance amount (PIA) is based on his or her lifetime earnings. The PIA is then adjusted to reflect the worker's age at retirement and number of qualifying dependents. In 1984 the average PIA for low earners was $361, for median earners $542, and for high earners $703.

AGE AT RETIREMENT

The PIA is permanently reduced for workers retiring before age 65 and is permanently increased for workers retiring past that age. The rates of adjustment are ⁵⁄₉ of 1% for each month of early retirement (6.66% per year) and ¼ of 1% for each month of delayed retirement (3% per year) up until age 70:

Age at retirement	PIA adjustment
62	80% PIA
63	87% PIA
64	93% PIA
65	100% PIA
66	103% PIA
67	106% PIA
68	109% PIA
69	112% PIA
70	115% PIA

The delayed retirement credit is scheduled to increase gradually to 8% a year between 1990 and 2008. However, the age for full retirement benefits is also scheduled to increase gradually to age 67, beginning in the year 2000. A person retiring at age 62 will then receive only 70% of the PIA.

DEPENDENTS

The spouse (and in some cases, the divorced spouse) of an individual who is receiving retirement benefits and their unmarried children who are under age 18 (under 19 if full-time high school students, and over 18 if severely disabled) may receive monthly benefits that are one-half of the retiree's PIA. Reduced spouses' benefits may be claimed at age 62.

Post-Retirement Earnings

Individuals can work while receiving Social Security retirement benefits, but earnings may reduce their monthly benefits. Retirees under age 65 in 1985 can earn $5,400 without causing any reduction in benefits; for retirees aged 65 to 70 in 1985, the limit is $7,320; there is no restriction for retirees after their seventieth birthday. (These levels are adjusted annually to keep pace with average wage increases.) For earnings that exceed these thresholds, $1 in benefits will be withheld for each $2 of surplus income.

In the year in which a worker retires, benefits will be paid for any month in which wages do not exceed $610 for workers 65 or older, and $450 for those under age 65.

Tax Liability

Beginning with the 1984 tax year, Social Security retirement benefits became subject to federal income tax for beneficiaries whose adjusted gross income and tax-exempt interest income exceed threshold levels. Recipients must total their adjusted gross income, tax-exempt interest income, and half the retirement benefits received during the year. If this total exceeds $25,000 for an individual ($32,000 for a couple filing jointly), then the *lesser* of the following must be declared as taxable income: one-half of the disability benefits received during the year, or one-half of the excess over the threshold level.

ESTIMATING SOCIAL SECURITY RETIREMENT BENEFITS

The Social Security Administration has developed two methods for calculating retirement benefits—the averaging method and the indexing method—and a retiree receives the higher of the two amounts.

Averaging Method

Step 1. Retirement benefits are based on average earnings over a period of years. The length of this period depends on the retiree's year of birth.

Year of birth	Length of averaging period
1917	23 years
1918	24 years
1919	25 years
1920	26 years
1921	27 years

Enter the length of retiree's averaging period: _____ years

Step 2. On the following worksheet, column A shows the maximum earnings covered by Social Security for a given year. In column B, list the retiree's earnings. Do not enter earnings that exceed the maximum covered earnings; enter 0 for a year of no earnings. Estimate earnings for future years up until the year in which the retiree will reach age 62.

Year	Column A	Column B	Year	Column A	Column B
1951	$ 3,600	$_____	1969	7,800	_____
1952	3,600	_____	1970	7,800	_____
1953	3,600	_____	1971	7,800	_____
1954	3,600	_____	1972	9,000	_____
1955	4,200	_____	1973	10,800	_____
1956	4,200	_____	1974	13,200	_____
1957	4,200	_____	1975	14,100	_____
1958	4,200	_____	1976	15,300	_____
1959	4,800	_____	1977	16,500	_____
1960	4,800	_____	1978	17,700	_____
1961	4,800	_____	1979	22,900	_____
1962	4,800	_____	1980	25,900	_____
1963	4,800	_____	1981	29,700	_____
1964	4,800	_____	1982	32,400	_____
1965	4,800	_____	1983	35,700	_____
1966	6,600	_____	1984	37,800	_____
1967	6,600	_____	1985	39,600*	_____
1968	7,800	_____			

* The maximum annual earnings covered by Social Security is expected to continue to rise each year to keep pace with rising national wage levels.

Step 3. Count the number of years for which earnings are reported above in column B. If this number exceeds the length of the averaging period determined in step 1, cross off the years of lowest earnings until the number of years remaining in column B matches that shown in step 1.

Step 4. Add up the earnings for the years remaining in column B.

Total averageable earnings: $_____

Step 5. Divide total averagable earnings (step 4) by number of years calculated in step 1.

Average annual earnings: $_____

Step 6. Use the following table of approximate monthly retirement benefits based on average annual earnings.

Approximate monthly benefit: $_____

Step 7. For retirees who have an eligible spouse or child, use the table to estimate dependents' benefits.

Approximate dependents' benefits: $_____

Approximate Monthly Social Security Benefits

Average Annual Earnings	For Workers				For Dependents[1]				Family Benefits[2]
	Retirement at 65	at 64	at 63	at 62	Spouse at 65 (or Child)	at 64	at 63	at 62	
$ 1,200	$156.70	$146.30	$135.90	$125.40	$ 78.40	$ 71.90	$ 65.40	$ 58.80	$235.10
2,600	230.10	214.80	199.50	184.10	115.10	105.50	95.90	86.40	345.20
3,000	251.80	235.10	218.30	201.50	125.90	115.40	104.90	94.50	384.90
3,400	270.00	252.00	234.00	216.00	135.00	123.80	112.50	101.30	434.90
4,000	296.20	276.50	256.80	237.00	148.10	135.70	123.40	111.10	506.20
4,400	317.30	296.20	275.00	253.90	158.70	145.40	132.20	119.10	562.50
4,800	336.00	313.60	291.20	268.80	168.00	153.90	140.00	126.00	612.70
5,200	353.20	329.70	306.20	282.60	176.60	161.80	147.20	132.50	662.70
5,600	370.60	345.90	321.20	296.50	185.30	169.80	154.40	139.00	687.10
6,000	388.20	362.40	336.50	310.60	194.10	177.80	161.70	145.60	712.10
6,400	405.60	378.60	351.60	324.50	202.80	185.80	169.00	152.10	737.10
6,800	424.10	395.90	367.60	339.30	212.10	194.30	176.70	159.10	762.30
7,200	446.00	416.30	386.60	356.80	223.00	204.30	185.80	167.30	788.90
7,600	465.60	434.60	403.60	372.50	232.80	213.30	194.00	174.60	814.70
8,000	482.60	450.50	418.30	386.10	241.30	221.10	201.10	181.00	844.50
8,400	492.90	460.10	427.20	394.40	246.50	225.80	205.40	184.90	862.60
8,800	505.10	471.50	437.80	404.10	252.60	231.40	210.50	189.50	883.80
9,200	516.00	481.60	447.20	412.80	258.00	236.40	215.00	193.50	903.00
9,400	520.40	485.80	451.10	416.40	260.20	238.40	216.80	195.20	910.40
9,600	524.60	489.70	454.70	419.70	262.30	240.30	218.50	196.80	918.00
9,800	530.40	495.10	459.70	424.40	265.20	243.00	221.00	198.90	928.00
10,000	534.70	499.10	463.50	427.80	267.40	245.00	222.80	200.60	935.70

1 *If a person is eligible for both a worker's benefit and a spouse's benefit, the check actually payable is limited to the larger of the two.*
2 *The maximum amount payable to a family is generally reached when a worker and two family members are eligible.*

Step 8. The benefit amounts derived in steps 6 and 7 are subject to cost-of-living increases. Calculate these increases by multiplying the amounts shown in steps 6 and 7 by the cost-of-living factor; beginning with the year in which the retiree reaches age 62:

1979	9.9%
1980	14.3%
1981	11.2%
1982	7.4%
1983	3.5%
1984	4.3%

Adjusted monthly retirement benefit: $_____

Adjusted dependents' benefits: $_____

Total benefits: _____

Note: *Total benefits cannot exceed the amount shown in the Family Benefits column after cost-of-living adjustments are applied to those figures.*

INDEXING METHOD

Step 1. The indexing method also requires retirees to calculate their earnings over a period of years.

Year of birth	Period of earnings
1917	23 years
1918	24 years
1919	25 years
1920	26 years
1921	27 years

Length of retiree's earnings period: _____ years

Step 2. On the following worksheet, column A shows the maximum earnings covered by Social Security for a given year. In column B, list the retiree's earnings. Do not enter earnings that exceed the maximum covered earnings; enter 0 for a year of no earnings. Estimate earnings for future years including any years of work past age 65 and up until the year in which the worker plans to retire.

Year Retiree Reaches Age 62

Year	A	B	C 1980	C 1981	C 1982	C 1983	D
1951	$ 3,600	$_____	3.8	4.1	4.5	4.9	$_____
1952	3,600	_____	3.6	3.9	4.2	4.6	_____
1953	3,600	_____	3.4	3.7	4.0	4.4	_____
1954	3,600	_____	3.3	3.6	4.0	4.4	_____
1955	4,200	_____	3.2	3.5	3.8	4.2	_____
1956	4,200	_____	3.0	3.2	3.5	3.9	_____
1957	4,200	_____	2.9	3.2	3.4	3.8	_____
1958	4,200	_____	2.9	3.1	3.4	3.7	_____
1959	4,800	_____	2.7	3.0	3.2	3.6	_____
1960	4,800	_____	2.6	2.9	3.1	3.4	_____
1961	4,800	_____	2.6	2.8	3.1	3.4	_____
1962	4,800	_____	2.5	2.7	2.9	3.2	_____
1963	4,800	_____	2.4	2.6	2.8	3.1	_____
1964	4,800	_____	2.3	2.5	2.7	3.0	_____
1965	4,800	_____	2.3	2.5	2.7	3.0	_____
1966	6,600	_____	2.1	2.3	2.5	2.8	_____
1967	6,600	_____	2.0	2.2	2.4	2.6	_____
1968	7,800	_____	1.9	2.1	2.2	2.5	_____
1969	7,800	_____	1.8	1.9	2.1	2.3	_____
1970	7,800	_____	1.7	1.9	2.0	2.2	_____
1971	7,800	_____	1.6	1.8	1.9	2.1	_____
1972	9,000	_____	1.5	1.6	1.8	1.9	_____
1973	10,800	_____	1.4	1.5	1.7	1.8	_____
1974	13,200	_____	1.3	1.4	1.6	1.7	_____
1975	14,100	_____	1.2	1.3	1.4	1.6	_____
1976	15,300	_____	1.1	1.2	1.4	1.5	_____
1977	16,500	_____	1.1	1.2	1.3	1.4	_____
1978	17,700	_____	1.0	1.1	1.2	1.3	_____
1979	22,900	_____	1.0	1.0	1.1	1.2	_____
1980	25,900	_____	1.0	1.0	1.0	1.1	_____

(Continued)

Year Retiree Reaches Age 62

Year	A	B	C 1980	C 1981	C 1982	C 1983	D
1981	29,700	$_____	1.0	1.0	1.0	1.0	$_____
1982	32,400	_____	1.0	1.0	1.0	1.0	_____
1983	35,700	_____	1.0	1.0	1.0	1.0	_____
1984	37,800	_____	1.0	1.0	1.0	1.0	_____
1985	39,600*	_____	1.0	1.0	1.0	1.0	_____

The maximum annual earnings covered by Social Security is expected to continue to rise each year to keep pace with rising national wage levels.

Step 3. Multiply earnings shown in column B by the appropriate factor shown in column C, and write the result in column D.

Step 4. If the number of years of earnings listed in column D exceeds the number of years shown in step 1, cross off the years of lowest earnings until the number of remaining years shown in column D matches that shown in step 1.

Step 5. Add up the earnings for the years remaining in column D.

Total indexed earnings: $_____

Step 6. Divide the total indexed earnings (step 5) by the number of years shown in step 1.

Average annual earnings: $_____

Step 7. Divide the average annual earnings (step 6) by 12 and round down to the next lower dollar.

Average monthly earnings: $_____

Step 8.

For workers born in 1918:

    a. Multiply the first $194 of average monthly earnings by 90%. $_____

    b. Multiply the next $977 of average monthly earnings by 32%. $_____

    c. Multiply remaining average monthly earnings by 15%. $_____

    d. Add figures calculated in steps a, b, and c. $_____

    e. To account for cost-of-living increases, multiply figure calculated in step d by 1.365.

Age 65 benefit: $_____

For workers born in 1919:

    a. Multiply the first $211 of average monthly earnings by 90%. $_____

    b. Multiply the next $1,063 of average monthly earnings by 32%. $_____

    c. Multiply remaining average monthly earnings by 15%. $_____

    d. Add figures calculated in steps a, b, and c. $_____

    e. To account for cost-of-living increases, multiply figure calculated in step d by 1.194.

Age 65 benefit: $_____

For workers born in 1920:

    a. Multiply the first $230 of average monthly earnings by 90%. $_____

    b. Multiply the next $1,158 of average monthly earnings by 32%. $_____

    c. Multiply remaining average monthly earnings by 15%. $_____

    d. Add figures calculated in steps a, b, and c. $_____

    e. To account for cost-of-living increases, multiply figure calculated in step d by 1.074.

Age 65 benefit: $_____

For workers born in 1921:

    a. Multiply first $254 of average monthly earnings by 90%. $_____

    b. Multiply the next $1,274 of average monthly earnings by 32%. $_____

    c. Multiply remaining average monthly earnings by 15%. $_____

    d. Add figures calculated in steps a, b, and c. $_____

Age 65 benefit: $_____

Step 9. The benefit calculated in step 8 is permanently reduced for a worker who chooses to receive retirement benefits before age 65. The following table shows the reduction factors, based on the number of months before age 65 that the worker begins to receive benefits.

Number of Months	Reduction Factor	Number of Months	Reduction Factor
1	.994	19	.894
2	.988	20	.888
3	.983	21	.883
4	.977	22	.877
5	.972	23	.872
6	.966	24	.866
7	.961	25	.861
8	.955	26	.855
9	.950	27	.850
10	.944	28	.844
11	.938	29	.838
12	.933	30	.833
13	.927	31	.827
14	.922	32	.822
15	.916	33	.816
16	.911	34	.811
17	.905	35	.805
18	.900	36	.800

Step 10. The benefit rate for a spouse at age 65 is one-half of the retiree's age 65 benefit. But if a spouse chooses to receive benefits before age 65, the monthly benefit is permanently reduced. The following table shows the reduction factors, based on the number of months before age 65 that the spouse begins to receive benefits.

Number of Months	Reduction Factor	Number of Months	Reduction Factor
1	.993	19	.868
2	.986	20	.861
3	.979	21	.854
4	.972	22	.847
5	.965	23	.840
6	.958	24	.833
7	.951	25	.826
8	.944	26	.819
9	.937	27	.812
10	.930	28	.805
11	.923	29	.798
12	.916	30	.791
13	.909	31	.784
14	.902	32	.777
15	.895	33	.770
16	.888	34	.763
17	.881	35	.756
18	.875	36	.750

DISABILITY BENEFITS

Disability benefits may be claimed by a worker who becomes disabled to the extent that medical evidence indicates that he or she cannot work for a year or longer. Monthly payments start after a five-month waiting period and continue for as long as the worker is disabled. After 24 months of receiving disability benefits, the disabled worker is eligible for Medicare, regardless of her or her age.

Eligibility

The number of quarters of covered work needed to qualify for disability benefits depends on the age of the worker at the time of disability:

- Under age 24: During the three-year period prior to the disability, six quarters of covered work.

- Age 24 through 30: Work credits for half of the quarters between the age of 21 and the time of the disability.

- Age 31 or older: During the ten-year period prior to the disability, 20 quarters of covered work. In addition, worker must have enough credits to be eligible for retirement benefits (40 quarters for workers born in 1929 and after).

A worker disabled by blindness does not have to meet the above work-credit requirements but does need at least one quarter of covered work for each year since 1950 or the year in which he or she reached age 21 (whichever is later) up until the year of blindness. A minimum of six quarters is required.

Dependents' Benefits

If a worker is receiving disability benefits, the following dependents may also qualify for monthly benefits:

- Unmarried child under age 18 (under 19 if a full-time high school student)

- Unmarried child 18 or older who was severely disabled before age 22 and continues to be disabled

- Spouse age 62 or older

- Spouse under age 62 who is caring for a child of the disabled worker if the child is under age 16 (or disabled) and receiving dependents' benefits based on the disabled worker's earnings.

Monthly Payments

The amount of a disabled worker's monthly benefits is based on his or her lifetime average earnings. In 1984 the average monthly benefit for a disabled worker was $452; the average payment for a disabled worker with a family was $855. Benefits are automatically adjusted each year to keep pace with the cost of living.

Tax Liability

Beginning with the 1984 tax year, disability benefits became subject to federal income tax for beneficiaries whose adjusted gross income and tax-exempt interest income exceed threshold levels. Recipients must total their adjusted gross income, tax-exempt interest income, and half the disability benefits received during the year. If this total exceeds $25,000 for an individual ($32,000 for a couple filing jointly), then the *lesser* of the following must be declared as taxable income:

- One-half of the disability benefits received during the year

- One-half of the excess over the threshold level.

SURVIVORS' BENEFITS

At an eligible worker's death, a lump-sum burial payment of $255 will be made to a surviving spouse or child. Monthly payments may also be claimed by the following relatives of a deceased worker:

- Unmarried child under age 18 (under 19 if a full-time high school student)

- Unmarried child age 18 or older who was severely disabled before age 22 and continues to be disabled

- Surviving spouse age 60 or older

- Surviving spouse or divorced spouse who is caring for the worker's child who is age 16 or younger (or disabled) and who is receiving dependents' benefits based on the deceased worker's earnings.

- Surviving spouse age 50 or older who becomes disabled within seven years after the worker's death or within seven years after spousal benefits as parent caring for the deceased's child end

- Dependent parents age 62 or older.

Under certain conditions divorced spouses and dependent grandchildren of the deceased worker may also receive benefits.

Eligibility

Work-credit requirements for survivors' benefits are lower than those for retirement benefits. If the deceased worker was born in 1929 or earlier, he or she need have accumulated one-quarter of covered work for each year after 1950 and up to the year of death. If the deceased worker was born in 1930 or later, he or she must have in addition accumulated one quarter of covered work for each year after turning 21 and up until the year of death.

MEDICARE

Medicare is a federal health insurance program that serves people aged 65 and older, people of any age who have permanent kidney failure, certain disabled persons, and certain spouses (including surviving spouses and divorced spouses) and dependent children and parents of eligible persons. Local Social Security offices take applications, assist in the filing of claims, and provide detailed information about all aspects of the program.

Medicare comprises a hospital insurance program and a medical insurance program, each of which has its own rules for eligibility and enrollment. Hospital insurance is financed by payroll and self-employment Social Security taxes, while medical insurance is paid for by enrollees' monthly premiums and general federal revenues.

Hospital Insurance

ELIGIBILITY

Eligibility for Medicare hospital insurance begins at age 65 for individuals who:

- Are entitled to monthly Social Security or railroad retirement benefits

- Have sufficient work credits to be insured under Social Security or the railroad retirement system

- Have sufficient work credits in federal employment to qualify

Disabled individuals under the age of 65 are eligible if they have been entitled to Social Security disability benefits for 24 months or are federal employees with sufficient work credits. The age requirement is also waived for those suffering permanent kidney damage who need maintenance dialysis or a kidney transplant if they are insured or receiving monthly benefits under Social Security or the railroad retirement system or are federal employees with sufficient work credits.

Under certain conditions, an eligible person's spouse, divorced spouse, surviving spouse, or dependent parents may be eligible for hospital insurance at age 65. Also, disabled surviving spouses under age 65, disabled surviving divorced spouses under age 65, and disabled children aged 18 or older may be eligible. In cases of permanent kidney failure, however, only the family member who has permanent kidney damage is eligible.

ELECTIVE COVERAGE

Individuals who are not eligible for hospital insurance may elect to purchase it at age 65. Those who choose to buy this insurance must also purchase Medicare medical insurance. In 1985 the basic monthly premiums are $174 for hospital insurance and $15.50 for medical insurance.

ENROLLMENT

Individuals who are receiving Social Security or railroad retirement checks will automatically be enrolled for hospital insurance when they turn 65; no application need be filed. Hospital insurance will also be automatically provided for disabled individuals of any age once they have been entitled to Social Security disability benefits for 24 months.

All other persons—including federal workers, individuals suffering permanent kidney damage, and disabled surviving spouses—must apply for coverage. Applications should be filed at a Social Security office about three months before the applicant's sixty-fifth birthday in order for coverage to begin at age 65. Both those who intend to retire at age 65 and those who intend to continue working should apply at this time.

BENEFITS

Medical hospital insurance helps pay for inpatient hospital care, inpatient care in a skilled nursing facility, home health care, and hospice care.

For limitations on length of stay and deductibles, contact a Social Security office.

Medical Insurance

ELIGIBILITY

Almost anyone who is 65 or older can enroll for Medicare medical insurance—no Social Security or federal work credits are required. In 1985 the basic monthly premium for this coverage is $15.50.

ENROLLMENT

Those receiving Social Security benefits under the railroad retirement system will be automatically enrolled for medical insurance—unless the individual declines coverage—when they become entitled to hospital insurance.

An application for medical insurance coverage must be filed by anyone who:

- Plans to continue working past age 65

- Is 65 but ineligible for hospital insurance

- Has permanent kidney failure

- Is a disabled surviving spouse between the ages of 50 and 65 who is not receiving disability checks

- Is eligible for Medicare on the basis of federal employment

- Lives in Puerto Rico or outside the U.S.

ENROLLMENT PERIOD

The seven-month initial enrollment period begins three months before the month in which an individual first becomes eligible for medical insurance and ends three months after that month.

Individuals who do not enroll during the initial enrollment period may enroll during the annual general enrollment period—January 1 through March 31. But their protection will not start until July 1 and their basic monthly premium will be 10% higher than the basic premium for *each* 12-month period in which they could have but did not enroll.

BENEFITS

Medicare medical insurance helps pay for doctors' services, outpatient emergency and clinic services, home health visits, and medical supplies and drugs furnished or administered in a doctor's office as part of treatment. Under *certain* conditions, medical insurance also covers ambulance transportation, artificial limbs and eyes, independent laboratory tests, oral surgery, outpatient physical therapy and speech pathology services, and X-ray and radiation treatments.

Medicare medical insurance *does not* cover custodial care; dentures and routine dental care; eyeglasses, hearing aids, and examinations to prescribe or fit them; personal comfort items in a hospital room; prescription drugs; private duty nurses; and routine physical checkups and tests directly related to such examinations.

In general, Medicare medical insurance will pay 80% of the approved charges for covered services after the insured meets the annual deductible; in 1985 the annual deductible is $75.

SUPPLEMENTAL HEALTH INSURANCE

Many private health insurers offer policies to supplement Medicare. Individuals receiving health care protection from the Veterans Administration, Indian Health Service, federal employees' health plan, or state medical assistance program should consult with the appropriate agency to determine whether they should also apply for Medicare. The issue of supplemental insurance is discussed in detail in "Guide to Health Insurance for People with Medicare," a free pamphlet available at all Social Security offices.

Individuals who work past age 65 should consult "Employed Medicare Beneficiaries Age 65 Through 69," a free pamphlet available at Social Security offices.

Source: U.S. Department of Health and Human Services, Social Security Administration and Health Care Financing Administration.

USE OF SKILLED NURSING FACILITIES BY THE AGED AND DISABLED
By Region

Area of Residence	Covered Days		Covered Charges			Reimbursements		
	Number (000)	Per 1,000 Enrolled	$ Amount (000)	$ Per Day	$ Amount (000)	% of Covered Charges	$ Per Enrollee (000)	$ Per Day
All Areas	7,758	309	554,003	71	328,081	59.2	13.08	42
United States	7,741	314	552,382	71	327,192	59.2	13.29	42
Northeast	1,812	306	136,395	75	80,488	59.0	13.61	44
North Central	2,371	361	170,784	72	98,853	57.8	15.03	42
South	2,237	281	139,860	63	78,597	56.2	9.86	35
West	1,320	319	105,319	80	69,240	65.7	16.76	52
New England	347	233	27,465	79	16,868	61.4	11.34	49
Connecticut	74	207	3,948	53	2,448	62.0	6.83	33
Maine	25	177	2,515	101	1,566	62.2	11.12	63
Massachusetts	120	170	12,103	101	7,573	62.5	10.75	63
New Hampshire	44	431	3,887	88	2,205	56.7	21.52	50
Rhode Island	68	552	4,046	60	2,571	63.5	20.89	38
Vermont	15	266	966	63	506	52.3	8.74	33
Middle Atlantic	1,466	331	108,931	74	63,620	58.4	14.37	43
New Jersey	215	256	18,002	84	11,007	61.1	13.10	51
New York	531	254	43,907	83	25,473	58.0	12.19	48
Pennsylvania	720	480	47,022	65	27,140	57.7	18.10	38
East North Central	1,928	437	133,369	69	74,896	56.1	16.98	39
Illinois	581	476	45,366	78	25,604	56.4	20.97	44
Indiana	203	353	12,590	62	6,855	54.4	11.91	34
Michigan	447	493	27,355	61	15,313	55.9	16.90	34
Ohio	610	533	42,300	69	23,850	56.3	20.85	39
Wisconsin	87	155	5,758	66	3,274	56.8	5.81	38
West North Central	443	205	37,415	84	23,957	64.0	11.06	54
Iowa	78	203	6,778	87	4,450	65.6	11.58	57
Kansas	33	110	2,283	69	1,274	55.7	4.23	37
Minnesota	57	119	5,302	94	3,702	69.8	7.80	65
Missouri	169	267	16,380	97	10,480	63.9	16.61	62
Nebraska	51	248	3,695	73	2,407	65.1	11.82	48
North Dakota	44	542	2,201	50	1,201	54.5	14.90	27
South Dakota	12	134	776	64	444	57.2	4.90	36
South Atlantic	1,363	333	81,498	60	46,078	56.5	11.27	34
Delaware	17	287	859	51	482	56.1	8.20	29
District of Columbia	13	188	820	65	482	58.7	7.25	38

Use of Skilled Nursing Facilities by the Aged and Disabled

Area of Residence	Covered Days		Covered Charges			Reimbursements		
	Number (000)	Per 1,000 Enrolled	$ Amount (000)	$ Per Day	$ Amount (000)	% of Covered Charges	$ Per Enrollee (000)	$ Per Day
Florida	644	416	39,086	61	22,406	57.3	14.47	35
Georgia	78	160	5,604	72	3,458	61.7	7.14	45
Maryland	116	311	6,689	58	3,992	59.6	10.69	34
North Carolina	228	396	12,107	53	6,574	54.3	11.40	29
South Carolina	91	337	4,312	47	2,283	52.9	8.42	25
Virginia	128	265	8,862	69	4,698	53.0	9.76	37
West Virginia	48	211	3,159	66	1,703	53.9	7.45	35
East South Central	658	419	37,503	57	19,235	51.2	12.25	29
Alabama	197	474	7,689	39	3,946	51.3	9.48	20
Kentucky	281	717	16,666	59	8,793	52.7	22.44	31
Mississippi	9	33	942	104	499	52.9	1.84	55
Tennessee	171	348	12,206	71	5,997	49.1	12.21	35
West South Central	216	93	20,858	97	13,284	63.6	5.74	62
Arkansas	13	43	1,079	84	481	44.6	1.62	37
Louisiana	51	137	4,410	86	2,718	61.6	7.24	53
Oklahoma	49	138	7,133	146	4,667	65.4	13.21	96
Texas	103	80	8,236	80	5,417	65.7	4.20	52
Mountain	239	232	15,596	65	10,510	67.3	10.20	44
Arizona	60	205	4,317	72	3,028	70.1	10.40	51
Colorado	41	172	3,044	74	2,091	68.6	8.72	51
Idaho	24	255	1,129	47	725	64.2	7.72	30
Montana	39	465	1,762	45	1,082	61.4	12.79	28
Nevada	27	419	1,803	67	1,181	65.5	18.41	44
New Mexico	10	92	767	75	436	56.8	3.92	43
Utah	33	312	2,579	77	1,847	71.6	17.19	55
Wyoming	4	105	194	49	118	60.9	3.13	30
Pacific	1,081	348	89,723	83	58,730	65.4	18.93	54
Alaska	1	94	128	125	88	68.9	8.05	86
California	772	336	69,054	89	45,227	65.4	19.68	59
Hawaii	45	620	3,750	84	2,325	62.0	32.24	52
Oregon	133	443	8,368	63	5,150	61.5	17.22	39
Washington	131	310	8,423	64	5,940	70.5	14.08	45
Puerto Rico	15	57	1,475	99	829	56.1	3.15	56

1 *Includes residence unknown, foreign, Guam, Virgin Islands, and other outlying areas.*
2 *Includes residence unknown.*

Source: Health Care Financing Administration.

USE OF SKILLED NURSING FACILITIES BY THE AGED AND DISABLED
1969–1980

Period Incurred	Covered Days of Care		Covered Charges (in Dollars)				Reimbursements			
	Number (000)	Per 1,000 Enrolled	Amount (000)	Per Day	Total Medicare (000)	Skilled Nursing Facility (000)	% of Covered Charges	% of Total Medicare Re-imbursements	$ Per Enrollee (000)	$ Per Day (000)
All Enrollees										
1969	17,572	878	432,179	25	6,284,009	335,037	77.5	5.3	16.74	19
1970	10,697	525	295,089	28	6,772,423	225,561	76.4	3.3	11.08	21
1971	7,481	361	229,912	31	7,486,953	178,703	77.7	2.4	8.62	24
1972	6,628	314	212,084	32	8,216,488	164,085	77.3	2.0	7.77	25
1973	8,629	370	282,091	33	9,639,206	212,761	75.4	2.2	9.13	25
1974	8,965	375	334,727	37	11,920,181	245,929	73.5	2.1	10.28	27
1975	8,874	360	420,305	47	14,746,886	261,058	62.1	1.8	10.59	29
1976	9,724	384	466,273	48	17,939,487	304,660	65.3	1.7	12.04	31
1977	9,612	368	497,553	52	21,094,334	312,703	62.8	1.5	11.98	33
1978	8,936	334	513,536	57	24,402,774	315,810	61.5	1.3	11.79	35
1979	8,294	302	535,718	65	28,267,017	323,721	60.4	1.1	11.79	39
1980	8,045	287	577,083	72	33,389,374	341,141	59.1	1.0	12.15	42
Annual % Rate of Change	−6.9	−9.7	2.7	10.1	16.4	0.2	−2.4	−14.1	−2.9	7.5
Aged										
1969	17,572	878	432,179	25	6,284,009	335,037	77.5	5.3	16.74	19
1970	10,697	525	295,089	28	6,772,423	225,561	76.4	3.3	11.08	21
1971	7,481	361	229,912	31	7,486,953	178,703	77.7	2.4	8.62	24
1972	6,628	314	212,084	32	8,216,488	164,085	77.3	2.0	7.77	25
1973	8,523	395	278,065	33	9,218,271	209,838	75.4	2.3	9.73	25
1974	8,688	395	322,952	37	10,789,062	237,634	73.5	2.2	10.80	27
1975	8,585	382	405,547	47	13,178,458	251,506	62.0	1.9	11.19	29
1976	9,407	410	448,658	48	15,883,884	293,505	65.4	1.8	12.81	31
1977	9,278	395	477,611	51	18,518,654	300,452	62.9	1.6	12.80	32
1978	8,622	359	492,828	57	21,272,391	303,294	61.5	1.4	12.65	35
1979	7,988	325	513,397	64	24,491,108	310,488	60.4	1.3	12.65	39
1980	7,758	309	554,003	71	28,985,547	328,081	59.2	1.1	13.07	42
Annual % Rate of Change	−7.2	−9.1	2.3	10.0	14.9	−0.2	2.4	−13.3	−2.2	7.5
Disabled										
1974	277	144	11,775	43	1,131,119	8,295	70.4	0.7	4.30	30
1975	289	133	14,758	51	1,568,428	9,552	64.7	0.6	4.41	33
1976	317	133	17,615	56	2,055,603	11,155	63.3	0.5	4.66	35
1977	334	128	19,942	60	2,575,680	12,251	61.4	0.5	4.68	37
1978	314	112	20,708	66	3,130,383	12,516	60.4	0.4	4.48	40
1979	306	105	22,321	73	3,775,909	13,233	59.2	0.4	4.55	43
1980	287	97	23,080	80	4,403,827	13,060	56.5	0.3	4.41	45
Annual % Rate of Change	0.6	−6.4	11.9	10.9	25.4	7.9	−3.6	−13.2	0.4	7.0

Note: *Data for July – Dec. 1973, the start of coverage for the disabled, included with all enrollees but not shown for the disabled.*

Source: Health Care Financing Administration

MONTHLY DISABILITY INSURANCE CASH BENEFITS

At End of Selected Month	Number				Amount (in Thousands of Dollars)			
	Total	Disabled Workers[1]	Wives and Husbands[2]	Children[3]	Total	Disabled Workers[1]	Wives and Husbands[2]	Children[3]
December								
1957	149,850	149,850			10,904	10,904		
1958[4]	268,057	237,719	12,231	18,107	20,425	19,516	415	494
1959	460,354	344,443	47,914	77,997	33,907	29,765	1,727	2,414
1960	687,451	455,371	76,599	155,481	48,000	40,668	2,636	4,697
1961	1,027,089	618,075	118,187	290,827	67,756	55,374	3,910	8,472
1962	1,275,105	740,867	147,066	387,172	82,498	66,673	4,767	11,058
1963	1,452,472	827,014	168,243	457,215	93,325	74,922	5,422	12,981
1964	1,563,366	894,173	179,344	489,849	101,205	81,473	5,781	13,951
1965	1,739,051	988,074	193,362	557,615	120,986	96,599	6,761	17,626
1966	1,970,322	1,097,190	219,559	653,573	135,685	107,627	7,577	20,482
1967	2,140,214	1,193,120	234,550	712,544	147,831	117,424	8,040	22,358
1968	2,335,134	1,295,300	253,198	786,636	181,949	144,892	9,687	27,370
1969	2,487,548	1,394,291	264,340	828,917	195,982	157,188	10,081	28,713
1970	2,664,995	1,492,948	283,447	888,600	242,400	196,010	12,060	34,330
1971	2,930,008	1,647,684	311,581	970,743	295,934	241,414	14,237	40,284
1972	3,271,486	1,832,916	350,139	1,088,431	401,462	328,675	19,044	53,743
1973	3,558,982	2,016,626	381,079	1,161,277	448,698	369,090	21,151	58,457
1974	3,911,334	2,236,882	411,660	1,262,792	556,748	460,078	25,479	71,191
1975	4,352,200	2,488,774	452,922	1,410,504	680,102	562,180	30,536	87,386
1976	4,623,827	2,670,244	473,909	1,479,674	790,246	654,656	34,586	101,004
1977	4,854,206	2,834,432	494,389	1,525,385	905,513	751,660	39,106	114,747
1978	4,868,576	2,879,828	491,535	1,497,213	997,284	830,118	42,324	124,842
1979	4,777,218	2,870,411	475,493	1,431,314	1,106,322	924,346	45,768	136,208
1980	4,682,172	2,861,253	462,204	1,358,715	1,261,723	1,060,792	51,065	149,866
1981	4,456,274	2,776,519	428,212	1,251,543	1,353,632	1,147,113	52,081	154,439
1982	3,973,465	2,603,713	365,883	1,003,869	1,322,899	1,147,186	47,288	128,425
1983	3,812,930	2,568,966	308,060	935,904	1,338,587	1,171,950	39,793	126,844
1984[5]	3,821,761	2,593,886	306,220	921,655	1,340,915	1,179,086	38,794	123,036

1 *Includes, from July 1957 through October 1960, disabled workers aged 50–64; beginning November 1960, includes disabled workers under age 65.*
2 *Mainly wives under age 65 with entitled children in their care.*
3 *Includes, beginning 1957, disabled persons aged 18 or older whose disability began before age 22 (age 18 before January 1973) and, beginning 1965, entitled full-time students aged 18–21. Beginning January 1973, students who attain age 22 before end of semester may continue to receive benefits until end of semester.*
4 *November data; December data not available.*
5 *October data.*

Source: *Social Security Bulletin.*

MINIMUM AND MAXIMUM MONTHLY RETIREMENT BENEFITS

Year of Attaining Age 65[1]	Minimum Benefit		Maximum Benefit[3]			
	Payable at the Time of Retirement	Payable Effective June 1983[2]	Payable at the Time of Retirement		Payable Effective June 1983[2]	
			Men	Women	Men	Women
1940	$ 10.00	$189.30	$ 41.20		$365.90	
1941	10.00	189.30	41.60		365.90	
1942	10.00	189.30	42.00		370.40	
1943	10.00	189.30	42.40		370.40	
1944	10.00	189.30	42.80		374.40	
1945	10.00	189.30	43.20		370.40	
1946	10.00	189.30	43.60		379.00	
1947	10.00	189.30	44.00		382.50	
1948	10.00	189.30	44.40		386.20	
1949	10.00	189.30	44.80		386.20	
1950	10.00	189.30	45.20		391.10	
1951	20.00	189.30	68.50		391.10	
1952	20.00	189.30	68.50		391.10	
1953	25.00	189.30	85.00		432.00	
1954	25.00	189.30	85.00		432.00	
1955	30.00	189.30	98.50		432.00	
1956	30.00	189.30	103.50		456.20	
1957	30.00	189.30	108.50		477.00	
1958	30.00	189.30	108.50		477.00	
1959	33.00	189.30	116.00		477.00	
1960	33.00	189.30	119.00		489.00	
1961	33.00	189.30	120.00		492.80	
1962	40.00	189.30	121.00	$123.00	497.30	$505.70
1963	40.00	189.30	122.00	125.00	501.40	513.30
1964	40.00	189.30	123.00	127.00	505.70	521.80
1965	44.00	189.30	131.70	135.90	505.70	521.80
1966	44.00	189.30	132.70	135.90	509.40	548.60
1967	44.00	189.30	135.90	140.00	521.80	568.30
1968	55.00[4]	189.30	156.00[4]	161.60[4]	529.80	548.60
1969	55.00	189.30	160.50	167.30	545.30	568.30
1970	64.00	189.30	189.80	196.40	560.40	580.10
1971	70.40	189.30	213.10	220.40	571.90	591.10
1972	70.40	189.30	216.10	224.70	580.10	602.90
1973	84.50	189.30	266.10	276.40	595.10	618.20
1974	84.50	189.30	274.60	284.90	613.90	667.10
1975	93.80	189.30	316.30	333.70	637.10	672.00
1976	101.40	189.30	364.00	378.80	678.40	706.10
1977	107.90	189.30	412.70	422.40	723.00	739.90
1978	114.30	189.30	459.80		760.50	
1979	121.80	189.30	503.40		781.80	

Minimum and Maximum Monthly Retirement

Year of Attaining Age 65[1]	Minimum Benefit		Maximum Benefit[3]			
	Payable at the Time of Retirement	Payable Effective June 1983[2]	Payable at the Time of Retirement		Payable Effective June 1983[2]	
			Men	Women	Men	Women
1980	133.90	189.30	572.00		808.20	
1981	153.10	189.30	677.00		836.90	
1982	170.30[5]	189.30	679.30[5]		755.00	
1983	166.40[5]	172.20	709.50		734.30	
1984	150.50[5]	150.50	703.60		703.60	

1 *Assumes retirement at beginning of year.*
2 *The final benefit amount payable after Supplemental Medical Insurance (SMI) premium or any other deductions is rounded to next lower dollar.*
3 *Benefit for both men and women shown in men's columns except where women's benefit appears separately.*
4 *Effective for February 1968.*
5 *Derived from transitional guarantee computation based on 1978 Primary Insurance Amount (PIA) table.*

Source: *Social Security Bulletin, Annual Statistical Supplement.*

CONTRIBUTIONS AND TAXES COLLECTED FOR SELECTED SOCIAL SECURITY AND RELATED PROGRAMS
(In Thousands of Dollars)

Calendar Years	Retirement, Disability, and Survivor					Unemployment		
	Old-Age and Survivors Insurance[1][2]	Disability Insurance[1][2]	Federal Civil Service[3]	Railroad Retirement[2][4]	Hospital Insurance under OASDHI[1][2][5]	State Unemployment Insurance[6]	Federal Unemployment Taxes[7]	Railroad Unemployment Insurance[8]
1950	2,667,077		677,730	546,097		1,191,438	223,693	23,356
1951	3,363,466		703,144	708,802		1,492,509	235,073	25,692
1952	3,818,911		748,277	633,792		1,367,675	265,615	25,270
1953	3,945,099		456,177	628,195		1,320,401	254,386	25,257
1954	5,163,263		459,961	604,204		1,135,314	285,307	24,479
1955	5,713,045		743,639	595,437		1,211,759	277,966	24,268
1956	6,171,931		1,119,769	628,681		1,472,410	291,959	59,337
1957	6,825,410	701,566	915,044	609,452		1,544,515	329,202	89,402
1958	7,565,797	965,509	1,462,195	534,888		1,490,014	336,171	107,902
1959	8,051,972	891,229	1,494,953	567,608		1,961,855	324,906	131,142
1960	10,866,294	1,009,926	1,610,266	596,370		2,292,070	339,687	166,553
1961	11,284,951	1,038,020	1,732,402	551,647		2,495,926	345,592	155,440
1962	12,058,809	1,046,192	1,819,903	557,723		2,962,611	454,037	152,771
1963	14,541,451	1,098,617	1,978,453	570,290		3,021,957	948,628	159,210
1964	15,688,879	1,153,945	2,161,404	610,619		3,044,082	844,752	156,997
1965	16,017,468	1,187,904	2,196,519	655,172		3,064,905	617,323	150,292
1966	20,579,611	2,005,619	2,381,174	718,583	1,874,152	3,033,916	557,561	147,187
1967	23,138,250	2,285,542	2,571,498	783,306	3,195,142	2,181,830	597,370	143,104
1968	23,718,648	3,315,641	2,966,149	852,274	4,169,959	2,562,751	601,084	136,710
1969	27,946,631	3,598,977	3,135,416	902,161	4,534,591	2,542,484	632,912	132,748
1970	30,256,144	4,480,914	3,890,842	953,454	4,943,781	2,521,608	891,367	129,066
1971	33,722,571	4,620,149	5,146,848	982,313	4,985,201	2,643,129	1,077,231	123,666
1972	37,781,320	5,106,908	5,512,174	1,062,095	5,792,367	3,920,060	1,235,885	118,678
1973	45,974,621	5,932,479	5,661,151	1,304,122	9,945,399	5,038,648	1,432,793	118,673
1974	52,081,072	6,825,505	7,421,679	1,483,288	10,849,635	5,282,356	1,374,808	119,222
1975	56,815,654	7,443,740	9,489,123	1,473,488	11,508,870	5,292,852	1,311,892	112,706
1976	63,361,747	8,232,877	10,841,461	1,634,791	12,871,989	7,799,634	1,634,562	137,675
1977	69,571,968	9,138,428	13,954,463	1,960,613	14,125,838	9,452,091	1,855,318	203,941

Contributions and Taxes Collected for Selected Social Security and Related Programs

Calendar Years	Retirement, Disability, and Survivor					Unemployment		
	Old-Age and Survivors Insurance[1][2]	Disability Insurance[1][2]	Federal Civil Service[3]	Railroad Retirement[2][4]	Hospital Insurance under OASDHI[1][2][5]	State Unemployment Insurance[6]	Federal Unemployment Taxes[7]	Railroad Unemployment Insurance[8]
1978	75,470,614	13,412,645	14,409,007	1,892,749	17,532,957	11,461,642	2,849,438	215,639
1979	87,919,452	15,114,241	16,540,695	2,267,472	20,959,833	12,377,804	2,943,959	201,565
1980	103,456,364	13,254,956	19,511,063	2,330,822	24,087,891	11,937,572	3,232,407	163,004
1981	122,626,590	16,737,722	22,484,581	2,583,746	33,227,212	10,848,484	3,284,885	188,959
1982	123,672,774	21,994,645	24,024,000	2,919,000	34,917,731	12,911,000	3,569,000	188,000
1983	132,715,994	17,547,260	25,567,000	2,790,000	37,594,691	15,140,000	4,394,000	164,000
1984[9]	13,254,634	1,258,035	17,307,000	296,000	3,475,342	130,000	127,000	38,000

1 Represents contributions of employees, employers, and the self-employed in employments covered by OASDHI under the Social Security Act, on an estimated basis, with suitable subsequent adjustments. Data for earlier years reflect former appropriation bases. Includes deposits by States under voluntary coverage agreements. Employee-tax refunds deducted. Excludes transfer from general revenues.

2 Excludes transfers between OASDHI system and railroad retirement account under the financial interchange provisions of the Railroad Retirement Act.

3 Represents employee and government contributions. Beginning 1968, also includes foreign service and contributory survivor programs for federal judiciary and Tax Court. For civil service, employee share includes voluntary contributions to purchase additional annuity; government share includes federal and District of Columbia agency contributions and, beginning 1968, federal payment for current unfunded liability.

4 Beginning 1959, net of tax refunds. Contributions for hospital insurance of railroad workers are collected and reported with railroad retirement contribution initially and are transferred once a year to the hospital insurance trust fund; data for that month only (the month in which the transfer occurs) are adjusted by the Treasury source to reflect the transfer.

5 Excludes reimbursement from Treasury general funds for cost of benefits for persons not insured for cash benefits under OASDHI or railroad retirement. Includes contributions for hospital insurance coverage of railroad workers (principal amount only), see footnote 4; and, beginning July 1973, premiums for voluntary coverage of uninsured individuals aged 65 or older.

6 Through 1952 represents deposits in state clearing accounts of contributions plus penalties and interest collected from employers and contributions from employees (three states in recent years), as reported by state agencies (to Department of Labor, 1950–52). Starting 1953, represents state deposits in (federal) unemployment trust fund.

7 Represents taxes paid by employers under the Federal Unemployment Tax Act. Beginning 1961, net of tax refunds. Includes tax proceeds for financing temporary extended unemployment compensation programs for 1958 and 1961.

8 Beginning 1947, also covers railroad temporary disability insurance.

9 September data.

Source: *Social Security Bulletin.*

BENEFICIARIES OF CASH PAYMENTS FROM SELECTED SOCIAL SECURITY AND RELATED PROGRAMS

(In Thousands)

At End of Selected Month	Retirement and Disability						Survivor			Railroad Temporary Disability[4]	Unemployment		Federal "Black Lung"[6]
	Retirement[1]	Disability	Railroad[2]	Federal Civil Service	Veterans	Hospitaliz-ation	Railroad	Federal Civil Service	Veterans[3]		State Laws[5]	Railroad	
December:													
1940	148		146	65	610	74	3		323		667	74	
1945	691		173	92	1,534	597	4	7	698		1,743	13	
1950	2,326		256	161	2,366	1,152	142	25	1,010	32	838	35	
1955	5,788		427	234	2,707	2,172	206	74	1,156	36	912	48	
1960	10,599	687	553	379	3,064	3,558	256	154	1,393	34	2,165	102	
1961	11,655	1,027	567	408	3,137	3,812	262	167	1,547	31	1,993	75	
1962	12,675	1,275	585	438	3,177	4,103	270	182	1,653	30	1,585	59	
1963	13,262	1,452	594	465	3,195	4,321	278	197	1,750	31	1,609	49	
1964	13,697	1,563	600	494	3,024	4,539	286	214	1,848	29	1,351	41	
1965	14,175	1,739	620	522	3,216	4,953	291	227	1,924	25	1,035	30	
1966	15,437	1,970	630	564	3,194	5,360	299	240	1,995	23	936	18	
1967	15,907	2,141	641	588	3,175	5,659	309	258	2,077	21	989	39	
1968	16,264	2,335	647	613	3,171	5,963	318	274	2,151	25	941	19	
1969	16,595	2,488	651	636	3,179	6,229	321	288	2,208	23	1,084	16	
1970	17,096	2,665	653	697	3,210	6,468	326	308	2,301	22	2,045	21	
1971	17,660	2,930	660	747	3,251	6,700	330	324	2,365	20	1,784	38	
1972	18,176	3,250	661	829	3,288	6,919	334	343	2,393	16	1,458	17	299
1973	19,151	3,561	660	924	3,267	7,160	335	358	2,360	14	1,462	8	461
1974	19,688	3,912	667	981	3,250	7,254	336	376	2,282	15	2,716	14	487
1975	20,364	4,352	694	1,029	3,244	7,368	337	391	2,259	19	2,845	37	482
1976	20,934	4,624	693	1,077	3,261	7,466	337	402	2,225	18	2,515	24	470
1977	21,634	4,854	695	1,129	3,289	7,594	338	418	2,191	17	2,114	22	457
1978	22,140	4,869	691	1,173	3,286	7,578	335	431	2,119	15	1,921	14	440
1979	22,730	4,777	689	1,230	3,235	7,618	333	430	1,925	13	2,267	18	419
1980	23,336	4,682	685	1,296	3,189	7,601	330	450	1,748	16	2,830	38	400
1981	23,935	4,456	680	1,338	3,145	7,615	326	467	1,374	16	3,191	52	376
1982	24,425	3,973	676	1,373	3,088	7,442	324	485	1,300	16	3,897	77	355

(Continued)

Beneficiaries of Cash Payments from Selected Social Security and Related Programs

At End of Selected Month	Retirement and Disability						Survivor			Railroad Temporary Disability[4]	Unemployment		
	Retirement[1]	Disability	Railroad[2]	Federal Civil Service	Veterans	Hospitalization	Railroad	Federal Civil Service	Veterans[3]		State Laws[5]	Railroad	Federal "Black Lung"[6]
1983	25,022	3,813	670	1,410	3,010	7,250	320	503	1,227	12	2,467	43	333
1984[8]	25,254	3,787	663	1,431	2,982	7,096	315	512	1,144	13	n/av.	17	319

1 Beginning October 1966, includes special benefits authorized by 1966 legislation for persons aged 72 and over and not insured under the regular or transitional provisions of the Social Security Act.
2 Includes auxiliaries or dependents.
3 Monthly number at end of quarter.
4 Average number during 14-day registration period.

5 Average weekly number in December. Includes regular State unemployment insurance, the federal employees' unemployment compensation program, and the exservicemen's compensation program through 1981. Excludes Federal employees' program thereafter.
6 Includes dependents and survivors.
7 Fewer than 500.
8 Data for August.

Source: Social Security Bulletin.

BENEFICIARIES' AVERAGE MONTHLY CASH PAYMENT FROM OLD AGE, SURVIVORS, AND DISABILITY INSURANCE

Period[1]	Retired Workers and Their Spouses and Children			Survivors of Deceased Workers				Disabled Workers and Their Spouses and Children			Persons with Special Age-72 Benefits[9]
	Retired Workers[2]	Wives and Husbands[2,3]	Children[4]	Widows and Widowers[2,5]	Children[4]	Widowed Mothers[6]	Parents[2]	Disabled Workers[7]	Wives and Husbands[8]	Children[4]	
				Average benefits in current-payment status at end of period							
1940	$22.60	$12.13	$9.70	$20.28	$12.22	$19.61	$13.09				
1950	43.86	23.60	17.05	36.54	28.43	34.24	36.69				
1960	74.04	38.72	28.25	57.68	51.37	59.24	60.31	$89.31	$34.41	$30.21	
1965	83.92	43.63	31.98	73.75	61.26	65.45	76.03	97.76	34.96	31.61	
1970	118.10	61.19	44.85	101.71	82.23	86.51	103.21	131.29	42.55	38.63	$45.22
1975	207.18	105.19	77.42	192.33	139.40	147.25	171.86	225.89	67.42	61.95	68.72
1978	263.19	132.77	105.69	238.84	182.12	190.36	213.95	288.25	86.11	83.38	82.96
1979	294.27	148.36	119.80	266.87	205.53	212.56	238.72	322.03	96.25	95.16	91.24
1980	341.41	171.95	140.49	308.12	239.52	246.20	276.07	370.74	110.48	110.30	104.41
1981	385.97	194.75	161.39	346.08	270.94	276.68	310.42	413.15	121.62	123.40	116.19
1982	419.25	212.49	165.45	375.28	285.38	302.81	335.36	440.60	129.24	127.93	124.75
1983	440.77	225.66	176.15	393.03	298.00	308.67	349.84	456.20	129.17	135.53	129.40

(Continued)

Beneficiaries' Average Monthly Cash Payment from Old Age, Survivors, and Disability Insurance

Period[1]	Retired Workers and Their Spouses and Children			Survivors of Deceased Workers				Disabled Workers and Their Spouses and Children			Persons with Special Age-72 Benefits[9]
	Retired Workers[2]	Wives and Husbands[2,3]	Children[4]	Widows and Widowers[2,5]	Children[4]	Widowed Mothers[6]	Parents[2]	Disabled Workers[7]	Wives and Husbands[8]	Children[4]	
Average benefits awarded during period											
1940	$22.71	$12.15	$10.60	$20.36	$12.46	$19.60	$13.09				
Jan.–Aug. 1950	29.03	15.02	14.08	21.65	14.35	22.65	14.65				
Sept.–Dec. 1950	33.24	19.72	11.22	36.89	27.95	35.42	37.99				
1960	81.73	40.25	30.37	62.10	50.87	65.93	70.14	$91.16	$35.38	$30.25	
Jan.–Aug. 1965	82.69	40.52	29.07	73.80	53.55	61.65	80.59	93.26	33.93	28.07	
Sept.–Dec. 1965	89.20	43.74	40.40	75.36	67.95	68.03	85.77	101.30	36.82	35.07	
1970	123.82	57.57	45.45	105.82	79.91	86.70	116.43	139.79	40.40	37.00	$45.18
1975[10]	213.00	99.69	84.17	195.46	142.03	154.98	203.12	241.18	69.86	65.07	68.41
1978[10]	278.80	129.14	114.50	241.76	185.20	204.10	267.00	324.30	92.71	90.80	82.43
1979[10]	317.40	146.45	132.30	265.15	208.60	217.30	295.00	363.00	105.45	105.50	90.49
1980[10]	363.10	169.60	155.10	307.75	238.80	240.60	309.30	406.30	113.67	116.80	102.89
1981[10]	402.08	189.44	192.86	339.65	263.75	262.07	346.72	429.29	113.58	119.58	115.16
1982[10]	412.52	203.48	189.66	367.83	279.10	275.87	348.87	444.35	120.09	125.86	122.97
1983[11]	421.84	211.81	185.31	389.12	287.55	291.45	368.65	447.43	123.71	127.12	128.55
1984[12]	409.57	206.55	180.28	399.98	294.38	296.09	379.61	444.88	119.98	121.72	129.42

1 Some years shown in several parts because of amendments changing the benefit provisions.
2 Persons aged 65 and over (and aged 62–64, beginning 1956 for women and 1961 for men).
3 Includes, beginning 1950, wife beneficiaries under age 65 with entitled children in their care and, beginning September 1965, entitled divorced wives.
4 Includes, beginning 1957, disabled persons aged 18 and over whose disability began before age 22 (age 18 before January 1973) and, beginning September 1965, entitled full-time students aged 18–21. Beginning January 1973, students who attain age 22 before end of semester may continue to receive benefits until end of semester.
5 Includes, beginning September 1965, widows aged 60–61 and entitled surviving divorced wives aged 60 and over; beginning March 1968, disabled widows 50–59 and disabled widowers aged 50–61 and; beginning January 1973, nondisabled widowers aged 60–61.
6 Includes, beginning 1950, surviving divorced mothers with entitled children in their care and, beginning June 1975, widowed fathers with entitled children in their care.
7 Includes, from July 1957 through October 1960, disabled workers aged 50–64; beginning November 1960, includes disabled workers under age 65.
8 Includes wife beneficiaries under age 65 with entitled children in their care, and beginning September 1965, entitled divorced wives.
9 Authorized by 1966 legislation for persons aged 72 and over not insured under the regular or transitional provisions of the Social Security Act.
10 Benefit amounts for awards before the June increase are used in the computation of the averages after conversion to the June rates.
11 Benefit amounts for awards before the December increase are used in the computation of the averages after conversion to the December rates.
12 October data.

Source: Social Security Bulletin.

CHAPTER 2

Taxation

CONTENTS

Tables are indicated by page numbers in italic type; accompanying charts, by a dagger: †

Federal, state, and municipal tax laws are extremely complicated, and both financial professionals and taxpayers should always consult a tax specialist before making decisions that can be expected to have tax-related ramifications.

The information presented here is of necessity abbreviated and largely pertains to issues of federal tax law. The discussions and tables are intended to serve as a quick reference guide and to acquaint readers with the spectrum of factors relevant to tax planning: the principal provisions of recent major tax acts—with special attention to the Tax Reform Act of 1984—and such topics as depreciation, the investment tax credit, income averaging, depletion, and capital gains.

2.01 Evolution of Tax Law

1950 to 1980—A BRIEF REVIEW

Since 1950, there has been an evolution in the nature of laws governing individual income taxes. The following summary of tax legislation provides an overview of the progression that led to the most recent tax legislation, the Tax Reform Act of 1984, a part of the Deficit Reduction Act.

1950

The standard tax rate was 3% and a graduated surtax ranged from 17% to 88%. The Revenue Act of 1950 increased tax rates by eliminating a series of percentage reductions in "tentative taxes" that were in effect during 1948 and 1949. Net combined taxes (standard plus surcharge) were limited to 87% of net income, compared to 77% in the previous year. The withholding tax rate was 18%.

1951

To help finance the war in Korea, the range of marginal surtax rates was increased to 19.2% to 89%, making marginal tax rates as high as 92%. Statutory reductions of the combined standard tax and surtax were eliminated, and the ceiling on combined taxes was raised to 89% of net income. Withholding tax rates were increased to 20%.

1954

Tax reform unified the standard tax and surtax into one rate structure. Marginal tax rates were slightly reduced, to a range of 20% to 91%. The earnings threshold for filing a return was raised from $600 to $1,200, and the definitions of dependent and head of household were broadened. The retirement income credit, credits for dividends received and for partially tax-exempt interest, and the deduction for dependent childcare were introduced. The withholding tax rate was reduced to 18%.

1962

The tax credit for investment in certain depreciable property was introduced. The rate was 7% of the qualified investment.

1964

The Revenue Act of 1964 lowered the tax range significantly. The new rates started at 16% and rose to 77%. It also introduced the income-averaging provision and reduced withholding rates to 14%.

1965

A further lowering of the tax rate range, from 14% up to 70%, legislated in 1964, became effective in 1965.

1966

Graduated withholding was initiated, with rates ranging from 14% to 30%.

1968

As U.S. involvement in Vietnam was nearing its peak, a 10% surcharge on income taxes was imposed, effective April 1, 1968.

1969

The investment tax credit began to be phased out, and the 10% surcharge was extended through 1969. The maximum withholding rate was raised to 33%.

1970

An additional 10% tax on tax preferences (minimum tax) was introduced. Depletion allowances were reduced, deductions for capital losses were limited, exemptions were increased, and the maximum withholding rate was reduced to 25%. In addition, a new minimum standard deduction (or low-income allowance) was allowed, and a 5% tax surcharge was continued through June 30.

1971

The investment tax credit was revived. The standard deduction was increased to 13% ($1,500 maximum). Taxes were lowered for single persons, and a maximum marginal tax of 60% was placed on earned income.

1972

The maximum tax rate on earned income was lowered to 50%.

1974

A tax rebate was approved.

1975

The Tax Reduction Act of 1975 constituted the largest tax cut Americans had received up to that date. A series of tax reductions was adopted as a temporary anti-recessionary measure. The standard deduction was increased to 16% ($2,300 maximum for a single return) and a credit of $30 per exemption was allowed. In addition, Congress approved earned income credits of up to $400 for heads of households (with dependents) whose adjusted gross income fell below $8,000. Purchase-of-residence credits of up to $2,000 were also approved, as was an increase in the investment tax credit from 7% to 10%.

Business also received temporary benefits from an increase in the investment tax credit to 10% and from higher surtax exemptions and accumulated earnings tax credits.

Major oil and gas producers suffered the loss of the percentage depletion allowance and radical changes in the tax treatment of overseas operations.

1976

Under the Tax Reform Act of 1976, some of the 1975 tax reductions were extended and modified. Childcare credits (instead of the childcare deduction) were allowed. The personal exemption credit became a general tax credit (the larger of $35 per exemption or 2% of the first $9,000 of taxable income). The minimum tax was expanded through broadened definitions, reductions, deductions, and an increase in the rate to 15%. The gift tax marital deduction was also expanded. The first $100,000 of gifts to a spouse qualified for an unlimited marital deduction. No part of the next $100,000 of gifts to a spouse qualified for the deduction. One-half of all gifts, in excess of $200,000 to a spouse qualified for the marital deduction.

1977

The Tax Reduction and Simplification Act of 1977 was part of the Administration's efforts to stimulate the economy. The Act increased the standard deduction for most individual taxpayers in the hope that a reduction in taxes would increase consumer spending. A new jobs tax credit was intended to encourage business to hire more employees. The Act also simplified procedures for filing individual income tax returns.

Beginning with 1977, the standard deduction became a flat $3,200 for married persons filing jointly and for surviving spouses, $2,200 for single persons, and $1,600 for married persons filing separately. The standard deduction was computed into the tax tables and rate schedules as a zero bracket, and taxpayers itemizing their deductions could take only those deductions that exceeded the flat standard deduction.

The new jobs tax credit for business allowed a tax credit of up to $100,000 a year for 1977 and 1978 for wages paid to new employees. The maximum credit for each new employee was $2,100 (50% of the first $4,200 of wages paid), with a 10% bonus credit for hiring disabled individuals referred through vocational rehabilitation programs.

The 20% tax rate on the first $25,000 of corporate taxable income and the 22% tax rate on the next $25,000 were continued through 1978, as were the general tax credit and the earned income credit for individuals.

The sick-pay exclusion and the retirement income credit were reinstated, but only for 1976. Taxpayers entitled to such benefits claimed them on amended 1976 returns.

1978

In 1978, a wide variety of changes were initiated through the Revenue Act of 1978 and the Energy Tax Act. The legislation provided significant tax reforms, new tax savings, options, deductions, and credits, as well as new pitfalls. The Energy Tax Act put a tax on gas-guzzling cars and meant higher car prices in subsequent years.

For individuals, tax rates were reduced for 1979 and later, and brackets were widened so that taxpayers would not so quickly move into higher brackets. The personal exemption deduction rose to $1,000 beginning in 1979. The top corporate rate was increased to 46% for 1979 and beyond, with new graduated rates for lower-income corporations.

Sellers of capital assets held more than a year became entitled to exclude 60% of the capital gains, for sales on or after November 1, 1978. Capital gains were not to adversely affect the maximum tax on earned income on or after that date, nor were they subject to the add-on 15% preference tax.

A new alternative minimum tax on capital gains and excess itemized deductions was introduced. The excluded portion of capital gains and adjusted itemized deductions was freed from the regular add-on preference tax, but subject to the new alternative minimum tax. With heavy capital gains or itemized deductions, taxpayers had to pay the higher of the regular tax or the alternative tax, scheduled at graduated rates with a 25% maximum, above an exclusion base of $20,000.

A gain of up to $100,000 on the sale of a prinicipal residence was made tax free for persons 55 or older. Also personal residence sales were no longer taxed as gains, as had been the case with the old add-on minimum tax. Credits for energy saving measures became applicable to qualified devices installed in a personal residence after April 19, 1977. Credits might also be taken in 1978 for work done after that date.

Tax shelter rules were broadened, causing more entities to be subject to the "at risk" rules—with real estate being an exception—that prevent deduction of more than the equity investment. Entertainment facilities, such as hunting lodges and yachts, no longer qualified as business deductions. Partnerships became subject to more stringent reporting requirements, with stiff penalties for the late filing of partnership returns.

A new targeted jobs credit was established and the investment credit was permanently set at 10%.

1980

The Installment Sales Revision Act of 1980 substantially changed rules for reporting gain under the installment method for sales of real property and casual sales of personal property, the rules for electing the installment method, and the rules governing installment sales to related parties. Among the major changes were:

- Elimination of the requirement that no more than 30% of the selling price be received in the tax year of sale to qualify for installment sale reporting for gains from sales of realty and non-dealer personal property.

- Elimination of the requirement that a deferred payment sale be for two or more payments.

- Elimination of the requirement that the selling price for casual sales of personal property exceed $1,000.

- Placement of the installment method on an automatic basis unless the taxpayer elects not to have the sale so treated.

- Adoption of special rules for situations involving installment sales to certain related parties who subsequently sell or dispose of the property and for situations involving installment sales of depreciable property between a taxpayer and his spouse or certain 80%-owned corporations or partnerships.

- Adoption of a general rule providing nonrecognition of gain treatment for a shareholder who receives installment obligations as a liquidating distribution from a corporation liquidating within 12 months of adopting a plan of complete liquidation.

The following tables illustrate the changes and escalating complexity of the history of tax legislation, and provide a review of the changing treatment of the various income groups.

SOURCES OF FEDERAL TAX REVENUES
Percentage Share by Type of Tax

Fiscal Year	Individual Income Taxes	Corporate Income Taxes	Social Insurance Taxes and Contribution	Excise Taxes, Gift and Estate Taxes, Other
1950	39.9%	26.5%	11.1%	22.6%
1955	43.9	27.3	12.0	16.7
1960	44.0	23.2	15.9	16.8
1965	41.8	21.8	19.1	17.4
1970	46.7	16.9	23.4	12.8
1975	43.6	14.5	30.8	11.2
1980	47.2	12.5	30.5	9.8
1981	47.7	10.2	30.5	11.6
1982	48.2	8.0	32.6	11.2
1983	48.1	6.2	34.8	10.9
1984*	43.8	9.9	35.7	10.6

* *Estimate.*

Source: Joint Committee on Taxation.

AVERAGE TAX ON INDIVIDUAL RETURNS

Adjusted Gross Income	1960	1965	1970	1974	1975	1976	1977	1978	1979	1980-present
	Average Tax (thousands of dollars)									
Under $5,000	.3	.2	.3	.2	.1	.2	.1	.1	.1	.2
$5,000–9,999	.8	.7	.8	.7	.6	.6	.5	.5	.5	.5
$10,000–14,999	1.7	1.4	1.5	1.4	1.3	1.3	1.2	1.2	1.2	1.2
$15,000–24,999	3.3	2.7	2.5	2.5	2.4	2.4	2.5	2.4	2.5	
$25,000–29,999	8.2	3.7	4.7	4.3	4.2	4.1	4.1	4.1	3.9	3.9
$30,000–49,999			7.8	6.9	6.7	6.7	6.6	6.6	6.3	6.4
$50,000–99,999	22.5	19.4	19.0	17.5	17.2	17.2	17.1	16.7	15.9	15.6
$100,000–499,999	68.9	63.0	60.6	57.2	56.3	57.8	57.7	57.4	56.9	56.7
$500,000–999,999	312	294	304	301	298	314	310	305	300	296
$1,000,000 and over	951	967	992	969	987	1,069	1,045	988	1,132	1,000
	Average Tax (dollars)									
All groups combined	821	922	1,415	1,836	2,025	2,201	2,482	2,740	2,992	3,387

Source: U.S. Dept. of Commerce, *Statistical Abstract of the United States 1982-83.*

TOTAL TAX AS A PERCENTAGE OF TAXABLE INCOME

Adjusted Gross Income	1960	1965	1970	1974	1975	1976	1977	1978	1979	1980-present
	Total Tax as % of Taxable Income									
Total	**23.0**	**19.5**	**20.9**	**21.6**	**21.1**	**21.2**	**17.6**	**18.3**	**18.5**	**19.6**
Under 5,000	19.9	15.3	15.8	15.4	12.8	12.5	4.4	4.2	2.3	2.9
5,000–9,999	20.4	16.3	17.2	16.9	15.3	14.3	8.6	8.8	8.0	8.1
10,000–14,999	21.4	17.6	18.4	18.0	17.0	16.1	11.8	11.3	12.3	12.3
15,000–24,999	24.2		20.4	19.6	18.8	18.3	15.1	15.2	15.2	15.5
25,000–29,999		22.1	23.1	21.9	21.2	20.9	18.1	18.1	17.5	17.7
30,000–49,999	30.8		27.0	25.0	24.4	24.4	21.9	21.7	21.0	21.2
50,000–99,999	42.0	35.8	36.1	33.6	33.3	33.6	31.5	30.9	29.9	29.9
100,000–499,999	53.7	47.7	49.8	46.1	45.7	46.7	45.1	44.5	43.9	43.9
500,000–999,999	59.0	53.7	62.5	60.0	59.1	62.2	60.5	59.1	57.4	57.0
1,000,000 and over	61.6	54.4	61.2	65.0	64.9	67.3	68.4	65.3	64.5	62.8

Note: *Total tax refers to income tax after credits; beginning in 1970, it includes the minimum tax, and from 1979 on, the alternative minimum tax. Data for years beginning with 1977 are not comparable to earlier years because of a change in the definition of taxable income.*

Source: U.S. Dept. of Commerce, *Statistical Abstract of the United States 1982-83.*

INDIVIDUAL INCOME TAX LIABILITY
(In Dollars)

Group and Revenue Act	Income Year or Period	Selected Net Income Groups — Single Exemption — Liability (Dollars)													
		$600	$1,000	$2,000	$3,000	$5,000	$6,000	$8,000	$10,000	$15,000	$20,000	$25,000	$50,000	$100,000	$1,000,000
1969	1970		53	208	391	792	1,018	1,511	2,065	3,788	5,934	8,423	22,770	56,435	702,179
1964	1969		56	222	425	856	1,098	1,628	2,224	4,077	6,380	9,053	24,453	60,584	753,577
	1968		56	219	415	836	1,073	1,591	2,174	3,984	6,235	8,847	23,897	59,207	736,450
	1965–1967		56	209	386	778	998	1,480	2,022	3,706	5,800	8,230	22,230	55,076	685,070
	1964		64	233	420	834	1,069	1,588	2,177	3,954	6,165	8,744	23,559	58,890	751,378
1954	1954–1963		80	280	488	944	1,204	1,780	2,436	4,448	6,942	9,796	26,388	66,798	869,478
1951	1952–1953		89	311	542	1,052	1,342	1,992	2,728	4,968	7,762	10,940	28,466	69,688	880,000
	1951		82	286	498	964	1,234	1,816	2,486	4,528	7,072	9,976	26,578	67,274	872,000
1950	1950		70	244	428	843	1,080	1,604	2,201	4,032	6,301	8,898	23,997	60,770	800,000
1948	1948–1949		66	232	409	811	1,040	1,546	2,124	3,894	6,089	8,600	23,201	58,762	770,000
1945	1946–1947	19	95	285	485	922	1,169	1,720	2,347	4,270	6,645	9,362	25,137	63,541	840,147
1944	1944–1945	23	115	345	585	1,105	1,395	2,035	2,755	4,930	7,580	10,590	27,945	69,870	900,000
1942	1943	17	107	333	574	1,105	1,401	2,052	2,783	4,968	7,626	10,644	28,058	69,665	899,500
	1942	15	89	273	472	920	1,174	1,742	2,390	4,366	6,816	9,626	25,811	64,641	854,616
1941	1941		21	117	221	483	649	1,031	1,493	2,994	4,929	7,224	20,882	53,214	733,139
1940	1940		4	44	84	172	255	449	686	1,476	2,666	4,253	14,709	44,268	718,404
1936,1938	1936–1939			32	68	140	216	378	560	1,104	1,834	2,804	9,334	33,354	680,184
1934	1934–1935			32	68	140	216	378	560	1,104	1,834	2,804	9,334	31,404	572,324
1932	1932–1933			40	80	160	240	420	600	1,140	1,800	2,640	8,720	30,220	571,220
1928	1929			2	6	13	22	52	90	285	555	922	4,250	14,930	230,930
	1928,1930–1931			6	17	40	56	101	154	386	694	1,099	4,664	15,844	240,844
1926	1925–1927			6	17	40	56	101	154	386	694	1,234	4,954	16,134	241,134
1924	1924			15	30	60	90	150	225	585	1,045	1,635	6,165	22,645	429,645
1921	1923			30	60	120	180	315	450	885	1,350	1,980	6,540	22,665	413,040
	1922			40	80	160	240	420	600	1,140	1,800	2,640	8,720	30,220	550,720
	1921			40	80	160	250	450	670	1,310	2,070	2,960	9,270	31,270	663,270
1918	1919–1920			40	80	160	250	450	670	1,310	2,070	2,960	9,270	31,270	663,270
	1918			60	120	240	370	650	950	1,790	2,750	3,840	11,150	35,150	703,150
1917	1917			20	40	120	170	275	395	770	1,220	1,820	5,220	16,220	475,220
1916	1916					40	60	100	140	240	340	490	1,340	3,940	102,940
1913	1913–1915					20	30	50	70	120	170	270	770	2,520	60,020

Source: U.S. Department of Commerce, *Historical Statistics of the United States.*

INDIVIDUAL INCOME TAX LIABILITY—EFFECTIVE RATES

Group and Revenue Act	Income Year or Period	Selected Net Income Groups													
		$600	$1,000	$2,000	$3,000	$5,000	$6,000	$8,000	$10,000	$15,000	$20,000	$25,000	$50,000	$100,000	$1,000,000
		Single Exemption — Effective Rate (%)													
1969	1970		5.3	10.4	13.0	15.8	17.0	18.9	20.6	25.3	29.7	33.7	45.5	56.4	70.2
	1969		5.6	11.1	14.2	17.1	18.3	20.4	22.2	27.2	31.9	36.2	48.9	60.6	75.4
1964	1968		5.6	11.0	13.8	16.7	17.9	19.9	21.7	26.6	31.2	35.4	47.8	59.2	73.6
	1965–1967		5.6	10.4	12.9	15.6	16.6	18.5	20.2	24.7	29.0	32.9	44.5	55.1	68.5
	1964		6.4	11.6	14.0	16.7	17.8	19.8	21.8	26.4	30.8	35.0	47.1	58.9	75.1
1954	1954–1963		8.0	14.0	16.3	18.9	20.1	22.2	24.4	29.7	34.7	39.2	52.8	66.8	86.9
1951	1952–1953		8.9	15.5	18.1	21.0	22.4	24.9	27.2	33.1	38.8	43.8	56.9	69.7	88.0
	1951		8.2	14.3	16.6	19.3	20.6	22.7	24.9	30.2	35.4	39.9	53.5	67.3	87.2
1950	1950		7.0	12.2	14.3	16.9	18.0	20.0	22.0	26.9	31.5	35.6	48.0	60.8	80.0
1948	1948–1949		6.6	11.6	13.6	16.2	17.3	19.3	21.2	26.0	30.4	34.4	46.4	58.8	77.0
1945	1946–1947	3.2	9.5	14.3	16.2	18.4	19.5	21.5	23.5	28.5	33.2	37.5	50.3	63.5	84.0
1944	1944–1945	3.8	11.5	17.3	19.5	22.1	23.3	25.4	27.6	32.9	37.9	42.4	55.9	69.9	90.0
1942	1943	2.8	10.7	16.7	19.1	22.1	23.4	25.7	27.8	33.1	38.1	42.6	56.1	69.7	90.0
	1942	2.5	8.9	13.7	15.7	18.4	19.6	21.8	23.9	29.1	34.1	38.5	51.6	64.6	85.5
1941	1941		2.1	5.9	7.4	9.7	10.8	12.9	14.9	20.0	24.6	28.9	41.8	53.2	73.3
1940	1940		.4	2.2	2.8	3.4	4.3	5.6	6.9	9.8	13.3	17.0	29.4	44.3	71.8
1936, 1938	1936–1939			1.6	2.3	2.8	3.6	4.7	5.6	7.4	9.2	11.2	18.7	33.4	68.0
1934	1934–1935			1.6	2.3	2.8	3.6	4.7	5.6	7.4	9.2	11.2	18.7	31.4	57.2
1932	1932–1933			2.0	2.7	3.2	4.0	5.3	6.0	7.6	9.0	10.6	17.4	30.2	57.1
1928	1929			.1	.2	.3	.4	.7	.9	1.9	2.8	3.7	8.5	14.9	23.1
	1928, 1930–1931			.3	.6	.8	.9	1.3	1.5	2.6	3.5	4.4	9.3	15.8	24.1
1926	1925–1927			.3	.6	.8	.9	1.3	1.5	2.6	3.5	4.9	9.9	16.1	24.1
1924	1924			.8	1.0	1.2	1.5	1.9	2.3	3.9	5.2	6.5	12.3	22.7	43.0
1921	1923			1.5	2.0	2.4	3.0	3.9	4.5	5.7	6.8	7.9	13.1	22.7	41.3
	1922			2.0	2.7	3.2	4.0	5.3	6.0	7.6	9.0	10.6	17.4	30.2	55.1
	1921			2.0	2.7	3.2	4.2	5.6	6.7	8.7	10.4	11.8	18.5	31.3	66.3
1918	1919–1920			2.0	2.7	3.2	4.2	5.6	6.7	8.7	10.4	11.8	18.5	31.3	66.3
	1918			3.0	4.0	4.8	6.2	8.1	9.5	11.9	13.8	15.4	22.3	35.2	70.3
1917	1917			1.0	1.3	2.4	2.8	3.4	4.0	5.1	6.1	7.3	10.4	16.2	47.5
1916	1916					.8	1.0	1.3	1.4	1.6	1.7	2.0	2.7	3.9	10.0
1913	1913–1915					.4	.5	.6	.7	.8	.9	1.1	1.5	2.5	6.0

Source: U.S. Department of Commerce, *Historical Statistics of the United States.*

The Economic Recovery Tax Act of 1981 (ERTA)

The Economic Recovery Tax Act of 1981 was intended to stimulate the economy by reducing personal and business taxes. The resulting tax cut affected individuals, corporations, partnerships, estates, and trusts.

INDIVIDUAL INCOME TAX PROVISIONS

- ERTA provided tax relief for individuals by reducing individual tax rates—by 1¼% in 1981, 10% in 1982, 19% in 1983, and 23% in 1984 and subsequent years. The top marginal tax rate was reduced from 70% to 50% beginning in January 1982. The maximum rate for long-term capital gains was reduced to 20% for sales or exchanges after June 1981.

- The Act adjusted the tax brackets, zero-bracket amount, and personal exemption for increases in the consumer price index, starting in 1985.

- ERTA introduced a new deduction against gross income for a two-earner married couple filing a joint return. This deduction equals a percentage of the first $30,000 of qualified income earned by whichever spouse has the lower earnings—in 1982, 5% or a maximum of $1,500; and 10% or a maximum of $3,000 in 1983 and subsequent years.

- Employment-related expenditures eligible for the childcare tax credit were increased from $2,000 to $2,400 for taxpayers with one dependent and from $4,000 to $4,800 for taxpayers with two or more dependents. In addition, the Act increased the rate of the childcare credit from 20% to 30% for taxpayers with incomes of $10,000 or less, with the rate decreasing by 1% for each $2,000 of income above $10,000 to a minimum of 20% for taxpayers with incomes above $28,000.

- The Act provided a deduction for charitable contributions for individual taxpayers not itemizing personal deductions. For 1982 and 1983, this was limited to 25% of the first $100 of contributions, with a maximum deduction of $25. For 1984 the contribution cap rose to $300, or a maximum deduction of $75. (For a married individual filing a separate return, the deduction limitation is one-half of these amounts). For 1985, the deduction applies to 50% of contributions, with no cap, and for 1986, the deduction applies to 100% of contributions. This provision expires after 1986.

- Beginning with 1981, the Act provided a new itemized deduction for up to $1,500 of expenses incurred in connection with the adoption of a child who has special needs that make him or her hard to place for adoption.

- ERTA extended from 18 months to 24 months the replacement period during which taxpayers must reinvest the proceeds from the sale of their principal residence in a new principal residence in order to be eligible for rollover nonrecognition treatment on gain from that sale. Also, the Act increased from $100,000 to $125,000 the maximum amount of capital gain on the sale of a principal residence that is excludable from gross income by a taxpayer age 55 or over.

- The system of deductions and exclusions for excess costs of living abroad was replaced by an exclusion for income earned abroad. The maximum amount excludable from income was $80,000 in 1983, increasing by increments of $5,000 to the permanent level of $95,000 in 1986 and thereafter. There is also an exclusion for excess housing costs.

CAPITAL COST RECOVERY PROVISIONS

- ERTA introduced the Accelerated Cost Recovery System (ACRS) for most tangible property placed in service after December 31, 1980. (See Depreciation, page 2.31.)

REHABILITATION EXPENDITURES

- ERTA initiated a three-tier system of investment credits to replace the 10% investment credit for expenditures to rehabilitate nonresidential structures, and authorized amortization and rapid depreciation provisions for certain rehabilitation of certified historic structures. Under the Act, the credit is 15% for rehabilitation of nonresidential buildings 30 to 39 years old, and 25% for certified historic structures. For expenditures to which the 15% and 20% credits apply, the basis for determining cost recovery deductions is reduced by the amount of the credit. The rehabilitation provisions generally apply to expenditures incurred after 1981.

INCENTIVES FOR RESEARCH

- ERTA provided a 25% income tax credit for certain qualified research expenditures incurred in carrying on the taxpayer's trade or business, to the extent such expenditures exceed a base period amount. This new credit applies to expenditures made after June 30, 1981, and before 1986.

- The Act allowed corporations a charitable deduction for contributions of newly manufactured scientific equipment to universities for research use; the deduction is limited to the taxpayer's basis plus 50% of the appreciation, not to exceed twice the basis.

OTHER BUSINESS PROVISIONS

- **Corporate rate reduction**: The Act reduced the tax rate on the first $25,000 of corporate taxable income from 17% to 16% in 1982, and 15% in subsequent years. It reduced the rate on the next $25,000 of taxable income from 20% to 19% in 1982, and 18% in subsequent years.

- **Incentive stock options**: The Act reinstated certain nonrecognition rules and capital gains characterization with respect to employee stock options that meet certain conditions. Under these rules, no gain or loss is recognized by the employees, and no deduction is allowed to the corporate employer, when the option is granted or when the option is exercised. The employee is allowed capital gains treatment on any gain on the sale of the stock.

- **Targeted jobs credit**: The targeted jobs tax credit was extended through 1982.

- **Accumulated earnings credit**: The Act increased from $150,000 to $250,000 the amount a corporation may accumulate, without showing a business purpose, that is exempt from the accumulated earnings tax, effective for taxable years after 1981.

- **Subchapter S corporations**: ERTA increased the maximum number of shareholders from 15 to 25, and allowed certain trusts to be qualified shareholders.

- **Inventory accounting**: The Act simplified LIFO ("last in / first out") inventory accounting for small businesses, allowing businesses with annual average gross receipts under $2 million for the previous three years to use a single dollar-value LIFO pool. Taxpayers switching to LIFO were given three years to take the inventory writedowns from prior years into income.

SAVINGS INCENTIVES

- **Interest and dividend exclusion**: Effective for 1982 and later years, the Act provided a $100 exclusion for dividends only (with $200 excludable on a joint return regardless of which spouse earned the dividends). Beginning in 1985, individuals can also exclude 15% of interest income to the extent such income exceeds non-business and nonmortgage interest deductions, up to a maximum interest exclusion of $450 ($900 on a joint return).

- **Qualified savings certificates**: The Act excluded from income interest on qualified savings certificates, not to exceed an aggregate amount of $1,000, or $2,000 on a joint return.

- **Individual Retirement Accounts**: See IRAS, page 1.69.

- **Self-Employed Retirement Savings**: See Keogh Accounts—HR-10s, page 1.84.

- **Employee stock ownership plans**: The Act terminated the additional investment tax credit for contributions to an employee stock ownership plan (ESOP) and substituted an income tax credit for contributions to an ESOP based on employee payroll. For 1983 and 1984, the credit is limited to 0.5% of compensation paid to employees under the plan; the limitation increases to 0.75% after 1984. The payroll-based ESOP credit expires at the end of 1987.

- **Dividend reinvestment plans**: The Act excluded from income up to $750 ($1,500 for a joint return) of stock distributions from public utilities that are reinvested in the stock of the utility under a qualified dividend reinvestment plan. Upon sale, gain will generally be treated as capital gain. The exclusion applies for the years 1982 through 1985.

ESTATE AND GIFT TAX PROVISIONS

- **Unified credit**: The Act increased the unified credit against the estate and gift taxes. As a result, the amount of cumulative transfers exempt from these taxes increased from $175,625 under prior law to $225,000 for gifts made and estates of decedents dying in 1982, $175,000 in 1983, $325,000 in 1984, $400,000 in 1985, $500,000 in 1986, and $600,000 in 1987 and subsequent years.

- **Rate reduction**: The Act reduced the top estate and gift tax rate from 70% to 65% for gifts made and estates of decedents dying in 1982, to 60% in 1983, 55% in 1984, and 50% in 1985 and subsequent years.

- **Marital deduction**: The Act removed the quantitative limits on the marital deduction under both the estate and gift taxes so that no transfer tax is imposed on transfers between spouses. Also, the Act made certain terminable interests eligible for the marital deduction and made such interests includible in the surviving spouse's gross estate.

- **Current use valuation**: The Act increased the maximum amount by which the gross estate may be reduced under the current use valuation rules from $500,000 to $600,000 for decedents dying in 1981, $700,000 in 1982, and $750,000 in 1983 and subsequent years.

- **Gift tax exclusion**: The Act increased from $3,000 to $10,000 the annual exclusion from the gift tax for gifts to a single recipient. It also provided an unlimited exclusion for certain gifts made to pay for qualifying medical expenses and school tuition.

- **Other provisions**: ERTA made other modifications to the estate and gift tax rules, including repeal of the rule that gifts made by a decedent within three years of death must be included in the decedent's gross estate; liberalization of the rules allowing deferral of the estate tax attributable to closely-held business; elimination of a step-up in basis if appreciated property is acquired by gift by the decedent within one year of the decedent's death and then is returned to the donor or the donor's spouse; repeal of the orphan's exclusions; annual filing of gift tax returns; one-year extension of the transition rule for certain wills or revocable trusts under the tax on generation-skipping transfers; and allowance of a charitable deduction for estate and gift tax purposes for certain bequests or gifts of copyrightable works of art, etc., when the donor retains the copyright.

The Equity and Fiscal Responsibility Act of 1982 (TEFRA)

The Tax Equity and Fiscal Responsibility Act of 1982, designed to increase revenue by approximately $98.3 billion over a three-year period, offered a combination of income tax and reform measures, as well as federal spending cuts. TEFRA also included more stringent policies governing a series of tax preferences, measures for improved tax collection and enforcement, and various excise tax increases.

Individual taxpayers were most affected by a new system of withholding on interest and dividends, strengthened tax compliance measures, and higher thresholds for medical expense and casualty loss deductions. Business taxpayers saw new restrictions on safe-harbor leasing, cutbacks in the use of accelerated depreciation and investment credits, and tougher rules governing mergers and liquidations.

INDIVIDUAL INCOME TAX PROVISIONS

This Act repealed the add-on minimum tax, added several new tax preferences to the alternative minimum tax, restructured the treatment of itemized deductions in the minimum tax, established a flat 20% rate for the minimum tax, and increased the minimum tax exemption from $20,000 to $30,000 for unmarried persons and $40,000 for married couples, beginning 1983.

The floor for itemizing medical expense deductions was raised from 3% of adjusted gross income to 5%, and a separate deduction for one-half of health insurance premiums up to $150 was established. Both measures became effective in 1983. Beginning in 1984, the threshold of 1% of adjusted gross income for the deductibility of expenditures for drugs was eliminated. Only prescription drugs and insulin are now eligible for this deduction.

TEFRA limited the itemized deduction for nonbusiness casualty and theft losses to amounts in excess of 10% of adjusted gross income, effective in 1983.

The income level at which the exclusion for unemployment compensation begins to be phased out was lowered from $20,000 to $12,000 on single returns and from $25,000 to $18,000 on joint returns, effective 1982.

BUSINESS TAX PROVISIONS

TEFRA scaled down the following corporate tax preferences by 15%:

- Excess bad debt reserves of financial institutions

- Interest incurred by financial institutions to carry tax-exempt obligations acquired after 1982

- DISC (Domestic International Sales Corporations)

- Percentage depletion for coal and iron ore

- Section 1250 recapture on real estate

- Rapid amortization of pollution control facilities

- Intangible drilling costs of integrated oil companies

- Mining exploration and development costs

The basis of assets for computing cost recovery deductions and gain or loss was reduced by one-half of the amount of the regular, energy, and historic structure investment tax credits.

The tax liability percentage that taxpayers may offset by the investment tax credit was reduced to 85% from 90%.

The acceleration of depreciation previously scheduled under ERTA 1981 for the period 1985 and 1986 was repealed.

Interest and taxes attributable to the construction period for nonresidential real estate owned by a corporation must be capitalized and written off over ten years.

TEFRA repealed safe-harbor leasing after 1983. From July 1, 1982 to January 1, 1984, a restricted form of safe-harbor leasing was in effect. In 1984, a more liberal form of prior law leasing was permitted.

Companies with foreign oil and gas extraction income were no longer to use tax benefits from that income to reduce taxes on other kinds of oil-related income, and certain oil-related income of their foreign subsidiaries became taxable.

In addition, new rules limited the extent to which businesses may use operations in U.S. possessions to avoid tax by transferring intangibles to their possession subsidiaries and allowing passive income to accumulate in a possession.

New restrictions were placed on industrial development bonds (IDBs), including a sunset of the small-issue exemption after 1986. Investments financed with IDBs were generally limited to straight-line depreciation over ACRS lives.

Rules restricting the issuance of tax-exempt bonds for both single-family and multi-family housing were liberalized.

New rules limited the tax benefits associated with mergers, acquisitions, and other corporate transactions.

TEFRA revised rules for determining whether costs are currently deductible or must be allocated to long-term contracts, with certain exceptions for construction contractors.

The percentage of current year tax liability that corporations must pay in estimated tax payments was increased from 80% to 90%.

Certain tax benefits associated with original issue discount, including zero-coupon bonds, were eliminated.

The Act extended the targeted jobs credit an additional two years and made the credit available for the summer employment of economically disadvantaged teenagers.

COMPLIANCE PROVISIONS

Beginning July 1, 1983, TEFRA imposed 10% withholding on dividends and interest, similar to wage withholdings. Exemptions are provided for persons 65 and older whose income is less than $22,000 for a married couple (not including exempt income such as social security). There is an additional exemption at a lower level of income for individuals under 65.

The Act also mandated additional reporting requirements, changes in penalty provisions, and modifications of voluntary withholding on pensions, partnership audits, among other compliance safeguards.

PENSION PROVISIONS

TEFRA reduced the limits on contributions to and benefits from qualified employee pension plans. It dropped the limit on annual additions under defined contribution plans from $45,475 to $30,000, and the limit on annual benefits in a defined benefit plan from $136,425 to $90,000. It also placed limits on loans from retirement plans. Rules were added to bring equality between corporate and noncorporate pension plans. A $100,000 cap was placed on the estate tax exclusion for annuities. Finally, TEFRA modified rules relating to retirement plans for church employees, state judicial retirement plans, profit-sharing contributions for disabled employees, and group trusts. It added a nondiscrimination rule for employer-provided group term life insurance.

EMPLOYMENT TAX PROVISIONS

The Act provided that certain direct sellers and certain salespeople who are licensed real estate agents would be treated as self-employed persons, rather than as employees. The Act also indefinitely extended the 1978 interim provisions relating to controversies on worker tax classifications, and it provided for reduced employment tax liabilities in specified employment tax reclassification cases.

Beginning in 1983, it increased the wage base subject to the federal unemployment tax (FUTA) to $7,000, and the FUTA rate was increased to 3.5%. It also implemented changes in the conditions that states must meet so that their employers may receive the maximum offset credit for state unemployment taxes. The definition of wages subject to FUTA was changed.

Beginning in 1983, federal employees became subject to the hospital insurance portion of the social security tax, and federal employment entered determinations of eligibility for Medicare.

INSURANCE PROVISIONS

TEFRA made several changes in the tax treatment of life insurance companies and annuities. Modified co-insurance provisions were repealed and the formula for revaluing preliminary term reserves was changed. In addition, provisions were adopted to reduce insurance company taxes for a two-year period. The Act also added rules relating to annuity contracts and flexible premium contracts.

EXCISE TAX PROVISIONS

TEFRA doubled the cigarette excise tax from 8¢ to 16¢ a pack on small cigarettes for the period January 1, 1983, through September 30, 1985, and imposed a floor stocks tax on cigarettes held on January 1, 1983, equal to the increase in tax rate.

The Act reauthorized the Airport and Airway Trust Fund through fiscal year 1987; aviation excise taxes, which were reduced in 1980, were reinstated effective September 1, 1982, through December 31, 1987.

TEFRA increased the excise tax on local and long-distance telephone services from 1% to 3% for 1983 through 1985.

It repealed the special windfall profit tax adjustment for transportation costs related to Alaskan oil and clarified the exemption for Alaskan native corporations.

The Act provided for certain additional refunds relating to the 1978 repeal of the excise tax on buses.

MISCELLANEOUS CHANGES

- The annual accrual accounting method was allowed for certain partnerships growing sugarcane.

- The Secretary of the Treasury was authorized to vary investment yield on savings bonds and to issue additional long-term debt.

- The income tax exclusion for National Research Service Awards was extended for two years.

- Rules disallowing deductions for certain payments to foreign government officials were changed.

- Rules under which veterans' organizations may qualify for tax-exempt status were modified.

- Rules limiting disclosure of tax information in nontax criminal investigations were revised.

- The definition of a lending or financial business under the personal holding company provisions was changed.

Subchapter S Corporation Election—1982

The Subchapter S Corporation Election allows small corporations to benefit from partnership-type taxation. This election is particularly useful to a corporation that distributes all its earnings, because the double taxation involved with regular corporations can be avoided. Similarly, if a corporation has losses, the losses can be passed through to individual shareholders, though each would be limited to the basis of his or her interest.

Eligibility for S corporation status is limited, but the Revision Act of 1982 liberalized these requirements, making it possible for more corporations to qualify. Some of the key requirements are:

- The corporation must have 35 or fewer shareholders.

- With limited exceptions for estates and trusts, all shareholders must be individuals; none of the shareholders can be nonresident aliens.

- The S corporation may have only one class of stock outstanding, with limited exceptions for varying voting rights.

- Passive income, such as dividends, interest, rent, gains on the sale of securities, cannot in general exceed 20% of gross receipts. However, S corporation law is complex, and professional counsel must be sought.

The following is a simple example contrasting tax treatment of a regular corporation and one using the Subchapter S election:

	Regular Corporation	Subchapter S
Assume taxable income all distributed to shareholders	$1,000,000	$1,000,000
Tax paid by corporation	439,750	-0-
Tax paid by individual (assume a 50% tax bracket)	280,125	500,000

2.02 **The Tax Reform Act of 1984 (TRA)**

On June 27, 1984, Congress passed the Deficit Reduction Act of 1984, which comprises the Tax Reform Act of 1984 and the Spending Reduction Act of 1984. The Tax Reform Act, discussed here, is a diverse collection of provisions affecting many areas of tax law. Although intended to increase tax revenues, TRA includes a few tax reductions. As the changes made are wide-ranging, only the key provisions of the Tax Reform Act of 1984 are covered in the following summary.

INDIVIDUAL INCOME TAX PROVISIONS

The Act reduced the benefits from *income averaging* by stiffening the qualifying requirements (see page 2.63).

Specific limits were imposed for write-offs on *automobiles* and *certain property not predominantly used for business* (see page 2.43).

The rules for *charitable contributions* were affected, particularly those applying to private foundations (see page 2.65).

Interest-free loans may now be subject to income tax, gift tax, or both (see page 2.61).

After 1984 contributions to IRAs must be made by the due date of the individual's tax return without extensions (see page 1.70).

Beginning in 1984, *personal casualty and theft losses* are netted and, if there are net gains for a year, all gains and losses are treated as capital and are not subject to the floor of 10% of adjusted gross income (see TEFRA, page 2.21). If there is a net loss, the gains and losses are ordinary and only the net losses are subject to the 10% floor. Losses to the extent of gains are deductible in full.

The *net interest exclusion* of $450 ($900 on a joint return), scheduled to become effective in 1985, has been repealed.

The rules governing *alimony* and *transfer of property between spouses* have been changed. Transfer of property between spouses or incident to divorce will generally not result in recognition of gain or loss. The transferor's basis will carry over to the transferee.

U.S. citizens living abroad are limited to an $80,000 exclusion of foreign earned income through 1987, $85,000 in 1988, $90,000 in 1989, and $95,000 thereafter.

INVESTMENT STRATEGIES AND FINANCIAL INSTRUMENTS

The holding period for a *long-term capital gain* has been reduced from more than one year to more than six months, generally for assets purchased after June 22, 1984 and before 1988 (see page 2.51).

Certain time limits have been imposed on the tax-free treatment of *like-kind exchanges* (see page 2.59).

The Act eliminates many tax advantages involving the use of *tax shelters* to defer income or to convert ordinary income and short-term capital gains to long-term capital gains.

The Act recharacterizes *market discounts*, which arise when the value of a bond declines after issuance, as interest income (rather than a capital gain) and limits the interest deduction allocable to the market discount.

EMPLOYEE BENEFITS

Qualifying employer-provided *fringe benefits* are to be excluded from the employee's gross income for income tax purposes, and from wages for employment tax purposes. Five categories of fringe benefits are affected:

1. No-additional-cost services (e.g., airline travel, hotel rooms),

2. Qualified employee discounts (e.g., meal discounts, clothing discounts),

3. Working condition fringe benefits (e.g., company cars for business, parking),

4. De minimis fringe benefits (e.g., office supplies, employee picnics), and

5. Athletic facilities.

The provision is generally effective as of January 1, 1985.

The Act repeals the $100,000 limit imposed by TEFRA on the *estate tax exclusion* for qualifying retirement benefits, including IRAs and qualified plan distributions. The provision is generally effective for decedents dying after 1984.

The definition of "key employee" under the rules for *top-heavy pension plans* has been changed to exclude officers who earn less than $45,000 a year (may increase after 1988), generally for plan years beginning in 1984. In addition, for plan years after 1983, employer contributions contributed to a Section 401(k) salary reduction agreement are taken into account to determine compliance with minimum employer contribution requirements, making it easier for employers with cash-or-deferred arrangements to satisfy the top-heavy rules.

The *cost-of-living increases* scheduled under TEFRA for *defined contribution and defined benefit plans* are postponed until 1988 when the limits will be adjusted for cost-of-living increases after 1984, using the formula then in effect for Social Security benefits.

The deductibility of contributions and the qualification rules for *funded welfare benefit plans*, including Voluntary Employee Beneficiary Associations (VEBAs; see page 1.92) and cafeteria plans are amended.

Excessive *"golden parachute"* arrangements for key personnel in the event of a hostile takeover are not deductible by the corporation and a nondeductible 20% excise tax is imposed on the recipient for contracts entered into after June 14, 1984.

EMPLOYEE STOCK OWNERSHIP PLANS (ESOPs)

The maximum tax credit for contributions to a tax credit ESOP is frozen at 0.5% of compensation paid or accrued through 1987.

For qualified stock sales to an eligible worker-owned cooperative (EWOC) or a leveraged ESOP, gain will not be recognized if the seller purchases, either 3 months before or 12 months after, securities of a domestic corporation that satisfies a passive income limitation.

Corporations are allowed a deduction for certain dividends paid on stock held by an ESOP, and banks, insurance companies, or other commercial lenders may exclude 50% of the interest received on loans to a leveraged ESOP when the proceeds are used to purchase employer securities.

ESOP provisions are generally effective for taxable years after date of enactment or for loans after date of enactment.

BUSINESS PROVISIONS

The ACRS *depreciation* period for real property has been increased from 15 years to 18 years (see page 2.31).

An alternative test for qualification for the *rehabilitation credit* has been provided to allow buildings of other than square or rectangular shape to qualify more easily (see page 2.41).

The scheduled increase in the Section 179 *first-year expense deduction* for certain property has been postponed (see page 2.43).

The Act delays the increased limit for the amount of used property eligible for the investment tax credit. The $125,000 limit will increase to $150,000 in 1987 (see page 2.39).

The Act requires all depreciation recapture in an *installment sale* to be recognized in the year of the sale, even if little or no payment is received (see page 2.57).

Tax benefits on *property leased to tax-exempt entities* have been restricted, primarily by limiting the benefits of ACRS. The provision is generally effective for property placed in service, and leases entered into, after May 23, 1983. There are various exceptions and transitional rules.

The Act imposes an additional 5% tax (up to $20,250) on corporate incomes in excess of $1 million; this surtax, in effect, *phases out the benefit of graduated corporate rates* for corporations with taxable income over $1 million (see page 2.72, note 2).

Beginning in 1985, the 15% reduction required for certain *corporate tax preferences* (see TEFRA, page 2.21) is increased to 20% except for percentage depletion. Only 59.83% (71.6% under prior law) of these tax preferences are to be included in the base of the add-on minimum tax for corporations (not applicable to Subchapter S corporations). *Deferred* foreign sales corporation income is also included as a tax preference item.

Under the Act, corporations distributing *appreciated property*, including dividend distributions, to shareholders will generally be subject to tax. Gain will be recognized as if the distributing corporation had sold the property and then distributed the proceeds. This provision is applicable for distributions on or after June 14, 1984, with some exceptions.

The Act delays the debut of finance leases, scheduled to begin in 1984 (see TEFRA, page 2.22), until 1988 and does not extend the *safe-harbor leasing* provisions that expired at the end of 1983.

The Act repeals three of the four exceptions to the TEFRA provision that property acquired using the proceeds of an *industrial development bond* (IDB) is subject to straight-line depreciation. Only IDB-financed qualified residential rental projects are still eligible for ACRS. In addition, volume limitations on IDBs were imposed and modifications made to small-issue IDBs.

Shareholders of a *Regulated Investment Company* or *Real Estate Investment Trust* must treat any recognized loss as a long-term capital loss to the extent that any distributions were treated as long-term capital gains unless the stock was held for more than six months. An exception is provided for dispositions of stock pursuant to a periodic redemption plan.

The Act tightens the rules for *collapsible corporations*. A corporation must now realize at least two-thirds of the potential taxable income that could be derived from the sale of collapsible property (previously one third) in order to qualify for the exception. If this requirement is not met, any gain realized from the sale of stock or liquidation is ordinary income rather than capital gain.

TAX ACCOUNTING PROVISIONS

Significant changes in tax accounting were devised to prevent the mismatching of income and deductions.

The Act extends the rules for *original issue discount* to certain transactions excepted under prior law, generally effective for debt instruments acquired after 1984.

Other changes in tax accounting affect:

- Market discount bonds
- Tax-exempt bonds
- Short-term obligations
- Deferred payments for use of property or services
- Capitalization of start-up expenses
- Construction period interest and taxes

ESTATE, GIFT, AND TRUST PROVISIONS

The 1984 *maximum gift and estate tax rate* of 55% is frozen until 1988, when it will drop to 50% (see page 2.73).

Under the Act, the *alternate valuation date* (six months after the date of death) may be used only when the total value of all property on the gross estate and the federal estate tax liability are reduced as a result of the election.

Multiple trusts established by substantially the same grantor for substantially the same beneficiary with a principal purpose of tax avoidance are to be treated as one trust for tax purposes for taxable years after March 1, 1984.

The Act changes the rules for *trusts* or *estates distributing property*. The trust or estate may deduct distributions of property only to the extent of the lesser of the property's basis or its fair market value, and the deduction amount is also the basis to the beneficiary. In order for the beneficiary to receive a stepped-up basis for the property, the trust or estate must elect to recognize gain or loss as if the property had been sold to the beneficiary. These rules apply to distributions made after June 1, 1984.

COMPLIANCE PROVISIONS

For *charitable contributions of property* exceeding $5,000, new appraisal and information reporting requirements are imposed.

Specific reporting requirements are imposed on taxpayers who, in connection with a trade or business, receive $600 or more of *mortgage interest* payments from an individual in a calendar year.

The Act makes certain requirements involving *tax shelter* registration, increases the penalty imposed on the organization or sale of abusive tax shelters, and applies an interest rate of 120% of the statutory rate to certain underpayments.

The Act separates income tax credits into three categories and generally tries to simplify the credit system.

An information return must be filed by a taxpayer who receives more than *$10,000 in cash* in one or more related transactions in the course of a trade or business.

Trustees of IRAs must file reports showing the total amount contributed each year and the taxable year to which the contribution relates. The penalty for failure to report has been increased from $10 to $50 per failure.

OTHER PROVISIONS

The 3% *telephone excise tax* is extended through 1987.

The taxation of *life insurance* companies and their products is revised.

Changes in *partnership taxations* include provisions affecting like-kind exchanges of partnership interests, transfers of partnership interests by corporations, tiered partnerships, retroactive allocations, allocation of certain liabilities to limited partners, dispositions of contributed property, and payments to partners for property or services.

Technical amendments have been made to clarify *Subchapter S corporation* rules.

TIMETABLE OF EFFECTIVE DATES

Many of the provisions of the Tax Reform Act of 1984 are scheduled to be implemented over the next several years. The following timetable summarizes the schedule.

Provisions Affecting Individuals	Effective Date
Foreign earned income exclusion	1984–87 $80,000 1988 $85,000 1989 $90,000 1990 $95,000
Keogh plan and SEP contribution limit increased	As of 1/1/84, up to $30,000 or 35% of earnings, whichever is less
First–year expensing of business property	1984–87 $5,000 1988–89 $7,500 1990 $10,000
Tax-free ceiling on estates	1984 $325,000 1985 $400,000 1986 $500,000 1987 $600,000
Maximum estate and gift tax rate	1984 55% over $3,000,000 1988 50% over $2,500,000
Attorneys' fees award in Tax Court	Cases begun after 1/1/86
Partial rollovers allowed for some distributions from qualified plans	7/19/86
Repeal of special carryover rule for capital losses incurred before 1970	Tax years beginning after 12/31/86

Provisions Affecting Corporations

Corporate tax rates	Surtax on income over $1,000,000, effective 1985
Targeted jobs credit changes	Extended through 1985
Payroll-based credit for ESOP	1984–88 0.5% 1988–90 0%
Postponement of NOL (net operating loss) rules for acquisitions and reorganizations	Tax years beginning after 1985 and reorganization plans adopted after 1985

2.03 Depreciation

The Economic Recovery Tax Act of 1981 (ERTA) introduced the accelerated cost recovery system (ACRS), which altered the nature of depreciation deductions. Changes to ERTA were made in 1982 by the Tax Equity and Fiscal Responsibility Act (TEFRA) and, in 1984, by the Tax Reform Act of 1984, a part of the Deficit Reduction Act of 1984. The following is a summary of key points of the depreciation rules for pre-1981 assets, ACRS initiated by ERTA in 1981, subsequent changes by TEFRA in 1982, and further amendments by the Tax Reform Act of 1984.

This summary is only a brief outline of the various depreciation laws. The depreciation rules are also affected by other areas of tax law, specifically the investment tax credit, the first-year expense deduction, and the limits on automobiles and property not predominantly used for business.

Pre-1981 Assets

Assets placed in service before January 1, 1981 can be depreciated using either the facts and circumstances approach or the class life asset depreciation range (ADR) system, which became effective in 1972. The facts and circumstances approach requires the taxpayer to estimate the useful life and salvage value of each asset; but considerable disagreement between the IRS and the taxpayer may arise concerning these estimates.

The second method, the ADR system, provides useful-life guidelines for classes of assets. (For sample depreciation ranges and comparisons with the ACRS recovery periods, see page 2.36).

The ADR guidelines helped avoid IRS disputes by providing the taxpayer with a framework for determining depreciation. Often, however, real estate was not depreciated as one unit but broken into components (e.g., roof, wiring, plumbing, etc.) with each component having a separate useful life. Complications arising from the use of component depreciation often resulted in problems with the IRS.

The Accelerated Cost Recovery System under ERTA

Beginning in 1981 and with specific changes effected by the Tax Reform Act of 1984, assets placed in service after December 31, 1980 are depreciated using ACRS, initially a part of the Economic Tax Recovery Act of 1981. ERTA shortened the depreciation period, reduced the number of asset classes, and simplified the depreciation computation. The recovery periods are 3, 5, 10, or 15 years. Three-year property includes automobiles and research and experimentation equipment. Most machinery and equipment, office furniture, greenhouses, and chicken houses are 5-year property. The 10-year class includes mobile homes, railroad tank cars, certain public utility property, and theme parks. Most real property, as well as certain public utility property, falls in the 15-year class. ACRS makes no distinction between new and used property and eliminates all salvage value.

The Tax Reform Act of 1984 extended the write-off period for real property, other than low-income housing, to 18 (from 15 years) for property placed in service after March 15, 1984. However, if the taxpayer or a qualified person entered into a binding contract to buy or construct or began construction of the property before March 16, 1984, this provision does not apply. This exception is for property placed in service before 1987. Special rules apply to building components.

Other changes by the Tax Reform Act of 1984 include immediate depreciation recapture on installment sales (see page 2.57), new rules for films, video tapes, and sound recordings, and restrictions on depreciation for automobiles and property not predominantly used in business (see page 2.43).

PERSONAL PROPERTY

ERTA provided three ACRS depreciation tables for personal property based on the date that property is placed in service. However, the Tax Equity and Fiscal Responsibility Act of 1982 subsequently repealed the 1985 and post-1985 tables that allowed for accelerated depreciation on personal property. The following table is relevant for personal property placed in service after December 31, 1980, except for specific limitations, imposed by the Tax Reform Act of 1984, on automobiles and property used for both business and personal purposes (see page 2.43). The table includes the half-year convention required by ERTA. All personal property is assumed to have been acquired in the middle of the year.

Depreciation of Personal Property

If the Recovery Year is:	Class of Investment			
	3-year	5-year	10-year	15-year public utility property
	Recovery Percentage			
1	25	15	8	5
2	38	22	14	10
3	37	21	12	9
4		21	10	8
5		21	10	7
6			10	7
7			9	6
8			9	6
9			9	6
10			9	6
11				6
12				6
13				6
14				6
15				6
Total	100	100	100	100

Note: *This depreciation table applies to property placed in service and leases entered into after June 18, 1984, except for contracts binding on June 18, 1984. The Tax Reform Act of 1984 places certain restrictions on automobiles and mixed-use property.*

REAL PROPERTY

There are three ACRS tables for real estate. The first table is for most real estate placed in service after 1980 through March 15, 1984 with exceptions, discussed previously, for binding contracts or construction. The second table is a result of the Tax Reform Act of 1984 and is applicable to most property placed in service after March 15, 1984. Both tables use the 175% declining-balance method, but the second table uses a mid-month convention, which treats all property as though it were placed in service in the middle of the month. The third table is for low-income housing and uses the 200% or double declining-balance method. All tables switch to straight-line depreciation when optimal to ensure the maximum deduction.

ACRS TABLES FOR REAL ESTATE
All Real Estate (except Low-Income Housing)
Placed in Service after 1980 and through March 15, 1984

If the Recovery Year Is:	Jan.	Feb.	Mar.	Apr.	May	June	July	Aug.	Sept.	Oct.	Nov.	Dec.
1	12	11	10	9	8	7	6	5	4	3	2	1
2	10	10	11	11	11	11	11	11	11	11	11	12
3	9	9	9	9	10	10	10	10	10	10	10	10
4	8	8	8	8	8	8	9	9	9	9	9	9
5	7	7	7	7	7	7	8	8	8	8	8	8
6	6	6	6	6	7	7	7	7	7	7	7	7
7	6	6	6	6	6	6	6	6	6	6	6	6
8	6	6	6	6	6	6	5	6	6	6	6	6
9	6	6	6	6	5	6	5	5	5	6	6	6
10	5	6	5	6	5	5	5	5	5	5	6	5
11	5	5	5	5	5	5	5	5	5	5	5	5
12	5	5	5	5	5	5	5	5	5	5	5	5
13	5	5	5	5	5	5	5	5	5	5	5	5
14	5	5	5	5	5	5	5	5	5	5	5	5
15	5	5	5	5	5	5	5	5	5	5	5	5
16	-	-	1	1	2	2	3	3	4	4	4	5

Note: *This table applies to properties involving binding contracts or construction on or before March 15, 1984 (see text). This table does not apply in short taxable years of less than twelve months.*

Source: *Treasury News Release R-345, September 10, 1981.*

All Real Estate (except Low-Income Housing)
Placed in Service after March 15, 1984

If the Recovery Year Is:	Jan.	Feb.	Mar.	Apr.	May	June	July	Aug.	Sept.	Oct.	Nov.	Dec.
1	9	9	8	7	6	5	4	4	3	2	1	0.4
2	9	9	9	9	9	9	9	9	9	10	10	10.0
3	8	8	8	8	8	8	8	8	9	9	9	9.0
4	7	7	7	7	7	8	8	8	8	8	8	8.0
5	7	7	7	7	7	7	7	7	7	7	7	7.0
6	6	6	6	6	6	6	6	6	6	6	6	6.0
7	5	5	5	5	6	6	6	6	6	6	6	6.0
8	5	5	5	5	5	5	5	5	5	5	5	5.0
9	5	5	5	5	5	5	5	5	5	5	5	5.0
10	5	5	5	5	5	5	5	5	5	5	5	5.0
11	5	5	5	5	5	5	5	5	5	5	5	5.0
12	5	5	5	5	5	5	5	5	5	5	5	5.0
13	4	4	4	5	4	4	5	4	4	4	5	5.0
14	4	4	4	4	4	4	4	4	4	4	4	4.0
15	4	4	4	4	4	4	4	4	4	4	4	4.0
16	4	4	4	4	4	4	4	4	4	4	4	4.0
17	4	4	4	4	4	4	4	4	4	4	4	4.0
18	4	3	4	4	4	4	4	4	4	4	4	4.0
19	1	1	1	2	2	2	3	3	3	3	3	3.6

Note: *This table applies to properties involving binding contracts or construction on or before March 15, 1984 (see text). This table does not apply in short taxable years of less than twelve months.*

Source: *Treasury News Release R-345, September 10, 1981.*

Low-Income Housing

If the Recovery Year Is:	Month the Property is Placed in Service											
	Jan.	Feb.	Mar.	Apr.	May	June	July	Aug.	Sept.	Oct.	Nov.	Dec.
	The Applicable Percentage Is:											
1	13	12	11	10	9	8	7	6	4	3	2	1
2	12	12	12	12	12	12	12	13	13	13	13	13
3	10	10	10	10	11	11	11	11	11	11	11	11
4	9	9	9	9	9	9	9	9	10	10	10	10
5	8	8	8	8	8	8	8	8	8	8	8	9
6	7	7	7	7	7	7	7	7	7	7	7	7
7	6	6	6	6	6	6	6	6	6	6	6	6
8	5	5	5	5	5	5	5	5	5	5	6	6
9	5	5	5	5	5	5	5	5	5	5	5	5
10	5	5	5	5	5	5	5	5	5	5	5	5
11	4	5	5	5	5	5	5	5	5	5	5	5
12	4	4	4	5	4	5	5	5	5	5	5	5
13	4	4	4	4	4	4	5	4	5	5	5	5
14	4	4	4	4	4	4	4	4	4	5	4	4
15	4	4	4	4	4	4	4	4	4	4	4	4
16	-	-	1	1	2	2	2	3	3	3	4	4

Note: *This table does not apply in short taxable years of less than twelve months.*

Source: *Treasury News Release R-345,* September 10, 1981.

THE STRAIGHT-LINE METHOD

Under ERTA, taxpayers may choose the straight-line method of depreciation for either personal or real property. This method allows an extended recovery period and is not a preference item for the alternative minimum tax. The allowable periods are:

Straight-Line Depreciation

Class of Property	Optional Recovery Periods
3-year	3, 5 or 12 years
5-year	5, 12 or 25 years
10-year	10, 25 or 35 years
15-year public utility	15, 35 or 45 years
15-year real property (effective through 3/15/84*)	15, 35 or 45 years
18-year real property (effective after 3-15-84*)	18, 35 or 45 years

See exceptions under the Tax Reform Act of 1984.

Another advantage involves the recapture rules. Recaptured gains due to depreciation are taxed, upon sale of the asset at ordinary income tax rates rather than at the capital gains rate. Because nonresidential property is subject to full recapture if the accelerated methods of depreciation are used, the straight-line method may be preferable.

Recapture Rules for ACRS Assets

Property Class	Recapture Rule
Real property using the straight-line method	No recapture
Residential property using the accelerated method	Recapture of amount of depreciation taken in excess of straight line
Nonresidential real property using accelerated methods	Full recapture
Substantial real property improvements using accelerated methods	Full recapture
Personal property	Full recapture

ANTI-CHURNING RULES

Churning transactions are those involving no real change in the owners and users of the property. These transactions were, in some instances, designed to convert pre-1981 assets into property that would qualify for ACRS write-offs. ERTA disallows ACRS benefits on property acquired through churning transactions.

ACRS RECOVERY PERIODS AND ADR CLASS LIVES

ADR Asset Guideline Class	Description of Assets Included[1]	Asset Depreciation Range (Years)		ACRS Recovery Period (Years)
		Lower Limit	Midpoint	
00.11	Office furniture, fixtures, and equipment	8	10	5
00.12	Information systems: includes computers and peripheral equipment used in normal business transactions and maintenance of business records	5	6	5
00.13	Data handling equipment (except computers—see Class 00.12): includes typewriters, calculators, accounting machines, and copiers	5	6	5
00.21	Airplanes (except commercial, contract, or freight) and helicopters	5	6	5
00.22	Automobiles (see specific limits, page 2.43), taxis	2.5	3	3
00.23	Buses	7	9	5
00.241	Light general purpose trucks, over-the-road use, weighing less than 13,000 lb.	3	4	3
00.242	Heavy general purpose trucks: includes ore trucks, over-the-road use, weighing more than 13,000 lb., and concrete mixers	5	6	5
00.3	Land improvements: includes improvements directly to or added to land, whether 1245 or 1250 property, provided such improvements are depreciable		20	5,15[+], 18[2]
01.1	Agriculture: includes machinery and equipment, grain bins, and fences used in production of crops, livestock, and dairies	8	10	5
01.21	Cattle, breeding or dairy	5.5	7	5
01.22	Horses, breeding or work	8	10	3,5[2]
01.3	Farm buildings	20	25	15[5],18
10.0	Mining: includes assets used in mining and quarrying of metallic and nonmetallic minerals and in primary preparation of such materials	8	10	5
13.0	Offshore drilling: includes floating, self-propelled and other drilling vessels, barges, platforms, drilling equipment, and support vessels. Does not include oil and gas production assets	6	7.5	5
13.1	Drilling of oil and gas wells: does not include assets used by integrated petroleum and natural gas producers for their own account	5	6	5
13.2	Exploration for and production of petroleum and natural gas deposits: includes assets used by producers for drilling and production including pipelines and related storage facilities; also includes offshore transportation facilities	11	14	5,15[5], 18[2]
13.3	Petroleum refining	13	16	5
15.0	Construction: does not include assets used in railroad construction	5	6	5
23.0	Manufacture of apparel and other finished products: does not include assets used in the manufacture of apparel from rubber and leather	7	9	5

ACRS Recovery Periods and ADR Class Lives

ADR Asset Guideline Class	Description of Assets Included[1]	Asset Depreciation Range (Years)		ACRS Recovery Period (Years)
		Lower Limit	Midpoint	
27.0	Printing, publishing, and allied industries: includes assets used in printing and publishing newspapers, books, and periodicals	9	11	5
33.4	Manufacture of primary steel mill products: includes assets used to smelt, refine, reduce, roll, draw, and alloy steel. Also, assets to manufacture basic products, all special tools, and land improvements	12	15	5
45.0	Air transport: includes assets (except helicopters) used in commercial and contract carrying of passengers and freight by air	9.5	12	5
48.11	Telephone central office buildings	36	45	15[5],18
48.12	Telephone central office equipment: includes central office switching and related equipment	16	20[4]	10
48.42	CATV-subscriber connection and distribution systems	8	10	5
49.11	Electric utility hydraulic production plant	40	50	15
49.23	Natural gas production plant	11	14	5
79.0	Recreation: includes assets used in the provision of entertainment services on payment of a fee, as in operation of bowling alleys, billiard establishments, theaters, and miniature golf courses	8	10	5
80.0	Theme and amusement parks, which are defined as combinations of amusements, rides, and attractions that are permanently situated on park land and open to the public	10	12.5	5,10[2]

1 *Specific depreciable assets used in all business activities, not property used for both business and personal use (see page 2.43), except as noted.*

2 *The ACRS recovery period depends upon a Section 1245 rather than a Section 1250 classification where ADR did not distinguish property as such in its guideline classes. Therefore, in order to determine the ACRS recovery period for an asset in this class, one must first determine if it is Section 1245 or Section 1250 property.*

3 *The normal ACRS recovery period for horses is 5 years. However, if the horse is more than 12 years old or is a racehorse that is more than 2 years old when placed in service, the recovery period is 3 years.*

4 *Treasury may change the midpoint ADR life for this class to 18 years, effective January 1, 1981, in which case the ACRS recovery period would be 5 years.*

5 *Generally, real property placed in service before March 16, 1984 has a 15-year ACRS life. Also, property under a binding contract to be bought or constructed or upon which construction has begun on or before March 15, 1984, to be placed in service before 1987 has a 15 year ACRS life.*

2.04 The Investment Tax Credit

The investment tax credit (ITC) was designed to encourage investment and boost productivity. It has an even greater tax advantage than depreciation or other deductions, as it allows a dollar-for-dollar reduction of tax liability. For example, if your tax is $20,000 and the credit is $8,000, the tax payable is reduced to $12,000. Tax credits are available for investment in qualified property and for qualified energy and rehabilitation expenditures.

Limitations

The credit is limited to 100% of the first $25,000 of tax liability, then 85% of the excess. In addition, under the Tax Reform Act of 1984, the credit is limited to a $1,000 maximum for automobiles and is not available for property not predominantly used in business (see page 2.43).

Qualified Property

The regular investment tax credit (ITC) applies to depreciable tangible personal property that must be either ACRS recovery property (see Depreciation, page 2.31) or other depreciable property with a useful life of *at least* 3 years. If only part of the property is depreciable, only that part qualifies for the credit. For example, if you use your car 80% for business and 20% for personal use, only 80% of the car's basis qualifies for the investment credit. The ITC for automobiles is further limited by a cap of $1,000 (generally effective after June 18, 1984) with the limit applied before the deduction for personal use. For example, if you buy a $30,000 car after June 18, 1984 and use it 75% for business, you can take a $750 ITC (75% of $1,000). For certain property not used more than 50% for business, the ITC is not available at all (generally effective after June 18, 1984, see page 2.43).

Certain depreciable real property, except for buildings and their structural components, may also qualify for the investment tax credit. In addition, used property may qualify up to a maximum of $125,000 of its cost ($150,000 in 1988).

The Credit Percentage

ACRS Property

Recovery period	Applicable percentage of cost	Credit
3-year*	60	10%
5-year	100	10
10-year public utility	100	10

Automobiles are limited to a $1,000 maximum credit.

Effects on Basis

If you take the full investment credit, the basis of the property for depreciation purposes is reduced by half the amount of the investment credit. However, you may choose to take a reduced investment credit and not reduce the property's depreciation basis. The reduced credit percentage is 4% of the full cost for 3-year ACRS property (with a $667 maximum for automobiles placed in service after June 18, 1984) and 8% of the full cost for all other ACRS property.

Examples of Applicable Percentage

Asset	Qualified Property	Recovery Period	Cost (Basis)	ITC	Basis for Depreciation
A	Office equipment	5 years	$20,000	$2,000	$19,000
B	Business automobile*	3 years	10,000	600	9,700
With optional reduced percentage:					
A	Office equipment	5 years	20,000	1,600	20,000
B	Business automobile*	3 years	10,000	400	10,000

* *Automobiles placed in service or leased after June 18, 1984, are generally subject to a $1,000 maximum ITC or $667 maximum reduced ITC (see page 2.43).*

CREDIT CARRYBACK AND CARRYOVER

If the credit is greater than the amount allowed for the year under the tax limitations, the excess may be carried back 3 years or forward 15 years.

Recapture

The investment credit may be subject to recapture if property is disposed of before the end of its recovery period or if it ceases to be qualified. Disposition includes sales, trade-ins, exchanges, gifts, and involuntary conversions, e.g., fire and theft. The amount of the credit recaptured is added back to the tax due in the year of disposition. Under the Tax Reform Act of 1984, if the business-use percentage of an automobile declines, part of the limited ITC on a luxury car is recaptured, and the unrecovered basis for post-recovery-period deductions is increased by half of the recapture amount. If, for example, the $30,000 car you used 75% for business is only used 60% for business in the third full year of service, the ITC recapture is $37 ($750 ITC × 15% [the difference between 75% and 60%] × 33% [recapture percentage—see below] and half of this amount, $19, is added to the unrecovered basis for post-recovery-period deductions.

ACRS PROPERTY RECAPTURE

If disposed of:	The percentage of credit recaptured is:	
	For 3-year property	For other property
Within 1 year	100	100
After 1 year	66	80
After 2 years	33	60
After 3 years	None	40
After 4 years	None	20
After 5 years	None	None

NON-ACRS PROPERTY RECAPTURE

If disposed of:	The percentage of credit recapture is:
Within 3 years	100
Within 4 or 5 years	66
Within 6 or 7 years	33
After 7 years	None

Energy Property

In addition to the regular investment credit, an energy investment credit is available. Only certain categories of energy property are eligible, and the property must be depreciable ACRS recovery property or have a useful life of at least three years. The rules for applicable percentage, carryback and carryforward, and recapture are the same as for the regular investment credit. Rates and effective dates are shown below.

ENERGY INVESTMENT CREDITS

Type of property	Energy percentage	Effective date Starts	Ends
General rule—not described below	10	10/1/78	12/31/82
Solar, wind, or geothermal	15	1/1/80	12/31/85
Ocean thermal	15	1/1/80	12/31/85
Qualified hydroelectric generating property	11	1/1/80	12/31/85
Qualified intercity buses	10	1/1/80	12/31/85
Biomass property	10	10/1/78	12/31/85
Cogeneration property	10	1/1/80	12/31/82

Rehabilitation Expenditures

For expenditures incurred in tax years after December 31, 1981, a separate percentage of the investment credit is available for the cost of rehabilitating qualified existing structures. The rehabilitation must meet certain requirements of substantiality. For expenditures incurred before 1984, at least 75% of the existing external walls of the building had to be retained as external walls. The Tax Reform Act of 1984 provides an alternative test to enable buildings of other than square or rectangular shape to qualify more easily for the credit. The alternative test requires that only 50% of the existing external walls be retained if certain other requirements are met.

For buildings:	The rehabilitation credit is:
At least 30 years old	15%
At least 40 years old	20
That are certified historic structures	25

The 15% and 20% credits only apply to nonresidential buildings, but the 25% credit is available for both nonresidential and residential structures. The 15% and 20% credits reduce the basis of the property by the full amount of the credit; the 25% credit reduces the basis by one-half.

Summary

The investment tax credit can provide a substantial direct reduction of tax liability, but taxpayers and their advisers must carefully ascertain that a particular business property is qualified, rather than being one of the exceptions (e.g., property acquired from a related party). Also, various basis consequences and recapture rules affect the use of the investment tax credit. Since the credit is not prorated according to the number of months the property is actually used, business owners may want to make business asset purchases later in the year. A tax accountant or attorney should be consulted on the proper application of this credit.

2.05 Expense Deduction For Depreciable Property

Section 179 Property

Certain depreciable property qualifies for a one-year expense deduction under Section 179. The deduction is subject to the following limits and married persons filing separately are only allowed half of these amounts:

1982 through 1987	$ 5,000
1988 and 1989	$ 7,500
1990 and after	$10,000

This option applies only to property acquired by purchase for use in trade or business, *not* property held for the production of income. The property must qualify for the investment tax credit (see page 2.39).

In addition, the Tax Reform Act of 1984 generally eliminated the expense deduction for property used for both business and personal purposes (e.g., transportation property, entertainment and recreation property, computers, etc.) if the qualified business use does not exceed 50% of total use. The Act also limited, *for automobiles*, the combined, first-year write-off of depreciation and the expense deduction to $4,000. These restrictions apply to property placed in service and leases entered into after June 18, 1984, with certain exceptions (see page 2.43).

The disadvantage of taking an expense deduction is that the amount expensed reduces the basis of the property for the ACRS deduction and the investment tax credit (see pages 2.31 and 2.39). For example, if you purchase $30,000 of business equipment in 1984 and elect the expense deduction of $5,000, the adjusted basis for ACRS depreciation and the investment tax credit is $25,000 ($30,000 − $5,000).

The expense deduction is also limited to the cost of the property purchased even if that cost is less than the deduction allowable. There is no carryover for unused deductions. However, the expense deduction can be allocated among more than one asset. For example, if you buy two pieces of business equipment in 1984, machine A for $2,500 and machine B for $10,000 and elect to completely expense machine A for the full $2,500, leaving a $2,500 deduction for machine B ($2,500 + $2,500 = $5,000), no ACRS deduction or ITC will be available for machine A: it has been completely expensed. The adjusted basis for ACRS and the ITC for machine B is $7,500 ($10,000 − $2,500).

The election to expense qualified property must be made by the tax return due date for the year the property was placed in service and must specify the assets to which it applies. The advantage of taking the deduction must be weighed against the disadvantage of a reduced ITC and ACRS depreciation. Consult a tax professional for an accurate comparison of the costs and benefits of taking the expense deduction.

Limits on Automobiles and Mixed-Use Property

The Tax Reform Act of 1984 imposed limitations on write-offs for automobiles and certain mixed-use property, that is, property used for both business and personal purposes. The new provisions depend on a more-than-50%-business-use test and are generally effective for property placed in service or leased after June 18, 1984, with an exception for binding contracts entered into on or before June 18, 1984. The new rules summarized below apply at the lessee level.

	Business use does not exceed 50% of total use	**More than 50% business use***
Depreciation	Straight-line basis over earnings and profits life (generally 5 years)	$4,000 maximum in first year $6,000 maximum in second and following years (subject to inflation adjustment after 1984)
Investment Tax Credit	None	$1,000 maximum ITC or $667 reduced ITC maximum (in lieu of the 50% basis adjustment)
First-year Expense Deduction (Section 179)	None	Limited to $4,000 total *including* depreciation deduction

---

* *The more-than-50%-business-use test must be met for both of the first two years. If the business use drops below this mark, all deductions and the ITC are subject to recapture. The recapture amount for ACRS and the expense deduction is the excess of fair market value over adjusted basis.*

Example: You buy a $40,000 car after June 18, 1984, and take the full investment credit. In 1984, 1985, and 1986, the business use of the car is 70% of the total use. The ITC is $700 (70% of $1,000). Assuming no inflation adjustment until 1986 and that, in 1986, the inflation-adjusted maximum increases to $6,300, the recovery deductions are $2,800 (70% of $4,000) in 1984, $4,200 (70% of $6,000) in 1985, and $4,410 (70% of $6,300) in 1986. The unrecovered basis of the car for post-recovery-period deductions is $23,350 ($40,000 – $350 ITC basis reduction – $16,300 [the sum of the 1984–86 limits before reduction for personal use]).

This summary provides only a brief description of the limits placed on automobiles and other mixed used property by the Tax Reform Act of 1984. Consultation with a tax professional will insure the correct application of the rules, complete with all exceptions and details.

2.06 Oil and Gas Depletion

Income tax law has long favored the exploitation of oil and gas supplies. Depletion allowances provide compensation for the investor who is basically reducing the value of his property by depleting its resources.

A depletion deduction for oil and gas wells is comparable to that for a depreciable asset. The taxpayer is allowed to recover his investment through annual tax deductions against ordinary income. In order to qualify for the depletion deduction, the taxpayer must own an economic interest in the deposit.

The two methods for computing the depletion deduction are cost depletion and percentage depletion. The higher deduction of the two must be used.

Cost Depletion

Cost depletion allows the taxpayer to deduct the cost per unit sold from his income. The cost per barrel of oil or per cubic foot of gas is determined by dividing the adjusted basis of the property by the number of recoverable units:

$$\text{cost depletion} = \frac{\text{adjusted basis}}{\text{recoverable units}} \times \text{units sold per year}$$

The maximum total depletion is the basis for the property.

Percentage Depletion

Percentage depletion allows the taxpayer to deduct from his property's gross income a fixed percentage, not to exceed 50% of the taxable income before deducting depletion. The Tax Reduction Act of 1975 established the following specified percentages for each calendar year:

1981	20%
1982	18%
1983	16%
1984 and thereafter	15%

While percentage depletion, like cost depletion, reduces the basis of the property, it has the advantage of continuing to be deductible as long as there is gross income from the property. Thus, total percentage depletion can exceed the basis of the property. Generally, the percentage depletion deduction will be greater than the cost depletion deduction.

The following examples provide a simple illustration of each method.

Cost Depletion

Basis of property	$500,000
Estimated reserves	1,000,000 units
Per unit cost	$.50 per unit
Units sold in one year	100,000
Cost depletion allowable ($.50 x 100,000)	$50,000

Percentage Depletion

Gross income (100,000 units x $3.50)	$350,000
Expenses before depletion	$200,000
Percentage depletion (16% of $350,000)	$56,000
Taxable income ceiling (50% of $150,000)	$75,000
Percentage depletion allowed	$56,000

Therefore the depletion deduction for this particular case would the $56,000 calculated by the percentage depletion method because that method yields the higher deduction.

2.07 **Alternative Minimum Tax**

Minimum taxes are designed for individuals in high tax brackets who shelter a large part of their income. The intent is to prevent such people from avoiding most or all taxation. Beginning in 1983, the add-on minimum tax was repealed, and the alternative minimum tax expanded. The new alternative minimum tax is payable in lieu of the regular tax only if it exceeds the taxpayer's regular tax liability.

In order to compute the alternative minimum tax, the minimum tax base must be determined by using the following formula: minimum taxable income = adjusted gross income + tax preference amounts − allowable deductions. This amount is then further reduced by an exemption allowance.

Tax Preference Items

The tax preference items that must be *added to* adjusted gross income (including five of the six old add-on minimum tax preferences plus six other preferences) are:

1. Accelerated depreciation in excess of straight-line depreciation on real property

2. Accelerated depreciation on personal property subject to a net lease

3. Excess of 60-month amortization of certified pollution control facilities over depreciation otherwise allowable

4. Percentage depletion in excess of the adjusted basis of the property

5. Excess of intangible drilling costs on oil, gas, and geothermal wells over net income from production

6. The long-term capital gains exclusion (other than from sale of personal residence)

7. The excess deduction where mining exploration costs, development expenditures, circulation expenditures, and research and development expenses are claimed as a current expense rather than amortized over a 10-year period; if these items are amortized over ten years (beginning with the year the expenditure is incurred), the minimum tax is avoided

8. The exclusion for All-Savers interest

9. Dividends excluded under the $100 dividend exclusion

10. The excess of the fair market value of an incentive stock option over the exercise price at the date of exercise

11. The regular net operating loss deduction

The preferences for excess itemized deductions and amortization of childcare facilities have been deleted.

Deductions

Deductions allowed in computing the minimum tax base are:

1. Medical expenses that exceed 10% of adjusted gross income

2. Personal casualty losses (under itemized deductions)

3. Charitable contributions

4. Income tax deduction for estate tax paid

5. Home mortgage interest

6. Investment interest expense to the extent of investment income

7. Net operating losses (NOLs) not attributable to preferences (a transitional rule permits pre-1983 regular tax NOLs to be carried forward as minimum tax NOLs (i.e., carried forward without reduction by preferences) until they are used up; the disadvantage is that these NOL carryforwards will still be subject to repealed add-on tax)

8. Wagering losses

Estates and trusts are allowed some additional deductions.

Exemptions

Once the tax preference items have been added and the allowable deductions subtracted, the minimum taxable income is subject to the following exemptions.

- $20,000 for trusts and estates or married filing separately

- $30,000 for single taxpayers

- $40,000 for married taxpayers filing jointly, or surviving spouse

All minimum taxable income in excess of the exemption is taxed at a 20% rate. Remember that this alternative minimum tax is imposed only to the extent that it exceeds the regular tax.

Credits

Other factors that may offset the alternative minimum tax include the foreign tax credit (to the extent of a minimum taxable income from a foreign source) and refundable credits. However, most tax credits, such as the investment tax credit and energy credits, are not offsetting.

In light of the changing minimum tax law, consultation with a tax adviser is necessary. Strategies such as the use of installment sales may reduce or eliminate the taxpayer's alternative minimum tax liability.

Example

For 1984, the Does, who have no dependents, have an adjusted gross income of $100,000, which includes $39,200 net long-term capital gain ($98,000 less the 60% deduction) as well as $800 in net dividends ($1,000 less the $200 exclusion). Their itemized deductions were: $15,000 for interest on a home mortgage; $3,000 for charitable contributions; $10,000 for deductible taxes; and $6,000 in miscellaneous deductions. They file jointly.

Regular tax calculation

Adjusted gross income		$100,000
Less: Personal exemptions	($ 2,000)	
Itemized deductions above zero bracket	(30,600)	
		(32,600)
Taxable income		67,400
Tax owed	$18,276	

Alternative minimum tax calculation

Adjusted gross income		$100,000
Plus tax preferences		
Capital gains deduction	$58,800	
Dividend-received exclusion	200	59,000
Alternative minimum tax base		$159,000
Less: Alternative minimum tax itemized		
deductions		
Housing interest	(15,000)	
Charitable contributions	(3,000)	
Exemption	(40,000)	(58,000)
Total subject to alternative minimum tax		$101,000
Tax at 20%	$20,200	

The Does pay a total tax of $20,200, since the alternative minimum tax owed is greater than the regular tax owed.

2.08 Capital Gains

A gain from the sale or trade of a capital asset is given special tax treatment. Capital assets generally include everything a taxpayer owns or uses for personal purposes, pleasure, or investment; for example,

- A personal residence

- An automobile

- Stock or bonds held by an investor

- Jewelry, stamps, antiques

- A patent held for investment

The following items, in contrast, are *not* capital assets:

- Inventory or stock in trade

- Depreciable property used in a trade or business

- Real property used in a trade or business

- Certain copyrights, compositions, or memorandums

- Certain accounts or notes receivable

A gain or loss from investment property is a capital gain or loss, but a loss of personal-use property is not deductible unless it is a casualty loss. Special rules apply to the sale of a principal residence. Usually the gain can be deferred as long as the seller buys a comparably priced or more expensive residence. A special $125,000 exclusion of gain, subject to certain limitations, may apply if the seller is 55 or older (see page 2.55).

Section 1231 Assets

Some depreciable property excluded from the capital assets category may receive capital gains treatment under Section 1231, for example,

- Depreciable personal property used in a trade or business and held for more than six months if acquired after June 22, 1984; property acquired before June 23, 1984 or after 1987 must be held for more than one year.

- Property for the production of rents or royalties and held for more than six months if acquired after June 22, 1984; property acquired before that date or after 1987 must be held for more than one year.

- Cattle and horses acquired for draft, breeding, dairy or sporting purposes and held for 24 months or longer.

In determining the treatment of Section 1231 sales or exchanges, any gain is first subject to depreciation recapture (see Depreciation, page 2.21). Recaptured gain is handled separately as ordinary income. Casualty and theft gains or losses are also handled separately (see page 2.25). Finally, Section 1231 asset gains and losses are netted. If net gains exceed net losses, all gains and losses are treated as long-term capital gains and losses. If, however, net losses exceed net gains, all gains and losses are treated as ordinary income. The Tax Reform Act of 1984 provides that net Section 1231 gain realized during 1985 and future years shall be taxable as ordinary income, *not* capital gain, to the extent that such gain does not exceed the sum of the net Section 1231 losses realized in the most recent five preceding taxable years after 1981. If net Section 1231 losses are used to recapture net Section 1231 gain, these losses cannot be used again to recapture other Section 1231 gains.

Capital Gains Treatment

All property, regardless of how it is acquired, has a cost basis—the price paid to acquire the property. For example, if an investor purchased a share of stock for $10 and it had increased in value to $100 when he decided to sell it, he would have a capital gain of $90, determined by comparing the selling price of $100 to the stock's cost basis, the $10 he paid for it.

The difference between the basis and the selling price is either a gain or a loss, and either short-term or long-term, depending upon the length of time the asset has been held (the holding period). Property acquired after June 22, 1984 must be held for more than six months in order to qualify any gain as a long-term gain, or loss as a long-term loss. Assets acquired before June 23, 1984, or after 1987 must be held for more than one year to qualify for long-term treatment.

Short-term gains are fully taxed as income at ordinary income tax rates, while only 40% of long-term gains are taxed at ordinary income tax rates. The rate at which long-term gains are taxed thus depends on the taxpayer's tax bracket. Since the ERTA reductions, the long-term capital gains tax can be a maximum of 20% of the gain (50% of the 40% that is taxed as ordinary income). Prior to ERTA, the maximum marginal tax rate was 70%, so the maximum long-term capital gains tax was 28% (70% of the 40% taxed as ordinary income).

The excess of net long-term gain over net short-term loss is called net capital gain, 40% of which is subject to tax. The excess of short-term gain over short-term loss is called short-term gain and is taxed as ordinary income.

A net short-term capital loss is deducted, dollar for dollar (subject to limitations and only up to $3,000), from ordinary income, but only one-half of a net long-term capital loss can be deducted. Thus, it takes $6,000 of net long-term loss to offset $3,000 of ordinary income. Any unused losses can be carried over indefinitely.

Tax Cost of Taking Short-Term Gains

Investors sometimes have to decide whether to take a profit on a short-term investment or risk a falling market while holding out for a long-term gain. The following table shows the potential tax advantage of letting short-term gains become long-term gains. The table does not reflect the alternative minimum tax.

After-Tax Profit On A $1,000 Net Capital Gain

Marginal Tax Bracket	Short-term	Long-term	Potential Long-term Advantage
23%	$ 770	$ 908	$ 138
24	760	904	144
25	750	900	150
26	740	896	156
27	730	892	162
28	720	888	168
29	710	884	174
30	700	880	180
31	690	876	186
32	680	872	192
33	670	868	198
34	660	864	204
35	650	860	210
36	640	856	216
37	630	852	222
38	620	848	228
39	610	844	234
40	600	840	240
41	590	836	246
42	580	832	252
44	560	824	264
45	550	820	270
48	520	808	288
49	510	804	294
50	500	800	300

2.09 **Sale of a Personal Principal Residence**

I f a personal principal residence is sold at a gain and another home purchased within 24 months, tax on the gain may be deferred indefinitely, provided the purchase price of the new home is greater than the selling price of the old. The deferred gain reduces the taxpayer's basis in the new residence. A loss on the sale of a residence is not deductible.

TAXPAYERS OVER 55

A taxpayer over age 55 may exclude the first $125,000 of gain on the sale of a principal residence; the exclusion is $62,500 for a married taxpayer filing a separate return. This provision can be used only once in a lifetime, regardless of the actual amount of gain. The property must have been the principal residence and occupied by the taxpayer for at least three years during the five-year period ending on the date of the sale. Unmarried persons 55 or over who sell their principal residence, held as joint tenants or tenants in common, can declare the exclusion in proportion to their undivided interest.

There is a transitional occupancy rule if the seller was 65 or over on the date of sale that occurred before July 26, 1981. In this situation, the taxpayer would qualify for the exclusion by having occupied the principal residence for five of the previous eight years, instead of three of the previous five years. In both situations, short temporary absences are counted as periods of use.

Gains on residences that are involuntarily converted, for example because of fire or condemnation, are eligible for the exclusion.

The Use of the Exclusion

Selling price	$230,000
Less selling expenses	- 5,000
Amount realized	225,000
Less adjusted basis of old residence	- 50,000
Realized gain	175,000
Less one-time exclusion	-125,000
Amount of gain not excluded	$ 50,000

PURCHASE OF A REPLACEMENT RESIDENCE

A taxpayer may elect the exclusion and nonrecognition of gain on the same sale, even if a replacement residence is bought. The adjusted basis of the new residence is equal to the cost of the new residence, less the gain not recognized due to electing the exclusion.

Example

Selling price	$230,000
Less selling expenses	(5,000)
Amount realized	$225,000
Less adjusted basis of old residence	(50,000)
Realized gain	$175,000
Less exclusion	(125,000)
Gain not excluded	$ 50,000

Adjustments to sales price

Amount realized	$225,000
Less fixing-up expenses	(5,000)
Adjusted sales price	$220,000

Recognition of gain

Adjusted sales price	$220,000
Less exclusion	(125,000)
Less cost of new residence	(85,000)
Gain recognized	(10,000)

Basic of new residence

Cost of new residence	$ 85,000
Plus gain not excluded	50,000
Less gain recognized	(10,000)
Basis of new residence	$ 45,000

2.10 Installment Sales

Tax on the gain from property sales may be deferred by an installment sale. However, the Tax Reform Act of 1984 (TRA) reduces and may eliminate the installment sales tax break when the gain involves depreciation. Under prior law, gain was not recognized until payments of principal were received, although ordinary income attributable to depreciation recapture was recognized before any capital gain. TRA provides for immediate taxation, in the year of sale, on all depreciation recapture income, even if no payments of principal are received.

Example: Equipment with an adjusted basis of $10,000 is sold for $25,000, to be paid in five annual installments of $5,000 each. Interest on the unpaid balance is charged at current rates. The recapture potential of the equipment is $6,000.

Previously, $3,000 of each installment payment was considered to be gain:

$$\frac{\$5,000 \text{ installment payment} \times \$15,000 \text{ gain}}{\$25,000 \text{ proceeds}} = \$3,000 \text{ gain}$$

The gain from the first two payments was treated as recapture income.

But under TRA, this $6,000 of recapture income is considered taxable in the year of the sale. The adjusted basis of the equipment for installment payments is increased to $16,000 ($10,000 adjusted basis + $6,000 recapture income), making the gross profit $9,000 ($25,000 proceeds −$16,000 adjusted basis for installments). Thus, $1,800 of each $5,000 installment payment received is regarded as income:

$$\frac{\$5,000 \text{ installment payment} \times \$9,000 \text{ gain}}{\$25,000 \text{ proceeds}} = \$1,800 \text{ gain}$$

The recognition of all depreciation recapture in the year of sale is applicable to installment sales made after June 6, 1984, with an exception for contracts binding on March 22, 1984.

Any sale with a deferred payment date is considered to be an installment sale, even if there is only one payment, and all deferred-payment contracts should specify a rate of interest that is at least 110% of the applicable federal rate:

For a debt instrument with a term of:	**The applicable federal rate is, in general:**
Less than three years	The federal short-term rate
Between three and nine years	The federal medium-term rate
Over nine years	The federal long-term rate

(The federal rates are based on average market yields and are announced twice a year by the Department of the Treasury.) If the interest rate on a deferred-payment contract is less than the safe-harbor rate of 110%, the IRS will inpute a rate of 120% of the applicable federal rate.

In certain circumstances, it might be preferable to forgo the installment sale treatment. For example, if a large capital loss is incurred, the investor might choose to sell the property and, electing out of an installment sale's tax deferral, report the entire gain in that year, regardless of when the payment would actually be made. The existing loss would balance out the gain and future installment payments would carry no tax obligation.

Note: Specific guidance on the use of installment sale treatments should be obtained from a tax professional.

2.11 Nontaxable Exchanges

The disposal of property through a reciprocal transfer for a similar piece of property is a nontaxable event. The transferor may pay cash or give other property along with the exchange, but there will be adjustments to basis and recognition of gain. Money or other property given or received as part of an exchange is called *boot*. A nontaxable exchange merely postpones the tax until the property is finally sold outright.

Some common nontaxable exchanges are:

- Securities for securities of the same corporation
- Transfers to a corporation controlled by the transferor
- Property held for productive use or investment for property of a like kind
- Exchanges of certain insurance policies
- Exchanges of stock and property in corporate reorganizations

Like-Kind Exchanges

Property held for productive use or investment can qualify for nonrecognition of gain or loss when exchanged for *like-kind* property. For example, a business-use automobile or truck with an adjusted basis of $10,000 is exchanged for another one with a fair market value of $12,000. While a $2,000 gain is realized, no gain is recognized. The basis of the new vehicle is $10,000, the same as that of the old one.

While personal-use property does not qualify for a like-kind exchange, property held for both business and personal use may qualify to the extent of the business portion. Also, trade or business property may be exchanged for investment property and vice versa. The like-kind qualification refers to the nature of the property, not its quality. Thus, an apartment house may be exchanged for a city lot, city real estate for a ranch, and improved for unimproved real estate.

Under the Tax Reform Act of 1984 (TRA), the transferor must identify the property to be received in a like-kind exchange within 45 days of the transfer date. Also, the property must be received by the earlier of the due date, including extension, of the transferor's tax return for the year of the transfer or within 180 days of the transfer date. These limits must be met in order for the exchange to qualify for tax-free treatment and are generally applicable to transfers made after the date of enactment of TRA. (Some exceptions have been made for transactions in process before enactment.)

Exchanges with Boot

Generally, if *boot* is given, the basis of the property acquired is equal to the basis of the property given plus the amount of the boot. If the boot is money, the gain or loss will not be recognized. For example, you exchange an apartment building with an adjusted basis of $125,000, plus $10,000 cash, for another apartment building with a fair market value of $165,000. The basis of your acquired apartment building is $135,000. No gain is recognized, and the fair market value is immaterial.

If cash boot is received, any gain will be recognized up to the amount of the boot received. The basis of the acquired property is the adjusted basis of the property given, decreased by the amount of cash received, and increased by the amount of gain recognized. For example, you exchange a business machine A with an adjusted basis of $8,000 for a business machine B with a fair market value of $7,500, plus $1,000 in cash. Your realized gain is $500, which is all recognized gain, because it is less than the $1,000 cash received. The basis of the acquired machine B is $8,000 − $1,000 + $500 = $7,500. Losses are not recognized if cash boot is received.

Different rules apply if the boot is property. The rules for nontaxable exchanges are very specific regarding the kinds of property that qualify. Rules pertaining to a principal residence are entirely separate. Some of the most common nontaxable exchanges involve business or investment property, the like-kind type of exchange. Under the Tax Reform Act of 1984, the like-kind rules do not apply to exchanges of interests in different partnerships. Taxpayers considering the use of a nontaxable exchange to defer recognized gain should consult a tax professional for advice on the specific changes in basis of the property and potential gain or loss consequences of such an exchange.

2.12 Interest-Free Loans

Interest-free loans (or Crown loans) have become an increasingly popular method of shifting income tax burdens to lower-bracket family members or of providing funds for the support of others, usually relatives. Under the Tax Reform Act of 1984, below–market interest rate loans have two tax consequences. First, the forgone interest constitutes a deductible expense for the borrower and income to the lender. Second, the loan represents a transfer from the lender to the borrower, by virtue of the lender's forgiving the borrower's obligation to pay the interest. This second aspect classifies the forgone interest as a gift subject to gift tax rules; but an individual may make an unlimited number of annual gifts of up to $10,000 per recipient without incurring any gift tax liability.

EXCEPTIONS

1. Interest income and expense will not be imputed for income or gift taxes on demand loans of $10,000 or less, provided the loan proceeds are not used to buy income-producing assets.

2. If a gift loan does not exceed $100,000, the imputed interest income and expenses will be limited to the borrower's net income from investments (i.e., interest, dividends, rents, royalties, short-term capital gains, etc.). If the borrower's investment income does not exceed $1,000, the imputed interest will be zero. This exception, however, does not apply to loans for which the principal purpose is tax avoidance.

These rules and exceptions apply to term loans made after June 6, 1984, and to demand loans outstanding on or after that date unless repaid within sixty days of the date of enactment (July 18, 1984) of the legislation.

Examples

1. Father lends son $1 million on January 1, 1985, with a stated interest rate of 0%, payable January 1, 1990. Interest rate on comparable U.S. obligations is 10%. The present value on January 1, 1985 of the $1 million—payable on January 1, 1990 and discounted at 10%—is approximately $614,000, which is considered the loan principal; the remaining $386,000 is treated as a gift. The gift portion is subject to gift taxes and the annual imputed interest ($100,000) constitutes income to the father and a deductible interest expense to the son.

   If this were a demand loan, the amount treated as a gift would be determined annually and would equal the amount of imputed interest—$100,000 for 1985.

2. Father lends daughter $125,000 on January 1, 1985, and this demand loan remains outstanding all year long. The daughter uses the money to purchase her principal residence, and she has no income from investments. The interest rate on comparable U.S. securities is 6%. The daughter would be able to deduct $7,600 (6% × $125,000) in interest expense, and the father would have to declare the same amount as taxable income. Also, the $7,500 of forgone interest would be treated as a taxable gift made on December 31, 1985. (Note that, had the loan been for less than $100,000, there would be no income tax consequences.)

2.13 Income Averaging

A taxpayer whose income rises sharply in any one year may be able to reduce his tax liability for that year by using income averaging. The Tax Reform Act of 1984, however, changed the rules for income averaging, making it more difficult to qualify and decreasing the potential benefits. The rules discussed here reflect these changes, effective for tax years beginning after 1983.

Eligibility

In order to be eligible to income average, the taxpayer must be and have been (throughout the three tax years immediately pending) a U.S. citizen and must meet the support test, which requires that the taxpayer provided at least half of his own support in all three base period years. Three exceptions exist:

1. The taxpayer is 25 or older in the current tax year and was not a full-time student (five or more months a year) for at least four tax years after age 21;

2. More than half of the current year's taxable income was received for work done in two or more base period years; and

3. The taxpayer's income is not more than 25% of the aggregate adjusted gross income reported on a joint return.

Calculation

Example: You and your spouse want to income average for 1984. Your combined taxable incomes were $25,000 in 1983, $20,000 in 1982, and $18,000 in 1981. Your average base period income is $21,000.

Step 1: Find the average of the previous three years' taxable income. Certain items such as premature payout from self-employed retirement funds are excluded from taxable income.

Step 2: Find *nonaverageable income* by multiplying the average base period income by 140%. In the example above, your nonaverageable income is $29,400. In order to use an income average, your 1984 taxable income must be over $32,400 (more than $3,000 greater than nonaverageable income).

Step 3: Find *averageable income* by subtracting nonaverageable income from your current year's taxable income. The remainder must be greater than $3,000. Using the example above, if your 1984 taxable income is $50,000, your *averageable income* is $20,600 ($50,000 − $29,400).

Step 4: Add 25% of averageable income to nonaverageable income and compute the tax on the total. From the example above, you add 25% of $20,600, or $5,150 to $29,400 and get a total of $34,550. The tax on $34,550 from the tables is $6,092.

Step 5: Find the tax on nonaverageable income. Following our example, the tax on $29,400 from the tables is $4,665.

Step 6: Subtract the tax in Step 5 from the tax in Step 4 and multiply the result by 4. Continuing with our example, $6,092 − $4,665 = $1,427, and $1,427 x 4 = $5,708.

Step 7: Find the total tax by adding the amounts in Step 5 and Step 6. Thus, in our example, $4,665 + $5,708 = $10,373. Using income averaging, your total 1984 tax is $10,373, compared with $11,368 using the tax tables for married couples filing jointly for $50,000 of taxable income. You save $995 by using income averaging.

Taxpayers who wish to income average must file Schedule G, Form 1040. Certain rules apply to married persons filing separately in a community property state and to married persons who were married to other spouses in base period years. Taxpayers should consult a tax professional to ensure appropriate and accurate application of the income averaging rules.

2.14 Charitable Contributions

The following discussion of charitable contributions applies to tax years after 1983. Charitable contributions may allow the taxpayer to donate pretax dollars to certain qualified organizations. Taxpayers who itemize deductions declare their charitable contributions on Schedule A. A special deduction for nonitemizers is limited, and married persons filing separately are only allowed half of the following amounts:

1983 25% of the first $100 of contributions
1984 25% of the first $300 of contributions
1985 50% of total contributions
1986 100% of total contributions

Qualified Organizations

In order to be deductible, a charitable contribution must be made to a qualified organization. Contributions to individuals are *not* deductible, even if the person is needy. Treasury Department Publication 78 lists qualified organizations, which include certain trusts, funds, community chests, corporations, veterans' organizations, fraternal organizations, cemetery organizations, and governmental units. Specific rules apply, so prospective donors should be sure that the organization is qualified.

Property

Contributions of property as well as money may be deductible. However, for taxable years after 1984, qualified appraisals must be obtained in certain instances for contributions of noncash property other than publicly traded securities. A contribution of the use of property or services is not an allowable deduction. Generally, the fair market value of the property is deductible, but for certain types of appreciated property (when the value is greater than the basis) special rules apply. The following table summarizes the rules.

DEDUCTION FOR CONTRIBUTIONS OF APPRECIATED PROPERTY

Type of property contributed	Recipient	Deduction
1. Property that, if sold, would result in ordinary income only (e.g., inventory and short-term capital assets)	Any qualified organization	Basis
2. Property that, if sold, would result in portion of ordinary income (e.g., Section 1245 asset)	Any qualified organization	Fair market value less amount recaptured if sold
3. Property, except for "qualified appreciated stock," that, if sold, would result in long-term capital gain	Private foundation	Fair market value less 40% appreciation

(Continued)

4. Qualified appreciated stock, which is, generally, any stock of a corporation for which market quotations are readily available on an established securities market and that is long-term capital gain property (effective for 1984 through 1994)	Private foundation	Fair market value
5. Tangible personal property put to unrelated use by the recipient and that, if sold, would result in long-term capital gain (e.g., a work of art contributed by a donor, not the creator)	Any qualified organization	Fair market value, less 40% appreciation
6. Property, other than those types listed in items 3, 4, and 5 above, that, if sold, would result in long-term capital gain if the 50% limit is elected	Any qualified organization (other than a private foundation)	Fair market value, less 40% appreciation
7. Other property, not described in items 3, 4, 5, or 6 above, that, if sold, would result in long-term capital gain	Any qualified organization	Fair market value

Limitations

The allowable deduction in any tax year for charitable contributions is limited to a percentage of the donor's adjusted gross income, before net operating loss carrybacks. Contributions over the limit may be carried over for five years (some restrictions prior to 1984).

THE 50% LIMIT

The 50% limit applies to donations to public charities. These charities include (but are not limited to) churches, most educational organizations, hospitals, certain medical research organizations, certain private foundations, state university funds, and funds that receive a substantial amount of their support from the government or general public.

THE 30% LIMIT

The 30% limit applies to donations of appreciated capital gains property that are not reduced by any amount of appreciation. *Capital gains property* is defined as a capital asset or a Section 1231 asset that, if sold, would result in long-term capital gains. Beginning in 1984, the 30% limit also applies to contributions by individuals of cash or ordinary income property to private nonoperating foundations and certain other organizations.

Example: Your adjusted gross income for 1984 was $30,000, and you contribute to the Red Cross stock worth $10,000 and held for two years. Your deduction is limited to $9,000 (30% of adjusted gross income) for 1984, but you have a $1,000 carryover for 1985.

THE 50% ELECTION

Although appreciated capital gains property donated to public charities and operating foundations is usually subject to a limit of 30% of adjusted gross income, a donor may elect to apply the more liberal 50% limitation by reducing the fair market value of the donation by 40% of the property's appreciation in value.

Example: Your adjusted gross income for 1984 was $30,000. On September 1, 1984, you contribute stock worth $20,000 to your local church (a qualified public charity). The stock had been purchased in 1972 for $9,000. You make the 50% election and thus reduce the amount of the donation to $15,600 ($20,000 − 40% of $11,000 appreciation, or $4,400). The allowable deduction for 1984 is $15,000 (50% of adjusted gross income), with a $600 carryover.

THE 20% LIMIT

The 20% limit applies to charitable contributions of capital gains property to qualified organizations that are not public charities—primarily private, nonoperating foundations. The 20% limit of adjusted gross income is actually a maximum. The allowable deduction may be even less than 20% if other donations are made, because the 50% limit still holds. The fair market value of the capital gains property must be reduced by 40% of the appreciation except for contributions of qualified appreciated stock (see table, pages 2.65–66), which are deductible at the stock's full fair market value.

Example: Your 1984 adjusted gross income is $24,000. You donate $10,000 to your local university (a public charity) and capital gains property (not qualified appreciated stock) with a fair market value of $3,000 to the Smith Foundation, a private, nonoperating foundation. The basis to you of the capital gain property is $1,000. The contribution of the property is thus $2,200 ($3,000 − 40% of $2,000 appreciation, or $800). Your allowable deduction is $12,000 for 1984 (50% of adjusted gross income) with a $200 carryover.

If in the above example, your donation to the Smith Foundation had been of qualified appreciated stock with a fair market value of $3,000, your allowable deduction for 1984 would still be $12,000, but with a $1,000 carryover. The stock contribution would be deductible at its full fair market value of $3,000.

SUMMARY OF LIMITS

Qualified Organization	Nature of Contribution	Percentage Limit
1. Public charities	Cash and property (including appreciated capital gains property after limit in 3 above applied)	50% of contribution base with 5-year carryover of excess
2. Other qualified organizations (generally private in nature) or public charities	Cash and property, except for capital gains property	Lesser of 30% of contribution base, or the difference between 50% of contribution base and contributions to charities; 5-year carryover of excess
3. Other qualified organizations (e.g., private, nonoperating foundations)	Capital gains property (after limit in 3, above, applied)	Lesser of 20% of contribution base, or the difference between 50% of contribution base and contributions to charities; 5-year carryover of excess
4. Public and private qualified organizations	Appreciated captial gain property (unless deduction reduced by election or otherwise)	30% of contribution base with 5-year carryover of excess

The charitable contribution deduction allows the taxpayer to direct pretax funds to qualified organizations of his choice. While many taxpayers will not be subject to the various limitations, persons planning to make substantial donations should consult a tax professional to ensure that the optimal tax benefits will be achieved.

2.15 Federal Tax Rate Schedules

SCHEDULE X—SINGLE INDIVIDUALS

Taxable Income		1983		1984	
Over	But Not Over	Pay	+% on Excess	Pay	+% on Excess
$ 0	$ 2,300	$ 0	0%	$ 0	0%
2,300	3,400	0	11	0	11
3,400	4,400	121	13	121	12
4,400	6,500	251	15	241	14
6,500	8,500	566	15	535	15
8,500	10,800	866	17	835	16
10,800	12,900	1,257	19	1,203	18
12,900	15,000	1,656	21	1,581	20
15,000	18,200	2,097	24	2,001	23
18,200	23,500	2,865	28	2,737	26
23,500	28,800	4,349	32	4,115	30
28,800	34,100	6,045	36	5,705	34
34,100	41,500	7,953	40	7,507	38
41,500	55,300	10,913	45	10,319	42
55,300	60,000	17,123	50	16,115	48
60,000	70,000	19,473	50	18,371	48
70,000	81,800	24,473	50	23,171	48
81,800	90,000	29,473	50	28,835	50
90,000	100,000	34,473	50	32,935	50
100,000	and over	39,473	50	37,935	50

Example:

Mr. Thomas, a single man, has gross income of $61,000 for 1984. He files a return as a single individual and claims itemized deductions of $5,000. His taxable income is $57,300 ($61,000 less $2,700 excess itemized deductions and less a $1,000 exemption). Referring to the 1984 schedule above, the tax on $55,300 is $16,115. The tax on the $2,000 balance at 48% is $960. The total tax is $17,075 ($16,115 plus $960).

Source: Reproduced with permission from the 1985 edition of *U.S. Master Tax Guide*, published and copyrighted by Commerce Clearing House, Inc., 4025 W. Peterson Ave., Chicago, Illinois 60646.

SCHEDULE Y—MARRIED INDIVIDUALS

Joint Returns and Surviving Spouses					
Taxable Income		1983		1984	
Over	But Not Over	Pay	+% on Excess	Pay	+% on Excess
$ 0	$ 3,400	$ 0	0%	$ 0	0%
3,400	5,500	0	11	0	11
5,500	7,600	231	13	231	12
7,600	11,900	504	15	483	14
11,900	16,000	1,149	17	1,085	16
16,000	20,200	1,846	19	1,741	18
20,200	24,600	2,644	23	2,497	22
24,600	29,900	3,656	26	3,465	25
29,900	35,200	5,034	30	4,790	28
35,200	45,800	6,624	35	6,274	33
45,800	60,000	10,334	40	9,772	38
60,000	85,600	16,014	44	15,168	42
85,600	109,400	27,278	48	25,920	45
109,400	120,000	38,702	50	36,630	49
120,000	162,400	44,002	50	41,824	49
162,400	200,000	65,202	50	62,600	50
200,000	and over	84,002	50	81,400	50

Example:

Mr. and Mrs. Foy file a joint return for 1984 showing a taxable income of $63,900. In the 1984 joint return schedule above, the tax on $60,000 is $15,168, and the tax on the $3,900 balance at 42% is $1,638. Therefore, their total tax for 1984 is $16,806 ($15,168 plus $1,638).

Source: Reproduced with permission from the 1985 edition of *U.S. Master Tax Guide*, published and copyrighted by Commerce Clearing House, Inc., 4025 W. Peterson Ave., Chicago, Illinois 60646.

Separate Returns — Married Individuals					
Taxable Income		1983		1984	
Over	But Not Over	Pay	+% on Excess	Pay	+% on Excess
$ 0	$ 2,300	$ 0	0%	$ 0	0%
1,700	2,750	0	11	0	11
2,750	3,800	115.50	13	115.50	12
3,800	5,950	252	15	241.50	14
5,950	8,000	574.50	17	542.50	16
8,000	10,100	923	19	870.50	18
10,100	12,300	1,322	23	1,248.50	22
12,300	14,950	1,828	26	1,732.50	25
14,950	17,600	2,517	30	2,395	28
17,600	22,900	3,312	35	3,137	33
22,900	30,000	5,167	40	4,886	38
30,000	42,800	8,007	44	7,584	42
42,800	54,700	13,639	48	12,960	45
54,700	81,200	19,351	50	18,315	49
81,200	100,000	27,001	50	31,300	50
100,000	and over	42,001	50	40,700	50

Source: Reproduced with permission from the 1985 edition of *U.S. Master Tax Guide*, published and copyrighted by Commerce Clearing House, Inc., 4025 W. Peterson Ave., Chicago, Illinois 60646.

SCHEDULE Z—HEADS OF HOUSEHOLDS

Taxable Income		1983		1984	
Over	But Not Over	Pay	+% on Excess	Pay	+% on Excess
$ 0	$ 2,300	$ 0	0%	$ 0	0%
2,300	4,400	0	11	0	11
4,400	6,500	231	13	231	12
6,500	8,700	504	15	483	14
8,700	11,800	834	18	791	17
11,800	15,000	1,392	19	1,318	18
15,000	18,200	2,000	21	1,894	20
18,200	23,500	2,672	25	2,534	24
23,500	28,800	3,997	29	3,806	28
28,800	34,100	5,534	34	5,290	32
34,100	44,700	7,336	37	6,986	35
44,700	60,600	11,258	44	10,696	42
60,600	81,800	18,254	48	17,374	45
81,800	108,300	28,430	50	26,914	48
108,300	120,000	41,680	50	39,634	50
120,000	150,000	47,530	50	45,484	50
150,000	200,000	62,530	50	60,484	50
200,000	and over	87,530	50	85,484	50

Example:

Mr. Green, a widower, maintains a home for himself and his two dependent children. During 1984 he has gross income of $56,000. He files a return as a head of household and claims itemized deductions of $3,250. His taxable income is $52,050 ($56,000 less $950 excess itemized deductions and less $3,000 exemptions). Referring to the schedule above, the tax on $10,696 is $12,498. The tax on the $7,350 balance at 42% is $3,087. Therefore, the total tax is $13,783 ($10,696 plus $3,087).

Source: Reproduced with permission from the 1985 edition of *U.S. Master Tax Guide*, published and copyrighted by Commerce Clearing House, Inc., 4025 W. Peterson Ave., Chicago, Illinois 60646.

CORPORATION INCOME TAX RATES

Corporations compute their tax liability by applying the appropriate tax rate to each increment of taxable income: 15% on the first $25,000 of taxable income, 18% on the next $25,000, 30% on the next $25,000, and so on.

Taxable Income		Tax years beginning in[1]		
Over	But Not Over	1982	1983	1984[2]
$ 0	$ 25,000	16%	15%	15%
25,000	50,000	19	18	18
50,000	75,000	30	30	30
75,000	100,000	40	40	40
100,000	and over	46	46	46

1 *The changes in rates require fiscal-year corporations whose tax year spans an effective date of rate change to follow the statutory procedure for tax proration specified in Code Sec. 21.*

2 *Phase-out of Graduated Rate for Large Corporations*
For tax years after 1983, the Tax Reform Act of 1984 limits the benefits of the graduated tax structure for corporations with taxable income over $1 million by imposing a 5% additional tax on income in excess of that amount. The additional corporate tax is limited to $20,250. Thus, all benefits of the graduated rates are eliminated for corporations with taxable income greater than or equal to $1,405,000. Fiscal-year corporations, whose tax year includes January 1, 1984, will not have to prorate the additional tax. Also, component members of a controlled group of corporations are treated as one corporation for the additional tax. The taxable income of all component members is taken into account, and the new tax is divided among them in the same manner as the benefits of the graduated rates are allocated.

Source: Reproduced with permission from the 1985 edition of *U.S. Master Tax Guide*, published and copyrighted by Commerce Clearing House, Inc., 4025 W. Peterson Ave., Chicago, Illinois 60646.

Other Provisions

A controlled group of corporations is subject to the same rates as those listed above but the group is entitled, in the aggregate, to only $25,000 of taxable income in each of the rate brackets below the 46% bracket.

- All the undistributed income of a personal holding company is subject to a 50% tax rate.

- The regular corporate rates apply to insurance companies. Certain small mutual insurance companies are subject to special rates.

- The first $100,000 of accumulated taxable income in excess of the $250,000 minimum accumulated earnings credit is subject to a tax of 27.5%; accumulated earnings over $100,000 are taxed at 38.5%. However, for personal service corporations in health, law, engineering, architecture, accounting, actuarial science, the performing arts, or consulting, the minimum accumulated earnings credit is $150,000.

- Foreign corporations that are not engaged in trade or business in the U.S. are generally taxed at a rate of 30% on their passive income, and their interest income from bank deposits and portfolio investments is generally exempt. The tax rates for domestic corporations are applied to foreign corporations that are engaged in trade or business in the U.S.

- The regular corporate tax rates apply to the "real estate investment trust taxable income" of real estate investment trusts and to the "investment company taxable income" of regulated investment companies.

ESTATE, GIFT, AND MISCELLANEOUS TAXES

The estates and gifts of U.S. residents and citizens are taxable at specified rates, shown in the various tables below. A different schedule of rates, also shown below, applies to the estates of nonresident aliens.

ESTATE TAXES

Estate taxes are computed by applying the unified rate schedule to the cumulated at death and lifetime transfers and subtracting the gift taxes payable. The unified rate schedule is effective for gifts made after December 31, 1976, and for estates of decedents dying after that date.

INCOME TAX RATE SCHEDULE FOR ESTATES AND TRUSTS

Taxable Income		1983		1984	
Over	But Not Over	Pay	+% on Excess	Pay	+% on Excess
$ 0	$ 3,400	$ 0	0%	$ 0	0%
1,050	2,100	115.50	13	115.50	12
2,100	4,250	252	15	241.50	14
4,250	6,300	574.50	17	542.50	16
6,300	8,400	923	19	870.50	18
8,400	10,600	1,322	23	1,248.50	22
10,600	13,250	1,828	26	1,732.50	25
13,250	15,900	2,517	30	2,395	28
15,900	21,200	3,312	35	3,137	33
21,200	28,300	5,167	40	4,886	38
28,300	41,100	8,007	44	7,584	42
41,100	53,000	13,639	48	12,960	45
53,000	60,000	19,351	50	18,315	49
60,000	70,000	22,851	50	21,745	49
70,000	79,500	27,851	50	26,645	49
79,500	90,000	32,601	50	31,300	50
90,000	100,000	37,851	50	36,550	50
100,000	......	42,851	50	41,550	50

Example:

An estate has taxable income of $27,500 for 1984. Referring to the schedule above, the tax on $21,200 is $4,886. The tax on the balance ($6,300) at 38% is $2,394. Therefore, the estate's total tax for 1984 is $7,280 ($4,886 plus $2,394).

Source: Reproduced with permission from the 1985 edition of *U.S. Master Tax Guide*, published and copyrighted by Commerce Clearing House, Inc., 4025 W. Peterson Ave., Chicago, Illinois 60646.

GIFT TAXES

Gift taxes are computed by applying the unified rate schedule to cumulative lifetime taxable transfers and subtracting the taxes payable for prior taxable periods. There is an annual $10,000 exclusion for gifts, and an annual maximum of $20,000 for spouses for gift-splitting.

The upper limits of the generation-skipping transfer tax are being reduced. For tax year 1983, the top tax rate was 60% and was applied to amounts in excess of $3,500,000. The top rate for 1984 through 1987 is reduced to 55% of transfers in excess of $3,000,000, and for 1988 and thereafter, the top tax rate will be 50%, to be applied to amounts in excess of $2,500,000. The determination of the tax on generation-skipping transfers is computed by using the following schedule.

UNIFIED TRANSFER TAX RATE SCHEDULE

If the Amount Is		Tentative Tax Is		
Over	But not Over	Tax	+ %	On Excess Over
$ 0	$ 10,000	$ 0	18%	$ 0
10,000	20,000	1,800	20	10,000
20,000	40,000	3,800	22	20,000
40,000	60,000	8,200	24	40,000
60,000	80,000	13,000	26	60,000
80,000	100,000	18,200	28	80,000
100,000	150,000	23,800	30	100,000
150,000	250,000	38,800	32	150,000
250,000	500,000	70,800	34	250,000
500,000	750,000	155,800	37	500,000
750,000	1,000,000	248,300	39	750,000
1,000,000	1,250,000	345,800	41	1,000,000
1,250,000	1,500,000	448,300	43	1,250,000
1,500,000	2,000,000	555,800	45	1,500,000
2,000,000	2,500,000	780,800	49	2,000,000
2,500,000	3,000,000	1,025,800	53	2,500,000
3,000,000	....	1,290,800	55	3,000,000

Note: *The cumulative transfers to which the tentative tax applies are the sum of (a) the amount of the taxable estate, and (b) the amount of the taxable gifts made by the decedent after 1976 other than gifts includible in the gross estate.*

UNIFIED CREDIT

The unified credit is subtracted from the taxpayer's estate or gift tax liability. The unified credit for estates of decedents dying during 1984 was $96,300. For decedents dying in 1985, the credit is $121,800. Any part of the credit used to offset gift taxes is not available to offset estate taxes. In addition, the amount of the unified credit will be reduced by 20% of any portion of the $30,000 specific gift tax exemption allowable under pre-1977 law that was used for gifts made after September 8, 1976, but before January 1, 1977. Thus, under this rule, the maximum reduction of the unified credit will be $6,000 (20% of $30,000). Generally, the unified credit amount is the same throughout an entire year; however, as a transitional rule, only $6,000 of the unified credit could be applied against gifts made after December 31, 1976, but before July 1, 1977.

DEATH TAX CREDIT FOR ESTATE TAX
Estates of Decedents Dying after 1976

Adjusted Taxable Estate*		Credit	+ %	Of excess Over
At Least	But Less Than			
$ 0	$ 40,000	$ 0	0 %	$ 0
40,000	90,000	0	.8	40,000
90,000	140,000	400	1.6	90,000
140,000	240,000	1,200	2.4	140,000
240,000	440,000	3,600	3.2	240,000
440,000	640,000	10,000	4	440,000
640,000	840,000	18,000	4.8	640,000
840,000	1,040,000	27,600	5.6	840,000
1,040,000	1,540,000	38,800	6.4	1,040,000
1,540,000	2,040,000	70,800	7.2	1,540,000

(Continued)

Death Tax Credit for Estate Tax

Adjusted Taxable Estate*		Credit	+ %	Of excess Over
At Least	But Less Than			
2,040,000	2,540,000	106,800	8	2,040,000
2,540,000	3,040,000	146,800	8.8	2,540,000
3,040,000	3,540,000	190,800	9.6	3,040,000
3,540,000	4,040,000	238,800	10.4	3,540,000
4,040,000	5,040,000	290,800	11.2	4,040,000
5,040,000	6,040,000	402,800	12	5,040,000
6,040,000	7,040,000	522,800	12.8	6,040,000
7,040,000	8,040,000	650,800	13.6	7,040,000
8,040,000	9,040,000	786,800	14.4	8,040,000
9,040,000	10,040,000	930,800	15.2	9,040,000
10,040,000	....	1,082,800	16	10,040,000

Note: *There is a limitation on the credit in estates of nonresident aliens dying after November 13, 1966. See Code Section 2102. This table may not be used in computing taxes on estates of certain members of the Armed Forces.*
* *The adjusted taxable estate is the taxable estate reduced by $60,000.*

Source: Reproduced with permission from the 1985 edition of *U.S. Master Tax Guide*, published and copyrighted by Commerce Clearing House, Inc., 4025 W. Peterson Ave., Chicago, Illinois 60646.

For estates of decedents dying in 1981 and thereafter, the credit is phased in as follows:

Year	Amount of Credit	Amount of Exemption Equivalent
1981	$ 47,000	$175,625
1982	62,800	225,000
1983	79,300	275,000
1984	96,300	325,000
1985	121,800	400,000
1986	155,800	500,000
1987 and thereafter	192,800	600,000

For gifts made in 1977, only $6,000 of the unified credit may be applied against gifts made after December 31, 1976, but before July 1, 1977.

ESTATES OF NONRESIDENT ALIENS DYING AFTER 1976

A separate estate tax rate schedule applies to nonresidents who are not citizens and who die after 1976. The amount of estate tax is determined by applying the rate schedule to the cumulative lifetime and deathtime transfers subject to U.S. transfer taxes and then subtracting gift taxes payable on post-1976 lifetime transfer. Gift tax for nonresident aliens should be computed in accordance with the rate schedule set forth in Section 2001(c) of the Tax Code.

TAXES ON ESTATES OF NONRESIDENT ALIENS

Taxable Estate	Tentative Tax		
	Credit =	+	Of Excess Over
$0 – $100,000	6%		
$100,000 – $ 500,000	$ 6,000	12%	$ 100,000
$500,000 – $1,000,000	$ 54,000	18	$ 500,000
$1,000,000 – $2,000,000	$144,000	24	$1,000,000
$2,000,000 and over	$384,000	30	$2,000,000

A $3,600 credit is allowed against the estate tax. For residents of a possession of the United States, who are not considered citizens, the credit allowable is the greater of $3,600 or that proportion of $15,075 that the value of that part of the decedent's property situated in the United States bears to the value of the entire gross estate wherever situated. The $15,075 figure is phased in over a five-year period. Expatriates are allowed a $13,000 credit against the estate tax.

Miscellaneous Taxes

SELF-EMPLOYMENT AND SOCIAL SECURITY TAXES

For a tax year beginning in 1984, a tax rate of 11.3% (14% less 2.7% credit) is imposed for social security and hospital insurance on self-employment income up to $37,800. For a tax year beginning in 1985, the rate increases to an effective rate of 11.8% (14% less 2.3% tax credit) and applies to a $39,600 earnings base. No tax is payable if annual net earnings are less than $400.

For the calendar year 1984, a tax rate of 7% (with a 0.3% credit for employees against 1984 taxes) is imposed, also for social security and hospital insurance, on employers and employees on wages up to $37,800. For 1985, the wage base goes to $39,600, and the tax rate is increased to 7.05% for both employers and employees.

Medicare B premiums ($14.60 a month for 1984) qualify as deductible medical expenses.

UNEMPLOYMENT COMPENSATION

A tax of 3.5% is imposed on the first $7,000 of wages paid in 1984 to a covered employee by an employer of one or more persons in covered employment in each of 20 days in the current or preceding year, each day being in a different week, or who has a payroll for covered employment of at least $1,500 in a calendar quarter (or $20,000 agricultural labor or $1,000 for domestic labor) in the current or preceding calendar year. The rate increases to 6.2% (before credits) for 1985.

RAILROAD RETIREMENT TAX

A railroad retirement tax of 9.75% applies to an employee's compensation up to $3,150 a month in 1984. In 1985, the rate, increased to 10.55%, applicable to monthly compensation of $3,300 or $39,600 annually (with a 0.3% tax credit against 1984 taxes).

WINDFALL PROFIT TAX

There is a federal excise tax on the windfall profit from domestically produced crude oil. Although the producer of the oil must pay the tax, the first purchaser of the oil generally must withhold the tax from the purchase price of the oil and deposit it. With limited exceptions, domestic crude oil falls into one of three tiers, taxed at 70% (tier one), 60% (tier two), and 30% (tier three). For newly discovered oil, the tax rate ranges from 22.5% in 1984 to 15% after 1988. Independent producers are entitled to special rates on limited quantities of tier one and tier two oil. A royalty owner is entitled to a limited exemption from tax of two barrels of oil per day until 1985 and of three barrels thereafter.

2.16 **Federal Tax Computation for Individuals**

Federal tax law is extremely complicated, and the rules change frequently. The generalized information given below and the ten-step tax computation form can be used to calculate a rough estimate of tax liability but cannot be substituted for consultation with a tax professional.

Who Must File a Return

Liability for taxes is determined according to income level and the circumstances of the taxpayer. Generally, individuals with gross incomes of less than $1,000 a year do not have to file a return, unless they

1. Could be claimed as a dependent on a parent's return and had $1,000 or more in income that was not earned income—for example, taxable interest and dividends.

2. Owe any special taxes, such as:

   • Social security tax on tips

   • Uncollected social security tax or RRTA tax on tips

   • Alternative minimum tax

   • Tax on an Individual Retirement Account (IRA)

   • Tax from recapture of investment credit

3. Received any advance earned income credit (EIC) payments.

4. Had net earnings from self-employment income of at least $400.

5. Had wages of $100 or more from a church or qualified church-controlled organization that is exempt from employer social security taxes.

People in the following categories must file a return. Requirements for filing are based on *total* income, not taxable income; thus, some individuals are required to file even though they owe no taxes.

Marital status at end of 1984	Filing status	Age at end of 1984	Gross income at least
Single (including divorced and legally separated)	Single or Head of household	Under 65 65 or over	$3,300 $4,300
Married with a dependent child and living apart from your spouse all year	Single or Head of household	Under 65 65 or over	$3,300 $4,300

(Continued)

Marital status at end of 1984	Filing status	Age at end of 1984	Gross income at least
Married and living with your spouse at end of 1984 (or on the date your spouse died)	Married, joint return	Under 65 (both spouses)	$5,400
		65 or over (one spouse)	$6,400
		65 or over (both spouses)	$7,400
	Married, separate return	Any age	$1,000
Married, not living with your spouse at end of 1984	Married, joint return	Any age	$1,000
	Married, separate return	Any age	$1,000
Widowed in 1983 or 1982 and not remarried in 1984	Single or Head of household	Under 65	$3,300
		65 or over	$4,300
	Qualifying widow(er) with dependent child	Under 65	$4,400
		65 or over	$5,400
Widowed before 1982 and not remarried in 1984	Single or Head of household	Under 65	$3,300
		65 or over	$4,300

Common Types of Income

Alimony received: periodic payments, but not lump-sum payments

Annuities (in whole or in part)

Bonuses

Business profits

Commissions

Compensation for personal services

Dividends ($100 exclusion; $200 for married couples filing jointly)

Expense allowance or reimbursement, if not accounted for to employer

Gains from sales or exchanges

Gambling winnings

Income received or receivable from estates or trusts

Interest received (except tax-exempt municipal bond income)

Jury fees

Partner's share of firm's profits

Pensions for past services

Prizes and awards (competitive)

Rents and royalties

Salary, wages, and tips

Common Deductions

Against their total income, taxpayers are allowed to declare a variety of deductions, the most common of which are:

Alimony paid, if taxable to spouse

Automobile expenses, to extent used in business

Bad business debts (nonbusiness debts are treated as short-term capital losses)

Contributions to Keogh Plan, Individual Retirement Account, or Simplified Employee Pension

Deduction for married couple if both spouses work

Depreciation of business equipment and buildings

Education expenses of employees, if reimbursed by employer (limited)

Entertainment expenses, if reimbursed (business only)

Interest penalty on early withdrawal from bank time deposits

Moving expenses of employees (subject to limitations)

Outside salesperson's business expenses

Property held for rent or royalties, related expenses

Rent or repairs of business property

Taxes: Federal excise taxes, stamp taxes, import duties (business only)

       Social Security (on business employer)

       State income, property, general sales, and gasoline taxes (business only)

Traveling expenses, including meals and lodging, while away from home overnight on business or to manage rental or royalty property

Zero Bracket Amount

The zero bracket amount is a minimum amount not subject to tax. It is based on filing status and is built into the tax tables and tax rate schedules. Starting in 1985, the ZBA is scheduled to be indexed to rise or fall with the consumer price index. For the 1984 tax year, the ZBA is:

Married taxpayers filing jointly	$3,400
Surviving spouses	3,400
Single taxpayers	2,300
Heads of household	2,300
Married taxpayers filing separately	1,700

Those ineligible to use the zero bracket amount include married persons filing separately, whose spouses elect to itemize; nonresident aliens; and U.S. citizens with excludable income from U.S. possessions.

Because the ZBA is incorporated into the tax schedules, taxpayers who itemize deductions must subtract the ZBA from those deductions.

Example 1

You and your spouse file jointly and have $6,000 in itemized deductions. You may deduct $2,600 ($6,000 − $3,400) from your adjusted gross income.

Example 2

You are single and have $2,000 in itemized deductions. You may not use any of these deductions, because they total less than your ZBA. One tax strategy would be to lump all itemized deductions into one year by paying early or deferring payment when possible.

Itemized Deductions

Itemized deductions, sometimes referred to as below-the-line deductions, are deductions from adjusted gross income. As mentioned, itemized deductions are only deductible to the extent they exceed the ZBA. Generally, these deductions involve personal expenses.

Automobile collision damage

Casualty and theft losses to nonbusiness property in excess of $100 (per casualty or loss) to the extent that they exceed 10% of adjusted gross income (special rules apply if the taxpayer also has casualty gains)

Charitable contributions (limitations)

Cooperative apartment, payments for, representing interest and taxes

Education expenses, to keep or improve skills in present job

Employment agency fees

Income-producing activities, related expenses

Income tax return, fee for preparing

Interest on personal loans (except to purchase tax-exempt securities, tax-exempt All-Savers Certificates, or a single-premium insurance, annuity or endowment contract); limit on minimum deposit life insurance; finance charges on credit cards and charge accounts

Investor's expenses, e.g., safe deposit rental, bond premium (amortized), custodian fees, investment advice

Medical expenses (limitations)

Mortgage points paid when you purchase a home

Mortgage prepayment penalty

Personal deductions are limited to state or local income, property, and general sales taxes; there is no deduction for federal income, estate, or gift taxes

Union dues

Personal Exemptions

Personal exemptions are deducted from adjusted gross income. In tax year 1984 each personal exemption is worth $1,000; starting in 1985, these exemptions are to be indexed to changes in the consumer price index.

Each individual filer is entitled to a personal exemption for him or herself. An additional exemption may be taken if the filer is over 65, and a third exemption if he or she is blind. Married couples filing jointly declare all the personal exemptions that each spouse is entitled to. For married couples filing separately, one spouse may claim the personal exemption(s) for the other if that other spouse had no gross income and is not the dependent of another taxpayer.

In addition to the above exemptions, a $1,000 exemption is allowed for each dependent. To qualify as a dependent, the person must meet five dependency tests (see p. 2.85).

Credits

Credits are particularly beneficial to the taxpayer because they reduce tax liability dollar for dollar, whereas deductions only reduce tax liability by the tax bracket percentage (e.g., for a taxpayer in the 30% tax bracket a deduction will reduce tax liability by 30%).

Common credits:

- Energy credit
- Credit for the elderly
- Childcare credit
- Investment credit
- Political contributions (maximum credit of $100 on a joint return, $50 for single persons)

Earned Income Credit

A tax credit known as the *earned income credit* is available for a low-income worker who maintains a household in the U.S. that is the principal place of abode of the worker and a child or children. In addition, the worker must be:

- A married person who files a joint return and is entitled to a dependency exemption for a son or a daughter, adopted child, or stepchild;
- A surviving spouse; or
- An individual who qualifies as a head of household and whose household includes a child or descendant of the child. Such child or descendant must be unmarried or, if married, must qualify as a dependent for whom the taxpayer is entitled to a dependency exemption. (See Dependent Status, page 2.85.)

The credit is 10% of earned income of up to $5,000—thus, the maximum credit is $500. (For tax years beginning after 1984, the credit is equal to 11% of earned income up to $5,000; thus the maximum credit will be $550.) Earned income includes wages, salaries, tips or other compensation, and earnings from self-employment. The amount of the allowable credit may be determined through the use of the table that appears on page 2.82. The credit is zero when adjusted gross income or earned income is $10,000 or more.

Under certain conditions specified in the tax code, a married person living apart from a spouse need not file a joint return to claim the credit. Also, the credit may be claimed only for a full 12-month tax year, except in the case of death.

The earned income credit is refundable to the extent that it reduces the tax below zero. An eligible taxpayer may elect to receive advance payment of the credit through his or her paychecks. Form W-5 is to be used by eligible employees in order to notify their employees that they choose to receive advance payments instead of waiting until they file their annual tax returns.

The advance payment is included on the taxpayer's Form W-2 and is shown on the return as part of the tax liability on Form 1040A and as an "other" tax due on Form 1040. The actual credit to which the taxpayer is entitled is treated as a payment. Any difference will be refunded to the taxpayer or has to be paid by the taxpayer to the IRS.

A taxpayer should use the worksheets that accompany the instructions to Forms 1040 and 1040A to determine eligibility for the earned income credit. If the taxpayer so qualifies, he can then use the following table to determine the amount of the credit.

1984 EARNED INCOME CREDIT TABLE

The earned income credit table is used in conjunction with the earned income credit worksheet appearing in the instructions that accompany Forms 1040 and 1040A. The worksheet is used only for the purpose of computing the earned income credit and is *not* to be filed with the taxpayer's income tax return. The credit so computed is entered on line 59, Form 1040, or on line 24b, Form 1040A.

If line 3 or 4 of the worksheet is—		Your earned income credit is—	If line 3 or 4 of the worksheet is—		Your earned income credit is—	If line 3 or 4 of the worksheet is—		Your earned income credit is—	If line 3 or 4 of the worksheet is—		Your earned income credit is—
Over	But not over		Over	But not over		Over	But not over		Over	But not over	
$0	$50	$3	$1,400	$1,450	$143	$2,800	$2,850	$283	$4,200	$4,250	$423
50	100	8	1,450	1,500	148	2,850	2,900	288	4,250	4,300	428
100	150	13	1,500	1,550	153	2,900	2,950	293	4,300	4,350	433
150	200	18	1,550	1,600	158	2,950	3,000	298	4,350	4,400	438
200	250	23	1,600	1,650	163	3,000	3,050	303	4,400	4,450	443
250	300	28	1,650	1,700	168	3,050	3,100	308	4,450	4,500	448
300	350	33	1,700	1,750	173	3,100	3,150	313	4,500	4,550	453
350	400	38	1,750	1,800	178	3,150	3,200	318	4,550	4,600	458
400	450	43	1,800	1,850	183	3,200	3,250	323	4,600	4,650	463
450	500	48	1,850	1,900	188	3,250	3,300	328	4,650	4,700	468
500	550	53	1,900	1,950	193	3,300	3,350	333	4,700	4,750	473
550	600	58	1,950	2,000	198	3,350	3,400	338	4,750	4,800	478
600	650	63	2,000	2,050	203	3,400	3,450	343	4,800	4,850	483
650	700	68	2,050	2,100	208	3,450	3,500	348	4,850	4,900	488
700	750	73	2,100	2,150	213	3,500	3,550	353	4,900	4,950	493
750	800	78	2,150	2,200	218	3,550	3,600	358	4,950	5,000	498
800	850	83	2,200	2,250	223	3,600	3,650	363	5,000	6,000	500
850	900	88	2,250	2,300	228	3,650	3,700	368	6,000	6,050	497
900	950	93	2,300	2,350	233	3,700	3,750	373	6,050	6,100	491
950	1,000	98	2,350	2,400	238	3,750	3,800	378	6,100	6,150	484
1,000	1,050	103	2,400	2,450	243	3,800	3,850	383	6,150	6,200	478
1,050	1,100	108	2,450	2,500	248	3,850	3,900	388	6,200	6,250	472
1,100	1,150	113	2,500	2,550	253	3,900	3,950	393	6,250	6,300	466
1,150	1,200	118	2,550	2,600	258	3,950	4,000	398	6,300	6,350	459
1,200	1,250	123	2,600	2,650	263	4,000	4,050	403	6,350	6,400	453
1,250	1,300	128	2,650	2,700	268	4,050	4,100	408	6,400	6,450	447
1,300	1,350	133	2,700	2,750	273	4,100	4,150	413	6,450	6,500	441
1,350	1,400	138	2,750	2,800	278	4,150	4,200	418	6,500	6,550	434

Earned Income Credit Table

If line 3 or 4 of the worksheet is—		Your earned income credit is—	If line 3 or 4 of the worksheet is—		Your earned income credit is—	If line 3 or 4 of the worksheet is—		Your earned income credit is—	If line 3 or 4 of the worksheet is—		Your earned income credit is—
Over	But not over		Over	But not over		Over	But not over		Over	But not over	
$6,550	$6,600	$428	$7,550	$7,600	$303	$8,550	$8,600	$178	$9,550	$9,600	$ 53
6,600	6,650	422	7,600	7,650	297	8,600	8,650	172	9,600	9,650	47
6,650	6,700	416	7,650	7,700	291	8,650	8,700	166	9,650	9,700	41
6,700	6,750	409	7,700	7,750	284	8,700	8,750	159	9,700	9,750	34
6,750	6,800	403	7,750	7,800	278	8,750	8,800	153	9,750	9,800	28
6,800	6,850	397	7,800	7,850	272	8,800	8,850	147	9,800	9,850	22
6,850	6,900	391	7,850	7,900	266	8,850	8,890	141	9,850	9,900	16
6,900	6,950	384	7,900	7,950	259	8,900	8,950	134	9,900	9,950	9
6,950	7,000	378	7,950	8,000	253	8,950	9,000	128	9,950	9,999	3
7,000	7,050	372	8,000	8,050	247	9,000	9,050	122			
7,050	7,100	366	8,050	8,100	241	9,050	9,100	116			
7,100	7,150	359	8,100	8,150	234	9,100	9,150	109			
7,150	7,200	353	8,150	8,200	228	9,150	9,200	103			
7,200	7,250	347	8,200	8,250	222	9,200	9,250	97			
7,250	7,300	341	8,250	8,300	216	9,250	9,300	91			
7,300	7,350	334	8,300	8,350	209	9,300	9,350	84			
7,350	7,400	328	8,350	8,400	203	9,350	9,400	78			
7,400	7,450	322	8,400	8,450	197	9,400	9,450	72			
7,450	7,500	316	8,450	8,500	191	9,450	9,500	66			
7,500	7,550	309	8,500	8,550	184	9,500	9,550	59			

Source: Reproduced with permission from *U.S. Master Tax Guide*, published and copyrighted by Commerce Clearing House, Inc., Chicago, Illinois 60646.

A SIMPLIFIED GUIDE TO FEDERAL TAX COMPUTATION

1. Add all sources of income (see list on page 2.78)

    $ _____
    1. Total Income

2. Add all deductions that can be taken against total income (see list on page 2.79)

    $ _____
    2. Deductions

3. Subtract deductions (line 2) from total income (line 1)

    $ _____
    3. Adjusted Gross Income

4. Determine the total of Schedule A itemized deductions (see page 2.80)

    $ _____
    4. Itemized Deductions

5. Deduct, from total itemized deductions (line 4), the Zero-Bracket Amount (ZBA) (see page 2.79); if itemized deductions do not exceed the ZBA, enter 0

    $ _____
    5. Excess Itemized Deductions

6. Determine personal exemption(s) (see page 2.80) and exemptions for dependents (see page 2.85)

    $ _____
    6. Personal Exemptions and Dependents

7. Subtract excess itemized deductions (line 5) *and* personal exemptions (line 6) from adjusted gross income (line 3)

    $ _____
    7. Taxable Income

8. Determine the taxes owed on taxable income (line 7) by consulting the federal tax rate schedules (see pages 2.69–71)

    $ _____
    8. Tax Owed

9. Determine the total amount of tax credits (see pages 2.39–42 and 2.48)

    $ _____
    9. Credits

10. Subtract, from taxes owed (line 8) the credits available (line 9)

    $ _____
    10. Tax Due

2.17 Dependent Status

A personal exemption (see page 2.80) may be claimed by a taxpayer for the support of others, generally family members. The requirements are quite specific, and all five listed below must be met to qualify for the exemption. Only one exemption—in 1984, worth $1,000—may be claimed for each dependent; the additional exemptions for old age and blindness may not be taken for dependents.

INCOME

The claimed dependent must have less than $1,000 of gross income for the calendar year in which the taxable year of the taxpayer begins, except where the dependent is a child of the taxpayer and either is under 19 at the close of such calendar year or is a full-time student.

SUPPORT

Over half of the dependent's support for that calendar year must have been furnished by the taxpayer. Exceptions exist for multiple support agreements, students, and children of divorced persons.

RELATIONSHIP

The dependent must fall within one of the following specified classes of relationship to the taxpayer, or his spouse if filing jointly:

- Son or daughter, descendent of either, or stepchild

- Brother or sister

- Brother or sister by the half blood

- Stepbrother or stepsister

- Mother or father, or ancestor of either

- Stepmother or stepfather

- Son or daughter of taxpayer's brother or sister

- Brother or sister of taxpayer's father or mother

- Son-in-law, daughter-in-law, father-in-law, mother-in-law, brother-in-law, or sister-in-law (the widow of a taxpayer's deceased wife's brother is not considered a sister-in-law)

- A person (other than the taxpayer's spouse) who, during the taxpayer's entire taxable year, lives in the taxpayer's home and is a member of the taxpayer's household (but not if the relationship between the person and the taxpayer is in violation of local law)

A legally adopted child or a child placed in the taxpayer's home for adoption by an authorized agency is considered to be a child by blood. The same status is given to a foster child who is cared for by the foster parent as his own child. The relationship of affinity, once existing, is not destroyed for income tax purposes by divorce or by the death of a spouse.

Assuming the support test is met, a full exemption may be claimed for a child born at any time during the taxable year, as long as the child lives momentarily and the birth is documented under state or local law as a live birth.

MARRIED DEPENDENT

The dependent must not have filed a joint return with his spouse (unless that filing was solely to claim a refund of tax withheld).

CITIZENSHIP

The dependent must be a citizen, national, or resident of the United States, a resident of Canada or Mexico at some time during the calendar year in which the tax year of the taxpayer begins, or an alien child adopted by and living with a U.S. citizen in a foreign country as a member of his household for the entire tax year.

2.18 **Tax Audits**

The IRS checks every return filed for mathematical accuracy, routinely checking more than a dozen simple errors. Taxpayers who forget, for instance, the 5% limitation on medical deductions, who claim a partial rather than full dependency exemption, or who use an incorrect tax rate schedule will have their returns corrected.

After the returns and refunds are processed, IRS computers grade the returns for their audit potential. Returns are compared to IRS norms; those that fall within these norms are less likely to be audited. Tax professionals are familiar with these IRS norms and can give taxpayers guidance in this area. While staying within these norms reduces the likelihood of an audit, taxpayers should not forgo deductions and credits to which they are entitled. However, taxpayers whose deductions fall below the IRS norms should not attempt to take credits and deductions beyond those actually earned.

Lowering the Probability of an Audit

1. File between April 1 and April 15. Many IRS insiders believe that later returns are less likely to be audited.

2. Avoid tax protest returns at all costs. The IRS has been known to go after a protester for as little as $25 in order to make an example of the person.

3. Avoid novel or tricky tax shelters. The IRS is actively working to shut down abusive tax-shelter investment schemes.

4. Other financial arrangements that are considered danger zones because the IRS tends to scrutinize them closely, include:

   Family estate trusts
   Barter
   Mail-order ministries
   Use of the wrong tax preparer
   No preparer on a complex return
   Selected occupations
   Home office
   Income-splitting schemes
   Children listed as payees of interest
   Interest-free loans to relatives
   Family businesses
   Vacation homes
   Financial losses
   Travel and entertainment

While legitimate deductions and credits should be considered safe, the taxpayer must have documentation to back up the return.

5. People who do not file returns at all are also considered worthy of the attention of the IRS.

Relatively Safe Deductions

Energy tax credits
Casualty losses
Charitable contributions (generally less than 2% of adjusted gross income)
Medical expenses
Sales tax
Mortgage interest
Other interest
Moving expenses
Political contributions (with reasonable limits)
Dues to professional organizations
Union dues
Capital gains and losses
Safe-deposit box rentals
Dividend exclusion
Personal retirement plans
Personal property taxes, and state and local taxes
Real estate taxes
Dependency exemptions
Alimony
Self-improvement expenses
Tax counseling

Probability of Being Audited

In general, the higher a taxpayer's income, the greater his risk of being audited. The following chart shows the likelihood of being audited:

Individual (based on adjusted gross income)	% Audited
Under $10,000, standard deductions	0.67
Under $10,000, itemized deductions	2.90
$10,000 to $50,000	2.63
$50,000 and over	10.40

Business Income	
Under $10,000	3.28
$10,000 to $30,000	2.03
$30,000 and over	6.68

Corporation (based on assets)	
Under $100,000	3.83
$100,000 to $1,000,000	9.26
$1,000,000 to $10,000,000	26.97
$10,000,000 to $100,000,000	42.14
$100,000,000 and over	78.52

Gift Tax	3.33

PATH OF A TAX AUDIT

At any stage of the procedure:

You may agree and arrange to pay.

You may ask the IRS to issue you a notice of deficiency so that you can file a petition with the Tax Court.

You may pay the tax and file a claim for a refund.

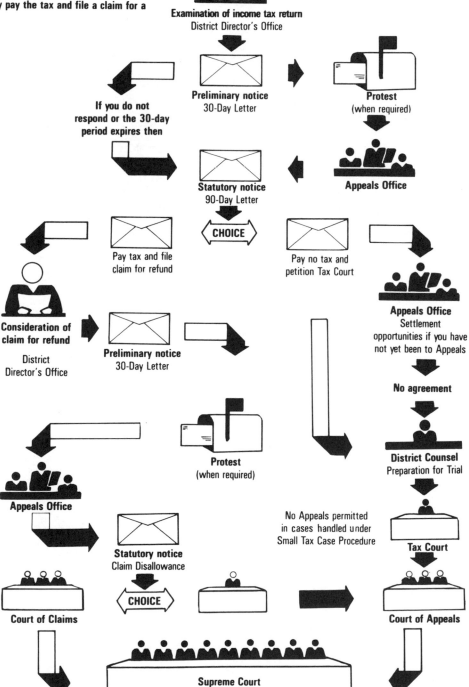

Examination of income tax return
District Director's Office

Preliminary notice
30-Day Letter

Protest
(when required)

If you do not respond or the 30-day period expires then

Statutory notice
90-Day Letter

Appeals Office

⟨ **CHOICE** ⟩

Pay tax and file claim for refund

Pay no tax and petition Tax Court

Appeals Office
Settlement opportunities if you have not yet been to Appeals

Consideration of claim for refund

District Director's Office

Preliminary notice
30-Day Letter

No agreement

Protest
(when required)

District Counsel
Preparation for Trial

Appeals Office

No Appeals permitted in cases handled under Small Tax Case Procedure

Tax Court

Statutory notice
Claim Disallowance

⟨ **CHOICE** ⟩

Court of Claims

Court of Appeals

Supreme Court

2.19 Filing Information for Federal Taxes

Due Dates for Federal Taxes, 1986–1987

**This day
1986**   **Annual Due Dates**

Each date shown is the prescribed last day for filing the return or making the payment of tax indicated. However, if such date falls on a Saturday, Sunday, or legal holiday, the due date is on the next succeeding day that is not a Saturday, Sunday, or legal holiday (national, in the District of Columbia, or statewide in the state where the return is to be filed).

Jan. 15

Final 1986 "estimation day" for individuals. Pay all of unpaid estimated 1985 tax, making any final amendments. Farmers and fishermen pay estimated tax for 1986.

Jan. 31

Employer's return on Form 941 for income and FICA taxes withheld from wages in last quarter of 1985.

Employees' statements (W-2, W-2P and 1099R) for amounts withheld in 1985 to be furnished by employer.

Individuals (other than farmers and fishermen) may file final 1986 income tax return instead of filing Jan. 15 estimate. Employers file federal unemployment tax Form 940 for 1985. Form 943 for wages paid for agricultural labor in 1985.

Note: If timely deposits in full payment of tax due were made, the due date of Forms 940, 941, and 943 is February 10.

Annual statements to recipients of dividends, interest, patronage dividends, interest on bearer certificates of deposit, original issue discount, proceeds from broker and barter exchange transactions, certain governmental payments including unemployment compensation and state and local tax refunds of $10 or more, and other payments of $600 or more by a person in a trade or business.

Feb. 28

Annual information returns on 1986 payments of dividends, interest, patronage dividends (aggregating $10 or more), interest on bearer certificates of deposit, original issue discount, salaries from which tax has not been withheld, direct sales of at least $5,000, and other payments of $600 or more by a person in a trade or business, proceeds from broker and barter exchange transactions, and certain government payments including unemployment compensation and state and local tax refunds of $10 or more.

Form 5452, return of nontaxable corporate distributions during 1985.

Return of information on distributions in liquidation during 1985 of $600 or more.

**This day
1986**

*Feb. 28
(cont.)*

Forms W-2 and W-2P "A" copies with transmittal form (Form W-3) to Social Security Administration.

Form 1099R "A" copy with transmittal form (Form W-3G) to IRS Service Center.

Mar. 1

Last day for farmers and fishermen to file 1985 calendar-year return instead of filing 1986 estimate on January 15.

Mar. 15

Due date of calendar-year corporations' 1986 income tax returns.

Returns on Forms 1042 and 1042S of tax withheld at the source from nonresident aliens and nonresident foreign corporations and partnerships.

Calendar-year corporations' 1986 information return (Form 5471) for foreign corporations. (Fiscal-year corporations file this form with their income tax returns.)

Apr. 15

Income tax and self-employment tax returns of individuals for calendar year 1985; partnership returns for calendar year 1985; and income tax returns of calendar-year decedents who died in 1985.

Payment of first installment of 1987 estimated income taxes by individuals (other than farmers and fishermen).

Calendar-year corporations' estimation date for 1987 taxes. Pay 25% of estimated tax when requirements are met before April 1, 1986.

Fiduciary income tax return due for calendar year 1985. Estate can pay 25% installment.

Individuals' information return (Form 5471) for foreign corporations. (Fiscal-year individuals file the form with their income tax returns.)

May 15

Annual information return by calendar-year organizations who are exempt or claiming exemption under Code Section 501.

Annual information returns for reporting foreign ownership of real property interests in the U.S. or the Virgin Islands.

June 15

Last day to file income tax returns of nonresident alien individuals not subject to withholding and nonresident foreign corporations for calendar year 1985. Also, by general extension, last day for returns of citizens abroad, other foreign corporations and partnerships, and domestic corporations whose records are abroad or whose principal income is from U.S. possessions.

Calendar-year corporations pay second installment (25%) of 1986 estimated tax.

Payment of second installment of 1986 estimated tax by individuals other than farmers and fishermen.

June 30

Last day for filing information return (Form 5498) for each person from whom IRA or SEP contributions were received during 1985. Also last day for providing statements for such persons.

Sept. 15

Payment of third installment (25%) of 1986 estimated tax by calendar-year corporations.

**This day
1986**

*Sept. 15
(cont.)*   Last day for exempt calendar-year farmers' cooperatives to file income tax returns.

Payment of third installment of 1986 estimated tax by individuals other than farmers and fishermen.

Dec. 15   Payment of last installment (25%) of 1986 estimated tax by calendar-year corporations.

**This day
1987**

Jan. 15   Final installment of 1986 estimated tax by individuals; payment of estimated tax in full by individuals who are first required to pay estimated tax; payment of estimated tax in full by farmers and fishermen who are not filing final returns by March 1, 1987.

Jan. 31   Final income tax return for 1986 by calendar-year individuals instead of payment of 1987 estimated tax otherwise due January 15.

Mar. 1   Final income tax return for 1986 by farmers and fishermen on calendar-year basis instead of paying estimated tax otherwise due January 15th.

Monthly Due Dates

*15th day of
each month*   If, at the end of a month, an employer's cumulative liability for payroll taxes (federal income tax, old-age benefits and hospital insurance taxes) is $500 or more but less than $3,000 at the end of any eighth-monthly period, the amount of cumulative liability is to be deposited by the 15th day of the following month.

If an employer's liability for payroll taxes for a quarter is less than $500, the total liability for the quarter is to be paid by the end of the following month, either with the return or by deposit.

*Last day of
the month*   Deposits with an authorized depositary are required when more than $100 in excise taxes is collected during either of the first two months in any quarter. Taxes for the third month, due at the end of the following month, may be paid in the same way or directly with quarterly return.

Eighth-Monthly Deposits

If, on the 3rd, 7th, 11th, 15th, 19th, 22nd, 25th, or the last day of the month, an employer's cumulative liability for payroll taxes is $3,000 or more, a deposit is required within the next three banking days after the close of the eighth-monthly period. Unless the undeposited tax liability is $10,000 or more, a "first-time three-banking-day depositor" may make a deposit within 15 days after the end of the month in which the tax liability reaches $3,000. If at least 95% of the actual tax liability for a deposit period is deposited, the deposit requirements are considered met. Any underpayment for a deposit period for the first or second month of a quarter is due with the first deposit after the 15th day of the next month.

Quarterly Due Dates

1st day, January, May, July, October—Employee status determination dates for wage withholding. Employer must honor new exemption certificate for first wage payment made on or after first status determination date that occurs at least 30 days from date new certificate was furnished.

15th day, April, June, September, December—Payments of estimated income tax of calendar-year corporations. Deposit payments, with federal tax deposit form (FTD Form), at a Federal Reserve Bank or authorized depositary.

15th day, April, June, September and January of next calendar year—Payments of current year's estimated income tax by individuals other than farmers and fishermen.

15th day, April, July, October and January of the next calendar year—Payments of income taxes covering preceding year for decedent's estate returns where installment method of payment is elected.

Last day, January, April, July, October—Quarterly return and payment (by depositary receipts or cash) of taxes withheld by employers and certain excise taxes collected during preceding quarter. If tax was deposited on time, return may be filed by 10th day of February, May, August and November.

Where to File Federal Income Tax Returns

Individual Taxpayers

Individual taxpayers report their income by filing IRS Form 1040 by April 15. Taxpayers whose taxable incomes are less than $50,000 and who do not wish to itemize their deductions may file their returns on Form 1040A, the so-called short form. Taxpayers must file their returns with the appropriate IRS Regional Service Center; no street address is needed.

Alabama
Atlanta, GA 31101

Alaska
Ogden, UT 84201

Arizona
Ogden, UT 84201

Arkansas
Austin, TX 73301

California
Fresno, CA 93888

Colorado
Ogden, UT 84201

Connecticut
Andover, MA 05501

Delaware
Philadelphia, PA 19255

District of Columbia
Phildelphia, PA 19255

Florida
Atlanta, GA 31101

Georgia
Atlanta, GA 31101

Hawaii
Fresno, CA 93888

Idaho
Ogden, UT 84201

Indiana
Memphis, TN 37501

Iowa
Kansas City, MO 64999

Kansas
Austin, TX 73301

Kentucky
Memphis, TN 37501

Louisiana
Austin, TX 73301

Maine
Andover, MA 05501

Maryland
Philadelphia, PA 19255

Massachusetts
Andover, MA 05501

Michigan
Cincinnati, OH 45999

Minnesota
Ogden, UT 84201

Mississippi
Atlanta, GA 31101

Missouri
Kansas City, MO 64999

Montana
Ogden, UT 84201

Nebraska
Ogden, UT 84201

Nevada
Ogden, UT 84201

New Hampshire
Andover, MA 05501

New Jersey
Holtsville, NY 00501

New Mexico
Austin, TX 73301

New York
New York City and Counties of Nassau, Rockland, Suffolk, and Westchester—Holtsville, NY 00501
All other Counties—Andover, MA 05501

North Carolina
Memphis, TN 37501

North Dakota
Ogden, UT 84201

Ohio
Cincinnati, OH 45999

Oklahoma
Austin, TX 73301

Oregon
Ogden, TX 84201

Pennsylvania
Philadelphia, PA 19255

Rhode Island
Andover, MA 05501

South Carolina
Atlanta, GA 31101

South Dakota
Ogden, UT 84201

Tennessee
Memphis, TN 37501

Texas
Austin, TX 73301

Utah
Ogden, UT 84201

Vermont
Andover, MA 05501

Virginia
Memphis, TN 37501

Washington
Ogden, UT 84201

West Virginia
Memphis, TN 37501

Wisconsin
Kansas City, MO 64999

Wyoming
Ogden, UT 84201

American Samoa
Philadelphia, PA 19255

Guam
Commissioner of Revenue and Taxation,
Agana, GU 96910

Puerto Rico
(or if excluding income under
Section 933) Philadelphia, PA 19255

Virgin Islands
Non-permanent resident
Philadelphia, PA 19255

Virgin Islands
Permanent resident
Department of Finance, Tax Division,
Charlotte Amalie, St. Thomas, VI 00801

A.P.O. or F.P.O. address of:
Miami — Atlanta, GA 31101
New York — Holtsville, NY 00501
San Francisco — Fresno, CA 93888
Seattle — Ogden, UT 84201

Foreign country
(U.S. citizens and those excluding income
under Section 911 or 931, or claiming the
housing deduction under Section 911)
Philadelphia, PA 19255

Corporations and Partnerships

The location of a corporation's or partnership's principal place of business or principal office or agency determines the Internal Revenue Service Center with which returns are to be filed. If a corporation or partnership is without a principal office or agency or principal place of business in the United States, returns are filed with the Philadelphia Service Center.

Estates and Trusts

A fiduciary of an estate or trust should file Form 1041 with the Internal Revenue Service Center for the state in which the fiduciary resides or has his principal place of business. However, a charitable or split-interest trust described in Code Section 4947(a), if located in Delaware, the District of Columbia, Maryland, Pennsylvania, Virginia, or outside the United States, should file with the Philadelphia Service Center.

2.20 State Taxes

This section consists of a number of tables summarizing various taxes and exemptions listed by state. Tax laws are constantly changing and, while these tables are useful as guidelines, they cannot be comprehensive. Tax professionals should be consulted about the applicability of the rates and provisions to individual situations.

STATE INCOME TAXES FOR INDIVIDUALS
Rates and Exemptions as of September 1, 1984

State	Taxable Income ($)		Rates	Personal Exemptions ($)		
				Single	Married or Head of Household	Credit per Dependent
Alabama[1]	First	1,000	2%	1,500	3,000	300
	1,001–6,000		4			
	over 6,000		5			
Arizona[1,2,4]	First	1,000	2	1,729	3,458	1,038
	1,001–2,000		3			
	2,001–3,000		4			
	3,001–4,000		5			
	4,001–5,000		6			
	5,001–6,000		7			
	over 6,000		8			
Arkansas[3]	First	2,999	1	17.50 (Tax credit)	35	6
	3,000–5,999		2.5			
	6,000–8,999		3.5			
	9,000–14,999		4.5			
	15,000–24,999		6			
	25,000 and over		7			
California[1,2,4,6]	First	3,120	1	38 (Tax credit)	76	12
	3,120–5,450		2			
	5,450–7,790		3			
	7,790–10,160		4	Heads of households have slightly lower tax rates.		
	10,160–12,500		5			
	12,500–14,850		6			
	14,850–17,170		7			
	17,170–19,520		8			
	19,520–21,860		9			
	21,860–24,200		10			
	over 24,200		11			
Colorado[1,4,6]	First	1,415	2.5	850	1,700	850
	1,415–2,831		3			
	2,831–4,246		3.5	Surtax on intangible income over $15,000, 2%. A credit equal to one half of 1% of net taxable income is allowed for income under $9,000.		
	4,246–5,661		4			
	5,661–7,076		4.5			
	7,076–8,492		5			
	8,492–9,907		5.5			
	9,907–11,322		6			
	11,322–12,738		6.5			
	12,738–14,153		7.5			
	14,153 and over		8			
Connecticut	7% capital gains tax; tax on dividends earned if federal adjusted gross income is greater than or equal to $20,000; tax ranges from 1% on $20,000 through 9% on $100,000 and over.				100	200

State Income Taxes for Individuals

State	Taxable Income ($)		Rates	Personal Exemptions ($)		
				Single	Married or Head of Household	Credit per Dependent
Delaware[3]	First	1,000	1.4%	600	1,200	600
	1,001–2,000		2.0			
	2,001–3,000		3.0	Exemptions apply only to adjusted		
	3,001–4,000		4.2	gross incomes of more than $20,000		
	4,001–5,000		5.2	and net capital gains of more than		
	5,001–6,000		6.2	$100 (or $200 on joint returns).		
	6,001–8,000		7.2			
	8,001–10,000		8.0			
	10,001–15,000		8.2			
	15,001–20,000		8.4			
	20,001–25,000		8.8			
	25,001–30,000		9.4			
	30,001–40,000		11.0			
	40,001–50,000		12.2			
	over 50,000		13.5			
District of Columbia[1,4]	First	1,000	2	750	1,500	750
	1,001–2,000		3			
	2,001–3,000		4			
	3,001–4,000		5			
	4,001–5,000		6			
	5,001–10,000		7			
	10,001–13,000		8			
	13,001–17,000		9			
	17,001–25,000		10			
	over 25,000		11			
Georgia[3,5]	First	1,000	1	1,500	3,000	700
	1,001–2,999		2			
	3,000–4,999		3	For married persons filing separately,		
				rates range from 1% on the first $500		
	5,000–6,999		4	to 6% on $5,000 or more. For single		
	7,000–10,000		5	persons rates range from 1% on the		
	over 10,000		6	first $8,750 to 6% on $7,000 or		
				more.		
Hawaii[1]	First	1,000	0	1,000	2,000	1,000
	1,001–2,000		2.25			
	2,001–3,000		3.25	Special tax rates for heads of		
	3,001–4,000		4.5	household.		
	4,001–5,000		5			
	5,001–7,000		6.5			
	7,001–11,000		7.5			
	11,001–21,000		8.5			
	21,001–29,000		9.5			
	29,001–41,000		10			
	41,001–61,000		10.5			
	over 61,000		11			

(Continued)

State Income Taxes for Individuals

State	Taxable Income ($)	Rates	Personal Exemptions ($)		
			Single	Married or Head of Household	Credit per Dependent
Idaho[2,3,4]	First 1,000 1,001–2,000 2,001–3,000 3,001–4,000 4,001–5,000 over 5,000	2% 4 4.5 5.5 6.5 7.5	Federal exemptions Each person (husband and wife filing jointly are deemed one person) filing return pays additional $10.		
Illinois	Total net income	2.5	1,000	2,000	1,000
Indiana[4]	Adjusted gross	3	1,000	*2,000 *Lesser of $1,000 or adjusted gross income of each spouse, but not less than $500.	500
Iowa[3,6]	First 1,023 1,024–2,046 2,047–3,069 3,070–4,092 4,093–7,161 7,162–9,207	0.5 1.25 2.75 3.5 5 6	15 (Tax credit) Net incomes $5,000 or less are not taxable On up to 14% over $76,725	30	10
Kansas[2,4]	First 2,000 2,001–3,000 3,001–5,000 5,001–7,000 7,001–10,000 10,001–20,000 20,001–25,000 over 25,000	2 3.5 4 5 6.5 7.5 8.5 9.0	1,000	2,000	1,000
Kentucky[3]	First 3,000 3,001–4,000 4,001–5,000 5,001–8,000 over 8,000	2 3 4 5 6	20 (Tax credit)	40	20
Louisiana[1,2]	First 10,000 10,001–50,000 over 50,000	2 4 7	4,500	9,000	1,000 Additional $100 credit for blindness allowed for dependents.

State Income Taxes for Individuals

State	Taxable Income ($)	Rates	Personal Exemptions ($)		
			Single	Married or Head of Household	Credit per Dependent
Maine[1,3]	First 2,000	1%	1,000	2,000	1,000
	2,001–4,000	2			
	4,001–6,000	3			
	6,001–8,000	6			
	8,001–10,000	7			
	10,001–15,000	8			
	15,001–25,000	9.2			
	over 25,000	10			
Maryland[1,3,4]	First 1,000	2	800	1,600	800
	1,001–2,000	3			
	2,001–3,000	4			
	over 3,000	5			
	An additional exemption of $800 is allowed for each dependent 65 or over.				
Massachusetts	Earned and business income.	5*	2,200	4,400	700
	Interest, dividends, and capital gains on intangibles.	10	The exemptions shown are those allowed against business income, including salaries and wages. A specific exemption of $2,200 is allowed for each taxpayer. In addition, a dependency exemption of $800 is allowed for a dependent spouse whose income from all sources is less than $2,200. In the case of a joint return the exemption is the lesser of either $4,400 or $2,200 plus the income of the spouse having the smaller income. *Plus 7.5% surtax.		
Michigan[4]	All taxable income	6.1 (1984)	1,500	3,000	1,500
Minnesota[1,3,4,6]	First 672	1.6	67	134	67
	672–1,344	2.2			
	1,344–2,687	3.5			
	2,687–4,030	5.8	An additional tax credit of $67 is allowed for each unmarried taxpayer aged 65 or older.		
	4,030–5,373	7.3			
	5,373–6,716	8.8			
	6,716–9,401	10.2			
	9,401–12,086	11.5			
	12,086–16,785	12.8			
	16,785–26,855	14			
	26,855–36,925	15			
	over 36,925	16			

(Continued)

State Income Taxes for Individuals

State	Taxable Income ($)		Rates	Personal Exemptions ($)		
				Single	Married or Head of Household	Credit per Dependent
Mississippi[3]	First	5,000	3%	6,000	9,500	1,500
	next 5,000		4			
	over 10,000		5			
Missouri[4]	First	1,000	1.5	1,200	2,400	400
	1,001–2,000		2			
	2,001–3,000		2.5	An additional $800 exemption is allowed an unmarried head of household.		
	3,001–4,000		3			
	4,001–5,000		3.5			
	5,001–6,000		4			
	6,001–7,000		4.5			
	7,001–8,000		5			
	8,001–9,000		5.5			
	over 9,000		6			
Montana[3] effective 12/82-1/84	First	1,200	2	960	1,920	960
	1,200–2,300		3			
	2,300–4,700		4	Additional surtax of 10% on tax liability.		
	4,700–7,000		5			
	7,000–9,400		6			
	9,400–11,700		7			
	11,700–16,400		8			
	16,400–23,500		9			
	23,500–41,100		10			
	over 41,100		11			
Nebraska[3,4] The tax imposed is a percentage of the taxpayer's federal income tax liability (not including surtax) before credits, with limited adjustments.			18	Federal exemptions		
New Hampshire	Interest and dividends (except interest on savings accounts). Commuter tax		5 4	$1,200 of each income is exempt; additional $1,200 exemptions are allowed to persons who are 65 or older, blind, or handicapped and unable to work.		
New Jersey[3]	First	20,000	2	1,000	2,000	1,000
	next 30,000		2.5			
	over 50,000		3.5	Additional credit of $1,000 allowed for the elderly and disabled.		

Commuter tax from 2% on net income under $1,000 to 14% on income over $23,000 (will cease after 12/31/90).

State Income Taxes for Individuals

State	Taxable Income ($)		Rates	Personal Exemptions ($)		
				Single	Married or Head of Household	Credit per Dependent
New Mexico[2,3,4]	First	2,000	0.7%			
	2,001–3,000		0.8	Federal exemptions		
	3,001–4,000		1.0			
	4,001–5,000		1.1	The income classes reported are for		
	5,001–6,000		1.3	individuals. For joint returns and		
	6,001–7,000		1.6	heads of households, a separate rate		
	7,001–8,000		2.0	schedule is provided. For taxpayers		
	8,001–10,000		2.5	with a gross income of less than		
	10,000–12,000		3.0	$9,000, a credit is allowed for state		
	12,001–14,000		3.6	and local taxes.		
	14,001–16,000		4.2			
	16,001–18,000		4.9			
	18,001–20,000		5.5			
	20,001–25,000		6.1			
	25,001–35,000		6.5			
	35,001–50,000		6.9			
	50,001–100,000		7.4			
	over 100,000		7.8			
New York[1,4]	First	1,000	2	800	1,600	800
	1,001–3,000		3			
	3,001–5,000		4	Income from unincorporated business		
	5,001–7,000		5	is taxed at 4½%.		
	7,001–9,000		6	The maximum tax rate on personal		
	9,001–11,000		7	service income is 10%.		
	11,001–13,000		8			
	13,001–15,000		9			
	15,001–17,000		10			
	17,001–19,000		11			
	19,001–21,000		12			
	21,001–23,000		13			
	over 23,000		14			
North Carolina[3,4]	First	2,000	3	1,100	2,200*	800
	2,001–4,000		4			
	4,001–6,000		5	*An additional exemption of $1,100		
	6,001–10,000		6	is allowed the spouse having the		
	over 10,000		7	lower income; joint returns are not permitted.		
North Dakota[3]	First	3,000	2	Federal exemptions		
	3,001–5,000		3			
	5,001–8,000		4			
	8,001–15,000		5			
	15,001–25,000		6			
	25,001–35,000		7			
	35,001–50,000		8			
	over 50,000		9			

(Continued)

State Income Taxes for Individuals

State	Taxable Income ($)	Rates	Personal Exemptions ($)		
			Single	Married or Head of Household	Credit per Dependent
Ohio[4]	First 5,000 5,001–10,000 10,001–15,000 15,001–20,000 20,001–40,000 40,001–80,000 80,001–100,000 over 100,000	0.5% 1 2 2.5 3 3.5 4 5	650	1,300	650
Taxpayers age 65 or older are allowed a $50 credit, or if they have received a lump-sum distribution from a pension, retirement or profit-sharing plan during the tax year, they are allowed a credit equal to 50 times the taxpayer's expected remaining life. Credit may not exceed tax otherwise due. Credit is also allowed for an amount paid during the school year for elementary and secondary education or instruction or training of dependents who do not have a high school diploma.					
Oklahoma[1,4]	First 2,000 2,001–5,000 5,001–7,500 7,501–10,000 10,001–12,500 12,501–15,000 over 15,000	0.5 1 2 3 4 5 6	1,000	2,000 Rates for single persons, married couples filing separately, and estates and trusts range from .5% on the first $1,000 to 6% over $7,500.	1,000
Nonresident aliens are taxed at a flat rate of 8% of Oklahoma taxable income.					
Oregon[3,4]	First 500 501–1,000 1,001–2,000 2,001–3,000 3,001–4,000 4,001,5,000 over 5,000	4.2 5.3 6.5 7.6 8.7 9.8 10.8	1,000	2,000 A credit is provided in an amount and equal to 25% of the federal retirement income tax credit to the extent that such a credit is based on taxable income in Oregon.	1,000
Pennsylvania	2.35% of specified classes of taxable income				
Rhode Island	27.5% of modified federal income tax liability		Federal exemptions		
South Carolina[1]	First 2,000 2,001–4,000 4,001–6,000 6,001–8,000 8,001–10,000 over 10,000	2 3 4 5 6 7	800	1,600	800
Tennessee	Interest and dividends	6	Dividends from corporations, 75% of whose property is taxable in Tennessee, are taxed at 4%.		

State Income Taxes for Individuals

State	Taxable Income ($)		Rates	Personal Exemptions ($)		
				Single	Married or Head of Household	Credit per Dependent
Utah[1]	First	1,500	2.25%	750	1,000	750
	1,501–3,000		3.75			
	3,001–4,500		4.75	Married taxpayers filing separately, single taxpayers, estates and trusts, pay rates ranging from 2.75% on first $750 of taxable income to 7.75% on taxable income over $3,750.		
	4,501–6,000		5.75			
	6,001–7,500		6.75			
	over 7,500		7.75			
Vermont[4]	Federal exemptions.					

The tax is imposed at a rate of 26% of the federal income tax liability of the taxpayer for the taxable year after certain credits (retirement income, investment, foreign tax, child and dependent care, and tax-free covenant bonds) but before any surtax on federal liability reduced by a percentage equal to the percentage of the taxpayer's adjusted gross income for the taxable year that is not Vermont income.

State	Taxable Income ($)		Rates	Single	Married or Head of Household	Credit per Dependent
Virginia[3]	First	3,000	2	600	1,200	600
	3,001–5,000		3			
	5,001–12,000		5			
	over 12,000		5.75			
West Virginia[1,3]	First	2,000	2.1	800	1,600	800
	2,001–4,000		2.3			
	4,001–6,000		2.8	For joint returns and a return of a surviving spouse, a separate rate schedule is provided.		
	6,001–8,000		3.2			
	8,001–10,000		3.5			
	10,001–12,000		4			
	12,001–14,000		5.3			
	14,001–16,000		5.9			
	16,001–18,000		6.8			
	18,001–20,000		7.4			
	20,001–22,000		8.2			
	22,001–26,000		9.2			
	26,001–32,000		10.5			
	32,001–38,000		11.6			
	38,001–44,000		12.6			
	44,001–60,000		12.9			
	over 60,000		13.0			
Wisconsin[1,4]	First	3,900	3.74	20 (Tax credit)	40	20
	3,900–7,700		5.72			
	7,700–11,700		7.70			
	11,700–15,500		9.02			
	15,000–19,400		9.57			
	19,400–25,800		10.01			
	25,800–51,600		10.45			
	over 51,600		11.0			

1 *A standard deduction and optional tax table are provided. In Louisiana, standard deduction is incorporated in tax tables.*
2 *Community property state in which, in general, one-half of the community income is taxable to each spouse.*
3 *A standard deduction is allowed.*

4 *A limited general tax credit for taxpayers filing joint returns and a credit for home improvements is allowed in Ohio; a limited tax credit is allowed for sales taxes in Colorado, Massachusetts, Nebraska, and Vermont; for property taxes and city income taxes in Michigan; for personal property taxes in Maryland and Wisconsin; for property taxes in Washington D.C. if household income is less than $10,000, and in N.Y. if household income is less than $12,000; for installation of solar energy devices in Arizona, California, Kansas, New Mexico, North Carolina, and Oregon; for property taxes paid on pollution control property in Colorado; for installation of insulation in residences in Idaho; and for making an existing building accessible to the handicapped in Kansas.*

5 *Tax credits are allowed: $15 for single persons or married persons filing separately if adjusted gross income (AGI) is $3,000 or less (for each dollar by which the federal AGI exceeds $3,000 the credit is reduced by $1 until no credit is allowed if federal AGI is $3,015 or more); $30 for heads of households or married persons filing jointly with $6,000 or less AGI (for each dollar by which federal AGI exceeds $6,000, credit is reduced by $1 until no credit is allowed if federal AGI is $6,030 or more).*

6 *Tax bracket adjusted for inflation.*

Source: *The World Almanac & Book of Facts, 1985 edition,* copyright © Newspaper Enterprise Association, Inc., 1985, New York, NY 10166.

STATE INCOME TAX RATES FOR CORPORATIONS
As of January 1, 1984

State or Other Jurisdiction	Number of Steps in Range	Tax Rate %	State or Other Jurisdiction	Number of Steps in Range	Tax Rate %
Alabama*			**Michigan**[13]		
Business corporations		5	**Minnesota**		
Banks & financial corps		6	$0 to $25,000		6
Alaska			Over $25,000		12
Business corporations:			**Mississippi**		
$0 to $10,000		1	$0 to $5,000		3
Over $90,000	10	9.4	Over $10,000	3	5
Banks & financial institutions		7[1]	**Missouri***		
Arizona*			Business corporations		5
$0 to $1,000		2.5	Banks & trust companies		7
Over $6,000	7	10.5	**Montana**		7.75[14]
Arkansas			**Nebraska**		
$0 to $3,000		1	$0 to $50,000		5
Over $25,000	5	6	Over $50,000	2	7[15]
California			**New Hampshire**		9.56[16]
Business corporations		9.6[2]	**New Jersey**		9[17]
Banks & financial corps		11.6[2]	**New Mexico**		
Colorado		5[3]	$0 to $1 million		4.8
Connecticut		11.5[4]	Over $2 million	3	7.2
Delaware		8.7	**New York**		
Florida		5[5]	Business corporations		10[18]
Georgia		6	Banks & financial corps		12[19]
Hawaii			**North Carolina**		6
Business corporations:			**North Dakota***		
$0 to $25,000		5.85[6]	Business corporations:		
Over $25,000	2	6.435	$0 to $3,000		3
Banks & financial corps		11.7	Over $50,000	6	10.5
Idaho		7.7[7]	Banks & financial corps		5[20]
Illinois		7.3[8]	**Ohio**		
Indiana[10]		7[9]	$0 to $25,000		5.1[21]
Iowa			Over $25,000	2	9.2[21]
Business corporations:			**Oklahoma**		4
$0 to $25,000		6	**Oregon**		7.5[22]
Over $250,000	4	12	**Pennsylvania**		10.5
Financial institutions		5	**Rhode Island**		8[23]
Kansas			**South Carolina**		
Business corporations		4.5[11]	Business corporations		6
Banks		4.25[11]	Banks		4.5
Trust companies & savings			Financial associations		8
& loan associations		4.5[11]	**South Dakota***		
Kentucky			Banks & financial corps		6[24]
$0 to $25,000		3	**Tennessee**		6
Over $100,000	4	6	**Utah**		4[25]
Louisiana*			**Vermont**		
$0 to $25,000		4	$0 to $10,000		5
Over $200,000	5	8	Over $250,000	4	7.5[26]
Maine			**Virginia**		6
$0 to $25,000		3.5	**West Virginia**		
Over $250,000	4	8.93	$0 to $50,000		6.9
Maryland		7	Over $50,000		8.05
Massachusetts			**Wisconsin**		7.9
Business corporations		9.4962[12]	**District of Columbia**		9.9[27]
Banks & trust companies		12.54			
Utility corporations		6.5			

---

* *Federal income tax is deductible.*

1 *Banks and other financial institutions are subject to a license tax.*

2 *Minimum tax is $200.*

3 *A credit was suspended for 1983 and 1984 but is scheduled to resume in 1985.*

(Continued)

4   Or 3.1 mills per dollar of capital stock and surplus (maximum tax $100,000), or $250, or 5% of 50% of net income of corporation plus salaries and other compensation paid to officers and certain shareholders, whichever is greater.

5   An exemption of $5,000 is allowed.

6   Taxes capital gains at 3.08%.

7   Minimum tax is $20. An additional tax of $10 is imposed on each return.

8   Includes 2.5% personal property tax replacement tax.

9   Consists of 3% basic rate plus a 4% supplemental tax.

10   50% of federal income tax is deductible.

11   Plus a surtax of 2.25% of taxable income in excess of $25,000 (2.125% for banks).

12   Rate includes a 14% surtax, as does the following: Plus a tax of $2.60 per $1,000 on taxable tangible property (or net worth allocable to state, for intangible property corporations). Minimum tax of $228 including surtax.
Corporations engaged exclusively in interstate or foreign commerce are taxed at 5% of net income, and are not subject to surtax.

13   Michigan imposes a single business tax (sometimes described as a business activities or value added tax) of 2.35% on the sum of federal taxable income of the business, compensation paid to employees, dividends, interest and royalties paid, and other items.

14   Minimum tax is $50; for small business corporations, $10.

15   Twenty-five and 35% of individual income tax rate, determined annually, imposed on net taxable income.

16   Business profits tax imposed on both corporations and unincorporated business; includes a 13.5% surtax.

17   This is the corporation business franchise tax rate, plus a net worth tax at millage rates ranging from 2 mills to 0.2 mill; minimum tax is $250. Corporations not subject to the franchise tax are subject to a 3% tax.

18   Or $250; 1.78 mills per dollar of capital; or 10% of 30% of net income plus salaries and other compensation to officers and stockholders owning more than 5% of the issued capital stock less $30,000 and any net loss, if any of these is greater than the tax computed on net income.

19   Minimum tax is $250 or 1.6 mills per dollar of capital stock; for savings institutions, the minimum tax is $250 or 2% of interest credited to depositors in preceding year.

20   Minimum tax is $50; plus an additional 2% tax.

21   Or 5,82 mills times the value of the taxpayer's issued and outstanding shares of stock as determined according to the total value of capital surplus, undivided profits, and reserves; minimum tax $50. An additional litter tax is imposed equal to 0.11% on the first $25,000 of income, 0.22% on income over $25,000, or 0.14 mills on net worth. Corporations manufacturing or selling litter stream products are subject to an additional 0.22% tax on income over $25,000 or 0.14 mills on net worth.

22   Minimum tax is $10.

23   Or, for business corporations, the tax is 40 cents per $100 of net worth, if greater than the tax computed on net income. For banks, if a greater tax results, the alternative tax is $2.50 per $10,000 of capital stock; minimum tax is $100.

24   Minimum tax is $200 per authorized location.

25   Minimum tax is $25. There is a graduated gross receipts tax on corporations not otherwise required to pay income or franchise taxes, ranging up to 1% on receipts in excess of $1 billion.

26   Minimum tax is $50.

27   Includes 10% surtax. Minimum tax is $100.

Source: The Book of the States 1984–1985.

STATE EXCISE TAX RATES
As of January 1, 1984

State or Jurisdiction	Sales and Gross Receipts (percent)	Cigarettes (cents per pack)	Distilled Spirits[1] ($ per gallon)	Motor Fuel[2] (cents per gallon)			
				Gasoline	Diesel	LPG	Gasohol
Alabama	4	16		11	12		8
Alaska		8	5.60	8	8		
Arizona	5[3]	13	2.50	12	12	12	12
Arkansas	4	21	2.50	9.5	10.5	7.5	
California	4.75	10	2.00[4]	9	9	6	9
Colorado	3.5	15	2.28[5]	12	13		7
Connecticut	7.5	26	3.00	14	14	14	13
Delaware		14	2.25	11	11	11	11
Florida	5[6]	21	6.50[7]	9.7[8]	9.7	9.7	4
Georgia	3	12	3.79[5]	7.5	7.5	7.5	7.5
Hawaii	4[9]	40% of wholesale	20% of wholesale	8.5	8.5	6	8.5
Idaho	4.5	9.1		14.5	14.5	14.5	10.5
Illinois	5	12	2.00	11	13.5	11	11
Indiana	5[10]	10.5	2.68	11.1	11.1	11.1	11.1
Iowa	4	18		13	15.5	13	10
Kansas	3	16	2.50	11	13	10	6
Kentucky	5	3.1	1.92	10[11]	10	10	6.5
Louisiana	3	11	2.50[5]	8	8	8	
Maine	5	20		14	14	14	14
Maryland	5	13	1.50[5]	13.5	13.5	13.5	10.5
Massachusetts	5	26	4.05	11	11	6.7	11
Michigan	4	21		15	15	15	11
Minnesota	6[12]	18	4.39[5]	17	17	17	9
Mississippi	6[13]	11		9	10	8	9
Missouri	4.125	13	2.00	7	7	7	7
Montana		16		15	17		8
Nebraska	4	18	2.75	15.4	15.4	15.4	10.4
Nevada	5.75[14]	15	2.05	12[15]	12	12	11
New Hampshire		17		14	14	14	9
New Jersey	6	25	2.80	8	8	4	8
New Mexico	3.75	12	3.94[5]	11	11	11	
New York	4	21	4.09[5]	8	10	8	8
North Carolina	3[16]	2		12	12	12	11
North Dakota	4[17]	18	4.05	13	13	13	8
Ohio	5	14		12	12	12	8.5
Oklahoma	2	18	4.00	6.58	6.58	6.58	6.58
Oregon		19		9	9	9	9
Pennsylvania	6	18		12	12	12	12
Rhode Island	6	23	2.50	13	13	13	13
South Carolina	4	7	2.96[5,18]	13	13	13	13
South Dakota	4	15	3.80	13	13	11	9
Tennessee	4.5[19]	13	4.00	9[20]	12	5	
Texas	4	18.5	2.00	5	6.5	5	
Utah	4.625	12		11	11	11	6

(Continued)

State Excise Rates

State or Jurisdiction	Sales and Gross Receipts (percent)	Cigarettes (cents per pack)	Distilled Spirits[1] ($ per gallon)	Motor Fuel[2] (cents per gallon)			
				Gasoline	Diesel	LPG	Gasohol
Vermont	4	17		13	14		13
Virginia	3	2.5		11[21]	11	11	3
Washington	6.5[22]	23		16	16		13.44
West Virginia	5[23]	17		15.35[8]	15.35	15.35	15.35
Wisconsin	5	25	3.25[5]	15	15	15	15
Wyoming	3	8		8			4
District of Columbia	6[24]	13	1.50	14.8			14.8

1 *Seventeen states have liquor monopoly systems (Alabama, Idaho, Iowa, Maine, Michigan, Mississippi, Montana, New Hampshire, Ohio, Oregon, Pennsylvania, Utah, Vermont, Virginia, Washington, West Virginia and Wyoming). (North Carolina has county-operated stores on a local option basis.) Some of the monopoly states impose taxes, generally expressed in terms of percentage of retail price. Only gallonage taxes imposed by states with license systems are reported in the table. Excise tax rates shown are general rates; some states tax distilled spirits manufactured in the state from state-grown products at lower rates.*

2 *Thirteen states and the District of Columbia have variable rate motor fuel taxes, under which the motor fuel tax rate is periodically changed by administrative action according to a statutory formula. The states that have these provisions, the variable on which the formula is based, and the dates that the rate changes become effective are: Indiana, retail price of motor fuel, January 1 and July 1. Kansas, retail price of motor fuel, July 1, beginning 1985. Kentucky, wholesale price of motor fuel, January 1, April 1, July 1 and October 1. Maryland, wholesale price of motor fuel, January 1 and July 1, beginning July 1, 1984. Massachusetts, wholesale price of motor fuel, January 1, April 1, July 1 and October 1. Michigan, highway maintenance costs and fuel consumption, January 1. Nebraska, price of fuel purchased by state government, January 1, April 1, July 1 and October 1. New Mexico, wholesale price of motor fuel, July 1. Ohio, highway maintenance costs and fuel consumption, March 1. Rhode Island, wholesale price of motor fuel, January 1, April 1, July 1 and October 1. Wisconsin, highway maintenance costs and fuel consumption, April 1, beginning in 1985. District of Columbia, consumer price index for Washington, D.C., June 1. See also Florida and West Virginia.*
Connecticut, New York, Pennsylvania, Rhode Island, and Virginia have gross receipts or franchise taxes on oil companies, which are not covered in this table.

3 *This rate is for retailers. Selected businesses are taxed at rates ranging from 0.46875 to 5%.*

4 *If not over 50% alcohol by weight; if over 50%, $4.00 per gallon.*

5 *In several states, the tax rate is expressed in metric units: Colorado — $0.6026 per liter; Georgia — $1.00 per liter; Louisiana — $0.66 per liter; Maryland — $0.3963 per liter; Minnesota — $1.16 per liter; New Mexico — $1.04 per liter; New York — $1.08 per liter; South Carolina — $0.7828925 per liter (includes 9% surcharge); and Wisconsin — $0.8586 per liter. One gallon equals 3.7854 liters.*

6 *Self-propelled or power-driven farm equipment is taxed at 3%.*

7 *On beverages containing 14 to 48% alcohol; the tax rate on beverages containing more than 48% alcohol is $9.53 per gallon.*

8 *The rates shown for Florida and West Virginia include motor fuel sales tax imposed on a cents-per-gallon basis.*

9 *Wholesalers and manufacturers, 0.5%; retailers, 4%.*

10 *In addition to the 4% sales tax, a gross income tax is imposed, under which wholesale and retail sales are taxed at 0.325% in 1984. Thereafter, the gross income tax will be reduced annually until 2010, when it goes out of existence.*

11 *Heavy equipment motor carriers pay a 12.2 cents per gallon tax on a use basis.*

12 *Farm machinery is taxed at 4%.*

13 *Among other rates imposed under the tax: aircraft, automobiles, trucks and truck tractors, 3%; manufacturing or processing machinery and farm tractors, 1.0%; contractors (on compensation exceeding $10,000), 2.5%.*

14 *Includes mandatory, statewide, state-collected 3.75% county and school sales tax.*

15 *Includes uniform local tax.*

16 *Motor vehicles, boats, railway cars and locomotives, and airplanes, 2% with a maximum tax of $300. A tax of 1% is imposed on various items used in agriculture and industry. On some items subject to the 1% rate, the maximum tax is $80 per article.*

17 *The tax on farm machinery, agricultural irrigation equipment and mobile homes is 2%. A 5% tax is imposed on alcoholic beverages.*

18 *Includes 9% surtax. In addition, there is a tax of $5.84 ($5.36 plus 9% surtax) per case on wholesale sales.*

19 *The tax on water sold to or used by manufacturers is 1%. The tax on various fuels is 1.5%.*

20 *Also subject to special privilege tax of 1.0 cents per gallon.*

21 *A 13 cents-per-gallon tax is imposed on motor carriers of property on a use basis.*

22 *Also has a gross income tax with rates varying from 0.01% to 1% according to type of business. Retailers are subject to a 0.4708% tax under the business and occupation tax.*

23 *Sales of mobile homes to be used by purchasers as their principal year-round residence and dwelling are taxed at 3%. West Virginia also has a gross income tax at rates ranging from 0.27 to 8.63%, according to type of business. Retailers are subject to a 0.55% rate under this tax.*

24 *District of Columbia: Parking charges are taxed at 12%; hotel lodging and accommodations at 10%; food or drink for immediate consumption at 8%; rental vehicles at 8%; and food or drink sold from vending machines at 2%.*

Source: *The Book of the States 1984-85*

STATE ESTATE, GIFT, AND INHERITANCE TAXES

State	Estate	Gift	Inheritance
Alabama	✓		
Alaska	✓		
Arizona	✓		
Arkansas	✓		
California	✓		
Colorado	✓	✓	
Connecticut	✓		✓
Delaware	✓	✓	✓
District of Columbia	✓		✓
Florida	✓		
Georgia	✓		
Hawaii	✓		
Idaho	✓		✓
Illinois	✓		
Indiana	✓		✓
Iowa	✓		✓
Kansas	✓		✓
Kentucky	✓		✓
Louisiana	✓	✓	✓
Maine	✓		✓
Maryland	✓		✓
Massachusetts	✓		✓
Michigan	✓		✓
Minnesota	✓	✓	✓
Mississippi	✓		
Missouri	✓		
Montana	✓		✓
Nebraska	✓		✓
Nevada			
New Hampshire	✓		✓
New Jersey	✓		✓
New Mexico	✓		
New York	✓	✓	
North Carolina	✓	✓	✓
North Dakota	✓		
Ohio	✓		
Oklahoma	✓		
Oregon	✓	✓	✓

(Continued)

State Estate, Gift, and Inheritance Taxes

State	Estate	Gift	Inheritance
Pennsylvania	√		√
Rhode Island	√	√	
South Carolina	√	√	
South Dakota			√
Tennessee	√	√	√
Texas	√		√
Utah	√		
Vermont	√		
Virginia	√	√	√
Washington	√		
West Virginia			√
Wisconsin	√	√	√
Wyoming	√		√

STATE ESTATE TAX RATES AND EXEMPTIONS
As of August, 1984

State	Rates (on Net Estate After Exemptions)[1]	Maximum Rate Applies Above	Exemption
Alabama	Maximum federal credit[2]	$10,040,000	$ 60,000
Alaska	Maximum federal credit[2]	10,040,000	60,000
Arizona	Maximum federal credit[2]	10,040,000	60,000[3]
Arkansas	Maximum federal credit[2]	10,040,000	60,000[3]
California	Maximum federal credit[2]	10,040,000	60,000
Colorado	Maximum federal credit[2]	10,040,000	60,000
Florida	Maximum federal credit[2]	10,040,000	60,000
Georgia	Maximum federal credit[2]	10,040,000	60,000
Illinois	Maximum federal credit[2]	10,000	60,000
Massachusetts	5% on first $50,000, to 16%	4,000,000	30,000[3,4]
Minnesota	7% on first $25,000, to 12%	925,000	225,000[3]
Mississippi	1% on first $60,000, to 16%[5]	10,000,000	175,625[3]
Missouri	Maximum federal credit[2]	10,040,000	60,000
New Mexico	Maximum federal credit[2]	10,040,000	60,000
New York	2% on first $50,000, to 21%[5,6]	10,100,000	[3,7,8]
North Dakota	Maximum federal credit[2]	10,040,000	60,000[3]
Ohio	2% on first $40,000, to 7%[5]	500,000	10,000[3,9]
Oklahoma	.5% on first $10,000, to 15%[5]	10,000,000	60,000[3,10,11]
Rhode Island	2% on first $25,000, to 9%[2]	1,000,000	25,000[3,12]
South Carolina	5% on first $40,000, to 7%[5]	100,000	120,000[3,12]
Texas	Maximum federal credit[2]	10,040,000	60,000
Utah	Maximum federal credit[2]	10,040,000	60,000[3]
Vermont	Maximum federal credit[2]	10,040,000	60,000[3]
Virginia	Maximum federal credit[2]	10,040,000	60,000[3]
Washington	Maximum federal credit[2]	10,040,000	60,000
Wyoming	Maximum federal credit[2]	10,000	60,000

Note: *From this list are excluded states in which an estate tax, in addition to their inheritance taxes, is levied to assure full absorption of the federal credit.*

1 *The rates generally are in addition to graduated absolute amounts.*

2 *Maximum federal credit allowed under the 1954 code for state estate taxes paid is expressed as a percentage of the taxable estate (after $60,000 exemption) in excess of $40,000, plus a graduated absolute amount. In Rhode Island on net estates above $250,000. A tax on nonresident estates is imposed on the proportionate share of the net estate which the property located in the state bears to the entire estate wherever situated.*

3 *Transfers to religious, charitable, educational, and municipal corporations are generally fully exempt. In Mississippi, limited to those located in United States or its possessions.*

4 *Applies to net estates above $60,000. Otherwise, exemption is equal to Massachusetts net estate.*

5 *An additional estate tax is imposed to assure full absorption of the federal credit. In New York, this applies only to residents. In Rhode Island it applies on net estates above $250,000.*

6 *On net estate before exemption. Marital deduction is one-half of adjusted gross estate or $250,000, whichever is greater. Orphans under age 21 receive deduction.*

7 *Insurance receives special treatment.*

8 *The specific exemptions are $20,000 of the net estate transferred to spouse and $5,000 to lineal ancestors and descendants and certain other named relatives. The credit is variable, ranging from the full amount of tax if estate tax is $2,750 or less to $500 if estate tax is $5,000 or more.*

9 *Property is exempt to the extent transferred to surviving spouse, not exceeding $60,000; for a child under 18, $14,000; and for each child 18 years of age and older, $6,000.*

10 *An estate valued at $100 or less is exempt.*

11 *Exemption is a total aggregate of $175,000 for father, mother, child, and named relatives.*

12 *Marital deduction is $175,000 in Rhode Island. In South Carolina, marital deduction is one-half of adjusted gross estate up to $250,000.*

Source: *World Almanac & Book of Facts,* 1985 edition, © Newspaper Enterprise Association, Inc., 1985, New York, NY 10166

STATE INHERITANCE TAX RATES AND EXEMPTIONS

State	Rates (percentage)[1]			Max. Rate Applies above ($1,000)	Exemptions ($1,000)[2]			
	Spouse, Child, or Parent	Brother or Sister	Other than Relative		Spouse	Child or Parent	Brother or Sister	Other than Relative
Connecticut[3]	2–8	4–10	8–14	1,000	100	20	6	1
Delaware	1–6	5–10	10–16	200	70	3	1	None
District of Columbia	1–8	5–23	5–23	1,000	5	5	1	1
Idaho	2–15	4–20	8–30	500	All	30[4]	10	10
Indiana	1–10	7–15	10–20	1,500[5]	All	10[4]	0.5	0.1
Iowa	1–8	5–10	10–15	150	150	15	None	None
Kansas	1–5	3–12.5	10–15	500	All	30	5	None
Kentucky	2–10	4–16	6–16	500	50	5	1	0.5
Louisiana	2–3	5–7	5–10	25	5[6]	5	1	0.5
Maine[7]	5–10	8–14	14–18	250[8]	50	25	1	1
Maryland[9]	1	10	10	[7]	.15	.15	0.15	0.15
Michigan	2–10[10]	2–10[10]	12–17[10]	750	65[4]	10	10	None
Montana	2–8	4–16	8–32	100	All	7	1.0	None
Nebraska	1	1	6–18	60	All	10	10	0.5
New Hampshire	[11]	15	15	[7]	[11]	[11]	None	None
New Jersey	2–16	11–16	15–16	3,200	5	15	0.5	0.5
North Carolina	1–12	4–16	8–17	3,000	3–15[12]	[13]	None	None
Oregon	12	12	12	[7]	14,15	14,15	14	None
Pennsylvania	6	15	15	[7]	None	None	None	None
South Dakota[16]	1.5–15	4–20	6–30	10	All	30[4]	0.5	0.1
Tennessee	5.5–9.5	5.5–9.5	6.5–16	440	120[17]	120	120	10
West Virginia	3–13	4–18	10–30	1,000	30	10	None	None
Wisconsin	2.5–12.5	5–25	10–30[16]	500	All	10	1	0.5

Note: *In addition to an inheritance tax, all states listed (except South Dakota) also levy an estate tax, generally to assure full absorption of the federal credit.*

1 *Rates generally apply to excess above graduated absolute amounts.*

2 *Generally, transfers to governments or to solely charitable, educational, scientific, religious, literary, public, and other similar organizations in the U.S. are wholly exempt. Some states grant additional exemptions either for insurance, homestead, joint deposits, support allowance, disinherited minor children, orphaned, incompetent, or blind children, and for previously or later taxed transfers. In many states, exemptions are deducted from the first bracket only.*

3 *There is a marital deduction equal to the greater of 250,000 or 50% of the value of the gross estate.*

4 *Exemption for child; $20,000 in Iowa; $30,000 in South Dakota; $10,000 in Indiana ($5,000 per parent). Exemption for minor child is: $50,000 in Idaho; $20,000 in Kentucky. In Michigan a widow receives $5,000 for every minor child to whom no property is transferred.*

5 *Additional credit of $1,200.*

6 *Community property state in which, in general, either all community property to the surviving spouse is exempt, or only one-half of the community property is taxable on the death of either spouse.*

7 *For persons dying after 6/30/81 but before 7/1/82, tax liability is 85% of calculated tax; for persons dying between 6/30/82 and 7/1/83, 75%; 65% between 6/30/83 and 7/1/84; 55% between 6/30/84 and 7/1/85; 45% between 6/30/85 and 7/1/86. Tax is scheduled to be replaced after 6/30/86.*

8 *In Maine, the maximum rate for any other relative applies above $150,000.*

9 *Where property of a decedent subject to administration in MD is 7,500 or less, no inheritance taxes are due.*

10 *No exemption if share exceeds amount stated.*

11 *Spouse entitled to another $10,000 exemption.*

12 *Spouses, minor children, parents, and minor adopted children in the decedent's line of succession are entirely exempt.*

13 *Credit.*

14 *Credits allowed on pro rata basis according to tax liability on the amount of credit unused by surviving spouse or beneficiaries.*

15 *Net taxable estates are allowed an exemption of $1,000,000 if the decedent died in 1982, $200,000 if death occurred in 1983 or 1984 and $500,000 if death occurs in 1985 or 1986.*

16 *Primary rate. If value of share exceeds $15,000 but less than $50,000, the tax liability is 2½ times the primary rate; between $50,000 and $100,000, 4 times the primary rate; over $100,000, 5 times the primary rate.*

17 *The rates range from 3 to 6% for a spouse or a child and from 3 to 12% for parents. Parent exemption is $3,000. Spouses exempt from tax.*

Source: Tax Foundation (compiled from Commerce Clearing House data).

INHERITANCE TAX OFFICIALS

Questions regarding inheritance tax laws should be addressed to the state in which the decedent resided.

State or Territory	Official or Department and Address
Alabama	State Department of Revenue Estate Tax Division Montgomery 36102
Alaska	Estate Tax Commissioner Department of Revenue Juneau 99801
Arizona	Estate Tax Commissioner State Capitol Building Phoenix 85026
Arkansas	Department of Revenue Estate and Inheritance Tax Division Little Rock 72203
California	Inheritance and Gift Tax Division Office of State Comptroller Sacramento 95805
Colorado	Department of Revenue Inheritance Tax Division Denver 80202
Connecticut	State Tax Department Inheritance Tax Division Hartford 06115
Delaware	Deputy Tax Commissioner Division of Revenue Wilmington 19899
District of Columbia	Government of the District of Columbia Finance Office Inheritance & Estate Tax Section Washington, D.C. 20013
Florida	Estate Tax Bureau, Department of Revenue Office of the State Comptroller Tallahassee 32304
Georgia	Department of Revenue Estate Tax Unit Atlanta 30304
Hawaii	Department of Taxation Inheritance Tax Unit Honolulu 96809
Idaho	Office of the State Tax Commission Inheritance Tax Division Boise 83707

State or Territory	Official or Department and Address
Illinois	Attorney General Inheritance Tax Department Springfield 60085
Indiana	Inheritance Tax Division Department of Revenue Indianapolis 46204
Iowa	Department of Revenue Inheritance Tax Division Des Moines 50319
Kansas	Inheritance Tax Division Department of Revenue Topeka 66625
Kentucky	Department of Revenue Property and Inheritance Tax Division Inheritance and Estate Tax Section Frankfort 40601
Louisiana	(Each parish) Inheritance Tax Collector (New Orleans only) Clerk of the Civil District Court Inheritance Tax Collector New Orleans (In general) Department of Revenue Baton Rouge 70825
Maine	Supervisor of Inheritance Tax Maine Bureau of Taxation Augusta 04330
Maryland	(Each county) Register of Wills and Orphans' Court (In general) Attorney General of Maryland Baltimore 21202
Massachusetts	Department of Revenue Estate Tax Division Boston 02109
Michigan	Department of Revenue Inheritance Tax Division Lansing 48924
Minnesota	Department of Revenue Inheritance & Gift Tax Division St. Paul 55145
Mississippi	Estate Tax Division State Tax Commission Jackson 39205
Missouri	Bureau of Inheritance Tax Department of Revenue Jefferson City 65101
Montana	Department of Revenue Inheritance Tax Bureau Helena 59601

State or Territory	Official or Department and Address
Nebraska	(Each county) County Treasurer (In general) Supervisor of Inheritance Tax Office of the State Tax Commissioner Lincoln 68509
Nevada	No inheritance tax law
New Hampshire	Department of Revenue Administration Inheritance Tax Division Concord 03301
New Jersey	Division of Taxation Transfer Inheritance Tax Bureau Trenton 08625
New Mexico	Bureau of Revenue Estate Tax Division Santa Fe 87501
New York	Department of Taxation and Finance Miscellaneous Tax Bureau Transfer and Estate Tax Section Albany 12227
North Carolina	State Department of Revenue Inheritance & Gift Tax Division Raleigh 27640
North Dakota	Office of State Tax Commissioner Estate Tax Deputy Bismarck 58501
Ohio	State Department of Taxation Estate Tax Division Columbus 43215
Oklahoma	Estate Tax Division Oklahoma Tax Commission Oklahoma City 73194
Oregon	Estate Audit Section, Audit Division State Office Building Salem 97310
Pennsylvania	Department of Revenue Bureau of County Collections Inheritance Tax Division Harrisburg 17127
Puerto Rico	Secretary of the Treasury San Juan 00905
Rhode Island	State Division of Taxation Inheritance and Gift Tax Section Providence 02908
South Carolina	Director, Estate Tax Division South Carolina Tax Commission Columbia 29214

State or Territory	Official or Department and Address
South Dakota	State Department of Revenue Division of Taxation, Inheritance Tax Department Pierre 57501
Tennessee	State Department of Revenue Inheritance, Estate and Gift Tax Division Nashville 43742
Texas	Office of the Comptroller of Public Accounts Inheritance Tax Division Austin 78774
Utah	State Tax Commission Inheritance Tax Division Salt Lake City 84101
Vermont	Commissioner of Taxes Department of Taxes Montpelier 05602
Virginia	Department of Taxation Division of Inheritance and Gift Taxes Richmond 23282
Washington	Supervisor of Inheritance Tax Department of Revenue Olympia 98504
West Virginia	Office of the State Tax Commissioner Inheritance Tax Division Charleston 25305
Wisconsin	Department of Revenue and Taxation Director of Inheritance and Gift Tax Division Madison 53701
Wyoming	Department of Revenue Inheritance Tax Division Cheyenne 82002

CHAPTER 3

Key Indicators

CONTENTS

Tables are indicated by page numbers in italics; accompanying charts by a dagger: †

Any well-reasoned financial planning strategy must begin with an understanding of the current performance of the domestic economy and assumptions about its future activity. This chapter presents historical data for those short- and long-term indicators that financial professionals most often use to make informed predictions about economic performance.

In this chapter key indicators are tabulated in ten categories:

1. **Interest Rates.** The cost of money, expressed in interest rates, affects all sectors of the economy and all investment decisions. Interest rates are affected by the perceived risk of the underlying security, the maturity date, and the perceived inflation risk.

2. **Stock Indicators.** While the Dow Jones Industrial Average is perhaps the best-known stock indicator, many investors also monitor the activity of several more broadly based indicators (such as Standard & Poor's 500 or the NYSE composite). Of primary interest to many investors and market technicians are historical highs and lows, the market's response to domestic business cycles, and seasonal variations in trading.

3. **Economic Indicators.** The general state of the domestic economy is most often represented by seven key measures: gross national product (GNP), money supply, federal budget surplus (or deficit), the index of leading economic indicators, balance of international current accounts, international trade balance, and foreign exchange rates. The index of leading economic indicators is the single measure most often used to predict the direction of the economy over the coming 6 to 12 months.

4. **Price Indexes.** Most often used as an index of inflation, price indexes measure the changing costs of selected goods and services. Of particular concern to investors is an investment's *real return*, the difference between the investment's nominal yield and the rate of inflation.

5. **Labor Force.** Labor statistics — including the unemployment rate and the length of the workweek — reflect productivity. Unemployment, in particular, is a key indicator of the nation's general economic health.

6. **Income Indicators.** Personal income affects patterns of consumer spending and savings. Periods of rising personal income signal the potential for increased demand for goods and services, although consumer spending also depends on levels of personal savings and borrowing.

7. **Tangibles and Collectibles.** During periods of inflation and economic uncertainty investors tend to rush toward tangibles (precious metals, gemstones, collectibles) in the hope that tangibles will hold their value or appreciate during hard times.

8. **Real Estate Indicators.** The real estate industry and sectors dependent on it (construction, household goods, etc.) form a large segment of the domestic economy. The performance of this industry is affected by the costs of construction and labor, mortgage rates, local housing supply and demand, and personal income.

9. **Limited Partnerships.** By far the largest volume of limited partnership investments are channeled into real estate and oil and gas drilling and income projects. Participation in these tax-advantaged enterprises has risen dramatically in recent years

10. **Futures and options.** Investment in futures and options, while still specialized, is growing. This section provides a brief introductory explanation of the markets in futures and options and directions on reading the quotations of trading activities that are published in the financial press.

3.01 **Interest Rates**

In any competitive market, interaction between supply and demand determines prices and quantities exchanged. Financial markets are no exception. The rate of interest is the price of credit, and it falls or rises according to the eagerness of lenders and borrowers for available funds. When lenders are motivated to lend and borrowers reluctant to borrow, the rate of interest falls; conversely, when borrowers are more eager to borrow than lenders are to lend, the rate of interest is likely to rise. In general, all interest rates tend to move up and down more or less together, although the differences among them may widen or narrow considerably according to market pressure.

Risk and Yield

While there is generally little concern about the federal government's ability to meet its obligations, individuals, corporations, and municipal governments have been known to default. Investors in the bonds of such issuers are consequently paid to bear more risk; thus, yields on corporate bonds tend to exceed those on government bonds. Similarly, yields vary with the financial strength of the individual issuer. Corporate bonds are rated from AAA (the most secure) to DDD (dead in default), and the highest-quality bonds offer the lowest yields.

Municipal bonds are the debt issued by county or city governments, districts, and authorities. The default risk on such instruments was traditionally considered quite low, but has recently become a consideration that has affected yields. Nevertheless, because income from municipals is tax-free, they still enjoy an advantage over other types of government bonds.

Residential mortgages, being the liabilities of individuals, carry somewhat more risk than corporate bonds. Although mortgages insured by the government are considered low-risk investments, they have historically paid higher yields than corporate bonds because of their relative illiquidity. But the establishment in 1970 of the Government National Mortgage Association (GNMA; "Ginnie Mae") and Federal Home Loan Mortgage Corporation (FHLMC; "Freddie Mac") provided a secondary market, and therefore greater liquidity, for mortgages. Recently, the Federal Housing Administration (FHA) mortgage rate has dropped below corporate rates, which some analysts attribute to the development of this secondary market.

PRIME RATES CHARGED BY LARGE COMMERCIAL BANKS

The prime interest rate is the rate of interest at which commercial banks lend money to their most creditworthy commercial customers, and interest rates on loans to financial intermediaries are often pegged to the prime. Changes in the prime rate are influenced by the federal monetary policy, inflation, the availability of excess reserves, and overall business conditions.

Date	Prime Rate		Date		Prime Rate	
	Low	High			Low	High
1929	5½	6	1971		5¼	6¾
1930	3½	6	1972		5	6
1931	2¾	5	1973		6	10
1932	3¼	4	1974		8¾	12
1933	1½	4	1975		7	10½
1934	1½		1976		6¼	7¼
1935	1½		1977		6½	7¾
1936	1½		1978		8	11¾
1937	1½		1979		11½	15¾
1938	1½		1980	Jan.	15¼	15¼
1939	1½			Feb.	15¼	16¾
1940	1½			Mar.	16¾	19½
1941	1½			Apr.	19½	19½
1942	1½			May	14	19
1943	1½			June	12	14
1944	1½			July	11	12
1945	1½			Aug.	11	11½
1946	1½			Sept.	11½	13
1947	1½	1¾		Oct.	13½	14½
1948	2			Nov.	14½	17¾
1949	2			Dec.	17¾	21½
1950	2	2¼	1981	Jan.	20½	
1951	2½	3		Feb.	19	19½
1952	3			Mar.	17½	18
1953	3	3¼		Apr.	17	18
1954	3	3¼		May	19	20½
1955	3	3½		June	20	
				July	20½	
1956	3½	4		Sept.	19	20
1957	4	4½		Oct.	18	
1958	3½	4½		Nov.	16	17½
1959	4	5		Dec.	15¾	
1960	4½	5	1982	Feb.	16½	17
1961	4½			Mar.	16½	16½
1962	4½			Apr.	16½	16½
1963	4½			May	16½	16½
1964	4½			June	16½	16½
1965	4½	5		July	15½	16½
1966	5	6		Aug.	13½	15½
1967	5½	6		Sept.	13½	13½
1968	6	6¾		Oct.	12	13½
1969	6¾	8½		Nov.	11½	12
1970	6¾	8½		Dec.	11½	11½

Prime Rates Charged By Large Commercial Banks

Date		Prime Rate		Date		Prime Rate	
		Low	High			Low	High
1983	Jan.	11	11½	1984	Mar.	11	11½
	Feb.	10½	11		Apr.	11½	12
	Mar.	10½	10½		May	12	12½
	Apr.	10½	10½		June	12½	13
	May	10½	10½		July	13	13
	June	10½	10½		Aug.	13	13
	July	10½	10½		Sept.	13	12¾
	Aug.	10½	11		Oct.	12	12¾
	Sept.	11	11		Nov.	11¼	12
	Oct.	11	11		Dec.	10¾	11¼
	Nov.	11	11	1985	Jan.	10½	10¾
	Dec.	11	11		Feb.	10½	10½
1984	Jan.	11	11		Mar.	10½	10½
	Feb.	11	11				

Source: *Economic Indicators.*

PRIME RATES CHARGED BY LARGE COMMERCIAL BANKS
(Monthly Average)

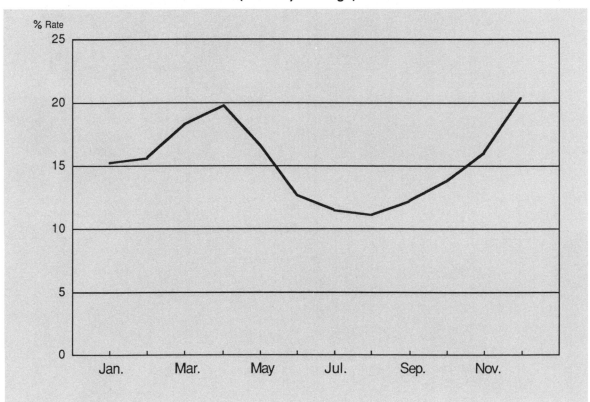

PRIME RATE
(Monthly Highs and Lows)

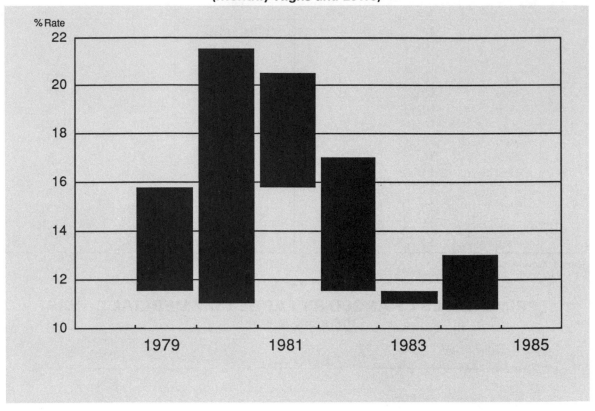

DISCOUNT RATE
Federal Reserve Bank of New York

The discount rate is the rate of interest the Federal Reserve banks and branches charge commercial banks to borrow funds. Such loans are made at the lender's discretion; banks that abuse their privileges may be denied new loans. Most banks are reluctant to borrow from the Federal Reserve and will do so only in the absence of other sources of funds. Generally, discount rates *follow* changes in the federal funds and T-bill rates rather than preceding them. The discount rate usually confirms current monetary policy and, as such, may affect short-term expectations.

Effective Date			Discount Rate % per Annum	Effective Date			Discount Rate % per Annum
1932	Dec.	31	2.5	1955	Sept.	13	2.25
1933	Mar.	3	3.5		Nov.	18	2.5
		4	3.5			23	2.5
	Apr.	7	3	1956	Apr.	13	2.75
	May	26	2.5			20	2.75
	Oct.	20	2		Aug.	24	3
1934	Feb.	2	1.5			31	3
	Mar.	16	1.5	1957	Aug.	9	3
1935	Jan.	11	1.5			23	3.5
	May	14	1.5		Nov.	15	3
1937	Aug.	27	1		Dec.	2	3
	Sept.	4	1	1958	Jan.	22	3
1942	Apr.	11	1		Jan.	24	2.75
	Oct.	15	1		Mar.	7	2.25
		30	1.5			13	2.25
1946	Apr.	25	1			21	2.25
	May	10	1		Apr.	18	1.75
1948	Jan.	12	1.25		May	9	1.75
		19	1.25		Aug.	12	1.75
	Aug.	13	1.5		Sept.	12	2
		23	1.5			23	2
1950	Aug.	21	1.75		Oct.	24	2
		25	1.75		Nov.	7	2.5
1953	Jan.	16	2	1959	Mar.	6	3
		23	2			16	3
1954	Feb.	5	1.75		May	29	3.5
		15	1.75		June	12	3.5
	Apr.	14	1.75		Sept.	11	4
		16	1.5			18	4
	May	21	1.5	1960	June	3	4
1955	Apr.	14	1.5			10	3.5
		15	1.75			14	3.5
	May	2	1.75		Aug.	12	3
	Aug.	4	1.75		Sept.	9	3
		5	2	1963	July	17	3.5
		12	2			26	3.5
	Sept.	9	2.25	1964	Nov.	24	4

(Continued)

DISCOUNT RATE

Effective Date			Discount Rate % per Annum	Effective Date			Discount Rate % per Annum
1964	Nov.	30	4	1974	Apr.	30	8
1965	June	30	4		Dec.	9	7.75
	Dec.	6	4.5			16	7.75
		13	4.5	1975	Jan.	6	7.75
1967	Apr.	7	4			10	7.25
		14	4			24	7.25
	Nov.	20	4.5		Feb.	5	6.75
		27	4.5			7	6.75
1968	Mar.	15	4.5		Mar.	10	6.25
		22	5			14	6.25
	Apr.	19	5.5		May	16	6
		26	5.5			23	6
	Aug.	16	5.5	1976	Jan.	19	5.5
		30	5.25			23	5.5
	Dec.	18	5.5		Nov.	22	5.25
		20	5.5			26	5.25
1969	Apr.	4	6	1977	Aug.	30	5.25
		8	6			31	5.75
1970	Nov.	11	6		Sept.	2	5.75
		13	5.75		Oct.	26	6
		16	5.75	1978	Jan.	9	6.5
	Dec.	1	5.25			20	6.5
		4	5.5		May	11	7
	Dec.	11	5.5		May	12	7
1971	Jan.	8	5.25		July	3	7.25
		15	5.25			10	7.25
		19	5.25		Aug.	21	7.75
		22	5		Sept.	22	8
		29	5		Oct.	16	8.5
	Feb.	13	5			20	8.5
		19	4.75		Nov.	1	9.5
	July	16	5			3	9.5
		23	5	1979	July	20	10
	Nov.	11	5		Aug.	17	10.5
		19	4.75			20	10.5
	Dec.	13	4.75		Sept.	19	11
		17	4.5			21	11
		24	4.5		Oct.	8	11
1973	Jan.	15	5			10	12
	Feb.	26	5.5	1980	Feb.	15	13
	Mar.	2	5.5			19	13
	Apr.	23	5.5		May	29	13
	May	4	5.75			30	12
		11	6		June	13	11
		18	6			16	11
	June	11	6.5		July	28	10
		15	6.5			29	10
	July	2	7		Sept.	26	11
	Aug.	14	7.5		Nov.	17	12
		23	7.5		Dec.	5	13
1974	Apr.	25	8			8	13

DISCOUNT RATE

Effective Date	Discount Rate % per Annum	Effective Date	Discount Rate % per Annum
1981 May 5	14	1982 Aug. 30	10
8	14	Oct. 12	9.5
Nov. 2	13	13	9.5
6	13	Nov. 22	9
Dec. 4	12	26	9
1982 July 20	11.5	Dec. 14	9
23	11.5	15	8.5
Aug. 2	11	17	8.5
3	11	1983 Jan.–Dec.	8.5
16	10.5	1984 Jan.–Dec.	8.75
27	10	1985 Apr. 6	8
		May 15	7.5

Source: *Federal Reserve Bulletin.*

FEDERAL FUNDS RATE

Federal funds are monies immediately available for loans within the Federal Reserve system, including excess reserves of the 12 member banks and 25 branches. The *federal funds rate* is the interest charged by member banks with excess reserves for short-term (usually overnight) loans to banks whose reserves fall below required levels, and it is determined by the supply of excess reserves and the demand for these funds. This very short-term rate and the number of federal funds transactions reflect the pressure that prevailing monetary policy is placing on the commercial banking system.

The federal funds rate usually remains below the *discount rate* (the rate the Federal Reserve system charges member banks for loans; see page 3.13.) However, during tight money periods, the federal funds rate may rise above the discount rate.

Traditionally the Federal Reserve has used the federal funds rate as a target in order to control the growth of the money supply. But on October 6, 1979 the Board of Governors of the Federal Reserve announced a new approach to monetary policy designed to more effectively restrain growth in the monetary aggregates. Instead of focusing on short-term variations in the federal funds rate, the Board decided to place greater emphasis on controlling the supply of bank reserves (see Money Supply, page 3.66).

Year	% Annual Rate	Year	% Annual Rate
1962	2.68	1975	5.82
1963	3.18	1976	5.05
1964	3.50	1977	5.54
1965	4.07	1978	7.94
1966	5.11	1979	11.20
1967	4.22	1980	13.36
1968	5.66	1981	16.38
1969	8.21	1982	12.26
1970	7.17	1983	9.09
1971	4.66	1984	10.23
1972	4.44		
1973	8.74		
1974	10.51		

Source: *Federal Reserve Bulletin.*

FEDERAL FUNDS RATE

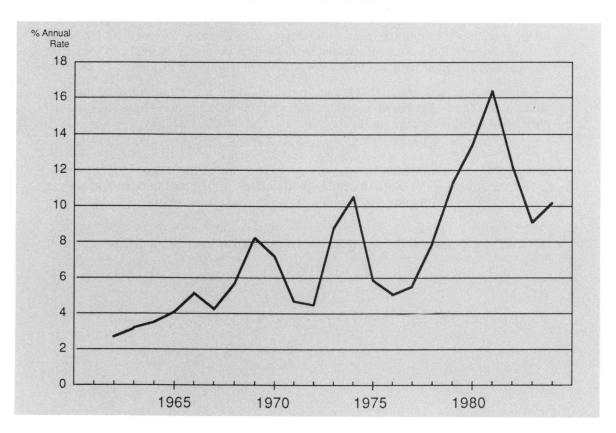

U.S. Treasury Bills

United States Treasury bills (T-bills) are government obligations with maturities of 3 months, 6 months, or 12 months, generally referred to as 13-week, 26-week, and 52-week bills, respectively. T-bills may be purchased by individual investors, banks, and securities dealers through auctions conducted by Federal Reserve banks and branches.

A minimum purchase of $10,000 is required, and larger purchases must be made in multiples of $5,000. T-bills are sold at a discount and redeemed at face value upon maturity, with yield being a function of the discount and the time to maturity:

$$\frac{\text{discount}}{\text{face value} - \text{discount}} \times \frac{365}{\text{days to maturity}} = \text{yield}$$

Exempt from state and local income taxes, the amount of the discount is, however, treated as a taxable interest (*not* as a capital gain) for federal income tax purposes; the tax liability is incurred in the year the tax bills are sold or reach maturity.

Prior to maturity, T-bills can be sold in the secondary market at prices reflecting current interest rates. Again, gains or losses must be reported as interest income or expenses.

THREE-MONTH TREASURY BILL RATES
New Issues

Year	% Rate	Year	% Rate	Year	% Rate
1931	1.402	1950	1.218	1969	6.677
1932	.879	1951	1.552	1970	6.458
1933	.515	1952	1.776	1971	4.348
1934	.256	1953	1.931	1972	4.071
1935	.137	1954	.953	1973	7.041
1936	.143	1955	1.753	1974	7.83
1937	.447	1956	2.658	1975	5.77
1938	.053	1957	3.267	1976	4.97
1939	.023	1958	1.839	1977	5.27
1940	.014	1959	3.405	1978	7.19
1941	.103	1960	2.928	1979	10.07
1942	.326	1961	2.378	1980	11.43
1943	.373	1962	2.778	1981	14.03
1944	.375	1963	3.157	1982	10.69
1945	.375	1964	3.549	1983	8.63
1946	.375	1965	3.954	1984	9.58
1947	.594	1966	4.881		
1948	1.040	1967	4.321		
1949	1.102	1968	5.339		

Source: *Federal Reserve Bulletin.*

THREE-MONTH TREASURY-BILL RATES
(New Issues)

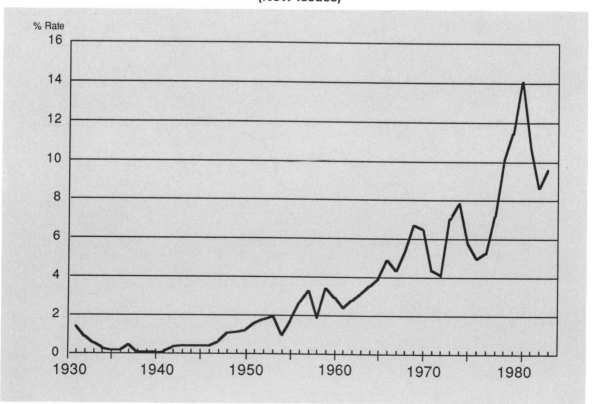

ONE-YEAR TREASURY BILL RATES
New Issues

Year	% Rate	Year	% Rate
1960	3.41	1974	7.70
1961	2.89	1975	6.28
1962	3.01	1976	5.52
1963	3.30	1977	5.71
1964	3.74	1978	7.74
1965	4.06	1979	9.75
1966	5.07	1980	10.89
1967	4.71	1981	13.14
1968	5.46	1982	11.10
1969	6.79	1983	8.86
1970	6.49	1984	9.91
1971	4.67		
1972	4.77		
1973	7.01		

Source: *Federal Reserve Bulletin.*

ONE-YEAR TREASURY-BILL RATES
(New Issues)

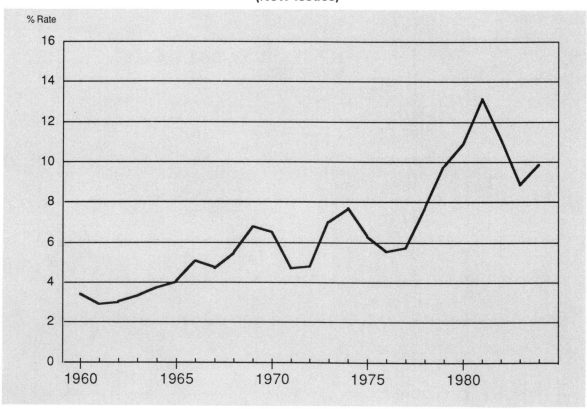

THREE- TO FIVE-YEAR TREASURY BONDS AND NOTES

Treasury notes are obligations of the United States government that have maturities that range from one to ten years; treasury bonds usually have even longer maturities. Backed by the full faith of the federal government, both are regarded as issues of the highest grade. Yields are conventionally considered to be those most closely approximating riskless rates and thus are generally lower than those of corporate bonds, for which the holder receives a risk premium. Treasury bonds are generally issued in minimum denominations of $1,000 (two-year notes) or $5,000 (four-year notes) and pay interest semiannually. Interest is subject to federal income tax, but exempt from state and local income taxes.

Year	% Annual Yield	Year	% Annual Yield	
1941	.73	1965	4.22	
1942	1.46	1966	5.16	
1943	1.34	1967	5.07	
1944	1.33	1968	5.59	
1945	1.18	1969	6.85	
1946	1.16	1970	7.37	
1947	1.32	1971	5.77	
1948	1.62	1972	5.85	
1949	1.43	1973	6.92	
1950	1.50	1974	7.81	
1951	1.93	1975	7.55	
1952	2.13	1976	6.94	
1953	2.56	1977	6.85	
1954	1.82	1978	8.30	
1955	2.50	1979	9.58	
1956	3.12			
1957	3.62		3-Year	5-Year
1958	2.90	1980	11.55	11.48
1959	4.33	1981	14.44	14.24
1960	3.99	1982	12.92	13.01
1961	3.60	1983	10.45	10.80
1962	3.57	1984	11.89	12.24
1963	3.72			
1964	4.06			

Source: *Federal Reserve Bulletin.*

TREASURY BONDS AND NOTES
(1941–1979)

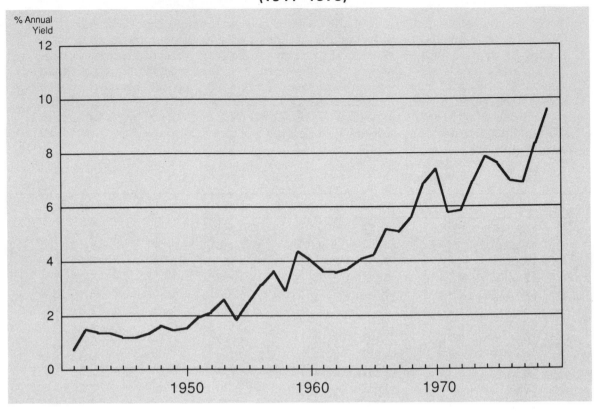

THREE- AND FIVE-YEAR TREASURY BONDS AND NOTES
(1980–1984)

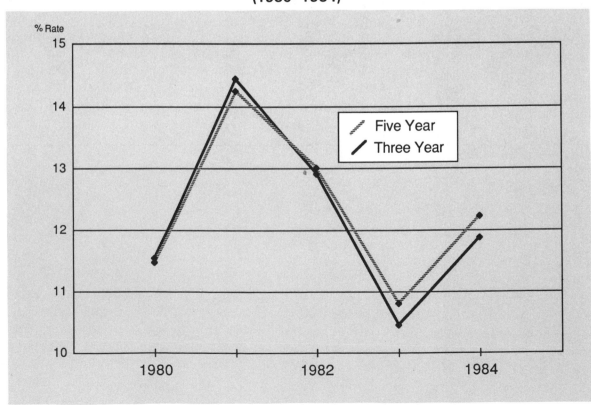

Municipal Bonds

Municipal bonds are the debt obligations of a county, city, town, village, tax district, or other civil division of a state. Such bonds are issued for a number of public purposes: school buildings and equipment, street improvements, parks and museums, bridges, sewers, and the like. While corporate bonds are paid out of earnings, some municipal bonds are backed by the "full faith and credit" of the jurisdiction and are paid off by tax revenues, others are backed only by revenues from the project itself.

Municipal bonds were traditionally considered to be almost risk-free, but this perception has changed and may force up rates. The tax-exempt status of interest payments on municipals is the most important influence on the yields. For an investor in the 50% tax bracket, a municipal bond yielding 4% tax-free would be as attractive as an 8% government bond. (For comparisons of tax-exempt yields and taxable yields, see page 4.8.)

HIGH-GRADE MUNICIPAL BONDS (AAA)

Year	% Annual Yield	Year	% Annual Yield
1920	4.98	1962	3.18
1925	4.09	1963	3.23
1930	4.07	1964	3.22
1935	3.40	1965	3.27
1940	2.50	1966	3.82
1941	2.10	1967	3.98
1942	2.36	1968	4.51
1943	2.06	1969	5.81
1944	1.86	1970	6.51
1945	1.67	1971	5.70
1946	1.64	1972	5.27
1947	2.01	1973	5.18
1948	2.40	1974	6.09
1949	2.21	1975	6.89
1950	1.98	1976	6.49
1951	2.00	1977	5.56
1952	2.19	1978	5.90
1953	2.72	1979	6.39
1954	2.37	1980	8.51
1955	2.53	1981	11.23
1956	2.93	1982	11.57
1957	3.60	1983	9.47
1958	3.56	1984	10.15
1959	3.95		
1960	3.73		
1961	3.46		

Source: *Economic Indicators.*

HIGH-GRADE MUNICIPAL BONDS
(AAA)

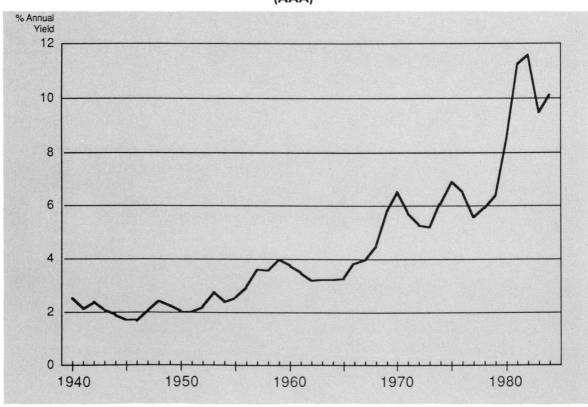

STATE AND LOCAL NOTES AND BONDS
Bond Buyer Series

Year	% Annual Yield	Year	% Annual Yield
1950	1.76	1968	4.42
1951	1.94	1969	5.66
1952	2.18	1970	6.35
1953	2.73	1971	5.52
1954	2.40	1972	5.25
1955	2.47	1973	5.19
1956	2.75	1974	6.17
1957	3.29	1975	7.05
1958	3.16	1976	6.64
1959	3.55	1977	5.68
1960	3.52	1978	6.03
1961	3.45	1979	6.52
1962	3.17	1980	8.59
1963	3.16	1981	11.33
1964	3.22	1982	11.66
1965	3.27	1983	9.51
1966	3.81	1984	10.10
1967	3.92		

Note: *The Bond Buyer Series consists of 20-year bonds of mixed quality issued by 20 state and local government units.*

Source: *Federal Reserve Bulletin.*

STATE AND LOCAL NOTES AND BONDS
(Bond Buyer Series)

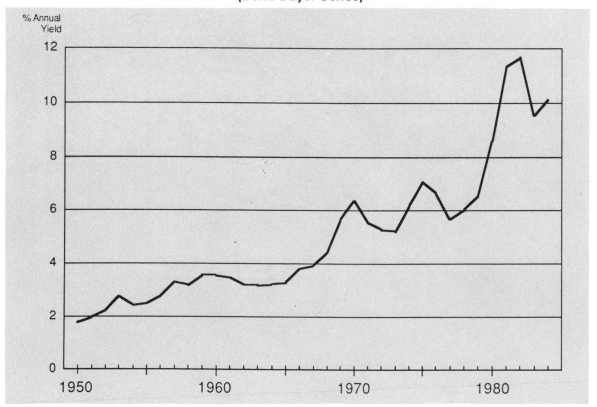

Corporate Bonds

Corporate bonds are obligations of nongovernment companies and are often graded according to the creditworthiness of the corporations issuing them. The degree of risk of a corporate bond depends on many factors, including the nature of the issuer, the industry, and the collateral offered, as well as the stability of earnings. The yields of AAA bonds — the most secure — are primarily influenced by market interest rates. In general, the higher the grade, the lower the yield.

LONG-TERM CORPORATE AAA BONDS
(Based on Yields to Maturity of Selected Long-Term Bonds)

Year	% Annual Yield	Year	% Annual Yield	Year	% Annual Yield
1920	6.12	1954	2.90	1972	7.21
1925	4.88	1955	3.06	1973	7.44
1930	4.55	1956	3.36	1974	8.57
1935	3.60	1957	3.89	1975	8.83
1940	2.84	1958	3.79	1976	8.43
1941	2.77	1959	4.38	1977	8.02
1942	2.83	1960	4.41	1978	8.73
1943	2.73	1961	4.35	1979	9.63
1944	2.72	1962	4.33	1980	11.94
1945	2.62	1963	4.26	1981	14.17
1946	2.53	1964	4.40	1982	13.79
1947	2.61	1965	4.49	1983	12.04
1948	2.82	1966	5.13	1984	12.71
1949	2.66	1967	5.51		
1950	2.62	1968	6.18		
1951	2.86	1969	7.03		
1952	2.96	1970	8.04		
1953	3.20	1971	7.39		

Sources: *Federal Reserve Bulletin; Economic Indicators.*

LONG-TERM CORPORATE AAA BONDS

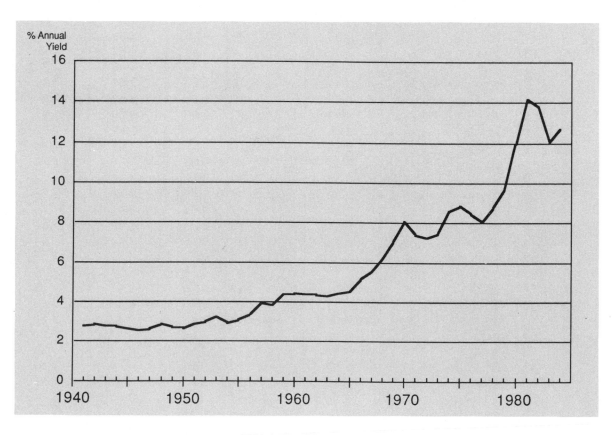

BARRON'S CONFIDENCE INDEX

Barron's Confidence Index is the ratio of Barron's average of the yield on 10 best grade corporate bonds to the yield on 10 intermediate grade corporate bonds. The ratio is high when investors are confidently buying bonds below top grade. It is low when they take refuge in top grade issues.

Date	Index	10 Intermediate Grade Bond Yield	10 Best Grade Bond Yield	Date	Index	10 Intermediate Grade Bond Yield	10 Best Grade Bond Yield
1976 Jan. 5	89.3	9.83	8.78	1976 Nov. 15	90.3	8.79	7.94
12	89.3	9.76	8.72	22	90.4	8.73	7.89
19	89.7	9.63	8.64	29	90.7	8.70	7.89
26	89.8	9.53	8.56	Dec. 6	90.1	8.66	7.80
Feb 2	89.3	9.48	8.47	13	90.4	8.56	7.74
9	89.2	9.48	8.46	20	89.8	8.55	7.68
16	89.6	9.45	8.47	27	89.4	8.55	7.64
23	89.6	9.36	8.39	1977 Jan. 3	88.6	8.52	7.55
Mar. 1	90.4	9.29	8.40	10	89.7	8.48	7.61
8	89.7	9.32	8.36	17	89.3	8.53	7.62
15	90.0	9.33	8.40	24	91.4	8.56	7.82
22	90.2	9.27	8.36	31	91.2	8.61	7.85
29	91.1	9.20	8.38	Feb. 7	91.6	8.55	7.83
Apr. 5	90.1	9.28	8.36	14	91.5	8.55	7.82
12	90.6	9.23	8.36	21	91.4	8.54	7.81
19	90.6	9.13	8.27	28	91.3	8.60	7.85
26	90.6	9.12	8.26	Mar. 7	91.3	8.58	7.83
May 3	90.5	9.18	8.31	14	91.3	8.59	7.84
10	90.1	9.20	8.29	21	91.5	8.59	7.86
17	90.2	9.26	8.35	28	91.1	8.59	7.83
24	91.1	9.28	8.45	Apr. 4	90.4	8.62	7.79
31	91.2	9.29	8.47	11	90.8	8.65	7.85
June 7	90.4	9.34	8.44	18	90.8	8.62	7.83
14	91.0	9.31	8.47	25	90.5	8.63	7.81
21	91.0	9.26	8.43	May 2	90.8	8.60	7.81
28	92.0	9.23	8.49	9	90.6	8.61	7.80
July 5	90.8	9.24	8.39	16	91.5	8.57	7.84
12	90.7	9.28	8.42	23	91.1	8.54	7.78
19	90.7	9.22	8.36	30	90.2	8.56	7.72
26	91.1	9.21	8.39	June 6	90.6	8.54	7.74
Aug. 2	91.6	9.13	8.36	13	90.5	8.49	7.68
9	91.4	9.09	8.31	20	90.3	8.46	7.64
16	91.6	9.03	8.27	27	90.5	8.44	7.64
23	91.8	8.98	8.24	July 4	91.2	8.39	7.65
30	90.7	8.96	8.13	11	91.8	8.39	7.70
Sept. 6	89.8	8.99	8.07	18	91.2	8.41	7.67
13	90.6	8.95	8.11	25	90.8	8.40	7.63
20	90.6	8.92	8.08	Aug. 1	89.7	8.47	7.60
27	91.9	8.79	8.08	8	90.4	8.44	7.63
Oct. 4	91.4	8.77	8.02	15	90.5	8.44	7.64
11	91.4	8.77	8.02	22	90.3	8.44	7.62
18	90.8	8.80	7.99	29	90.0	8.44	7.60
25	90.6	8.81	7.98	Sept. 4	91.2	8.82	8.04
Nov. 1	91.6	8.78	8.04	5	90.5	8.42	7.62
8	91.0	8.76	7.97	12	89.9	8.44	7.59

Barron's Confidence Index

Date	Index	10 Intermediate Grade Bond Yield	10 Best Grade Bond Yield	Date	Index	10 Intermediate Grade Bond Yield	10 Best Grade Bond Yield
1977 Sept. 19	90.3	8.43	7.61	1978 Sept. 4	91.8	9.07	8.33
26	90.0	8.49	7.64	11	91.7	9.04	8.29
Oct. 3	90.2	8.48	7.65	18	91.5	9.02	8.25
10	91.2	8.50	7.75	25	91.5	9.04	8.27
17	90.8	8.58	7.79	Oct. 2	91.5	9.08	8.31
24	92.4	8.59	7.94	9	91.9	9.13	8.39
31	92.8	8.62	8.00	16	91.9	9.11	8.37
Nov. 7	91.5	8.67	7.93	23	93.2	9.18	8.56
14	91.2	8.67	7.91	30	94.1	9.27	8.72
21	92.2	8.60	7.93	Nov. 6	92.7	9.44	8.75
28	91.9	8.56	7.87	13	92.7	9.40	8.71
Dec. 5	91.0	8.58	7.81	20	92.0	9.45	8.69
12	91.4	8.57	7.83	27	94.0	9.36	8.80
19	91.5	8.61	7.88	Dec. 4	93.4	9.46	8.84
26	91.1	8.65	7.88	11	92.2	9.49	8.75
1978 Jan. 2	91.0	8.67	7.89	18	91.9	9.56	8.79
9	91.9	8.68	7.98	25	91.2	9.71	8.86
16	91.7	8.78	8.05	1979 Jan. 1	90.8	9.81	8.91
23	91.4	8.81	8.04	8	91.4	9.84	8.99
30	90.6	8.87	8.04	15	91.3	9.86	9.00
Feb. 6	91.5	8.80	8.05	22	91.1	9.80	8.93
13	91.6	8.82	8.08	29	91.5	9.75	8.92
20	91.3	8.82	8.05	Feb. 5	92.7	9.65	8.95
27	91.2	8.85	8.07	12	92.7	9.65	8.95
Mar. 6	90.8	8.83	8.02	19	92.4	9.68	8.95
13	90.1	8.83	7.96	26	91.4	9.77	8.93
20	90.7	8.86	8.04	Mar. 5	91.4	9.81	8.97
27	90.7	8.86	8.04	12	92.1	9.78	9.01
Apr. 3	90.6	8.87	8.04	19	91.7	9.84	9.02
10	91.4	8.91	8.14	26	91.4	9.83	8.99
17	90.7	8.94	8.11	Apr. 2	91.1	9.83	8.96
24	91.2	8.96	8.17	9	90.7	9.88	8.96
May 1	91.2	8.96	8.17	16	90.7	9.91	8.99
8	90.6	9.01	8.16	23	90.0	9.94	8.95
15	90.8	9.04	8.21	30	90.7	9.94	9.02
22	91.8	9.01	8.29	May 7	90.8	9.99	9.07
29	91.8	9.11	8.36	14	91.8	10.03	9.21
June 5	91.7	9.15	8.39	21	92.1	9.96	9.17
12	91.2	9.16	8.35	28	91.4	9.96	9.10
19	91.0	9.20	8.37	June 4	91.7	9.91	9.09
26	92.5	9.10	8.42	11	91.4	9.84	8.99
July 3	91.9	9.15	8.41	18	91.4	9.76	8.92
10	92.5	9.22	8.53	25	91.5	9.70	8.88
17	92.3	9.25	8.54	July 2	91.8	9.67	8.88
24	92.4	9.23	8.53	9	92.7	9.65	8.95
31	92.6	9.21	8.53	16	92.7	9.68	8.97
Aug. 7	92.1	9.16	8.44	23	93.3	9.67	9.02
14	92.6	9.09	8.42	30	93.3	9.68	9.03
21	91.9	9.10	8.36	Aug. 6	93.3	9.67	9.02
28	91.7	9.11	8.35	13	92.4	9.65	8.92

(Continued)

Barron's Confidence Index

Date	Index	10 Intermediate Grade Bond Yield	10 Best Grade Bond Yield	Date	Index	10 Intermediate Grade Bond Yield	10 Best Grade Bond Yield
1979 Aug. 20	93.0	9.64	8.97	1980 Aug. 4	88.7	11.96	10.61
27	92.7	9.68	8.97	11	87.1	12.28	10.69
Sept. 3	93.0	9.74	9.06	18	87.2	12.32	10.74
10	92.4	9.79	9.05	25	88.1	12.48	10.99
17	91.2	9.93	9.06	Sept. 1	88.0	12.61	11.10
24	92.1	9.94	9.15	8	90.0	12.37	11.13
Oct. 1	91.0	10.06	9.16	15	90.8	12.51	11.36
8	90.8	10.26	9.32	22	90.7	12.63	11.46
15	90.0	10.67	9.60	29	88.5	12.77	11.30
22	89.3	10.82	9.66	Oct. 6	89.5	12.93	11.57
29	89.4	11.25	10.06	13	89.4	12.87	11.50
Nov. 5	92.0	11.22	10.33	20	89.9	12.73	11.45
12	92.6	11.22	10.39	27	91.8	12.75	11.71
19	90.9	11.28	10.25	Nov. 3	92.4	12.98	11.99
26	92.3	11.31	10.44	10	91.3	13.02	11.89
Dec. 3	91.5	11.26	10.30	17	90.9	13.09	11.90
10	90.9	11.27	10.24	24	87.8	13.51	11.86
17	91.3	11.38	10.39	Dec. 1	86.9	13.60	11.82
24	89.2	11.64	10.38	8	86.0	13.68	11.77
31	89.2	11.77	10.50	15	89.3	13.78	12.31
1980 Jan. 7	90.0	11.81	10.63	22	87.4	14.05	12.28
14	90.9	11.67	10.61	29	84.0	13.69	11.50
21	90.6	11.74	10.63	1981 Jan. 5	86.1	13.82	11.90
28	91.7	11.91	10.92	12	87.3	13.65	11.92
Feb. 4	90.1	12.17	10.97	19	87.7	13.17	11.55
11	90.7	12.32	11.18	26	88.7	13.31	11.81
18	90.2	12.61	11.38	Feb. 2	86.0	13.50	11.69
25	92.3	12.99	11.99	9	86.7	13.58	11.78
Mar. 3	89.8	13.28	11.93	16	87.4	13.63	11.91
10	92.3	13.27	12.25	23	87.4	13.71	11.99
17	93.6	13.28	12.43	Mar. 2	86.7	13.81	11.98
24	91.9	13.25	12.18	9	88.3	13.77	12.16
31	90.0	13.42	12.08	16	86.4	13.78	11.91
Apr. 7	90.5	13.50	12.22	23	86.3	13.61	11.74
14	89.5	13.31	11.91	30	87.0	13.66	11.88
21	85.5	13.02	11.13	Apr. 6	87.0	13.89	2.08
28	87.3	12.64	11.03	13	88.3	13.97	12.33
May 5	86.5	12.41	10.73	20	90.1	14.02	12.63
12	85.7	12.10	10.37	27	90.3	14.05	12.69
19	86.8	12.12	10.52	May 4	90.4	14.34	12.97
26	88.8	11.94	10.60	11	90.2	14.59	13.16
June 2	88.5	11.94	10.57	18	91.6	14.51	13.29
9	87.4	11.87	10.38	25	90.5	14.39	13.02
16	86.9	11.77	10.23	June 1	89.4	14.30	12.79
23	88.4	11.30	9.99	8	89.0	14.18	12.62
30	89.3	11.24	10.04	15	88.5	14.21	12.58
July 7	89.3	11.57	10.33	22	88.2	13.86	12.37
14	89.6	11.58	10.38	29	90.0	13.89	12.50
21	89.4	11.70	10.46	July 6	89.5	14.11	12.63
28	88.6	11.86	10.51	13	90.5	14.13	12.79

Barron's Confidence Index

Date	Index	10 Intermediate Grade Bond Yield	10 Best Grade Bond Yield	Date	Index	10 Intermediate Grade Bond Yield	10 Best Grade Bond Yield
1981 July 20	90.3	14.10	12.73	1982 July 5	90.2	15.06	13.59
27	91.7	14.21	13.03	12	91.7	14.93	13.69
Aug. 3	92.2	14.32	13.20	19	90.5	14.92	13.51
10	92.9	14.27	13.26	26	90.9	14.77	13.42
17	91.9	14.26	13.11	Aug. 2	89.3	15.00	13.39
24	90.8	14.54	13.20	9	89.2	14.81	13.21
31	89.7	14.72	13.21	16	90.5	14.70	13.31
Sept. 7	90.8	14.67	13.32	23	87.9	14.28	12.56
14	93.9	14.66	13.76	30	88.3	14.16	12.50
21	93.1	14.56	13.56	Sept. 6	89.5	14.14	12.66
28	93.1	14.69	13.67	13	88.8	14.00	12.43
Oct. 5	91.5	15.19	13.90	20	87.4	14.14	12.36
12	91.6	15.09	13.82	27	88.9	13.82	12.29
19	93.1	14.77	13.75	Oct. 4	88.6	13.77	12.20
26	90.1	15.23	13.72	11	88.9	13.67	12.16
Nov. 2	90.1	15.23	13.72	18	88.2	13.18	11.62
9	90.6	14.86	13.46	25	87.4	13.13	11.47
16	90.0	14.52	13.07	Nov. 1	85.2	13.35	11.38
23	88.8	14.38	12.77	8	85.9	13.02	11.19
30	88.7	14.40	12.78	15	87.0	12.91	11.23
Dec. 7	87.7	14.43	12.65	22	86.5	12.89	11.15
14	88.1	14.58	12.84	29	87.1	12.82	11.17
21	88.9	14.83	13.18	Dec. 6	86.7	12.98	11.26
28	88.8	14.99	13.31	13	87.3	12.89	11.25
1982 Jan. 4	88.6	15.13	13.41	20	88.0	12.74	11.21
11	89.5	15.25	13.65	27	87.9	12.77	11.22
18	91.7	15.31	14.04	1983 Jan. 7	87.4	12.80	11.19
25	91.4	15.28	13.96	14	88.6	12.68	11.24
Feb. 1	90.5	15.27	13.82	21	89.3	12.63	11.28
8	91.4	15.03	13.74	28	88.6	12.81	11.35
15	90.6	15.19	13.77	Feb. 4	89.5	12.76	11.42
22	89.0	15.39	13.70	11	88.7	12.81	11.36
Mar. 1	89.3	15.02	13.42	18	88.5	12.67	11.22
8	88.5	14.94	13.23	25	88.3	12.55	11.08
15	87.7	15.00	13.15	Mar. 4	87.0	12.35	10.75
22	88.0	15.12	13.30	11	89.1	12.29	10.95
29	87.8	15.05	13.21	18	88.7	12.26	10.87
Apr. 5	88.1	15.10	13.30	25	90.1	12.08	10.89
12	89.3	15.07	13.45	31	89.5	12.03	10.77
19	89.4	14.93	13.35	Apr. 8	89.6	12.12	10.86
26	88.4	14.91	13.18	15	89.9	11.93	10.72
May 3	89.2	14.70	13.11	22	91.6	11.73	10.74
10	89.5	14.64	13.10	29	91.1	11.67	10.63
17	88.8	14.59	12.96	May 6	91.2	11.48	10.48
24	88.5	14.59	12.92	13	90.7	11.53	10.46
31	88.6	14.60	12.94	20	91.2	11.71	10.68
June 7	87.5	14.82	12.97	27	90.2	11.89	10.72
14	88.2	14.88	13.13	June 3	89.9	11.99	10.78
21	90.5	14.71	13.31	10	91.5	12.08	11.05
28	89.4	14.95	13.37	17	90.1	12.17	10.97

(Continued)

Barron's Confidence Index

Date	Index	10 Intermediate Grade Bond Yield	10 Best Grade Bond Yield	Date	Index	10 Intermediate Grade Bond Yield	10 Best Grade Bond Yield
1983 June 24	91.1	12.10	11.02	1984 June 1	91.5	14.06	12.87
July 1	91.1	12.17	11.09	8	91.5	13.89	12.71
8	91.3	12.36	11.28	15	90.8	14.04	12.75
15	89.9	12.48	11.22	22	88.0	14.18	12.48
22	91.2	12.50	11.40	29	89.1	14.19	12.64
29	91.5	12.55	11.48	July 6	91.7	14.18	13.01
Aug 5	91.3	12.75	11.64	13	91.2	14.18	12.93
12	90.3	12.85	11.60	20	91.9	14.14	12.99
19	90.0	12.68	11.41	27	90.4	14.06	12.71
26	89.6	12.64	11.32	Aug. 3	91.0	13.84	12.60
Sept. 2	89.9	12.72	11.44	10	90.2	13.84	12.49
9	90.5	12.71	11.50	17	90.5	13.73	12.43
16	90.4	12.67	11.46	24	90.9	13.64	12.40
23	89.2	12.62	11.26	31	92.2	13.35	12.31
30	89.4	12.58	11.25	Sept. 7	91.1	13.53	12.32
Oct. 7	91.6	12.36	11.32	14	91.2	13.42	12.24
14	92.9	12.43	11.55	21	91.2	13.24	12.08
21	93.3	12.37	11.54	28	91.6	13.36	12.24
28	93.7	12.42	11.64	Oct. 5	93.1	13.40	12.48
Nov. 4	91.2	12.51	11.41	12	93.6	13.42	12.56
11	91.8	12.50	11.47	19	92.5	13.33	12.33
18	91.1	12.55	11.43	26	92.5	13.01	12.03
25	90.7	12.61	11.44	Nov. 2	92.5	12.96	11.99
Dec. 2	91.3	12.60	11.50	9	92.3	12.92	11.92
9	89.3	12.82	11.45	16	92.1	13.04	12.01
16	90.3	13.17	11.89	23	92.1	12.87	11.86
23	91.6	12.94	11.85	30	94.2	12.44	11.72
30	91.0	12.92	11.76	Dec. 7	93.9	12.48	11.72
1984 Jan. 6	91.2	12.95	11.81	14	91.6	12.78	11.70
13	90.5	12.80	11.59	21	91.8	12.69	11.65
20	91.6	12.68	11.62	28	92.5	12.71	11.76
27	91.1	12.64	11.52				
Feb. 3	92.1	12.61	11.61				
10	91.6	12.66	11.60				
17	90.6	12.67	11.48				
24	91.0	12.72	11.58				
Mar. 2	92.3	12.83	11.84				
9	91.9	12.91	11.87				
16	92.9	12.90	11.99				
23	92.0	13.09	12.05				
30	92.1	13.05	12.02				
Apr. 6	92.5	13.31	12.31				
13	90.3	13.32	12.03				
19	92.1	13.52	12.45				
27	92.1	13.49	12.42				
May 4	91.7	13.52	12.40				
11	89.5	13.85	12.39				
18	91.3	13.99	12.77				
25	91.0	14.03	12.77				

Source: *Dow Jones Investor's Handbook, 1985.*

COMMERCIAL PAPER
Six-Month

Year	% per Annum	Year	% per Annum	Year	% per Annum
1929	5.85	1953	2.52	1969	7.83
1933	1.73	1954	1.58	1970	7.71
1939	0.59	1955	2.18	1971	5.11
1940	0.56	1956	3.31	1972	4.73
1941	0.53	1957	3.81	1973	8.15
1942	0.66	1958	2.46	1974	9.84
1943	0.69	1959	3.97	1975	6.32
1944	0.73	1960	3.85	1976	5.34
1945	0.75	1961	2.97	1977	5.61
1946	0.81	1962	3.26	1978	7.99
1947	1.03	1963	3.55	1979	10.91
1948	1.44	1964	3.97	1980	12.29
1949	1.49	1965	4.38	1981	14.76
1950	1.45	1966	5.55	1982	11.89
1951	2.16	1967	6.10	1983	8.89
1952	2.33	1968	5.90	1984	10.16

Note: *Bank discount basis; prior to November 1979, data are for four- to six-month commercial paper.*

Source: *The Economic Report of the President, 1985.*

GNMA INTEREST RATES

The Government National Mortgage Association is a federal institution set up to encourage mortgage lending by providing guarantees of repayment. The GNMA issues long-term securities, known as "Ginnie Maes," the interest rates of which are a bellwether for the housing industry. Although GNMA mortgages have 30-year terms, the average mortgage is repaid within 8 to 12 years (upon sale of the property).

The initial investment is $25,000 and may be increased thereafter in increments of $10,000. The trading price of the securities is based on the bid price of three New York dealers at the close of business every Friday. The securities are for immediate delivery, and yields are based on a 30-year mortgage with a 12-year prepayment. The monthly figures given here are simple averages of the Friday prices.

Period		% Interest Rate	Period		% Interest Rate	Period		% Interest Rate
1971	Aug.	7.75	1974	Sept.	9.75	1977	Oct.	8.20
	Sept.	7.52		Oct.	9.38		Nov.	8.22
	Oct.	7.38		Nov.	8.84		Dec.	8.32
	Nov.	7.21		Dec.	8.77	1978	Jan.	8.58
	Dec.	7.11	1975	Jan.	8.53		Feb.	8.66
1972	Jan.	7.00		Feb.	8.32		Mar.	8.63
	Feb.	6.98		Mar.	8.32		Apr.	8.76
	Mar.	6.95		Apr.	8.65		May	8.94
	Apr.	7.05		May	8.60		June	9.09
	May	7.10		June	8.42		July	9.18
	June	7.06		July	8.57		Aug.	8.98
	July	7.08		Aug.	8.87		Sept.	9.09
	Aug.	7.11		Sept.	9.09		Oct.	9.33
	Sept.	7.20		Oct.	8.82		Nov.	9.43
	Oct.	7.25		Nov.	8.67		Dec.	9.61
	Nov.	7.14		Dec.	8.62	1979	Jan.	9.70
	Dec.	7.16	1976	Jan.	8.44		Feb.	9.68
1973	Jan.	7.20		Feb.	8.40		Mar.	9.73
	Feb.	7.24		Mar.	8.38		Apr.	9.86
	Mar.	7.38		Apr.	8.26		May	10.02
	Apr.	7.47		May	8.48		June	9.81
	May	7.58		June	8.45		July	9.81
	June	7.71		July	8.44		Aug.	9.97
	July	8.04		Aug.	8.36		Sept.	10.40
	Aug.	8.56		Sept.	8.25		Oct.	11.30
	Sept.	8.30		Oct.	8.16		Nov.	11.58
	Oct.	7.96		Nov.	7.90		Dec.	11.56
	Nov.	7.99		Dec.	7.41	1980	Jan.	11.96
	Dec.	7.94	1977	Jan.	7.80		Feb.	13.02
1974	Jan.	7.97		Feb.	7.96		Mar.	13.69
	Feb.	7.94		Mar.	8.04		Apr.	13.17
	Mar.	8.18		Apr.	8.00		May	11.54
	Apr.	8.61		May	8.06		June	10.89
	May	8.80		June	7.94		July	11.53
	June	8.98		July	7.98		Aug.	12.33
	July	9.27		Aug.	8.06		Sept.	12.86
	Aug.	9.61		Sept.	8.05		Oct.	13.24

GNMA Interest Rates

Period		% Interest Rate	Period		% Interest Rate	Period		% Interest Rate
1980	Nov.	13.69	1982	Apr.	15.56	1983	Sept.	12.78
	Dec.	13.71		May	15.26		Oct.	12.58
1981	Jan.	13.65		June	15.89		Nov.	12.62
	Feb.	14.16		July	15.54		Dec.	12.65
	Mar.	14.15		Aug.	14.31	1984	Jan.	12.35
	Apr.	15.05		Sept.	13.51		Feb.	12.31
	May	15.55		Oct.	12.86		Mar.	12.70
	June	15.35		Nov.	11.85		Apr.	13.01
	July	15.97		Dec.	12.00		May	13.67
	Aug.	16.63	1983	Jan.	11.89		June	14.14
	Sept.	17.33		Feb.	12.20		July	13.88
	Oct.	16.90		Mar.	11.82		Aug.	13.56
	Nov.	15.10		Apr.	11.78		Sept.	13.36
	Dec.	15.39		May	11.54		Oct.	13.09
1982	Jan.	16.22		June	12.03		Nov.	12.71
	Feb.	16.24		July	12.80		Dec.	12.54
	Mar.	15.83		Aug.	13.22	1985	Jan.	12.26

Source: Mortgage Bankers Association of America.

AVERAGE ANNUAL YIELD ON SAVINGS DEPOSITS
In Savings Associations

Deposits in savings accounts and certificates issued by banks and thrift institutions offer security of principal and interest. Because of their safety, convenience, and liquidity, as well as, in some cases, government restrictions, these deposits generally offer lower yields than other interest-bearing instruments. All interest is treated as regular taxable income by federal, state, and local governments.

Year	% Yield	Year	% Yield	Year	% Yield
1930	5.3	1949	2.4	1968	4.68
1931	5.1	1950	2.5	1969	4.80
1932	4.1	1951	2.6	1970	5.06
1933	3.4	1952	2.7	1971	5.33
1934	3.5	1953	2.8	1972	5.40
1935	3.1	1954	2.9	1973	5.55
1936	3.2	1955	2.9	1974	5.98
1937	3.5	1956	3.0	1975	6.24
1938	3.5	1957	3.3	1976	6.32
1939	3.4	1958	3.38	1977	6.41
1940	3.3	1959	3.53	1978	6.52
1941	3.1	1960	3.86	1979	7.31
1942	3.0	1961	3.90	1980	8.69
1943	2.9	1962	4.08	1981	10.70
1944	2.8	1963	4.17	1982	11.03
1945	2.5	1964	4.19	1983	9.83
1946	2.2	1965	4.23	1984	10.14*
1947	2.3	1966	4.45		
1948	2.3	1967	4.67		

* *For savings and loan institutions only.*

Source: U.S. League of Savings Institutions, *Savings & Loan Sourcebook, 1983.*

AVERAGE ANNUAL YIELD ON SAVINGS DEPOSITS
(In Savings Associations)

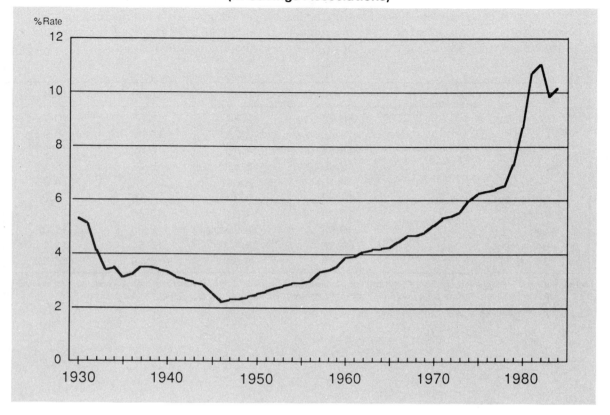

FOREIGN SHORT-TERM INTEREST RATES

In most countries the 1980s have so far been a period of volatile but declining short-term interest rates. Real interest rates can be determined by comparing the nominal rates shown here with the consumer price indexes shown on page 3.87–88.

Country or Type	1981	1982	1983	1984
Eurodollars	16.79	12.24	9.57	10.75
United Kingdom	13.86	12.21	10.06	9.91
Canada	18.84	14.38	9.48	11.29
Germany	12.05	8.81	5.73	5.96
Switzerland	9.15	5.04	4.11	4.35
Netherlands	11.52	8.26	5.58	6.08
France	15.28	14.61	12.44	11.66
Italy	19.98	19.99	18.95	17.08
Belgium	15.28	14.10	10.51	11.41
Japan	7.58	6.84	6.49	6.32

Note: *Rates are averages of daily figures, expressed in percentages per annum, for three-month interbank loans, except for: Canada, rates on finance company paper; Belgium, rates on three-month Treasury bills; and Japan, the Gensaki rate.*

Source: *Federal Reserve Bulletin.*

3.02 Stock Market Indicators

Savings accounts, bonds, and mortgages are *fixed-dollar investments,* that is, the yield is predetermined. But stockholders buy direct ownership in a corporation, and the performance of their investments depends on the success or failure of the company; thus stocks are called *variable-dollar investments.*

Common stock represents ownership in a company. Holders of common stock have the greatest control over the management of the company but the last claim on its earnings and assets — and therein lies their risk. However, after the fixed claims of the senior securities (bonds, debentures, and preferred stock) have been met, common stockholders are entitled to share in all the company's further earnings. Other benefits of stock ownership include the possibility of long-term capital appreciation (as the company becomes more profitable, the stock becomes more valuable), dividends, and liquidity, which permits a quick profit or a quick retreat.

A stock's market value is affected by a variety of factors, including competition, the quality of the company's management, the market in which it sells its products or services, and changes in technology or government regulations. Interest rates and foreign exchange rates also exert a major impact, as do broad business cycles, changing consumer habits, and demographic patterns.

Stocks are generally undervalued when the economic outlook is bleak, earnings are down, and unemployment high. At those times many investors are attracted to the high interest rates on Certificates of Deposit (CDs) and T-bills; this provides an opportunity for the bargain hunter who diligently seeks out well-managed companies with prospects for future growth. When the economy is particularly good — when inflation and interests are down and earnings up — stock prices are at their peak. Some investors see this as the time to sell stocks purchased in gloomier days and invest in T-bills, CDs, or real estate.

No one can consistently predict the performance of the stock market. However, some analysts believe that certain long-term trends follow established patterns. Patterns do change, but the following generalizations are often made.

- Interest rates are the single most powerful force for the stock market as a whole. When interest rates go down, the stock market tends to go up, and vice versa.

- The stock market tends to rally in the summertime, suggesting that prices in June will be lower than in September or at the end of the year.

- January, and the first five days in particular, are believed by some to set the pattern for the following year.

The Dow Jones Averages

The Dow Jones Industrial Average (DJIA), the oldest and most widely used stock market average, is currently based on the stocks of the 30 corporations, which represent 15% of the total value of shares traded on the New York Stock Exchange (NYSE). (The components have changed over the years to reflect consumer tastes, technological development, and

American involvement in international business.) The average is determined by dividing the closing prices of the component stocks by a divisor that factors in stock splits and dividends.

The Dow Jones Transportation Average (DJTA) tracks the stocks of 20 major transportation companies, and the Dow Jones Utilities Average (DJUA) tracks 15 major utility companies. Components of both these averages are also changed from time to time to reflect current trends in the market.

How to Read Quotations from the New York and American Stock Exchanges

Stock quotations are printed in most newspapers in an eleven-column format.

(1)	(2)	(3)	(4)	(5)	(6)	(7)	(8)	(9)	(10)	(11)
52-week				Yld	P-E	Sales				Net
High	Low	Stock	Div.	(%)	Ratio	100s	High	Low	Last	Chg.
24⅞	18¼	Goldm pf	2.50	10	...	10	24¼	24¼	24¼	− ⅛
27⅝	23	GorRup	1.12	4.4	10	1	25½	25½	25½	...
25¾	19¾	GouldT	1.40r	6.1	8	2	23	23	23	+ ¼
30¼	26½	GouldT pf	3.25	12	...	158	26⅝	d26	26⅝	−2¾
13	8⅝	GrahCp	.32	2.8	...	10	11⅝	11½	11⅝	+ ¼

Columns 1 and 2 — the highest and lowest prices paid per share in the past 52 weeks, shown in one-eighths of a dollar (12 ⅛ = $12.125).

Column 3 — an abbreviation of the company's name.

Column 4 — the regular dividend paid.

Column 5 — the yield (computed by dividing the annual dividend by the current price of the stock; stock that sells for $30.00 a share and pays an annual dividend of $3.00 a share yields 10%).

Column 6 — the price-earnings ratio (computed by dividing the current price of the stock by the company's most current annual earnings per share; see page 3.55 for further discussion of the p/e ratio).

Column 7 — number of shares traded that day (in hundreds of shares).

Columns 8, 9, and 10 — the highest, the lowest, and closing price paid per share on that day.

Column 11 — the difference between the day's closing price and that at the close of the previous trading day.

Explanations of other symbols in the quotations are usually given at the end of the listing. In the example shown here: pf = preferred shares; r = dividends paid or declared in the preceding twelve months; d = a new 52-week low.

OVER-THE-COUNTER MARKET (OTC)

Securities not listed on major exchanges are traded over-the-counter by broker-dealers who are members of the National Association of Securities Dealers Automated Quotations (NASDAQ) system. Some 3,000 stocks — mostly industrials — are traded on this market.

How to Read the NASDAQ Over-the-Counter Quotations

Newspapers generally print quotations for the national over-the-counter market (generally, the better-capitalized and longer-established OTC stocks) in an eight-column format.

(1) 365-day High	(2) Low	(3) Stock	(4) Sales (100s)	(5) High	(6) Low	(7) Last	(8) Net Chg.
23¼	14¾	South Trust	287	23	22¼	23	+¼
14¾	8½	SP Drug 10i	66	14¼	14	14	...
5⅝	1¾	Space Mirhv	104	2⅝	2½	2⅝	...

Columns 1 and 2 — the highest and lowest prices paid for the stock in the previous 52 weeks.

Column 3 — an abbreviated name for the company and an indication of the kind of business.

Column 4 — the number of shares traded that day (in hundreds of shares).

Columns 5, 6, and 7 — the highest, the lowest, and the closing price paid per share on that day.

Column 8 — the net change in the closing bid price from that of the previous trading day.

This listing also indicates that SP Drug paid a 10% stock dividend in the past year.

How to Read Other OTC Quotations

OTC stocks not listed in the NASDAQ network are generally listed in a ''Bid and Asked'' format, reflecting the buying and selling prices that dealers in those securities are willing to accept.

(1) Stock	(2) Div.	(3) Sales (100s)	(4) Bid	(5) Asked	(6) Net Chg.
ComrceBcsh	2	50	46	46½	+1
ComrClHs	1.92	59	76	77	+1

Columns 1 and 2 — an abbreviated name for the company and the annual regular dividend, when appropriate.

Column 3 — number of shares sold that day, in hundreds.

Column 4 — bid price (the price at which a broker-dealer will buy the stock from an investor).

Column 5 — ask price (price at which a broker-dealer will sell the stock).

Column 6 — net change in the closing bid price from that of the previous day.

THE 65 COMPONENTS OF THE DOW JONES AVERAGES

Industrial Average

Allied Corporation	Inco
Aluminum Company of America	IBM
American Brands	International Harvester
American Can	International Paper
American Express	Merck
AT&T	3M
Bethlehem Steel	Owens-Illinois
Chevron	Procter & Gamble
DuPont	Sears Roebuck
Eastman Kodak	Texaco
Exxon	Union Carbide
General Electric	United Technologies
General Foods	US Steel
General Motors	Westinghouse
Goodyear	Woolworth

Transportation Average

AMR	NWA
Burlington Northern	Overnite Transportation
Canadian Pacific	Pan Am
Carolina Freight	Rio Grande Industries
Consolidated Freight	Santa Fe Southern Pacific
CSX	Transway International
Delta Air Lines	TWA
Eastern Air Lines	UAL
Federal Express	Union Pac
Norfolk Southern	USAir Group

Utility Average

American Electric Power	Niagara Mohawk Power
Cleveland Electric Illumination	Pacific Gas & Electric
Columbia Gas System	Panhandle Eastern
Commonwealth Edison	Peoples Energy
Consolidated Edison	Philadelphia Electric
Consolidated Natural Gas	Public Service Electric & Gas
Detroit Edison	Southern California Edison
Houston Industries	

DOW JONES AVERAGES
Annual Highs & Lows

Year	Industrials		Transportation		Utilities	
	High	Low	High	Low	High	Low
1908	87.67	58.62	120.05	86.04		
1909	100.53	79.91	134.46	113.90		
1910	98.34	73.62	129.90	105.59		
1911	87.06	72.94	123.86	109.80		
1912	94.15	80.15	124.35	114.92		
1913	88.57	72.11	118.10	100.50		
1914	83.43	71.42	109.43	89.41		
1915	99.21	54.22	108.28	87.85		
1916	110.15	84.96	112.28	99.11		
1917	99.18	65.95	105.76	70.75		
1918	89.07	73.38	92.91	77.21		
1919	119.62	79.15	91.13	73.63		
1920	109.88	66.75	85.37	67.83		
1921	81.50	63.90	77.56	65.52		
1922	103.43	78.59	93.99	74.43		
1923	105.38	85.76	90.63	76.78		
1924	120.51	88.33	99.50	80.23		
1925	159.39	115.00	112.93	92.82		
1926	166.64	135.20	123.23	102.41		
1927	202.40	152.73	144.82	119.92		
1928	300.00	191.33	152.70	132.60		
1929	381.17	198.69	189.11	128.07	144.61	64.72
1930	294.07	157.51	157.94	91.65	108.62	55.14
1931	194.36	73.79	111.58	31.42	73.40	30.55
1932	88.78	41.22	41.20	13.23	36.11	16.53
1933	108.67	50.16	56.53	23.42	37.73	19.33
1934	110.74	85.51	52.97	33.19	31.03	16.83
1935	148.44	96.71	41.84	27.31	29.78	14.46
1936	184.90	143.11	59.89	40.66	36.08	28.63
1937	194.40	113.64	64.46	28.91	37.54	19.65
1938	158.41	98.95	33.98	19.00	25.19	15.14
1939	155.62	121.44	35.90	24.14	27.10	20.71
1940	152.80	111.84	32.67	22.14	26.45	18.03
1941	139.59	106.34	30.88	24.25	20.65	13.51
1942	119.71	92.92	29.28	23.31	14.94	10.58
1943	145.82	119.26	38.30	27.59	22.30	14.69
1944	152.53	134.22	48.40	33.45	26.37	21.74
1945	195.82	151.35	64.89	47.03	39.15	26.15
1946	212.50	163.12	63.31	44.69	43.74	33.20
1947	186.85	163.21	53.42	41.16	37.55	32.28
1948	193.16	165.39	64.95	48.13	36.04	31.65
1949	200.52	161.60	54.29	41.03	41.31	33.36
1950	235.47	196.81	77.89	51.24	44.26	37.40
1951	276.37	238.99	90.08	72.39	47.22	41.47
1952	292.00	256.35	112.63	82.03	52.64	47.53
1953	293.79	255.49	112.21	90.56	53.88	47.87
1954	404.39	279.87	146.23	94.84	62.47	52.22

Dow Jones Averages

Year	Industrials		Transportation		Utilities	
	High	Low	High	Low	High	Low
1955	488.40	388.20	167.83	137.84	66.68	61.39
1956	521.05	462.35	181.23	150.44	71.77	63.03
1957	520.77	419.79	157.67	95.67	74.61	62.10
1958	583.65	436.89	157.91	99.89	91.00	68.94
1959	679.36	574.46	173.56	146.65	94.70	85.05
1960	685.47	566.05	160.43	123.37	100.07	85.02
1961	734.91	610.25	152.92	131.06	135.90	99.75
1962	726.01	535.76	149.83	114.86	130.85	103.11
1963	767.21	646.69	179.46	142.03	144.37	129.19
1964	891.71	766.08	224.91	178.81	155.71	137.30
1965	969.26	840.59	249.55	187.29	163.32	149.84
1966	995.15	744.32	271.72	184.34	152.39	118.96
1967	943.08	786.41	274.49	205.16	140.43	120.97
1968	985.21	825.13	279.48	214.58	141.30	119.79
1969	968.85	769.93	279.88	169.03	139.95	106.31
1970	842.00	631.16	183.31	116.69	121.84	95.86
1971	950.82	797.97	248.33	169.70	128.39	108.03
1972	1036.27	889.15	275.71	121.24	124.14	105.06
1973	1051.70	788.31	228.10	151.97	120.72	84.42
1974	891.66	577.60	202.45	125.93	95.09	57.93
1975	881.81	632.04	174.57	146.47	87.07	72.02
1976	1014.79	858.71	237.03	175.69	108.38	84.52
1977	999.75	800.85	246.64	199.60	118.67	104.97
1978	907.74	742.12	261.49	199.31	110.98	96.35
1979	879.61	796.67	271.77	205.78	109.74	98.24
1980	1000.17	759.13	425.68	233.69	117.34	96.04
1981	1024.05	824.01	447.38	335.48	117.81	101.28
1982	1070.55	776.92	464.55	292.12	122.83	103.22
1983	1287.20	1027.04	612.57	434.24	140.70	119.51
1984	1286.64	1086.57	612.63	444.03	149.93	122.25

Note: *The industrial average was composed of 12 stocks when the New York Stock Exchange closed in July 1914, because of World War I. In September 1916, a new list of 20 stocks was adopted and computed back to the opening of the Exchange on December 12, 1914. On October 1, 1928 the number of stocks comprising the industrial average was increased to 30. On March 7, 1928 transportation components were increased to 20 from 12. Since June 2, 1938 the utility average has been based on 15 stocks instead of 20.*

Source: *Dow Jones Investor's Handbook, 1985.*

DOW JONES INDEXES
(Average of Annual Highs and Lows)

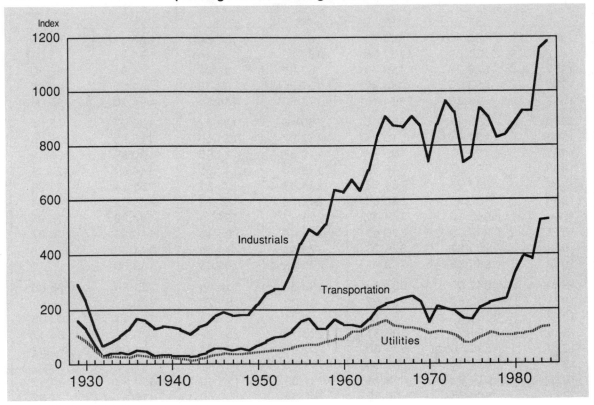

DOW JONES INDUSTRIAL AVERAGES
(Annual Highs and Lows)

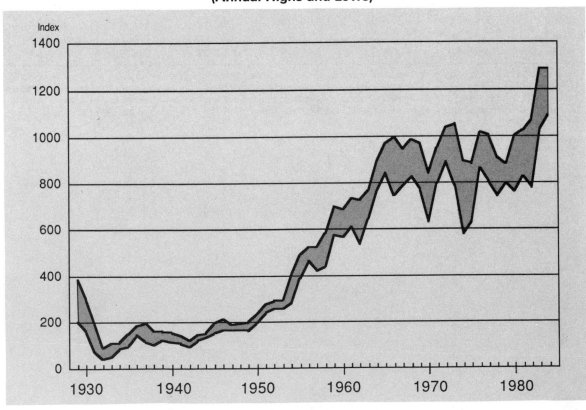

DOW JONES TRANSPORTATION AVERAGES
(Annual Highs and Lows)

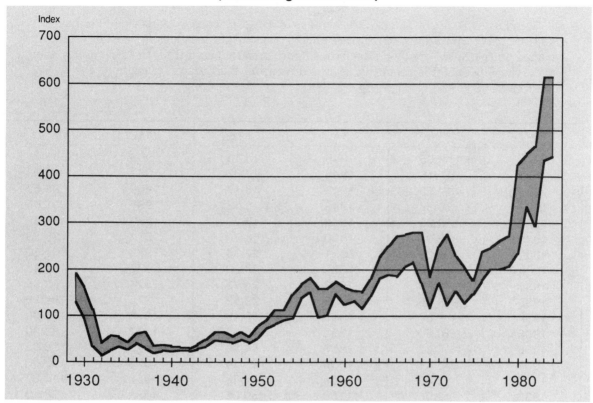

DOW JONES UTILITIES AVERAGES
(Annual Highs and Lows)

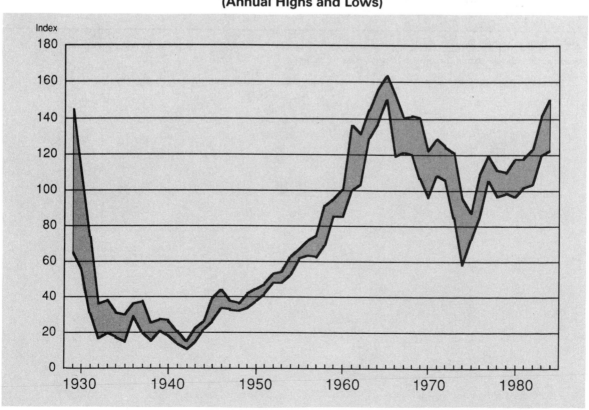

STANDARD & POOR'S 500 STOCK INDEX

Standard & Poor's 500 Stock Index tracks 500 leading corporations — 400 industrials, 40 financial corporations, 40 utilities, and 20 transportation stocks — most of which are traded on the New York Stock Exchange. More broadly based than the Dow Jones Averages, the S & P 500 is generally regarded as a more accurate reflector of the overall market.

Year	Average	Year	Average	Year	Average
1924	9.05	1945	15.16	1966	85.26
1925	11.15	1946	17.08	1967	91.93
1926	12.59	1947	15.17	1968	98.69
1927	15.34	1948	15.53	1969	97.84
1928	19.95	1949	15.23	1970	83.22
1929	26.02	1950	18.40	1971	98.29
1930	21.03	1951	22.34	1972	109.20
1931	13.66	1952	24.50	1973	107.40
1932	6.93	1953	24.73	1974	82.85
1933	8.96	1954	29.69	1975	86.16
1934	9.84	1955	40.49	1976	102.00
1935	10.60	1956	46.62	1977	98.20
1936	15.47	1957	44.38	1978	96.02
1937	15.41	1958	46.24	1979	103.00
1938	11.49	1959	57.38	1980	118.80
1939	12.06	1960	55.85	1981	128.10
1940	11.02	1961	68.27	1982	119.71
1941	9.82	1962	62.38	1983	160.41
1942	8.67	1963	69.87	1984	160.50
1943	11.50	1964	81.37		
1944	12.47	1965	88.17		

Note: *Annual average for 1941–43 = 10.*

Sources: Standard & Poor's Corporation; *Federal Reserve Bulletin.*

STANDARD & POOR'S 500 STOCK INDEX
(Annual Average)

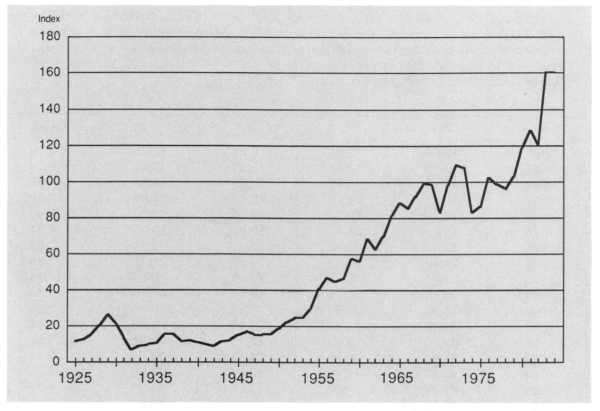

NEW YORK STOCK EXCHANGE
Composite Stock Index

The NYSE Composite Index represents price movements of all the common stocks — over 2,000 — listed on the New York exchange. The index is weighted according to the number of shares listed for each issue, and point values are also converted to dollars and cents to provide a measure of price action. (The base for the index sets $50.00 to represent prices at the close of trading on December 31, 1965.)

Year	Open	High	Low	Close	Change
1950	10.06	12.01	9.85	12.01	+ 2.10
1951	12.28	13.89	12.28	13.60	+ 1.59
1952	13.70	14.49	13.31	14.49	+ 0.89
1953	14.65	14.65	12.62	13.60	− 0.89
1954	13.70	19.40	13.70	19.40	+ 5.80
1955	19.05	23.71	19.05	23.71	+ 4.31
1956	23.56	25.90	22.55	24.35	+ 0.64
1957	24.43	26.30	20.92	21.11	− 3.24
1958	21.71	28.85	21.45	28.85	+ 7.74
1959	29.54	32.39	28.94	32.15	+ 3.30
1960	31.99	31.99	28.38	30.94	− 1.21
1961	31.17	38.60	31.17	38.39	+ 7.45
1962	37.34	38.02	28.20	33.81	− 4.58
1963	34.41	39.92	34.41	39.92	+ 6.11
1964	40.47	46.49	40.47	45.65	+ 5.73
1965	45.37	50.00	43.64	50.00	+ 4.35
1966	49.86	51.06	39.37	43.72	− 6.28
1967	43.74	54.16	43.74	53.83	+10.11
1968	53.68	61.27	48.70	58.90	+ 5.07
1969	58.94	59.32	49.31	51.53	− 7.37
1970	52.10	52.36	37.69	50.23	− 1.30
1971	49.73	57.76	49.60	56.43	+ 6.20
1972	56.23	65.14	56.23	64.48	+ 8.05
1973	65.06	65.48	49.05	51.82	−12.66
1974	51.98	53.37	32.89	36.13	+15.69
1975	37.06	51.24	37.06	47.64	+11.51
1976	48.04	57.88	48.04	57.88	+10.24
1977	57.69	57.69	49.78	52.50	− 5.38
1978	51.82	60.38	48.37	53.62	+ 1.12
1979	53.93	63.39	53.88	61.95	+ 8.33
1980	60.69	81.02	55.30	77.86	+15.91
1981	78.26	79.14	64.96	71.11	− 6.75
1982	81.33	82.35	58.80	81.03	+ 9.92
1983	79.79	99.63	79.79	95.18	+14.15
1984	95.18	98.12	85.13	96.38	+ 1.30

Note: *December 31, 1965 = 50.*

Source: *Dow Jones Investor's Handbook,* 1985.

NEW YORK STOCK EXCHANGE
(Composite Stock Index)

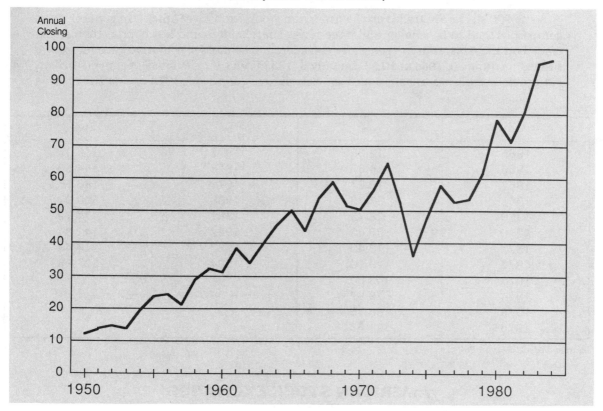

AMERICAN STOCK EXCHANGE
Total Index

Some 900 stocks are traded on the American Stock Exchange (Amex). In general, these companies tend to be smaller and have fewer shareholders and less capital than stocks traded on the NYSE; thus are generally considered to be more speculative. The index was started on June 30, 1965 at 10.90. On July 5, 1983 it was recalculated, which effectively cut previous readings in half; under the new system August 31, 1973 equals 100.

Year	Index	Year	Index
1965	12.05	1977	116.18
1966	14.67	1978	144.56
1967	19.67	1979	186.56
1968	27.72	1980	300.94
1969	28.73	1981	171.79
1970	96.63	1982	141.31
1971	113.40	1983	216.48
1972	129.10	1984	207.96
1973	103.80		
1974	79.97		
1975	83.15		
1976	101.63		

Source: *Federal Reserve Bulletin.*

AMERICAN STOCK EXCHANGE
(Total Index)

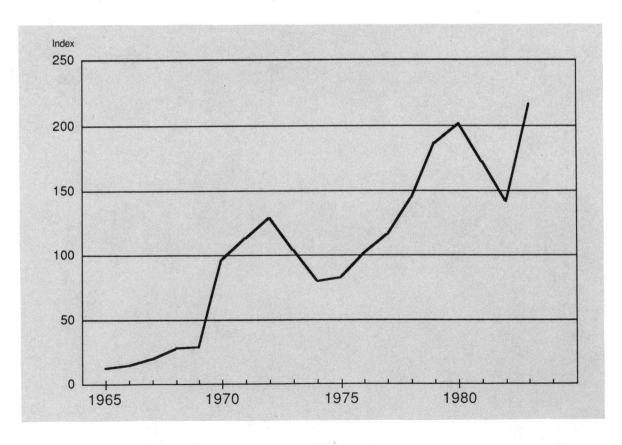

OVER-THE-COUNTER
Annual NASDAQ Indexes

Category	High	Low	Last	% Change
1977 Composite	**105.05**	**93.66**	**105.05**	**7.3**
Industrials	109.43	96.29	109.43	9.3
Financial	105.65	97.04	105.53	3.9
Insurance	115.01	96.14	114.51	8.8
Utilities	101.68	87.04	101.03	16.2
Banks	96.02	89.64	95.28	2.8
Transportation	104.40	91.60	97.68	−3.6
1978 Composite	**139.25**	**99.09**	**117.98**	**12.3**
Industrials	155.79	101.91	126.85	15.9
Financial	129.97	101.10	114.43	8.90
Insurance	144.14	106.71	127.24	11.1
Utilities	116.73	93.23	106.04	5.0
Banks	111.56	93.96	102.33	7.4
Transportation	128.71	92.92	100.53	2.9
1979 Composite	**152.29**	**117.84**	**151.14**	**28.1**
Industrials	175.18	126.88	175.18	38.1
Financial	139.50	114.18	130.92	14.4
Insurance	166.31	126.58	162.03	27.3
Utilities	130.41	106.27	130.41	23.0
Banks	115.81	102.09	108.24	5.8
Transportation	133.42	100.76	118.47	17.8
1980 Composite	**208.15**	**124.09**	**202.34**	**33.9**
Industrials	274.70	145.03	261.36	49.2
Financial	154.07	106.35	154.07	17.7
Insurance	184.71	128.74	166.81	3.0
Utilities	165.92	106.01	165.70	27.1
Banks	118.58	91.99	118.39	9.4
Transportation	179.20	100.55	164.19	39.0
1981 Composite	**223.47**	**175.03**	**195.84**	**−3.2**
Industrials	283.03	204.62	229.29	−12.3
Financial	182.10	154.61	176.20	14.4
Insurance	204.77	166.10	194.31	16.5
Utilities	190.59	148.69	181.67	9.6
Banks	144.06	118.59	143.13	20.9
Transportation	201.71	155.99	167.88	2.2
1982 Composite	**240.70**	**159.14**	**232.41**	**18.7**
Industrials	281.64	177.70	273.58	19.3
Financial	216.40	154.45	207.50	15.8
Insurance	236.76	163.78	226.40	16.5
Utilities	316.17	168.02	286.23	57.6
Banks	160.73	127.84	156.37	9.2
Transportation	205.81	145.26	195.48	16.5

(Continued)

Over-The-Counter

Category	High	Low	Last	% Change
1983 Composite	**328.91**	**230.59**	**278.60**	**19.9**
Industrials	408.42	270.55	323.68	18.3
Financial	284.39	206.86	277.53	33.7
Insurance	287.34	217.33	257.63	13.8
Utilities	391.37	257.12	269.39	−5.9
Banks	203.75	155.68	203.75	30.3
Transportation	293.76	194.27	280.80	43.6
1984 Composite	**287.90**	**231.93**	**247.35**	**−11.2**
Industrials	336.16	250.18	260.73	−19.4
Financial	298.62	252.34	298.62	+7.6
Insurance	283.91	226.87	283.11	+9.9
Utilities	280.54	194.33	238.66	−11.4
Banks	229.77	192.99	229.77	+12.8
Transportation	290.70	194.33	239.29	−14.8

Source: *Dow Jones Investor's Handbook*, 1985.

NASDAQ OVER-THE-COUNTER INDEXES
(Annual Highs and Lows)

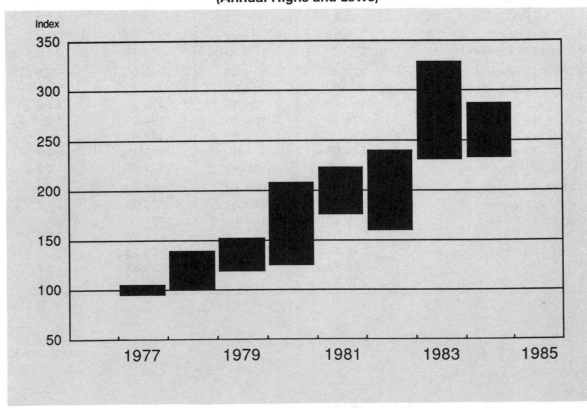

PRICE/EARNINGS RATIOS FOR COMMON STOCKS
Standard & Poor's 500

Price-earnings ratios (the current market price of the stock divided by the annual earnings) are used to make comparisons among stocks and to track the performance of any specific stock. In general, investors are prepared to pay higher prices in relation to earnings for the stock of fast-growing companies.

Year	P/E	Year	P/E
1950	6.84	1969	16.53
1951	9.60	1970	15.48
1952	10.54	1971	18.48
1953	9.86	1972	18.18
1954	11.43	1973	14.04
1955	12.44	1974	8.62
1956	13.95	1975	10.93
1957	12.18	1976	11.24
1958	19.46	1977	9.27
1959	16.89	1978	8.31
1960	17.01	1979	7.43
1961	21.10	1980	7.90
1962	16.50	1981	8.36
1963	17.61	1982	8.62
1964	18.05	1983	12.45
1965	17.04	1984, Sept.	10.04
1966	14.88		
1967	17.51		
1968	17.12		

Sources: *Federal Reserve Bulletin; Economic Indicators.*

PRICE/EARNINGS RATIOS FOR COMMON STOCKS
Standard & Poor's 500

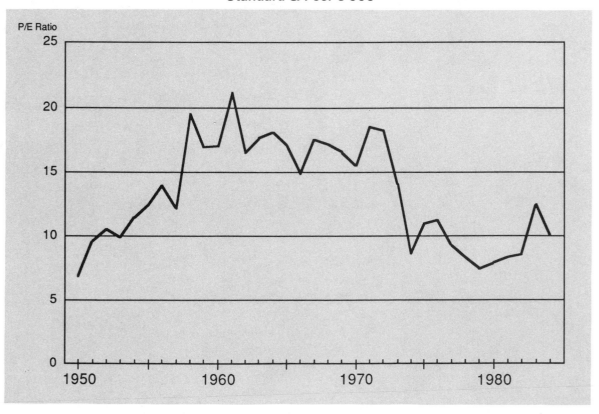

COMMON STOCK YIELDS
Dividend/Price Ratio (Standard & Poor's 500)

The current yield is equal to the annual dividends on either common or preferred stock expressed as a percentage of price.

Year	% Annual Yield	Year	% Annual Yield
1950	14.61	1969	6.05
1951	10.42	1970	6.46
1952	9.49	1971	5.41
1953	10.14	1972	5.50
1954	8.75	1973	7.12
1955	8.04	1974	11.60
1956	7.17	1975	9.15
1957	8.21	1976	8.90
1958	5.14	1977	10.79
1959	5.92	1978	12.03
1960	5.88	1979	13.46
1961	4.74	1980	12.66
1962	6.06	1981	11.96
1963	5.68	1982	11.60
1964	5.54	1983	8.03
1965	5.87	1984, Sept.	9.96
1966	6.72		
1967	5.71		
1968	5.84		

Sources: *Federal Reserve Bulletin; Economic Indicators.*

PREFERRED STOCK YIELDS
Dividend/Price Ratio

Dividends on preferred stock must be paid before dividends on common stock. However, preferred stock dividends are subordinate to the claims of bondholders. Regular dividends are due and frequently are cumulative, which means that any omitted dividend payment must be paid before any dividend is paid on the common stock. Preferred stock also has a prior claim on the assets of the company in event of liquidation. However, because all these prior claims are fixed, preferred stock — unlike common stock — cannot benefit from appreciation due to rising corporate earnings.

Year	% Annual Yield	Year	% Annual Yield
1920	6.79	1970	7.22
1925	5.90	1971	6.75
1930	4.95	1972	7.27
1935	4.63	1973	7.23
1940	4.14	1974	8.23
1945	3.70	1975	8.38
1950	3.85	1976	7.97
1955	4.01	1977	7.60
1960	4.75	1978	8.25
1961	4.66	1979	9.07
1962	4.50	1980	10.57
1963	4.30	1981	12.36
1964	4.32	1982	12.53
1965	4.33	1983	11.02
1966	4.97	1984	11.59
1967	5.34		
1968	5.78		
1969	6.41		

Note: *Ratio based on a sample of 10 issues: 4 public utilities, 4 industrials, 1 financial, 1 transportation.*

Source: *Federal Reserve Bulletin.*

CORPORATE PROFITS
(Billions of Dollars)

Year	Corporate Profits Before Taxes	Corporate Tax Liability	Corporate Profits After Taxes		
			Total	Dividend Payments	Undistributed Profits
1956	48.8	21.7	27.2	11.3	15.9
1957	47.2	21.2	26.0	11.7	14.2
1958	41.4	19.0	22.3	11.6	10.8
1959	52.1	23.7	28.5	12.6	15.9
1960	49.7	23.0	26.7	13.4	13.2
1961	50.3	23.1	27.2	13.8	13.5
1962	55.4	24.2	31.2	15.2	16.0
1963	58.6	26.0	32.6	15.8	16.8
1964	64.8	27.6	37.2	17.2	19.9
1965	77.8	31.3	46.5	19.8	26.7
1966	84.2	34.3	49.9	20.8	29.1
1967	79.8	33.2	46.6	21.4	25.3
1968	87.6	39.9	47.8	23.6	24.2
1969	84.9	40.1	44.8	24.3	20.5
1970	74.0	34.8	39.3	24.7	14.6
1971	86.6	37.5	49.0	22.9	26.1
1972	100.6	41.6	58.9	24.4	34.5
1973	125.6	49.0	76.6	27.0	49.6
1974	136.7	51.6	85.1	29.9	55.2
1975	132.1	50.6	81.5	30.8	50.7
1976	166.3	63.8	102.5	37.4	65.1
1977	194.7	72.7	122.0	40.8	81.2
1978	229.1	83.2	145.9	47.0	98.9
1979	252.7	87.6	165.1	52.7	112.4
1980	234.6	84.8	149.8	58.6	91.2
1981	221.2	81.1	140.0	66.5	73.5
1982	165.5	60.7	104.8	69.2	35.6
1983	203.2	75.8	127.4	72.9	54.5
1984	236.2	90.0	146.2	80.5	65.7

Note: *Quarterly data seasonally adjusted.*

Source: *Economic Indicators.*

CORPORATE PROFITS

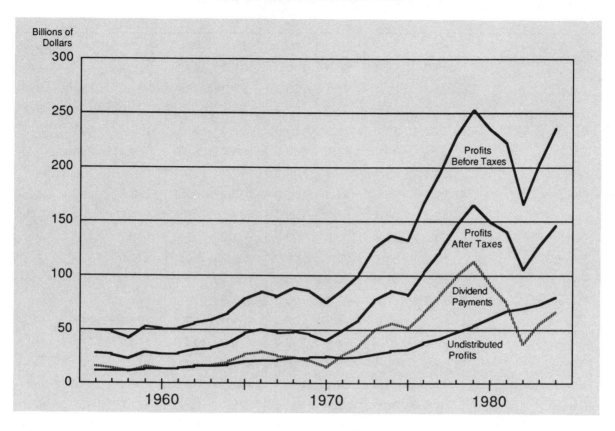

INTERNATIONAL STOCK INDEXES

Country	1977	1978	1979	1980	1981	1982	1983–Q4	1984 Mar.	1984 June
Australia	48.0	54.4	66.9	100.0	104.2	79.5	115.2	117.0	—
Austria[1]	101.5	95.1	96.8	100.0	89.1	79.4	87.2	78.8	86.8
Belgium	92.0	93.0	102.0	100.0	81.0	96.0	130.0	145.0	149.0
Canada	46.2	50.6	73.3	100.0	97.4	77.9	116.4	114.4	—
Chile	7.9	22.7	37.2	100.0	82.9	65.0	58.1	70.6	—
Colombia	60.4	89.4	115.7	100.0	117.7	150.6	—	—	—
Finland	79.5	76.9	93.9	100.0	102.9	137.7	256.0	286.1	303.8
France[2]	52.1	68.1	87.2	100.0	88.1	85.4	134.0	129.0	—
Germany, Fed. Rep. of	104.0	109.0	105.5	100.0	101.2	99.0	147.7	149.5	147.3
India[3]	69.7	81.0	92.7	100.0	122.7	120.1	132.0	133.4	—
Ireland	62.8	95.0	101.7	100.0	103.7	84.9	126.0	146.4	143.4
Israel[4]	17.5	26.0	37.2	100.0	2544.5	997.4	1,894.1	3,312.4	—
Italy	63.0	63.9	78.7	100.0	151.7	123.1	152.9	174.9	—
Japan[5]	79.5	87.6	94.9	100.0	116.3	115.8	146.1	171.5	—
Netherlands	107.5	108.1	106.7	100.0	105.6	107.3	170.1	190.1	—
New Zealand	70.0	71.0	77.0	100.0	142.0	139.0	230.0	256.0	—
Norway	69.0	59.0	83.0	100.0	98.0	92.0	161.0	195.0	195.0
Pakistan[6]	82.6	93.8	108.3	100.0	98.9	108.4	154.2	186.8	—
Peru	42.7	63.6	59.1	100.0	112.4	100.7	—	—	—
Philippines[7]	86.9	110.3	132.8	100.0	79.7	65.2	59.0	54.0	—
Spain[5]	154.3	124.5	107.2	100.0	127.3	116.8	126.3	148.6	153.6
Sweden	87.0	92.0	92.0	100.0	149.0	185.0	397.0	437.0	401.0
Switzerland	99.0	95.3	105.5	100.0	91.0	98.7	125.8	129.7	121.7
United Kingdom[8]	73.1	82.4	93.6	100.0	112.8	130.7	169.9	195.1	188.4
United States	80.6	78.9	85.4	100.0	107.2	99.3	138.8	132.2	129.5
Venezuela	217.5	151.7	122.7	100.0	86.8	112.1	—	—	—
Zimbabwe	47.4	44.5	82.6	100.0	47.8	34.8	26.0	25.6	21.5

Note: *Prices at year end, unless specified otherwise.*
1 *Friday quotations in Vienna.*
3 *Daily quotations in four cities.*
5 *General Index.*
7 *Commercial and industrial quotations.*

2 *Quotations on the Paris stock exchange.*
4 *End of month quotations.*
6 *Last Friday of the month quotations.*
8 *Last Tuesday of the month quotations.*

Source: International Monetary Fund.

3.03 Economic Indicators

Among the most important measures of the nation's economic condition are: gross national product (GNP), money supply, federal budget surplus or deficit, the index of leading economic indicators, U.S. current account balance in international transactions, trade balance, and foreign exchange rates.

Money Supply and GNP

Changes in money supply have both immediate and delayed effects on spending and GNP. Thus the Federal Reserve must carefully monitor the short- and long-term repercussions of any expansionary monetary policy it initiates. By studying changes in the money supply, investors can estimate future changes in the GNP and possibly anticipate business expansions or cutbacks.

Federal Deficits and GNP

Another critical element influencing the GNP is the national debt. Budget deficits require the federal government to either print or borrow more money. If it borrows, we acquire a national debt in the form of government bonds. If the federal debt grows at a faster rate than the GNP, taxes may have to be increased to meet the interest payments on the bonds. Such tax increases can reduce work incentives, decrease production, and eventually slow down the economy. A higher budget deficit absorbs capital otherwise available for investment spending, resulting in less production and less consumption. Ultimately, higher interest rates shift resources away from private investment and into the hands of government.

International Factors and GNP

U.S. transactions with other countries and foreign exchange rates also affect the GNP. A deficit in the U.S. balance of payments means that we are paying out more money abroad than we are taking in. When the dollar is strong, foreign goods become less expensive here, and U.S. consumers enjoy import bargains at the expense of domestic products. In addition, the prices of United States products become less competitive in overseas markets. These two factors cause reductions in domestic production and a slowing or declining GNP.

CYCLICAL ECONOMIC INDICATORS

Series (and Unit of Measure)	1974	1975	1976	1977	1978	1979	1980	1981	1982	1983	1984	1985[1]
Leading Indicators: Composite (1967 = 100)	**121.2**	**115.7**	**130.9**	**139.4**	**145.8**	**145.1**	**138.2**	**140.9**	**136.8**	**156.0**	**165.8**	**167.5**
Net business formation (1967 = 100)	109.2	107.0	115.6	123.2	128.2	128.3	122.4	118.6	113.2	114.8	117.1	118.0
New building permits (1967 = 100)[2]	92.2	80.9	111.8	144.9	145.4	123.6	96.7	80.0	80.7	129.4	133.3	129.3
Stock prices (1941-43 = 100)[3]	82.8	86.2	102.0	98.2	96.0	103.0	118.8	128.0	119.7	160.4	160.5	180.9
Initial state unemployment insurance claims (000)[4]	351	468	381	368	338	379	480	446	578	426	366	402
Change in sensitive materials prices (%)[5,6]	-0.1	-0.3	1.1	4	1.3	0.9	0	-0.6	-0.7	1.0	-0.2	-0.8
Change in credit outstanding (% annual rate)[6,7]	10.5	3.5	10.1	15.4	14.6	13.4	6.2	7.3	1.9	5.7	15.2	10.6
Vendor performance (%)[6,8]	66	30	54	55	64	63	40	45	37	54	61	48
Average workweek hours[9]	40.0	39.5	40.1	40.3	40.4	40.4	40.2	39.7	38.9	40.1	40.7	39.9
Change in inventories (annual rate; $ billions)[10,11]	10	-17	8	13	20	9	-8	1	-16	2	21.3	6.8
Contracts and orders for plant and equipment ($ billions)[11]	149	117	132	146	172	186	170	169	149	161	184.9	18.6
New orders for consumer goods and materials ($ billions)[11]	396	342	391	433	458	450	400	399	353	409	448	437.8
Money supply (M2) ($ billions)[11]	753	754	805	852	859	836	796	789	814	886	917	955
Coincident Indicators:												
Composite (1967 = 100)	**126.4**	**116.2**	**124.8**	**133.6**	**144.0**	**150.2**	**144.8**	**146.0**	**136.3**	**139.9**	**154.4**	**157.9**
Industrial production (1967 = 100)	129.3	117.8	130.5	138.2	146.1	152.5	147.1	151.0	138.6	147.6	163.3	164.9
Employees on nonagricultural payrolls (000,000)	78.3	76.9	79.4	82.5	86.7	89.8	90.4	91.2	89.6	90.1	94.2	96.2
Personal income (annual rate; $ billions)[11,12]	882	867	909	956	1,012	1,047	1,043	1,075	1,072	1,095	1,177	1,202
Manufacturing and trade sales ($ billions)[11]	167.2	156.9	168.2	179.7	190.1	184.2	188.7	190.9	152.5	161.7	176.1	180.0

(Continued)

Cyclical Economic Indicators

Series (and Unit of Measure)	1974	1975	1976	1977	1978	1979	1980	1981	1982	1983	1984	1985[1]
Lagging Indicators: Composite (1967 = 100)	**117.0**	**110.9**	**103.5**	**106.4**	**114.0**	**122.6**	**124.6**	**122.4**	**123.0**	**111.7**	**117.4**	**125.3**
Labor costs (%)[13]	99.0	104.6	100.0	100.2	99.6	98.7	102.0	100.2	101.0	95.4	90.1	88.9
Labor costs (1967 = 100)[14]	127.9	143.6	143.2	154.3	164.4	175.9	196.4	209.0	228.0	219.6	218.5	223.3
Ratio of consumer installment credit to personal income (%)[6]	13.6	13.0	12.9	13.6	14.4	14.9	14.3	13.3	13.1	12.7	13.8	15.0
Average prime rate charged by banks (%)	10.8	7.9	6.8	6.8	6.8	9.1	12.7	15.3	14.9	10.8	12.0	10.5
Average duration of employment (weeks)[4]	9.8	14.2	15.8	14.3	11.9	10.8	11.9	13.7	15.6	20.0	18.2	15.9
Ratio of inventories to sales[15]	1.6	1.7	1.6	1.6	1.6	1.6	1.7	1.7	1.7	1.6	1.5	1.6
Commercial and industrial loans outstanding ($000,000)[11,16]	96	90	80	79	82	87	89	92	106	104	115	126

1 *February.*
2 *Authorized for private housing units.*
3 *Standard and Poor's index of 500 common stocks.*
4 *A decrease in this series is considered an upward movement.*
5 *Producer price index of selected crude and intermediate materials and spot market price index of raw industrial materials.*
6 *Differences, rather than percentage change, are shown for this series.*
7 *Business and consumer borrowing.*
8 *Companies receiving slower deliveries.*
9 *For manufacturing production workers.*
10 *On hand and on order.*
11 *In 1972 dollars.*
12 *Less transfer payments.*
13 *Per unit of manufacturing output; actual data as a percentage of trend.*
14 *Per unit of manufacturing output; index of actual data.*
15 *For manufacturing and trade; in constant 1972 dollars.*
16 *Includes commercial paper issued by nonfinancial companies.*

Source: U.S. Bureau of Economic Analysis, *Business Conditions Digest.*

GROSS NATIONAL PRODUCT
(Billions of Dollars)

| Year or Quarter | Gross National Product | Personal Consumption Expenditures | Gross Private Domestic Investment | Net Exports of Goods and Services | | | Gov't. Purchases of Goods and Services | | | | | Final Sales |
| | | | | Net Exports | Exports | Imports | Total | Federal | | | State and Local | |
								Total	Nat'l. Defense	Non-Defense		
1929	103.4	77.3	16.2	1.1	7.0	5.9	8.8	1.4	—	—	7.4	101.7
1933	55.8	45.8	1.4	.4	2.4	2.0	8.2	2.1	—	—	6.1	57.4
1939	90.9	67.0	9.3	1.2	4.6	3.4	13.5	5.2	1.2	3.9	8.3	90.5
1940	100.0	71.0	13.1	1.8	5.4	3.6	14.2	6.1	2.2	3.9	8.1	97.8
1941	125.0	80.8	17.9	1.5	6.1	4.7	24.9	16.9	13.7	3.2	8.0	120.6
1942	158.5	88.6	9.9	.2	5.0	4.8	59.8	52.0	49.4	2.6	7.8	156.7
1943	192.1	99.4	5.8	−1.9	4.6	6.5	88.9	81.3	79.7	1.6	7.5	192.8
1944	210.6	108.2	7.2	−1.7	5.5	7.2	97.0	89.4	87.4	2.0	7.6	211.6
1945	212.4	119.5	10.6	−.5	7.4	7.9	82.8	74.6	73.5	1.1	8.2	213.5
1946	209.8	143.8	30.7	7.8	15.1	7.3	27.5	17.6	14.8	2.8	9.9	203.5
1947	233.1	161.7	34.0	11.9	20.2	8.3	25.5	12.7	9.0	3.7	12.8	233.5
1948	259.5	174.7	45.9	6.9	17.5	10.5	32.0	16.7	10.7	6.0	15.3	254.8
1949	258.3	178.1	35.3	6.5	16.3	9.8	38.4	20.4	13.2	7.2	18.0	261.4
1950	286.5	192.0	53.8	2.2	14.4	12.2	38.5	18.7	14.0	4.7	19.8	279.7
1951	330.8	207.1	59.2	4.4	19.7	15.3	60.1	38.3	33.5	4.8	21.8	320.5
1952	348.0	217.1	52.1	3.2	19.1	15.9	75.6	52.4	45.8	6.5	23.2	344.8
1953	366.8	229.7	53.3	1.3	18.0	16.7	82.5	57.5	48.6	8.9	25.0	366.3
1954	366.8	235.8	52.7	2.5	18.7	16.2	75.8	47.9	41.1	6.8	27.8	368.4
1955	400.0	253.7	68.4	3.0	21.0	18.0	75.0	44.5	38.4	6.0	30.6	394.1
1956	421.7	266.0	71.0	5.3	25.0	19.8	79.4	45.9	40.2	5.7	33.5	417.0
1957	444.0	280.4	69.2	7.3	28.1	20.8	87.1	50.0	44.0	5.9	37.1	442.6
1958	449.7	289.5	61.9	3.3	24.2	21.0	95.0	53.9	45.6	8.3	41.1	451.2
1959	487.9	310.8	78.1	1.4	24.8	23.4	97.6	53.9	45.6	8.3	43.7	482.2
1960	506.5	324.9	75.9	5.5	28.9	23.4	100.3	53.7	44.5	9.3	46.5	503.6
1961	524.6	335.0	74.8	6.6	29.9	23.3	108.2	57.4	47.0	10.4	50.8	522.2
1962	565.0	355.2	85.4	6.4	31.8	25.4	118.0	63.7	51.1	12.7	54.3	558.8
1963	596.7	374.6	90.9	7.6	34.2	26.6	123.7	64.6	50.3	14.3	59.0	590.7
1964	637.7	400.5	97.4	10.1	38.8	28.8	129.8	65.2	49.0	16.2	64.6	632.1
1965	691.1	430.4	113.5	8.8	41.1	32.3	138.4	67.3	49.4	17.8	71.1	681.2
1966	756.0	465.1	125.7	6.5	44.6	38.1	158.7	78.8	60.3	18.5	79.8	741.9
1967	799.6	490.3	122.8	6.3	47.3	41.0	180.2	90.9	71.5	19.5	89.3	789.3
1968	873.4	536.9	133.3	4.3	52.4	48.1	199.0	98.0	76.9	21.2	101.0	865.5
1969	944.0	581.8	149.3	4.2	57.5	53.3	208.8	97.6	76.3	21.2	111.2	934.2
1970	992.7	621.7	144.2	6.7	65.7	59.0	220.1	95.7	73.6	22.2	124.4	989.5
1971	1,077.6	672.2	166.4	4.1	68.8	64.7	234.9	96.2	70.2	26.0	138.7	1,070.0
1972	1,185.9	737.1	195.0	.7	77.5	76.7	253.1	101.7	73.1	28.5	151.4	1,175.7
1973	1,326.4	812.0	229.8	14.2	109.6	95.4	270.4	102.0	72.8	29.1	168.5	1,307.9
1974	1,434.2	888.1	228.7	13.4	146.2	132.8	304.1	111.0	77.0	33.9	193.1	1,420.1
1975	1,549.2	976.4	206.1	26.8	154.9	128.1	339.9	122.7	83.0	39.7	217.2	1,556.1
1976	1,718.0	1,084.3	257.9	13.8	170.9	157.1	362.1	129.2	86.0	43.2	232.9	1,706.2
1977	1,918.3	1,204.4	324.1	−4.0	182.7	186.7	393.8	143.4	92.8	50.6	250.4	1,895.3
1978	2,163.9	1,346.5	386.6	−1.1	218.7	219.8	431.9	153.6	100.3	53.3	278.3	2,137.4
1979	2,417.8	1,507.2	423.0	13.2	281.4	268.1	474.4	168.3	111.8	56.5	306.0	2,403.5
1980	2,631.7	1,668.1	401.9	23.9	338.8	314.8	537.8	197.0	131.2	65.9	340.8	2,641.5
1981	2,957.8	1,849.1	484.2	28.0	369.9	349.9	596.5	228.9	153.7	75.2	367.6	2,931.7

Gross National Product

Year or Quarter	Gross National Product	Personal Consumption Expenditures	Gross Private Domestic Investment	Net Exports of Goods and Services			Gov't. Purchases of Goods and Services					Final Sales
				Net Exports	Exports	Imports	Total	Federal			State and Local	
								Total	Nat'l. Defense	Non-Defense		
1982	3,069.3	1,984.9	414.9	19.0	348.4	329.4	650.5	258.9	179.5	79.4	391.5	3,095.4
Q1	3,026.0	1,931.3	436.2	27.7	359.4	331.7	630.9	249.8	168.4	81.4	381.1	3,043.1
Q2	3,061.2	1,960.9	431.2	35.5	366.3	330.8	633.7	245.0	175.3	69.7	388.7	3,072.1
Q3	3,080.1	2,001.3	415.9	6.6	346.3	339.7	656.3	261.6	183.3	78.2	394.7	3,095.5
Q4	3,109.6	2,046.1	376.2	6.3	321.7	315.4	681.0	279.4	191.0	88.4	401.6	3,170.8
1983	3,304.8	2,155.9	471.6	−8.3	336.2	344.4	685.5	269.7	200.5	69.3	415.8	3,318.3
Q1	3,173.8	2,070.4	405.0	19.6	328.5	308.9	678.8	273.0	194.7	78.3	405.8	3,216.8
Q2	3,267.0	2,141.6	449.6	−6.5	328.1	334.5	682.2	270.5	199.3	71.3	411.6	3,286.4
Q3	3,346.6	2,181.4	491.9	−16.4	342.0	358.4	689.8	269.2	200.9	68.3	420.6	3,350.9
Q4	3,431.7	2,230.2	540.0	−29.8	346.1	375.9	691.4	266.3	207.2	59.1	425.1	3,419.0
1984	3,662.8	2,341.8	637.8	−64.2	364.3	428.5	747.4	295.4	221.5	73.9	452.0	3,604.6
Q1	3,553.3	2,276.5	623.8	−51.5	358.9	410.4	704.4	267.6	213.4	54.2	436.8	3,479.5
Q2	3,644.7	2,332.7	627.0	−58.7	362.4	421.1	743.7	296.4	220.8	75.6	447.4	3,594.1
Q3	3,694.6	2,361.4	662.8	−90.6	368.6	459.3	761.0	302.0	220.3	81.7	458.9	3,622.8
Q4	3,758.7	2,396.5	637.8	−56.0	367.2	423.2	780.5	315.7	231.6	84.1	464.8	3,722.1

Note: *Quarterly data are seasonally adjusted; data for the third and fourth quarters of 1984 are preliminary.*

Sources: *Economic Report of the President,* February 1983; *Economic Indicators.*

GROSS NATIONAL PRODUCT

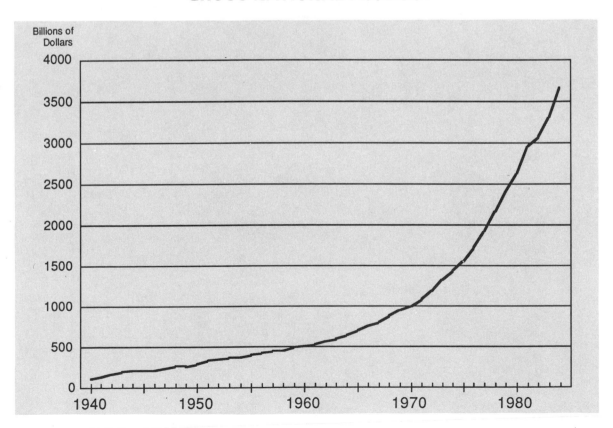

Money Supply

The Federal Reserve Bank monitors three principal measures of money supply:

- M1, the narrowest measure, is reported weekly and consists of currency in the hands of the public, demand deposits, interest-bearing accounts against which checks can be written (NOW accounts), credit-union share drafts, demand deposits at mutual savings banks, and travelers' checks.

- M2 is a broader indicator, reported monthly, that includes the M1 supply and money market mutual funds, overnight repurchase agreements issued by commercial banks, certain overnight Eurodollars, and savings and small time deposits (under $100,000). M2 is one of the factors in the government's monthly index of leading economic indicators. In recent decades, a prolonged fall in M2 has signaled an economic decline.

- M3, also reported monthly, includes the M2 supply plus large time deposits (over $100,000), term repurchase agreements, term Eurodollars, and institution-only money market mutual funds.

The Federal Reserve periodically specifies target growth rates for these money supply measures; targets are revised to meet certain objectives such as controlling inflation while keeping pace with economic growth. The growth ranges for 1984 were 4% to 8% for M1 and 6% to 9% for M2 and M3.

MONEY SUPPLY
(Billions of Dollars)

Year (Dec.)	M1	% Change	M2 (excluding Nonbank Thrift)	% Change	M2 (including Nonbank Thrift)	% Change
1920	$ 23.73	—	$ 34.80	—	$ 41.55	—
1925	25.66	8.1	42.05	20.8	52.55	26.5
1930	25.76	0.4	45.73	8.8	61.09	16.3
1935	25.88	0.5	39.07	−14.6	53.21	−12.9
1940	39.65	53.2	55.20	41.3	70.00	31.6
1945	99.23	150.3	126.63	129.4	147.83	111.2
1950	114.14	15.0	150.81	19.1	183.81	24.3
1955	134.44	17.8	183.69	21.8	240.53	30.9
1960	141.59	5.3	210.67	14.7	303.99	26.4
1961	143.93	1.7	221.24	5.0	324.62	6.8
1962	147.00	2.1	233.92	5.7	348.63	7.4
1963	151.28	2.9	249.15	6.5	377.76	8.4
1964	157.22	3.9	264.73	6.3	407.55	7.9
1965	163.79	4.2	285.89	8.0	442.07	8.4
1966	171.05	4.4	308.02	7.7	473.10	7.1
1967	177.77	3.9	331.78	7.7	508.47	7.5
1968	190.41	7.1	361.60	9.0	551.18	8.4
1969	201.77	6.0	385.17	6.5	564.80	2.5
1970	209.98	4.1	401.29	4.2	608.78	7.8
1971	235.20	12.0	473.00	17.9	727.90	19.6
1972	255.70	8.7	525.50	11.1	822.80	13.0
1973	270.50	5.8	571.40	8.7	919.50	11.8
1974	283.10	4.7	624.00	9.2	981.60	6.8
1975	291.10	2.8	664.70	6.5	1,023.00	4.2
1976	310.40	6.6	740.50	11.4	1,163.50	13.7
1977	335.30	8.0	809.50	9.3	1,286.40	10.6
1978	363.00	8.3	875.80	8.2	1,388.90	8.0
1979	389.00	7.2	—	—	1,497.90	7.8
1980	414.80	6.6	—	—	1,631.40	8.9
1981	441.80	6.5	—	—	1,794.40	10.0
1982	480.80	8.8	—	—	1,954.90	8.9
1983	528.00	9.8	—	—	2,188.80	12.0
1984	558.50	5.8	—	—	2,371.40	8.3

Note: *Figures are seasonally adjusted; percentage changes for 1920 through 1960 are calculated on five-year averages.*

Sources: *Federal Reserve Bulletin; Economic Indicators.*

MONEY SUPPLY

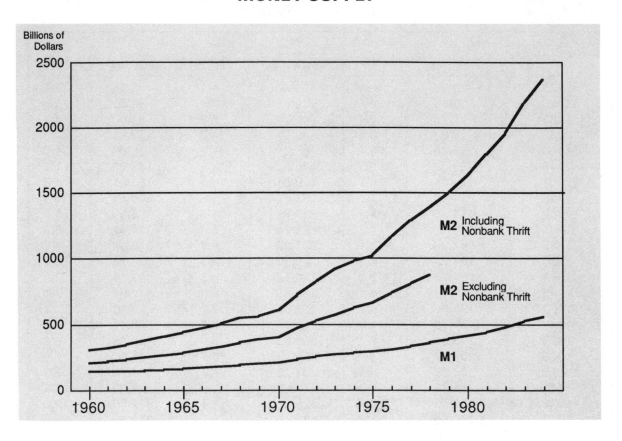

MONEY SUPPLY M–1

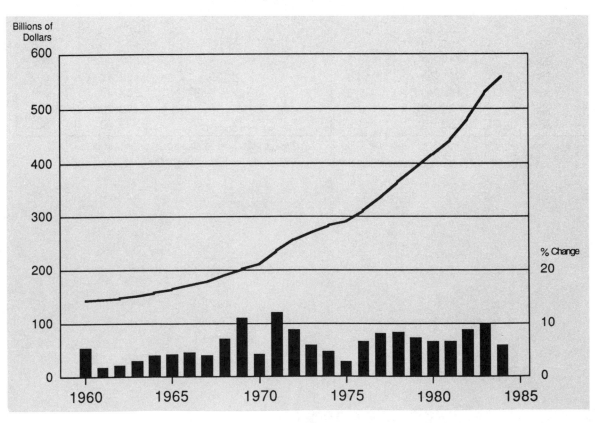

MONEY SUPPLY M–2
(Excluding Nonbank Thrift)

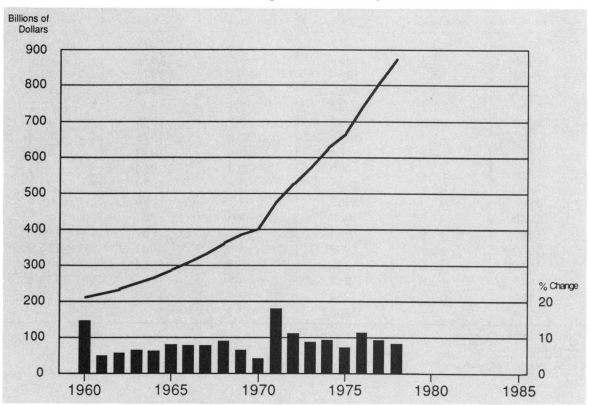

MONEY SUPPLY M–2
(Including Nonbank Thrift)

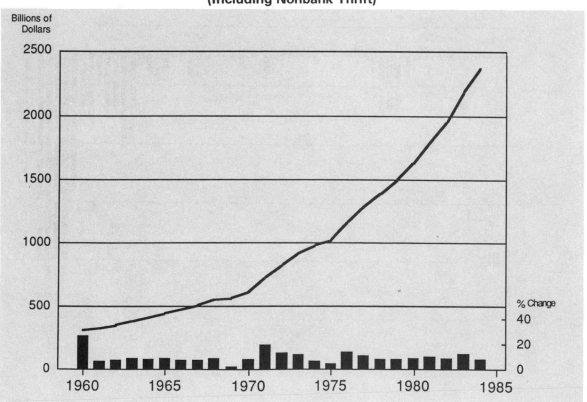

FEDERAL BUDGET DEFICIT OR SURPLUS
(Billions of Dollars)

Year	Deficit/Surplus	Year	Deficit/Surplus	Year	Deficit/Surplus
1934	− 3.6	1952	− 1.5	1970	− 2.8
1935	− 2.8	1953	− 6.5	1971	− 23.0
1936	− 4.4	1954	− 1.2	1972	− 23.4
1937	− 2.8	1955	− 3.0	1973	− 14.8
1938	− 1.2	1956	4.1	1974	− 4.7
1939	− 3.9	1957	3.2	1975	− 45.2
1940	− 3.1	1958	− 2.9	1976[1]	− 79.4
1941	− 5.0	1959	− 12.9	1977	− 44.9
1942	− 20.8	1960	0.3	1978	− 48.8
1943	− 54.9	1961	− 3.4	1979	− 27.7
1944	− 47.0	1962	− 7.1	1980	− 59.6
1945	− 47.5	1963	− 4.8	1981	− 57.9
1946	− 15.9	1964	− 5.9	1982	− 110.7
1947	3.9	1965	− 1.6	1983	− 195.4
1948	12.0	1966	− 3.8	1984	− 175.4
1949	0.6	1967	− 8.7	1985[2]	− 209.8
1950	− 3.1	1968	− 25.2	1986[2]	− 178.5
1951	6.1	1969	3.2		

1 *Includes transition quarter.*
2 *Estimate.*

Source: *Economic Indicators.*

FEDERAL BUDGET DEFICIT OR SURPLUS

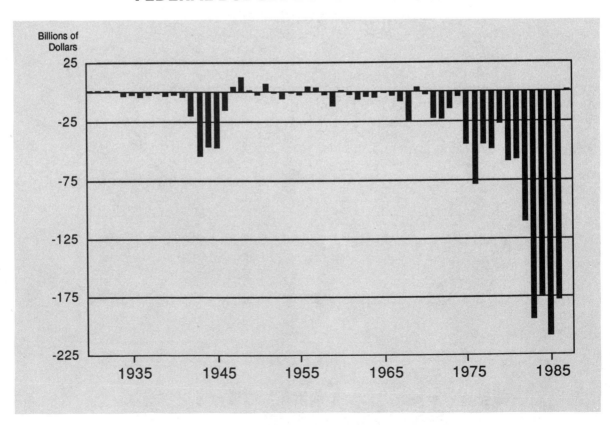

FOREIGN EXCHANGE RATES

Up until 1976 the International Monetary Fund supervised a system of fixed exchange rates, with each country's currency having a specified value for international exchange. Since then, exchange rates have been allowed to fluctuate in response to supply and demand. Other things being equal, an excess supply of dollars increases the demand for and relative value of other currencies. Conversely, an overabundance of other currencies can lower their value relative to the dollar.

Period	Australia (Dollar)[1]	Austria (Schilling)	Belgium (Franc)	Brazil (Cruzeiro)	Canada (Dollar)	China, P.R. (Yuan)	Denmark (Krone)	Finland (Markka)	France (Franc)	Germany (Deutschemark)	Greece (Drachma)	Hong Kong (Dollar)
1981	114.95	15.948	37.194	92.374	1.1990	1.7031	7.1350	4.3128	5.4396	2.2631	n/av.	5.5678
1982	101.65	17.060	45.780	179.22	1.2344	1.8978	8.3443	4.8086	6.5793	2.428	66.872	6.0697
1983	90.14	17.968	51.121	573.27	1.2325	1.9809	9.1483	5.5636	7.6203	2.5539	87.895	7.2569
1984	87.94	20.005	57.749	1841.50	1.2953	2.3308	10.354	6.0007	8.7355	2.8454	112.73	7.8188

Period	India (Rupee)	Ireland (Pound)[1]	Israel (Shekel)	Italy (Lira)	Japan (Yen)	Malaysia (Ringgit)	Mexico (Peso)	Netherlands (Guilder)	New Zealand (Dollar)	Norway (Krone)	Philippines (Peso)	Portugal (Escudo)
1981	8.6807	161.32	n/av.	1138.60	220.63	2.3048	24.547	2.4998	86.848	5.7430	7.8113	61.739
1982	9.4846	142.05	24.407	1354.00	249.06	2.3395	72.990	2.6719	75.101	6.4567	8.5324	80.101
1983	10.1040	124.81	55.865	1519.30	237.55	2.3204	155.01	2.8543	66.790	7.3012	11.0940	111.610
1984	11.348	108.64	n/av.	1756.10	237.45	2.3448	192.31	3.2083	57.837	8.1596	n/av.	147.70

Period	Singapore (Dollar)	South Africa (Rand)[1]	South Korea (Won)	Spain (Peseta)	Sri Lanka (Rupee)	Sweden (Krona)	Switzerland (Franc)	Taiwan (Dollar)	Thailand (Baht)	U.K. (Pound)[1]	Venezuela (Bolivar)	U.S. (Dollar)[2]
1981	2.1053	114.77	n/av.	92.396	18.967	5.0659	1.9674	n/av.	21.731	202.43	4.2781	102.94
1982	2.1406	92.297	731.93	110.09	20.756	6.2838	2.0327	n/av.	23.014	174.80	4.2981	116.57
1983	2.1136	89.95	776.04	143.500	23.510	7.6717	2.1006	n/av.	22.991	151.59	10.6840	125.34
1984	2.1325	69.534	807.91	160.78	25.428	8.2708	2.3500	39.633	23.582	133.66	n/av.	138.19

Note: *Rates are averages of certified noon buying rates in New York for cable transfers, quoted in currency units per dollar.*
1 *Value in U.S. cents.*
2 *Index of weighted-average exchange value of U.S. dollar against currencies of other G-10 countries plus Switzerland. March 1973 = 100. Weights are 1972-76 global trade of each of the ten countries. Series revised as of August 1978.*

Source: *Federal Reserve Bulletin.*

U.S. INTERNATIONAL TRANSACTIONS
(Millions of Dollars)

Period	Merchandise[1,2] Exports	Imports	Net Balance	Military Transactions Direct Expenditures	Sales	Net Balance	Net Investment Income Private[3]	U.S. Government	Net Travel and Transportation Expenditures	Other Services, Net	Balance on Goods and Services[1]	Remittances, Pensions, and Other Unilateral Transfers	Current Account Balance
1966	29,390	(25,463)	3,927	(3,764)	829	(2,935)	5,331	44	(1,382)	315	5,300	(2,890)	2,410
1967	30,680	(26,821)	3,859	(4,378)	1,240	(3,138)	5,848	40	(1,752)	365	5,220	(3,081)	2,139
1968	33,588	(32,964)	624	(4,535)	1,395	(3,140)	6,157	63	(1,558)	344	2,489	(2,875)	(386)
1969	36,414	(35,807)	607	(4,856)	1,528	(3,328)	3,471	(156)	(1,763)	1,878	1,020	(2,976)	(1,956)
1970	42,469	(39,866)	2,603	(4,855)	1,501	(3,355)	3,631	(112)	(2,023)	2,220	2,966	(3,248)	(281)
1971	43,311	(45,579)	(2,268)	(4,819)	1,926	(2,893)	5,659	(956)	(2,315)	2,537	(237)	(3,642)	(3,879)
1972	49,388	(55,797)	(6,409)	(4,784)	1,163	(3,621)	6,208	(1,888)	(3,024)	2,803	(5,930)	(3,779)	(9,710)
1973	71,379	(70,424)	955	(4,658)	2,342	(2,317)	8,188	(3,009)	(2,862)	3,222	4,177	(3,841)	335

Period	Exports	Imports	Net Balance	Net Military Transactions	Investment Income[4] Receipts	Payments	Net	Net Travel and Transportation Expenditures	Other Services, Net	Balance on Goods and Services[1]	Remittances, Pensions, and Other Unilateral Transfers	Current Account Balance
1974	98,306	(103,811)	(5,505)	(1,653)	27,587	(12,084)	15,503	(3,184)	3,986	9,147	(7,186)	1,962
1975	107,088	(98,185)	8,903	(746)	25,351	(12,564)	12,787	(2,792)	4,598	22,749	(4,613)	18,136
1976	114,745	(124,228)	(9,483)	559	29,286	(13,311)	15,975	(2,558)	4,711	9,205	(4,998)	4,207
1977	120,816	(151,907)	(31,091)	1,528	32,179	(14,217)	17,962	(3,565)	5,272	(9,894)	(4,617)	(14,511)
1978	142,054	(176,020)	(33,966)	621	42,245	(21,680)	20,565	(3,573)	6,013	(10,340)	(5,106)	(15,446)
1979	184,473	(212,028)	(27,555)	(1,778)	64,132	(32,914)	31,218	(2,935)	5,735	4,686	(5,649)	(964)
1980	224,269	(249,781)	(25,512)	(2,237)	72,506	(42,063)	30,443	(997)	7,277	8,975	(7,077)	1,898
1981	237,085	(265,086)	(28,001)	(1,115)	86,411	(52,359)	34,052	(144)	8,048	13,128	(6,833)	6,294
1982	211,198	(247,667)	(36,469)	195	83,862	(56,059)	27,803	(1,008)	8,339	(1,141)	(8,058)	(9,119)
1983	200,257	(261,312)	(61,055)	515	77,003	(53,495)	23,508	(4,584)	8,704	(32,912)	(8,651)	(41,563)
1984	220,343	(327,778)	(107,435)	(1,635)	87,620	(69,505)	18,115	(8,806)	(9,311)	(90,449)	(11,199)	(101,647)

Note: *Debits shown in parentheses.* 1 *Excludes military grants.*
2 *Adjusted from census data for differences in timing and coverage.*
3 *Includes fees and royalties from U.S. direct investments abroad or from foreign direct investments in the United States.*
4 *Fees and royalties from U.S. direct investments abroad or from foreign direct investments in the U.S. are excluded from investment income and included in other services, net.*

Source: *Economic Indicators.*

U.S. TRADE BALANCE
Merchandise Imports and Exports
(Millions of Dollars)

| | Merchandise Exports[1] | | | | | Merchandise Imports | | | | | | Merchandise Trade Balance | | |
| | Total Domestic and Foreign Exports | Domestic Exports | | | | General Imports[3] | | | | Total (c.i.f.[4] Value) | Exports (f.a.s.[5]) less Imports (customs value) | Exports (f.a.s.) less Imports (f.a.s.) | Exports (f.a.s.) less Imports (c.i.f.) |
		Total[2]	Food, Beverages, and Tobacco	Crude Materials and Fuels	Manufactured Goods	Total[2]	Food, Beverages, and Tobacco	Crude Materials and Fuels	Manufactured Goods				
				F.a.s. Value									
Monthly average:													
1975	8,971	8,847	1,399	1,266	5,913	8,209	827	2,716	4,257	8,823		762	148
1976	9,602	9,462	1,436	1,341	6,437	10,290	991	3,457	5,398	11,042		−688	−1,440
1977	10,103	9,919	1,330	1,548	6,679	12,533	1,186	4,463	6,379	13,368		−2,430	−3,265
1978	11,973	11,762	1,717	1,746	7,873	14,563	1,312	4,325	8,360	15,504		−2,590	−3,530
1979	15,155	14,886	2,049	2,352	9,716	17,455	1,478	5,949	9,352	18,519		−2,300	−3,364
1980	18,386	18,043	2,534	2,810	11,991	20,406	1,546	7,831	10,427	21,415		−2,020	−3,030
						Customs Value							
1981	19,473	19,075	2,767	2,752	12,857	21,748	1,529	7,739	11,873	22,779	−2,275		−3,306
1982	17,683	17,256	2,248	2,793	11,643	20,329	1,485	6,200	12,002	21,240	−2,647		−3,558
1983	16,707	16,326	2,248	2,463	11,034	21,504	1,568	5,670	13,621	22,490	−4,797		−5,783
1984	18,155	17,670	2,276	2,624	11,929	27,144	1,802	6,063	18,460	28,431	−8,988		−10,276

1 Department of Defense shipments of grant-aid military supplies and equipment under the Military Assistance Program are excluded.

2 Includes commodities and transactions not classified according to kind.

3 Total arrivals of imported goods other than shipments in transit.

4 C.i.f.: customs, insurance, freight — a price quotation that includes the cost of the goods, the shipping insurance, and the freight charges to a specific destination, e.g., "c.i.f. Khartoum."

5 F.a.s.: free alongside ship — a price quotation meaning that the seller assumes all costs of getting the shipment, usually for export, to the designated port, e.g., "f.a.s. Vladivostok."

Source: Department of Commerce, Bureau of the Census.

3.04 **Price Indexes and Comparisons**

From 1949 through 1984, the cost of living increased at an average rate of approximately 4% a year. Prices in the past ten years however, have increased at an average annual rate of nearly 8%. Regardless of the rate at which they rise, in the long run prices continue to go up.

Long-term price indicators are particularly important in financial planning. Because of inflation, $10,000 set aside today will not have the same buying power thirty years from now unless invested in vehicles that keep pace with — or preferably keep ahead of — inflation. One of the most important comparisons investors can make is between the consumer price index (CPI) and yields on various investments, such as T-bills, corporate bonds, stocks, and tangibles. If an investment's net yield does not exceed the rate of inflation, in real terms its yield is negative.

PRODUCER PRICE INDEXES FOR MAJOR COMMODITY GROUPS

Dating from 1890 and formerly known as the *wholesale price index,* the *producer price index* is the oldest continuous statistical series published by the Bureau of Labor Statistics. The index measures average changes in prices, at all stages of processing, of all commodities, produced or imported for sale in primary markets in the U.S.

The index has undergone several revisions and is now based on approximately 3,500 commodity price series instead of the approximately 1,900 included in the 1947–1960 period and the 900 included before 1947. Prices used in constructing the index are collected from sellers, if possible, and generally apply to the first significant large-volume commercial transaction for each commodity: the manufacturer's or other producer's selling price, the importer's selling price, or the selling price on an organized exchange or at a central market.

The weights used in the index represent the total net selling value of commodities produced or processed in this country, or imported. Values are f.o.b. production point and exclude excise taxes, interplant transfers, military products, and goods sold directly at retail from producing establishments. Beginning in January 1976, the weights are values of net shipments of commodities as derived from the industrial censuses of 1972 and other data. For January 1967 through December 1975, weights are based on 1963 shipment values. Alaska and Hawaii are not included before 1961. 1967 = 100.

Year	All Commodities	Farm Products	Processed Foods & Feeds	Industrial Commodities	
				Total	Energy*
1913	36.0	43.7	—	37.2	—
1914	35.2	43.5	—	35.2	—
1915	35.8	43.7	—	36.1	—
1916	44.1	51.7	—	46.8	—
1917	60.6	78.9	—	61.0	—
1918	67.6	90.6	—	65.9	—
1919	71.4	96.4	—	68.6	—
1920	79.6	92.2	—	85.7	—
1921	50.3	54.1	—	55.7	—
1922	49.9	57.4	—	54.4	—
1923	51.9	60.4	—	55.6	—
1924	50.5	61.1	—	53.1	—
1925	53.3	67.1	—	54.6	—
1926	51.6	61.3	—	53.2	71.5
1927	49.3	60.8	—	50.0	63.2
1928	50.0	64.8	—	49.3	60.4
1929	49.1	64.1	—	48.6	59.4
1930	44.6	54.2	—	45.2	56.2
1931	37.6	39.7	—	39.9	48.3
1932	33.6	29.5	—	37.3	50.3
1933	34.0	31.4	—	37.8	47.6
1934	38.6	40.0	—	41.6	52.4
1935	41.3	48.1	—	41.4	52.6
1936	41.7	49.5	—	42.2	54.5
1937	44.5	52.9	—	45.2	55.5
1938	40.5	42.0	—	43.4	54.6
1939	39.8	40.0	—	43.3	52.3
1940	40.5	41.4	—	44.0	51.4
1941	45.1	50.3	—	47.3	54.6
1942	50.9	64.8	—	50.7	56.2
1943	53.3	75.0	—	51.5	57.8
1944	53.6	75.5	—	52.3	59.5

Producer Price Indexes for Major Commodity Groups

Year	All Commodities	Farm Products	Processed Foods & Feeds	Industrial Commodities	
				Total	Energy*
1945	54.6	78.5	—	53.0	60.1
1946	62.3	90.9	—	58.0	64.4
1947	76.5	109.4	82.9	70.8	76.9
1948	82.8	117.5	88.7	76.9	90.5
1949	78.7	101.6	80.6	75.3	86.2
1950	81.8	106.7	83.4	78.0	87.1
1951	91.1	124.2	92.7	86.1	90.3
1952	88.6	117.2	91.6	84.1	90.1
1953	87.4	106.2	87.4	84.8	92.6
1954	87.6	104.7	88.9	85.0	91.3
1955	87.8	98.2	85.0	86.9	91.2
1956	90.7	96.9	84.9	90.8	94.0
1957	93.3	99.5	87.4	93.3	99.1
1958	94.6	103.9	91.8	93.6	95.3
1959	94.8	97.5	89.4	95.3	95.3
1960	94.9	97.2	89.5	95.3	96.1
1961	94.5	96.3	91.0	94.8	97.2
1962	94.8	98.0	91.9	94.8	96.7
1963	94.5	96.0	92.5	94.7	96.3
1964	94.7	94.6	92.3	95.2	93.7
1965	96.6	98.7	95.5	96.4	95.5
1966	99.8	105.9	101.2	98.5	97.8
1967	100.0	100.0	100.0	100.0	100.0
1968	102.5	102.5	101.2	102.5	98.9
1969	106.5	108.8	107.3	106.0	101.0
1970	110.4	111.0	112.0	110.0	105.9
1971	114.0	112.9	114.5	114.1	115.2
1972	119.1	125.0	120.8	117.9	118.6
1973	134.7	176.3	148.1	125.9	134.3
1974	160.1	187.7	170.9	153.8	208.3
1975	174.9	186.7	182.6	171.5	245.1
1976	183.0	191.0	178.0	182.4	265.6
1977	194.2	192.5	186.1	195.1	302.2
1978	209.3	212.5	202.6	209.4	322.5
1979	235.6	241.4	222.5	236.5	408.1
1980	268.8	249.4	241.2	274.8	574.0
1981	293.4	254.9	248.7	304.1	694.5
1982	299.3	242.4	251.5	312.3	693.2
1983	303.1	248.2	256.0	315.8	665.9
1984	310.3	255.7	265.3	322.6	657.0

* *Fuels and related products and power.*

Sources: *Statistical Abstract of the United States, 1982-83* and *Historical Statistics of the U.S.*

CONSUMER PRICE INDEX
Annual Change

The consumer price index (CPI) is a monthly measure of the average changes in prices for a specified market basket of goods and services. Since 1978 the Bureau of Labor Statistics has published CPIs for two population groups: all urban consumers (80% of the total noninstitutional population) and urban wage earners and clerical workers (about 50% of the population).

The CPI is based on prices of housing, food, clothing, fuel, transportation, drugs, doctors' and dentists' fees, entertainment and other common goods and services. Though known as a cost-of-living index, the CPI actually measures only changes in prices, which are but one factor affecting living costs. Also, the CPI measures only the average change in prices for each region and does not reflect differences in prices among cities.

A new treatment of home ownership costs was introduced into the CPI for all urban consumers (CPI-U) in January 1983; the CPI for urban wage earners and clerical workers (CPI-W) will be similarly modified in 1985.

Year	% Annual Change	Year	% Annual Change
1929–33	24.0	1966	2.9
1933–41	13.8	1967	2.9
1941–45	22.2	1968	4.2
1948	7.8	1969	5.4
1949	1.0	1970	5.9
1950	1.0	1971	4.3
1951	7.9	1972	3.3
1952	2.2	1973	6.2
1953	0.8	1974	11.0
1954	0.5	1975	9.1
1955	0.4	1976	5.8
1956	1.5	1977	6.5
1957	3.6	1978	7.7
1958	2.7	1979	11.1
1959	0.8	1980	13.5
1960	1.6	1981	10.4
1961	1.0	1982	6.1
1962	1.1	1983	3.2
1963	1.2	1984	4.3
1964	1.3		
1965	1.7		

Note: *This index includes all items; not seasonally adjusted.*

Sources: *U.S. Department of Commerce; Bureau of Labor Statistics; Federal Reserve Bulletin.*

CONSUMER PRICE INDEX

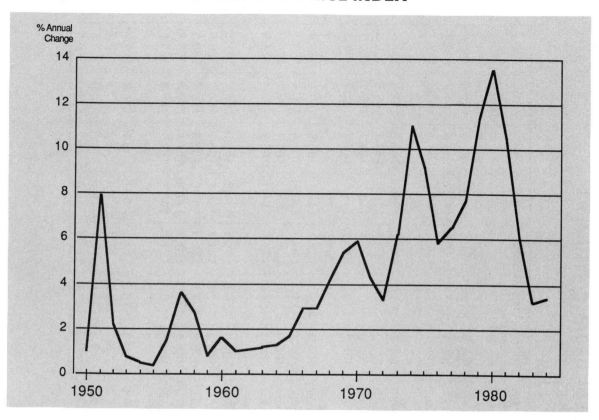

CONSUMER PRICE INDEXES FOR URBAN CONSUMERS
By Region

Region	1973	1974	1975	1976	1977	1978	1979	1980	1981	1982	1983	1984
All items:												
Northeast	73.3	81.4	87.9	92.9	98.1	104.3	114.7	129.4	143.3	150.8	157.1	164.5
Midwest	71.5	79.3	86.2	91.2	97.4	105.3	118.2	134.0	146.6	157.0	162.6	168.6
South	70.3	78.8	86.5	91.3	97.4	105.4	117.4	132.9	147.2	156.6	161.7	168.4
West	69.7	77.1	85.1	90.2	96.9	105.1	117.3	134.6	148.5	157.5	160.0	167.4
Food:												
Northeast	72.5	83.1	89.8	92.8	98.0	107.2	118.0	128.6	138.9	144.8	147.8	153.6
Midwest	72.2	82.8	88.6	92.0	97.9	108.0	119.8	130.0	139.4	144.1	145.9	150.9
South	71.8	80.9	89.8	92.0	98.0	107.9	120.1	130.4	140.7	146.1	149.5	155.9
West	71.0	81.1	88.3	90.2	97.1	108.0	120.2	130.2	141.0	147.7	152.3	158.3
Housing:												
Northeast	n/av.	n/av.	n/av.	n/av.	n/av.	104.3	115.2	132.3	148.7	156.9	163.6	171.5
Midwest	n/av.	n/av.	n/av.	n/av.	n/av.	106.1	121.1	140.0	153.5	168.4	175.4	181.1
South	n/av.	n/av.	n/av.	n/av.	n/av.	106.0	119.0	136.8	153.2	165.1	168.7	174.5
West	n/av.	n/av.	n/av.	n/av.	n/av.	105.1	117.8	138.5	154.1	163.7	163.4	171.9
Population-size class:[1]												
Less than 75,000	n/av.	n/av.	n/av.	n/av.	n/av.	104.9	116.6	131.3	144.8	156.0	160.7	167.2
75,000 to 384,999	n/av.	n/av.	n/av.	n/av.	n/av.	105.4	117.8	133.1	146.4	155.7	160.1	166.6
385,000 to 1,249,999	n/av.	n/av.	n/av.	n/av.	n/av.	105.2	117.8	134.0	148.6	156.9	161.6	168.5
1,250,000 to 4,000,000	n/av.	n/av.	n/av.	n/av.	n/av.	105.1	117.2	133.5	147.8	157.4	162.9	169.8
Over 4,000,000	n/av.	n/av.	n/av.	n/av.	n/av.	104.5	115.4	131.1	143.8	152.1	157.4	164.5
Annual % change, all items:												
Northeast	6.4	11.1	8.0	5.7	5.6	6.3	10.0	12.7	10.7	5.2	4.6	4.7[2]
Midwest	5.9	10.9	8.7	5.8	6.8	8.1	12.3	13.3	9.4	7.1	3.6	3.7[2]
South	6.5	12.1	9.8	5.5	6.7	8.2	11.4	13.3	10.8	6.4	3.3	4.1[2]
West	5.8	10.6	10.4	6.0	7.4	8.5	11.6	14.8	10.3	6.1	1.6	4.6[2]

1 These data represent the consumer price indexes for all items by urban population-size classes as shown.
2 Figures for 1984 show change from December, 1983.

Source: *U.S. Statistical Abstracts.*

CONSUMER PRICE INDEX FOR URBAN CONSUMERS
(By Region, All Items)

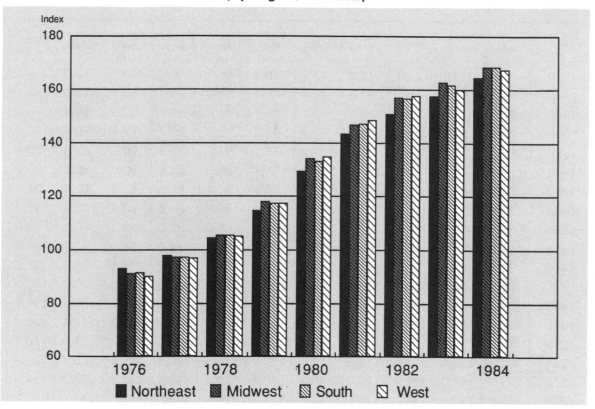

CONSUMER PRICE INDEX FOR URBAN CONSUMERS
(Percentage Change by Region, All Items)

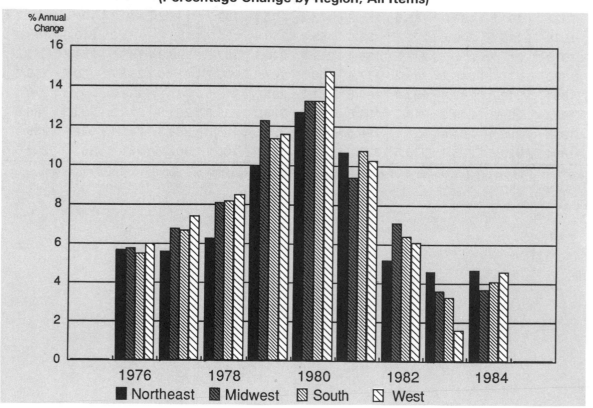

CONSUMER PRICE INDEX
For Urban Consumers

Period	All Items	Food & Beverages	Housing	Apparel & Upkeep	Transpor- tation	Medical Care	Entertain- ment	Other Goods & Services	Personal Care	All Services	All Items Less Med. Care
1940	42.0	35.2	52.4	42.8	42.7	36.8	46.1	48.3	40.2	43.6	—
1945	53.9	50.7	59.1	61.5	47.8	42.1	62.4	56.9	55.1	48.7	—
1950	72.1	74.5	72.8	79.0	68.2	53.7	74.4	69.9	68.3	58.9	—
1955	80.2	81.6	82.3	84.1	77.4	64.8	76.7	79.8	77.9	70.5	—
1960	88.7	88.0	90.2	89.6	89.6	79.1	87.3	87.8	90.1	83.8	89.4
1961	89.6	89.1	90.9	90.4	90.6	81.4	89.3	88.5	90.6	85.2	90.3
1962	90.6	89.9	91.7	90.9	92.5	83.5	91.3	89.1	92.2	86.2	91.2
1963	91.7	91.2	92.7	91.9	93.0	85.6	92.8	90.6	93.4	88.5	92.3
1964	92.9	92.4	93.8	92.4	94.3	87.3	95.0	92.0	94.5	90.2	93.5
1965	94.5	94.4	94.9	93.7	95.9	89.5	95.9	94.2	95.2	92.2	94.9
1966	97.2	99.1	97.2	96.1	97.2	93.4	97.5	97.2	97.1	95.8	97.7
1967	100.0	100.0	100.0	100.0	100.0	100.0	100.0	100.0	100.0	100.0	100.0
1968	104.2	103.6	104.2	105.2	103.2	106.1	104.7	104.6	104.2	105.2	104.1
1969	109.8	108.9	110.8	111.5	107.2	113.4	108.7	109.1	109.3	112.5	109.7
1970	116.3	114.9	118.9	116.1	112.7	120.6	113.4	116.0	113.2	121.6	116.1
1971	121.3	118.4	124.3	119.8	118.6	128.4	119.3	120.9	116.8	128.4	120.9
1972	125.3	123.3	129.2	122.3	119.9	132.5	122.8	125.5	119.8	133.3	124.9
1973	133.1	141.4	135.0	126.8	123.8	137.7	125.9	129.0	125.2	139.1	132.9
1974	147.7	161.7	150.6	136.2	137.7	150.5	133.8	137.2	137.3	152.0	147.7
1975	161.2	175.4	166.8	142.3	150.6	168.6	144.4	147.4	150.7	166.6	160.9
1976	170.5	180.8	177.2	147.6	165.5	184.7	151.2	153.3	160.5	180.4	169.7
1977	181.5	188.0	186.5	154.2	177.2	202.4	167.7	172.2	170.9	194.3	180.3
1978	195.3	206.2	202.6	159.5	185.8	219.4	176.2	183.2	182.0	210.8	193.9
1979	217.7	228.7	227.5	166.4	212.8	240.1	187.7	196.3	195.5	234.4	216.2
1980	247.0	248.7	263.2	177.4	250.5	267.2	203.7	213.6	212.7	270.9	245.6
1981	272.3	267.8	293.2	186.6	281.3	295.1	219.0	233.3	229.8	306.2	270.8
1982	289.1	278.2	314.7	191.8	291.5	328.7	235.8	259.9	248.3	333.3	286.8
1983	298.4	284.4	323.1	196.5	298.4	357.3	246.0	288.3	261.1	344.9	295.1
1984	311.1	295.1	336.5	200.2	311.7	379.5	255.1	307.7	271.4	363.0	307.3

Note: *1967 = 100; yearly data are annual averages; annual data from* CPI Detailed Report; *monthly data from* Bureau of Labor Statistics News.

Source: *Social Security Bulletin.*

CONSUMER PRICE INDEX
U.S. City Average and Selected Areas

Area	All Urban Consumers				Urban Wage Earners and Clerical Workers			
	1982	1983	1984	1985	1982	1983	1984	1985
U.S. City Average[1]	**282.5**	**293.1**	**305.2**	**316.1**	**282.1**	**292.1**	**302.7**	**312.6**
Anchorage (10/67 = 100)	253.0	257.6	271.5	278.3	248.6	250.6	264.0	271.7
Atlanta[2]	282.2	296.1	307.3	318.2	284.1	297.8	309.7	316.0
Baltimore	282.1	291.4	307.6	315.2	282.3	289.7	303.8	315.1
Boston	274.0	286.2	297.3	309.4	274.3	283.9	295.1	307.8
Buffalo	264.3	277.8	288.2	303.4	262.7	275.1	285.6	289.8
Chicago – Northwestern Indiana	275.4	294.0	305.4	315.1	275.9	292.8	298.3	302.5
Cincinnati – Kentucky – Indiana	285.7	306.0	318.4	325.1	288.4	305.2	313.4	318.9
Cleveland	281.6	317.6	330.7	339.7	281.2	315.0	314.6	318.6
Dallas – Fort Worth	295.1	303.3	317.6	330.7	291.0	299.4	313.5	325.0
Denver – Boulder	305.4	327.5	343.5	350.6	310.5	323.9	336.2	346.2
Detroit	280.8	292.6	301.3	310.9	277.8	288.0	307.9	301.2
Honolulu	258.3	269.9	278.4	289.8	259.3	271.0	288.2	297.6
Houston	302.7	318.1	320.7	333.4	298.8	316.1	317.9	330.9
Kansas City, Missouri – Kansas	273.5	290.6	303.0	313.7	272.0	288.6	300.0	304.0
Los Angeles – Long Beach, Anaheim	285.6	285.6	299.1	313.0	289.6	288.0	297.9	308.1
Miami (11/77 = 100)	155.2	157.9	165.0	168.6	156.4	159.2	165.9	169.8
Milwaukee	291.3	305.0	314.0	324.6	295.3	303.5	327.5	343.4
Minneapolis – St. Paul, Minnesota – Wisconsin	298.7	306.1	317.5	327.9	298.3	306.1	312.5	323.8
New York – Northeastern N.J.	286.5	282.6	297.3	308.4	267.5	280.8	290.2	302.0
Northeast Pennsylvania (Scranton)	272.5	278.9	291.0	301.5	274.5	282.6	293.2	301.0
Philadelphia – N.J.	275.7	282.1	294.4	306.3	275.1	282.5	296.7	309.4
Pittsburgh	281.8	302.1	314.3	322.1	282.6	301.7	302.6	304.6
Portland, Oregon – Washington	288.4	286.6	295.1	306.8	285.5	281.7	289.5	297.4
St. Louis, Missouri – Illinois	278.4	291.1	300.9	313.3	277.1	285.3	296.8	310.4
San Diego	323.1	324.9	346.2	364.1	317.4	313.6	329.2	329.1
San Francisco – Oakland	294.0	293.9	307.3	325.8	292.7	293.6	306.1	321.5
Seattle – Everett	295.9	297.5	308.7	319.5	291.9	291.4	297.3	306.7
Washington, D.C. – Maryland – Virginia	278.0	289.0	303.7	314.6	281.8	292.9	308.3	317.7

Note: Areas include the entire portion of the Standard Metropolitan Statistical Area, as defined for the 1970 census, except that the Standard Consolidated Area is used for New York and Chicago; 1967 = 100 unless otherwise specified; January unless otherwise specified.

1 Average of 85 cities.
2 December of the previous year; e.g., under 1982, the Atlanta index is as of December 1981.

Source: *Monthly Labor Review.*

INDEXES OF MEDICAL CARE PRICES

Year	Index Total	Avg. Annual % Change	Med. Care Services	Professional Services			Hospital Room	Med. Care Commodities[2]
				Total[1]	Physicians	Dental		
1960	79.1	4.1[3]	74.9	n/av.	77.0	82.1	57.3	104.5
1965	89.5	2.5	87.3	n/av.	88.3	92.2	75.9	100.2
1970	120.6	6.3	124.2	119.7	121.4	119.4	145.4	103.6
1971	128.4	6.5	133.3	127.5	129.8	127.0	163.1	105.4
1972	132.5	3.2	138.2	132.1	133.8	132.3	173.9	105.6
1973	137.7	3.9	144.3	136.4	138.2	136.4	182.1	105.9
1974	150.5	9.3	159.1	148.2	150.9	146.8	201.5	109.6
1975	168.6	12.0	179.1	164.5	169.4	161.9	236.1	118.8
1976	184.7	9.5	197.1	179.4	188.5	172.2	268.8	126.0
1977	202.4	9.6	216.7	194.1	206.0	185.1	299.5	134.1
1978	219.4	8.4	235.3	209.2	223.3	199.3	331.7	143.9
1979	240.1	9.5	258.5	228.5	245.5	217.0	368.2	154.7
1980	267.2	11.3	288.9	255.0	274.3	242.3	416.3	168.7
1981	295.1	10.4	318.6	280.1	303.5	264.4	476.8	187.4
1982	326.9	11.8	353.4	301.6	330.1	281.7	549.2	206.3
1983	355.1	8.6	384.1	323.4	356.0	300.4	612.0	223.7
1984, Nov.	385.6		416.1	353.4	387.0	334.3	680.8	245.6

Note: *1967 = 100. 1960 excludes Alaska and Hawaii. Differences in data between this table and the one above are the result of compilation from different sources.*
1 *Includes other services, not shown separately.*   2 *Prior to 1978, covers drugs and prescriptions only.*
3 *Change from 1955.*

Source: U.S. Bureau of Labor Statistics.

INDEX OF MEDICAL CARE PRICES

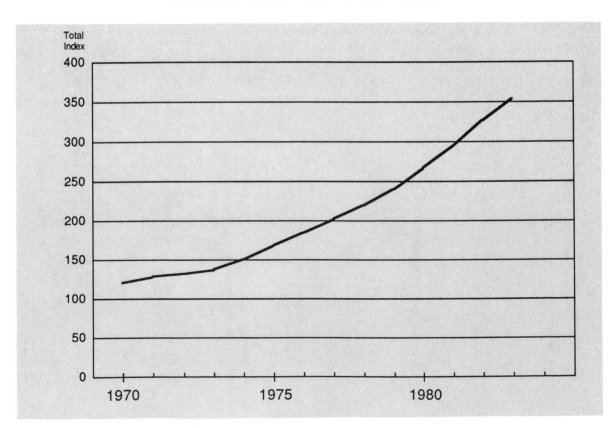

MEDICAL CARE COMPONENT OF THE CONSUMER PRICE INDEX

Period	All Medical Care	Medical Care Commodities		Professional Services				Other Medical Care Services	
		All Commodities	Prescription Drugs	All Services	Professional Services	Physicians	Dentists	All Other Services	Hospital Room
1977	202.4	134.1	122.1	216.7	194.1	206.0	158.1	244.2	299.5
1978	219.4	143.9	132.1	235.3	209.2	223.3	199.3	267.0	331.6
1979	240.1	154.7	142.6	258.5	228.5	245.5	217.0	295.2	368.2
1980	267.2	168.7	155.8	288.9	255.0	274.3	242.3	330.4	416.3
1981	295.1	187.4	173.4	318.6	280.1	303.5	264.4	365.9	476.8
1982	326.9	206.3	193.7	353.4	301.6	330.1	281.7	418.2	549.2
1983	357.3	223.3	213.8	387.0	323.0	352.3	302.7	464.4	619.7
1984	379.5	239.7	234.3	410.3	346.1	376.8	327.9	488.0	670.9

Note: *1967 = 100; yearly data are annual averages; 1972 = 100, beginning February 1977, for hospital service charges.*

Sources: *Social Security Bulletin; CPI Detailed Report.*

ENERGY COSTS IN 25 SELECTED U.S. CITIES
Typical Gas and Electric Rates, January 1, 1985

City	Gas/70 Therms	Electric/500 Kwh	Total Bill
Seattle	$46.88	$ 9.92	$ 56.80
Memphis	32.39	25.58	57.97
New Orleans	37.15	29.50	66.65
San Jose	31.07	36.85	67.92
Los Angeles	34.93	36.51	71.44
San Francisco	31.07	40.54	71.61
San Antonio	36.29	36.86	73.15
Denver	36.79	37.11	73.90
St. Louis	46.26	28.67	74.93
Dallas	35.99	40.27	76.26
Cleveland	38.33	43.47	81.80
Milwaukee	47.38	35.45	82.83
Jacksonville	43.45	39.80	83.25
Detroit	46.26	37.37	83.63
Houston	43.06	40.58	83.64
Columbus	47.11	36.73	83.84
Indianapolis	52.72	31.36	84.08
Phoenix	43.89	43.76	87.65
Chicago	45.16	43.72	88.88
Washington, D.C.	61.98	27.26	89.24
Baltimore	50.26	41.04	91.30
San Diego	38.28	65.00	103.28
Boston	54.83	53.99	108.82
Philadelphia	54.89	53.99	108.88
New York	61.98	74.50	129.62

Note: *All figures include minimum customer charges, base rates, and fuel or energy charges; taxes not included.*

Source: Pacific Gas & Electric Company.

CONSUMER PRICE INDEXES IN MAJOR INDUSTRIAL COUNTRIES

Year	United States	Canada	Japan	European Community[1]	France	West Germany	Italy	United Kingdom
1960	88.7	85.9	68.3	79.2	78.0[2]	82.9	74.1	79.0
1961	89.6	86.7	71.8	81.1	80.6[2]	84.8	75.7	81.6
1962	90.6	87.7	76.7	84.5	85.4	87.4	79.2	85.1
1963	91.7	89.2	82.5	87.6	89.5	89.9	85.1	86.8
1964	92.9	90.9	85.8	90.8	92.5	92.0	90.1	89.6
1965	94.5	93.1	91.6	94.2	94.8	95.0	94.2	93.9
1966	97.2	96.5	96.3	97.5	97.4	98.4	96.4	97.6
1967	100.0	100.0	100.0	100.0	100.0	100.0	100.0	100.0
1968	104.2	104.0	105.3	103.7	104.5	101.6	101.4	104.8
1969	109.8	108.8	110.9	108.0	111.3	103.5	104.1	110.3
1970	116.3	112.4	119.3	113.3	117.1	107.1	109.2	117.4
1971	121.3	115.6	126.5	120.3	123.5	112.7	114.4	128.5
1972	125.3	121.2	132.3	127.6	131.1	119.0	121.0	137.7
1973	133.1	130.3	147.9	138.3	140.7	127.2	134.0	150.2
1974	147.7	144.5	184.0	156.4	160.0	136.1	159.7	174.3
1975	161.2	160.1	205.8	176.7	178.9	144.2	186.8	216.5
1976	170.5	172.1	224.9	195.2	196.1	150.4	218.1	252.4
1977	181.5	185.9	243.0	214.7	214.5	155.9	255.2	292.4
1978	195.4	202.5	252.3	229.9	233.9	160.2	286.2	316.6
1979	217.4	221.0	261.3	250.7	259.1	166.8	328.5	359.0
1980	246.8	243.5	282.2	281.4	294.2	175.9	398.0	423.6
1981	272.4	273.9	296.2	313.4	332.7	186.3	472.4	473.9
1982	289.1	303.5	304.1	344.3	373.1	196.2	549.4	514.7
1983	298.4	321.0	309.7	n/av.	407.9	203.3	631.8	538.3
1984	311.1	335.0	316.6	n/av.	439.5	208.2	689.8	565.1

Note: *1967=100.*

1 *Consists of Belgium-Luxembourg, Denmark, France, Greece, Ireland, Italy, Netherlands, United Kingdom, and West Germany. Industrial production prior to July 1981 excludes data for Greece, which joined the Common Market in 1981.*

2 *Data for 1960 and 1961 are for Paris only.*

Sources: *Economic Report of the President, 1984; Economic Indicators.*

ANNUAL CHANGES IN INTERNATIONAL CONSUMER PRICES
(In Percentages)

Country	1965-70 Average	1970-75 Average	1975-80 Average	1970	1973	1974	1975	1976	1977	1978	1979	1980	1981	1982	1983
United States	4.2	6.7	8.9	5.9	6.2	11.0	9.1	5.8	6.5	7.7	11.3	13.5	10.4	6.2	3.2
Australia	3.1	10.2	10.6	3.9	9.5	15.1	15.1	13.5	12.3	7.9	9.1	10.1	9.7	11.1	10.1
Canada	3.8	7.3	8.7	3.3	7.6	10.8	10.8	7.5	8.0	9.0	9.1	10.2	12.4	10.8	5.8
Japan	5.5	11.5	6.5	7.7	11.7	24.5	11.8	9.3	8.1	3.8	3.6	8.0	4.9	2.6	1.8
New Zealand	1.9	10.2	14.8	6.5	8.2	11.1	14.7	16.9	14.3	12.0	13.8	17.1	15.4	16.1	5.5
Austria	3.3	7.3	5.3	4.4	7.6	9.5	8.4	7.3	5.5	3.6	3.7	6.4	6.8	5.4	3.3
Belgium	3.5	8.4	6.4	3.9	7.0	12.7	12.8	9.2	7.1	4.5	4.5	6.6	7.6	8.7	7.7
Denmark	6.4	9.3	10.4	5.8	9.3	15.3	9.6	9.0	11.1	10.0	9.6	12.3	11.7	10.1	6.9
Finland	4.7	11.7	10.7	2.8	10.7	16.9	17.9	14.4	12.2	7.8	7.5	11.6	12.0	9.3	8.5
France	4.3	8.8	10.4	5.2	7.3	13.7	11.8	9.6	9.4	9.1	10.8	13.6	13.4	11.8	9.6
Germany, Fed. Rep. of	2.6	6.1	4.1	3.4	6.9	7.0	6.0	4.5	3.7	2.7	4.1	5.4	6.3	5.3	3.3
Greece	2.5	12.3	16.3	3.2	15.5	26.9	13.4	13.3	12.1	12.6	19.0	24.9	24.5	21.0	20.5
Ireland	5.3	13.3	14.1	8.2	11.4	17.0	20.9	18.0	13.6	7.6	13.2	18.2	20.5	17.1	10.5
Italy	3.0	11.3	16.6	5.0	10.8	19.1	17.0	16.8	18.4	12.1	14.7	21.2	17.8	16.5	14.7
Luxembourg	3.0	7.2	6.1	4.6	6.1	9.5	10.7	9.8	6.7	3.1	4.5	6.3	8.1	9.4	8.6
Netherlands	4.8	8.6	6.0	3.6	8.0	9.6	10.2	8.8	6.4	4.1	4.2	6.5	6.7	5.9	2.8
Norway	4.9	8.4	8.4	10.6	7.5	9.4	11.7	9.1	9.1	8.1	4.8	10.8	13.7	11.4	8.4
Portugal*	5.5	15.4	21.8	6.3	11.5	29.2	20.4	19.3	27.2	22.5	23.8	16.6	20.0	22.7	25.1
Spain	5.1	12.1	18.6	5.7	11.4	15.7	16.9	17.7	24.5	19.8	15.6	15.6	14.6	14.4	12.2
Sweden	4.5	8.0	10.5	7.0	6.7	9.9	9.8	10.3	11.4	10.0	7.3	13.7	12.1	8.6	8.9
Switzerland	3.5	7.7	2.3	3.6	8.7	9.8	6.7	1.7	1.3	1.1	3.6	4.0	6.5	5.7	3.0
Turkey*	8.1	18.6	50.1	7.9	14.0	23.9	21.2	17.4	26.0	61.9	63.5	94.3	37.6	32.7	28.8
United Kingdom	4.6	13.0	14.4	6.4	9.2	16.0	24.2	16.5	15.8	8.3	13.4	18.0	11.9	8.6	4.6

* Excludes rent.

Source: *Main Economic Indicators*, Organization for Economic Development and Co-operation, Paris, France.

CONSUMER PRICE INDEXES
Selected Items and Selected Countries
1975 and 1982

Country	Total		Food¹		Clothing		Housing²		Transportation		Average Annual % Change 1975-82			
	1975	1982	1975	1982	1975	1982	1975	1982	1975	1982	Food¹	Clothing	Housing²	Trans.
United States	161.2	289.1	175.4	285.7	142.3	191.8	164.5	314.7	150.6	291.5	7.2	4.4	9.7	9.9
Canada	160.1	303.4	180.1	346.4	136.9	221.0	160.7	307.2	150.3	314.9	9.8	7.1	9.7	11.1
Austria	157.2	229.0	149.4	206.3	141.7	188.2	174.4	271.4	161.4	247.2	4.7	4.1	6.5	6.3
France	178.9	373.1	182.8	378.6	166.2	319.4	180.6	402.3	192.0	431.7	11.0	9.8	12.1	12.3
Germany, F.R.	144.1	196.1	135.0	177.1	143.2	196.2	153.7	217.4	151.0	206.1	4.0	4.6	5.1	4.5
Italy	186.9	553.2	185.2	517.7	194.6	594.3	173.6	539.1	207.5	660.8	15.8	17.3	17.6	18.0
Netherlands	175.3	268.7	155.9	220.4	190.6	277.9	173.9	289.6	167.8	253.9	5.1	5.5	7.6	6.1
Sweden	164.3	329.3	169.5	364.5	141.9	219.6	177.0	389.1	n/av.	n/av.	11.6	6.4	11.9	n/av.
United Kingdom	216.5	514.7	243.8	517.3	187.5	314.0	208.7	538.5	224.4	535.3	12.2	7.6	14.5	13.2
Australia	178.7	360.3	165.8	343.1	184.1	345.8	199.6	396.5	n/av.	n/av.	10.9	9.4	10.3	n/av.
Japan	204.5	303.8	220.9	309.0	217.5	310.6	174.3	242.8	170.2	274.6	4.9	5.2	4.8	7.1

Note: 1967 = 100

1 Restaurant meals, alcohol, and tobacco are included for some countries; excluded for others.

2 Includes shelter, utilities, and household furnishings and operations; actual coverage and measurement methods vary significantly from country to country.

Source: U.S. Bureau of Labor Statistics, *Handbook of Labor Statistics.*

CONSUMER PRICE INDEXES
Selected Items and Selected Countries
1983–1984

Country	1983	1984	% Change
United States			
All items	120.9	126.1	+ 4.3
Food	114.6	119.0	+ 3.8
Durable goods	120.2	126.7	+ 5.4
Beverages and tobacco	129.3	135.3	+ 4.6
Fuel and electricity[1]	132.9	139.0	+ 4.6
Services (less rent)[2]	128.3	135.3	+ 5.5
Rent	123.7	129.7	+ 4.9
New York: all items	121.7	127.8	+ 5.0
Canada			
All items	131.9	137.6	+ 4.5
Food	123.9	130.8	+ 5.6
Durable goods	120.2	124.1	+ 3.2
Beverages and tobacco	146.8	158.8	+ 8.2
Fuel and electricity	160.7	169.4	+ 5.4
Services (less rent)	135.1	140.6	+ 4.1
Rent	132.7	137.6	+ 3.7
Montreal: all items	132.4	137.9	+ 4.2
Japan			
All items	109.7	112.1	+ 2.2
Food	109.2	111.9	+ 2.5
Durable goods	101.1	101.1	—
Beverages and tobacco	113.9	121.8	+ 6.9
Fuel and electricity	111.2	111.0	− 0.2
Services (less rent)	112.6	116.1	+ 3.1
Rent	110.3	113.2	+ 2.6
Tokyo: all items	110.3	113.3	+ 2.7
Australia			
All items	134.2	139.5	+ 3.9
Food	129.6	136.7	+ 5.5
All goods (less food)	131.5	140.2	+ 6.6
Fuel and electricity	158.0	166.5	+ 5.4
Services (less rent)	148.3	142.3	− 4.0
Rent	131.7	141.2	+ 7.2
Sydney: all items	134.2	138.5	+ 3.2
New Zealand			
All items	143.9	152.8	+ 6.2
Food	136.4	144.4	+ 5.9
All goods (less food)	135.8	144.6	+ 6.5
Beverages and tobacco	148.9	157.1	+ 5.5
Fuel and electricity	130.2	132.3	+ 1.6
Services (less rent)	145.6	152.1	+ 4.5
Rent	165.6	177.8	+ 7.4
Wellington: all items	144.9	154.1	+ 6.3
Austria			
All items	116.3	122.9	+ 5.7
Food[4]	113.4	119.8	+ 5.6
Rent	127.1	136.0	+ 7.0

Consumer Price Indexes

Country	1983	1984	% Change
Austria (continued)			
Other goods and services	116.6	123.0	+ 5.5
Fuel and electricity	126.7	136.4	+ 7.7
Belgium[3]			
All items	126.0	134.0	+ 6.3
Food[4,5]	126.0	135.9	+ 7.9
All goods (less food)[4]	128.1	135.9	+ 6.1
Services (less rent)[5]	122.3	128.8	+ 5.3
Rent	129.9	139.4	+ 7.3
Denmark			
All items	132.0	140.0	+ 6.1
Food	130.0	142.0	+ 9.2
All goods (less food)	130.0	137.0	+ 5.4
Beverages and tobacco	127.0	137.0	+ 7.7
Fuel and electricity	146.0	146.0	–
Services (less rent)[2]	153.0	162.0	+ 5.9
Rent[2]	130.0	140.0	+ 7.7
Finland			
All items	133.0	142.0	+ 6.8
Food[6]	136.0	146.0	+ 7.4
Rent[7]	136.0	143.0	+ 5.1
Other goods and services[6,7]	131.0	141.0	+ 7.6
Beverages and tobacco	140.0	148.0	+ 5.7
France			
All items	139.0	149.3	+ 7.4
Food[4]	140.5	152.6	+ 8.6
All goods (less food)[4]	137.0	147.4	+ 7.6
Fuel and electricity	150.7	162.8	+ 8.0
Services (less rent)	139.8	148.6	+ 6.3
Rent	138.1	149.1	+ 8.0
Paris: all items	137.9	148.2	+ 7.5
Germany, Federal Republic of			
All items	115.6	118.4	+ 2.4
Food[8]	114.3	116.0	+ 1.5
All goods (less food)[8]	115.5	118.4	+ 2.5
Fuel and electricity	124.5	128.8	+ 3.4
Services (less rent)	117.6	120.3	+ 2.3
Rent	115.6	120.0	+ 3.8
Greece			
All items	181.0	214.4	+ 18.5
Food	185.9	219.9	+ 18.3
Iceland[9]			
All items[10]	422.0	550.0	+ 13.0
Food	372.0	501.0	+ 34.7
Home ownership	389.0	467.0	+ 20.1
Ireland			
All items	155.8	169.3	+ 8.7
Food	140.6	154.3	+ 9.7
Housing	141.5	154.4	+ 9.7

(Continued)

Consumer Price Indexes

Country	1983	1984	% Change
Ireland (continued)			
Other goods and services	163.8	177.2	+ 8.2
Beverages and tobacco	183.6	195.2	+ 6.3
Fuel and electricity	153.9	165.6	+ 7.6
Italy			
All items	157.3	174.3	+ 8.7
Food	149.5	163.3	+ 9.2
All goods (less food)	158.4	174.6	+ 10.2
Beverages and tobacco	168.8	182.6	+ 8.2
Fuel and electricity	181.7	201.9	+ 11.1
Services (less rent)	166.7	186.8	+ 12.1
Rent	160.1	196.5	+ 22.7
Luxembourg			
All items[10,11]	128.4	135.7	+ 5.7
Food[11]	129.4	138.1	+ 6.7
Fuel and electricity[12]	151.6	147.1	− 3.0
Netherlands			
All items	116.2	120.0	+ 3.3
Food	111.9	115.5	+ 3.2
All goods (less food)	116.3	119.9	+ 3.1
Fuel and electricity	146.4	153.5	+ 4.8
Services (less rent)	113.4	116.2	+ 2.5
Rent[13]	124.1	130.2	+ 4.9
Norway			
All items	137.0	146.0	+ 6.6
Food	144.0	153.0	+ 6.4
All goods (less food)	132.0	140.0	+ 6.1
Fuel and electricity	140.0	151.0	+ 7.9
Home-produced goods	141.0	150.0	+ 6.4
Imported goods	125.0	131.0	+ 5.6
Services (less rent)	146.0	155.0	+ 6.2
Rent	136.0	146.0	+ 9.4
Portugal			
All items (less rent)	184.3	238.3	+ 29.3
Food	188.3	248.1	+ 31.8
Lisbon: all items (less rent)	184.1	235.8	+ 28.1
Spain			
All items	147.0	163.6	+ 11.3
Food[14]	144.6	163.1	+ 12.8
Rent	137.9	145.5	+ 5.5
Sweden			
All items	133.0	143.0	+ 7.5
Food	144.0	161.0	+ 11.8
Housing	125.0	133.0	+ 6.4
Other goods and services	132.0	142.0	+ 7.6
Fuel and electricity	149.0	162.0	+ 8.7
Switzerland			
All items[13]	115.9	119.2	+ 2.8
Food	120.6	125.2	+ 3.8

Consumer Price Indexes

Country	1983	1984	% Change
Switzerland (continued)			
All goods (less food)	109.0	113.2	+ 3.0
Beverages and tobacco	115.7	116.6	+ 0.8
Fuel and electricity	108.9	113.4	+ 4.1
Services (less rent)	118.5	124.2	+ 4.8
Rent[13]	120.5	123.5	+ 2.5
Turkey			
Istanbul: (84 items)	235.2	342.4	+ 45.6
United Kingdom (Great Britain)			
All items	127.1	133.4	+ 5.0
Food	121.4	128.5	+ 5.8
All goods (less food)	126.7	131.3	+ 3.6
Beverages and tobacco	146.2	158.7	+ 8.5
Fuel and electricity	148.6	152.9	+ 2.9
Services (less rent)	131.5	136.3	+ 3.7
Rent	136.2	148.7	+ 9.2
Yugoslavia			
All items	265.0	405.0	+ 52.8
Food	294.0	435.0	+ 48.0
Durable goods	255.0	426.0	+ 67.1
Services (less rent)	209.0	307.0	+ 46.9
Rent	179.0	218.0	+ 21.8
O.E.C.D. Total[15]			
All items	125.4	132.1	+ 5.3

Note: *For All Items: 1980 = 100.*
1 *Including water, telephone, and sewerage services.*
2 *House repairs included in Services (less rent).*
3 *From 1984, new index.*
4 *Beverages included in Food.*
5 *Restaurant meals included in Services.*
6 *Restaurant meals included in Other goods and services.*
7 *Fuel and electricity included in Rent.*
8 *Beverages and tobacco included in Food.*
9 *From 1984, new index; prior to 1984, Reykjavik only.*
10 *Excluding rent.*
11 *Excluding restaurant meals.*
12 *Including water.*
13 *Excluding house repair.*
14 *Including beverages and tobacco and excluding restaurant meals.*
15 *The country weights used in the aggregate indexes are based on the private consumption and exchange rates of the previous year.*

Source: O.E.C.D., Department of Economics and Statistics, *Labor Forces Statistics.*

3.05 The Labor Force

Estimates of the U.S. labor force, total employment, and unemployment are published monthly by the Bureau of Labor Statistics of the Department of Labor. These are based on a sample survey of households conducted by the Bureau of the Census, as part of the various series on labor statistics, and also include data on hours, earnings, and wage rates. Labor data are used as current economic indicators for purposes of analyzing the labor force and business conditions, and as measures of progress that inform program planning in the public and private sectors.

The unemployment rate is considered a *lagging* indicator; that is, declines in unemployment generally follow — rather than predict — gains in the gross national product (GNP). The growth cycle begins with increased production and subsequent increases in spending; these then result in increased employment, as producers hire more workers to keep up with demand. If demand exceeds production, prices rise and set off an inflationary phase. In turn, an environment of inflationary expectations sets the stage for wage negotiations predicated on the rising cost of living. If wages increase faster than productivity, employers raise prices to cover the difference, and higher prices then prompt demands for even higher wages — a sequence known as a *wage-price spiral*.

UNEMPLOYMENT RATE
Civilian Labor Force

Year	%	Year	%	Year	%	Year	%
1900	5.0	1922	6.7	1944	1.2	1966	3.8
1901	4.0	1923	2.4	1945	1.9	1967	3.8
1902	3.7	1924	5.0	1946	3.9	1968	3.6
1903	3.9	1925	3.2	1947	3.9	1969	3.5
1904	5.4	1926	1.8	1948	3.8	1970	4.9
1905	4.3	1927	3.3	1949	5.9	1971	5.9
1906	1.7	1928	4.2	1950	5.3	1972	5.6
1907	2.8	1929	3.2	1951	3.3	1973	4.9
1908	8.0	1930	8.7	1952	3.0	1974	5.6
1909	5.1	1931	15.9	1953	2.9	1975	8.5
1910	5.9	1932	23.6	1954	5.5	1976	7.7
1911	6.7	1933	24.9	1955	4.4	1977	7.1
1912	4.6	1934	21.7	1956	4.1	1978	6.1
1913	4.3	1935	20.1	1957	4.3	1979	5.8
1914	7.9	1936	16.9	1958	6.8	1980	7.1
1915	8.5	1937	14.3	1959	5.5	1981	7.6
1916	5.1	1938	19.0	1960	5.5	1982	9.7
1917	4.6	1939	17.2	1961	6.7	1983	9.6
1918	1.4	1940	14.6	1962	5.5	1984	7.5
1919	1.4	1941	9.9	1963	5.7		
1920	5.2	1942	4.7	1964	5.2		
1921	11.7	1943	1.9	1965	4.5		

Source: *Economic Indicators.*

UNEMPLOYMENT RATE
(Civilian Labor Force)

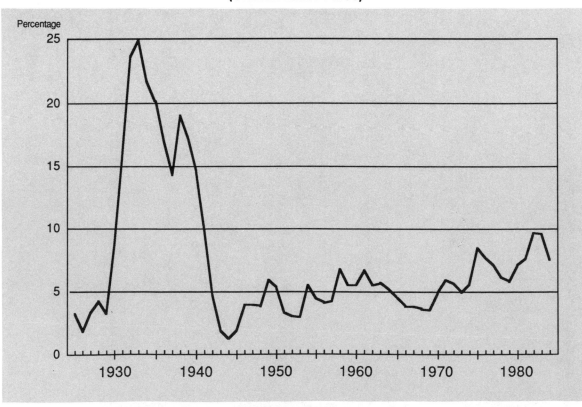

EMPLOYMENT TRENDS
Job Openings to 1990 and Current Earnings

Occupation	Number of Jobs, 1981 (000)	% Change 1980–90	Median Weekly Earnings[1] (dollars)
Industry			
Assemblers	1,145	19 to 31	236
Blue-collar worker supervisors	1,790	16 to 25	394
Compositors	128	−2 to 10	394
Machine tool operators	1,020[1]	18 to 21	274
Machinist, all-round	557	16 to 29	356
Photographic process workers	85	6 to 16	230
Printing press operators	163	9 to 17	320
Tool-and-die makers	170	8 to 24	433
Welders	709	22 to 37	334
Office			
Accountants	1,096	25 to 34	379
Bank officers, managers	680	26 to 33	411
Bank tellers	558	25 to 29	189
Bookkeepers	1,922	15 to 24	227
Cashiers	1,621	28 to 36	168
Collection workers	90	22 to 34	233
Computer operators	551	22 to 30	260
Computer programmers	357	49 to 60	422
Computer systems analysts	209	68 to 80	519
Insurance claim representatives	186	39 to 43	270
Lawyers	548	25 to 39	546
Librarians	276	3 to 5	320
Library assistants	149	3 to 4	203
Personnel and labor relations	432	15 to 22	402
Postal clerks	263	−29	400
Purchasing agents	260	16 to 24	390
Receptionists	660	22 to 31	200
Secretaries	3,587	28 to 37	229
Stenographers	72	−2 to −8	275
Telephone operators	301	4 to 15	240
Typists	1,011	18 to 25	213
Service			
Barbers	106	7 to 22	327[2]
Bartenders	309	19 to 26	195
Correction officers	103	47 to 49	313[3]
Cooks and chefs	1,360	22 to 28	171
Cosmetologists	564	14 to 29	179
Firefighters	210	17 to 19	362
Food counter workers	460	48	141
Guards	593	23 to 24	232
Meatcutters	173	11 to 18	316
Police officers	503	17 to 19	363
Waiters and waitresses	1,442	21 to 28	150

(Continued)

Employment Trends

Occupation	Number of Jobs, 1981 (000)	% Change 1980–90	Median Weekly Earnings[1] (dollars)
Educational			
K-6 teachers	1,389	18 to 19	322
Secondary school teachers	1,213	−14	351
College and university faculty	691	− 9	444
Sales			
Advertising workers	126	n/av.	334
Auto sales workers	157	26 to 36	179
Real estate agents, brokers	546	34 to 46	326
Retail trade sales workers	2,380	19 to 27	178
Construction			
Carpenters	1,082	18 to 27	325
Construction laborers	768	n/av.	250
Electricians (construction)	628	20 to 28	419
Painters	473	14 to 25	271
Plumbers, pipefitters	482	20 to 28	404
Roofers	133	15 to 24	267
Transportation			
Airplane mechanics	119	15 to 22	427
Airplane pilots	80	15 to 23	530
Airline reservation agents	86	0 to 7	339[2]
Flight attendants	56	15 to 22	365[2]
Busdrivers (local)	355	27 to 29	298
Truckdrivers (local)	1,843	23 to 31	314
Truckdrivers (long-distance)	575	23 to 31	517
Science & Technology			
Aerospace engineers	68	43 to 52	n/av.
Chemical engineers	65	23 to 32	575
Chemists	134	18 to 24	467
Civil engineers	183	26 to 31	505
Drafters	332	20 to 39	343
Electrical engineers	370	35 to 47	549
Industrial engineers	231	26 to 38	530
Mathematicians	40[1]	11 to 14	508[4]
Mechanical engineers	247	29 to 41	540
Mechanics and Repairers			
Appliance repairers	77	16 to 29	385[5]
Automobile mechanics	1,013	24 to 33	285
Business machine operators	73	60 to 74	327
Computer service technicians	97	93 to 112	395
Industrial machinery repairers	507	17 to 26	334[5]
Shoe repairers	16	12 to 17	200[2]
Telephone, PBX installers and repairers	318	15 to 30	412
TV, radio service technicians	83	31 to 43	336

Employment Trends

Occupation	Number of Jobs, 1981 (000)	% Change 1980–90	Median Weekly Earnings[1] (dollars)
Health & Medicine			
Dentists	127	23	352
Dental assistants	139	38 to 42	183
Dental hygienists	54	67	351
Dietitians	62	38 to 46	291
Health service administrators	216	43 to 53	431
Medical laboratory workers	205	35 to 43	304[6]
Nurses, registered	1,311	40 to 47	332
Nurses, licensed practical	395	42	227
Operating room technicians	31.5	39 to 45	
Pharmacists	147	10 to 20	463
Physical therapists	244	51 to 59	305
Physicians, osteopaths	436	32	501
Radiology technologists	102	36 to 43	290
Veterinarians	36	31 to 43	656[3]
Social Science			
Economists	157	26 to 32	536
Political scientists	15	14	413[7]
Psychologists	115	22 to 27	394
Sociologists	21	6 to 8	500[8]
Social Service			
School counselors	53	0	396
Social workers	383	20 to 24	309
Design			
Architects	91	33 to 41	428
Interior designers	35	25	—[9]
Communications			
Newspaper reporters	57	22 to 32	351
Public relations workers	121	18 to 26	402

1 *Average median weekly earnings of wage and salary workers employed full-time; annual averages for 1981.*
2 *1980 annual average based on reports in* Occupational Outlook Handbook, 1982–83.
3 *1980 average for federal government workers.*
4 *Average starting salary for Ph.D. holders in 1980.*
5 *1980 average salary based on a 35-hour week.*
6 *1980 average salary for medical technologists working in hospitals, medical centers, and medical schools.*
7 *1979–80 average salary for professors.*
8 *1979 average salary for doctoral sociologists.*
9 *1980 average salary ranged from $15,000 to $25,000 for moderately experienced workers.*

Source: *The World Almanac,* 1984.

3.06 Income Indicators

Personal income is considered a *coincident indicator* of economic activity. Since consumer spending is a function of personal income and levels of personal savings and borrowing, changes in real personal income affect consumer demand for goods and services.

PERSONAL INCOME PER CAPITA
By Region and State

Region, Division, and State	Current Dollars					Constant 1972 Dollars				
	1970	1980	1981	1982	1983*	1970	1980	1981	1982	1983*
United States	3,945	9,530	10,582	11,100	11,675	4,265	5,303	5,441	5,407	5,471
Regions:										
Northeast	4,423	10,097	11,276	12,047	12,814	4,781	5,635	5,797	5,868	6,005
Midwest	3,984	9,588	10,587	10,958	11,493	4,308	5,350	5,443	5,338	5,386
South	3,391	8,620	9,711	10,208	10,700	3,665	4,810	4,993	4,972	5,014
West	4,207	10,255	11,317	11,603	12,368	4,548	5,723	5,819	5,652	5,796
New England	4,306	9,989	11,149	11,958	12,845	4,655	5,574	5,732	5,825	6,019
Maine	3,303	7,672	8,480	4,031	9,619	3,571	4,281	4,365	4,399	4,507
New Hampshire	3,781	9,010	10,043	10,721	11,620	4,088	5,028	5,164	5,222	5,445
Vermont	3,530	7,833	8,882	9,478	10,036	3,816	4,371	4,567	4,617	4,703
Massachusetts	4,349	10,089	11,287	12,153	13,089	4,702	5,630	5,803	5,920	6,134
Rhode Island	3,924	9,174	10,138	10,751	11,504	4,242	5,119	5,212	5,237	5,391
Connecticut	4,913	11,536	12,871	13,810	14,826	5,311	6,438	6,617	6,727	6,947
Mid-Atlantic	4,460	10,133	11,319	12,077	12,804	4,822	5,655	5,802	5,883	6,000
New York	4,695	10,283	11,523	12,389	13,146	5,076	5,738	5,924	6,035	6,160
New Jersey	4,737	10,975	12,269	13,169	14,957	5,121	6,124	6,308	6,414	6,587
Pennsylvania	3,928	9,389	10,425	10,934	11,510	4,246	5,239	5,360	5,326	5,394
E. North Central	4,085	9,734	10,657	11,307	11,589	4,416	5,432	5,479	5,376	5,435
Ohio	3,971	9,431	10,278	10,667	11,254	4,293	5,263	5,284	5,196	5,274
Indiana	3,735	8,900	9,760	9,994	10,567	4,038	4,967	5,028	4,868	4,952
Illinois	4,515	10,470	11,621	12,091	12,626	4,881	5,843	5,975	5,889	5,917
Michigan	4,044	9,872	10,653	10,942	11,574	4,372	5,509	5,477	5,330	5,424
Wisconsin	3,774	9,344	10,238	10,725	11,132	4,808	5,214	5,264	5,224	5,216
W. North Central	3,736	9,235	10,420	10,768	11,242	4,039	5,153	5,367	5,245	5,268
Minnesota	3,893	9,691	10,683	11,115	11,666	4,209	5,408	5,493	5,433	5,467
Iowa	3,792	9,335	10,733	10,754	11,048	4,099	5,209	5,518	5,238	5,177
Missouri	3,706	8,720	9,767	10,188	10,790	4,006	4,866	5,022	4,962	5,056
North Dakota	3,216	8,761	10,896	10,830	11,350	3,477	4,889	5,602	5,275	5,319
South Dakota	3,140	8,028	9,220	9,582	9,704	3,395	4,480	4,740	4,667	5,547
Nebraska	3,748	9,139	10,311	10,641	10,940	4,052	5,100	5,301	5,183	5,126
Kansas	3,777	9,943	11,222	11,717	12,285	4,083	5,549	5,770	5,707	5,757
South Atlantic	3,605	8,787	9,805	10,357	11,020	3,897	4,903	5,041	5,045	5,164
Delaware	4,505	10,066	11,044	11,810	12,442	4,870	5,617	5,628	5,753	5,830
Maryland	4,322	10,384	11,533	12,237	12,994	4,672	5,795	5,930	5,961	6,089
Washington, D.C.	4,775	12,732	14,088	15,064	16,409	5,162	7,105	7,243	7,338	7,689
Virginia	3,712	9,305	10,385	11,056	11,835	4,013	5,193	5,339	5,385	5,546
West Virginia	3,043	7,664	8,306	8,758	8,937	3,290	4,277	4,270	4,266	4,188
North Carolina	3,220	7,753	8,646	9,048	9,656	3,481	4,326	4,445	4,407	4,525
South Carolina	2,975	7,298	8,109	8,475	8,954	3,216	4,073	4,169	4,128	4,196
Georgia	3,323	8,060	9,009	9,573	10,283	3,592	4,498	4,632	4,663	4,819
Florida	3,779	9,022	10,362	10,907	11,592	4,085	5,135	5,328	5,313	5,432
E. South Central	2,951	7,439	8,268	8,628	9,056	3,190	4,151	4,251	4,203	4,244
Kentucky	3,096	7,642	8,550	8,893	9,162	3,347	4,265	4,396	4,332	4,293
Tennessee	3,097	7,660	8,513	8,899	9,362	3,348	4,275	4,377	4,335	4,387
Alabama	2,903	7,481	8,284	8,647	9,235	3,138	4,175	4,259	4,212	4,328
Mississippi	2,556	6,678	7,390	7,725	8,072	2,763	3,727	3,799	3,763	3,783

Personal Income per Capita

Region, Division, and State	Current Dollars					Constant 1972 Dollars				
	1970	1980	1981	1982	1983*	1970	1980	1981	1982	1983*
W. South Central	3,340	9,086	10,436	10,915	11,173	3,611	5,070	5,366	5,317	5,236
Arkansas	2,773	7,166	8,149	8,424	9,040	2,998	3,999	4,190	4,103	4,236
Louisiana	3,041	8,525	9,778	10,211	10,406	3,288	4,757	5,027	4,974	4,876
Oklahoma	3,337	9,188	10,602	11,247	11,187	3,608	5,127	5,451	5,478	5,242
Texas	3,536	9,538	10,950	11,423	11,702	3,823	5,323	5,630	5,564	5,484
Mountain	3,611	9,010	10,022	10,449	10,864	3,904	5,028	5,152	5,090	5,091
Montana	3,428	8,361	9,245	9,544	9,999	3,706	4,666	4,753	4,649	4,686
Idaho	3,315	8,044	8,834	8,937	9,342	3,584	4,489	4,542	4,353	4,378
Wyoming	3,686	11,040	12,135	12,211	11,969	3,985	6,161	6,239	5,948	5,609
Colorado	3,887	10,042	11,360	12,202	12,580	4,202	5,604	5,841	5,943	5,895
New Mexico	3,072	7,889	8,695	9,135	9,560	3,321	4,402	4,470	4,450	4,480
Arizona	3,688	8,833	9,805	10,067	10,719	3,987	4,929	5,041	4,904	5,023
Utah	3,220	7,656	8,458	8,820	9,031	3,481	4,272	4,349	4,296	4,232
Nevada	4,691	10,758	11,778	12,022	12,516	5,071	6,003	6,056	5,856	5,865
Pacific	4,394	10,701	11,786	12,297	12,920	4,750	5,972	6,060	5,990	6,054
Washington	4,046	10,198	11,117	11,466	12,051	4,374	5,691	5,716	5,585	5,647
Oregon	3,711	9,356	9,979	10,231	10,920	4,012	5,221	5,131	4,983	5,117
California	4,510	10,920	12,081	12,616	13,239	4,875	6,094	6,211	6,145	6,204
Alaska	4,726	12,916	14,819	16,598	16,820	5,109	7,208	7,619	8,086	7,882
Hawaii	4,674	10,222	11,044	11,614	12,101	5,053	5,704	5,679	5,656	5,671

* *Preliminary figures.*

Source: U.S. Bureau of Economic Analysis, *Survey of Current Business*, and unpublished data.

PERSONAL INCOME PER CAPITA
Ranking by State

Region, Division and State	1970	1980	1981	1982	1983*
New England:					
Maine	37	42	44	41	40
New Hampshire	20	29	29	26	19
Vermont	32	40	38	38	36
Massachusetts	10	12	11	10	6
Rhode Island	16	27	28	27	23
Connecticut	1	2	2	2	2
Mid-Atlantic:					
New York	4	9	9	6	5
New Jersey	2	4	3	3	3
Pennsylvania	15	20	24	22	22
E. North Central:					
Ohio	14	19	26	29	25
Indiana	25	30	34	34	33
Illinois	7	7	7	9	8
Michigan	13	16	20	21	21
Wisconsin	23	23	27	25	27
W. North Central:					
Minnesota	17	17	19	19	18
Iowa	19	24	18	24	28
Missouri	28	33	33	33	31
North Dakota	40	32	17	23	23
South Dakota	41	38	36	33	38
Nebraska	24	28	25	28	29
Kansas	22	15	12	12	12
South Atlantic:					
Delaware	9	13	15	13	11
Maryland	11	8	8	8	7
Virginia	26	21	22	19	16
West Virginia	45	43	46	46	49
North Carolina	38	41	41	40	39
South Carolina	47	48	49	48	48
Georgia	35	36	37	36	35
Florida	21	25	23	20	20
E. South Central:					
Kentucky	43	46	42	43	45
Tennessee	42	44	43	44	45
Alabama	48	47	47	47	44
Mississippi	50	50	50	50	50
W. South Central:					
Arkansas	49	49	48	49	46
Louisiana	46	34	32	31	34
Oklahoma	34	26	21	17	26
Texas	31	18	16	16	17

Personal Income per Capita

Region, Division and State	1970	1980	1981	1982	1983*
Mountain:					
Montana	33	35	35	37	37
Idaho	36	37	39	42	43
Wyoming	30	3	4	5	15
Colorado	18	14	10	7	9
New Mexico	44	39	40	39	41
Arizona	29	31	31	32	32
Utah	39	45	45	45	47
Nevada	5	6	6	11	10
Pacific:					
Washington	12	11	13	15	14
Oregon	27	22	30	30	30
California	8	5	5	4	4
Alaska	3	1	1	1	1
Hawaii	6	10	14	14	13

* *Estimated.*

Source: U.S. Bureau of Economic Analysis, *Survey of Current Business.*

INCOME BY HOUSEHOLDS
(1984)

Characteristic	Total Households (000)	% Distribution of Households by Income Level								Median Income (dollars)
		Under $5,000	$5,000- 9,999	$10,000- 14,999	$15,000- 19,999	$20,000- 24,999	$25,000- 34,999	$35,000- 49,999	$50,000 and over	
Total	85,407	9.2	13.7	13.0	12.0	10.8	17.0	14.0	10.3	20,885
White	74,376	7.7	12.8	12.8	12.1	11.1	17.7	14.7	11.1	21,902
Black	9,236	21.1	20.9	15.3	11.6	8.4	11.7	8.0	3.1	12,429
Spanish origin*	4,326	12.5	19.3	15.4	13.2	12.1	13.5	9.4	4.6	15,906
Northeast	18,199	9.3	13.9	11.7	11.0	10.3	16.8	15.6	11.4	21,818
Midwest	21,456	9.1	13.2	13.1	11.9	11.5	18.2	13.7	9.3	21,068
South	28,809	10.6	14.3	13.9	12.6	10.6	16.0	12.7	9.3	19,386
West	16,943	7.0	13.2	12.8	12.1	10.7	17.2	15.0	12.0	22,217
Nonfarm	83,589	9.1	13.7	13.0	11.9	10.8	17.1	14.1	10.4	20,971
Farm	1,818	12.8	15.2	16.2	13.0	11.3	13.8	11.3	6.6	17,367
Marital status:										
Male householder	59,361	4.6	9.2	11.5	11.8	11.8	20.1	17.7	13.3	25,467
Married, wife present	47,579	2.7	7.5	10.5	11.5	12.0	21.4	19.5	15.0	27,370
Married, wife absent	1,282	16.1	18.6	13.6	10.5	10.4	15.4	8.4	6.9	15,775
Widowed	1,664	16.3	26.2	18.7	12.2	6.3	8.2	6.9	5.1	11,727
Divorced	3,345	9.4	12.6	13.4	12.9	11.8	18.0	13.8	8.2	20,631
Single (never married)	5,491	11.7	14.4	16.2	14.6	12.3	15.1	9.5	6.1	17,442
Female householder	26,046	19.7	24.0	16.6	12.3	8.5	9.8	5.8	3.3	11,667
Married, husband present	2,510	3.5	8.6	11.7	11.0	12.2	19.8	17.9	15.2	26,409
Married, husband absent	2,564	28.7	26.7	16.0	10.3	6.9	7.4	2.5	1.5	8,851
Widowed	9,484	23.7	32.3	16.8	9.2	6.0	6.7	3.3	2.0	8,806
Divorced	6,037	16.4	21.3	17.3	15.7	10.4	11.3	5.6	2.1	13,486
Single (never married)	5,450	19.8	18.3	17.8	15.4	9.9	10.3	6.2	2.5	13,251
Age of householder:										
15–24 years	5,510	15.9	20.0	20.4	14.8	12.1	10.9	4.5	1.3	13,402
25–34 years	19,808	7.2	10.0	13.1	14.3	13.9	21.1	14.4	6.0	21,746
35–44 years	16,596	5.2	7.3	9.2	10.9	11.0	21.2	19.8	15.3	27,679
45–54 years	12,471	6.0	7.5	8.8	8.4	8.9	19.0	20.9	20.4	30,352
55–64 years	13,121	9.2	12.2	11.5	11.1	10.5	17.0	15.2	13.4	22,778
65 years and over	17,901	15.3	27.3	18.2	12.6	8.3	9.0	5.6	3.7	11,718
Size of household:										
One	19,954	21.4	25.5	17.6	12.4	8.4	8.7	3.9	2.0	10,747
Two	26,890	6.2	12.8	14.6	13.7	11.9	17.5	13.9	9.4	21,065
Three	15,134	5.9	8.8	10.4	11.7	11.6	20.0	18.6	13.0	25,707
Four	13,593	4.1	7.1	8.2	9.2	11.5	23.0	20.5	16.4	29,187
Five	6,070	4.5	7.6	9.5	10.5	10.9	19.7	20.1	17.1	28,029
Six	2,372	4.5	10.3	10.8	10.8	8.7	20.7	17.8	16.4	26,888
Seven or more	1,394	5.5	12 7	13.4	10.2	11.4	15.9	16.1	14.9	23,423
Education of householder:										
Elementary school	12,860	21.2	27.3	17.6	11.4	7.3	8.4	4.9	2.0	10,370
Less than 8 years	6,895	23.9	30.1	16.5	11.0	6.5	6.6	3.9	1.5	9,221
8 years	5,964	18.0	24.1	18.9	11.8	8.2	10.4	6.0	2.6	11,811
High school	41,391	9.4	14.9	15.0	13.4	12.0	17.4	12.2	5.6	18,883
1–3 years	10,975	15.7	21.3	16.9	12.4	9.8	13.1	7.7	3.1	13,705
4 years	30,416	7.1	12.6	14.4	13.7	12.8	19.0	13.8	6.5	20,800
College	31,156	4.0	6.5	8.5	10.3	10.6	19.9	20.3	19.9	29,982
1–3 years	13,766	5.9	9.5	11.5	12.0	12.0	20.8	17.6	10.7	24,606
4 years or more	17,390	2.5	4.2	6.1	9.0	9.4	19.2	22.3	27.1	34,709
Tenure:										
Owner occupied	55,157	5.9	10.4	11.0	10.9	10.8	19.3	17.6	14.1	25,485
Renter occupied	28,704	14.8	19.6	16.7	14.1	10.9	13.0	7.6	3.3	14,621
Occupier paid no cash rent	1,546	23.5	23.6	17.2	12.4	8.6	7.9	4.7	2.1	10,722

Note: *Data for households as of March 1984.*
* *Persons of Spanish origin may be of any race.*

Source: U.S. Bureau of the Census, *Current Population Reports.*

FEDERAL MINIMUM HOURLY WAGE RATES

Effective Date	Minimum Rates for Non-farm Workers	Effective Date	Minimum Rates for Non-farm Workers
Oct. 24, 1938	$ .25	Feb. 1, 1968	$1.60
Oct. 24, 1940	.30	May 1, 1974	2.00
Oct. 24, 1945	.40	Jan. 1, 1975	2.10
Jan. 25, 1950	.75	Jan. 1, 1976	2.30
Mar. 1, 1956	1.00	Jan. 1, 1978	2.65
Sept. 3, 1961	1.15	Jan. 1, 1979	2.90
Sept. 3, 1963	1.25	Jan. 1, 1980	3.10
Feb. 1, 1967	1.40	Jan. 1, 1981	3.35

Note: *The Fair Labor Standards Act of 1938 and subsequent amendments provide for minimum wage coverage applicable to specified nonsupervisory employment categories. Exempt from coverage are executives and administrators or professionals.*

Source: U.S. Department of Labor.

AVERAGE WEEKLY HOURS OF WORK
Private Nonagricultural Industries

Period	Hours	Period	Hours	Period	Hours
1962	38.7	1970	37.1	1978	35.8
1963	38.8	1971	37.0	1979	35.7
1964	38.7	1972	37.1	1980	35.3
1965	38.8	1973	37.1	1981	35.2
1966	38.6	1974	36.6	1982	34.8
1967	38.0	1975	36.1	1983	35.0
1968	37.8	1976	36.1	1984	35.3
1969	37.7	1977	36.0		

Note: *Figures for production or nonsupervisory workers; monthly data seasonally adjusted.*

Sources: *Economic Indicators;* U.S. Department of Labor.

AVERAGE WEEKLY EARNINGS
Private Nonagricultural Industries

Period	Average Gross Weekly Earnings				% Change from a Year Earlier, Total Private Nonagricultural	
	Total Private Nonagricultural		Manufacturing	Construction	Retail Trade	Current Dollars	1977 Dollars
	Current Dollars	1977 Dollars	Current Dollars				
1975	163.53	184.16	190.79	266.08	108.86	5.7	−3.1
1976	175.45	186.85	209.32	283.73	114.60	7.3	1.5
1977	189.00	189.00	228.90	295.65	121.66	7.7	1.2
1978	203.70	189.31	249.27	318.69	130.20	7.8	.2
1979	219.91	183.41	269.34	342.99	138.62	8.0	−3.1
1980	235.10	172.74	288.62	367.78	147.38	6.9	−5.8
1981	255.20	170.13	318.00	399.26	158.03	8.5	−1.5
1982	267.26	168.09	330.26	426.82	163.85	4.7	−1.2
1983	280.70	171.37	354.08	443.42	171.05	5.0	2.0
1984	294.05	173.48	373.22	454.73	176.70	4.8	1.3

Note: *For production or nonsupervisory workers; weekly earnings seasonally adjusted. 1977 dollars = current dollars ÷ consumer price index (1977 = 100 base).*

Sources: U.S. Department of Labor, Bureau of Labor Statistics; *Economic Indicators.*

EXPECTED LIFETIME EARNINGS FOR MALES
(Data for 1979, Thousands of Dollars)

Age and Years of School Completed	Discount Rate of 0% with Annual Productivity Increase of				Discount Rate of 3% with Annual Productivity Increase of				Discount Rate of 5% with Annual Productivity Increase of			
	0%	1%	2%	3%	0%	1%	2%	3%	0%	1%	2%	3%
All Males												
Age 18: Less than 12 yrs.	601	772	1,001	1,311	300	369	460	580	200	240	291	356
High school, 4 yrs.	861	1,104	1,430	1,872	432	531	660	830	289	346	419	512
College, 1-3 yrs.	957	1,242	1,627	2,151	461	574	724	921	299	363	446	553
College, 4 yrs.	1,190	1,560	2,062	2,748	553	698	890	1,145	349	430	534	671
College, 5 yrs. or more	1,301	1,712	2,273	3,042	596	756	968	1,251	373	462	576	726
Age 25: Less than 12 yrs.	563	685	840	1,038	326	384	456	545	237	273	318	372
High school, 4 yrs.	803	976	1,196	1,478	466	548	650	777	339	391	454	531
College, 1-3 yrs.	918	1,124	1,386	1,725	522	618	738	889	375	435	508	598
College, 4 yrs.	1,165	1,434	1,780	2,226	650	774	930	1,127	461	538	632	749
College, 5 yrs. or more	1,273	1,574	1,962	2,465	699	837	1,011	1,231	490	574	679	810
Age 35: Less than 12 yrs.	441	505	581	672	298	335	378	429	235	261	292	327
High school, 4 yrs.	624	715	823	952	422	474	535	607	333	370	413	462
College, 1-3 yrs.	736	846	977	1,134	493	556	629	716	388	432	482	542
College, 4 yrs.	956	1,102	1,277	1,486	635	717	815	930	496	553	620	699
College, 5 yrs. or more	1,065	1,229	1,427	1,664	704	796	906	1,036	548	613	688	776
Age 45: Less than 12 yrs.	283	308	336	368	219	236	255	277	186	199	215	231
High school, 4 yrs.	401	438	478	523	308	334	361	392	261	281	303	327
College, 1-3 yrs.	483	528	579	635	369	400	434	472	312	336	363	392
College, 4 yrs.	639	699	767	843	486	527	573	624	409	441	477	517
College, 5 yrs. or more	715	784	862	949	541	588	641	699	454	491	531	576
Age 55: Less than 12 yrs.	121	126	132	138	105	109	114	119	96	99	103	108
High school, 4 yrs.	178	186	194	203	154	161	168	175	141	146	152	158
College, 1-3 yrs.	230	240	251	262	200	208	217	226	182	189	197	205
College, 4 yrs.	298	312	327	342	257	268	280	293	233	243	253	264
College, 5 yrs. or more	352	368	386	404	303	316	330	345	274	286	298	311
Year-round Full-time Workers												
Age 18: Less than 12 yrs.	845	1,091	1,427	1,888	419	516	644	814	281	336	406	497
High school, 4 yrs.	1,041	1,343	1,753	2,315	519	638	795	1,003	349	417	503	615
College, 1-3 yrs.	1,155	1,501	1,973	2,622	561	696	874	1,112	371	446	543	670
College, 4 yrs.	1,392	1,830	2,433	3,266	648	815	1,039	1,338	414	507	626	784
College, 5 yrs. or more	1,503	1,978	2,629	3,529	696	878	1,120	1,445	442	542	673	844
Age 25: Less than 12 yrs.	776	954	1,184	1,483	438	519	621	751	315	365	426	503
High school, 4 yrs.	954	1,170	1,451	1,815	541	640	764	922	390	451	526	620
College, 1-3 yrs.	1,075	1,326	1,650	2,073	600	714	857	1,039	428	498	584	691
College, 4 yrs.	1,329	1,650	2,069	2,616	725	869	1,051	1,284	510	596	705	840
College, 5 yrs. or more	1,444	1,792	2,244	2,834	789	945	1,143	1,396	555	649	767	915
Age 35: Less than 12 yrs.	614	712	829	971	403	457	521	597	313	350	394	445
High school, 4 yrs.	750	868	1,011	1,183	493	559	636	729	384	429	482	544
College, 1-3 yrs.	864	1,002	1,169	1,371	565	641	732	840	438	491	552	625
College, 4 yrs.	1,097	1,277	1,495	1,759	709	808	925	1,066	545	613	692	786
College, 5 yrs. or more	1,196	1,390	1,624	1,908	777	884	1,011	1,163	600	673	759	861
Age 45: Less than 12 yrs.	410	452	499	552	307	335	366	401	256	278	301	328
High school, 4 yrs.	501	552	609	673	375	409	447	489	313	339	368	401
College, 1-3 yrs.	586	646	713	788	439	478	523	573	366	396	430	468
College, 4 yrs.	762	841	929	1,030	567	619	678	744	471	511	556	606
College, 5 yrs. or more	820	904	999	1,105	612	667	730	801	509	552	600	653
Age 55: Less than 12 yrs.	203	213	224	235	173	181	190	199	156	163	171	178
High school, 4 yrs.	249	261	274	288	212	222	233	244	191	200	209	219
College, 1-3 yrs.	297	311	327	343	253	265	278	291	228	239	249	261
College, 4 yrs.	388	407	428	450	330	346	363	380	297	311	325	340
College, 5 yrs. or more	422	443	465	488	360	377	395	414	324	339	354	371

Note: *Estimates of expected lifetime earnings from the specified age to age 64 calculated by summing the product of the mean earnings at each age from a specified age to age 64, the probability of surviving to each age from the starting age, and the probability of being employed at each age. Discount rates (the difference between interest rates and the rate of inflation) used to deflate future earnings into present value (constant 1981 dollars). Productivity rates represent growth in real earnings, adjusting for inflation.*

Source: U.S. Department of Commerce, *Statistical Abstract of the United States, 1982–83.*

3.07 Tangibles and Collectibles

Historically, tangibles and collectibles have done well when the mood of the economy has been bleak or uncertain. Specific conditions that favor investment in tangibles include rising inflation, increasing taxes, political uncertainty, a consuming society, and increasing government regulation. Under such conditions, and most specifically during periods of rapid inflation, carefully selected tangibles can offer the investor a greater hedge against inflation. However, because tangibles and collectibles do not yield interest or dividends, their value depends entirely on future price appreciation.

PERFORMANCE OF TANGIBLES AND SELECTED INVESTMENTS

	1984 (CPI = +4.3%)		1983 (CPI = +3.9%)		1982 (CPI = +6.6%)		1978 (CPI = +8.1%)		1973 (CPI = +8.5%)		1968 (CPI = +7.3%)	
	% Return	Rank	% Return	Rank	% Return	Rank	% Return	Rank	% Return	Rank	% Return	Rank
Tangibles												
Gold	−4.0	12	28.6	4	−34.0	13	17.5	3	15.5	5	16.6	4
Silver	−25.2	15	109.5	1	−44.5	14	19.7	2	17.3	4	12.6	6
Diamonds	0.0	7	0	9	0	5	5.4	12	10.3	7	10.1	7
Coins	7.4	3	16.8	5	−27.8	12	13.2	6	25.7	1	17.9	2
U.S. stamps	−4.0	13	−6.2	13	−3.0	9	21.8	1	19.2	3	16.8	3
Old masters	14.3	1	1.7	8	−22.0	11	4.1	13	8.4	10	7.8	11
Chinese ceramics	3.0	6	0	10	−0.5	6	13.1	7	4.0	13	14.2	5
Selected Investments												
Stocks	−1.0	10	51.8	2	−10.5	10	14.8	5	7.5	11	5.7	13
Bonds	−7.2	14	39.0	3	11.4	2	7.2	10	6.6	12	6.4	12
T-bills	9.4	2	10.8	6	16.2	1	12.8	8	10.1	8	8.8	10
Oil	0.0	8	−14.7	14	6.3	3	16.2	4	25.4	2	20.4	1
Farmland	−0.7	9	−5.7	12	−0.9	7	7.0	11	11.7	6	10.0	8
Housing	5.5	4	2.1	7	3.4	4	7.4	9	9.2	9	8.6	9
Foreign exchange	−3.0	11	−4.3	11	−1.9	8	−2.8	14	1.4	14	3.1	14

Note: *Annual change in consumer price index (CPI) shown for comparison.*

Source: Salomon Brothers.

U.S. GOLD PRICES
(Dollars per Troy Ounce)

Year	Price	Year	Price	Year	Price
1968	39.26	1974	161.08	1980	612.56
1969	41.51	1975	161.49	1981	459.70
1970	36.41	1976	125.32	1982	376.01
1971	41.25	1977	148.31	1983	423.83
1972	58.60	1978	193.55	1984	360.29
1973	97.81	1979	307.50		

Source: U.S. Department of Commerce, *Survey of Current Business,* March 1984.

U.S. GOLD PRICES
(Dollars per Troy Ounce)

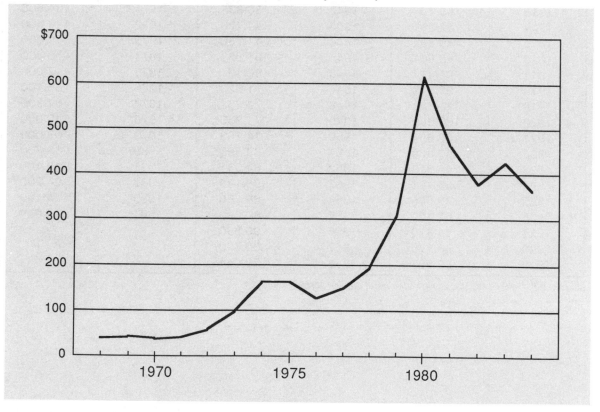

AVERAGE PRICE OF SILVER IN NEW YORK
(Cents per Troy Ounce)

Year	Average Price	Year	Average Price	Year	Average Price
1901	58.950	1930	38.154	1959	91.202
1902	52.160	1931	28.700	1960	91.375
1903	53.570	1932	27.892	1961	92.449
1904	57.221	1933	34.727	1962	108.375
1905	60.352	1934	47.973	1963	127.912
1906	66.791	1935	64.273	1964	129.300
1907	65.327	1936	45.087	1965	129.300
1908	52.864	1937	44.883	1966	129.300
1909	51.502	1938	43.225	1967	154.967
1910	53.486	1939	39.082	1968	214.500
1911	53.304	1940	34.773	1969	179.100
1912	60.835	1941	34.783	1970	177.100
1913	59.791	1942	38.333	1971	154.600
1914	54.811	1943	44.750	1972	168.500
1915	49.684	1944	44.750	1973	256.000
1916	65.601	1945	51.928	1974	470.800
1917	81.417	1946	80.151	1975	442.000
1918	96.772	1947	71.820	1976	435.400
1919	111.122	1948	74.361	1977	462.300
1920	100.900	1949	71.930	1978	540.000
1921	62.654	1950	74.169	1979	1,109.000
1922	67.528	1951	89.368	1980	2,063.300
1923	64.873	1952	84.941	1981	1,048.100
1924	66.781	1953	85.188	1982	794.700
1925	69.065	1954	85.250	1983	1,144.100
1926	62.107	1955	89.099	1984	814.050
1927	56.370	1956	90.830		
1928	58.176	1957	90.820		
1929	52.993	1958	89.044		

Source: U.S. Department of Commerce, *Survey of Current Business.*

AVERAGE PRICE OF SILVER IN NEW YORK
(Cents per Troy Ounce)

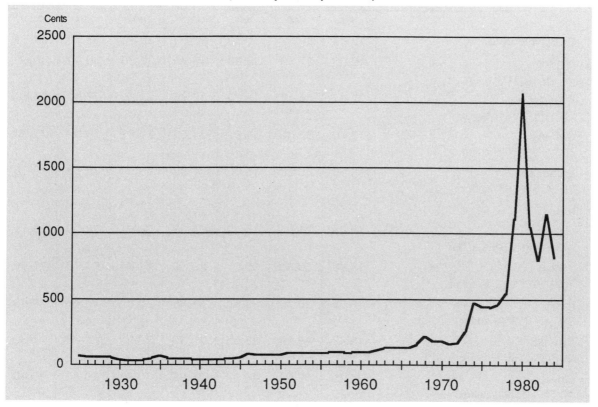

OFFICIAL SALES PRICE OF OPEC CRUDE OIL
U.S. Dollars per Barrel

	1979	1980	1981	1982	1983	1984	1985[1]
OPEC average[2]	18.67	30.87	34.50	33.63	29.31	28.70	28.59
Algeria 42° API 0.10% sulfur	19.65	37.59	39.58	35.79	31.30	30.50	30.50
Ecuador 28° API 0.93% sulfur	22.41	34.42	34.50	32.96	27.50	27.50	27.50
Gabon 29° API 1.26% sulfur	18.20	31.09	34.83	34.00	29.82	29.00	29.00
Indonesia 35° API 0.09% sulfur	18.35	30.55	35.00	34.92	29.95	29.53	29.53
Iran							
Light 34° API 1.35% sulfur	19.45	34.54	36.60	31.05	28.61	28.00	29.11
Heavy 31° API 1.60% sulfur	18.49	33.60	35.57	29.15	27.44	27.10	27.55
Iraq[3] 35° API 1.95% sulfur	18.56	30.30	36.66	34.86	30.32	29.43	29.43
Kuwait 31° API 2.50% sulfur	18.48	29.84	35.08	32.30	27.68	27.30	27.30
Libya 40° API 0.22% sulfur	21.16	36.07	40.08	35.69	30.91	30.40	30.40
Nigeria 34° API 0.16% sulfur	20.86	35.50	38.48	35.64	30.22	29.12	27.90
Qatar 40° API 1.17% sulfur	19.72	31.76	37.12	34.56	29.95	29.49	29.49
Saudi Arabia							
Berri 39° API 1.16% sulfur	19.33	30.19	34.04	34.68	29.96	29.52	29.27
Light 34° API 1.70% sulfur	17.26	28.67	32.50	34.00	29.46	29.00	29.00
Medium 31° API 2.40% sulfur	16.79	28.12	31.84	32.40	27.86	27.40	27.65
Heavy 27° API 2.85% sulfur	16.41	27.67	31.13	31.00	26.46	26.00	26.50
UAE 39° API 0.75% sulfur	19.81	31.57	36.42	34.74	30.38	29.56	29.31
Venezuela 26° API 1.52% sulfur	17.22	28.44	32.88	32.88	28.69	27.88	27.88

Note: *F.o.b. prices set by the government for direct sales and, in most cases, for the producing company buy-back oil. American Petroleum Institute (API) classifications of viscosity and sulfur content are given in each category.*

1 *January data.*
2 *Weighted by the volume of production.*
3 *Beginning in 1981 the price of Kirkuk (Mediterranean) is used in calculating the OPEC average official sales price.*

Source: Central Intelligence Agency, Directorate of Intelligence.

AVERAGE ANNUAL PRICE AT WELL OF CRUDE PETROLEUM
U.S Domestic Production

Year	Price per 42-Gallon Barrel	Year	Price per 42-Gallon Barrel
1905	$ .62	1970	$ 3.18
1910	.61	1975	7.67
1915	.64	1976	8.14
1920	3.07	1977	8.57
1925	1.68	1978	9.00
1930	1.19	1979	12.64
1935	.97	1980	21.59
1940	1.02	1981	31.77
1945	1.22	1982	28.52
1950	2.51	1983	26.19
1955	2.77	1984	26.31
1960	2.88		
1965	2.86		

Source: U.S. Department of Commerce.

AVERAGE ANNUAL PRICE AT WELL OF CRUDE PETROLEUM
(U.S. Domestic Production Price per 42-Gallon Barrel)

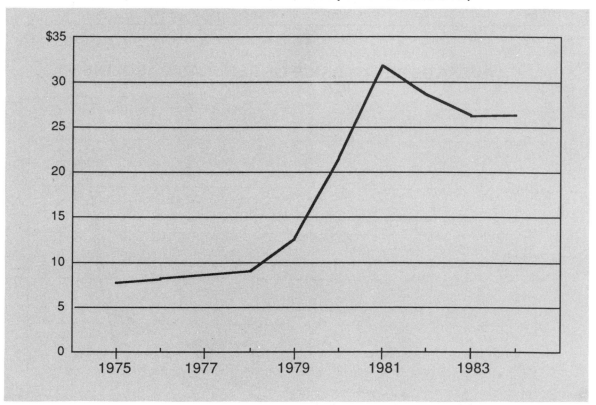

AVERAGE RETAIL PRICE OF REGULAR GASOLINE
U.S. City Average

Year	Cents per Gallon		Year	Cents per Gallon	
	Excluding Taxes	**Including Taxes**		**Excluding Taxes**	**Including Taxes**
1947	16.93	23.11	1967	22.55	33.16
1948	19.54	25.88	1968	22.93	33.71
1949	20.27	26.79	1969	23.85	34.84
1950	20.08	26.76	1970	24.55	35.69
1951	20.31	27.15	1971	25.20	36.43
1952	20.04	27.36	1972	24.46	36.13
1953	21.28	28.69	1973	26.88	38.82
1954	21.56	29.04	1974	40.41	52.41
1955	21.42	29.07	1975	45.5	56.70
1956	21.57	29.93	1976	47.4	59.47
1957	22.11	30.96	1977	50.7	63.07
1958	21.47	30.38	1978	53.1	62.60
1959	21.18	30.49	1979	74.33	85.70
1960	20.99	31.13	1980	107.35	119.10
1961	20.53	30.76	1981	n/av.	131.10
1962	20.36	30.64	1982	n/av.	122.20
1963	20.11	30.42	1983	n/av.	115.70
1964	19.98	30.35	1984	n/av.	121.23
1965	20.70	31.15			
1966	21.57	32.08			

Source: U.S. *Statistical Abstract.*

AVERAGE RETAIL PRICE OF REGULAR GASOLINE
(U.S. City Average)

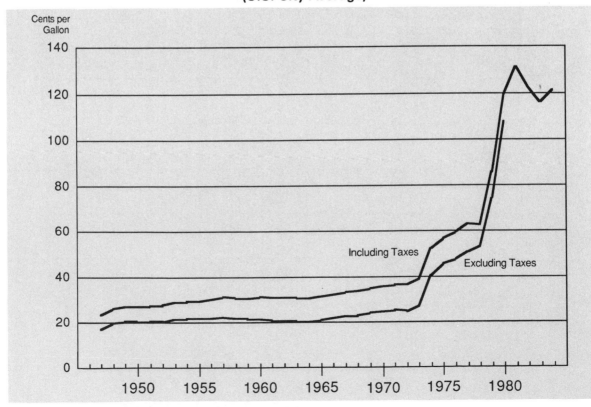

3.08 Real Estate Indicators

The role of real estate in individual and institutional portfolios has expanded over the years largely because of the increasing number of real estate investment vehicles: real estate investment trusts (REITs), limited partnerships, GNMAs, and possibly, soon, real estate-backed certificates of deposits (CDs). Real estate can provide a number of tax benefits and has typically been an excellent hedge against inflation.

Mortgage Rates

In making portfolio decisions, investors should compare yields on mortgages with those on bonds and other debt instruments. Mortgage rates run counter to home prices: high rates keep home prices in check by limiting the affordability of housing.

Housing Prices

Location is such a critical factor in real estate pricing that indicators for new and existing homes provide only broad guidelines as a basis for comparison. Purchases within specific neighborhoods must be individually evaluated.

Housing Payments and Affordability

Monthly housing payments are determined by prevailing mortgage rates and home prices. In recent years actual payments have increased somewhat, but payments as a percentage of income have risen dramatically. When the affordability index falls below 100, as it has since 1979, a median family income is insufficient to purchase a median-priced existing home.

Construction Costs

Construction costs exert considerable influence on the price of new structures, which is also reflected in the prices of existing structures.

Housing Demand

Demand for housing, often reflected in housing starts, is influenced by many factors, among them the number of new households formed and vacancy rates. New household formation, in turn, is affected not only by actual population trends but also by changes in the sociocultural and economic climate of marriage and divorce, the birthrate, and lifestyles.

Building Permits

Building permits usually are quickly transformed into housing starts — and housing starts typically help ignite an economic recovery.

TERMS OF CONVENTIONAL FIRST MORTGAGES ON NEW HOMES

Year	Contract Rate	Fees and Charges*	Maturity	Loan/Price	Purchase Price
1963	5.84%	.64%	24.0 yrs.	73.3%	$22,500
1964	5.78	.57	24.8	74.1	23,700
1965	5.74	.49	25.0	73.9	25,100
1966	6.14	.71	24.7	73.0	26,600
1967	6.33	.81	25.2	73.6	28,000
1968	6.83	.89	25.5	73.9	30,700
1969	7.66	.91	25.5	72.8	34,100
1970	8.27	1.03	25.1	71.7	35,500
1971	7.60	.87	26.2	74.3	36,300
1972	7.45	.88	27.2	76.8	37,300
1973	7.78	1.11	26.3	77.3	37,100
1974	8.71	1.30	26.3	75.8	40,100
1975	8.75	1.54	26.8	74.7	44,600
1976	8.76	1.44	27.2	74.2	48,400
1977	8.80	1.33	27.9	76.3	54,300
1978	9.33	1.39	28.0	75.2	62,800
1979	10.50	1.66	28.5	73.8	74,400
1980	12.30	2.09	28.1	73.2	83,200
1981	14.10	2.66	27.7	74.8	90,300
1982	14.47	2.95	27.6	76.6	94,600
1983	12.20	2.40	26.7	77.0	92,600
1984	11.87	2.63	27.8	78.7	96,600

Note: *Weighted averages are based on sample surveys of mortgages from major institutional lenders; compiled by the Federal Home Loan Bank Board and the Federal Deposit Insurance Corporation.*

* *Includes all fees, commissions, discounts, and "points" paid, by the borrower or seller, to obtain a loan.*

Source: *Federal Reserve Bulletin.*

NEW HOME MORTGAGE YIELDS
FHLBB Series

Year	% Annual Yield	Year	% Annual Yield	Year	% Annual Yield
1963	5.84	1971	7.74	1979	10.78
1964	5.78	1972	7.60	1980	12.66
1965	5.76	1973	7.95	1981	14.70
1966	6.25	1974	8.92	1982	15.14
1967	6.46	1975	9.01	1983	12.57
1968	6.97	1976	8.99	1984	12.38
1969	7.81	1977	9.02		
1970	8.44	1978	9.54		

Note: *Average effective interest rates on loans closed, assuming prepayment at the end of ten years.*

Sources: *Federal Reserve Bulletin; Economic Indicators.*

NEW HOME MORTGAGE YIELDS
(FHLBB Series)

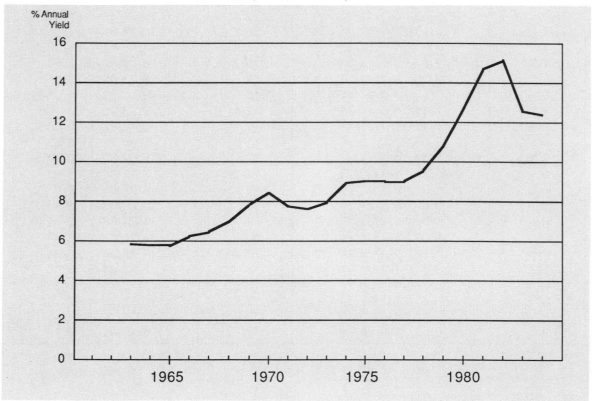

FHA/VA MAXIMUM INTEREST RATES ON HOME MORTGAGES

Rate	Period	Rate	Period
5–5 ½	11/27/34–6/23/35	9 ½	6/29/78–4/22/79
5	6/24/35–7/31/39	10	4/23/79–9/24/79
4 ½	8/01/39–4/23/50	10 ½	9/25/79–10/25/79
4 ¼	4/24/50–5/01/53	11 ½	10/26/79–2/10/80
4 ½	5/02/53–12/02/56	12	2/11/80–2/27/80
5	12/03/56–8/04/57	13	2/28/80–4/02/80
5 ¼	8/05/57–9/22/59	14	4/03/80–4/27/80
5 ¾	9/23/59–2/01/61	13	4/28/80–5/14/80
5 ½	2/02/61–5/28/61	11 ½	5/15/80–8/19/80
5 ¼	5/29/61–2/06/66	12	8/20/80–9/21/80
5 ½	2/07/66–4/10/66	13	9/22/80–11/23/80
5 ¾	4/11/66–10/02/66	13 ½	11/24/80–3/07/81
6	10/03/66–5/06/68	14	3/08/81–4/12/81
6 ¾	5/07/68–1/23/69	14 ½	4/13/81–5/07/81
7 ½	1/24/69–1/04/70	15 ½	5/08/81–8/16/81
8 ½	1/05/70–12/01/70	16 ½	8/17/81–9/13/81
8	12/02/70–1/12/71	17 ½	9/14/81–10/10/81
7 ½	1/13/71–1/17/71	16 ½	10/11/81–11/15/81
7	1/18/71–7/06/73*	15 ½	11/16/81–8/08/82
7 ¾	7/07/73–8/24/73*	15	8/09/82–8/22/82
8 ½	8/25/73–1/21/74	14	8/23/82–9/23/82
8 ¼	1/22/74–4/14/74	13 ½	9/24/82–10/12/82
8 ½	4/15/74–5/12/74	12 ½	10/13/82–11/14/82
8 ¾	5/13/74–7/07/74	12	11/15/82–5/08/83
9	7/08/74–8/13/74	11 ½	5/09/83–6/08/83
9 ½	8/14/74–11/24/74	12	6/09/83–7/08/83
9	11/25/74–1/20/75	12 ½	7/11/83–7/29/83
8 ½	1/21/75–3/02/75	13 ½	8/01/83–8/22/83
8	3/03/75–4/27/75	13	8/23/83–10/31/83
8 ½	4/28/75–9/01/75	12 ½	11/01/83–3/20/84
9	9/02/75–1/04/76	13	3/21/84–5/07/84
8 ¾	1/05/76–3/29/76	13 ½	5/08/84–5/28/84
8 ½	3/30/76–10/17/76	14	5/29/84–8/12/84
8	10/18/76–5/30/77	13 ½	8/13/84–10/21/84
8 ½	5/31/77–2/27/78	13	10/22/84–11/20/84
8 ¾	2/28/78–5/22/78	12 ½	11/21/84–3/24/85
9	5/23/78–6/28/78	13	3/26/85–4/18/85

Note: *As of November 1, 1983, the FHA rate was no longer set by the Department of Housing and Urban Development, but became determined by market conditions. Rates listed after that date are Veterans Administration rates.*

*   *FHA authority lapsed on 6/30/73 and was renewed on 8/20/73.*

Source: Mortgage Bankers Association of America, Economics Department.

REGIONAL HOUSING PRICES

Movements in sales prices can be usefully compared to the consumer price index (CPI). For example, from 1982 to 1983 the median home price in the U.S. rose 3.7%, the CPI by 3.2%, which means that the rise in median home prices exceeded inflation. Home price movements vary considerably by region, however. During the same 1982–1983 period, the median prices rose by 13.7% in the Northeast, by 2.7% in the Midwest, and by 3.0% in the South, while declining by 4% in the West.

Median and mean sales prices are shown for the United States and for each of the four standard census regions:

Northeast	**Midwest**	**South**	**West**
Connecticut	Illinois	Alabama	Alaska
Maine	Indiana	Arkansas	Arizona
Massachusetts	Iowa	Delaware	California
New Hampshire	Kansas	District of Columbia	Colorado
New Jersey	Michigan	Florida	Hawaii
New York	Minnesota	Georgia	Idaho
Pennsylvania	Missouri	Kentucky	Montana
Rhode Island	Nebraska	Louisiana	Nevada
Vermont	North Dakota	Maryland	New Mexico
	Ohio	Mississippi	Oregon
	South Dakota	North Carolina	Utah
	Wisconsin	Oklahoma	Washington
		South Carolina	Wyoming
		Tennessee	
		Texas	
		Virginia	
		West Virginia	

SALES PRICE OF EXISTING SINGLE-FAMILY HOMES
By Region

Year	United States		Northeast		Midwest		South		West	
	Median	Average (Mean)	Median	Average (Mean)	Median	Average (Mean)	Median	Average (Mean)	Median	Average (Mean)
1968	$20,100	$22,300	$21,400	$24,200	$18,200	$19,900	$19,000	$22,000	$22,900	$ 25,200
1969	21,800	23,700	23,700	26,600	19,000	21,100	20,300	23,500	23,900	26,700
1970	23,000	25,700	25,200	28,400	20,100	22,600	22,200	25,300	24,300	27,400
1971	24,800	28,000	27,100	30,600	22,100	24,300	24,300	27,800	26,500	29,700
1972	26,700	30,100	29,800	33,600	23,900	25,700	26,400	30,100	28,400	32,300
1973	28,900	32,900	32,800	36,800	25,300	28,100	29,000	33,200	31,000	35,400
1974	32,000	35,800	35,800	39,700	27,700	30,600	32,300	36,200	34,800	39,000
1975	35,300	39,000	39,300	43,600	30,100	33,100	34,800	38,800	39,600	44,100
1976	38,100	42,200	41,800	45,900	32,900	35,900	36,500	40,900	46,100	50,300
1977	42,900	47,900	44,400	49,100	36,700	40,200	39,800	45,000	57,300	63,200
1978	48,700	55,500	47,900	55,200	42,200	45,700	45,100	51,300	66,700	75,500
1979	55,700	64,200	53,600	63,300	47,800	51,600	51,300	59,000	77,400	89,400
1980	62,200	72,800	60,800	71,700	51,900	56,300	58,300	67,700	89,300	104,700
1981	66,400	78,300	63,700	76,000	54,300	58,900	64,400	75,400	96,200	111,400
1982	67,800	80,500	63,500	75,400	55,100	60,700	67,100	78,700	98,900	114,200
1983	70,300	83,100	72,200	85,400	56,600	62,900	69,200	81,500	94,900	111,000
1984	72,400	86,000	78,700	94,800	57,100	63,700	71,300	84,000	95,800	112,700

Note: *Data are not seasonally adjusted.*

Source: National Association of Realtors.

SALES PRICE OF EXISTING SINGLE-FAMILY HOMES
(United States)

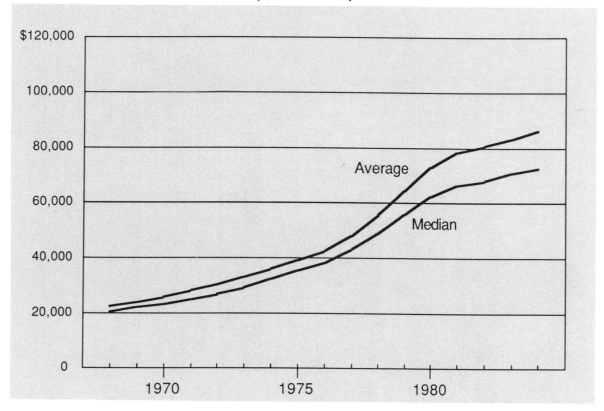

AVERAGE SALES PRICE OF EXISTING SINGLE-FAMILY HOMES
(By Region 1981–1984)

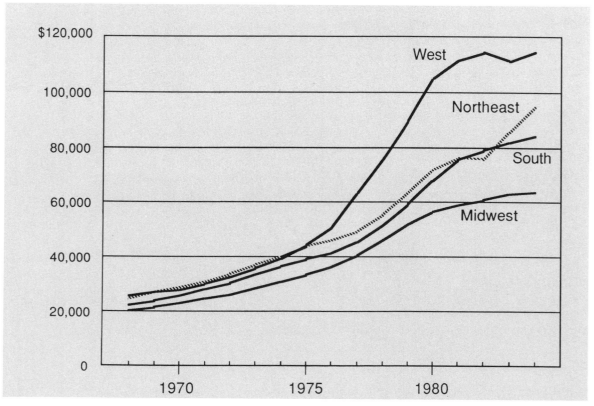

AVERAGE SALES PRICE OF EXISTING SINGLE-FAMILY HOMES
(By Region)

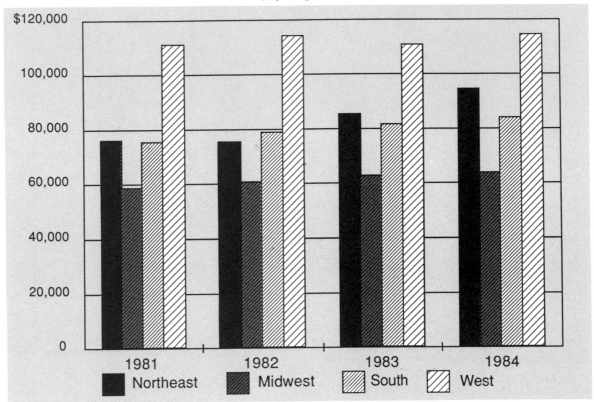

MEDIAN SALES PRICE OF EXISTING SINGLE-FAMILY HOMES
In Metropolitan Areas (Thousands of Dollars)

Sales prices of existing single-family homes vary greatly across the country. Similarly, quarterly and annual movement in local sales prices may lag behind or move ahead of the consumer price index (CPI) in different regions.

Area	1981	1982	1983	1984	1984[1]			
					I	II	III	IV
Albany	46.1	47.1	49.4	52.9	52.0	53.4	52.4	53.8
Anaheim/Santa Ana[1]	131.4	133.0	134.9	133.7	133.5	135.1	134.9	130.6
Atlanta	n/av.	55.3	63.0	66.2	67.9	63.9	64.6	68.5
Baltimore	57.7	62.0	n/av.	66.1	64.2	67.7	65.2	66.6
Birmingham	59.2	60.6	62.8	65.1	65.0	65.7	66.6	61.7
Boston	n/av.	80.2	82.6	100.0	89.4	95.6	102.0	104.8
Chicago	7.3	73.0	76.4	79.5	77.8	80.3	77.5	77.8
Cincinnati	n/av.	n/av.	57.2	58.9	58.7	59.7	59.6	57.2
Cleveland	n/av.	n/av.	n/av.	62.7	59.8	62.9	65.4	61.4
Columbus	55.0	57.8	59.4	59.9	60.2	61.1	60.4	57.4
Dallas/Ft. Worth	67.3	74.0	76.0	82.2	81.0	84.3	83.4	80.0
Denver	n/av.	76.2	78.3	82.7	79.6	82.4	85.0	82.7
Detroit	48.5	47.5	47.5	48.5	48.1	49.6	48.0	47.9
Ft. Lauderdale	72.8	74.2	73.9	73.1	69.9	71.4	76.0	73.5
Houston	72.7	77.2	79.9	77.6	78.4	77.6	79.6	74.8
Indianapolis	49.7	50.6	52.8	53.1	50.6	55.5	54.2	51.5
Kansas City	46.1	58.1	58.8	59.1	60.8	59.6	57.6	58.9
Los Angeles[1]	111.4	113.4	112.7	115.3	114.2	117.0	115.3	114.5
Louisville	47.6	46.0	47.4	48.9	47.9	49.3	49.5	48.3
Memphis	55.9	59.3	61.6	64.1	62.0	64.4	65.2	64.5
Miami	n/av.	n/av.	n/av.	79.5	79.8	78.7	82.1	77.8
Milwaukee	64.5	65.8	68.0	68.2	69.8	68.1	69.6	64.1
Minneapolis/St. Paul	69.7	72.4	73.6	74.0	73.4	73.8	75.1	73.6
Nashville	n/av.	n/av.	61.0	62.9	60.0	63.9	64.0	62.8
New York Met. Area[2]	73.8	70.5	88.9	105.3	100.6	105.4	106.9	107.7
Oklahoma City	54.1	58.4	61.6	63.9	62.1	65.4	63.6	64.4
Philadelphia	59.2	58.1	59.6	60.3	59.8	62.0	59.8	59.5
Providence	50.0	49.7	54.7	59.6	56.5	60.8	61.4	59.3
Rochester	45.9	49.5	54.8	59.7	55.4	60.3	62.1	60.4
St. Louis	n/av.	57.0	58.9	61.8	57.5	62.4	64.4	61.9
Salt Lake City	62.9	64.6	64.3	65.8	64.0	65.1	67.1	66.7
San Antonio	53.6	58.3	62.6	67.5	64.5	68.7	71.6	62.6
San Diego[1]	97.4	98.6	98.9	100.2	96.3	98.9	102.9	104.9
San Francisco[1]	121.6	124.9	129.5	129.9	126.6	130.5	132.6	130.4
San Jose[1]	109.0	122.6	127.6	123.1	125.0	124.0	121.6	119.0
Tampa	51.9	53.9	55.5	58.4	55.6	58.2	60.8	58.6
Washington, D.C.	88.3	87.2	89.4	93.0	91.3	95.5	92.9	91.7

Note: *Prices are not seasonally adjusted.*
2 *Including Long Island and Newark.*

1 *Provided by the California Association of Realtors.*

Source: National Association of Realtors.

MEDIAN SALES PRICE OF NEW PRIVATELY OWNED SINGLE-FAMILY HOMES

Year	U.S.	Northeast	Midwest	South	West
1965	$20,000	$21,500	$21,600	$17,500	$21,600
1967	22,700	25,400	25,100	19,400	24,100
1968	24,700	27,700	27,400	21,500	25,100
1969	25,600	31,600	27,600	22,800	25,300
1970	23,400	30,300	24,400	20,300	24,000
1971	25,200	30,600	27,200	22,500	25,500
1972	27,600	31,400	29,300	25,800	27,500
1973	32,500	37,100	32,900	30,900	32,400
1974	35,900	40,100	36,100	34,500	35,800
1975	39,300	44,000	39,600	37,300	40,600
1976	44,200	47,300	44,800	40,500	47,200
1977	48,800	51,600	51,500	44,100	53,500
1978	55,700	58,100	59,200	50,300	61,300
1979	62,900	65,500	63,900	57,300	69,600
1980	64,600	69,500	63,400	59,600	72,300
1981	68,900	76,000	65,900	64,400	77,800
1982	69,300	78,200	68,900	66,100	75,000
1983	75,300	82,200	79,500	70,900	80,700
1984	79,800	88,500	85,600	71,600	87,700

Source: U.S. Department of Commerce, *Construction Review.*

HOUSING AFFORDABILITY

The indicator of housing affordability is a measure of the relationship between the costs of ownership (sales price, mortgage rates) and family income. If the affordability index is 100 or more, then a family earning the median income can qualify for the median-priced existing home. But since 1979 the index has been below 100; for example, in 1983 a family earning the median income ($24,700) had only 83.6% of the income needed to buy the median-priced existing home ($70,300). However, after dipping to a low of 68.9 in 1981, the index has risen steadily through 1984, to 88.7.

Year	Median-Priced Existing Single-family Home	Mortgage Rate[1]	Monthly P & I Payment	Payment as % of Income	Median Family Income	Qualifying Income[2]	Affordability Index[3]
1977	$42,900	9.02%	$277	20.7%	$16,010	$13,279	120.6%
1978	48,700	9.58	330	22.4	17,640	15,834	111.4
1979	55,700	10.92	422	25.7	19,680	20,240	97.2
1980	62,200	12.95	549	31.3	21,023	25,328	79.9
1981	66,400	15.12	677	36.3	22,388	32,485	68.9
1982	67,800	15.38	702	35.4	23,800	33,713	70.6
1983	70,300	12.85	616	29.9	24,700	29,546	83.6
1984	72,400	12.49	618	28.2	26,300	29,650	88.7

1 *Effective rate established by the Federal Home Loan Bank Board, on loans closed on existing homes.*
2 *Based on current lending requirements of the Federal National Mortgage Association, using a 20% down payment.*
3 *Index equals 100 when median family income equals qualifying income.*

Source: *Existing Home Sales,* National Association of Realtors.

AVERAGE MONTHLY PAYMENT OF PRINCIPAL AND INTEREST
For New Homes with a 10% Down Payment

The monthly housing payment is important for the homeowner and determines the affordability of housing. Between 1963 and 1982, the average monthly payment increased by more than 700%. Substantial increases in the late 1970s and early 1980s largely reflect sharp rises in interest rates. In 1983, the easing of the recession and the Federal Reserve's "tight" money policy led to a drop in nominal mortgage rates and a corresponding decrease of 16.4% in the average monthly payment.

Year	Payment	Index	Year	Payment	Index
1963	$122	100	1975	$ 324	266
1964	123	101	1976	348	285
1965	125	102	1977	392	321
1966	138	113	1978	470	385
1967	145	119	1979	601	493
1968	160	131	1980	784	643
1969	186	152	1981	964	790
1970	203	166	1982	1,040	852
1971	196	161	1983	870	713
1972	209	171	1984	886	726
1973	238	195			
1974	289	237			

Source: *Mortgage Banking Magazine.*

INCOME NEEDED TO QUALIFY FOR FIXED-RATE, LEVEL-PAYMENT MORTGAGE

Mortgage rates determine the amount of annual income a prospective homeowner must earn to qualify for a loan. For example, if the prevailing mortgage rate is 13%, a borrower would need an annual income of approximately $49,779 to qualify for a $112,500 mortgage. Although criteria vary among lenders, most assume that mortgage payments should not exceed approximately one-third of the borrower's annual income.

Loan Amount	12%	13%	14%	15%	16%	17%
$ 36,000	14,812	15,929	17,063	18,217	19,366	20,533
45,000	18,515	19,912	21,330	22,770	24,210	25,567
54,000	22,218	23,894	25,597	27,323	29,053	30,797
67,500	27,773	29,867	31,996	34,156	36,316	38,494
90,000	37,030	39,823	42,660	45,450	48,420	51,330
112,500	46,288	49,779	53,319	56,900	60,514	64,155
135,000	55,545	59,735	63,983	68,280	72,617	76,986

Note: *Based on 30% payment-to-income ratio; 10% down payment, 30-year term.*

Source: *Mortgage Banking Magazine.*

NEW HOUSEHOLD FORMATION
(Millions)

Year	Number of U.S. Households	Average Annual Increase in No. of Households	Year	Number of U.S. Households	Average Annual Increase in No. of Households
1960	52.8	n/av.	1976	72.9	1.80
1963	55.3	.83	1977	74.1	1.20
1965	57.4	1.05	1978	76.0	1.90
1967	59.2	.90	1979	77.3	1.30
1970	63.4	1.40	1980	80.8	4.50
1972	66.7	1.65	1981	82.4	1.20
1973	68.3	1.60	1982	83.5	1.10
1974	69.9	1.60	1983	85.4	1.90
1975	71.1	1.20	1984*	87.4	2.00

* *Estimate.*

Source: Predicasts, Inc.

NEW HOUSEHOLD FORMATION
(In Millions)

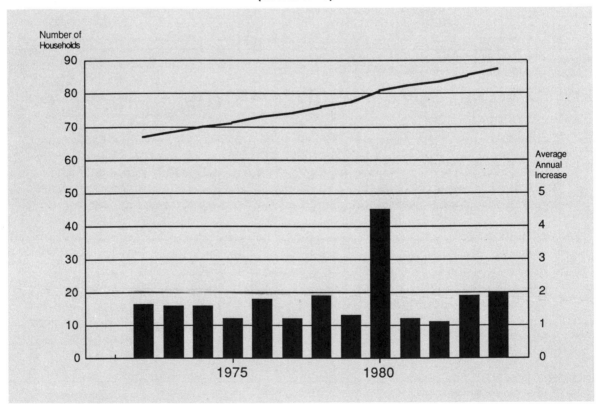

CONSTRUCTION PERMITS

The table below emphasizes the importance of location in real estate investment. Building permits, an indication of real estate growth, vary signficantly from region to region and even from city to city. A negative percentage change in one year may be a reaction to overbuilding in previous years; a large growth spurt may reflect shortages from underbuilding or increases in population or business activity. Economic conditions also affect the number of permits issued.

Region	% Change 1981–1982	% Change 1982–83
New England	0.8	−11.4
Middle Atlantic	−10.8	−0.8
North Central	5.1	8.2
West North Central	29.6	11.0
East South Atlantic	129.7	−44.1
East South Central	−3.0	40.5
West South Central	0.5	14.8
Mountain	−1.0	41.0
Pacific	3.8	23.1

Source: Reprinted with the permission of *Dun's Business Month* (formerly *Dun's Review*), May 1984, Copyright 1984, Dun & Bradstreet Publications Corporation.

TOP 10 CITIES FOR CONSTRUCTION PERMITS

City	Permits 1983 (millions)	Permits 1982 (millions)	% Change 1982–83
Los Angeles	$2,160	$1,737	24.4
Dallas	1,917	1,479	29.6
Houston	1,639	2,884	−43.2
New York	1,349	1,347	0.1
San Diego	1,151	719	60.1
San Francisco	1,122	1,172	−4.2
Anchorage	999	562	77.7
Oklahoma City	961	637	50.8
Austin	894	739	20.9
Phoenix	845	644	31.1
Chicago	779	835	−6.7

Source: Reprinted with the permission of *Dun's Business Month* (formerly *Dun's Review*), May 1984, Copyright 1984, Dun & Bradstreet Publications Corporation.

HOUSING STARTS
Including Farm Housing, but Excluding Mobile Homes (Thousands)

Year	Total	Single-Family	Multi-Family
1935	221	183	38
1940	603	486	117
1945	326	118	25
1950	1,952	n/av.	n/av.
1951	1,491	n/av.	n/av.
1952	1,504	n/av.	n/av.
1953	1,438	n/av.	n/av.
1954	1,551	n/av.	n/av.
1955	1,646	n/av.	n/av.
1956	1,349	n/av.	n/av.
1957	1,224	n/av.	n/av.
1958	1,382	n/av.	n/av.
1959	1,554	1,251	303
1960	1,296	1,009	288
1961	1,365	989	376
1962	1,492	996	496
1963	1,635	1,013	622
1964	1,561	972	589
1965	1,510	965	544
1966	1,196	780	417
1967	1,322	845	477
1968	1,545	900	645
1969	1,500	811	688
1970	1,469	815	654
1971	2,052.2	1,151.0	901.2
1972	2,356.6	1,309.2	1,047.4
1973	2,045.3	1,132.0	913.3
1974	1,337.7	888.1	449.6
1975	1,160.4	892.2	268.2
1976	1,537.5	1,162.4	385.1
1977	1,987.1	1,450.9	536.2
1978	2,020.3	1,433.3	587.0
1979	1,745.1	1,194.1	551.0
1980	1,292.2	852.2	440.0
1981	1,084.2	705.4	378.8
1982	1,062.2	662.6	399.6
1983	1,703.0	1,067.6	635.5
1984	1,749.5	1,084.2	665.4

Source: *Economic Indicators.*

HOUSING STARTS

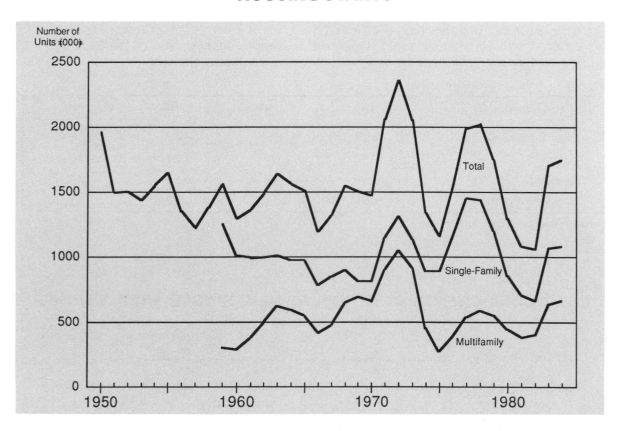

COST COMPONENTS OF A TYPICAL NEW SINGLE-FAMILY HOME

In home building the costs of labor and materials as a percentage of total costs have declined, while land prices and financing costs have each doubled over the last 35 years. The combined cost of overhead and profit, however, has barely changed.

Component	1949	1969	1982	1984
Labor & materials	69%	55%	45%	47%
Land	11	21	24	25
Financing	5	7	15	11
Overhead & profit	15	17	16	17

Source: *Contra Costa Times,* July 3, 1984.

COST COMPONENTS OF A TYPICAL NEW SINGLE-FAMILY HOME

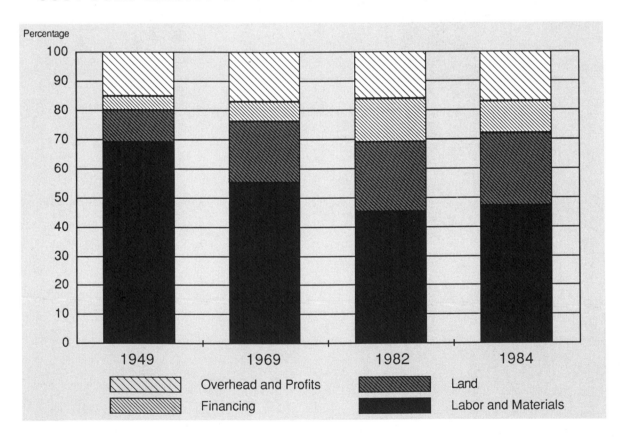

INDEX OF CONSTRUCTION COSTS
"Boeckh Index" The American Appraisal Company

Year	Small Residential Structures	Apartments, Hotels, and Office Buildings	Commercial and Factory Buildings
1920	16.0	15.0	14.3
1925	12.9	12.4	12.0
1930	13.2	12.4	12.1
1935	10.9	10.9	10.6
1940	13.7	13.4	13.0
1945	19.0	17.5	16.8
1950	29.1	26.8	25.7
1951	31.4	28.9	27.7
1952	32.2	29.9	28.7
1953	32.8	30.8	29.7
1954	32.5	31.1	30.0
1955	33.5	32.0	31.0
1956	34.9	33.5	32.7
1957	35.6	34.6	33.8
1958	36.0	35.2	34.5
1959	37.2	36.4	35.7
1960	37.8	37.1	36.3
1961	37.9	37.6	36.6
1962	38.5	38.5	37.4
1963	39.3	39.4	38.2
1964	40.4	40.5	39.3
1965	41.7	41.9	40.7
1966	43.5	43.6	42.4
1967	46.2	46.2	45.2
1968	49.5	49.5	48.2
1969	53.6	53.7	51.7
1970	56.5	57.5	55.6
1971	n/av.	n/av.	n/av.
1972	n/av.	n/av.	n/av.
1973	73.5	71.3	69.8
1974	79.4	77.9	77.3
1975	84.7	85.6	85.3
1976	91.7	92.4	92.6
1977	100.0	100.0	100.0
1978	109.0	106.5	107.5
1979	119.0	114.7	117.1
1980	128.9	125.1	127.7
1981	136.0	137.4	140.1
1982	147.5	150.0	151.9
1983	156.2	159.6	159.9
1984	165.1	166.8	166.2

Note: *1977 = 100. Average of 20 cities for types shown. Weights based on surveys of building costs. Wage rates used for both common and skilled labor. Reflects payment of sales taxes and Social Security payroll taxes.*

Sources: U.S. Department of Commerce, *Construction Review* and *Historical Statistics of the U.S.*

CONSUMER PRICE INDEXES OF RESIDENTIAL RENTS
In Selected Metropolitan Areas

Greater Metropolitan Area	1970	1975	1976	1977	1978	1979	1980	1981	1982	1983	1984[2]
Anchorage[1]	n/av.	125.5	143.2	152.9	160.4	161.1	158.3	169.1	206.6	239.3	250.3[3]
Atlanta	109.9	129.0	131.2	135.3	140.0	152.3	168.2	188.4	199.9	214.2	226.6
Baltimore	106.9	127.4	135.5	143.9	154.6	163.5	173.8	187.7	204.6	221.5	231.9[3]
Boston	115.4	149.6	156.7	166.2	174.2	183.0	198.8	222.5	245.5	262.0	274.5[3]
Buffalo	109.3	140.8	149.3	156.8	162.7	169.2	177.2	185.2	195.6	206.5	214.8
Chicago	107.6	132.8	137.7	142.7	150.6	160.6	172.2	185.0	199.2	210.2	220.1
Cincinnati	105.7	120.1	124.0	133.4	142.9	155.2	169.1	183.5	191.8	200.2	205.3[3]
Cleveland	107.5	123.7	130.8	139.8	149.7	158.9	170.9	179.7	190.5	199.8	206.5
Dallas	110.1	122.1	129.2	140.3	155.5	172.6	191.2	211.1	228.6	247.7	258.3
Denver-Boulder	n/av.	130.3	133.5	139.7	152.3	168.8	186.8	204.9	228.5	244.0	252.6[3]
Detroit	111.5	135.9	141.5	150.8	162.6	176.5	194.1	206.1	214.3	220.2	226.7
Honolulu	118.1	150.4	156.8	163.5	174.1	187.3	206.1	224.8	240.7	253.0	270.2
Houston	106.9	125.3	140.1	155.8	163.0	172.1	182.8	198.8	223.6	230.4	226.7
Kansas City	106.3	119.2	124.0	131.3	139.6	149.2	160.3	174.0	187.2	199.2	214.7
Los Angeles-Long Beach-Anaheim	111.9	134.8	144.3	157.2	171.7	188.5	211.3	235.2	257.9	274.8	293.9
Milwaukee	109.8	136.9	144.1	152.5	159.6	168.7	179.6	192.7	208.8	221.0	229.7
Minneapolis-St. Paul	114.2	132.8	141.5	150.6	160.5	175.8	195.2	214.3	231.1	244.5	252.3
New York	110.9	153.7	162.5	171.4	180.1	188.7	202.5	217.6	232.6	247.4	258.7
Northeast Pennsylvania	113.1	155.9	166.3	178.2	186.2	207.2	220.7	229.3	238.1	251.7	257.7[3]
Philadelphia	112.5	146.4	155.7	166.1	174.4	182.4	194.5	210.2	229.6	246.4	260.4
Pittsburgh	109.0	129.0	137.0	149.2	162.7	173.9	185.3	198.5	211.6	223.6	233.0
Portland	109.3	135.8	145.2	157.9	172.6	188.5	202.6	217.1	222.5	271.1	231.4[3]
St. Louis	105.6	116.1	120.4	127.0	136.8	149.0	165.6	179.2	191.8	202.4	215.0[3]
San Diego	123.6	148.7	158.3	170.2	185.6	205.5	225.3	243.2	263.5	286.4	309.3[3]
San Francisco-Oakland	119.3	144.8	153.3	164.7	177.3	190.3	214.3	236.1	258.8	284.4	306.0
Seattle	109.1	130.8	141.1	153.6	168.0	195.1	226.1	239.8	245.2	247.6	253.8[3]
Washington, DC	109.4	140.3	149.0	158.4	168.0	181.2	197.2	215.5	233.8	251.2	262.8[3]

Note: *Data represent annual averages of monthly figures, except as indicated; 1967 = 100.*
1 *Oct. 1967 = 100.* **2** *June data.* **3** *May data.*

Source: U.S. Bureau of Labor Statistics, *Monthly Labor Review.*

NATIONWIDE RENTAL AND HOMEOWNER VACANCY RATES

Year	Rental Vacancy Rate				Homeowner Vacancy Rate			
	Q1	Q2	Q3	Q4	Q1	Q2	Q3	Q4
1960	8.0	8.0	8.3	8.4	1.2	1.3	1.3	1.3
1965	8.5	8.2	7.8	8.5	1.7	1.5	1.6	1.5
1966	8.3	7.4	7.4	7.7	1.5	1.5	1.4	1.3
1967	7.3	6.9	7.0	6.2	1.4	1.3	1.4	1.3
1968	6.1	6.2	5.9	5.4	1.1	1.1	1.2	1.2
1969	5.6	5.7	5.5	5.1	1.0	1.0	1.1	1.0
1970	5.4	5.4	5.3	5.2	1.0	1.0	1.1	1.1
1971	5.3	5.3	5.6	5.6	1.0	0.9	1.0	1.0
1972	5.3	5.5	5.8	5.6	1.0	1.0	0.9	1.0
1973	5.7	5.8	5.8	5.8	1.0	0.9	1.1	1.2
1974	6.2	6.3	6.2	6.0	1.2	1.1	1.2	1.3
1975	6.1	6.3	6.2	5.4	1.2	1.2	1.4	1.2
1976	5.5	5.8	5.7	5.3	1.2	1.2	1.3	1.2
1977	5.1	5.3	5.4	5.1	1.3	1.3	1.1	1.0
1978	5.0	5.1	5.0	5.0	1.0	0.9	1.0	1.1
1979[1]	5.1	5.5	5.7	5.4	1.1	1.1	1.2	1.3
1979[2]	4.8	5.0	5.2	5.0	1.0	1.1	1.1	1.1
1980	5.2	5.6	5.7	5.0	1.3	1.4	1.4	1.4
1981	5.2	5.0	5.0	5.0	1.3	1.3	1.5	1.4
1982	5.3	5.1	5.3	5.5	1.4	1.6	1.5	1.6
1983	5.7	5.5	5.8	5.5	1.4	1.5	1.6	1.6
1984	5.6	5.5	6.0	6.3	1.6	1.7	1.7	1.7

1 *1979 revised rates.*   **2** *Rates as published in 1979 before revisions in processing were employed.*

Source: U.S. Department of Commerce, Bureau of the Census, *Housing Vacancies.*

QUOTED OFFICE RENTAL RATES

Class A Space
($ per Square Foot per Year)

City	Existing Buildings				Buildings Under Construction			
	Central Business District		Other Districts		Central Business District		Other Districts	
	Avg.	Range	Avg.	Range	Avg.	Range	Avg.	Range
Atlanta	18.05	13.25–25.00	16.38	12.00–22.00	21.77	19.00–25.00	18.83	14.75–23.00
Baltimore	21.50	19.00–24.00	15.00	13.00–17.00	23.00	22.00–24.50	16.00	13.75–22.00
Boston	33.83	22.00–60.00	16.76	9.00–30.00	36.16	26.00–50.00	22.80	16.00–34.00
Chicago	19.25	17.00–32.00	14.75	13.50–20.00	24.50	22.00–33.00	19.25	18.50–26.00
Cleveland	18.50	16.50–23.00	14.50	12.00–17.00	23.00	18.00–28.00	15.50	13.50–17.50
Dallas	20.84	17.75–24.60	17.95	12.50–24.50	30.00	25.00–35.00	20.75	16.00–26.25
Denver	22.00	18.00–25.00	20.00	18.00–24.00	29.00	25.00–31.00	22.00	20.00–26.00
Fort Worth	16.88	14.70–20.00	14.68	12.35–18.25		n/av.	16.00	14.00–20.00
Hartford	22.50	14.00–28.50	15.00	11.00–19.50	25.00	21.00–27.00	19.00	13.50–24.00
Houston	21.40	15.00–30.00	20.19	15.00–32.00		n/av.	17.78	14.50–23.50
Kansas City	16.00	12.50–18.00	15.00	11.50–25.00	20.00	19.00–22.50	21.00	15.00–25.00
Los Angeles	27.00	20.00–34.00	21.30	15.00–27.60	30.00	26.00–34.00	25.20	22.20–28.50
Manhattan	43.09	28.75–77.75	33.51	21.75–48.75	50.75	44.75–62.75	42.75	38.75–54.75
Miami	28.50	20.00–37.00	20.00	12.00–28.00	32.50	25.00–40.00	22.50	14.00–31.00
New Orleans	22.00	20.00–24.00	20.00	18.50–22.00	24.00	23.00–25.00		n/av.
Philadelphia	21.00	18.00–28.00	16.00	12.00–18.50	28.00	27.00–30.00	18.00	17.00–22.00
Pittsburgh	21.75	17.00–28.50	16.00	14.00–17.50	20.90	15.00–28.00	17.25	14.00–18.00
San Diego	21.00	14.40–35.00	21.80	15.40–42.00	22.20	19.20–24.00	17.40	11.40–22.20
San Francisco	32.00	22.00–39.00		n/av.	39.00	30.00–44.00		n/av.
Stamford, Conn.	28.50	20.50–41.00	26.50	19.50–41.50	32.50	30.50–36.50	26.50	19.50–31.50
Washington, D.C.	27.50	17.00–36.50	17.88	13.25–24.00	33.40	22.50–43.50	21.31	13.50–30.00
White Plains, N.Y.	26.50	24.00–29.00	25.00	22.00–29.00	27.00	26.00–29.00	25.00	24.00–27.00

Note: *See the Glossary of Rental Space Data, page 3.137.*

Source: The Office Network, Inc.

GLOSSARY FOR OFFICE SPACE DATA

Absorption

The net increase, or decrease, in square feet of occupied office space in a market over a given period.

Available for lease

In existing buildings, space currently available to lease, including sublease space. In buildings under construction, any space that has not been preleased.

Building classification class A

Building has excellent location and access to attract the highest quality tenants. Must be well managed. Structure is of high quality finish, usually new or competitive with new buildings.

CBD: Central business district

The generally accepted downtown area. In New York City, CBD refers to midtown Manhattan.

Contiguous space

A block of adjoining office space in a building.

Existing buildings

Office buildings currently occupied or available for occupancy.

Market surveyed

Includes multi-tenant office buildings measured in rentable area. Excludes solely owner-occupied, government, and medical buildings. Both existing buildings and those under construction are surveyed.

Operating costs

The annual cost per square foot to operate a building. Includes energy, janitorial, and other costs, and taxes.

Outside CBD/suburban

The market area outside of the downtown area. In New York City, Outside CBD refers to downtown Manhattan (Wall Street area).

Prelease

The leasing of office space in buildings not yet available for occupancy.

Rentable area

The floor area of an office building less any vertical penetration of the floors. No deductions are made for columns and projections necessary to the building.

Rental rates

Annual rental costs per square foot measured on rentable basis. Rates include operating costs and typical buildout and lease terms. An average rate is a typical rate, not necessarily a mathematical average.

Sublease space

Space already under lease to a tenant who in turn subleases it to a second tenant, usually requiring approval of the landlord.

Under construction

Office buildings underway (ground broken) but not yet ready for occupancy.

Usable area

The actual area of an office building that can be occupied, excluding all common areas, corridors, and vertical penetrations of floors.

Vacancy

Office space that is physically vacant.

Source: The Office Network, Inc.

3.09 Limited Partnerships

Limited partnerships are, essentially, the investment enterprises of groups of investors who pool their resources to put money directly into various businesses, principally oil and gas drilling, agriculture, equipment leasing, and real estate. A limited partnership consists of a general partner (the management that forms and runs the company) and limited partners (individuals who invest funds to keep the company operating).

Limited partnerships may be organized to offer investors current income, capital gains, or tax shelter. *Public limited partnerships* are registered with the Securities and Exchange Commission and the securities commissions of those states in which they are offered. Public offerings have minimum investment requirements and investor suitability standards. (See also Chapter 5, Section 5.08.) *Private limited partnerships* are exempt from registration, but must comply with Regulation D (see page 3.143). Private offerings are limited to 35 accredited investors, have higher investor suitability standards, and may not be sold across state lines.

NUMBER OF SPONSORS AND PUBLICLY REGISTERED PROGRAMS

	Sponsors of Publicly Registered Programs[1]			Publicly Registered Programs		
	1982	1983	1984	1982	1983	1984
Real Estate	n/av.	89	100	n/av.	133	142
Leveraged	n/av.	89	100	n/av.	133	142
Unleveraged	n/av.	30	40	n/av.	43	68
Mortgage loans	n/av.	13	21	n/av.	18	23
FREITs[2]	n/av.	3	7	n/av.	3	8
Total	75	94	133	122	197	241
Oil and Gas						
Drilling	93	65	58	103	72	64
Income	18	40	29	24	43	42
Royalty and completion	6	4	3	8	6	3
Combination[3]	0	10	7	0	10	7
Total	99	103	81	135	131	116
Equipment Leasing	10	15	17	13	21	24
Miscellaneous	26	56	67	23	70	81
Total	186	252	275	293	419	462

1 *Sponsor total adjusted to reflect participation of some sponsors in more than one category.*
2 *Finite-life REITs.*
3 *Includes programs that allocate significant portions of capital to both drilling operations and property purchases.*

Source: Robert A. Stanger & Co.

REAL ESTATE PROGRAM SALES
By Investment Description (Millions of Dollars)

Investment	1981	1982	1983	1984	% Change 1983–84	% Share of 1984 Real Estate Market
Leveraged	$ n/av.	$1,492.0	$2,549.8	$2,380.9	−6.6	41.9
Unleveraged	n/av.	456.2	920.9	1,953.3	112.1	34.3
Mortgage Loans	n/av.	317.5	875.1	938.7	7.3	16.5
FREITs[1]	n/av.	205.6	128.7	413.0	220.9	7.3
Total[2]	$1,600.0	2,471.3	4,474.5	5,685.9	27.0	100.0
Commercial, residential	$ 603.6	856.5	1,533.1	2,263.8	47.7	39.7
Commercial	356.2	270.9	788.6	857.9	8.8	15.1
Residential	342.9	390.0	583.0	431.6	−26.2	7.6
Subsidized housing	66.0	107.3	168.0	196.1	16.7	3.5
Mini warehouse	73.0	100.3	164.1	278.0	69.4	4.9
Commercial net lease	32.3	173.1	182.6	244.6	34.0	4.3
Hotels, motels	38.5	47.1	51.1	54.6	6.8	1.0
Mobile home	—[2]	3.0	0.2	7.6	3,700.0	0.1
Mortgage loans	356.2	317.5	875.1	938.7	7.3	16.5
FREITs[1]	—[2]	205.6	128.7	413.0	220.9	7.3
Total	$1,600.0	2,471.3	4,474.5	5,685.9	27.0	100.0

1 *Self-liquidating (finite-life) REITs only.*
2 *1981 sales included in residential category.*

Source: *Stanger's Tax Shelter Yearbook.*

NASD DIRECT PARTICIPATION PROGRAM FILINGS

	Product	Number	Dollars Registered		Product	Number	Dollars Registered
1971	Oil & gas	155	740,093,579	**1978**	Oil & gas	95	1,613,397,975
	Real estate	139	523,534,085		Real estate	70	782,671,171
	Vintage & farming	7	30,226,611		Vintage & farming	2	27,700,000
	Cattle feeding & breeding	22	244,915,620		Cattle feeding & breeding	14	22,325,000
	Miscellaneous	11	29,915,620		Miscellaneous	29	162,815,950
	Total	334	1,568,405,895		Total	210	2,608,910,096
	REIT	71	2,540,358,976		REIT	10	226,806,011
1972	Oil & gas	230	1,110,607,895	**1979**	Oil & gas	110	2,086,572,625
	Real estate	207	787,735,062		Real estate	74	910,176,295
	Vintage & farming	20	34,568,034		Vintage & farming	0	-0-
	Cattle feeding & breeding	31	193,512,000		Cattle feeding & breeding	5	43,255,000
	Miscellaneous	19	55,256,800		Miscellaneous	59	649,321,000
	Total	507	2,181,679,791		Total	233	3,430,316,920
	REIT	62	1,417,807,823		REIT	18	246,247,500
1973	Oil & gas	228	908,615,170	**1980**	Oil & gas	110	3,935,248,259
	Real estate	207	849,436,163		Real estate	131	1,988,299,203
	Vintage & farming	29	59,894,880		Vintage & farming	0	-0-
	Cattle feeding & breeding	47	397,111,000		Cattle feeding & breeding	5	53,700,000
	Miscellaneous	28	205,712,000		Miscellaneous	59	649,321,000
	Total	504	2,352,769,213		Total	349	6,626,568,462
	REIT	51	1,320,457,871		REIT	10	141,926,250
1974	Oil & gas	158	868,006,102	**1981**	Oil & gas	211	2,086,572,625
	Real estate	94	521,457,932		Real estate	159	3,587,570,079
	Vintage & farming	17	29,666,600		Vintage & farming	0	-0-
	Cattle feeding & breeding	18	142,561,010		Cattle feeding & breeding	5	70,500,000
	Miscellaneous	19	98,446,190		Miscellaneous	94	1,474,030,748
	Total	306	1,628,137,834		Total	469	12,231,858,175
	REIT	13	122,983,560		REIT	9	348,442,250
1975	Oil & gas	121	575,994,990	**1982**	Oil & gas	144	5,246,028,475
	Real estate	67	341,425,001		Real estate	203	4,644,674,287
	Vintage & farming	4	2,465,150		Vintage & farming	1	30,000,000
	Cattle feeding & breeding	8	27,845,000		Cattle feeding & breeding	3	110,625,000
	Miscellaneous	33	57,457,300		Miscellaneous	101	1,534,323,291
	Total	242	1,005,187,441		Total	452	11,565,651,053
	REIT	10	138,911,490		REIT	12	402,120,825
1976	Oil & gas	119	757,772,513	**1983**	Oil & gas	136	7,993,695,048
	Real estate	44	272,705,500		Real estate	222	7,116,198,286
	Vintage & farming	3	2,750,000		Vintage & farming	0	-0-
	Cattle feeding & breeding	5	35,980,000		Cattle feeding & breeding	4	67,975,000
	Miscellaneous	25	111,438,000		Miscellaneous	110	2,849,829,800
	Total	196	1,180,596,013		Total	472	18,027,698,134
	REIT	8	118,134,420		REIT	12	925,885,625
1977	Oil & gas	85	$ 1,202,651,745	**1984**	Oil & gas	98	3,565,708,000
	Real estate	47	292,973,320		Real estate	247	10,230,786,000
	Vintage & farming	2	17,500,000		Vintage & farming	0	-0-
	Cattle feeding & breeding	14	57,237,500		Miscellaneous*	100	3,596,205,000
	Miscellaneous	34	250,030,575		Total	445	17,392,699,000
	Total	182	1,820,393,140		REIT	18	1,763,498,000
	REIT	9	81,246,762				

* *Includes cattle feeding and breeding.*

Source: National Association of Securities Dealers, Inc.

DUE DILIGENCE

Before advising an investor to put money into any investment program, a financial professional must determine the credibility of the sponsor — a process often referred to as due diligence. The following list of questions provides a guideline for such research.

The Sponsor

- Who is the sponsor? What is the general history of the sponsor's organization? The sucess of previous programs? Reputation within the industry? About the organization: its age; net worth and composition of the net worth; earnings; numbers of stockholders and stockholder-employees; growth pattern; and its reputation in the industry?

- Who are the decision makers in the sponsor's organization? Do their education and experience qualify them relative to the program being offered and its future management?

- Does management have operational experience in areas critical to the success of the program or is their expertise mainly in raising money? (The ability to raise money is not a guarantee that an organization knows how to manage money or the assets acquired.)

- What is the sponsor's track record regarding the amount, consistency, and sources of cash distributions back to investors?

- What banking relations does the issuer or sponsor maintain? What is its line of credit? What is its policy on cash reserves?

- What are the issuer's fiduciary activities? Are internal auditing procedures, investor relations programs, including financial reporting and communications relative to tax data, asset acquisition, and sales and other significant events included? (Examination of investor communications from previous programs will provide some insight.)

- Has the sponsor even been involved in SEC, state, or NASD investigations?

- Are all relevant risk factors disclosed and fully described in the offering material?

- What is the sponsor's general philosophy regarding risk?

- How accessible is the management?

- What percentage of the distributions has come from operations and what percentage from contributed capital?—in this program?—in other programs of the sponsor?

The Program

The following points pertain to specific types of programs.

OIL AND GAS

- Consider the sponsor's record of both cash distributions and total expected return. The economics of a 2-to-1 program that produces a large amount of recoverable reserves and, therefore, cash returns, in the early years may be superior to a 3-to-1 program with long-lived gas reserves providing little cash in the early years.

- Look at program size. On average, sponsors with annual fundraising under $10 million exceeded both the annual industry total expected return ratio and the average for sponsors raising more than $10 million (1976 to 1981).

- The odds of investing in a program that returns three times the amount invested are about 1 in 4. The odds of not recovering the original investment are about 1 in 3. About 4 out of 10 programs will return more than $2.00 per dollar invested, and 1 out of 10 will return more than $5.00 for each dollar invested.

REAL ESTATE

- Is the program structured so that investors are equity owners of existing income-producing properties, rather than lenders?

- Is the program's portfolio geographically diversified so that it has holdings in several areas, rather than in one city or region?

- Is the program's portfolio functionally diversified so that it includes different kinds of income properties (apartments, office buildings, shopping centers, and business or industrial parks)?

- Have distributions and tax benefits been realized as originally anticipated in this program and in other programs having the same sponsor?

- Who is responsible for the selection of properties, and what are his or her qualifications?

- In selecting properties in previous programs, how well has management anticipated economic trends and conditions?

- What has been management's timing on the purchase of properties, i.e., in identifying markets where rent increases were possible?

- What kind of emphasis is placed on property management?

- Who is, or will be, managing the properties in the program? Is the staff adequate in number, skill, and experience?

- What kinds of cash flows to investors have been produced by properties the sponsor has managed previously or is now managing?

- Does the property management group have a proprietary attitude? How effective are they? Are they market-oriented and cost-conscious?

PRIVATE PLACEMENT PROGRAMS

In contrast to public programs, private placements or private programs are tax-sheltered investments not registered with the Securities and Exchange Commission (SEC). They are offered and sold subject to the private offering exemption first established under the Securities Act of 1933, as modified by some registration exemptions granted by the securities regulation authorities of one or more states. The broad-based and far-reaching Regulation D was adopted by the SEC on March 8, 1982, and become effective April 15, 1982. This regulation has eased the burdens of making an exempt offering of limited partnership interests under the Securities Act of 1933.

Small businesses can now raise needed financing under three new exemptive rules that entirely replace Rules 240, 242, and 146. Regulation D brings together these replacements—Rules 504, 505, and 506—in a single, coherent regulation that contains uniform terms and conditions, and a uniform notice of sales form. The regulation, with its three expanded exemptions, represents a major effort by the SEC to assist capital formation and reduce the burdens imposed by the federal securities law.

Rules regulating private placements fall into six major categories:

- number of investors,

- nature (qualifications) of investors,

- issuer qualifications,

- information requirements,

- aggregate offering price limitation, and

- limitations on manner of offering.

The following analysis is abbreviated to include only key points relating to programs qualifying under Regulation D. The accompanying chart provides additional detail as to how the new regulation affects private placement offerings. Financial professionals should refer to the regulations in their entirety to assure a complete understanding of private placement procedures.

Number of Investors

A private placement under the new Rule 506 may have no more than 35 purchasers who are not accredited and an unlimited number of accredited investors. Accredited investors are those:

- With a net worth (either individual or joint, including home, automobile, and furnishings) of $1,000,000 or more

- With a gross income of $200,000 for the current and most recent two years

- Who make a cumulative investment of $150,000 within five years of the date of purchase and whose net worth is at least five times the investment

- Any entity 100% owned by accredited investors

Nature of Investors

Generally speaking, investors should not be participating in a private offering unless they are in the top tax bracket. The issuer must determine before any sale that the purchaser, either alone or in conjunction with a representative, has the knowledge and experience in financial and business matters to evaluate the merits and risks of the prospective investment. The issuer must also determine whether the purchaser can bear the economic risk of the investment.

Qualifications of Issuer

Some limited partnership offerings qualify for private placement treatment (Rule 505). However, this option is limited to program sponsors who have not been subject to the reporting requirements of Sections 13 and 15(d) of the Exchange Act for 36 consecutive months preceding the offering in reliance of this rule.

Information Requirements

If only accredited purchasers are involved, no specific information is required. However, if 60% or more of the offering is purchased by accredited institutional investors and all others purchase on the same or better terms, such other purchasers would receive information only upon written request. In all other instances, the type of information to be provided would be tiered according to the size of the offering:

1. Offerings up to $1.5 million—information similar to Regulation A with one year's audited financial statements, if these are obtainable without undue burden or expense; if they are not, an audit of the balance sheet only

2. Offerings of $1.5 million to $5 million—disclosure similar to Form S-18 with one year's audited financial statements

3. Offerings over $5,000,000—information that would be required to be included in a registration statement that the issuer would be entitled to use

Aggregate Offering Price Limitations

Programs qualifying under:

Rule 504	$500,000	Unlimited number of investors
Rule 505	$5,000,000 (12 months)	35 plus unlimited accredited investors
Rule 506	*Unlimited*	35 plus those purchasing in excess of $150,000

Offering Limitations

Under both Rules 505 and 506, no general solicitation is permitted. However, under Rule 504, no general solicitation is permitted *except* in states that require delivery of a disclosure document.

REGULATION D COMPARISON

	Old Rule 240	New Rule 504	Old Rule 242	New Rule 505	Old Rule 146	New Rule 506	Section 4(6)
Aggregate offering price limitation	$100,000	$500,000	$2,000,000 (6 months)	$5,000,000 (12 months)	Unlimited	Unlimited	$5,000,000
Number of investors	100 (total shareholders)	Unlimited	35 + unlimited accredited	35 + unlimited accredited	35 + those purchasing more than $150,000	35 + unlimited accredited	Unlimited accredited only
Qualification of investor	None required	None required	Accredited or none required	Accredited or none required	Offeree and purchaser must be sophisticated or wealthy (with representative)	Purchaser must be sophisticated (alone or with representative)	Accredited
Commissions	Prohibited	Permitted	Permitted	Permitted	Permitted	Permitted	Permitted
Limitations	No general solicitation permitted	No general solicitation unless registered in states that require delivery of a disclosure document	No general solicitation permitted	No general solicitation permitted	No general solicitation permitted	No general solicitation permitted	No general solicitation permitted
Limitations on resale	Restricted	Restricted unless registered in states that require delivery of a disclosure document	Restricted	Restricted	Restricted	Restricted	Restricted
Qualifications of issuer	No companies having more than 100 shareholders at completion of offering	No reporting or investment companies	No non-North American issuers, investment companies, oil and gas companies, or issuers disqualified under Regulation A	No investment companies or issuers disqualified under Regulation A	None	None	None
Notice of sales	Form 240 required as a condition of rule except for first $100,000 under rule—3 copies filed in Regional Office within 10 days after end of month in which sale made	For D required as a condition of exemption—5 copies filed with Commission 15 days after first sale, every 6 months after first sale, 30 days after last sale	Form 242 required as a condition of rule—5 copies filed with Commission 10 days after first sale, every 6 months after first sale, 10 days after last sale	See requirement under Rule 504	Form 146 required as a condition of rule—3 copies filed in Regional Office at time of first sale except for offerings below $50,000 in 12 months	See requirement under Rule 504	Form 4(6) required as condition of exemption—5 copies filed with Commission 10 days after first sale, every 6 months after first sale, 10 days after completion

(Continued)

Regulation D Comparison

	Old Rule 240	New Rule 504	Old Rule 242	New Rule 505	Old Rule 146	New Rule 506	Section 4(6)
Information requirements	No information specified	No information specified	1. If purchased solely by accredited, no information specified 2. If purchased by any non-accredited, must furnish: (a) (nonreporting companies) information in Part I of Form S-18 with 1 year audited financials (b) (reporting companies) most recent annual report, def. proxy statement and recent periodic reports	1. If purchased solely by accredited, no information specified 2. If purchased by nonaccredited, must furnish: (a) (nonreporting companies) *i* offerings up to $5,000,000 — information in Part I of Form S-18 or available registration, 2 years financials, 1 year audited — if undue effort or expense, issuers other than limited partnerships only balance sheet as of 120 days before offering must be audited—if limited partnership and undue effort or expense, financials may be tax basis *ii* offerings over $5,000,000 —information in Part I of available registration—if undue effort or expense, issuers other than limited partnerships only balance sheet as of 120 days before offering must be audited—if limited partnership and undue effort or expense, financials may be tax basis (b) (reporting companies) *i* Rule 14a-3 annual report to shareholders, definitive proxy statement and 10-K, if requested, plus subsequent reports and other updating information, *or* *ii* information in most recent Form S-1 or Form 10 or Form 10-K plus subsequent reports and other updating information (c) Issuers must make available prior to sale: *i* exhibits *ii* written information given to accredited investors *iii* opportunity to ask questions and receive answers	Must furnish (unless offeree has access via economic bargaining power) 1. Below $1,500,000 — information may be limited to Part II, Form 1-A of Regulation A 2. Other offerings (a) (nonreporting) information in registration available to issuer—unaudited financials if audit requirements entail unreasonable effort or expense (b) (reporting companies) recent Form S-1 or Form 10, def. proxy statements and periodic reports	See requirements under Rule 505	No information specified

3.10 **Futures and Options**

COMMODITY AND FINANCIAL FUTURES

Futures contracts are legally binding agreements, made at a commodity exchange and traded through brokerage firms. They call for the purchase or sale of a physical commodity or financial instrument on a specified future date. All terms and conditions of these contracts are standardized by the commodity exchanges, except the price of a contract, which is established at open auction in the exchange's trading area (the "pit"). Only a small percentage of futures contracts results in the actual delivery of a commodity; some 95% of contracts are closed out before the delivery date.

The basic function of futures markets is to offer price or interest-rate protection for individuals and businesses exposed to adverse fluctuations in commodities or financial instruments; futures markets permit the transfer of risk. Prices for contracts are also an expression of expected future price levels. This price discovery element contributes to economic forecasting and planning by both business and government.

Like the stock markets, the futures markets respond to both broad influences of political, social, and economic circumstances and to specific market conditions and technical market factors.

How to Read Futures Quotations

Summaries of each trading day's activities are reported by major newspapers. Currently, the largest active markets for futures in the U.S. are:

- Grains and oils: corn, oats, soybeans, soybean meal, soybean oil, wheat

- Livestock: feeder cattle, live beef cattle, live hogs, pork bellies

- Food and fibers: cocoa, coffee, cotton, orange juice, domestic sugar, world sugar

- Metals, petroleum, and lumber: aluminum, copper, gold, palladium, platinum, silver, New York gasoline (leaded regular), heating oil (no. 2), crude oil, lumber

- Financial instruments: bank certificates of deposit (CDs), Eurodollars, GNMA certificates, U.S. Treasury bills, U.S. Treasury bonds, U.S. Treasury notes, British pound, Canadian dollar, Japanese yen, Swiss franc, West German mark

- Stock indexes: NYSE composite, Standard & Poor's 500, Value Line, Major Market Index

The heading for each entry shows the name of the commodity or financial instrument, the exchange on which the futures are traded (here, CBT = Chicago Board of Trade), the unit of delivery, and the monetary unit in which prices are quoted.

| (1) | (2) | (3) | (4) | (5) | (6) | (7) Lifetime | | (8) |
	Open	High	Low	Settle	Change	High	Low	Open Interest
CORN (CBT) 5,000 bu.; ¢ per bu.								
May	232	233	232	232½	½	253	211	55,389
July	234	234½	233¼	233¼	−¾	254½	214	42,988
Sept	215	216¼	214¼	215	...	285	207	9,377
Dec	202	202	200	200	−2	238	193	25,666

Est vol. 12,000; vol. Tues. 13,456; open int. 152,398, −128

Column 1 — month: the month during which the contract is to be fulfilled

Column 2 — open: the price at which the first bid and offer were made, or the first transaction completed

Column 3 — high: the top price at which the contract was traded during the day

Column 4 — low: the lowest price at which the contract was traded during the day

Column 5 — settlement price: technical adjustment of the closing prices during the last period of trading

Column 6 — net change: increase or decrease from the previous trading day's settlement price

Column 7 — lifetime high and low: the highest and lowest prices at which the contract has traded during its lifetime

Column 8 — open interest: total of all currently outstanding positions (one side only)

OPTIONS

Options give their buyer the right, but not the obligation, to purchase (in the case of a *call* option) or to sell (a *put* option) an underlying security or instrument at a predetermined price (*exercise* or *strike price*) any time before the option's maturity date. For this right the purchaser pays a premium—which is determined at auction on the trading floor—that reflects the underlying instrument's current market price relative to the strike price, the duration of the option (its *time value*), and the volatility in the price fluctuation of the underlying instrument.

Options on stocks are traded in 100-share blocks at a per-share premium. For example, if an investor buys a ZYZ Nov 60 call at $3, he or she will pay $300 (plus commissions) for the right to purchase 100 shares of ZYZ at $60 a share before the Saturday following the third Friday in November. If the investor does not exercise the option, it simply expires and has no economic value.

Investors may also purchase options on futures contracts for various stock indexes (Standard and Poor's 500, Major Market Index, etc.) and commodities (sugar, gold, etc.).

How to Read Options Quotations

Options quotations are printed in the major daily newspapers. Stock options are reported in the following form:

(1)	(2)	(3)	(4) Sales	(5) Open Int.	(6) High	(7) Low	(8) Last	(9) Net Chg.	(10) Stock Close
AAB	May	30	454	1678	5½	4½	5¼	$-3/16$	35
AAB	May	30p	213	981	2	1¼	1¼	$-¼$	35

Column 1 — name of company or instrument

Column 2 — month in which option expires

Column 3 — strike price (p=put)

Column 4 — sales: number of options traded that day

Column 5 — open interest: total number of outstanding options

Column 6 — high: highest price at which the option traded during the day

Column 7 — low: lowest price at which option traded during the day

Column 8 — last: closing price

Column 9 — net change: change since previous trading day's close

Column 10 — stock close: price at which stock closed

Source: Chicago Mercantile Exchange.

CHAPTER 4

Measures, Calculations, and Formulas

CONTENTS

Tables are indicated by page numbers in italic type.

4.04 Compounding and Amortization Tables (continued)

The tables, calculations, formulas, and concepts presented here can be helpful in answering many questions that often arise concerning various types of investments:

- How does an investor compare the return on a tax-exempt security to one with a taxable yield?

- How long can a saver make periodic withdrawals from a savings account at a specific rate?

- What return is required to maintain purchasing power under various inflation and tax rates?

- How do real estate investors use the capitalization concept to accurately evaluate income-producing property?

- How long will it take money to double or triple at various interest rates?

Many of the table and formulas will be useful in applying some of the investment strategies discussed elsewhere in the book, such as risk return relationships and financial ratios.

4.01 **Yields**

YIELDS ON SECURITIES
Taxable and Tax-Exempt

This table shows the equivalent taxable yield for joint returns on securities before federal income taxes compared with tax-exempt yields (the yield on purchases of tax-exempt obligations made at par). The interest on state and municipal securities is exempt from present federal income taxes. Under current law, the maximum federal tax rate is 50%. However, as recently as 1980, the maximum rate was 70%.

Example: For investors in the 40% tax bracket, an 11.67% return on a taxable security equals the 7% return on a tax-exempt one.

Tax-Exempt Yield	Federal Income Tax Brackets								
	32%	40%	45%	48%	50%	55%	60%	66%	70%
2.50	3.68	4.17	4.55	4.81	5.00	5.56	6.25	7.35	8.33
3.00	4.41	5.00	5.45	5.77	6.00	6.67	7.50	8.82	10.00
3.25	4.78	5.42	5.91	6.25	6.50	7.22	8.13	9.56	10.83
3.50	5.15	5.83	6.36	6.73	7.00	7.78	8.75	10.29	11.67
3.75	5.51	6.25	6.82	7.21	7.50	8.33	9.38	11.03	12.50
4.00	5.88	6.67	7.27	7.69	8.00	8.89	10.00	11.76	13.33
4.10	6.03	6.83	7.45	7.88	8.20	9.11	10.25	12.06	13.67
4.20	6.18	7.00	7.64	8.08	8.40	9.33	10.50	12.35	14.00
4.25	6.25	7.08	7.73	8.17	8.50	9.44	10.63	12.50	14.17
4.30	6.32	7.17	7.82	8.27	8.60	9.56	10.75	12.65	14.33
4.40	6.47	7.33	8.00	8.46	8.80	9.78	11.00	12.94	14.67
4.50	6.62	7.50	8.18	8.65	9.00	10.00	11.25	13.24	15.00
4.60	6.76	7.67	8.36	8.85	9.20	10.22	11.50	13.53	15.33
4.70	6.91	7.83	8.55	9.04	9.40	10.44	11.75	13.82	15.67
4.75	6.99	7.92	8.64	9.13	9.50	10.56	11.88	13.97	15.83
4.80	7.06	8.00	8.73	9.23	9.60	10.67	12.00	14.12	16.00
4.90	7.21	8.17	8.91	9.42	9.80	10.89	12.25	14.41	16.33
5.00	7.35	8.33	9.09	9.62	10.00	11.11	12.50	14.71	16.67
5.10	7.50	8.50	9.27	9.81	10.20	11.33	12.75	15.00	17.00
5.20	7.65	8.67	9.45	10.00	10.40	11.56	13.00	15.29	17.33
5.25	7.72	8.75	9.55	10.10	10.50	11.67	13.12	15.44	17.50
5.30	7.79	8.83	9.64	10.19	10.60	11.78	13.25	15.59	17.67
5.40	7.94	9.00	9.82	10.38	10.80	12.00	13.50	15.88	18.00
5.50	8.09	9.17	10.00	10.58	11.00	12.22	13.75	16.18	18.33
5.60	8.24	9.33	10.18	10.77	11.20	12.44	14.00	16.47	18.67
5.70	8.38	9.50	10.36	10.96	11.40	12.67	14.25	16.76	19.00
5.75	8.46	9.58	10.45	11.06	11.50	12.78	14.38	16.91	19.17
5.80	8.53	9.67	10.55	11.15	11.60	12.89	14.50	17.06	19.33
5.90	8.68	9.83	10.73	11.35	11.80	13.11	14.75	17.35	19.67
6.00	8.82	10.00	10.91	11.54	12.00	13.33	15.00	17.65	20.00
6.10	8.97	10.17	11.09	11.73	12.20	13.56	15.25	17.94	20.33
6.20	9.12	10.33	11.27	11.92	12.40	13.78	15.50	18.24	20.67
6.25	9.19	10.42	11.36	12.02	12.50	13.89	15.63	18.38	20.83
6.30	9.26	10.50	11.45	12.12	12.60	14.00	15.75	18.53	21.00
6.40	9.41	10.67	11.64	12.31	12.80	14.22	16.00	18.82	21.33

(Continued)

Yields on Securities

Tax-Exempt Yield	Federal Income Tax Brackets								
	32%	40%	45%	48%	50%	55%	60%	66%	70%
6.50	9.56	10.83	11.82	12.50	13.00	14.44	16.25	19.12	21.67
6.60	9.71	11.00	12.00	12.69	13.20	14.67	16.50	19.41	22.00
6.70	9.85	11.17	12.18	12.88	13.40	14.89	16.75	19.71	22.33
6.75	9.93	11.25	12.27	12.98	13.50	15.00	16.87	19.85	22.50
6.80	0.00	11.33	12.36	13.08	13.60	15.11	17.00	20.00	22.67
6.90	10.15	11.50	12.55	13.27	13.80	15.33	17.25	20.29	23.00
7.00	10.29	11.67	12.73	13.46	14.00	15.56	17.50	20.59	23.33
7.10	10.44	11.83	12.91	13.65	14.20	15.78	17.75	20.88	23.67
7.20	10.59	12.00	13.09	13.85	14.40	16.00	18.00	21.18	24.00
7.25	10.66	12.08	13.18	13.94	14.50	16.11	18.13	21.32	24.17
7.30	10.74	12.17	13.27	14.04	14.60	16.22	18.25	21.47	24.33
7.40	10.88	12.33	13.45	14.23	14.80	16.44	18.50	21.76	24.67
7.50	11.03	12.50	13.64	14.42	15.00	16.67	18.75	22.06	25.00
7.75	11.40	12.92	14.09	14.90	15.50	17.22	19.37	22.79	25.83
8.00	11.76	13.33	14.55	15.38	16.00	17.78	20.00	23.53	26.67
8.25	12.13	13.75	15.00	15.87	16.50	18.33	20.63	24.26	27.50
8.50	12.50	14.17	15.45	16.35	17.00	18.89	21.25	25.00	28.33
8.75	12.87	14.58	15.91	16.83	17.50	19.44	21.87	25.74	29.17
9.00	13.24	15.00	16.36	17.31	18.00	20.00	22.50	26.47	30.00

TAXABLE YIELDS ON SECURITIES
Versus Tax-Exempt Bonds

Example: A couple making $34,000 in 1984 would have to obtain a return of 11.11% on a taxable security to equal the 8% yield on a tax-exempt bond.

Joint Return Taxable Income 1981–1984	% Tax Rate	Tax-Exempt Bond Yields — Taxable Equivalent Yields														
		6%	6½%	7%	7½%	8%	8½%	9%	9½%	10%	10½%	11%	11½%	12%	12½%	13%
$20,200 – 24,600	28	8.33	9.03	9.72	10.42	11.11	11.81	12.5	13.19	13.89	14.58	15.28	15.97	16.67	17.36	18.06
	25	8.0	8.67	9.33	10.0	10.67	11.33	12.0	12.67	13.33	14.0	14.67	15.33	16.0	16.67	17.33
	23	7.79	8.44	9.09	9.74	10.39	11.04	11.69	12.34	12.99	13.64	14.29	14.94	15.58	16.23	16.88
	22	7.69	8.33	8.97	9.62	10.26	10.90	11.54	12.18	12.82	13.46	14.10	14.74	15.38	16.03	16.67
24,600 – 29,900	32	8.82	9.56	10.29	11.03	11.76	12.5	13.24	13.97	14.71	15.44	16.18	16.91	17.65	18.38	19.12
	29	8.45	9.15	9.86	10.56	11.27	11.97	12.68	13.38	14.08	14.79	15.49	16.20	16.90	17.61	18.31
	26	8.12	8.78	9.46	10.14	10.81	11.49	12.16	12.84	13.51	14.19	14.86	15.54	16.22	16.89	17.57
	25	8.0	8.67	9.33	10.0	10.67	11.33	12.0	12.67	13.33	14.0	14.67	15.33	16.0	16.67	17.33
29,900 – 35,200	37	9.52	10.32	11.11	11.90	12.70	13.49	14.29	15.08	15.87	16.67	17.46	18.25	19.05	19.84	20.63
	33	8.96	9.70	10.45	11.19	11.94	12.69	13.43	14.18	14.93	15.67	16.42	17.16	17.91	18.66	19.40
	30	8.57	9.29	10.0	10.71	11.43	12.14	12.86	13.57	14.29	15.0	15.71	16.43	17.14	17.86	18.57
	28	8.33	9.03	9.72	10.42	11.11	11.81	12.5	13.19	13.89	14.58	15.28	15.97	16.67	17.36	18.06
35,200 – 45,800	43	10.53	11.40	12.28	13.16	14.03	14.91	15.79	16.67	17.54	18.42	19.30	20.18	21.05	21.93	22.81
	39	9.84	10.66	11.48	12.30	13.11	13.93	14.75	15.57	16.39	17.21	18.03	18.85	19.67	20.49	21.31
	35	9.23	10.0	10.77	11.54	12.30	13.08	13.85	14.62	15.38	16.15	16.92	17.69	18.46	19.23	20.0
	33	8.96	9.70	10.45	11.19	11.94	12.69	13.43	14.18	14.93	15.67	16.42	17.16	17.91	18.66	19.40
45,800 – 60,000	49	11.76	12.75	13.73	14.71	15.69	16.67	17.65	18.63	19.61	20.59	21.57	22.55	23.5	24.51	25.49
	44	10.71	11.61	12.50	13.39	14.29	15.18	16.07	16.96	17.86	18.75	19.64	20.54	21.43	22.32	23.21
	40	10.0	10.83	11.67	12.50	13.33	14.17	15.0	15.83	16.67	17.50	18.33	19.17	20.0	20.83	21.67
	38	9.68	10.48	11.29	12.10	12.90	13.71	14.52	15.32	16.13	16.94	17.74	18.55	19.35	20.16	20.97
60,000 – 85,600	54	13.0	14.13	15.22	16.30	17.39	18.48	19.57	20.65	21.74	22.83	23.91	25.0	26.09	27.17	28.26
	49	11.76	12.75	13.73	14.71	15.69	16.67	17.65	18.63	19.61	20.59	21.57	22.55	23.5	24.51	25.49
	44	10.71	11.61	12.50	13.39	14.29	15.18	16.0	16.96	17.86	18.75	19.64	20.54	21.43	22.32	23.21
	42	10.34	11.21	12.07	12.93	13.79	14.66	15.52	16.38	17.24	18.10	18.97	19.83	20.69	21.55	22.41
85,600 – 109,400	59	14.63	15.85	17.07	18.29	19.51	20.73	21.95	23.17	24.39	25.61	26.83	28.05	29.27	30.49	31.71
	50	12.0	13.0	14.0	15.0	16.0	17.0	18.0	19.0	20.0	21.0	22.0	23.0	24.0	25.0	26.0
	48	11.54	12.5	13.46	14.42	15.38	16.35	17.31	18.27	19.23	20.19	21.15	22.12	23.08	24.04	25.0
	45	10.91	11.82	12.73	13.64	14.55	15.45	16.36	17.27	18.18	19.09	20.0	20.91	21.82	22.73	23.64

(Continued)

Taxable Yields on Securities

Joint Return Taxable Income 1981–1984	% Tax Rate	Tax-Exempt Bond Yields														
		6%	6½%	7%	7½%	8%	8½%	9%	9½%	10%	10½%	11%	11½%	12%	12½%	13%
		Taxable Equivalent Yields														
109,400 – 162,400	64	16.67	18.06	19.44	20.83	22.22	23.61	25.0	26.39	27.78	29.17	30.56	31.94	33.33	34.72	36.11
	50	12.0	13.0	14.0	15.0	16.0	17.0	18.0	19.0	20.0	21.0	22.0	23.0	24.0	25.0	26.0
	49	11.76	12.75	13.73	14.71	15.69	16.67	17.65	18.63	19.61	20.59	21.57	22.55	23.5	24.51	25.49
162,400 – 215,400	68	18.75	20.31	21.88	23.44	25.0	25.56	28.13	29.69	31.25	32.81	34.38	35.94	37.5	39.06	40.63
	50	12.0	13.0	14.0	15.0	16.0	17.0	18.0	19.0	20.0	21.0	22.0	23.0	24.0	25.0	26.0
215,400 and over	70	20.0	21.67	23.33	25.0	26.67	28.3	30.0	31.67	33.33	35.0	36.67	38.33	40.0	41.67	43.33
	50	12.0	13.0	14.0	5.0	16.0	17.0	18.0	19.0	20.0	21.0	22.0	23.0	24.0	25.0	26.0

Source: Drexel Burnham Lambert, Inc.

SAVINGS WITHDRAWAL SCHEDULES

Years of Monthly Withdrawals from a Specific Amount

Example: If you have a deposit of $100,000 at 9% interest, you can withdraw $1,000 per month for 15 years.

Principal Amount	Monthly Withdrawal	Interest Rate (%)*						Principal Amount	Monthly Withdrawal	Interest Rate (%)*					
		5	6	7	8	9	10			5	6	7	8	9	10
$50,000	300	23	29	—	—	—	—	$100,000	600	23	29	—	—	—	—
	400	14	16	18	22	30	—		700	18	20	25	—	—	—
	500	10	11	12	13	15	17		800	14	16	18	22	30	—
	600	8	9	9	10	10	11		900	12	13	14	16	19	26
	700	7	7	7	8	9	9		1000	10	11	12	13	15	17
	800	6	6	6	6	7	7		1100	9	10	10	11	12	14

* A dash indicates that monthly interest earned exceeds monthly withdrawal.

Years of Monthly Withdrawals by Amount of Withdrawal

Example: If you have a $60,000 deposit at 7% interest, you can withdraw $800 a month for 8 years.

Monthly Withdrawal	Principal Amount	Interest Rate (%)*						Monthly Withdrawal	Principal Amount	Interest Rate (%)*					
		5	6	7	8	9	10			5	6	7	8	9	10
$300	40,000	16	18	21	27	—	—		100,000	23	29	—	—	—	—
	50,000	23	29	—	—	—	—		110,000	28	—	—	—	—	—
$400	40,000	10	11	12	13	15	17	$700	40,000	5	5	5	6	6	6
	50,000	14	16	18	22	30	—		50,000	7	7	7	8	8	9
	60,000	19	23	29	—	—	—		60,000	8	9	9	10	11	12
	70,000	26	—	—	—	—	—		70,000	10	11	12	13	15	17
$500	40,000	8	8	9	9	10	11		80,000	12	14	15	17	21	30
	50,000	10	11	12	13	15	17		90,000	15	17	19	24	—	—
	60,000	13	15	17	20	25	—		100,000	18	20	25	—	—	—
	70,000	17	20	24	—	—	—		110,000	21	25	—	—	—	—
	80,000	22	26	—	—	—	—	$800	40,000	—	—	—	5	5	4
	90,000	27	—	—	—	—	—		50,000	6	6	6	6	7	7
$600	40,000	6	6	7	7	7	8		60,000	7	7	8	8	9	9
	50,000	8	9	9	10	10	11		70,000	9	9	10	10	11	13
	60,000	10	11	12	13	15	17		80,000	10	11	12	13	15	17
	70,000	13	14	16	18	23	—		90,000	12	13	15	17	20	27
	80,000	16	18	21	27	—	—		100,000	14	16	18	22	30	—
	90,000	19	23	29	—	—	—		110,000	17	19	23	—	—	—

* A dash indicates that monthly interest earned exceeds monthly withdrawal.

Years of Monthly Withdrawals Given a Specific Interest Rate

Example: If your account pays 8% interest, and you have $70,000, you can withdraw $600 a month for 18 years.

Interest	Principal Amount	Monthly Withdrawal*						Interest	Principal Amount	Monthly Withdrawal*					
		300	400	500	600	700	800			300	400	500	600	700	800
5%	40,000	16	10	8	6	5	—	8%	40,000	27	13	9	7	6	5
	50,000	23	14	10	8	7	6		50,000	—	22	13	10	8	6
	60,000	—	19	13	10	8	7		60,000	—	—	20	13	10	8
	70,000	—	26	17	13	10	9		70,000	—	—	—	18	13	10
	80,000	—	—	22	16	12	10		80,000	—	—	—	27	17	13
	90,000	—	—	27	19	15	12		90,000	—	—	—	—	24	17
	100,000	—	—	—	23	18	14		100,000	—	—	—	—	—	22
	110,000	—	—	—	28	21	17	9%	40,000	—	15	10	7	6	5
6%	40,000	18	11	8	6	5	—		50,000	—	30	15	10	8	7
	50,000	29	16	11	9	7	6		60,000	—	—	25	15	11	9
	60,000	—	23	15	11	9	7		70,000	—	—	—	23	15	11
	70,000	—	—	20	14	11	9		80,000	—	—	—	—	21	15
	80,000	—	—	26	18	14	11		90,000	—	—	—	—	—	20
	90,000	—	—	—	23	17	13		100,000	—	—	—	—	—	30
	100,000	—	—	—	29	20	16	10%	40,000	—	17	11	8	6	5
	110,000	—	—	—	—	25	19		50,000	—	—	17	11	9	7
7%	40,000	21	12	9	7	5	—		60,000	—	—	—	17	12	9
	50,000	—	18	12	9	7	6		70,000	—	—	—	—	17	13
	60,000	—	29	17	12	9	8		80,000	—	—	—	—	30	17
	70,000	—	—	24	16	12	10		90,000	—	—	—	—	—	27
	80,000	—	—	—	21	15	12								
	90,000	—	—	—	29	19	15								
	100,000	—	—	—	—	25	18								
	110,000	—	—	—	—	—	23								

* *A dash indicates that monthly interest earned exceeds monthly withdrawal.*

Calculation   To calculate values not listed in the above tables, use the tables giving present value of an annuity (see page 4.27).

Example 1:   You want $14,400 per year ($1,200/month) for 10 years. How much principal must you have on deposit if you can earn 10% interest annually?

Looking at the table, for 10% interest for 10 years, you will need $6.145 to earn $1 a year, so you need $88,488 ($14,400 x 6.145) to withdraw $14,400 a year for 10 years. The table allows for the payment to be withdrawn at the end of the year, so if you want it at the beginning of the year, use the Present Value of $1 Table and divide by .909 (10 years, 10%).

Example 2:   You have $125,000 in an account at 11% interest. If you withdraw $20,000 per year, how long will your money last?

Divide the principal by the annual payment ($125,000/$20,000) to get the factor of 6.25. Look at the table under 11%, and choose the nearest factor, which is 6.207. Your money will last approximately 11 years.

Any good financial calculator will also enable you to do these calculations. Many calculators allow you to set the payment period for monthly or annually and to indicate beginning or end of period as payout time. Generally, once you have done several calculations, the calculator becomes much easier and quicker to use than the tables.

TAX-SAVINGS YIELD BASED ON INVESTMENT
WRITE-OFF AND TAX BRACKET

Percentage Write-off	Tax Bracket and Tax-Saving Yield as a Percentage				
	30%	35%	40%	45%	50%
15	4.5	5.25	6.0	6.75	7.5
20	6.0	7.00	8.0	9.00	10.0
25	7.5	8.75	10.0	11.25	12.5
30	9.0	10.50	12.0	13.50	15.0
35	10.5	12.25	14.0	15.75	17.5
40	12.0	14.00	16.0	18.00	20.0
45	13.5	15.75	18.0	20.25	22.5
50	15.0	17.50	20.0	22.50	25.0
55	16.5	19.25	22.0	24.75	27.5
60	18.0	21.00	24.0	27.00	30.0
65	19.5	22.75	26.0	29.25	32.5
70	21.0	24.50	28.0	31.50	35.0
75	22.5	26.25	30.0	33.75	37.5
80	24.0	28.00	32.0	36.00	40.0
85	25.5	29.75	34.0	38.25	42.5
90	27.0	31.50	36.0	40.50	45.0
95	28.5	33.25	38.0	42.75	47.5
100	30.0	35.00	40.0	45.00	50.0

Source: F. J. Nammacher and Associates.

4.02 **Measures**

PURCHASING POWER AND INFLATION

This table illustrates the rate of return required for an investor to maintain current purchasing power under various rates of inflation and taxation. For example, at an 8% rate of inflation, an investor will have to earn 16% on a taxable investment, at a 50% marginal tax rate.

Marginal Tax Rate (%)	Inflation Rate (%)						
	2	4	6	8	10	12	14
0	2.0	4.0	6.0	8.0	10.0	12.0	14.0
10	2.2	4.5	6.7	8.9	11.1	13.3	15.6
15	2.4	4.7	7.1	9.4	11.8	14.1	16.4
20	2.5	5.0	7.5	10.0	12.5	15.0	17.4
25	2.7	5.4	8.0	10.7	13.3	16.0	18.6
30	2.9	5.7	8.6	11.4	14.3	17.1	20.2
35	3.1	6.2	9.2	12.3	15.4	18.5	21.6
40	3.3	6.7	10.0	13.3	16.7	20.2	23.4
45	3.6	7.3	10.9	14.5	18.2	21.8	25.4
50	4.0	8.0	12.0	16.0	20.0	24.0	28.0

Source: F. J. Nammacher and Associates.

CAPITALIZATION (CAP) RATES

Capitalization (cap) rates are useful in evaluating the market price of income-producing real property. The cap rate is the ratio, expressed as a percentage, of a property's annual net operating income to its market price:

Annual rents − (operating expenses + vacancy allowance)
= Net operating income
Net operating income ÷ market price = Cap rate

For example, a property whose annual net operating income is $100,000 and whose market price is $1,250,000 has a cap rate of 8%.

By obtaining rents and selling prices for several properties within an area and calculating the cap rates, investors can get a general feel for the marketplace, a guideline for determining how well one property compares to another.

Factors Affecting the Capitalization Rate

Real estate income is generally capitalized anywhere from 5 to 15 times, with more secure properties falling into the 10 to 15 range. Factors affecting the cap rate include:

• Investor demand for, and the existing supply of, the particular type of property;

• Stability and security of future income; and

• Capitalization rates or price-earning ratios of investments other than real estate with comparable risk factors.

High demand, good stability, and security decrease the cap rate; lower demand and higher risk raise it. There are a variety of factors to consider in determining the appropriate cap rate for a property, many of which might be interpreted differently on a case by case basis. It is therefore important to make a thorough study of the demographics, as well as specific data relating to the property in question, before selecting a cap rate.

Demand

Location is a key consideration in determining demand. In a major business district, even a few feet may make one location preferable to another. Access to mass transportation becomes increasingly important as the cost of private transportation becomes higher. Proximity to major employers is another important factor. Likewise, property that is experiencing growth is preferable to one without a growth pattern.

In addition, the age of the building, degree of obsolescence, size of the parcel, quality of the leases, existing financing on the building, and operating costs all influence both demand and risk. Other factors to consider include the purpose of the building. Fad properties have more inherent risk than those with ongoing value. For example, skateboard parks and discos were popular and successful for a time, but are no longer.

THE RULE OF 72 (DOUBLING)

How long does it take $1 to become $2 at various rates of return? Simply divide the rate of return into 72. For example, at 5% per annum, an investment will double in 14.4 years (72 ÷ 5).

THE RULE OF 115 (TRIPLING)

How long does it take $1 to become $3 at various rates of return? Divide the rate of return into 115. For example, at 5% per annum, an investment will triple in 23 years (115 ÷ 5).

CAPITAL ASSET PRICING MODEL

The Capital Asset Pricing Model (CAPM) offers an explanation of the relationship between risk and return. Rational investors will not take on additional risk without being compensated. They require an additional return or risk premium above the risk-free rate. In the CAPM, the expected risk premium varies in direct proportion to beta (defined below). Thus, the expected return on an investment would be determined as follows:

$$r = r_f + b(r_m - r_f)$$

Where r is the expected return; r_f is the risk-free rate; $r_m - r_f$ is the expected risk premium on the market, and b is beta.

The risk-free rate can be thought of as the U.S. Treasury bill rate and has a beta of 0. Thus, it is easy to determine r_f by observing the current market T-bill rate. The market portfolio can be considered a portfolio of risky assets such as the S & P 500. A mutual or index fund best approximates the market portfolio. Over the past 50 years, the average risk premium on the market, the difference between the return on the market and the risk-free rate ($r_m - r_f$) has been 8.8% annually. The beta of the market portfolio is 1. Thus, if the T-bill rate is 8%, the expected return on the market portfolio is approximately 16.8% (8% + 1(8.8%)).

BETA

Beta is a measure of systematic or market risk. Systematic risk cannot be eliminated by diversification, while unsystematic risk, the volatility or variability of each individual stock or investment, can be diversified away. Thus, investors are only compensated for the systematic risk they bear, and beta is the only relevant measure of risk that affects return. An investor holding an undiversified portfolio is bearing some unsystematic risk and not being compensated for it. To avoid this, many people buy mutual funds.

Mathematically, beta is the covariance of the stock and the market over the variance of the market. This number, beta, shows how sensitive an investment is to market movements. A stock with a beta of 2 will swing twice as far as the market; for every percentage point the market rises or drops, the stock will rise or drop two points. An investment with a beta of .5 will swing only half as far as the market, and a negative beta investment moves opposite the market.

Betas for different stocks or projects can be difficult to estimate. Fortunately, the betas for many stocks have been calculated and are available at stock brokerage firms or in Value Line.

Once beta is known, the capital asset pricing model is easy to apply

expected return = risk-free rate + beta × (return on the market − risk-free rate)

The relationship is a simple linear one. As beta increases, return increases proportionately. Thus, the CAPM provides a method for assessing the increased return expected by investors for bearing increased risk.

MEASURES OF FINANCIAL STRENGTH

A. **Coverage Ratios:** designed to measure the relationship between a company's earnings and its obligations to pay interest, preferred stock dividends, and any sinking-fund obligations. The principal ratios are:

Fixed charge coverage — equal to earnings before interest and taxes, divided by interest.

Coverage of interest and sinking-funds — equal to earnings before interest, taxes, and depreciation divided by interest plus sinking-fund requirements.

Coverage of interest and preferred dividends — equal to earnings before interest divided by interest plus (preferred dividends divided by (1.0 − tax rate)).

Alternative fixed charge coverage — equal to earnings before interest as a percentage of the principal amount of long-term debt or debt plus preferred stock.

B. **Liquidity Measures:** measures needed because a company may be generating a lot of bookkeeping earnings, while remaining cash poor.

Current ratio — equal to current assets divided by current liabilities.

Acid test (or quick asset) ratio — equal to sum of cash (and equivalents) plus accounts receivable divided by current liabilities.

Cash ratio — cash (and equivalents) divided by current liabilities.

Working capital to sales — equal to (current assets minus current liabilities) as a percentage of sales.

Cash flow to debt — equal to cash flow as a percentage of principal amount of debt.

Days to sell inventory — equal to average inventory divided by average daily cost of goods sold.

Receivables collection period — equal to average receivables divided by average daily sales.

Internal funding of capital expenditures — equal to capital expenditures as a percentage of the sum of retained earnings plus depreciation.

MEASURES OF STOCK AND BOND PRICES

Price-earnings ratio — equal to price divided by net available for common stock per share.

Relative p/e — equal to price-earnings ratio of a particular stock expressed as a percentage of the price-earnings ratio of a broad market index, such as the S & P 500 Index.

Price-book value — equal to price divided by stockholders' equity per share.

Current yield — equal to annual dividend rate on stock (common or preferred) as a percentage of price, or annual coupon rate on bond as a percentage of price.

Yield to maturity — equal to discount rate, which equates price with future interest and principal payments.

4.03 **Calculations**

NET PRESENT VALUE

Present value is a measure of the current worth of a sum of money to be paid out or received in the future. To account for the foregone earning power of a future payment, the dollar amount of that payment must be discounted by an appropriate rate of compound interest over the period in question. For example, if an investor can earn 10% a year, the receipt of $1,000 a year from now has a present value of $909, since $909 invested today for one year at 10% will yield $1,000.

The present value (PV) of a single future value (FV) is easily calculated:

$$PV = \frac{FV}{(1 + i)^n}$$

where *i* represents the interest rate for period *n*. (Note: if *n* is a number of months, then *i* must be expressed as a monthly—not an annual—rate of interest.)

To calculate the present value of a series of future cash flows, one can use the *net present value* method (NPV). The first step is to list the series of cash flows for each year (or each month) of the future period. (Note: NPV calculations use actual cash flows, not accounting flows—which would, for example, reflect depreciation.) Here are the expected cash flows for a small office building now selling for $250,000, which the prospective buyer intends to sell after the fifth year of ownership:

Year	Cash Flow	
0	− $250,000	(cost of building)
1	10,000	
2	15,000	
3	25,000	
4	35,000	
5	365,000	($40,000 from operations + $325,000 for the sale)

Next, the investor has to discount these cash flows by a specific interest rate (often called the *discount rate* or *opportunity cost*). If a five-year certificate of deposit for $250,000 is paying 12%, then 12% might be a reasonable discount rate. (Note: NPV calculations do not account for the effect of taxation on investments. For an investor in the 50% bracket, the after-tax return on a 12% certificate would be only 6%.)

The actual calculations may be easily done on a financial calculator (see page 4.20) or, with patience, by hand. The formula for calculating NPV is:

$$NPV = CF_0 + \frac{CF_1}{(1 + i)} + \frac{CF_2}{(1 + i)^2} + \ldots + \frac{CF_n}{(1 + i)^n}$$

where CF_0 is the cash flow for period 0 (the initial investment cost), CF_1 is the cash flow for period one, and so on, and *i* is the discount rate. Thus the NPV for the office building is:

$$- 250,000 + \frac{10,000}{1.12} + \frac{15,000}{(1.12)^2} + \frac{25,000}{(1.12)^3} + \frac{35,000}{(1.12)^4} + \frac{365,000}{(1.12)^5} = \$18,035$$

Since in this case NPV is a positive value, the rate of return on these expected cash flows exceeds the opportunity cost of 12%. When NPV is 0 (as it would be in this example for *i* = 13.7%), then the selected discount rate represents the exact rate of return on the cash flows. When NPV is a negative value (as it would be in this example for *i* = 15%), then the return on the cash flows does not meet the opportunity cost.

INTERNAL RATE OF RETURN

Internal rate of return (IRR) is the discount rate for which the NPV of a series of cash flows will be 0:

$$CF_0 + \frac{CF_1}{(1 + IRR)} + \frac{CF_2}{(1 + IRR)^2} + \cdots + \frac{CF_n}{(1 + IRR)^n} = 0$$

IRR can be calculated on a financial calculator or estimated from the formula.

For example, to return to the office building, the calculation of IRR would be as follows:

Step 1. List the cash flows:

Year	Cash Flow
0	− $250,000
1	10,000
2	15,000
3	25,000
4	35,000
5	365,000

Step 2. Plug these cash flow values into the formula:

$$-250,000 + \frac{10,000}{(1 + IRR)} + \frac{15,000}{(1 + IRR)^2} + \frac{25,000}{(1 + IRR)^3} + \frac{35,000}{(1 + IRR)^4} + \frac{365,000}{(1 + IRR)^5} = 0$$

Step 3. Try different rates. In the given example, for IRR = 12%, NPV = $18,035; so the IRR is greater than 12%. For IRR = 15%, NPV = − $12,043; so IRR is less than 15%. Repeated trials show that for IRR = 13.7%, NPV = 0, so the internal rate of return for this series of cash flows is 13.7%.

In many cases, the IRR method will give the same results as the NPV analysis, but projects with the same IRR may have different NPVs. For example:

Project	Cash Flows		IRR	NPV at 10%
	C_0	C_1		
A	− 500	800	60%	227
B	500	− 800	60%	− 227

Although the IRRs for projects A and B are the same, the NPV method shows project A to exceed the opportunity cost of 10%, while project B does not.

Also, if short-term interest rates differ from long-term interest rates, the IRR method cannot be used, whereas the NPV method can be adjusted to reflect different interest rates in each period.

NPV USING A CALCULATOR

NPV can be calculated on many financial calculators. With the Hewlett-Packard 12C (HP-12C), the general procedure is:

1. Determine the cash flows of the investment for each period, including period 0 (the initial outlay).

2. Clear registers by pressing [f] CLEAR [REG].

3. Key in the amount of the initial investment, and press [CHS] if the amount is negative. Press [g] [CFo].

4. Key in the amount for the first period. Again, if the amount is negative, press CHS , and if the amount is 0, key in 0. Press g CFj .

5. Repeat step 4 for each cash flow in the following periods up to 20 periods (in addition to the initial outlay).

   Note: If 2 or more cash flows are equal, problems involving more than 20 cash flows may be solved.

6. Enter the interest rate, using i if the periods are years; if the periods are months use g 12÷ .

7. Press f NPV to find the net present value of the investment. If the NPV is negative, the return is less than the opportunity cost, and an alternative investment with an NPV of 0 or greater should generally be chosen. If two or more investments have positive NPVs, the one with the highest NPV should generally be selected.

Consult appropriate manuals for other calculators.

ADDITIONAL PRESENT VALUE FORMULAS

Present value of a perpetuity:

$$PV = \frac{C}{i}$$

where C is a cash flow to be paid in perpetuity and i is the discount rate.

Present value of a growing perpetuity:

$$PV = \frac{C}{i-g}$$

where the cash flow C, increases at a steady rate, g, in perpetuity.

Average Return on Book Value

Although net present value is generally the best method for determining the present value of future cash flows, there are alternative methods, the most useful of which is average return on book value.

$$\text{Average Book Rate of Return} = \frac{\text{Average Annual Income}}{\text{Average Annual Investment}}$$

Example:

Cash Flows

	Year 1	Year 2	Year 3
Revenue	$20,000	$18,000	$16,000
Out-of-pocket cost	−10,000	− 9,000	− 8,000
Cash flow	$10,000	$ 9,000	$ 8,000
Depreciation	− 5,000	− 5,000	− 5,000
Net Income	$ 5,000	$ 4,000	$ 3,000

Average Annual Income = $4,000

	Year 0	Year 1	Year 2	Year 3
Gross book value of investment	$15,000	$15,000	$15,000	$15,000
Accumulated depreciation	− 0	− 5,000	−10,000	−15,000
Net book value of investment	$15,000	$10,000	$ 5,000	$ 0

Average Annual Investment = $7,500

$$\text{Average Book Rate of Return} = \frac{\text{Average Annual Income}}{\text{Average Annual Investment}} = \frac{\$4,000}{\$7,500} = 0.53 \text{ or } 53\%$$

Note: With the average return on book value method, the cash flows are based on accounting income, not actual cash inflows and outflows; and all cash flows are treated equally. (No allowance is made for the opportunity cost of money.)

PERCENTAGE CHANGE

To calculate the percentage of change between data for two years, subtract year A from year B and divide the result by year A.

Example:

Year A	153.3
Year B	182.7

Step 1: $182.7 - 153.3 = 29.4$

Step 2: $\dfrac{29.4}{153.3} = .192$ or 19.2% increase

4.04 Compounding and Amortization Tables

PRESENT VALUE OF $1

Example: You own a bond that will pay you $1,000 at the end of five years. How much is it worth today if a similar type of investment today pays 8% a year compounded annually (your opportunity cost)? The worth or price today is $681.00 ($1,000 × .681).

Year	1%	2%	3%	4%	5%	6%	7%	8%	9%	10%	11%	12%
1	0.990	0.980	0.971	0.962	0.952	0.943	0.935	0.926	0.917	0.909	0.901	0.893
2	0.980	0.961	0.943	0.925	0.907	0.890	0.873	0.857	0.842	0.826	0.812	0.797
3	0.971	0.942	0.915	0.889	0.864	0.840	0.816	0.794	0.772	0.751	0.731	0.712
4	0.961	0.924	0.888	0.855	0.823	0.792	0.763	0.735	0.708	0.683	0.659	0.636
5	0.951	0.906	0.863	0.822	0.784	0.747	0.713	0.681	0.650	0.621	0.593	0.567
6	0.942	0.888	0.837	0.790	0.746	0.705	0.666	0.630	0.596	0.564	0.535	0.507
7	0.933	0.871	0.813	0.760	0.711	0.665	0.623	0.583	0.547	0.513	0.482	0.452
8	0.923	0.853	0.789	0.731	0.677	0.627	0.582	0.540	0.502	0.467	0.434	0.404
9	0.914	0.837	0.766	0.703	0.645	0.592	0.544	0.500	0.460	0.424	0.391	0.361
10	0.905	0.820	0.744	0.676	0.614	0.558	0.508	0.463	0.422	0.386	0.352	0.322
11	0.896	0.804	0.722	0.650	0.585	0.527	0.475	0.429	0.388	0.350	0.317	0.287
12	0.887	0.788	0.701	0.625	0.557	0.497	0.444	0.397	0.356	0.319	0.286	0.257
13	0.879	0.773	0.681	0.601	0.530	0.469	0.415	0.368	0.326	0.290	0.258	0.229
14	0.870	0.758	0.661	0.577	0.505	0.442	0.388	0.340	0.299	0.263	0.232	0.205
15	0.861	0.743	0.642	0.555	0.481	0.417	0.362	0.315	0.275	0.239	0.209	0.183
16	0.853	0.728	0.623	0.534	0.458	0.394	0.339	0.292	0.252	0.218	0.188	0.163
17	0.844	0.714	0.605	0.513	0.436	0.371	0.317	0.270	0.231	0.198	0.170	0.146
18	0.836	0.700	0.587	0.494	0.416	0.350	0.296	0.250	0.212	0.180	0.153	0.130
19	0.828	0.686	0.570	0.475	0.396	0.331	0.277	0.232	0.194	0.164	0.138	0.116
20	0.820	0.673	0.554	0.456	0.377	0.312	0.258	0.215	0.178	0.149	0.124	0.104
25	0.780	0.610	0.478	0.375	0.295	0.233	0.184	0.146	0.116	0.092	0.074	0.059
30	0.742	0.552	0.412	0.308	0.231	0.174	0.131	0.099	0.075	0.057	0.044	0.033
40	0.672	0.453	0.307	0.208	0.142	0.097	0.067	0.046	0.032	0.022	0.015	0.011
50	0.608	0.372	0.228	0.141	0.087	0.054	0.034	0.021	0.013	0.009	0.005	0.003

(Continued)

Present Value of $1

Year	13%	14%	15%	16%	17%	18%	19%	20%	25%	30%	35%	40%	50%
1	0.885	0.877	0.870	0.862	0.855	0.847	0.840	0.833	0.800	0.769	0.741	0.714	0.667
2	0.783	0.769	0.756	0.743	0.731	0.718	0.706	0.694	0.640	0.592	0.549	0.510	0.444
3	0.693	0.675	0.658	0.641	0.624	0.609	0.593	0.579	0.512	0.455	0.406	0.364	0.296
4	0.613	0.592	0.572	0.552	0.534	0.516	0.499	0.482	0.410	0.350	0.301	0.260	0.198
5	0.543	0.519	0.497	0.476	0.456	0.437	0.419	0.402	0.320	0.269	0.223	0.186	0.132
6	0.480	0.456	0.432	0.410	0.390	0.370	0.352	0.335	0.262	0.207	0.165	0.133	0.088
7	0.425	0.400	0.376	0.354	0.333	0.314	0.296	0.279	0.210	0.159	0.122	0.095	0.059
8	0.376	0.351	0.327	0.305	0.285	0.266	0.249	0.233	0.168	0.123	0.091	0.068	0.039
9	0.333	0.300	0.284	0.263	0.243	0.225	0.209	0.194	0.134	0.094	0.067	0.048	0.026
10	0.295	0.270	0.247	0.227	0.208	0.191	0.176	0.162	0.107	0.073	0.050	0.035	0.017
11	0.261	0.237	0.215	0.195	0.178	0.162	0.148	0.135	0.086	0.056	0.037	0.025	0.012
12	0.231	0.208	0.187	0.168	0.152	0.137	0.124	0.112	0.069	0.043	0.027	0.018	0.008
13	0.204	0.182	0.163	0.145	0.130	0.116	0.104	0.093	0.055	0.033	0.020	0.013	0.005
14	0.181	0.160	0.141	0.125	0.111	0.099	0.088	0.078	0.044	0.025	0.015	0.009	0.003
15	0.160	0.140	0.123	0.108	0.095	0.084	0.074	0.065	0.035	0.020	0.011	0.006	0.002
16	0.141	0.123	0.107	0.093	0.081	0.071	0.062	0.054	0.028	0.015	0.008	0.005	0.002
17	0.125	0.108	0.093	0.080	0.069	0.060	0.052	0.045	0.023	0.012	0.006	0.003	0.001
18	0.111	0.095	0.081	0.069	0.059	0.051	0.044	0.038	0.018	0.009	0.005	0.002	0.001
19	0.098	0.083	0.070	0.060	0.051	0.043	0.037	0.031	0.014	0.007	0.003	0.002	0
20	0.087	0.073	0.061	0.051	0.043	0.037	0.031	0.026	0.012	0.005	0.002	0.001	0
25	0.047	0.038	0.030	0.024	0.020	0.016	0.013	0.010	0.004	0.001	0.001	0	0
30	0.026	0.020	0.015	0.012	0.009	0.007	0.005	0.004	0.001	0	0	0	0
40	0.008	0.005	0.004	0.003	0.002	0.001	0.001	0.001	0	0	0	0	0
50	0.009	0.005	0.003	0.002	0.001	0.001	0.001	0	0	0	0	0	0

COMPOUND SUM OF $1

THE FINANCIAL DESK BOOK

Example: You invest $100 in a savings account that pays 7% a year compounded annually. At the end of the tenth year you will have $196.70 in your account ($100 x 1.967).

Year	1%	2%	3%	4%	5%	6%	7%	8%	9%	10%	11%
1	1.010	1.020	1.030	1.040	1.050	1.060	1.070	1.080	1.090	1.100	1.110
2	1.020	1.040	1.061	1.082	1.103	1.124	1.145	1.166	1.188	1.210	1.232
3	1.030	1.061	1.093	1.125	1.158	1.191	1.225	1.260	1.295	1.331	1.368
4	1.041	1.082	1.126	1.170	1.216	1.262	1.311	1.360	1.412	1.464	1.518
5	1.051	1.104	1.159	1.217	1.276	1.338	1.403	1.469	1.539	1.611	1.685
6	1.062	1.126	1.194	1.265	1.340	1.419	1.501	1.587	1.677	1.772	1.870
7	1.072	1.149	1.230	1.316	1.407	1.504	1.606	1.714	1.828	1.949	2.076
8	1.083	1.172	1.267	1.369	1.477	1.594	1.718	1.851	1.993	2.144	2.305
9	1.094	1.195	1.305	1.423	1.551	1.689	1.838	1.999	2.172	2.358	2.558
10	1.105	1.219	1.344	1.480	1.629	1.791	1.967	2.159	2.367	2.594	2.839
11	1.116	1.243	1.384	1.539	1.710	1.898	2.105	2.332	2.580	2.853	3.152
12	1.127	1.268	1.426	1.601	1.796	2.012	2.252	2.518	2.813	3.138	3.498
13	1.138	1.294	1.469	1.665	1.886	2.133	2.410	2.720	3.066	3.452	3.883
14	1.149	1.319	1.513	1.732	1.980	2.261	2.579	2.937	3.342	3.797	4.310
15	1.161	1.346	1.558	1.801	2.079	2.397	2.759	3.172	3.642	4.177	4.785
16	1.173	1.373	1.605	1.873	2.183	2.540	2.952	3.426	3.970	4.595	5.311
17	1.184	1.400	1.653	1.948	2.292	2.693	3.159	3.700	4.328	5.054	5.895
18	1.196	1.428	1.702	2.206	2.407	2.854	3.380	3.996	4.717	5.560	6.544
19	1.208	1.457	1.754	2.107	2.527	3.026	3.617	4.316	5.142	6.116	7.263
20	1.220	1.486	1.806	2.191	2.653	3.207	3.870	4.661	5.604	6.727	8.062
25	1.282	1.641	2.094	2.666	3.386	4.292	5.427	6.848	8.623	10.835	13.585
30	1.348	1.811	2.427	3.243	4.322	5.743	7.612	10.063	13.268	17.449	22.892
40	1.489	2.208	3.262	4.801	7.040	10.286	14.974	21.725	31.409	45.259	65.001
50	1.645	2.692	4.384	7.107	11.467	18.420	29.457	46.902	74.358	117.390	184.570

(Continued)

Compound Sum of $1

Year	12%	13%	14%	15%	16%	17%	18%	19%	20%	25%	30%
1	1.120	1.130	1.140	1.150	1.160	1.170	1.180	1.190	1.200	1.250	1.300
2	1.254	1.277	1.300	1.323	1.346	1.369	1.392	1.416	1.440	1.563	1.690
3	1.405	1.443	1.482	1.521	1.561	1.602	1.643	1.685	1.728	1.953	2.197
4	1.574	1.630	1.689	1.749	1.811	1.874	1.939	2.005	2.074	2.441	2.856
5	1.762	1.842	1.925	2.011	2.100	2.192	2.288	2.386	2.488	3.052	3.713
6	1.974	2.082	2.195	2.313	2.436	2.565	2.700	2.840	2.986	3.815	4.827
7	2.211	2.353	2.502	2.660	2.826	3.001	3.185	3.379	3.583	4.768	6.276
8	2.476	2.658	2.853	3.059	3.278	3.511	3.759	4.021	4.300	5.960	8.157
9	2.773	3.004	3.252	3.518	3.803	4.108	4.435	4.785	5.160	7.451	10.604
10	3.106	3.395	3.707	4.046	4.411	4.807	5.234	5.696	6.192	9.313	13.786
11	3.479	3.836	4.226	4.652	5.117	5.624	6.176	6.777	7.430	11.642	17.922
12	3.896	4.335	4.818	5.350	5.936	6.580	7.288	8.064	8.916	14.552	23.298
13	4.363	4.898	5.492	6.153	6.886	7.699	8.599	9.596	10.699	18.190	30.288
14	4.887	5.535	6.261	7.076	7.988	9.007	10.147	11.420	12.839	22.737	39.374
15	5.474	6.254	7.138	8.137	9.266	10.539	11.974	13.590	15.407	28.422	51.186
16	6.130	7.067	8.137	9.358	10.748	12.330	14.129	16.172	18.488	35.527	66.542
17	6.866	7.986	9.276	10.761	12.468	14.426	16.672	19.244	22.186	44.409	86.504
18	7.690	9.024	10.575	12.375	14.463	16.879	19.673	22.091	26.623	55.511	112.460
19	8.613	10.197	12.056	14.232	16.777	19.748	23.214	27.252	31.948	69.389	146.190
20	9.646	11.523	13.743	16.367	19.461	23.106	27.393	32.429	38.338	86.736	190.050
25	17.000	21.231	26.462	32.919	40.874	50.658	62.669	77.388	95.396	264.700	705.640
30	29.960	39.116	50.950	66.212	85.850	111.070	143.370	184.680	237.380	807.790	2,620.000
40	93.051	132.780	188.880	267.860	378.720	533.870	750.380	1,051.700	1,469.800	7,523.200	36,119.000
50	289.000	450.740	700.230	1,083.700	1,670.700	2,566.200	3,927.400	5,988.900	9,100.400	70,065.000	497,929.000

PRESENT VALUE OF AN ANNUITY OF $1

Example: You receive a note that promises to pay you $500 a year for 7 years. How much is it worth today if a loan of similar risk pays a 12% a year rate compounded annually? The note is worth $2,282.00 ($500 x 4.564) today.

| Year | | | | | | Percent | | | | | | |
	1%	2%	3%	4%	5%	6%	7%	8%	9%	10%	11%	12%
1	0.990	0.980	0.971	0.962	0.952	0.943	0.935	0.926	0.917	0.909	0.901	0.893
2	1.970	1.942	1.913	1.886	1.859	1.833	1.808	1.783	1.759	1.736	1.713	1.690
3	2.941	2.884	2.829	2.775	2.723	2.673	2.624	2.577	2.531	2.487	2.444	2.402
4	3.902	3.808	3.717	3.630	3.546	3.465	3.387	3.312	3.240	3.170	3.102	3.037
5	4.853	4.713	4.580	4.452	4.329	4.212	4.100	3.993	3.890	3.791	3.696	3.605
6	5.795	5.601	5.417	5.242	5.076	4.917	4.767	4.623	4.486	4.355	4.231	4.111
7	6.728	6.472	6.230	6.002	5.786	5.582	5.389	5.206	5.033	4.868	4.712	4.564
8	7.652	7.325	7.020	6.733	6.463	6.210	5.971	5.747	5.535	5.335	5.146	4.968
9	8.566	8.162	7.786	7.435	7.108	6.802	6.515	6.247	5.995	5.759	5.537	5.328
10	9.471	8.983	8.530	8.111	7.722	7.360	7.024	6.710	6.418	6.145	5.889	5.650
11	10.368	9.787	9.253	8.760	8.306	7.887	7.499	7.139	6.805	6.495	6.207	5.938
12	11.255	10.575	9.954	9.385	8.863	8.384	7.943	7.536	7.161	6.814	6.492	6.194
13	12.134	11.348	10.635	9.986	9.394	8.853	8.358	7.904	7.487	7.103	6.750	6.424
14	13.004	12.106	11.296	10.563	9.899	9.295	8.745	8.244	7.786	7.367	6.982	6.628
15	13.865	12.849	11.938	11.118	10.380	9.712	9.108	8.559	8.061	7.606	7.191	6.811
16	14.718	13.578	12.561	11.652	10.838	10.106	9.447	8.851	8.313	7.824	7.379	6.974
17	15.562	14.292	13.166	12.166	11.274	10.477	9.763	9.122	8.544	8.022	7.549	7.102
18	16.398	14.992	13.754	12.659	11.690	10.828	10.059	9.372	8.756	8.201	7.702	7.250
19	17.226	15.678	14.324	13.134	12.085	11.158	10.336	9.604	8.950	8.365	7.839	7.366
20	18.046	16.351	14.877	13.590	12.462	11.470	10.594	9.818	9.129	8.514	7.963	7.469
25	22.023	19.523	17.413	15.622	14.094	12.783	11.654	10.675	9.823	9.077	8.422	7.843
30	25.808	22.396	19.600	17.292	15.372	13.765	12.409	11.258	10.274	9.427	8.694	8.055
40	32.835	27.355	23.115	19.793	17.159	15.046	13.332	11.925	10.757	9.779	8.951	8.244
50	39.196	31.424	25.730	21.482	18.256	15.762	13.801	12.233	10.962	9.915	9.042	8.304

(Continued)

Present Value of an Annuity of $1

Year	13%	14%	15%	16%	17%	18%	19%	20%	25%	30%	35%	40%	50%
1	0.885	0.877	0.870	0.862	0.855	0.847	0.840	0.833	0.800	0.769	0.741	0.714	0.667
2	1.668	1.647	1.626	1.605	1.585	1.566	1.547	1.528	1.440	1.361	1.289	1.224	1.111
3	2.361	2.322	2.283	2.246	2.210	2.174	2.140	2.106	1.952	1.816	1.696	1.589	1.407
4	2.974	2.914	2.855	2.798	2.743	2.690	2.639	2.589	2.362	2.166	1.997	1.849	1.605
5	3.517	3.433	3.352	3.274	3.199	3.127	3.058	2.991	2.689	2.436	2.220	2.035	1.737
6	3.998	3.889	3.784	3.685	3.589	3.498	3.410	3.326	2.951	2.643	2.385	2.168	1.824
7	4.423	4.288	4.160	4.039	3.922	3.812	3.706	3.605	3.161	2.802	2.508	2.263	1.883
8	4.799	4.639	4.487	4.344	4.207	4.078	3.954	3.837	3.329	2.925	2.598	2.331	1.922
9	5.132	4.946	4.772	4.607	4.451	4.303	4.163	4.031	3.463	3.019	2.665	2.379	1.948
10	5.426	5.216	5.019	4.833	4.659	4.494	4.339	4.192	3.571	3.092	2.715	2.414	1.965
11	5.687	5.453	5.234	5.029	4.836	4.656	4.486	4.327	3.656	3.147	2.752	2.438	1.977
12	5.918	5.660	5.421	5.197	4.988	4.793	4.611	4.439	3.725	3.190	2.779	2.456	1.985
13	6.122	5.842	5.583	5.342	5.118	4.910	4.715	4.533	3.780	3.223	2.799	2.469	1.990
14	6.302	6.002	5.724	5.468	5.229	5.008	4.802	4.611	3.824	3.249	2.814	2.478	1.993
15	6.462	6.142	5.847	5.575	5.324	5.092	4.876	4.675	3.859	3.268	2.825	2.484	1.995
16	6.604	6.265	5.954	5.668	5.405	5.162	4.938	4.730	3.887	3.283	2.834	2.489	1.997
17	6.729	6.373	6.047	5.749	5.475	5.222	4.988	4.775	3.910	3.295	2.840	2.492	1.998
18	6.840	6.467	6.128	5.818	5.534	5.273	5.033	4.812	3.928	3.304	2.844	2.494	1.999
19	6.938	6.550	6.198	5.877	5.584	5.316	5.070	4.843	3.942	3.311	2.848	2.496	1.999
20	7.025	6.623	6.259	5.929	5.628	5.353	5.101	4.870	3.954	3.316	2.850	2.497	1.999
25	7.330	6.873	6.464	6.097	5.766	5.467	5.195	4.948	3.985	3.329	2.856	2.499	2.000
30	7.496	7.003	6.566	6.177	5.829	5.517	5.235	4.979	3.995	3.332	2.857	2.500	2.000
40	7.634	7.105	6.642	6.233	5.871	5.548	5.258	4.997	3.999	3.333	2.857	2.500	2.000
50	7.675	7.133	6.661	6.246	5.880	5.554	5.262	4.999	4.000	3.333	2.857	2.500	2.000

COMPOUND SUM OF AN ANNUITY OF $1

Example: You invest $2,000 a year in a retirement plan paying 9% a year compounded annually. At the end of the twentieth year, you will have $102,320 saved ($2,000 x 51.160).

Period	1%	2%	3%	4%	5%	Percent 6%	7%	8%	9%	10%	11%
1	1.000	1.000	1.000	1.000	1.000	1.000	1.000	1.000	1.000	1.000	1.000
2	2.010	2.020	2.030	2.040	2.050	2.060	2.070	2.080	2.090	2.100	2.110
3	3.030	3.060	3.091	3.122	3.153	3.184	3.215	3.246	3.278	3.310	3.342
4	4.060	4.122	4.184	4.246	4.310	4.375	4.440	4.506	4.573	4.641	4.710
5	5.101	5.204	5.309	5.416	5.526	5.637	5.751	5.867	5.985	6.105	6.228
6	6.152	6.308	6.468	6.633	6.802	6.975	7.153	7.336	7.523	7.716	7.913
7	7.214	7.434	7.662	7.898	8.142	8.394	8.654	8.923	9.200	9.487	9.783
8	8.286	8.583	8.892	9.214	9.549	9.897	10.260	10.637	11.028	11.436	11.859
9	9.369	9.755	10.159	10.583	11.027	11.491	11.978	12.488	13.021	13.579	14.164
10	10.462	10.950	11.464	12.006	12.578	13.181	13.816	14.487	15.193	15.937	16.722
11	11.567	12.169	12.808	13.486	14.207	14.972	15.784	16.645	17.560	18.531	19.561
12	12.683	13.412	14.192	15.026	15.917	16.870	17.888	18.977	20.141	21.384	22.713
13	13.809	14.680	15.618	16.627	17.713	18.882	20.141	21.495	22.953	24.523	26.212
14	14.947	15.974	17.086	18.292	19.599	21.015	22.550	24.215	26.019	27.975	30.095
15	16.097	17.293	18.599	20.024	21.579	23.276	25.129	27.152	29.361	31.772	34.405
16	17.258	18.639	20.157	21.825	23.657	25.673	27.888	30.324	33.003	35.950	39.190
17	18.430	20.012	21.762	23.698	25.840	20.213	30.840	33.750	36.974	40.545	44.501
18	19.615	21.412	23.414	25.645	28.132	30.906	33.999	37.450	41.301	45.599	50.396
19	20.811	22.841	25.117	27.671	30.539	33.760	37.379	41.446	46.018	51.159	56.939
20	22.019	24.297	26.870	29.778	33.066	36.786	40.995	45.762	51.160	57.275	64.203
25	28.243	32.030	36.459	41.646	47.727	54.865	63.249	73.106	84.701	98.347	114.410
30	34.785	40.588	47.575	56.085	66.439	79.058	94.461	113.280	136.310	164.490	199.020
40	48.886	60.402	75.401	95.026	120.800	154.760	199.640	259.060	337.890	442.590	581.830
50	64.463	84.579	112.800	152.670	209.350	290.340	406.530	573.770	815.080	1,163.900	1,668.800

(Continued)

Compound Sum of an Annuity of $1

Period	12%	13%	14%	15%	16%	17%	18%	19%	20%	25%	30%
						Percent					
1	1.000	1.000	1.000	1.000	1.000	1.000	1.000	1.000	1.000	1.000	1.000
2	2.120	2.130	2.140	2.150	2.160	2.170	2.180	2.190	2.200	2.250	2.300
3	3.374	3.407	3.440	3.473	3.506	3.539	3.572	3.606	3.640	3.813	3.990
4	4.779	4.850	4.921	4.993	5.066	5.141	5.215	5.291	5.368	5.766	6.187
5	6.353	6.480	6.610	6.742	6.877	7.014	7.154	7.297	7.442	8.207	9.043
6	8.115	8.323	8.536	8.754	8.977	9.207	9.442	9.683	9.930	11.259	12.756
7	10.089	10.405	10.730	11.067	11.414	11.772	12.142	12.523	12.916	15.073	17.583
8	12.300	12.757	13.233	13.727	14.240	14.773	15.327	15.902	16.499	19.842	23.858
9	14.776	15.416	16.085	16.786	17.519	18.285	19.086	19.923	20.799	25.802	32.015
10	17.549	18.420	19.337	20.304	21.321	22.393	23.521	24.701	25.959	33.253	42.619
11	20.655	21.814	23.045	23.349	25.733	27.200	28.755	30.404	32.150	42.566	56.405
12	24.133	25.650	27.271	29.002	30.850	32.824	34.931	37.180	39.581	54.208	74.327
13	28.029	29.985	32.089	34.352	36.786	39.404	42.219	45.244	48.497	68.760	97.625
14	32.393	34.883	37.581	40.505	43.672	47.103	50.818	54.841	59.196	86.949	127.910
15	37.280	40.417	43.842	47.580	51.660	56.110	60.965	66.261	72.035	109.690	167.290
16	42.753	46.672	50.980	55.717	60.925	66.649	72.939	79.850	87.442	138.110	218.470
17	48.884	53.739	59.118	65.075	71.673	78.979	87.068	96.022	105.930	173.640	285.010
18	55.750	61.725	68.394	75.836	84.141	93.406	103.740	115.270	128.120	218.050	371.520
19	63.440	70.749	78.969	88.212	98.603	110.290	123.410	138.170	154.740	273.560	483.970
20	72.052	80.947	91.025	102.440	115.380	130.030	146.630	165.420	186.690	342.950	630.170
25	133.330	155.620	181.870	212.790	249.210	292.110	342.600	402.040	471.980	1,054.800	2,348.800
30	241.330	293.200	356.790	434.750	530.310	647.440	790.950	966.700	1,181.900	3,227.200	8,730.000
40	767.090	1,013.700	1,342.000	1,779.100	2,360.800	3,134.500	4,163.210	5,529.800	7,343.900	30,089.000	120,393.000
50	2,400.000	3,459.500	4,994.500	7,217.700	10,436.000	15,090.000	21,813.000	31,515.000	45,497.000	280,256.000	165,976.000

CONSTANT ANNUAL PERCENTAGE
Percentage Paid Off in Monthly Payments (Paydown)

Constant Annual %	Interest Rate %	Percentage Paid Off In				Full Term
		5 Yrs	10 Yrs	15 Yrs	20 Yrs	
10	9	6.3	16.1	31.5	93.4	25 yrs., 9 mos.
	9 ½	3.2	8.3	16.5	50.8	31 yrs., 8 mos.
10 ½	9	9.4	24.2	47.3	83.5	21 yrs., 9 mos.
	9 ½	6.4	16.6	33.0	59.3	24 yrs.,11 mos.
	10	3.2	8.5	17.3	55.3	30 yrs., 7 mos.
11	9	12.6	32.3	63.1		19 yrs., 1 mos.
	9 ½	9.6	24.9	49.5	89.0	21 yrs., 1 mos.
	10	6.5	17.1	34.5	63.3	24 yrs., 1 mos.
	10 ½	3.3	8.8	18.1	33.8	29 yrs., 7 mos.
11 ½	9	15.7	40.3	78.8		17 yrs., 1 mos.
	9 ½	12.7	33.2	66.0		18 yrs., 6 mos.
	10	9.7	25.6	51.8	94.9	20 yrs., 6 mos.
	10 ½	6.5	17.6	36.2	67.5	23 yrs., 5 mos.
	11	3.3	9.0	18.9	36.1	28 yrs., 8 mos.
12	9	18.9	48.4	94.6		15 yrs., 6 mos.
	9 ½	15.9	41.5	82.5		16 yrs., 7 mos.
	10	12.9	34.1	69.1		18 yrs., 0 mos.
	10 ½	9.8	26.4	54.3		19 yrs.,11 mos.
	11	6.6	18.1	37.9	72.1	22 yrs., 9 mos.
	11 ½	3.4	9.3	19.9	38.5	27 yrs.,10 mos.
12 ½	9	22.0	56.4			14 yrs., 3 mos.
	9 ½	19.1	49.8	99.0		15 yrs., 1 mos.
	10	16.1	42.7	86.3		16 yrs., 2 mos.
	10 ½	13.1	35.1	72.3		17 yrs., 7 mos.
	11	9.9	27.1	56.8		19 yrs., 5 mos.
	11 ½	6.7	18.6	39.7	77.1	22 yrs., 1 mos.
	12	3.4	9.6	20.8	41.2	27 yrs., 0 mos.
13	9	25.1	64.5			13 yrs., 2 mos.
	9 ½	22.3	58.1			13 yrs.,11 mos.
	10	19.4	51.2			14 yrs., 9 mos.
	10 ½	16.3	43.9	90.4		15 yrs.,10 mos.
	11	13.3	36.2	75.8		17 yrs., 2 mos.
	11 ½	10.1	27.9	59.6		18 yrs.,11 mos.
	12	6.8	19.2	41.6	8.24	21 yrs., 6 mos.
	12 ½	3.4	9.9	21.8	44.1	26 yrs., 3 mos.
13 ½	9	28.3	72.6			12 yrs., 4 mos.
	9 ½	25.5	66.4			12 yrs.,11 mos.
	10	22.6	59.7			13 yrs., 7 mos.
	10 ½	19.6	52.7			14 yrs., 5 mos.
	11	16.6	45.2	94.7		15 yrs., 5 mos.
	11 ½	13.4	37.2	79.4		16 yrs., 9 mos.
	12	10.2	28.8	62.4		18 yrs., 5 mos.
	12 ½	6.9	19.7	43.7	88.2	21 yrs., 0 mos.
	13	3.5	10.2	22.9	47.2	25 yrs., 6 mos.
14	9	31.4	80.6			11 yrs., 6 mos.
	9 ½	28.7	74.7			12 yrs., 0 mos.
	10	25.8	68.3			12 yrs., 7 mos.

(Continued)

Constant Annual Percentage

Constant Annual %	Interest Rate %	Percentage Paid Off In				Full Term
		5 Yrs	10 Yrs	15 Yrs	20 Yrs	
	10 ½	22.9	61.5			13 yrs., 4 mos.
	11	19.9	54.2			14 yrs., 1 mos.
	11 ½	16.8	46.5	99.3		15 yrs., 1 mos.
	12	13.6	38.3	83.3		16 yrs., 4 mos.
	12 ½	10.3	29.6	65.5		18 yrs., 0 mos.
	13	7.0	20.3	45.8	94.4	20 yrs., 5 mos.
	13 ½	3.5	10.5	24.0	50.6	24 yrs.,10 mos.
14 ½	9	34.6	88.7			10 yrs.,10 mos.
	9 ½	31.8	83.0			11 yrs., 4 mos.
	10	29.0	76.8			11 yrs., 9 mos.
	10 ½	26.2	70.3			12 yrs., 4 mos.
	11	23.2	63.3			13 yrs., 0 mos.
	11 ½	20.1	55.9			13 yrs.,10 mos.
	12	17.0	47.9			14 yrs., 9 mos.
	12 ½	13.8	39.5	83.7		16 yrs., 0 mos.
	13	10.5	30.5	68.7		17 yrs., 7 mos.
	13 ½	7.1	21.0	48.1		20 yrs., 0 mos.
	14	3.6	10.8	25.2	54.2	24 yrs., 3 mos.
15	9	37.7	96.8			10 yrs., 3 mos.
	9 ½	35.0	91.2			10 yrs., 8 mos.
	10	32.3	85.4			11 yrs., 1 mos.
	10 ½	29.4	79.1			11 yrs., 7 mos.
	11	26.5	72.3			12 yrs., 1 mos.
	11 ½	23.5	65.2			12 yrs., 9 mos.
	12	20.4	57.5			13 yrs., 6 mos.
	12 ½	17.2	49.4			14 yrs., 5 mos.
	13	14.0	40.7	91.6		15 yrs., 7 mos.
	13 ½	10.6	31.4	72.1		17 yrs., 2 mos.
	14	7.2	21.6	50.5		19 yrs., 6 mos.
	14 ½	3.6	11.1	26.5		23 yrs., 8 mos.
15 ½	9	40.9				9 yrs., 9 mos.
	9 ½	38.2	99.5			10 yrs., 1 mos.
	10	35.5	93.9			10 yrs., 5 mos.
	10 ½	32.7	87.8			10 yrs.,10 mos.
	11	29.8	81.4			11 yrs., 4 mos.
	11 ½	26.9	74.5			11 yrs.,11 mos.
	12	23.8	67.1			12 yrs., 6 mos.
	12 ½	20.7	59.2			13 yrs., 3 mos.
	13	17.5	50.8			14 yrs., 2 mos.
	13 ½	14.2	41.9	96.2		15 yrs., 4 mos.
	14	10.8	32.4	75.7		16 yrs.,10 mos.
	14 ½	7.3	22.2	53.0		19 yrs., 1 mos.
	15	3.7	11.5	27.9	62.4	23 yrs., 1 mos.
16	9	44.0				9 yrs., 3 mos.
	9 ½	41.4				9 yrs., 7 mos.
	10	38.7				9 yrs.,11 mos.
	10 ½	36.0	96.6			10 yrs., 3 mos.
	11	33.1	90.4			10 yrs., 8 mos.
	11 ½	30.2	83.8			11 yrs., 1 mos.

Constant Annual Percentage

Constant Annual %	Interest Rate %	Percentage Paid Off In				Full Term
		5 Yrs	10 Yrs	15 Yrs	20 Yrs	
	12	27.2	76.7			11 yrs., 8 mos.
	12 ½	24.1	69.1			12 yrs., 3 mos.
	13	21.0	61.0			13 yrs., 0 mos.
	13 ½	17.7	52.4			13 yrs.,10 mos.
	14	14.4	43.2			15 yrs., 0 mos.
	14 ½	10.9	33.4	79.50		16 yrs., 6 mos.
	15	7.4	22.9	55.7		18 yrs., 8 mos.
16 ½	9	47.1				8 yrs.,10 mos.
	9 ½	44.6				9 yrs., 1 mos.
	10	41.9				9 yrs., 5 mos.
	10 ½	39.2				9 yrs., 9 mos.
	11	36.4	99.5			10 yrs., 1 mos.
	11 ½	33.6	93.1			10 yrs., 6 mos.
	12	30.6	86.3			10 yrs.,11 mos.
	12 ½	27.6	79.0			11 yrs., 5 mos.
	13	24.5	71.2			12 yrs., 0 mos.
	13 ½	21.3	62.9			12 yrs., 9 mos.
	14	18.0	54.0			13 yrs., 7 mos.
	14 ½	14.6	44.5			14 yrs., 8 mos.
	15	11.1	34.4	83.6		16 yrs., 2 mos.
17	9	50.3				8 yrs., 5 mos.
	9 ½	47.8				8 yrs., 8 mos.
	10	45.2				8 yrs.,11 mos.
	10 ½	42.5				9 yrs., 3 mos.
	11	39.8				9 yrs., 7 mos.
	11 ½	36.9				9 yrs.,11 mos.
	12	34.0	95.8			10 yrs., 3 mos.
	12 ½	31.0	88.8			10 yrs., 9 mos.
	13	28.0	81.3			11 yrs., 3 mos.
	13 ½	24.8	73.3			11 yrs.,10 mos.
	14	21.5	64.8			12 yrs., 6 mos.
	14 ½	18.2	55.6			13 yrs., 4 mos.
	15	14.8	45.9			14 yrs., 5 mos.
18	9	56.6				7 yrs., 9 mos.
	9 ½	54.1				8 yrs., 0 mos.
	10	51.6				8 yrs., 2 mos.
	10 ½	49.0				8 yrs., 5 mos.
	11	46.4				8 yrs., 8 mos.
	11 ½	43.7				8 yrs.,11 mos.
	12	40.8				9 yrs., 3 mos.
	12 ½	37.9				9 yrs., 7 mos.
	13	35.0				9 yrs.,11 mos.
	13 ½	31.9	94.3			10 yrs., 4 mos.
	14	28.7	86.4			10 yrs.,10 mos.
	14 ½	25.5	77.9			10 yrs., 5 mos.
	15	21.1	68.8			12 yrs., 1 mos.
19	9	62.9				7 yrs., 2 mos.
	9 ½	60.5				7 yrs., 4 mos.
	10	58.1				7 yrs., 7 mos.

(Continued)

Constant Annual Percentage

Constant Annual %	Interest Rate %	Percentage Paid Off In				Full Term
		5 Yrs	10 Yrs	15 Yrs	20 Yrs	
	10 ½	55.6				7 yrs., 9 mos.
	11	53.0				7 yrs.,11 mos.
	11 ½	50.4				8 yrs., 2 mos.
	12	47.6				8 yrs., 5 mos.
	12 ½	44.8				8 yrs., 8 mos.
	13	41.9				8 yrs.,11 mos.
	13 ½	39.0				9 yrs., 3 mos.
	14	35.9				9 yrs., 8 mos.
	14 ½	32.8				10 yrs., 0 mos.
	15	29.5				10 yrs., 6 mos.
20	9	69.1				6 yrs., 9 mos.
	9 ½	66.9				6 yrs.,10 mos.
	10	64.5				7 yrs., 0 mos.
	10 ½	62.1				7 yrs., 2 mos.
	11	59.6				7 yrs., 4 mos.
	11 ½	57.1				7 yrs., 6 mos.
	12	51.7				7 yrs., 9 mos.
	12 ½	51.7				7 yrs.,11 mos.
	13	48.9				8 yrs., 2 mos.
	13 ½	46.1				8 yrs., 5 mos.
	14	43.1				8 yrs., 8 mos.
	14 ½	40.0				9 yrs., 0 mos.
	15	36.9				9 yrs., 4 mos.

COMPOUNDED SAVINGS INTEREST RATES

Nominal Annual % Rate	The True Annual Rate If Compounded . . .				
	Semi-Annually	Quarterly	Monthly	Weekly	Daily
3.00	3.0225	3.0339	3.0415	3.0445	3.0453
3.25	3.2764	3.2898	3.2988	3.3023	3.3032
3.50	3.5306	3.5462	3.5566	3.5607	3.5617
3.75	3.7851	3.8030	3.8151	3.8197	3.8209
4.00	4.0400	4.0604	4.0741	4.0794	4.0808
4.25	4.2951	4.3182	4.3337	4.3397	4.3413
4.50	4.5506	4.5765	4.5939	4.6007	4.6024
4.75	4.8064	4.8352	4.8547	4.8623	4.8642
5.00	5.0625	5.0945	5.1161	5.1245	5.1267
5.25	5.3189	5.3542	5.3781	5.3874	5.3898
5.50	5.5756	5.6144	5.6407	5.6509	5.6536
5.75	5.8326	5.8751	5.9039	5.9151	5.9180
6.00	6.0900	6.1363	6.1677	6.1799	6.1831
6.25	6.3476	6.3980	6.4321	6.4454	6.4488
6.50	6.6056	6.6601	6.6971	6.7115	6.7152
6.75	6.8639	6.9227	6.9627	6.9783	6.9823
7.00	7.1225	7.1859	7.2290	7.2457	7.2500
7.25	7.3814	7.4495	7.4958	7.5138	7.5185
7.50	7.6406	7.7135	7.7632	7.7825	7.7875
7.75	7.9001	7.9781	8.0312	8.0519	8.0573
8.00	8.1600	8.2432	8.2999	8.3220	8.3277
8.25	8.4201	8.5087	8.5692	8.5927	8.5988
8.50	8.6806	8.7747	8.8390	8.8641	8.8706
8.75	8.9414	9.0413	9.1095	9.1362	9.1430
9.00	9.2025	9.3083	9.3806	9.4089	9.4162
9.25	9.4639	9.5758	9.6524	9.6823	9.6900
9.50	9.7256	9.8438	9.9247	9.9563	9.9645
9.75	9.9876	10.1123	10.1977	10.2310	10.2397
10.00	10.2500	10.3812	10.4713	10.5064	10.5155
11.00	11.3025	11.4621	11.5718	11.6148	11.6259
12.00	12.3600	12.5508	12.6825	12.7340	12.7474
13.00	13.4225	13.6475	13.8032	13.8643	13.8802
14.00	14.4900	14.7523	14.9342	15.0057	15.0242
15.00	15.5625	15.8650	16.0754	16.1583	16.1798

RETURN ON INVESTMENT

The following three tables may be used in a variety of ways to estimate results of long-term savings, investments, and retirement funding

For example, the first table, which shows how a $10,000 investment grows at various interest rates, can be used to calculate the value of a tax-exempt bond portfolio, tax-deferred annuity, or tax-deferred retirement account.

The second and third tables can be used to determine how much money an investor needs to save to fund a long-term goal such as retirement or a child's college education.

$10,000 Lump Sum at Rates Compounded Annually
End-of-Year Values

%	5th Year	10th Year	15th Year	20th Year	25th Year	30th Year	35th Year	40th Year
1	10,510	11,046	11,609	12,201	12,824	13,478	14,166	14,888
2	11,040	12,189	13,458	14,859	16,406	18,113	19,998	22,080
3	11,592	13,439	15,579	18,061	20,937	24,272	28,138	32,620
4	12,166	14,802	18,009	21,911	26,658	32,433	39,460	48,010
5	12,762	16,288	20,789	26,532	33,863	43,219	55,160	70,399
6	13,382	17,908	23,965	32,071	42,918	57,434	76,860	102,857
7	14,025	19,671	27,590	38,696	54,274	76,122	106,765	149,744
8	14,693	21,859	31,721	46,609	68,484	100,626	147,853	217,245
9	15,386	23,673	36,424	56,044	86,230	132,676	204,139	314,094
10	16,105	25,937	41,772	67,274	108,347	174,494	281,024	452,592
11	16,850	28,394	47,845	80,623	135,854	228,922	385,748	650,008
12	17,623	31,058	54,735	96,462	170,000	299,599	527,996	930,509
13	18,424	33,945	62,542	115,230	212,305	391,158	720,685	1,327,815
14	19,254	37,072	71,379	137,434	264,619	509,501	981,001	1,888,835
15	20,113	40,455	81,370	163,665	329,189	662,117	1,331,755	2,678,635
16	21,003	44,114	92,655	194,607	408,742	858,498	1,803,140	3,787,211
17	21,924	48,068	105,387	231,055	506,578	1,110,646	2,435,034	5,338,687
18	22,877	52,338	119,737	273,930	626,686	1,433,706	3,279,972	7,503,783
19	23,863	56,946	135,895	324,294	773,880	1,846,753	4,407,006	10,516,675
20	24,883	61,917	154,070	383,375	953,962	2,373,763	5,906,682	14,697,715

Lump Sum Required to Equal $100,000 at the End of a Specified Period

%	5 Years	10 Years	15 Years	20 Years	25 Years	30 Years	35 Years	40 Years
1	95,147	90,529	86,135	81,954	77,977	74,192	70,591	67,165
2	90,573	82,348	74,301	67,297	60,953	55,207	50,003	45,289
3	86,261	74,409	64,186	55,367	47,761	41,199	35,538	30,656
4	82,193	67,556	55,526	45,639	37,512	30,832	25,341	20,829
5	78,353	61,391	48,102	37,689	29,530	23,138	18,129	14,205
6	74,726	55,839	41,727	31,180	23,300	17,411	13,011	9,722
7	71,299	50,835	36,245	25,842	18,425	13,137	9,367	6,678
8	68,058	46,319	31,524	21,455	14,602	9,938	6,763	4,603
9	64,993	42,241	27,454	17,843	11,597	7,537	4,899	3,184
10	62,092	38,554	23,940	14,864	9,230	5,731	3,558	2,209
11	59,345	35,218	20,900	12,403	7,361	4,368	2,592	1,538
12	56,743	32,197	18,270	10,367	5,882	3,340	1,894	1,075
13	54,276	29,460	15,989	8,678	4,710	2,557	1,388	753
14	51,937	26,974	14,010	7,276	3,780	1,963	1,019	529
15	49,718	24,718	12,289	6,100	3,040	1,510	751	373
16	47,611	22,683	10,792	5,139	2,447	1,165	555	264
17	45,611	20,804	9,489	4,329	1,974	900	411	187
18	43,711	19,107	8,352	3,651	1,596	697	395	133
19	41,905	17,560	7,359	3,084	1,292	541	227	95
20	40,188	16,151	6,491	2,610	1,048	421	169	68

Approximate Annual Investment Required to Equal $100,000 at the End of a Specified Period

%	5 Years	10 Years	15 Years	20 Years	25 Years	30 Years	35 Years	40 Years
1	19,380	9,464	6,151	4,497	3,506	2,768	2,378	2,026
2	18,841	8,954	5,669	4,036	3,061	2,417	1,961	1,624
3	18,290	8,470	5,220	3,613	2,663	2,041	1,606	1,288
4	17,751	8,009	4,802	3,229	2,309	1,714	1,306	1,011
5	17,236	7,572	4,414	2,880	1,966	1,433	1,054	788
6	16,736	7,157	4,053	2,565	1,720	1,193	847	610
7	16,254	6,764	3,719	2,280	1,478	989	676	468
8	15,783	6,392	3,410	2,024	1,267	817	537	357
9	15,332	6,039	3,125	1,793	1,083	673	425	272
10	14,890	5,704	2,861	1,587	924	553	335	205
11	14,467	5,388	2,618	1,403	787	453	264	155
12	14,055	5,088	2,395	1,239	670	370	206	116
13	13,658	4,805	2,190	1,070	569	302	168	87
14	13,270	4,536	2,001	964	482	246	126	65
15	12,898	4,283	1,828	849	409	200	99	49
16	12,537	4,043	1,669	747	346	165	77	37
17	12,185	3,817	1,523	657	293	132	60	28
18	11,846	3,603	1,390	578	247	107	47	20
19	11,517	3,401	1,268	508	209	87	36	15
20	11,198	3,210	1,157	446	177	71	28	11

MORTGAGE AMORTIZATION

The amortization tables, showing annual interest rates from 8% to 18% by ½% increments, on the following pages are given for monthly payments in arrears. Tables are given at each interest rate for 5, 10, 15, 20, 25, 30 and 40 year loans. The tables use level monthly payments, and the factors are per $100 of loan amount. The terms used in the tables are defined below.

Monthly payment The amount per $100 of loan paid per month.

Example: On a $100,000 loan made at 8% for 20 years, the payment is $836.44 per month:
$$\frac{\$100,000}{100} \times .836440$$

Example: On an $85,000 loan made at 12% for 30 years, the monthly payment is $874.32:
$$\frac{\$85,000}{100} \times 1.028613$$

Annual interest The amount of interest paid that year for each $100 of loan.

Example: On a $100,000 loan made at 10% for 15 years, $9,863.54 of interest is paid in the *first* year. In the *tenth* year, $5,466.20 of interest is paid.

Annual principal The amount of principal paid that year for each $100 of loan.

Example: On a $125,000 loan made at 13% for 25 years, $708.78 of principal is paid in the *first* year. In the *fifteenth* year, $4,331.85 of principal is paid.

Year-end balance The amount still owed at the end of that year for each $100 of loan.

Example: On a $115,000 loan made at 13.50% for 10 years, $109,158.46 is still owed at the end of the first year. At the end of the fifth year, $76,104.57 is still owed.

Annual constant The amount paid each year, (i.e., the monthly payments x 12) for each $100 of loan.

Example: On a $150,000 loan made at 15% for 40 years, the annual payment is $22,560.

MORTGAGE AMORTIZATION TABLES
8%

5 YEARS
Monthly Payment: 2.027639
Annual Constant: 24.34

Year	Annual		Year End Balance
	Interest	Principal	
1	7.387663	16.944010	83.055990
2	5.981318	18.350355	64.705635
3	4.458248	19.873425	44.832210
4	2.808764	21.522910	23.309300
5	1.022373	23.309300	0.000000

10 YEARS
Monthly Payment: 1.213276
Annual Constant: 14.56

Year	Annual		Year End Balance
	Interest	Principal	
1	7.754066	6.805245	93.194755
2	7.189234	7.370077	85.824678
3	6.577522	7.981790	77.842888
4	5.915037	8.644274	69.198614
5	5.197566	9.361745	59.836869
6	4.420546	10.138765	49.698104
7	3.579034	10.980278	38.717826
8	2.667676	11.891635	26.826191
9	1.680676	12.878635	13.947556
10	0.611756	13.947556	0.000000

15 YEARS
Monthly Payment: 0.955652
Annual Constant: 11.47

Year	Annual		Year End Balance
	Interest	Principal	
1	7.869978	3.597847	96.402153
2	7.571358	3.896467	92.505686
3	7.247954	4.219871	88.285815
4	6.897706	4.570119	83.715696
5	6.518389	4.949436	78.766260
6	6.107588	5.360237	73.406023
7	5.662691	5.805134	67.600889
8	5.180868	6.286957	61.313932
9	4.659053	6.808772	54.505160
10	4.093929	7.373896	47.131264
11	3.481899	7.985926	39.145337
12	2.819071	8.648754	30.496583
13	2.101229	9.366596	21.129987
14	1.323806	10.144019	10.985968
15	0.481857	10.985968	0.000000

20 YEARS
Monthly Payment: 0.836440
Annual Constant: 10.04

Year	Annual		Year End Balance
	Interest	Principal	
1	7.923615	2.113666	97.886334
2	7.748181	2.289100	95.597234
3	7.558187	2.479094	93.118140
4	7.352424	2.684857	90.433283
5	7.129582	2.907699	87.525584
6	6.888244	3.149037	84.376547
7	6.626876	3.410405	80.966142
8	6.343814	3.693467	77.272675
9	6.037258	4.000023	73.272652
10	5.705258	4.332023	68.940629
11	5.345702	4.691579	64.249050
12	4.956303	5.080977	59.168073
13	4.534585	5.502696	53.665377
14	4.077864	5.959417	47.705960
15	3.583235	6.454046	41.251914
16	3.047552	6.989728	34.262185
17	2.467408	7.569872	26.692313
18	1.839113	8.198168	18.494145
19	1.158669	8.878612	9.615533
20	0.421748	9.615533	0.000000

25 YEARS
Monthly Payment: 0.771816
Annual Constant: 9.27

Year	Annual		Year End Balance
	Interest	Principal	
1	7.952690	1.309104	98.690896
2	7.844035	1.417759	97.273137
3	7.726362	1.535432	95.737704
4	7.598922	1.662873	94.074832
5	7.460904	1.800890	92.273941
6	7.311431	1.950363	90.323578
7	7.149552	2.112242	88.211336
8	6.974237	2.287557	85.923778
9	6.784371	2.477424	83.446355
10	6.578746	2.683049	80.763306
11	6.356054	2.905740	77.857566
12	6.114879	3.146915	74.710651
13	5.853687	3.408108	71.302543
14	5.570816	3.690979	67.611564
15	5.264466	3.997328	63.614236
16	4.932690	4.329105	59.285131
17	4.573376	4.688418	54.596713
18	4.184240	5.077555	49.519158
19	3.762806	5.498989	44.020169
20	3.306392	5.955402	38.064767
21	2.812097	6.449698	31.615069
22	2.276775	6.985020	24.630049
23	1.697022	7.564773	17.065276
24	1.069149	8.192645	8.872631
25	0.389164	8.872631	0.000000

(Continued)

Mortgage Amortization Tables
8%

30 YEARS				**40** YEARS			
Monthly Payment: 0.733765				Monthly Payment: 0.695312			
Annual Constant: 8.81				Annual Constant: 8.35			

30 YEARS — Monthly Payment: 0.733765, Annual Constant: 8.81

Year	Annual Interest	Annual Principal	Year End Balance
1	7.969811	0.835364	99.164636
2	7.900476	0.904699	98.259937
3	7.825387	0.979788	97.280149
4	7.744065	1.061110	96.219039
5	7.655993	1.149182	95.069857
6	7.560611	1.244563	93.825293
7	7.457313	1.347862	92.477432
8	7.345441	1.459733	91.017698
9	7.224284	1.580891	89.436808
10	7.093071	1.712104	87.724704
11	6.950967	1.854208	85.870496
12	6.797069	2.008106	83.862391
13	6.630397	2.174778	81.687613
14	6.449892	2.355283	79.332330
15	6.254404	2.550770	76.781560
16	6.042692	2.762483	74.019076
17	5.813407	2.991768	71.027309
18	5.565092	3.240083	67.787226
19	5.296167	3.509008	64.278217
20	5.004921	3.800254	60.477963
21	4.689501	4.115674	56.362289
22	4.347902	4.457272	51.905017
23	3.977951	4.827224	47.077793
24	3.577294	5.227881	41.849912
25	3.143382	5.661793	36.188119
26	2.673456	6.131719	30.056401
27	2.164527	6.640648	23.415752
28	1.613356	7.191819	16.223934
29	1.016439	7.788736	8.435197
30	0.369977	8.435197	0.000000

40 YEARS — Monthly Payment: 0.695312, Annual Constant: 8.35

Year	Annual Interest	Annual Principal	Year End Balance
1	7.987112	0.356628	99.643372
2	7.957512	0.386228	99.257143
3	7.925455	0.418285	98.838858
4	7.890738	0.453003	98.385855
5	7.853139	0.490602	97.895254
6	7.812419	0.531321	97.363932
7	7.768320	0.575421	96.788512
8	7.720560	0.623180	96.165331
9	7.668836	0.674904	95.490427
10	7.612820	0.730921	94.759507
11	7.552153	0.791587	93.967920
12	7.486452	0.857288	93.110632
13	7.415298	0.928443	92.182189
14	7.338237	1.005503	91.176686
15	7.254781	1.088959	90.087727
16	7.164398	1.179342	88.908385
17	7.066513	1.277227	87.631158
18	6.960504	1.383236	86.247922
19	6.845696	1.498044	84.749878
20	6.721359	1.622381	83.127497
21	6.586702	1.757038	81.370459
22	6.440869	1.902871	79.467588
23	6.282932	2.060809	77.406779
24	6.111886	2.231855	75.174924
25	5.926643	2.417097	72.757827
26	5.726025	2.617715	70.140112
27	5.508756	2.834984	67.305127
28	5.273454	3.070287	64.234840
29	5.018621	3.325119	60.909721
30	4.742638	3.601102	57.308619
31	4.443748	3.899992	53.408627
32	4.120051	4.223689	49.184938
33	3.769487	4.574254	44.610684
34	3.389826	4.953914	39.656770
35	2.978654	5.365087	34.291683
36	2.533354	5.810386	28.481297
37	2.051095	6.292646	22.188651
38	1.528808	6.814932	15.373719
39	0.963172	7.380568	7.993151
40	0.350589	7.993151	0.000000

MORTGAGE AMORTIZATION TABLES
8.5%

5 YEARS — Monthly Payment: 2.051653 — Annual Constant: 24.62

Year	Interest	Principal	Year End Balance
1	7.856931	16.762906	83.237094
2	6.375243	18.244595	64.992499
3	4.762586	19.857251	45.135247
4	3.007386	21.612452	23.522796
5	1.097042	23.522796	0.000000

10 YEARS — Monthly Payment: 1.239857 — Annual Constant: 14.88

Year	Interest	Principal	Year End Balance
1	8.245551	6.632732	93.367268
2	7.659278	7.219005	86.148264
3	7.021184	7.857099	78.291165
4	6.326687	8.551595	69.739569
5	5.570804	9.307478	60.432091
6	4.748108	10.130175	50.301916
7	3.852692	11.025590	39.276326
8	2.878131	12.000152	27.276174
9	1.817426	13.060856	14.215317
10	0.662965	14.215317	0.000000

15 YEARS — Monthly Payment: 0.984740 — Annual Constant: 11.82

Year	Interest	Principal	Year End Balance
1	8.367680	3.449195	96.550805
2	8.062802	3.754072	92.796733
3	7.730977	4.085898	88.710835
4	7.369820	4.447054	84.263780
5	6.976741	4.840134	79.423647
6	6.548917	5.267957	74.155690
7	6.083278	5.733597	68.422093
8	5.576480	6.240395	62.181698
9	5.024886	6.791989	55.389709
10	4.424536	7.392339	47.997371
11	3.771120	8.045754	39.951616
12	3.059949	8.756926	31.194690
13	2.285916	9.530958	21.663732
14	1.443466	10.373409	11.290323
15	0.526551	11.290323	0.000000

20 YEARS — Monthly Payment: 0.867823 — Annual Constant: 10.42

Year	Interest	Principal	Year End Balance
1	8.423650	1.990229	98.009771
2	8.247731	2.166147	95.843623
3	8.056264	2.357615	93.486008
4	7.847872	2.566007	90.920002
5	7.621060	2.792818	88.127183
6	7.374201	3.039678	85.087505
7	7.105521	3.308358	81.779147
8	6.813092	3.600787	78.178360
9	6.494815	3.919064	74.259296
10	6.148405	4.265473	69.993823
11	5.771376	4.642502	65.351320
12	5.361021	5.052857	60.298463
13	4.914395	5.499484	54.798979
14	4.428290	5.985588	48.813391
15	3.899219	6.514660	42.298731
16	3.323382	7.090497	35.208234
17	2.696647	7.717232	27.491002
18	2.014514	8.399365	19.091637
19	1.272086	9.141793	9.949844
20	0.464035	9.949844	0.000000

25 YEARS — Monthly Payment: 0.805227 — Annual Constant: 9.67

Year	Interest	Principal	Year End Balance
1	8.453615	1.209110	98.790890
2	8.346741	1.315984	97.474907
3	8.230420	1.432305	96.042602
4	8.103817	1.558908	94.483694
5	7.966024	1.696701	92.786993
6	7.816051	1.846674	90.940319
7	7.652822	2.009903	88.930416
8	7.475165	2.187560	86.742856
9	7.281804	2.380921	84.361936
10	7.071353	2.591372	81.770563
11	6.842299	2.820426	78.950137
12	6.592999	3.069726	75.880411
13	6.321663	3.341062	72.539349
14	6.026344	3.636381	68.902968
15	5.704921	3.957804	64.945163
16	5.355087	4.307638	60.637525
17	4.974331	4.688394	55.949131
18	4.559919	5.102806	50.846325
19	4.108878	5.553847	45.292477
20	3.617968	6.044757	39.247720
21	3.083666	6.579059	32.668662
22	2.502137	7.160588	25.508074
23	1.869207	7.793518	17.714556
24	1.180330	8.482395	9.232161
25	0.430564	9.232161	0.000000

(Continued)

Mortgage Amortization Tables
8.5%

30 YEARS	Monthly Payment: 0.768913		Annual Constant: 9.23

| Year | Annual | | Year End |
	Interest	Principal	Balance
1	8.470999	0.755962	99.244038
2	8.404179	0.822783	98.421255
3	8.331453	0.895509	97.525746
4	8.252298	0.974664	96.551081
5	8.166146	1.060816	95.490266
6	8.072380	1.154582	94.335684
7	7.970325	1.256637	93.079047
8	7.859250	1.367712	91.711336
9	7.738357	1.488605	90.222731
10	7.606778	1.620184	88.602546
11	7.463568	1.763394	86.839153
12	7.307700	1.919262	84.919891
13	7.138055	2.088907	82.830984
14	6.953414	2.273547	80.557437
15	6.752454	2.474508	78.082928
16	6.533729	2.693232	75.389696
17	6.295672	2.931290	72.458406
18	6.036573	3.190389	69.268018
19	5.754572	3.472390	65.795627
20	5.447644	3.779318	62.016309
21	5.113586	4.113375	57.902934
22	4.750002	4.476960	53.425974
23	4.354279	4.872683	48.553291
24	3.923578	5.303384	43.249907
25	3.454807	5.772155	37.477753
26	2.944601	6.282361	31.195392
27	2.389298	6.837664	24.357728
28	1.784910	7.442051	16.915676
29	1.127101	8.099861	8.815815
30	0.411147	8.815815	0.000000

40 YEARS	Monthly Payment: 0.733094		Annual Constant: 8.80

| Year | Annual | | Year End |
	Interest	Principal	Balance
1	8.488147	0.308982	99.691018
2	8.460835	0.336293	99.354724
3	8.431110	0.366019	98.988706
4	8.398757	0.398371	98.590334
5	8.363545	0.433584	98.156751
6	8.325220	0.471909	97.684842
7	8.283508	0.513621	97.171221
8	8.238108	0.559021	96.612200
9	8.188696	0.608433	96.003767
10	8.134916	0.662213	95.341555
11	8.076382	0.720746	94.620808
12	8.012675	0.784454	93.836354
13	7.943336	0.853792	92.982562
14	7.867869	0.929260	92.053302
15	7.785731	1.011398	91.041904
16	7.696332	1.100796	89.941108
17	7.599032	1.198097	88.743011
18	7.493131	1.303998	87.439013
19	7.377870	1.419259	86.019754
20	7.252420	1.544709	84.475045
21	7.115882	1.681247	82.793798
22	6.967275	1.829854	80.963944
23	6.805532	1.991596	78.972348
24	6.629493	2.167635	76.804712
25	6.437894	2.359235	74.445478
26	6.229359	2.567770	71.877708
27	6.002392	2.794737	69.082971
28	5.755362	3.041766	66.041205
29	5.486498	3.310631	62.730574
30	5.193868	3.603261	59.127313
31	4.875373	3.921756	55.205557
32	4.528725	4.268404	50.937154
33	4.151437	4.645692	46.291462
34	3.740800	5.056328	41.235134
35	3.293867	5.503262	35.731872
36	2.807429	5.989700	29.742172
37	2.277994	6.519135	23.223036
38	1.701761	7.095368	16.127669
39	1.074595	7.722534	8.405135
40	0.391994	8.405135	0.000000

MORTGAGE AMORTIZATION TABLES
9%

5 YEARS
Monthly Payment: 2.075836
Annual Constant: 24.92

| Year | Annual | | Year End Balance |
	Interest	Principal	
1	8.327024	16.583002	83.416998
2	6.771424	18.138602	65.278395
3	5.069898	19.840128	45.438267
4	3.208757	21.701269	23.736998
5	1.173028	23.736998	0.000000

10 YEARS
Monthly Payment: 1.266758
Annual Constant: 15.21

| Year | Annual | | Year End Balance |
	Interest	Principal	
1	8.737701	6.463392	93.536608
2	8.131390	7.069703	86.466905
3	7.468203	7.732890	78.734016
4	6.742805	8.458288	70.275727
5	5.949359	9.251734	61.023994
6	5.081483	10.119610	50.904383
7	4.132193	11.068900	39.835484
8	3.093854	12.107239	27.728245
9	1.958112	13.242981	14.485264
10	0.715829	14.485264	0.000000

15 YEARS
Monthly Payment: 1.014267
Annual Constant: 12.18

| Year | Annual | | Year End Balance |
	Interest	Principal	
1	8.865862	3.305337	96.694663
2	8.555798	3.615401	93.079262
3	8.216649	3.954550	89.124712
4	7.845685	4.325514	84.799198
5	7.439922	4.731277	80.067921
6	6.996095	5.175104	74.892817
7	6.510635	5.660564	69.232253
8	5.979635	6.191564	63.040689
9	5.398824	6.772375	56.268314
10	4.763528	7.407671	48.860643
11	4.068637	8.102562	40.758081
12	3.308561	8.862638	31.895444
13	2.477185	9.694014	22.201429
14	1.567819	10.603380	11.598050
15	0.573149	11.598050	0.000000

20 YEARS
Monthly Payment: 0.899726
Annual Constant: 10.80

| Year | Annual | | Year End Balance |
	Interest	Principal	
1	8.924001	1.872710	98.127290
2	8.748328	2.048383	96.078906
3	8.556176	2.240536	93.838370
4	8.345998	2.450714	91.387657
5	8.116104	2.680608	88.707049
6	7.864644	2.932067	85.774982
7	7.589596	3.207115	82.567867
8	7.288747	3.507965	79.059902
9	6.959676	3.837036	75.222866
10	6.599735	4.196976	71.025890
11	6.206030	4.590682	66.435208
12	5.775392	5.021319	61.413889
13	5.304358	5.492354	55.921535
14	4.789137	6.007574	49.913961
15	4.225585	6.571126	43.342835
16	3.609168	7.187543	36.155291
17	2.934927	7.861784	28.293507
18	2.197437	8.599274	19.694233
19	1.390766	9.405945	10.288288
20	0.508424	10.288288	0.000000

25 YEARS
Monthly Payment: 0.839196
Annual Constant: 10.08

| Year | Annual | | Year End Balance |
	Interest	Principal	
1	8.954725	1.115631	98.884369
2	8.850071	1.220285	97.664084
3	8.735600	1.334756	96.329327
4	8.610391	1.459966	94.869362
5	8.473436	1.596920	93.272441
6	8.323634	1.746723	91.525719
7	8.159779	1.910577	89.615141
8	7.980554	2.089803	87.525339
9	7.784516	2.285840	85.239498
10	7.570088	2.500268	82.739230
11	7.335546	2.734810	80.004420
12	7.079002	2.991355	77.013065
13	6.798392	3.271964	73.741101
14	6.491459	3.578897	70.162204
15	6.155734	3.914622	66.247581
16	5.788515	4.281841	61.965741
17	5.386849	4.683507	57.282233
18	4.947504	5.122852	52.159381
19	4.466945	5.603411	46.555970
20	3.941306	6.129050	40.426920
21	3.366359	6.703997	33.722923
22	2.737478	7.332878	26.390045
23	2.049604	8.020753	18.369292
24	1.297202	8.773155	9.596137
25	0.474219	9.596137	0.000000

(Continued)

Mortgage Amortization Tables
9%

30 YEARS	Monthly Payment: 0.804623 Annual Constant: 9.66		

| Year | Annual | | Year End Balance |
	Interest	Principal	
1	8.972274	0.683197	99.316803
2	8.908186	0.747286	98.569517
3	8.838085	0.817386	97.752131
4	8.761409	0.894063	96.858068
5	8.677539	0.977932	95.880136
6	8.585803	1.069669	94.810468
7	8.485460	1.170011	93.640456
8	8.375705	1.279766	92.360690
9	8.255654	1.399817	90.960873
10	8.124342	1.531130	89.429744
11	7.980711	1.674760	87.754984
12	7.823607	1.831864	85.923120
13	7.651766	2.003706	83.919414
14	7.463804	2.191667	81.727747
15	7.258211	2.397260	79.330487
16	7.033331	2.622140	76.708347
17	6.787357	2.868115	73.840232
18	6.518308	3.137164	70.703068
19	6.224020	3.431451	67.271617
20	5.902126	3.753345	63.518271
21	5.550037	4.105435	59.412836
22	5.164918	4.490553	54.922283
23	4.743674	4.911798	50.010486
24	4.282913	5.372558	44.637927
25	3.778930	5.876541	38.761386
26	3.227670	6.427802	32.333584
27	2.624698	7.030774	25.302811
28	1.965163	7.690309	17.612502
29	1.243759	8.411713	9.200789
30	0.454682	9.200789	0.000000

40 YEARS	Monthly Payment: 0.771361 Annual Constant: 9.26		

| Year | Annual | | Year End Balance |
	Interest	Principal	
1	8.989157	0.267181	99.732819
2	8.964094	0.292244	99.440575
3	8.936679	0.319659	99.120916
4	8.906693	0.349645	98.771272
5	8.873894	0.382444	98.388828
6	8.838018	0.418320	97.970508
7	8.798777	0.457561	97.512947
8	8.755854	0.500483	97.012463
9	8.708906	0.547432	96.465031
10	8.657553	0.598785	95.866246
11	8.601383	0.654955	95.211290
12	8.539943	0.716395	94.494896
13	8.472740	0.783598	93.711298
14	8.399234	0.857104	92.854194
15	8.318831	0.937507	91.916687
16	8.230887	1.025451	90.891236
17	8.134692	1.121646	89.769590
18	8.029474	1.226864	88.542726
19	7.914386	1.341952	87.200774
20	7.788502	1.467836	85.732938
21	7.650808	1.605530	84.127408
22	7.500199	1.756139	82.371269
23	7.335461	1.920877	80.450392
24	7.155269	2.101069	78.349323
25	6.958174	2.298164	76.051159
26	6.742591	2.513747	73.537412
27	6.506784	2.749554	70.787858
28	6.248857	3.007481	67.780377
29	5.966734	3.289604	64.490773
30	5.658147	3.598191	60.892582
31	5.320612	3.935726	56.956856
32	4.951413	4.304925	52.651931
33	4.547582	4.708756	47.943175
34	4.105868	5.150470	42.792705
35	3.622718	5.633620	37.159085
36	3.094246	6.162092	30.996993
37	2.516199	6.740139	24.256855
38	1.883928	7.372410	16.884444
39	1.192345	8.063993	8.820451
40	0.435887	8.820451	0.000000

MORTGAGE AMORTIZATION TABLES
9.5%

5 YEARS — *Monthly Payment: 2.110186* *Annual Constant: 25.21*

Year	Annual Interest	Annual Principal	Year End Balance
1	8.797931	16.404303	83.595697
2	7.169844	18.032390	65.563307
3	5.380172	19.822061	45.741246
4	3.412881	21.789353	23.951893
5	1.250340	23.951893	0.000000

10 YEARS — *Monthly Payment: 1.293976* *Annual Constant: 15.53*

Year	Annual Interest	Annual Principal	Year End Balance
1	9.230493	6.297214	93.702786
2	8.605509	6.922197	86.780588
3	7.918498	7.609209	79.171379
4	7.163302	8.364404	70.806975
5	6.333156	9.194551	61.612424
6	5.420619	10.107088	51.505335
7	4.417514	11.110193	40.395143
8	3.314855	12.212852	28.182290
9	2.102759	13.424948	14.757342
10	0.770365	14.757342	0.000000

15 YEARS — *Monthly Payment: 1.044225* *Annual Constant: 12.54*

Year	Annual Interest	Annual Principal	Year End Balance
1	9.364493	3.166203	96.833797
2	9.050255	3.480441	93.353356
3	8.704830	3.825866	89.527490
4	8.325122	4.205574	85.321916
5	7.907729	4.622967	80.698948
6	7.448911	5.081786	75.617163
7	6.944556	5.586141	70.031022
8	6.390145	6.140552	63.890471
9	5.780710	6.749986	57.140484
10	5.110790	7.419906	49.720578
11	4.374382	8.156314	41.564264
12	3.564888	8.965809	32.598455
13	2.675053	9.855643	22.742812
14	1.696904	10.833792	11.909020
15	0.621676	11.909020	0.000000

20 YEARS — *Monthly Payment: 0.932131* *Annual Constant: 11.19*

Year	Annual Interest	Annual Principal	Year End Balance
1	9.424636	1.760939	98.239061
2	9.249867	1.935708	96.303354
3	9.057752	2.127822	94.175532
4	8.846571	2.339003	91.836529
5	8.614431	2.571143	89.265385
6	8.359251	2.826323	86.439062
7	8.078745	3.106829	83.332233
8	7.770400	3.415174	79.917059
9	7.431452	3.754122	76.162937
10	7.058865	4.126710	72.036227
11	6.649299	4.536276	67.499952
12	6.199084	4.986490	62.513462
13	5.704187	5.481387	57.032075
14	5.160173	6.025401	51.006674
15	4.562166	6.623408	44.383266
16	3.904809	7.280765	37.102500
17	3.182211	8.003364	29.099137
18	2.387896	8.797678	20.301459
19	1.514748	9.670826	10.630632
20	0.554942	10.630632	0.000000

25 YEARS — *Monthly Payment: 0.873697* *Annual Constant: 10.49*

Year	Annual Interest	Annual Principal	Year End Balance
1	9.455988	1.028372	98.971628
2	9.353924	1.130435	97.841192
3	9.241731	1.242628	96.598564
4	9.118404	1.365956	95.232608
5	8.982836	1.501524	93.731083
6	8.833813	1.650547	92.080536
7	8.670000	1.814360	90.266177
8	8.489929	1.994430	88.271746
9	8.291987	2.192373	86.079373
10	8.074399	2.409961	83.669413
11	7.835217	2.649143	81.020269
12	7.572295	2.912064	78.108205
13	7.283280	3.201080	74.907125
14	6.965581	3.518779	71.388346
15	6.616350	3.868010	67.520336
16	6.232460	4.251900	63.268436
17	5.810469	4.673891	58.594545
18	5.346597	5.137763	53.456782
19	4.836686	5.647674	47.809108
20	4.276168	6.208192	41.600916
21	3.660020	6.824340	34.776576
22	2.982721	7.501639	27.274936
23	2.238201	8.246159	19.028777
24	1.419790	9.064570	9.964207
25	0.520153	9.964207	0.000000

(Continued)

Mortgage Amortization Tables
9.5%

| **30** YEARS | Monthly Payment: 0.840854
 Annual Constant: 10.10 |

Year	Annual		Year End Balance
	Interest	Principal	
1	9.473609	0.616641	99.383359
2	9.412409	0.677842	98.705517
3	9.345135	0.745116	97.960401
4	9.271184	0.819067	97.141335
5	9.189893	0.900357	96.240978
6	9.100535	0.989715	95.251262
7	9.002308	1.087942	94.163320
8	8.894333	1.195918	92.967402
9	8.775641	1.314610	91.652793
10	8.645169	1.445082	90.207711
11	8.501748	1.588502	88.619208
12	8.344093	1.746157	86.873051
13	8.170791	1.919459	84.953592
14	7.980289	2.109961	82.843630
15	7.770881	2.319370	80.524261
16	7.540689	2.549561	77.974699
17	7.287651	2.802599	75.172100
18	7.009500	3.080751	72.091350
19	6.703743	3.386508	68.704842
20	6.367640	3.722610	64.982232
21	5.998180	4.092070	60.890161
22	5.592052	4.498198	56.391963
23	5.145617	4.944634	51.447329
24	4.654874	5.435377	46.011953
25	4.115426	5.974825	40.037128
26	3.522439	6.567812	33.469316
27	2.870599	7.219651	26.249665
28	2.154067	7.936184	18.313481
29	1.366419	8.723831	9.589650
30	0.500600	9.589650	0.000000

| **40** YEARS | Monthly Payment: 0.810062
 Annual Constant: 9.73 |

Year	Annual		Year End Balance
	Interest	Principal	
1	9.490130	0.230608	99.769392
2	9.467243	0.253496	99.515896
3	9.442084	0.278654	99.237242
4	9.414429	0.306310	98.930932
5	9.384028	0.336711	98.594221
6	9.350610	0.370128	98.224093
7	9.313876	0.406863	97.817230
8	9.273496	0.447243	97.369987
9	9.229108	0.491631	96.878356
10	9.180315	0.540424	96.337932
11	9.126679	0.594060	95.743873
12	9.067720	0.653019	95.090854
13	9.002910	0.717829	94.373025
14	8.931667	0.789072	93.583953
15	8.853353	0.867385	92.716568
16	8.767267	0.953471	91.763097
17	8.672638	1.048101	90.714996
18	8.568616	1.152122	89.562873
19	8.454271	1.266468	88.296405
20	8.328577	1.392162	86.904244
21	8.190408	1.530330	85.373913
22	8.038527	1.682212	83.691701
23	7.871571	1.849167	81.842534
24	7.688046	2.032693	79.809841
25	7.486306	2.234433	77.575408
26	7.264544	2.456195	75.119213
27	7.020772	2.699966	72.419247
28	6.752807	2.967931	69.451316
29	6.458247	3.262491	66.188824
30	6.134453	3.586286	62.602539
31	5.778523	3.942216	58.660323
32	5.387267	4.333471	54.326851
33	4.957181	4.763558	49.563293
34	4.484409	5.236330	44.326964
35	3.964716	5.756023	38.570941
36	3.393445	6.327294	32.243647
37	2.765476	6.955263	25.288385
38	2.075183	7.645556	17.642829
39	1.316380	8.404358	9.238471
40	0.482268	9.238471	0.000000

MORTGAGE AMORTIZATION TABLES
10%

5 YEARS Monthly Payment: 2.124704 Annual Constant: 25.50

Year	Annual Interest	Annual Principal	Year End Balance
1	9.269642	16.226812	83.773188
2	7.570482	17.925971	65.847217
3	5.693399	19.803055	46.044162
4	3.619760	21.876693	24.167469
5	1.328985	24.167469	0.000000

10 YEARS Monthly Payment: 1.321507 Annual Constant: 15.86

Year	Annual Interest	Annual Principal	Year End Balance
1	9.723904	6.134184	93.865816
2	9.081575	6.776513	87.089303
3	8.371986	7.486103	79.603200
4	7.588093	8.269996	71.333204
5	6.722116	9.135972	62.197232
6	5.765461	10.092628	52.104604
7	4.708631	11.149458	40.955146
8	3.541137	12.316952	28.638194
9	2.251391	13.606698	15.031497
10	0.826592	15.031497	0.000000

15 YEARS Monthly Payment: 1.074605 Annual Constant: 12.90

Year	Annual Interest	Annual Principal	Year End Balance
1	9.863544	3.031717	96.968283
2	9.546084	3.349177	93.619106
3	9.195381	3.699880	89.919225
4	8.807956	4.087306	85.831920
5	8.379961	4.515300	81.316619
6	7.907150	4.988111	76.328508
7	7.384830	5.510432	70.818077
8	6.807816	6.087446	64.730631
9	6.170381	6.724881	58.005750
10	5.466198	7.429064	50.576686
11	4.688278	8.206984	42.369703
12	3.828899	9.066362	33.303340
13	2.879533	10.015729	23.287612
14	1.830755	11.064507	12.223105
15	0.672156	12.223105	0.000000

20 YEARS Monthly Payment: 0.965022 Annual Constant: 11.59

Year	Annual Interest	Annual Principal	Year End Balance
1	9.925521	1.654738	98.345262
2	9.752249	1.828011	96.517250
3	9.560832	2.019428	94.497823
4	9.349371	2.230888	92.266934
5	9.115768	2.464491	89.802443
6	8.857704	2.722556	87.079887
7	8.572617	3.007643	84.072244
8	8.257677	3.322583	80.749661
9	7.909759	3.670501	77.079160
10	7.525410	4.054850	73.024311
11	7.100814	4.479446	68.544865
12	6.631758	4.948502	63.596363
13	6.113585	5.466675	58.129688
14	5.541152	6.039107	52.090581
15	4.908779	6.671481	45.419100
16	4.210188	7.370072	38.049028
17	3.438445	8.141815	29.907213
18	2.585891	8.994369	20.912844
19	1.644063	9.936197	10.976647
20	0.603613	10.976647	0.000000

25 YEARS Monthly Payment: 0.908701 Annual Constant: 10.91

Year	Annual Interest	Annual Principal	Year End Balance
1	9.957375	0.947034	99.052966
2	9.858208	1.046201	98.006764
3	9.748657	1.155752	96.851012
4	9.627634	1.276775	95.574238
5	9.493939	1.410469	94.163768
6	9.346245	1.558164	92.605604
7	9.183085	1.721324	90.884280
8	9.002840	1.901569	88.982711
9	8.803720	2.100689	86.882022
10	8.583751	2.320658	84.561364
11	8.340748	2.563661	81.997703
12	8.072299	2.832110	79.165593
13	7.775740	3.128669	76.036924
14	7.448127	3.456282	72.580642
15	7.086210	3.818199	68.762443
16	6.686394	4.218015	64.544428
17	6.244713	4.659696	59.884732
18	5.756782	5.147627	54.737105
19	5.217758	5.686651	49.050454
20	4.622291	6.282118	42.768336
21	3.964471	6.939937	35.828398
22	3.237769	7.666640	28.161759
23	2.434972	8.469437	19.692322
24	1.548111	9.356298	10.336024
25	0.568385	10.336024	0.000000

(Continued)

Mortgage Amortization Tables
10%

30 YEARS	Monthly Payment: 0.877572	Annual Constant: 10.54

Year	Interest	Principal	Year End Balance
1	9.974980	0.555879	99.444121
2	9.916773	0.614086	98.830035
3	9.852470	0.678389	98.151646
4	9.781433	0.749425	97.402221
5	9.702959	0.827900	96.574320
6	9.616267	0.914592	95.659728
7	9.520497	1.010362	94.649367
8	9.414699	1.116160	93.533207
9	9.297823	1.233036	92.300171
10	9.168708	1.362151	90.938019
11	9.026072	1.504786	89.433233
12	8.868502	1.662357	87.770876
13	8.694431	1.836428	85.934448
14	8.502133	2.028726	83.905722
15	8.289699	2.241160	81.664563
16	8.055020	2.475838	79.188724
17	7.795768	2.735091	76.453633
18	7.509368	3.021491	73.432142
19	7.192978	3.337880	70.094262
20	6.843459	3.687400	66.406862
21	6.457340	4.073519	62.333343
22	6.030789	4.500070	57.833273
23	5.559573	4.971286	52.861987
24	5.039014	5.491845	47.370142
25	4.463946	6.066912	41.303230
26	3.828661	6.702197	34.601032
27	3.126854	7.404005	27.197027
28	2.351558	8.179301	19.017726
29	1.495078	9.035781	9.981945
30	0.548914	9.981945	0.000000

40 YEARS	Monthly Payment: 0.849146	Annual Constant: 10.19

Year	Interest	Principal	Year End Balance
1	9.991057	0.198694	99.801306
2	9.970251	0.219500	99.581806
3	9.947267	0.242484	99.339322
4	9.921875	0.267876	99.071446
5	9.893825	0.295926	98.775520
6	9.862838	0.326913	98.448607
7	9.828606	0.361145	98.087462
8	9.790789	0.398962	97.688500
9	9.749013	0.440738	97.247762
10	9.702862	0.486889	96.760873
11	9.651878	0.537873	96.223000
12	9.595556	0.594195	95.628805
13	9.533336	0.656415	94.972389
14	9.464600	0.725151	94.247239
15	9.388668	0.801083	93.446155
16	9.304784	0.884967	92.561188
17	9.212116	0.977635	91.583553
18	9.109745	1.080006	90.503547
19	8.996654	1.193097	89.310451
20	8.871721	1.318030	87.992421
21	8.733707	1.456044	86.536377
22	8.581240	1.608511	84.927866
23	8.412807	1.776943	83.150922
24	8.226738	1.963013	81.187909
25	8.021185	2.168566	79.019344
26	7.794108	2.395643	76.623701
27	7.543253	2.646498	73.977203
28	7.266130	2.923621	71.053582
29	6.959989	3.229762	67.823820
30	6.621790	3.567961	64.255859
31	6.248178	3.941573	60.314286
32	5.835444	4.354307	55.959979
33	5.379491	4.810260	51.149720
34	4.875794	5.313957	45.835763
35	4.319354	5.870397	39.965366
36	3.704646	6.485105	33.480261
37	3.025571	7.164180	26.316081
38	2.275388	7.914363	18.401718
39	1.446650	8.743100	9.658617
40	0.531134	9.658617	0.000000

MORTGAGE AMORTIZATION TABLES
10.5%

5 YEARS   *Monthly Payment: 2.149390*
Annual Constant: 25.80

Year	Annual Interest	Annual Principal	Year End Balance
1	9.742146	16.050535	83.949465
2	7.973321	17.819359	66.130106
3	6.009566	19.783114	46.346992
4	3.829399	21.963281	24.383711
5	1.408970	24.383711	0.000000

10 YEARS   *Monthly Payment: 1.349350*
Annual Constant: 16.20

Year	Annual Interest	Annual Principal	Year End Balance
1	10.217914	5.974286	94.025714
2	9.559527	6.632673	87.393041
3	8.828583	7.363616	80.029424
4	8.017087	8.175112	71.854312
5	7.116162	9.076038	62.778274
6	6.115951	10.076249	52.702025
7	5.005514	11.186686	41.515339
8	3.772702	12.419497	29.095842
9	2.404031	13.788169	15.307673
10	0.884527	15.307673	0.000000

15 YEARS   *Monthly Payment: 1.105399*
Annual Constant: 13.27

Year	Annual Interest	Annual Principal	Year End Balance
1	10.362986	2.901801	97.098199
2	10.043198	3.221589	93.876610
3	9.688168	3.576619	90.299991
4	9.294012	3.970775	86.329215
5	8.856419	4.408368	81.920847
6	8.370601	4.894186	77.026661
7	7.831245	5.433542	71.593119
8	7.232450	6.032337	65.560782
9	6.567666	6.697121	58.863661
10	5.829620	7.435167	51.428494
11	5.010239	8.254548	43.173946
12	4.100559	9.164228	34.009718
13	3.090630	10.174158	23.835560
14	1.969402	11.295385	12.540175
15	0.724612	12.540175	0.000000

20 YEARS   *Monthly Payment: 0.998380*
Annual Constant: 11.99

Year	Annual Interest	Annual Principal	Year End Balance
1	10.426628	1.553930	98.446070
2	10.255380	1.725179	96.720891
3	10.065259	1.915299	94.805592
4	9.854187	2.126372	92.679220
5	9.619853	2.360705	90.318514
6	9.359695	2.620863	87.697651
7	9.070867	2.909691	84.787960
8	8.750209	3.230350	81.557610
9	8.394213	3.586345	77.971265
10	7.998986	3.981573	73.989692
11	7.560203	4.420356	69.569336
12	7.073064	4.907494	64.661842
13	6.532241	5.448317	59.213525
14	5.931818	6.048741	53.164784
15	5.265226	6.715333	46.449452
16	4.525173	7.455385	38.994066
17	3.703564	8.276995	30.717072
18	2.791411	9.189148	21.527924
19	1.778735	10.201824	11.326100
20	0.654459	11.326100	0.000000

25 YEARS   *Monthly Payment: 0.944182*
Annual Constant: 11.34

Year	Annual Interest	Annual Principal	Year End Balance
1	10.458859	0.871321	99.128679
2	10.362836	0.967344	98.161334
3	10.256232	1.073949	97.087386
4	10.137879	1.192302	95.895084
5	10.006483	1.323697	94.571387
6	9.860607	1.469573	93.101814
7	9.698655	1.631525	91.470288
8	9.518855	1.811325	89.658963
9	9.319241	2.010939	87.648024
10	9.097629	2.232552	85.415472
11	8.851594	2.478587	82.936885
12	8.578445	2.751736	80.185149
13	8.275194	3.054986	77.130163
14	7.938524	3.391656	73.738507
15	7.564752	3.765429	69.973078
16	7.149789	4.180392	65.792686
17	6.689095	4.641085	61.151601
18	6.177631	5.152549	55.999052
19	5.609803	5.720378	50.278674
20	4.979397	6.350783	43.927891
21	4.279519	7.050661	36.877229
22	3.502512	7.827669	29.049561
23	2.639876	8.690305	20.359256
24	1.682174	9.648006	10.711250
25	0.618931	10.711250	0.000000

(Continued)

Mortgage Amortization Tables
10.5%

30 YEARS	Monthly Payment: 0.914739 Annual Constant: 10.98		

Year	Annual		Year End Balance
	Interest	Principal	
1	10.476368	0.500504	99.499496
2	10.421211	0.555661	98.943835
3	10.359975	0.616897	98.326939
4	10.291991	0.684881	97.642058
5	10.216514	0.760357	96.881701
6	10.132721	0.844151	96.037550
7	10.039692	0.937179	95.100370
8	9.936412	1.040460	94.059911
9	9.821749	1.155122	92.904789
10	9.694451	1.282420	91.622368
11	9.553124	1.423748	90.198620
12	9.396222	1.580650	88.617971
13	9.222029	1.754843	86.863128
14	9.028639	1.948232	84.914896
15	8.813937	2.162934	82.751962
16	8.575575	2.401297	80.350665
17	8.310943	2.665928	77.684736
18	8.017149	2.959723	74.725014
19	7.690977	3.285894	71.439119
20	7.328860	3.648011	67.791108
21	6.926837	4.050035	63.741073
22	6.480509	4.496363	59.244711
23	5.984994	4.991877	54.252834
24	5.434872	5.541999	48.710834
25	4.824125	6.152747	42.558088
26	4.146071	6.830801	35.727287
27	3.393293	7.583578	28.143708
28	2.557557	8.419315	19.724394
29	1.629719	9.347153	10.377241
30	0.599631	10.377241	0.000000

40 YEARS	Monthly Payment: 0.888570 Annual Constant: 10.67		

Year	Annual		Year End Balance
	Interest	Principal	
1	10.491930	0.170913	99.829087
2	10.473095	0.189749	99.639338
3	10.452184	0.210660	99.428678
4	10.428968	0.233875	99.194804
5	10.403195	0.259649	98.935155
6	10.374580	0.288263	98.646892
7	10.342813	0.320031	98.326861
8	10.307544	0.355299	97.971562
9	10.268389	0.394454	97.577108
10	10.224919	0.437924	97.139184
11	10.176658	0.486185	96.652998
12	10.123079	0.539764	96.113234
13	10.063595	0.599248	95.513985
14	9.997556	0.665288	94.848698
15	9.924239	0.738605	94.110093
16	9.842842	0.820001	93.290092
17	9.752475	0.910368	92.379723
18	9.652149	1.010694	91.369029
19	9.540767	1.122076	90.246953
20	9.417111	1.245733	89.001220
21	9.279827	1.383017	87.618203
22	9.127413	1.535430	86.082773
23	8.958204	1.704640	84.378134
24	8.770346	1.892497	82.485637
25	8.561787	2.101057	80.384580
26	8.330243	2.332600	78.051980
27	8.073182	2.589661	75.462319
28	7.787793	2.875051	72.587268
29	7.470952	3.191891	69.395377
30	7.119195	3.543648	65.851729
31	6.728673	3.934171	61.917558
32	6.295114	4.367730	57.549828
33	5.813775	4.849069	52.700760
34	5.279391	5.383453	47.317307
35	4.686115	5.976728	41.340579
36	4.027459	6.635384	34.705195
37	3.296217	7.366626	27.338569
38	2.484390	8.178454	19.160115
39	1.583096	9.079748	10.080367
40	0.582476	10.080367	0.000000

MORTGAGE AMORTIZATION TABLES
11%

5 YEARS
Monthly Payment: 2.174242
Annual Constant: 26.10

Year	Annual Interest	Annual Principal	Year End Balance
1	10.215432	15.875475	84.124525
2	8.378341	17.712567	66.411958
3	6.328663	19.762244	46.649714
4	4.041799	22.049108	24.600605
5	1.490302	24.600605	0.000000

10 YEARS
Monthly Payment: 1.377500
Annual Constant: 16.54

Year	Annual Interest	Annual Principal	Year End Balance
1	10.712498	5.817503	94.182497
2	10.039304	6.490698	87.691799
3	9.288208	7.241794	80.450006
4	8.450196	8.079805	72.370200
5	7.515210	9.014791	63.355409
6	6.472029	10.057972	53.297437
7	5.308132	11.221869	42.075568
8	4.009551	12.520451	29.555117
9	2.560699	13.969303	15.585814
10	0.944187	15.585814	0.000000

15 YEARS
Monthly Payment: 1.136597
Annual Constant: 13.64

Year	Annual Interest	Annual Principal	Year End Balance
1	10.862791	2.776372	97.223628
2	10.541513	3.097650	94.125978
3	10.183056	3.456107	90.669871
4	9.783120	3.856043	86.813828
5	9.336903	4.302260	82.511567
6	8.839050	4.800113	77.711455
7	8.283587	5.355576	72.355878
8	7.663846	5.975317	66.380561
9	6.972389	6.666774	59.713787
10	6.200918	7.438245	52.275541
11	5.340173	8.298991	43.976551
12	4.379823	9.259340	34.717211
13	3.308343	10.330820	24.386390
14	2.112873	11.526291	12.860100
15	0.779064	12.860100	0.000000

20 YEARS
Monthly Payment: 1.032188
Annual Constant: 12.39

Year	Annual Interest	Annual Principal	Year End Balance
1	10.927929	1.458332	98.541668
2	10.759173	1.627088	96.914580
3	10.570888	1.815373	95.099208
4	10.360815	2.025446	93.073762
5	10.126433	2.259828	90.813934
6	9.864928	2.521332	88.292602
7	9.573163	· 2.813098	85.479504
8	9.247634	3.138627	82.340877
9	8.884436	3.501825	78.839052
10	8.479209	3.907052	74.932001
11	8.027089	4.359171	70.572829
12	7.522651	4.863610	65.709220
13	6.959840	5.426421	60.282799
14	6.331901	6.054360	54.228439
15	5.631297	6.754963	47.473476
16	4.849621	7.536640	39.936836
17	3.977490	8.408771	31.528065
18	3.004436	9.381824	22.146240
19	1.918783	10.467478	11.678762
20	0.707498	11.678762	0.000000

25 YEARS
Monthly Payment: 0.980113
Annual Constant: 11.77

Year	Annual Interest	Annual Principal	Year End Balance
1	10.960417	0.800939	99.199061
2	10.867734	0.893623	98.305437
3	10.764325	0.997032	97.308405
4	10.648949	1.112408	96.195997
5	10.520223	1.241134	94.954863
6	10.376600	1.384757	93.570107
7	10.216358	1.544999	92.025107
8	10.037572	1.723785	90.301323
9	9.838098	1.923259	88.378063
10	9.615541	2.145816	86.232247
11	9.367229	2.394128	83.838119
12	9.090183	2.671173	81.166946
13	8.781078	2.980279	78.186667
14	8.436204	3.325153	74.861514
15	8.051421	3.709936	71.151579
16	7.622112	4.139245	67.012334
17	7.143123	4.618234	62.394100
18	6.608706	5.152650	57.241449
19	6.012448	5.748909	51.492540
20	5.347191	6.414166	45.078374
21	4.604951	7.156406	37.921968
22	3.776820	7.984537	29.937431
23	2.852859	8.908498	21.028932
24	1.821977	9.939379	11.089553
25	0.671804	11.089553	0.000000

(Continued)

Mortgage Amortization Tables
11%

30 YEARS	Monthly Payment: 0.952323
	Annual Constant: 11.43

Year	Annual Interest	Annual Principal	Year End Balance
1	10.977755	0.450126	99.549874
2	10.925667	0.502214	99.047660
3	10.867551	0.560330	98.487330
4	10.802710	0.625170	97.862160
5	10.730366	0.697514	97.164645
6	10.649651	0.778230	96.386415
7	10.559595	0.868286	95.518130
8	10.459118	0.968763	94.549367
9	10.347014	1.080867	93.468500
10	10.221937	1.205944	92.262556
11	10.082387	1.345494	90.917062
12	9.926688	1.501193	89.415869
13	9.752971	1.674909	87.740960
14	9.559153	1.868728	85.872232
15	9.342906	2.084975	83.787257
16	9.101635	2.326246	81.461011
17	8.832445	2.595436	78.865575
18	8.532104	2.895777	75.969798
19	8.197008	3.230873	72.738925
20	7.823135	3.604746	69.134179
21	7.405998	4.021883	65.112296
22	6.940590	4.487290	60.625006
23	6.421326	5.006555	55.618451
24	5.841974	5.585907	50.032544
25	5.195579	6.232302	84.800242
26	4.474384	6.953497	36.846746
27	3.669734	7.758147	29.088598
28	2.771970	8.655911	20.432688
29	1.770318	9.657563	10.775125
30	0.652756	10.775125	0.000000

40 YEARS	Monthly Payment: 0.928294
	Annual Constant: 11.14

Year	Annual Interest	Annual Principal	Year End Balance
1	10.992746	0.146787	99.853213
2	10.975760	0.163773	99.689440
3	10.956808	0.182725	99.506715
4	10.935663	0.203869	99.302846
5	10.912072	0.227461	99.075385
6	10.885750	0.253782	98.821602
7	10.856383	0.283150	98.538453
8	10.823617	0.315916	98.222537
9	10.787060	0.352473	97.870064
10	10.746272	0.393261	97.476803
11	10.700764	0.438768	97.038035
12	10.649991	0.489542	96.548492
13	10.593341	0.546191	96.002301
14	10.530137	0.609396	95.392905
15	10.459618	0.679915	94.712990
16	10.380939	0.758594	93.954396
17	10.293156	0.846377	93.108019
18	10.195214	0.944319	92.163700
19	10.085938	1.053595	91.110106
20	9.964018	1.175515	89.934590
21	9.827988	1.311545	88.623046
22	9.676218	1.463315	87.159731
23	9.506885	1.632648	85.527083
24	9.317957	1.821576	83.705507
25	9.107166	2.032367	81.673140
26	8.871983	2.267550	79.405590
27	8.609585	2.529948	76.875641
28	8.316822	2.822711	74.052930
29	7.990181	3.149352	70.903579
30	7.625742	3.513791	67.389788
31	7.219130	3.920403	63.469385
32	6.765465	4.374067	59.095318
33	6.259304	4.880229	54.215088
34	5.694569	5.444964	48.770124
35	5.064484	6.075049	42.695076
36	4.361487	6.778046	35.917030
37	3.577139	7.562394	28.354636
38	2.702028	8.437505	19.917131
39	1.725649	9.413883	10.503247
40	0.636286	10.503247	0.000000

MORTGAGE AMORTIZATION TABLES
11.5%

5 YEARS
Monthly Payment: 2.199261
Annual Constant: 26.40

Year	Annual Interest	Annual Principal	Year End Balance
1	10.689492	15.701637	84.298363
2	8.785522	17.605607	66.692756
3	6.650678	19.740451	46.952304
4	4.256964	22.134165	24.818139
5	1.572990	24.818139	0.000000

10 YEARS
Monthly Payment: 1.405954
Annual Constant: 16.88

Year	Annual Interest	Annual Principal	Year End Balance
1	11.207637	5.663816	94.336184
2	10.520847	6.350606	87.985578
3	9.750777	7.120677	80.864901
4	8.887328	7.984125	72.880776
5	7.919179	8.952275	63.928502
6	6.833632	10.037821	53.890680
7	5.616452	11.255001	42.635679
8	4.251679	12.619775	30.015905
9	2.721413	14.150040	15.865865
10	1.005589	15.865865	0.000000

15 YEARS
Monthly Payment: 1.168190
Annual Constant: 14.02

Year	Annual Interest	Annual Principal	Year End Balance
1	11.362933	2.655345	97.344655
2	11.040947	2.977330	94.367325
3	10.679918	3.338359	91.028966
4	10.275111	3.743167	87.285799
5	9.821217	4.197060	83.088739
6	9.312285	4.705993	78.382746
7	8.741639	5.276639	73.106107
8	8.101797	5.916480	67.189627
9	7.384369	6.633909	60.555718
10	6.579946	7.438332	53.117386
11	5.677979	8.340299	44.777087
12	4.666639	9.351638	35.425448
13	3.532666	10.485612	24.939837
14	2.261188	11.757090	13.182747
15	0.835531	13.182747	0.000000

20 YEARS
Monthly Payment: 1.066430
Annual Constant: 12.80

Year	Annual Interest	Annual Principal	Year End Balance
1	11.429397	1.367758	98.632242
2	11.263544	1.533612	97.098630
3	11.077579	1.719577	95.379053
4	10.869064	1.928091	93.450962
5	10.635265	2.161890	91.289072
6	10.373116	2.424040	88.865032
7	10.079178	2.717977	86.147055
8	9.749598	3.047557	83.099497
9	9.380054	3.417102	79.682396
10	8.965698	3.831457	75.850938
11	8.501098	4.296057	71.554881
12	7.980161	4.816994	66.737886
13	7.396056	5.401100	61.336786
14	6.741122	6.056034	55.280753
15	6.006771	6.790384	48.490368
16	5.183374	7.613782	40.876587
17	4.260132	8.537024	32.339563
18	3.224938	9.572218	22.767345
19	2.064217	10.732938	12.034407
20	0.762748	12.034407	0.000000

25 YEARS
Monthly Payment: 1.016469
Annual Constant: 12.20

Year	Annual Interest	Annual Principal	Year End Balance
1	11.462029	0.735599	99.264401
2	11.372831	0.824797	98.439604
3	11.272816	0.924811	97.514793
4	11.160674	1.036953	96.477840
5	11.034934	1.162693	95.315146
6	10.893947	1.303681	94.011466
7	10.735863	1.461764	92.549701
8	10.558611	1.639017	90.910684
9	10.359865	1.837763	89.072921
10	10.137019	2.060609	87.012312
11	9.887151	2.310477	84.701835
12	9.606984	2.590644	82.111191
13	9.292844	2.904784	79.206408
14	8.940612	3.257016	75.949392
15	8.545668	3.651959	72.297433
16	8.102834	4.094793	68.202639
17	7.606302	4.591325	63.611314
18	7.049561	5.148066	58.463248
19	6.425310	5.772317	52.690930
20	5.725363	6.472265	46.218666
21	4.940540	7.257087	38.961578
22	4.060551	8.137077	30.824502
23	3.073854	9.123773	21.700728
24	1.967512	10.230116	11.470613
25	0.727015	11.470613	0.000000

(Continued)

Mortgage Amortization Tables
11.5%

30 YEARS	Monthly Payment: 0.990291 Annual Constant: 11.89		

| Year | Annual | | Year End Balance |
	Interest	Principal	
1	11.479127	0.404371	99.595629
2	11.430093	0.453404	99.142225
3	11.375113	0.508384	98.633841
4	11.313467	0.570030	98.063811
5	11.244346	0.639151	97.424660
6	11.166843	0.716655	96.708005
7	11.079942	0.803556	95.904450
8	10.982503	0.900994	95.003456
9	10.873249	1.010248	93.993208
10	10.750747	1.132750	92.860457
11	10.613391	1.270107	91.590351
12	10.459378	1.424119	90.166232
13	10.286691	1.596807	88.569425
14	10.093063	1.790434	86.778991
15	9.875956	2.007541	84.771449
16	9.632523	2.250974	82.520475
17	9.359571	2.523926	79.996549
18	9.053522	2.829976	77.166573
19	8.710361	3.173137	73.993437
20	8.325588	3.557909	70.435528
21	7.894159	3.989339	66.446189
22	7.410414	4.473083	61.973106
23	6.868011	5.015486	56.957620
24	6.259837	5.623661	51.333960
25	5.557915	6.305582	45.028378
26	4.813305	7.070193	37.958185
27	3.955978	7.927519	30.030666
28	2.994692	8.888805	21.141861
29	1.916842	9.966656	11.175205
30	0.708292	11.175205	0.000000

40 YEARS	Monthly Payment: 0.968282 Annual Constant: 11.62		

| Year | Annual | | Year End Balance |
	Interest	Principal	
1	11.493502	0.125880	99.874120
2	11.478238	0.141144	99.732975
3	11.461123	0.158259	99.574716
4	11.441932	0.177450	99.397266
5	11.420415	0.198967	99.198299
6	11.396288	0.223094	98.975205
7	11.369236	0.250146	98.725058
8	11.338904	0.280479	98.444579
9	11.304893	0.314490	98.130090
10	11.266758	0.352624	97.777466
11	11.223999	0.395383	97.382082
12	11.176055	0.443327	96.938755
13	11.122298	0.497085	96.441670
14	11.062021	0.557361	95.884310
15	10.994436	0.624946	95.259363
16	10.918656	0.700727	94.558637
17	10.833686	0.785696	93.772941
18	10.738413	0.880969	92.891971
19	10.631587	0.987795	91.904176
20	10.511808	1.107574	90.796602
21	10.377504	1.241878	89.554724
22	10.226915	1.392467	88.162256
23	10.058065	1.561317	86.600939
24	9.868741	1.750641	84.850298
25	9.656459	1.962923	82.887375
26	9.418437	2.200946	80.686429
27	9.151552	2.467831	78.218598
28	8.852304	2.767078	75.451520
29	8.516770	3.102612	72.348907
30	8.140549	3.478833	68.870074
31	7.718708	3.900674	64.969400
32	7.245715	4.373667	60.595733
33	6.715367	4.904015	55.691718
34	6.120710	5.498673	50.193045
35	5.453944	6.165438	44.027607
36	4.706327	6.913055	37.114552
37	3.868055	7.751327	29.363224
38	2.928134	8.691248	20.671976
39	1.874239	9.745143	10.926833
40	0.692550	10.926833	0.000000

MORTGAGE AMORTIZATION TABLES
12%

5 YEARS — Monthly Payment: 2.224445 — Annual Constant: 26.70

Year	Annual Interest	Annual Principal	Year End Balance
1	11.164313	15.529024	84.470976
2	9.194844	17.498493	66.972482
3	6.975597	19.717740	47.254742
4	4.474894	22.218443	25.036298
5	1.657039	25.036298	0.000000

10 YEARS — Monthly Payment: 1.434709 — Annual Constant: 17.22

Year	Annual Interest	Annual Principal	Year End Balance
1	11.703309	5.513204	94.486796
2	11.004097	6.212417	88.274379
3	10.216207	7.000307	81.274072
4	9.328393	7.888121	73.385952
5	8.327982	8.888532	64.497420
6	7.200694	10.015820	54.481600
7	5.930437	11.286077	43.195523
8	4.499080	12.717434	30.478089
9	2.886191	14.330323	16.147766
10	1.068747	16.147766	0.000000

15 YEARS — Monthly Payment: 1.200168 — Annual Constant: 14.41

Year	Annual Interest	Annual Principal	Year End Balance
1	11.863385	2.538632	97.461368
2	11.541423	2.860594	94.600774
3	11.178628	3.223389	91.377385
4	10.769821	3.632195	87.745189
5	10.309168	4.092849	83.652340
6	9.790092	4.611924	79.040416
7	9.205185	5.196832	73.843584
8	8.546096	5.855920	67.987664
9	7.803419	6.598598	61.389066
10	6.966552	7.435465	53.953601
11	6.023549	8.378468	45.575133
12	4.960949	9.441067	36.134066
13	3.763586	10.638431	25.495635
14	2.414366	11.987650	13.507985
15	0.894032	13.507985	0.000000

20 YEARS — Monthly Payment: 1.101086 — Annual Constant: 13.22

Year	Annual Interest	Annual Principal	Year End Balance
1	11.931008	1.282025	98.717975
2	11.768416	1.444618	97.273357
3	11.585202	1.627832	95.645525
4	11.378752	1.834282	93.811243
5	11.146119	2.066914	91.744329
6	10.883983	2.329051	89.415278
7	10.588601	2.624433	86.790845
8	10.255757	2.957277	83.833568
9	9.880700	3.332333	80.501235
10	9.458077	3.754957	76.746278
11	8.981854	4.231179	72.515099
12	8.445235	4.767799	67.747301
13	7.840559	5.372475	62.374826
14	7.159195	6.053839	56.320987
15	6.391416	6.821617	49.499369
16	5.526264	7.686769	41.812600
17	4.551390	8.661644	33.150956
18	3.452876	9.760157	23.390799
19	2.215044	10.997989	12.392810
20	0.820224	12.392810	0.000000

25 YEARS — Monthly Payment: 1.053224 — Annual Constant: 12.64

Year	Annual Interest	Annual Principal	Year End Balance
1	11.963674	0.675015	99.324985
2	11.878066	0.760624	98.564360
3	11.781599	0.857090	97.707270
4	11.672899	0.965791	96.741479
5	11.550412	1.088277	95.653202
6	11.412392	1.226298	94.426904
7	11.256866	1.381823	93.045080
8	11.081616	1.557073	91.488007
9	10.884141	1.754549	89.733458
10	10.661620	1.977070	87.756388
11	10.410878	2.227812	85.528576
12	10.128336	2.510354	83.018222
13	9.809960	2.828730	80.189492
14	9.451206	3.187484	77.002009
15	9.046953	3.591736	73.410273
16	8.591431	4.047258	69.363014
17	8.078138	4.560552	64.802462
18	7.499746	5.138944	59.663518
19	6.847999	5.790691	53.872827
20	6.113594	6.525095	47.347732
21	5.286049	7.352641	39.995091
22	4.353550	8.285140	31.709951
23	3.302787	9.335903	22.374048
24	2.118761	10.519929	11.854119
25	0.784570	11.854119	0.000000

(Continued)

Mortgage Amortization Tables
12%

30 YEARS	Monthly Payment: 1.028613 Annual Constant: 12.35			**40 YEARS**	Monthly Payment: 1.008500 Annual Constant: 12.11		

Year	Annual Interest	Annual Principal	Year End Balance	Year	Annual Interest	Annual Principal	Year End Balance
1	11.980472	0.362879	99.637121	1	11.994199	0.107801	99.892199
2	11.934450	0.408902	99.228219	2	11.980527	0.121472	99.770727
3	11.882591	0.460760	98.767459	3	11.965121	0.136878	99.633849
4	11.824155	0.519196	98.248262	4	11.947762	0.154238	99.479611
5	11.758308	0.585044	97.663219	5	11.928200	0.173799	99.305812
6	11.684109	0.659242	97.003977	6	11.906158	0.195841	99.109971
7	11.600501	0.742850	96.261127	7	11.881321	0.220679	98.889292
8	11.506289	0.837062	95.424065	8	11.853333	0.248666	98.640626
9	11.400129	0.943222	94.480842	9	11.821796	0.280203	98.360422
10	11.280504	1.062847	93.417996	10	11.786259	0.315740	98.044682
11	11.145709	1.197642	92.220353	11	11.746216	0.355784	97.688898
12	10.993818	1.349533	90.870820	12	11.701093	0.400906	97.287992
13	10.822663	1.520688	89.350132	13	11.650248	0.451751	96.836241
14	10.629802	1.713549	87.636583	14	11.592955	0.509045	96.327196
15	10.412481	1.930870	85.705713	15	11.528395	0.573604	95.753592
16	10.167598	2.175753	83.529960	16	11.455648	0.646351	95.107241
17	9.891659	2.451693	81.078268	17	11.373674	0.728325	94.378916
18	9.580723	2.762629	78.315639	18	11.281305	0.820695	93.558221
19	9.230352	3.112999	75.202640	19	11.177220	0.924779	92.633442
20	8.835546	3.507805	71.694835	20	11.059935	1.042065	91.591377
21	8.390668	3.952683	67.742152	21	10.927775	1.174225	90.417152
22	7.889369	4.453982	63.288170	22	10.778854	1.323146	89.094007
23	7.324493	5.018858	58.269312	23	10.611046	1.490954	87.603053
24	6.687976	5.655375	52.613937	24	10.421956	1.680044	85.923010
25	5.970733	6.372618	46.241319	25	10.208884	1.893115	84.029894
26	5.162525	7.180826	39.060493	26	9.968790	2.133210	81.896684
27	4.251817	8.091534	30.968959	27	9.698245	2.403754	79.492930
28	3.225608	9.117743	21.851216	28	9.393389	2.708610	76.784320
29	2.069250	10.274101	11.577114	29	9.049869	3.052130	73.732190
30	0.766237	11.577114	0.000000	30	8.662783	3.439217	70.292973
				31	8.226604	3.875395	66.417578
				32	7.735107	4.366892	62.050686
				33	7.181276	4.920724	57.129962
				34	6.557205	5.544795	51.585167
				35	5.853986	6.248013	45.337154
				36	5.061582	7.040418	38.296736
				37	4.168680	7.933319	30.363417
				38	3.162537	8.939462	21.423955
				39	2.028789	10.073210	11.350745
				40	0.751254	11.350745	0.000000

MORTGAGE AMORTIZATION TABLES
12.5%

5 YEARS — Monthly Payment: 2.249794 — Annual Constant: 27.00

Year	Annual Interest	Annual Principal	Year End Balance
1	11.639885	15.357640	84.642360
2	9.606287	17.391239	67.251121
3	7.303408	19.694118	47.557003
4	4.695591	22.301935	25.255069
5	1.742457	25.255069	0.000000

10 YEARS — Monthly Payment: 1.463762 — Annual Constant: 17.57

Year	Annual Interest	Annual Principal	Year End Balance
1	12.199493	5.365647	94.634353
2	11.488996	6.076144	88.558209
3	10.684417	6.880724	81.677485
4	9.773299	7.791842	73.885643
5	8.741534	8.823607	65.062037
6	7.573147	9.991994	55.070043
7	6.250046	11.315094	43.754949
8	4.751746	12.813394	30.941555
9	3.055047	14.510093	16.431462
10	1.133678	16.431462	0.000000

15 YEARS — Monthly Payment: 1.232522 — Annual Constant: 14.80

Year	Annual Interest	Annual Principal	Year End Balance
1	12.364122	2.426143	97.573857
2	12.042862	2.747403	94.826454
3	11.679062	3.111203	91.715251
4	11.267089	3.523176	88.192075
5	10.800564	3.989701	84.202373
6	10.272263	4.518002	79.684372
7	9.674007	5.116258	74.568114
8	8.996532	5.793733	68.774381
9	8.229349	6.560916	62.213465
10	7.360579	7.429686	54.783779
11	6.376769	8.413496	46.370283
12	5.262687	9.527578	36.842706
13	4.001083	10.789182	26.053524
14	2.572422	12.217843	13.835681
15	0.954584	13.835681	0.000000

20 YEARS — Monthly Payment: 1.136141 — Annual Constant: 13.64

Year	Annual Interest	Annual Principal	Year End Balance
1	12.432740	1.200946	98.799054
2	12.273716	1.359971	97.439083
3	12.093634	1.540053	95.899030
4	11.889706	1.743981	94.155049
5	11.658775	1.974912	92.180137
6	11.397265	2.236422	89.943716
7	11.101127	2.532560	87.411156
8	10.765775	2.867911	84.543245
9	10.386018	3.247669	81.295576
10	9.955974	3.677712	77.617864
11	9.468986	4.164700	73.453163
12	8.917513	4.716174	68.736990
13	8.293016	5.340671	63.396319
14	7.585826	6.047861	57.348458
15	6.784992	6.848695	50.499763
16	5.878115	7.755572	42.744191
17	4.851152	8.782534	33.961657
18	3.688204	9.945483	24.016174
19	2.371262	11.262424	12.753750
20	0.879937	12.753750	0.000000

25 YEARS — Monthly Payment: 1.090354 — Annual Constant: 13.09

Year	Annual Interest	Annual Principal	Year End Balance
1	12.465337	0.618912	99.381088
2	12.383384	0.700866	98.680222
3	12.290578	0.793672	97.886550
4	12.185483	0.898767	96.987783
5	12.066472	1.017778	95.970004
6	11.931701	1.152548	94.817456
7	11.779085	1.305164	93.512292
8	11.606261	1.477989	92.034303
9	11.410551	1.673698	90.360605
10	11.188927	1.895323	88.465282
11	10.937956	2.146294	86.318988
12	10.653752	2.430498	83.888490
13	10.331915	2.752335	81.136156
14	9.967462	3.116788	78.019368
15	9.554749	3.529501	74.489867
16	9.087386	3.996863	70.493004
17	8.558138	4.526112	65.966892
18	7.958808	5.125442	60.841450
19	7.280117	5.804133	55.037318
20	6.511557	6.572693	48.464625
21	5.641227	7.443023	41.021602
22	4.655651	8.428599	32.593004
23	3.539569	9.544680	23.048323
24	2.275701	10.808549	12.239774
25	0.844475	12.239774	0.000000

(Continued)

Mortgage Amortization Tables
12.5%

30 YEARS
Monthly Payment: 1.067258
Annual Constant: 12.81

Year	Annual Interest	Annual Principal	Year End Balance
1	12.481781	0.325312	99.674688
2	12.438704	0.368389	99.306298
3	12.389923	0.417170	98.889129
4	12.334683	0.472410	98.416719
5	12.272129	0.534964	97.881755
6	12.201291	0.605802	97.275953
7	12.121073	0.686020	96.589933
8	12.030233	0.776860	95.813072
9	11.927364	0.879729	94.933344
10	11.810874	0.996219	93.937124
11	11.678959	1.128134	92.808990
12	11.529576	1.277518	91.531472
13	11.360412	1.446681	90.084791
14	11.168848	1.638245	88.446546
15	10.951918	1.855175	86.591370
16	10.706263	2.100830	84.490540
17	10.428079	2.379014	82.111526
18	10.113060	2.694033	79.417493
19	9.756326	3.050767	76.366726
20	9.352356	3.454737	72.911989
21	8.894893	3.912200	68.999789
22	8.376855	4.430238	64.569552
23	7.790221	5.016872	59.552679
24	7.125906	5.681187	53.871492
25	6.373626	6.433467	47.438025
26	5.521732	7.285361	40.152664
27	4.557033	8.250060	31.902604
28	3.464593	9.342500	22.560103
29	2.227496	10.579597	11.980506
30	0.826587	11.980506	0.000000

40 YEARS
Monthly Payment: 1.048919
Annual Constant: 12.59

Year	Annual Interest	Annual Principal	Year End Balance
1	12.494836	0.092196	99.907804
2	12.482628	0.104405	99.803399
3	12.468803	0.118229	99.685170
4	12.453148	0.133885	99.551285
5	12.435419	0.151613	99.399672
6	12.415343	0.171689	99.227982
7	12.392609	0.194424	99.033558
8	12.366864	0.220169	98.813390
9	12.337710	0.249323	98.564067
10	12.304696	0.282337	98.281730
11	12.267310	0.319723	97.962008
12	12.224974	0.362059	97.599949
13	12.177031	0.410002	97.189947
14	12.122740	0.464292	96.725655
15	12.061261	0.525772	96.199882
16	11.991640	0.595393	95.604490
17	11.912800	0.674232	94.930257
18	11.823521	0.763512	94.166746
19	11.722420	0.864613	93.302133
20	11.607931	0.979101	92.323031
21	11.478283	1.108750	91.214281
22	11.331466	1.255566	89.958715
23	11.165209	1.421824	88.536891
24	10.976937	1.610096	86.926796
25	10.763734	1.823298	85.103497
26	10.522300	2.064732	83.038765
27	10.248897	2.338136	80.700629
28	9.939290	2.647743	78.052886
29	9.588686	2.998346	75.054540
30	9.191657	3.395375	71.659165
31	8.742055	3.844978	67.814187
32	8.232918	4.354114	63.460073
33	7.656364	4.930669	58.529404
34	7.003464	5.583569	52.945835
35	6.264110	6.322923	46.622912
36	5.426854	7.160179	39.462733
37	4.478731	8.108302	31.354431
38	3.405062	9.181971	22.172460
39	2.189221	10.397811	11.774649
40	0.812384	11.774649	0.000000

MORTGAGE AMORTIZATION TABLES
13%

5 YEARS — Monthly Payment: 2.275307 — Annual Constant: 27.31

Year	Annual Interest	Annual Principal	Year End Balance
1	12.116199	15.187488	84.812512
2	10.019832	17.283855	67.528656
3	7.634099	19.669589	47.859068
4	4.919057	22.384631	25.474437
5	1.829251	25.474437	0.000000

10 YEARS — Monthly Payment: 1.493107 — Annual Constant: 17.92

Year	Annual Interest	Annual Principal	Year End Balance
1	12.696169	5.221120	94.778880
2	11.975485	5.941804	88.837076
3	11.155323	6.761966	82.075110
4	10.221952	7.695337	74.379774
5	9.159746	8.757543	65.622230
6	7.950920	9.966369	55.655862
7	6.575238	11.342051	44.313810
8	5.009666	12.907623	31.406188
9	3.227995	14.689294	16.716894
10	1.200395	16.716894	0.000000

15 YEARS — Monthly Payment: 1.265242 — Annual Constant: 15.19

Year	Annual Interest	Annual Principal	Year End Balance
1	12.865122	2.317784	97.682216
2	12.545192	2.637714	95.044502
3	12.181102	3.001804	92.042699
4	11.766756	3.416150	88.626548
5	11.295216	3.887690	84.738859
6	10.758589	4.424317	80.314541
7	10.147889	5.035017	75.279524
8	9.452893	5.730013	69.549512
9	8.661965	6.520941	63.028571
10	7.761864	7.421042	55.607529
11	6.737519	8.445387	47.162142
12	5.571781	9.611125	37.551017
13	4.245134	10.937772	26.613245
14	2.735366	12.447540	14.165705
15	1.017201	14.165705	0.000000

20 YEARS — Monthly Payment: 1.171576 — Annual Constant: 14.06

Year	Annual Interest	Annual Principal	Year End Balance
1	12.934572	1.124337	98.875663
2	12.779377	1.279532	97.596132
3	12.602760	1.456149	96.139983
4	12.401764	1.657144	94.482838
5	12.173024	1.885884	92.596954
6	11.912711	2.146197	90.450757
7	11.616466	2.442442	88.008314
8	11.279330	2.779579	85.228736
9	10.895658	3.163251	82.065484
10	10.459026	3.599882	78.465602
11	9.962125	4.096783	74.368819
12	9.396636	4.662272	69.706547
13	8.753091	5.305817	64.400730
14	8.020716	6.038192	58.362537
15	7.187249	6.871659	51.490878
16	6.238737	7.820171	43.670707
17	5.159300	8.899609	34.771098
18	3.930865	10.128044	24.643054
19	2.532866	11.526043	13.117011
20	0.941897	13.117011	0.000000

25 YEARS — Monthly Payment: 1.127835 — Annual Constant: 13.54

Year	Annual Interest	Annual Principal	Year End Balance
1	12.967004	0.567020	99.432980
2	12.888736	0.645287	98.787693
3	12.799666	0.734358	98.053335
4	12.698301	0.835723	97.217612
5	12.582944	0.951080	96.266532
6	12.451664	1.082360	95.184172
7	12.302263	1.231761	93.952411
8	12.132240	1.401784	92.550627
9	11.938748	1.595275	90.955352
10	11.718548	1.815475	89.139876
11	11.467954	2.066070	87.073806
12	11.182769	2.351255	84.722552
13	10.858219	2.675804	82.046748
14	10.488872	3.045152	79.001596
15	10.068542	3.465482	75.536114
16	9.590193	3.943831	71.592283
17	9.045816	4.488208	67.104075
18	8.426297	5.107726	61.996349
19	7.721265	5.812758	56.183590
20	6.918916	6.615108	49.568483
21	6.005816	7.528208	42.040275
22	4.966679	8.567345	33.472930
23	3.784107	9.749917	23.723014
24	2.438302	11.095722	12.627292
25	0.906732	12.627292	0.000000

(Continued)

Mortgage Amortization Tables
13%

30 YEARS	*Monthly Payment: 1.106200* *Annual Constant: 13.28*			**40** YEARS	*Monthly Payment: 1.089514* *Annual Constant: 13.08*		
Year	**Annual**		**Year End Balance**	**Year**	**Annual**		**Year End Balance**
	Interest	**Principal**			**Interest**	**Principal**	
1	12.983046	0.291349	99.708651	1	12.995417	0.078753	99.921247
2	12.942830	0.331564	99.377087	2	12.984547	0.089623	99.831624
3	12.897063	0.377331	98.999756	3	12.972176	0.101994	99.729630
4	12.844980	0.429415	98.570342	4	12.958097	0.116073	99.613557
5	12.785706	0.488688	98.081654	5	12.942076	0.132094	99.481463
6	12.718252	0.556143	97.525511	6	12.923842	0.150328	99.331135
7	12.641486	0.632908	96.892603	7	12.903092	0.171078	99.160057
8	12.554124	0.720270	96.172333	8	12.879478	0.194692	98.965365
9	12.454703	0.819691	95.352641	9	12.852604	0.221566	98.743799
10	12.341559	0.932835	94.419806	10	12.822021	0.252149	98.491650
11	12.212798	1.061597	93.358210	11	12.787216	0.286954	98.204696
12	12.066263	1.208131	92.150079	12	12.747607	0.326563	97.878133
13	11.899502	1.374893	90.775186	13	12.702531	0.371639	97.506494
14	11.709722	1.564673	89.210513	14	12.651232	0.422938	97.083556
15	11.493746	1.780648	87.429865	15	12.592853	0.481317	96.602239
16	11.247959	2.026436	85.403430	16	12.526416	0.547754	96.054485
17	10.968245	2.306149	83.097280	17	12.450808	0.623362	95.431123
18	10.649921	2.624473	80.472807	18	12.364764	0.709406	94.721717
19	10.287659	2.986735	77.486072	19	12.266843	0.807327	93.914390
20	9.875392	3.399002	74.087070	20	12.155405	0.918765	92.995625
21	9.406220	3.868175	70.218895	21	12.028586	1.045584	91.950041
22	8.872286	4.402108	65.816787	22	11.884261	1.189909	90.760133
23	8.264652	5.009742	60.807044	23	11.720015	1.354155	89.405978
24	7.573145	5.701250	55.105795	24	11.533098	1.541072	87.864907
25	6.786187	6.488207	48.617587	25	11.320380	1.753790	86.111117
26	5.890604	7.383791	41.233797	26	11.078300	1.995870	84.115247
27	4.871401	8.402993	32.830804	27	10.802805	2.271365	81.843882
28	3.711515	9.562879	23.267924	28	10.489283	2.584887	79.258996
29	2.391527	10.882867	12.385057	29	10.132485	2.941685	76.317311
30	0.889338	12.385057	0.000000	30	9.726437	3.347733	72.969577
				31	9.264341	3.809829	69.159748
				32	8.738461	4.335709	64.824039
				33	8.139992	4.934178	59.889861
				34	7.458915	5.615255	54.274606
				35	6.683828	6.390342	47.884264
				36	5.801753	7.272417	40.611847
				37	4.797923	8.276247	32.335600
				38	3.655532	9.418638	22.916962
				39	2.355454	10.718716	12.198247
				40	0.875923	12.198247	0.000000

MORTGAGE AMORTIZATION TABLES
13.5%

5 YEARS
Monthly Payment: 2.300985
Annual Constant: 27.62

Year	Annual Interest	Principal	Year End Balance
1	12.593244	15.018572	84.981428
2	10.435459	17.176356	67.805072
3	7.967655	19.644160	48.160912
4	5.145292	22.466524	25.694389
5	1.917427	25.694389	0.000000

10 YEARS
Monthly Payment: 1.522743
Annual Constant: 18.28

Year	Annual Interest	Principal	Year End Balance
1	13.193316	5.079599	94.920401
2	12.463507	5.809407	89.110994
3	11.628844	6.644071	82.466923
4	10.674261	7.598654	74.868269
5	9.582528	8.690386	66.177883
6	8.333942	9.938973	56.238910
7	6.905966	11.366949	44.871961
8	5.272826	13.000089	31.871872
9	3.405045	14.867870	17.004002
10	1.268912	17.004002	0.000000

15 YEARS
Monthly Payment: 1.298319
Annual Constant: 15.58

Year	Annual Interest	Principal	Year End Balance
1	13.366361	2.213462	97.786538
2	13.048343	2.531480	95.255059
3	12.684634	2.895189	92.359870
4	12.268669	3.311153	89.048717
5	11.792941	3.786881	85.261836
6	11.248863	4.330959	80.930876
7	10.626615	4.953207	75.977669
8	9.914966	5.664857	70.312812
9	9.101071	6.478752	63.834061
10	8.170240	7.409583	56.424478
11	7.105672	8.474151	47.950327
12	5.888153	9.691669	38.258658
13	4.495708	11.084115	27.174543
14	2.903204	12.676619	14.497925
15	1.081898	14.497925	0.000000

20 YEARS
Monthly Payment: 1.207375
Annual Constant: 14.49

Year	Annual Interest	Principal	Year End Balance
1	13.436484	1.052012	98.947988
2	13.285337	1.203159	97.744828
3	13.112474	1.376023	96.368806
4	12.914774	1.573722	94.795084
5	12.688671	1.799826	92.995258
6	12.430082	2.058414	90.936844
7	12.134340	2.354156	88.582688
8	11.796108	2.692388	85.890300
9	11.409281	3.079215	82.811084
10	10.966876	3.521620	79.289464
11	10.460909	4.027587	75.261878
12	9.882248	4.606248	70.655630
13	9.220448	5.268048	65.387582
14	8.463564	6.024932	59.362650
15	7.597935	6.890561	52.472089
16	6.607938	7.880558	44.591531
17	5.475703	9.012793	35.578738
18	4.180795	10.307701	25.271037
19	2.699842	11.788654	13.482382
20	1.006114	13.482382	0.000000

25 YEARS
Monthly Payment: 1.165645
Annual Constant: 13.99

Year	Annual Interest	Principal	Year End Balance
1	13.468660	0.519078	99.480922
2	13.394082	0.593657	98.887265
3	13.308789	0.678950	98.208315
4	13.211241	0.776498	97.431818
5	13.099678	0.888060	96.543757
6	12.972087	1.015652	95.528105
7	12.826163	1.161575	94.366530
8	12.659275	1.328464	93.038066
9	12.468408	1.519330	91.518736
10	12.250119	1.737619	89.781116
11	12.000468	1.987271	87.793846
12	11.714948	2.272791	85.521055
13	11.388406	2.599333	82.921723
14	11.014948	2.972790	79.948932
15	10.587834	3.399904	76.549028
16	10.099355	3.888384	72.660644
17	9.540694	4.447045	68.213600
18	8.901767	5.085972	63.127628
19	8.171043	5.816696	57.310932
20	7.335332	6.652406	50.658526
21	6.379552	7.608187	43.050339
22	5.286450	8.701289	34.349050
23	4.036297	9.951442	24.397608
24	2.606529	11.381210	13.016399
25	0.971340	13.016399	0.000000

(Continued)

Mortgage Amortization Tables
13.5%

30 YEARS	Monthly Payment: 1.145412	Annual Constant: 13.75

Year	Annual		Year End Balance
	Interest	Principal	
1	13.484261	0.260685	99.739315
2	13.446807	0.298139	99.441176
3	13.403972	0.340974	99.100202
4	13.354983	0.389963	98.710239
5	13.298955	0.445991	98.264248
6	13.234878	0.510068	97.754180
7	13.161594	0.583352	97.170827
8	13.077781	0.667165	96.503662
9	12.981927	0.763020	95.740643
10	12.872300	0.872646	94.867997
11	12.746923	0.998023	93.869974
12	12.603533	1.141413	92.728561
13	12.439541	1.305405	91.423156
14	12.251988	1.492958	89.930197
15	12.037488	1.707458	88.222739
16	11.792170	1.952777	86.269962
17	11.511605	2.233341	84.036622
18	11.190731	2.554215	81.482407
19	10.823756	2.921190	78.561217
20	10.404056	3.340890	75.220327
21	9.924055	3.820891	71.399436
22	9.375091	4.369855	67.029581
23	8.747254	4.997692	62.031889
24	8.029214	5.715732	56.316157
25	7.208009	6.536937	49.779220
26	6.268818	7.476128	42.303092
27	5.194690	8.550256	33.752836
28	3.966237	9.778709	23.974126
29	2.561286	11.183660	12.790466
30	0.954480	12.790466	0.000000

40 YEARS	Monthly Payment: 1.130261	Annual Constant: 13.57

Year	Annual		Year End Balance
	Interest	Principal	
1	13.495943	0.067191	99.932809
2	13.486290	0.076844	99.855965
3	13.475249	0.087885	99.766080
4	13.462622	0.100512	99.667569
5	13.448181	0.114953	99.552616
6	13.431666	0.131468	99.421148
7	13.412777	0.150357	99.270791
8	13.391175	0.171959	99.098831
9	13.366468	0.196666	98.902165
10	13.338213	0.224921	98.677244
11	13.305897	0.257237	98.420007
12	13.268939	0.294195	98.125812
13	13.226670	0.336464	97.789348
14	13.178329	0.384805	97.404543
15	13.123043	0.440092	96.964452
16	13.059813	0.503321	96.461130
17	12.987498	0.575636	95.885494
18	12.904794	0.658340	95.227154
19	12.810207	0.752927	94.474228
20	12.702031	0.861103	93.613125
21	12.578313	0.984821	92.628303
22	12.436819	1.126315	91.501988
23	12.274996	1.288138	90.213850
24	12.089924	1.473210	88.740640
25	11.878261	1.684873	87.055767
26	11.636188	1.926946	85.128821
27	11.359335	2.203799	82.925022
28	11.042705	2.520429	80.404594
29	10.680584	2.882550	77.522044
30	10.266436	3.296698	74.225345
31	9.792784	3.770350	70.454995
32	9.251081	4.312053	66.142943
33	8.631550	4.931584	61.211358
34	7.923007	5.640127	55.571231
35	7.112665	6.450469	49.120762
36	6.185897	7.377237	41.743525
37	5.125977	8.437157	33.306368
38	3.913773	9.649361	23.657007
39	2.527406	11.035728	12.621280
40	0.941855	12.621280	0.000000

MORTGAGE AMORTIZATION TABLES
14%

5 YEARS — Monthly Payment: 2.326825 — Annual Constant: 27.93

Year	Interest	Principal	Year End Balance
1	13.071009	14.850892	85.149108
2	10.853146	17.068755	68.080353
3	8.304064	19.617837	48.462515
4	5.374296	22.547605	25.914910
5	2.006991	25.914910	0.000000

10 YEARS — Monthly Payment: 1.552664 — Annual Constant: 18.64

Year	Interest	Principal	Year End Balance
1	13.690914	4.941058	95.058942
2	12.953007	5.678966	89.379976
3	12.104898	6.527074	82.852902
4	11.130132	7.501840	75.351062
5	10.009792	8.622180	66.728881
6	8.722138	9.909834	56.819047
7	7.242183	11.389789	45.429258
8	5.541209	13.090763	32.338494
9	3.586208	15.045765	17.292730
10	1.339243	17.292730	0.000000

15 YEARS — Monthly Payment: 1.331741 — Annual Constant: 15.99

Year	Interest	Principal	Year End Balance
1	13.867817	2.113079	97.886921
2	13.552246	2.428651	95.458269
3	13.189546	2.791351	92.666919
4	12.772680	3.208217	89.458702
5	12.293558	3.687338	85.771364
6	11.742884	4.238013	81.533351
7	11.109970	4.870926	76.662425
8	10.382536	5.598360	71.064064
9	9.546466	6.434431	64.629633
10	8.585535	7.395362	57.234272
11	7.481097	8.499800	48.734471
12	6.211719	9.769178	38.965294
13	4.752770	11.228126	27.737168
14	3.075939	12.904958	14.832210
15	1.148687	14.832210	0.000000

20 YEARS — Monthly Payment: 1.243521 — Annual Constant: 14.93

Year	Interest	Principal	Year End Balance
1	13.938459	0.983790	99.016210
2	13.791538	1.130712	97.885498
3	13.622675	1.299574	96.585924
4	13.428594	1.493655	95.092268
5	13.205529	1.716721	93.375547
6	12.949150	1.973100	91.402448
7	12.654484	2.267766	89.134682
8	12.315811	2.606439	86.528243
9	11.926560	2.995690	83.532553
10	11.479177	3.443072	80.089480
11	10.964982	3.957268	76.132213
12	10.373996	4.548254	71.583959
13	9.694750	5.227500	66.356459
14	8.914065	6.008185	60.348274
15	8.016790	6.905460	53.442814
16	6.985515	7.936735	45.506079
17	5.800227	9.122023	36.384056
18	4.437925	10.484324	25.899732
19	2.872175	12.050075	13.849657
20	1.072592	13.849657	0.000000

25 YEARS — Monthly Payment: 1.203761 — Annual Constant: 14.45

Year	Interest	Principal	Year End Balance
1	13.970297	0.474836	99.525164
2	13.899384	0.545749	98.979416
3	13.817881	0.627252	98.352164
4	13.724206	0.720927	97.631237
5	13.616541	0.828592	96.802646
6	13.492797	0.952335	95.850310
7	13.350574	1.094559	94.755752
8	13.187110	1.258022	93.497729
9	12.999235	1.445898	92.051831
10	12.783301	1.661831	90.390000
11	12.535120	1.910013	88.479988
12	12.249875	2.195258	86.284730
13	11.922031	2.523102	83.761628
14	11.545225	2.899907	80.861721
15	11.112147	3.332985	77.528736
16	10.614393	3.830740	73.697996
17	10.042302	4.402830	69.295166
18	9.384775	5.060358	64.234808
19	8.629050	5.816082	58.418726
20	7.760465	6.684668	51.734058
21	6.762163	7.682969	44.051089
22	5.614773	8.830360	35.220729
23	4.296029	10.149103	25.071626
24	2.780341	11.664791	13.406835
25	1.038298	13.406835	0.000000

(Continued)

Mortgage Amortization Tables
14%

30 YEARS	Monthly Payment: 1.184872 Annual Constant: 14.22

Year	Annual		Year End Balance
	Interest	Principal	
1	13.985422	0.233039	99.766961
2	13.950620	0.267841	99.499120
3	13.910620	0.307841	99.191279
4	13.864646	0.353815	98.837465
5	13.811807	0.406654	98.430810
6	13.751076	0.467385	97.963426
7	13.681276	0.537185	97.426241
8	13.601052	0.617409	96.808832
9	13.508847	0.709614	96.099218
10	13.402872	0.815589	95.283629
11	13.281070	0.937391	94.346237
12	13.141078	1.077383	93.268854
13	12.980179	1.238282	92.030573
14	12.795252	1.423209	90.607364
15	12.582707	1.635754	88.971610
16	12.338420	1.880041	87.091569
17	12.057651	2.160810	84.930759
18	11.734951	2.483510	82.447249
19	11.364059	2.854402	79.592847
20	10.937777	3.280684	76.312163
21	10.447833	3.770628	72.541535
22	9.884719	4.333742	68.207793
23	9.237510	4.980951	63.226842
24	8.493644	5.724817	57.502025
25	7.638689	6.579772	50.922253
26	6.656052	7.562409	43.359844
27	5.526666	8.691795	34.668049
28	4.228616	9.989845	24.678204
29	2.736713	11.481748	13.196456
30	1.022005	13.196456	0.000000

40 YEARS	Monthly Payment: 1.171140 Annual Constant: 14.06

Year	Annual		Year End Balance
	Interest	Principal	
1	13.996418	0.057263	99.942737
2	13.987866	0.065815	99.876923
3	13.978037	0.075643	99.801279
4	13.966741	0.086940	99.714339
5	13.953757	0.099924	99.614415
6	13.938834	0.114847	99.499568
7	13.921682	0.131998	99.367570
8	13.901970	0.151711	99.215859
9	13.879313	0.174368	99.041491
10	13.853272	0.200409	98.841082
11	13.823343	0.230338	98.610744
12	13.788944	0.264737	98.346007
13	13.749407	0.304273	98.041734
14	13.703967	0.349714	97.692020
15	13.651739	0.401941	97.290078
16	13.591713	0.461968	96.828110
17	13.522722	0.530959	96.297151
18	13.443427	0.619254	95.686897
19	13.352290	0.701390	94.985507
20	13.247543	0.806137	94.179370
21	13.127153	0.926528	93.252842
22	12.988784	1.064897	92.187945
23	12.829750	1.223931	90.964014
24	12.646965	1.406715	89.557299
25	12.436884	1.616797	87.940502
26	12.195428	1.858253	86.082249
27	11.917913	2.135768	83.946481
28	11.598953	2.454728	81.491754
29	11.232359	2.821322	78.670432
30	10.811017	3.242664	75.427768
31	10.326751	3.726930	71.700838
32	9.770164	4.283517	67.417321
33	9.130455	4.923226	62.494095
34	8.395210	5.658471	56.835624
35	7.550162	6.503518	50.332106
36	6.578914	7.474767	42.857339
37	5.462617	8.591064	34.266275
38	4.179610	9.8740/1	24.392204
39	2.704996	11.348684	13.043520
40	1.010161	13.043520	0.000000

MORTGAGE AMORTIZATION TABLES
14.5%

5 YEARS
Monthly Payment: 2.352828
Annual Constant: 28.24

| Year | Annual | | Year End Balance |
	Interest	Principal	
1	13.549483	14.684454	85.315546
2	11.272874	16.961063	68.354483
3	8.643309	19.590628	48.763855
4	5.606070	22.627868	26.135987
5	2.097950	26.135987	0.000000

10 YEARS
Monthly Payment: 1.582868
Annual Constant: 19.00

| Year | Annual | | Year End Balance |
	Interest	Principal	
1	14.188945	4.805470	95.194530
2	13.443927	5.550488	89.644042
3	12.583405	6.411010	83.233032
4	11.589472	7.404943	75.828089
5	10.441444	8.552971	67.275118
6	9.115431	9.878984	57.396135
7	7.583839	11.410575	45.985559
8	5.814797	13.179618	32.805941
9	3.771490	15.222925	17.583016
10	1.411398	17.583016	0.000000

15 YEARS
Monthly Payment: 1.365501
Annual Constant: 16.39

| Year | Annual | | Year End Balance |
	Interest	Principal	
1	14.369470	2.016540	97.983460
2	14.056836	2.329175	95.654285
3	13.695731	2.690279	92.964006
4	13.278643	3.107368	89.856638
5	12.796891	3.589119	86.267519
6	12.240450	4.145560	82.121959
7	11.597742	4.788268	77.333691
8	10.855391	5.530619	71.803072
9	9.997950	6.388061	65.415011
10	9.007575	7.378436	58.036575
11	7.863656	8.522354	49.514221
12	6.542390	9.843620	39.670601
13	5.016281	11.369730	28.300871
14	3.253571	13.132440	15.168432
15	1.217578	15.168432	0.000000

20 YEARS
Monthly Payment: 1.279998
Annual Constant: 15.36

| Year | Annual | | Year End Balance |
	Interest	Principal	
1	14.440482	0.919491	99.080509
2	14.297928	1.062045	98.018464
3	14.133274	1.226700	96.791764
4	13.943092	1.416881	95.374883
5	13.723425	1.636548	93.738335
6	13.469702	1.890271	91.848064
7	13.176644	2.183330	89.664734
8	12.838150	2.521823	87.142911
9	12.447179	2.912795	84.230116
10	11.995592	3.364381	80.865736
11	11.473994	3.885979	76.979757
12	10.871530	3.488443	72.491314
13	10.175663	5.184310	67.307004
14	9.371912	5.988062	61.318942
15	8.443550	6.916423	54.402519
16	7.371260	7.988713	46.413806
17	6.132727	9.227246	37.186561
18	4.702178	10.657795	26.528766
19	3.049843	12.310130	14.218635
20	1.141338	14.218635	0.000000

25 YEARS
Monthly Payment: 1.242163
Annual Constant: 14.91

| Year | Annual | | Year End Balance |
	Interest	Principal	
1	14.471904	0.434051	99.565949
2	14.404611	0.501344	99.064605
3	14.326885	0.579070	98.485535
4	14.237108	0.668846	97.816688
5	14.133414	0.772541	97.044147
6	14.013642	0.892313	96.151835
7	13.875302	1.030653	95.121182
8	13.715515	1.190440	93.930742
9	13.530955	1.375000	92.555741
10	13.317781	1.588174	90.967567
11	13.071558	1.834397	89.133170
12	12.787161	2.118794	87.014376
13	12.458673	2.447282	84.567095
14	12.079258	2.826697	81.740398
15	11.641020	3.264935	78.475463
16	11.134840	3.771115	74.704348
17	10.550184	4.355771	70.348577
18	9.874885	5.031070	65.317508
19	9.094892	5.811063	59.506444
20	8.193971	6.711984	52.794461
21	7.153377	7.752578	45.041883
22	5.951453	8.954502	36.087381
23	4.563189	10.342766	25.744614
24	2.959694	11.946261	13.798354
25	1.107601	13.798354	0.000000

(Continued)

Mortgage Amortization Tables
14.5%

30 YEARS — Monthly Payment: 1.224556 — Annual Constant: 14.70

Year	Interest	Principal	Year End Balance
1	14.486527	0.208144	99.791856
2	14.454257	0.240414	99.551442
3	14.416985	0.277687	99.273755
4	14.373933	0.320738	98.953018
5	14.324208	0.370463	98.582554
6	14.266773	0.427898	98.154656
7	14.200433	0.494238	97.660418
8	14.123809	0.570862	97.089556
9	14.035305	0.659366	96.430190
10	13.933080	0.761591	95.668599
11	13.815007	0.879665	94.788934
12	13.678628	1.016044	93.772891
13	13.521105	1.173566	92.599324
14	13.339161	1.355511	91.243814
15	13.129009	1.565663	89.678151
16	12.886275	1.808396	87.869756
17	12.605910	2.088761	85.780995
18	12.282078	2.412593	83.368402
19	11.908041	2.786630	80.581772
20	11.476015	3.218656	77.363116
21	10.977010	3.717661	73.645455
22	10.400641	4.294030	69.351424
23	9.734914	4.959757	64.391667
24	8.965977	5.728695	58.662973
25	8.077826	6.616845	52.046128
26	7.051981	7.642690	44.403438
27	5.867094	8.827577	35.575862
28	4.498508	10.196163	25.379698
29	2.917742	11.776929	13.602769
30	1.091902	13.602769	0.000000

40 YEARS — Monthly Payment: 1.212133 — Annual Constant: 14.55

Year	Interest	Principal	Year End Balance
1	14.496844	0.048751	99.951249
2	14.489286	0.056309	99.894940
3	14.480556	0.065039	99.829901
4	14.470473	0.075122	99.754779
5	14.458826	0.086769	99.668010
6	14.445374	0.100221	99.567789
7	14.429836	0.115759	99.452030
8	14.411890	0.133706	99.318324
9	14.391160	0.154435	99.163889
10	14.367218	0.178378	98.985511
11	14.339563	0.206033	98.779479
12	14.307620	0.237975	98.541504
13	14.270726	0.274869	98.266634
14	14.228111	0.317484	97.949150
15	14.178890	0.366705	97.582445
16	14.122038	0.423557	97.158888
17	14.056372	0.489224	96.669664
18	13.980525	0.565071	96.104593
19	13.892919	0.652677	95.451916
20	13.791731	0.753865	94.698052
21	13.674855	0.870740	93.827311
22	13.539859	1.005736	92.821575
23	13.383935	1.161661	91.659915
24	13.203836	1.341759	90.318156
25	12.995816	1.549779	88.768376
26	12.755546	1.790050	86.978327
27	12.478025	2.067571	84.910756
28	12.157478	2.388117	82.522639
29	11.787236	2.758360	79.764279
30	11.359592	3.186003	76.578276
31	10.865649	3.679946	72.898330
32	10.295127	4.250468	68.647862
33	9.636155	4.909441	63.738421
34	8.875018	5.670578	58.067843
35	7.995878	6.549718	51.518126
36	6.980440	7.565155	43.952970
37	5.807573	8.738022	35.214948
38	4.452871	10.092724	25.122224
39	2.888142	11.657453	13.464771
40	1.080825	13.464771	0.000000

MORTGAGE AMORTIZATION TABLES
15%

5 YEARS — Monthly Payment: 2.378993 — Annual Constant: 28.55

Year	Annual Interest	Annual Principal	Year End Balance
1	14.028658	14.519258	85.480742
2	11.694622	16.853294	68.627447
3	8.985378	19.562538	49.064910
4	5.840612	22.707304	26.357606
5	2.190310	26.357606	0.000000

10 YEARS — Monthly Payment: 1.613350 — Annual Constant: 19.37

Year	Annual Interest	Annual Principal	Year End Balance
1	14.687388	4.672807	95.327193
2	13.936213	5.423982	89.903212
3	13.064284	6.295911	83.607300
4	12.052188	7.308007	76.299293
5	10.877392	8.482803	67.816491
6	9.513744	9.846451	57.970039
7	7.930882	11.429313	46.540726
8	6.093568	13.266627	33.274100
9	3.960898	15.399297	17.874803
10	1.485392	17.874803	0.000000

15 YEARS — Monthly Payment: 1.399587 — Annual Constant: 16.80

Year	Annual Interest	Annual Principal	Year End Balance
1	14.871301	1.923744	98.076256
2	14.562050	2.232995	95.843261
3	14.203086	2.591959	93.251302
4	13.786417	3.008628	90.242673
5	13.302767	3.492279	86.750395
6	12.741367	4.053678	82.696716
7	12.089720	4.705325	77.991391
8	11.333318	5.461728	72.529663
9	10.455320	6.339725	66.189938
10	9.436181	7.358865	58.831073
11	8.253210	8.541835	50.289238
12	6.880071	9.914974	40.374264
13	5.286195	11.508851	28.865413
14	3.436095	13.358951	15.506462
15	1.288583	15.506462	0.000000

20 YEARS — Monthly Payment: 1.316790 — Annual Constant: 15.81

Year	Annual Interest	Annual Principal	Year End Balance
1	14.942537	0.858938	99.141062
2	14.804459	0.997016	98.144045
3	14.644184	1.157291	96.986754
4	14.458144	1.343331	95.643423
5	14.242197	1.559278	94.084146
6	13.991536	1.809938	92.274207
7	13.700581	2.100894	90.173313
8	13.362852	2.438623	87.734690
9	12.970833	2.830642	84.904048
10	12.515794	3.285681	81.618368
11	11.987606	3.813869	77.804499
12	11.374510	4.426965	73.377534
13	10.662855	5.138620	68.238914
14	9.836799	5.964676	62.274238
15	8.877950	6.923525	55.350713
16	7.764962	8.036513	47.314200
17	6.473056	9.328419	37.985781
18	4.973471	10.828004	27.157777
19	3.232820	12.568655	14.589123
20	1.212352	14.589123	0.000000

25 YEARS — Monthly Payment: 1.280831 — Annual Constant: 15.37

Year	Annual Interest	Annual Principal	Year End Balance
1	14.973475	0.396493	99.603507
2	14.909737	0.460231	99.143276
3	14.835752	0.534215	98.609061
4	14.749875	0.620092	97.988969
5	14.650192	0.719775	97.269194
6	14.534485	0.835482	96.433712
7	14.400178	0.969790	95.463922
8	14.244279	1.125688	94.338234
9	14.063320	1.306647	93.031587
10	13.853271	1.516697	91.514890
11	13.609455	1.760513	89.754377
12	13.326444	2.043523	87.710854
13	12.997939	2.372028	85.338826
14	12.616625	2.753343	82.585483
15	12.174012	3.195955	79.389528
16	11.660248	3.709719	75.679809
17	11.063894	4.306073	71.373735
18	10.371673	4.998294	66.375441
19	9.568175	5.801793	60.573649
20	8.635510	6.734457	53.839192
21	7.552916	7.817051	46.022141
22	6.296290	9.073678	36.948463
23	4.837655	10.532312	26.416151
24	3.144538	12.225429	14.190722
25	1.179245	14.190722	0.000000

(Continued)

Mortgage Amortization Tables
15%

30 YEARS	Monthly Payment: 1.264444		
	Annual Constant: 15.18		

Year	Annual Interest	Annual Principal	Year End Balance
1	14.987573	0.185755	99.814245
2	14.957712	0.215616	99.598628
3	14.923051	0.250278	99.348351
4	14.882817	0.290511	99.057840
5	14.836116	0.337212	98.720628
6	14.781908	0.391420	98.329208
7	14.718986	0.454343	97.874865
8	14.645948	0.527380	97.347485
9	14.561169	0.612159	96.735325
10	14.462762	0.710567	96.024759
11	14.348535	0.824793	95.199966
12	14.215946	0.957383	94.242583
13	14.062042	1.111286	93.131297
14	13.883398	1.289930	91.841366
15	13.676036	1.497293	90.344074
16	13.435339	1.737989	88.606085
17	13.155950	2.017379	86.588706
18	12.831647	2.341681	84.247025
19	12.455211	2.718117	81.528908
20	12.018261	3.155067	78.373841
21	11.511070	3.662258	74.711582
22	10.922346	4.250983	70.460600
23	10.238981	4.934347	65.526252
24	9.445762	5.727566	59.798686
25	8.525030	6.648298	53.150388
26	7.456286	7.717042	45.433346
27	6.215737	8.957591	36.475755
28	4.775764	10.397565	26.078190
29	3.104308	12.069020	14.009170
30	1.164158	14.009170	0.000000

40 YEARS	Monthly Payment: 1.253224		
	Annual Constant: 15.04		

Year	Annual Interest	Annual Principal	Year End Balance
1	14.997226	0.041464	99.958536
2	14.990561	0.048129	99.910407
3	14.982824	0.055866	99.854541
4	14.973843	0.064847	99.789695
5	14.963419	0.075271	99.714424
6	14.951318	0.087371	99.627052
7	14.937273	0.101417	99.525636
8	14.920970	0.117720	99.407916
9	14.902046	0.136644	99.271272
10	14.880080	0.158610	99.112663
11	14.854583	0.184107	98.928556
12	14.824987	0.213703	98.714852
13	14.790633	0.248057	98.466796
14	14.750757	0.287933	98.178862
15	14.704470	0.334220	97.844643
16	14.650743	0.387947	97.456696
17	14.588378	0.450311	97.006385
18	14.515989	0.522701	96.483684
19	14.431962	0.606727	95.876957
20	14.334428	0.704261	95.172695
21	14.221215	0.817475	94.355221
22	14.089802	0.948887	93.406333
23	13.937264	1.101425	92.304908
24	13.760205	1.278484	91.026424
25	13.554683	1.484006	89.542417
26	13.316122	1.722567	87.819850
27	13.039212	1.999478	85.820372
28	12.717787	2.320903	83.499469
29	12.344691	2.693998	80.805471
30	11.911619	3.127071	77.678400
31	11.408928	3.629762	74.048639
32	10.825428	4.213262	69.835377
33	10.148127	4.890563	64.944813
34	9.361946	5.676743	59.268070
35	8.449384	6.589305	52.678765
36	7.390124	7.648566	45.030199
37	6.160582	8.878107	36.152092
38	4.733386	10.305303	25.846788
39	3.076762	11.961927	13.884861
40	1.153828	13.884861	0.000000

MORTGAGE AMORTIZATION TABLES
15.5%

5 YEARS
Monthly Payment: 2.405319
Annual Constant: 28.87

Year	Annual Interest	Annual Principal	Year End Balance
1	14.508522	14.355307	85.644693
2	12.118369	16.745461	68.899232
3	9.330256	19.533574	49.365658
4	6.077923	22.785907	26.579752
5	2.284078	26.579752	0.000000

10 YEARS
Monthly Payment: 1.644105
Annual Constant: 19.73

Year	Annual Interest	Annual Principal	Year End Balance
1	15.186226	4.543038	95.456962
2	14.429812	5.299453	90.157509
3	13.547455	6.181810	83.975699
4	12.518186	7.211079	76.764621
5	11.317544	8.411721	68.352900
6	9.916996	9.812269	58.540631
7	8.283256	11.446008	47.094623
8	6.377500	13.351764	33.742859
9	4.154436	15.574828	18.168031
10	1.561233	18.168031	0.000000

15 YEARS
Monthly Payment: 1.433990
Annual Constant: 17.21

Year	Annual Interest	Annual Principal	Year End Balance
1	15.373290	1.834594	98.165406
2	15.067831	2.140053	96.025353
3	14.711513	2.496371	93.528982
4	14.295868	2.912016	90.616965
5	13.811018	3.396866	87.220100
6	13.245441	3.962443	83.257657
7	12.585696	4.622188	78.635469
8	11.816104	5.391780	73.243689
9	10.918374	6.289510	66.954179
10	9.871173	7.336711	59.617468
11	8.649613	8.558271	51.059197
12	7.224664	9.983220	41.075977
13	5.562462	11.645422	29.430555
14	3.623504	13.584380	15.846175
15	1.361709	15.846175	0.000000

20 YEARS
Monthly Payment: 1.353881
Annual Constant: 16.25

Year	Annual Interest	Annual Principal	Year End Balance
1	15.444611	0.801957	99.198043
2	15.311086	0.935483	98.262560
3	15.155328	1.091240	97.171320
4	14.973637	1.272931	95.898389
5	14.761695	1.484874	94.413515
6	14.514464	1.732105	92.681411
7	14.226069	2.020499	90.660911
8	13.889656	2.356912	88.303999
9	13.497231	2.749337	85.554663
10	13.039468	3.207100	82.347562
11	12.505487	3.741081	78.606481
12	11.882598	4.363970	74.242511
13	11.155999	5.090570	69.151941
14	10.308421	5.938147	63.213794
15	9.319721	6.926847	56.286947
16	8.166404	8.080164	48.206783
17	6.821060	9.425509	38.781274
18	5.251716	10.994852	27.786422
19	3.421077	12.825491	14.960931
20	1.285638	14.960931	0.000000

25 YEARS
Monthly Payment: 1.319745
Annual Constant: 15.84

Year	Annual Interest	Annual Principal	Year End Balance
1	15.475002	0.361941	99.638059
2	15.414739	0.422204	99.215855
3	15.344442	0.492501	98.723354
4	15.262441	0.574502	98.148852
5	15.166786	0.670156	97.478696
6	15.055206	0.781737	96.696958
7	14.925047	0.911896	95.785062
8	14.773216	1.063727	94.721335
9	14.596106	1.240837	93.480499
10	14.389507	1.447436	92.033063
11	14.148510	1.688433	90.344630
12	13.867386	1.969557	88.375074
13	13.539456	2.297487	86.077587
14	13.156925	2.680018	83.397569
15	12.710703	3.126240	80.271329
16	12.190185	3.646757	76.624572
17	11.583002	4.253941	72.370631
18	10.874722	4.962221	67.408410
19	10.048514	5.788429	61.619982
20	9.084743	6.752200	54.867782
21	7.960504	7.876439	46.991343
22	6.649080	9.187863	37.803480
23	5.119304	10.717639	27.085842
24	3.334821	12.502121	14.583720
25	1.253223	14.583720	0.000000

(Continued)

Mortgage Amortization Tables
15.5%

30 YEARS	Monthly Payment: 1.304517 Annual Constant: 15.66		

| Year | Annual | | Year End Balance |
	Interest	Principal	
1	15.488560	0.165643	99.834357
2	15.460980	0.193223	99.641133
3	15.428808	0.225395	99.415739
4	15.391280	0.262923	99.152816
5	15.347504	0.306699	98.846117
6	15.296438	0.357765	98.488352
7	15.236871	0.417332	98.071020
8	15.167385	0.486818	97.584202
9	15.086330	0.567873	97.016329
10	14.991779	0.662424	96.353905
11	14.881486	0.772717	95.581188
12	14.752829	0.901374	94.679814
13	14.602751	1.051452	93.628362
14	14.427684	1.226519	92.401843
15	14.223469	1.430734	90.971109
16	13.985252	1.668950	89.302159
17	13.707373	1.946830	87.355328
18	13.383226	2.270977	85.084352
19	13.005110	2.649093	82.435258
20	12.564037	3.090166	79.345092
21	12.049525	3.604678	75.740414
22	11.449347	4.204856	71.535558
23	10.749240	4.904963	66.630596
24	9.932566	5.721637	60.908959
25	8.979916	6.674287	54.234671
26	7.868649	7.785554	46.449118
27	6.572357	9.081846	37.367272
28	5.060233	10.593970	26.773303
29	3.296341	12.357862	14.415441
30	1.238762	14.415441	0.000000

40 YEARS	Monthly Payment: 1.294400 Annual Constant: 15.54		

| Year | Annual | | Year End Balance |
	Interest	Principal	
1	15.497567	0.035233	99.964767
2	15.491700	0.041099	99.923668
3	15.484857	0.047942	99.875726
4	15.476875	0.055924	99.819802
5	15.467564	0.065236	99.754566
6	15.456702	0.076097	99.678469
7	15.444032	0.088768	99.589701
8	15.429252	0.103547	99.486154
9	15.412011	0.120788	99.365366
10	15.391900	0.140899	99.224466
11	15.368441	0.164359	99.060107
12	15.341075	0.191725	98.868383
13	15.309153	0.223647	98.644736
14	15.271916	0.260884	98.383853
15	15.228479	0.304321	98.079532
16	15.177809	0.354990	97.724542
17	15.118704	0.414096	97.310446
18	15.049757	0.483043	96.827403
19	14.969330	0.563469	96.263935
20	14.875513	0.657286	95.606648
21	14.766075	0.766724	94.839924
22	14.638416	0.894384	93.945540
23	14.489501	1.043298	92.902242
24	14.315793	1.217007	91.685235
25	14.113161	1.419638	90.265597
26	13.876792	1.656007	88.609590
27	13.601068	1.931732	86.677858
28	13.279435	2.253364	84.424494
29	12.904251	2.628549	81.795945
30	12.466598	3.066201	78.729744
31	11.956077	3.576723	75.153022
32	11.360554	4.172246	70.980776
33	10.665876	4.866923	66.113853
34	9.855536	5.677264	60.436589
35	8.910273	6.622526	53.814063
36	7.807625	7.725174	46.088889
37	6.521387	9.011413	37.077476
38	5.020990	10.511810	26.565667
39	3.270777	12.262022	14.303644
40	1.229155	14.303644	0.000000

MORTGAGE AMORTIZATION TABLES
16%

5 YEARS — Monthly Payment: 2.431806 — Annual Constant: 29.19

Year	Annual Interest	Annual Principal	Year End Balance
1	14.989065	14.192604	85.807396
2	12.544094	16.637575	69.169822
3	9.677926	19.503743	49.666079
4	6.318000	22.863668	26.802411
5	2.379258	26.802411	0.000000

10 YEARS — Monthly Payment: 1.675131 — Annual Constant: 20.11

Year	Annual Interest	Annual Principal	Year End Balance
1	15.685440	4.416135	95.583865
2	14.924669	5.176906	90.406960
3	14.032839	6.068735	84.338225
4	12.987374	7.114201	77.224024
5	11.761804	8.339770	68.884254
6	10.325106	9.776469	59.107785
7	8.640905	11.460669	47.647115
8	6.666567	13.435008	34.212108
9	4.352107	15.749467	18.462641
10	1.638934	18.462641	0.000000

15 YEARS — Monthly Payment: 1.468701 — Annual Constant: 17.63

Year	Annual Interest	Annual Principal	Year End Balance
1	15.875420	1.748989	98.251011
2	15.574120	2.050289	96.200723
3	15.220915	2.403493	93.797229
4	14.806864	2.817545	90.979684
5	14.321483	3.302926	87.676758
6	13.752485	3.871924	83.804835
7	13.085466	4.538943	79.265892
8	12.303539	5.320870	73.945021
9	11.386908	6.237501	67.707520
10	10.312369	7.312040	60.395480
11	9.052718	8.571691	51.823789
12	7.576066	10.048343	41.775446
13	5.845030	11.779379	29.996067
14	3.815787	13.808622	16.187445
15	1.436964	16.187445	0.000000

20 YEARS — Monthly Payment: 1.391256 — Annual Constant: 16.70

Year	Annual Interest	Annual Principal	Year End Balance
1	15.946693	0.748378	99.251622
2	15.817770	0.877302	98.374320
3	15.666636	1.028435	97.345885
4	15.489467	1.205605	96.140281
5	15.281776	1.413295	94.726986
6	15.038307	1.656764	93.070221
7	14.752895	1.942177	91.128045
8	14.418314	2.276757	88.851288
9	14.026096	2.668976	86.182312
10	13.566309	3.128762	83.053550
11	13.027315	3.667756	79.385794
12	12.395467	4.299604	75.086190
13	11.654771	5.040300	70.045890
14	10.786475	5.908597	64.137293
15	9.768596	6.926475	57.210818
16	8.575367	8.119705	49.091113
17	7.176579	9.518493	39.572621
18	5.536820	11.158251	28.414370
19	3.614580	13.080492	15.333878
20	1.361193	15.333878	0.000000

25 YEARS — Monthly Payment: 1.358889 — Annual Constant: 16.31

Year	Annual Interest	Annual Principal	Year End Balance
1	15.976481	0.330186	99.669814
2	15.919600	0.387067	99.282747
3	15.852919	0.453747	98.829000
4	15.774752	0.531915	98.297085
5	15.683118	0.623548	97.673537
6	15.575699	0.730967	96.942570
7	15.449775	0.856892	96.085678
8	15.302158	1.004509	95.081169
9	15.129110	1.177557	93.903613
10	14.926251	1.380415	92.523197
11	14.688446	1.618220	90.904977
12	14.409674	1.896993	89.007984
13	14.082878	2.223789	86.784195
14	13.699784	2.606883	84.177313
15	13.250694	3.055973	81.121340
16	12.724239	3.582427	77.538912
17	12.107091	4.199575	73.339337
18	11.383627	4.923039	68.416298
19	10.535531	5.771135	62.645163
20	9.541333	6.765333	55.879830
21	8.375864	7.930803	47.949027
22	7.009618	9.297048	38.651979
23	5.408008	10.898658	27.753320
24	3.530488	12.776179	14.977141
25	1.329525	14.977141	0.000000

(Continued)

Mortgage Amortization Tables
16%

30 YEARS	Monthly Payment: 1.344757 Annual Constant: 16.14		

| Year | Annual | | Year End Balance |
	Interest	Principal	
1	15.989487	0.147597	99.852403
2	15.964060	0.173024	99.679379
3	15.934253	0.202831	99.476548
4	15.899311	0.237773	99.238775
5	15.858350	0.278734	98.960041
6	15.810332	0.326752	98.633289
7	15.754042	0.383042	98.250247
8	15.688055	0.449029	97.801219
9	15.610701	0.526383	97.274836
10	15.520020	0.617064	96.657772
11	15.413718	0.723366	95.934407
12	15.289104	0.847980	95.086426
13	15.143021	0.994063	94.092364
14	14.971773	1.165310	92.927053
15	14.771025	1.366059	91.560994
16	14.535692	1.601392	89.959602
17	14.259819	1.877265	88.082338
18	13.936422	2.200662	85.881675
19	13.557312	2.579772	83.301903
20	13.112892	3.024192	80.277711
21	12.591912	3.545172	76.732539
22	11.981183	4.155901	72.576638
23	11.265242	4.871842	67.704796
24	10.425966	5.711118	61.993679
25	9.442107	6.694977	55.298702
26	8.288758	7.848326	47.450377
27	6.936721	9.200363	38.250014
28	5.351767	10.785317	27.464697
29	3.493772	12.643312	14.821385
30	1.315699	14.821385	0.000000

40 YEARS	Monthly Payment: 1.335648 Annual Constant: 16.03		

| Year | Annual | | Year End Balance |
	Interest	Principal	
1	15.997869	0.029912	99.970088
2	15.992716	0.035065	99.935023
3	15.986676	0.041106	99.893917
4	15.979594	0.048187	99.845730
5	15.971293	0.056488	99.789241
6	15.961562	0.066220	99.723022
7	15.950154	0.077627	99.645394
8	15.936781	0.091000	99.554394
9	15.921104	0.106677	99.447717
10	15.902727	0.125054	99.322663
11	15.881184	0.146598	99.176065
12	15.855929	0.171852	99.004213
13	15.826324	0.201457	98.802756
14	15.791619	0.236162	98.566594
15	15.750935	0.276846	98.289748
16	15.703243	0.324539	97.965209
17	15.647334	0.380447	97.584762
18	15.581794	0.445987	97.138775
19	15.504964	0.522818	96.615957
20	15.414898	0.612884	96.003073
21	15.309316	0.718466	95.284607
22	15.185545	0.842237	94.442371
23	15.040452	0.987329	93.455041
24	14.870364	1.157417	92.297624
25	14.670975	1.356807	90.940817
26	14.437237	1.590545	89.350272
27	14.163232	1.864549	87.485723
28	13.842025	2.185757	85.299967
29	13.465483	2.562299	82.737668
30	13.024074	3.003708	79.733960
31	12.506623	3.521159	76.212801
32	11.900030	4.127752	72.085050
33	11.188939	4.838843	67.246207
34	10.355347	5.672434	61.573772
35	9.378152	6.649629	54.924143
36	8.232616	7.795166	47.128978
37	6.889736	9.138045	37.990932
38	5.315518	10.712264	27.278668
39	3.470108	12.557674	14.720994
40	1.306787	14.720994	0.000000

MORTGAGE AMORTIZATION TABLES
16.5%

5 YEARS
Monthly Payment: 2.458452
Annual Constant: 29.51

Year	Annual		Year End Balance
	Interest	Principal	
1	15.470277	14.031148	85.968852
2	12.971777	16.529649	69.439203
3	10.028373	19.473052	49.966151
4	6.560843	22.940582	27.025569
5	2.475857	27.025569	0.000000

10 YEARS
Monthly Payment: 1.706423
Annual Constant: 20.48

Year	Annual		Year End Balance
	Interest	Principal	
1	16.185013	4.292063	95.707937
2	15.420733	5.056343	90.651594
3	14.520359	5.956717	84.694877
4	13.459658	7.017418	77.677459
5	12.210079	8.266996	69.410463
6	10.737991	9.739085	59.671378
7	9.003770	11.473306	48.198072
8	6.960740	13.516336	34.681737
9	4.553912	15.923164	18.758572
10	1.718504	18.758572	0.000000

15 YEARS
Monthly Payment: 1.503709
Annual Constant: 18.05

Year	Annual		Year End Balance
	Interest	Principal	
1	16.377674	1.666829	98.333171
2	16.080865	1.963638	96.369533
3	15.731204	2.313300	94.056233
4	15.319279	2.725225	91.331008
5	14.834003	3.210500	88.120508
6	14.262315	3.782188	84.338320
7	13.588828	4.455675	79.882645
8	12.795414	5.249089	74.633556
9	11.860719	6.183784	68.449772
10	10.759584	7.284919	61.164852
11	9.462372	8.582131	52.582721
12	7.934168	10.110335	42.472386
13	6.133840	11.910664	30.561722
14	4.012930	14.031573	16.530149
15	1.514354	16.530149	0.000000

20 YEARS
Monthly Payment: 1.428901
Annual Constant: 17.15

Year	Annual		Year End Balance
	Interest	Principal	
1	16.448772	0.698035	99.301965
2	16.324474	0.822333	98.479632
3	16.178043	0.968764	97.510867
4	16.005537	1.141271	96.369597
5	15.802313	1.344494	95.025102
6	15.562902	1.583906	93.441196
7	15.280858	1.865949	91.575247
8	14.948592	2.198215	89.377031
9	14.557160	2.589647	86.787384
10	14.096027	3.050781	83.736603
11	13.552780	3.594028	80.142575
12	12.912798	4.234010	75.908565
13	12.158856	4.987952	70.920613
14	11.270660	5.876147	65.044465
15	10.224306	6.922502	58.121963
16	8.991629	8.155179	49.966785
17	7.539451	9.607356	40.359428
18	5.828687	11.318120	29.041308
19	3.813291	13.333517	15.707791
20	1.439016	15.707791	0.000000

25 YEARS
Monthly Payment: 1.398245
Annual Constant: 16.78

Year	Annual		Year End Balance
	Interest	Principal	
1	16.477908	0.301028	99.698972
2	16.424305	0.354631	99.344341
3	16.361156	0.417780	98.926561
4	16.286763	0.492173	98.434389
5	16.199123	0.579813	97.854575
6	16.095876	0.683059	97.171516
7	15.974245	0.804691	96.366825
8	15.830955	0.947980	95.418845
9	15.662150	1.116785	94.302059
10	15.463286	1.315649	92.986410
11	15.229011	1.549925	91.436485
12	14.953019	1.825917	89.610569
13	14.627881	2.151054	87.459514
14	14.244847	2.534089	84.925426
15	13.793607	2.985329	81.940097
16	13.262015	3.516921	78.423176
17	12.635763	4.143172	74.280004
18	11.897996	4.880939	69.399064
19	11.028857	5.750079	63.648985
20	10.004951	6.773985	56.875000
21	8.798720	7.980216	48.894785
22	7.377698	9.401238	39.493547
23	5.703637	11.075299	28.418249
24	3.731480	13.047456	15.370792
25	1.408143	15.370792	0.000000

(Continued)

Mortgage Amortization Tables
16.5%

30 YEARS	Monthly Payment: 1.385148
	Annual Constant: 16.63

Year	Annual		Year End Balance
	Interest	Principal	
1	16.490355	0.131422	99.868578
2	16.466953	0.154824	99.713754
3	16.439384	0.182393	99.531361
4	16.406906	0.214871	99.316490
5	16.368644	0.253133	99.063357
6	16.323569	0.298208	98.765148
7	16.270467	0.351310	98.413839
8	16.207910	0.413867	97.999972
9	16.134214	0.487563	97.512409
10	16.047395	0.574382	96.938027
11	15.945115	0.676662	96.261365
12	15.824623	0.797154	95.464212
13	15.682676	0.939101	94.525110
14	15.515452	1.106325	93.418785
15	15.318451	1.303326	92.115459
16	15.086370	1.535407	90.580052
17	14.812963	1.808814	88.771237
18	14.490870	2.130907	86.640331
19	14.111424	2.510353	84.129977
20	13.664410	2.957367	81.172610
21	13.137797	3.483980	77.688631
22	12.517411	4.104366	73.584265
23	11.786555	4.835222	68.749043
24	10.925556	5.696221	63.052821
25	9.911240	6.710537	56.342285
26	8.716307	7.905470	48.436815
27	7.308595	9.313182	39.123633
28	5.650215	10.971562	28.152071
29	3.696529	12.925248	15.226823
30	1.394954	15.226823	0.000000

40 YEARS	Monthly Payment: 1.376959
	Annual Constant: 16.53

Year	Annual		Year End Balance
	Interest	Principal	
1	16.498138	0.025374	99.974626
2	16.493620	0.029892	99.944734
3	16.488297	0.035215	99.909519
4	16.482026	0.041486	99.868033
5	16.474639	0.048873	99.819160
6	16.465936	0.057576	99.761584
7	16.455684	0.067828	99.693756
8	16.443605	0.079906	99.613849
9	16.429377	0.094135	99.519714
10	16.412614	0.110898	99.408817
11	16.392867	0.130645	99.278172
12	16.369603	0.153909	99.124263
13	16.342197	0.181315	98.942948
14	16.309911	0.213601	98.729347
15	16.271875	0.251637	98.477710
16	16.227067	0.296445	98.181265
17	16.174279	0.349233	97.832033
18	16.112092	0.411420	97.420613
19	16.038831	0.484681	96.935932
20	15.952525	0.570987	96.364945
21	15.850850	0.672661	95.692284
22	15.731071	0.792441	94.899843
23	15.589962	0.933549	93.966294
24	15.423727	1.099785	92.866509
25	15.227890	1.295621	91.570888
26	14.997182	1.526330	90.044557
27	14.725391	1.798121	88.246436
28	14.405203	2.118309	86.128127
29	14.027999	2.495512	83.632615
30	13.583628	2.939884	80.692731
31	13.060129	3.463383	77.229348
32	12.443411	4.080101	73.149247
33	11.716875	4.806637	68.342610
34	10.860966	5.662546	62.680064
35	9.852647	6.670865	56.009198
36	8.664778	7.858734	48.150465
37	7.265388	9.258124	38.892341
38	5.616811	10.906700	27.985641
39	3.674676	12.848836	15.136804
40	1.386707	15.136804	0.000000

MORTGAGE AMORTIZATION TABLES
17%

5 YEARS
Monthly Payment: 2.485258
Annual Constant: 29.83

Year	Annual Interest	Annual Principal	Year End Balance
1	15.952148	13.870943	86.129057
2	13.401396	16.421695	69.707362
3	10.381582	19.441509	50.265853
4	6.806449	23.016641	27.249211
5	2.573879	27.249211	0.000000

10 YEARS
Monthly Payment: 1.737977
Annual Constant: 20.86

Year	Annual Interest	Annual Principal	Year End Balance
1	16.684926	4.170792	95.829208
2	15.917952	4.937766	90.891441
3	15.009937	5.845781	85.045660
4	13.934947	6.920772	78.124889
5	12.662274	8.193444	69.931444
6	11.155567	9.700151	60.231293
7	9.371790	11.483928	48.747365
8	7.259990	13.595728	35.151637
9	4.759848	16.095870	19.055767
10	1.799951	19.055767	0.000000

15 YEARS
Monthly Payment: 1.539004
Annual Constant: 18.47

Year	Annual Interest	Annual Principal	Year End Balance
1	16.880037	1.588015	98.411985
2	16.588014	1.880038	96.531948
3	16.242290	2.225761	94.306187
4	15.832991	2.635060	91.671126
5	15.348426	3.119626	88.551501
6	14.774752	3.693299	84.858202
7	14.095585	4.372466	80.485735
8	13.291525	5.176527	75.309208
9	12.339604	6.128447	69.180761
10	11.212634	7.255418	61.925343
11	9.878422	8.589629	53.335714
12	8.298860	10.169191	43.166523
13	6.428830	12.039221	31.127302
14	4.214917	14.253134	16.874168
15	1.593884	16.874168	0.000000

20 YEARS
Monthly Payment: 1.466801
Annual Constant: 17.61

Year	Annual Interest	Annual Principal	Year End Balance
1	16.950839	0.650768	99.349232
2	16.831168	0.770438	98.578794
3	16.689491	0.912115	97.666679
4	16.521761	1.079846	96.586833
5	16.323186	1.278421	95.308412
6	16.088095	1.513512	93.794900
7	15.809773	1.791834	92.003066
8	15.480269	2.121337	89.881729
9	15.090173	2.511434	87.370295
10	14.628341	2.973266	84.397029
11	14.081582	3.520025	80.877004
12	13.434278	4.167328	76.709676
13	12.667941	4.933665	71.776011
14	11.760681	5.840926	65.935085
15	10.686583	6.915024	59.020061
16	9.414967	8.186639	50.833422
17	7.909512	9.692094	41.141328
18	6.127216	11.474390	29.666937
19	4.017171	13.584436	16.082501
20	1.519105	16.082501	0.000000

25 YEARS
Monthly Payment: 1.437797
Annual Constant: 17.26

Year	Annual Interest	Annual Principal	Year End Balance
1	16.979280	0.274279	99.725721
2	16.928843	0.324716	99.401005
3	16.869130	0.384429	99.016576
4	16.798437	0.455122	98.561453
5	16.714743	0.538816	98.022637
6	16.615660	0.637899	97.384738
7	16.498355	0.755204	96.629534
8	16.359479	0.894080	95.735454
9	16.195065	1.058494	94.676961
10	16.000417	1.253142	93.423819
11	15.769975	1.483584	91.940235
12	15.497156	1.756403	90.183832
13	15.174168	2.079391	88.104441
14	14.791785	2.461774	85.642667
15	14.339085	2.914474	82.728194
16	13.803138	3.450421	79.277773
17	13.168634	4.084925	75.192848
18	12.417450	4.836109	70.356739
19	11.528130	5.725429	64.631309
20	10.475271	6.778288	57.853021
21	9.228799	8.024760	49.828261
22	7.753112	9.500447	40.327815
23	6.006059	11.247500	29.080314
24	3.937737	13.315822	15.764492
25	1.489067	15.764492	0.000000

(Continued)

Mortgage Amortization Tables
17%

30 YEARS	Monthly Payment: 1.425675 Annual Constant: 17.11

Year	Annual		Year End Balance
	Interest	Principal	
1	16.991166	0.116938	99.883062
2	16.969662	0.138442	99.744620
3	16.944204	0.163900	99.580720
4	16.914064	0.194040	99.386680
5	16.878382	0.229722	99.156957
6	16.836138	0.271967	98.884991
7	16.786125	0.321979	98.563012
8	16.726916	0.381188	98.181824
9	16.656819	0.451286	97.730538
10	16.573831	0.534273	97.196265
11	16.475582	0.632522	96.563743
12	16.359267	0.748837	95.814906
13	16.221562	0.886542	94.928364
14	16.058534	1.049570	93.878794
15	15.865527	1.242577	92.636216
16	15.637027	1.471077	91.165140
17	15.366508	1.741596	89.423544
18	15.046243	2.061861	87.361683
19	14.667084	2.441020	84.920663
20	14.218201	2.889903	82.030760
21	13.686772	3.421333	78.609427
22	13.057617	4.050487	74.558940
23	12.312766	4.795338	69.763601
24	11.430943	5.677162	64.086440
25	10.386960	6.721145	57.365295
26	9.150997	7.957108	49.408188
27	7.687750	9.420354	39.987834
28	5.955425	11.152679	28.835155
29	3.904540	13.203564	15.631591
30	1.476514	15.631591	0.000000

40 YEARS	Monthly Payment: 1.418324 Annual Constant: 17.02

Year	Annual		Year End Balance
	Interest	Principal	
1	16.998375	0.021508	99.978492
2	16.994420	0.025463	99.953030
3	16.989738	0.030145	99.922885
4	16.984194	0.035688	99.887197
5	16.977632	0.042251	99.844945
6	16.969862	0.050021	99.794925
7	16.960664	0.059219	99.735706
8	16.949774	0.070109	99.665596
9	16.936881	0.083002	99.582595
10	16.921618	0.098265	99.484330
11	16.903548	0.116335	99.367995
12	16.882155	0.137728	99.230267
13	16.856828	0.163055	99.067212
14	16.826843	0.193040	98.874173
15	16.791345	0.228538	98.645635
16	16.749319	0.270564	98.375071
17	16.699564	0.320319	98.054752
18	16.640660	0.379223	97.675529
19	16.570924	0.448958	97.226571
20	16.488365	0.531518	96.695053
21	16.390623	0.629260	96.065793
22	16.274907	0.744976	95.320817
23	16.137912	0.881971	94.438847
24	15.975725	1.044158	93.394689
25	15.783713	1.236170	92.158519
26	15.556392	1.463491	90.695028
27	15.287268	1.732615	88.962413
28	14.968654	2.051228	86.911185
29	14.591450	2.428432	84.482753
30	14.144882	2.875001	81.607752
31	13.616193	3.403690	78.204062
32	12.990283	4.029600	74.174462
33	12.249272	4.770610	69.403851
34	11.371997	5.647886	63.755965
35	10.333397	6.686486	57.069480
36	9.103808	7.916075	49.153404
37	7.648107	9.371776	39.781629
38	5.924715	11.095168	28.686461
39	3.884405	13.135478	15.550983
40	1.468900	15.550983	0.000000

MORTGAGE AMORTIZATION TABLES
17.5%

5 YEARS
Monthly Payment: 2.512221
Annual Constant: 30.15

Year	Annual Interest	Annual Principal	Year End Balance
1	16.434667	13.711990	86.288010
2	13.832931	16.313726	69.974284
3	10.737536	19.409120	50.565164
4	7.054817	23.091840	27.473325
5	2.673332	27.473325	0.000000

10 YEARS
Monthly Payment: 1.769788
Annual Constant: 21.24

Year	Annual Interest	Annual Principal	Year End Balance
1	17.185163	4.052288	95.947712
2	16.416275	4.821176	91.126536
3	15.501497	5.735954	85.390582
4	14.413148	6.824304	78.566279
5	13.118293	8.119159	70.447120
6	11.577749	9.659702	60.787418
7	9.744901	11.492550	49.294868
8	7.564285	13.673166	35.621702
9	4.969915	16.267536	19.354166
10	1.883285	19.354166	0.000000

15 YEARS
Monthly Payment: 1.574578
Annual Constant: 18.90

Year	Annual Interest	Annual Principal	Year End Balance
1	17.382493	1.512446	98.487554
2	17.095519	1.799420	96.688133
3	16.754093	2.140846	94.547288
4	16.347886	2.547053	92.000235
5	15.864604	3.030335	88.969899
6	15.289623	3.605316	85.364583
7	14.605544	4.289395	81.075188
8	13.791666	5.103272	75.971915
9	12.823363	6.071576	69.900339
10	11.671332	7.223607	62.676732
11	10.300712	8.594227	54.082505
12	8.670029	10.224910	43.857594
13	6.729937	12.165002	31.692592
14	4.421729	14.473210	17.219382
15	1.675557	17.219382	0.000000

20 YEARS
Monthly Payment: 1.504942
Annual Constant: 18.06

Year	Annual Interest	Annual Principal	Year End Balance
1	17.452885	0.606418	99.393582
2	17.337822	0.721481	98.672101
3	17.200927	0.858376	97.813726
4	17.038058	1.021245	96.792480
5	16.844285	1.215018	95.577462
6	16.613745	1.445558	94.131905
7	16.339463	1.719840	92.412064
8	16.013137	2.046166	90.365898
9	15.624894	2.434409	87.931490
10	15.162985	2.896318	85.035172
11	14.613433	3.445870	81.589302
12	13.959608	4.099695	77.489607
13	13.181725	4.877578	72.612028
14	12.256245	5.803058	66.808970
15	11.155163	6.904141	59.904829
16	9.845159	8.214144	51.690685
17	8.286593	9.772710	41.917976
18	6.432303	11.627000	30.290976
19	4.226176	13.833127	16.457848
20	1.601455	16.457848	0.000000

25 YEARS
Monthly Payment: 1.477530
Annual Constant: 17.74

Year	Annual Interest	Annual Principal	Year End Balance
1	17.480595	0.249761	99.750239
2	17.433205	0.297151	99.453087
3	17.376823	0.353533	99.099554
4	17.309743	0.420613	98.678941
5	17.229935	0.500421	98.178519
6	17.134984	0.595372	97.583147
7	17.022017	0.708339	96.874808
8	16.887616	0.842741	96.032068
9	16.727713	1.002644	95.029424
10	16.537470	1.192887	93.836537
11	16.311129	1.419227	92.417310
12	16.041843	1.688514	90.728796
13	15.721461	2.008895	88.719901
14	15.340290	2.390067	86.329834
15	14.886795	2.843562	83.486273
16	14.347252	3.383104	80.103168
17	13.705336	4.025020	76.078148
18	12.941622	4.788734	71.289414
19	12.033000	5.697357	65.592058
20	10.951973	6.778383	58.813675
21	9.665831	8.064525	50.749150
22	8.135655	9.594702	41.154448
23	6.315140	11.415217	29.739231
24	4.149197	13.581159	16.158072
25	1.572285	16.158072	0.000000

(Continued)

Mortgage Amortization Tables
17.5%

30 YEARS	Monthly Payment: 1.466325 Annual Constant: 17.60

| Year | Annual | | Year End |
	Interest	Principal	Balance
1	17.491921	0.103981	99.896019
2	17.472192	0.123711	99.772308
3	17.448719	0.147184	99.625123
4	17.420792	0.175111	99.450012
5	17.387566	0.208337	99.241675
6	17.348035	0.247867	98.993808
7	17.301005	0.294898	98.698910
8	17.245050	0.350852	98.348057
9	17.178479	0.417424	97.930634
10	17.099276	0.496627	97.434007
11	17.005045	0.590857	96.843150
12	16.892935	0.702968	96.140182
13	16.759553	0.836350	95.303833
14	16.600862	0.995040	94.308792
15	16.412062	1.183841	93.124951
16	16.187438	1.408465	91.716487
17	15.920193	1.675709	90.040777
18	15.602241	1.993661	88.047116
19	15.223961	2.371942	85.675174
20	14.773904	2.821998	82.853175
21	14.238454	3.357449	79.495726
22	13.601405	3.994497	75.501229
23	12.843483	4.752420	70.748809
24	11.941750	5.654152	65.094657
25	10.868922	6.726981	58.367676
26	9.592533	8.003370	50.364306
27	8.073960	9.521943	40.842364
28	6.267250	11.328652	29.513711
29	4.117733	13.478170	16.035541
30	1.560362	16.035541	0.000000

40 YEARS	Monthly Payment: 1.459733 Annual Constant: 17.52

| Year | Annual | | Year End |
	Interest	Principal	Balance
1	17.498585	0.018217	99.981783
2	17.495128	0.021673	99.960110
3	17.491016	0.025786	99.934324
4	17.486123	0.030678	99.903646
5	17.480302	0.036499	99.867147
6	17.473377	0.043425	99.823722
7	17.465137	0.051664	99.772058
8	17.455335	0.061467	99.710591
9	17.443672	0.073130	99.637462
10	17.429796	0.087005	99.550456
11	17.413287	0.103514	99.446942
12	17.393647	0.123155	99.323788
13	17.370279	0.146523	99.177265
14	17.342478	0.174324	99.002941
15	17.309401	0.207400	98.795541
16	17.270048	0.246753	98.548788
17	17.223229	0.293572	98.255215
18	17.167526	0.349275	97.905940
19	17.101254	0.415547	97.490393
20	17.022408	0.494394	96.995999
21	16.928600	0.588201	96.407798
22	16.816994	0.699807	95.707990
23	16.684211	0.832590	94.875400
24	16.526234	0.990567	93.884833
25	16.338282	1.178519	92.706314
26	16.114668	1.402133	91.304181
27	15.848625	1.668176	89.636005
28	15.532103	1.984699	87.651306
29	15.155522	2.361279	85.290027
30	14.707489	2.809312	82.480714
31	14.174446	3.342356	79.138358
32	13.540261	3.976540	75.161818
33	12.785746	4.731056	70.430762
34	11.888067	5.628734	64.802028
35	10.820061	6.696740	58.105288
36	9.549410	7.967391	50.137897
37	8.037664	9.479137	40.658759
38	6.239076	11.277725	29.381034
39	4.099222	13.417580	15.963454
40	1.553347	15.963454	0.000000

MORTGAGE AMORTIZATION TABLES
18%

5 YEARS
Monthly Payment: 2.539343
Annual Constant: 30.48

Year	Annual Interest	Annual Principal	Year End Balance
1	16.917824	13.554288	86.445712
2	14.266359	16.205754	70.239958
3	11.096219	19.375893	50.864065
4	7.305943	23.166170	27.697894
5	2.774219	27.697894	0.000000

10 YEARS
Monthly Payment: 1.801852
Annual Constant: 21.63

Year	Annual Interest	Annual Principal	Year End Balance
1	17.685708	3.936516	96.063484
2	16.915654	4.706570	91.356915
3	15.994964	5.627260	85.729655
4	14.894169	6.728055	79.001600
5	13.578040	8.044184	70.957416
6	12.004451	9.617773	61.339643
7	10.123040	11.499184	49.840459
8	7.873591	13.748633	36.091826
9	5.184108	16.438116	19.653710
10	1.968514	19.653710	0.000000

15 YEARS
Monthly Payment: 1.610421
Annual Constant: 19.33

Year	Annual Interest	Annual Principal	Year End Balance
1	17.885028	1.440024	98.559976
2	17.603333	1.721719	96.838257
3	17.266534	2.058519	94.779738
4	16.863850	2.461202	92.318536
5	16.382394	2.942658	89.375878
6	15.806757	3.518295	85.857583
7	15.118515	4.206538	81.651045
8	14.295639	5.029413	76.621632
9	13.311795	6.013258	70.608374
10	12.135492	7.189560	63.418814
11	10.729084	8.595969	54.822845
12	9.047556	10.277497	44.545348
13	7.037091	12.287962	32.257386
14	4.633342	14.691710	17.565676
15	1.759377	17.565676	0.000000

20 YEARS
Monthly Payment: 1.543312
Annual Constant: 18.52

Year	Annual Interest	Annual Principal	Year End Balance
1	17.954904	0.564835	99.435165
2	17.844412	0.675327	98.759839
3	17.712305	0.807433	97.952406
4	17.554357	0.965381	96.987024
5	17.365511	1.154228	95.832797
6	17.139723	1.380015	94.452781
7	16.869767	1.649971	92.802810
8	16.547002	1.972736	90.830074
9	16.161099	2.358639	88.471435
10	15.699707	2.820031	85.651404
11	15.148057	3.371681	82.279723
12	14.488495	4.031243	78.248480
13	13.699911	4.819827	73.428653
14	12.757065	5.762673	67.665979
15	11.629782	6.889957	60.776023
16	10.281981	8.237757	52.538265
17	8.670526	9.849212	42.689053
18	6.743841	11.775897	30.913155
19	4.440261	14.079477	16.833678
20	1.686060	16.833678	0.000000

25 YEARS
Monthly Payment: 1.517430
Annual Constant: 18.21

Year	Annual Interest	Annual Principal	Year End Balance
1	17.981852	0.227308	99.772692
2	17.937386	0.271773	99.500919
3	17.884223	0.324937	99.175983
4	17.820659	0.388500	98.787482
5	17.744661	0.464498	98.322984
6	17.653797	0.555362	97.767622
7	17.545158	0.664001	97.103620
8	17.415267	0.793892	96.309728
9	17.259968	0.949192	95.360537
10	17.074288	1.134871	94.225666
11	16.852287	1.356872	92.868793
12	16.586858	1.622301	91.246492
13	16.269507	1.939653	89.306839
14	15.890075	2.319084	86.987755
15	15.436420	2.772739	84.215016
16	14.894022	3.315137	80.899879
17	14.245521	3.963638	76.936240
18	13.470161	4.738998	72.197242
19	12.543127	5.666032	66.531210
20	11.434748	6.774411	59.756799
21	10.109550	8.099609	51.657190
22	8.525120	9.684040	41.973151
23	6.630746	11.578414	30.394737
24	4.365797	13.843362	16.551375
25	1.657784	16.551375	0.000000

(Continued)

Mortgage Amortization Tables
18%

| **30** YEARS | Monthly Payment: 1.507085
Annual Constant: 18.09 |

Year	Annual Interest	Annual Principal	Year End Balance
1	17.992623	0.092402	99.907598
2	17.974547	0.110477	99.797121
3	17.952936	0.132089	99.665032
4	17.927097	0.157928	99.507105
5	17.896203	0.188821	99.318283
6	17.859266	0.225758	99.092525
7	17.815104	0.269920	98.822605
8	17.762303	0.322722	98.499883
9	17.699173	0.385852	98.114032
10	17.623693	0.461332	97.652700
11	17.533448	0.551576	97.101124
12	17.425550	0.659475	96.441649
13	17.296544	0.788480	95.653169
14	17.142303	0.942721	94.710448
15	16.957890	1.127134	93.583314
16	16.737402	1.347622	92.235691
17	16.473783	1.611242	90.624450
18	16.158595	1.926430	88.698020
19	15.781750	2.303275	86.394745
20	15.331188	2.753837	83.640908
21	14.792487	3.292537	80.348371
22	14.148407	3.936618	76.411753
23	13.378333	4.706692	71.705062
24	12.457619	5.627406	66.077656
25	11.356796	6.728229	59.349427
26	10.040632	8.044393	51.305035
27	8.467003	9.618022	41.687013
28	6.585543	11.499482	30.187531
29	4.336035	13.748989	16.438542
30	1.646483	16.438542	0.000000

| **40** YEARS | Monthly Payment: 1.501182
Annual Constant: 18.02 |

Year	Annual Interest	Annual Principal	Year End Balance
1	17.998769	0.015419	99.984581
2	17.995753	0.018435	99.966146
3	17.992147	0.022041	99.944105
4	17.987835	0.026353	99.917752
5	17.982680	0.031508	99.886244
6	17.976516	0.037672	99.848572
7	17.969147	0.045041	99.803532
8	17.960336	0.053852	99.749680
9	17.949802	0.064386	99.685294
10	17.937207	0.076981	99.608313
11	17.922148	0.092040	99.516273
12	17.904143	0.110045	99.406229
13	17.882616	0.131571	99.274657
14	17.856879	0.157309	99.117348
15	17.826106	0.188082	98.929267
16	17.789314	0.224874	98.704393
17	17.745325	0.268863	98.435530
18	17.692730	0.321458	98.114072
19	17.629847	0.384341	97.729732
20	17.554663	0.459525	97.270207
21	17.464772	0.549416	96.720791
22	17.357296	0.656892	96.063900
23	17.228796	0.785392	95.278508
24	17.075159	0.939028	94.339479
25	16.891468	1.122719	93.216760
26	16.671844	1.342344	91.874416
27	16.409257	1.604931	90.269485
28	16.095304	1.918884	88.350601
29	15.719935	2.294253	86.056348
30	15.271137	2.743050	83.313298
31	14.734547	3.279641	80.033657
32	14.092989	3.921198	76.112458
33	13.325932	4.688256	71.424202
34	12.408824	5.605364	65.818838
35	11.312313	6.701875	59.116963
36	10.001304	8.012884	51.104079
37	8.433838	9.580349	41.523730
38	6.559748	11.454440	30.069290
39	4.319051	13.695136	16.374154
40	1.640034	16.374154	0.000000

CHAPTER 5

Key Rankings

CONTENTS

Tables are indicated by page numbers in italics; accompanying charts by a dagger: †

5.07 The Biggest   5.53

5.08 Publicly Registered Investment Programs   5.87

5.09 Quality of Life   5.101

This section focuses on a broad range of leaders — in size, performance, or quality — with emphasis on investment sponsor rankings and the performance of various stock, mutual fund, money market fund, and pension fund programs. We also list the largest industrial corporations, insurance companies, banks, real estate brokers, and 1984's biggest deals.

In looking at the performance rankings, however, keep in mind that past performance is no guarantee of continued success, though a company's successful track record is at least an indication that it might have the capacity to do well in the future. By studying the mutual fund rankings, an investor can judge the performance of various companies over 10-year, 5-year, and 1-year intervals. This information can help identify those funds that maintained their positions over the long term and those that shone brightly before sinking back down into the ranks.

Included as a matter of interest are a number of other leaders — best-paid occupations with the greatest demand, best retirement cities and states, zip codes with the highest income and fastest growth, and so on. This kind of information can be applied to a variety of decisions — when selecting a profession, considering a place to retire, or pinpointing an area for marketing luxury products.

5.01 **Stocks**

Common stocks are traded on several different exchanges. The stocks of the largest companies are generally traded on the New York Stock Exchange, while those of smaller companies are more frequently traded on the American Stock Exchange. A number of regional exchanges trade stocks of local corporations, as well as stocks also listed on both the New York and American Exchanges.

The Over-the-Counter Market (OTC) does not have a specific location, but consists of a telephone and wire network linking brokers and dealers. Small or newer companies are generally traded on the OTC. The National Association of Securities Dealers Automated Quote System (NASDAQ) provides trading information for many but not all of the OTC stocks.

Large institutional traders such as mutual and pension funds and insurance companies often make direct trades of large blocks of stock. Information on these transactions is available through the Instinet System.

MAJOR STOCK EXCHANGES

United States

AMERICAN STOCK EXCHANGE, INC.
86 Trinity Place
New York, New York 10006

BOSTON STOCK EXCHANGE, INC.
53 State Street
Boston, Massachusetts 02109

THE CINCINNATI STOCK EXCHANGE, INC.
205 Dixie Terminal Building
Cincinnati, Ohio 45202

INTERMOUNTAIN STOCK EXCHANGE, INC.
39 Exchange Place
Salt Lake City, Utah 84111

MIDWEST STOCK EXCHANGE, INC.
120 South LaSalle Street
Chicago, Illinois 60603

NEW YORK STOCK EXCHANGE, INC.
11 Wall Street
New York, New York 10005

PACIFIC STOCK EXCHANGE, INC.
301 Pine Street
San Francisco, California 94104

618 South Spring Street
Los Angeles, California 90014

PHILADELPHIA STOCK EXCHANGE, INC.
17th Street & Stock Exchange Place
Philadelphia, Pennsylvania 19103

SPOKANE STOCK EXCHANGE, INC.
225 Peyton Building
Spokane, Washington 99201

Canada

ALBERTA STOCK EXCHANGE
201 Sun Oil Building
500 Fourth Avenue, S.W.
Calgary, Alberta T2P 2V6

MONTREAL STOCK EXCHANGE
The Stock Exchange Tower
800 Victoria Square
Montreal, Quebec H4Z 1A9

TORONTO STOCK EXCHANGE
234 Bay Street
Toronto, Ontario M5J 1R1

VANCOUVER STOCK EXCHANGE
536 Howe Street
Vancouver, B.C. V6C 2E1

WINNIPEG STOCK EXCHANGE
167 Lombard Avenue
Winnipeg, Manitoba R3B OT

STOCK PERFORMANCE

The following three tables show stock performances. The first table shows total return to investors for 1984; the second shows total return to investors for the ten years between 1974 and 1984; the third shows return on stockholders' equity for 1984. The ten-year figures are average annual averages, compounded. The tables for total return to stockholders include both price appreciation and dividend yield. The figures shown assume sales at the end of 1984 of stock owned at the end of 1974 and 1983. It has also been assumed that any proceeds from cash dividends, the sales of rights and warrant offerings, and stock received in spinoffs were reinvested at the end of the year in which they were received.

Returns are adjusted for stock splits, stock dividends, recapitalizations, and corporate reorganizations as they occur. However, the costs of brokerage commissions and taxes are not reflected. If companies have more than one class of shares outstanding, only the more widely held and actively traded have been considered. Results are listed as not available (n/av.) if shares are not publicly traded or are traded on only a limited basis.

The median figures refer only to results of companies listed in the *Fortune 500* (see page 5.56 for a list of the top 100) and no attempt has been made to calculate medians in groups with fewer than four companies.

TOTAL RETURN TO INVESTORS
1984

The Ten Highest	Sales Rank	Percentage Return	The Industry Medians, cont'd.	Sales Rank	Percentage Return
Tyson Foods	364	118.67	Soaps, cosmetics		5.67
Mattel	334	105.00	Petroleum refining		2.74
Hasbro Bradley	373	101.87	Glass, concrete, abrasives, gypsum		2.25
Harcourt Brace Jovanovich	376	69.91	Chemicals		1.59
Macmillan	446	68.36	Shipbuilding; railroad and transportation equipment		.91
Avco	176	59.29	Motor vehicles and parts		−1.46
Data General	279	57.72	Metal products		−1.74
Digital Equipment	65	53.82	Paper, fiber, and wood products		−3.70
Management Assistance	487	51.75	Measuring, scientific, photographic equipment		−5.23
G.D. Searle	266	50.77	Musical instruments; toys; sporting goods		−6.00
The Five Lowest			Electronics, appliances		−6.02
Storage Technology	340	−83.49	Apparel		−6.93
Tosco	189	−80.00	Office equipment (includes computers)		−7.60
Allis-Chalmers	253	−64.66	Rubber, plastic products		−8.17
Inspiration Resources	329	−58.89	Mining, crude-oil production		−8.41
Oak Industries	490	−57.45	Industrial and farm equipment		−8.86
The Industry Medians			Textiles, vinyl flooring		−10.20
Publishing; printing		16.44	Metal manufacturing		−21.67
Beverages		16.44	Furniture		n/av.
Food		16.31	Jewelry, silverware		n/av.
Tobacco		15.82	Leather		n/av.
Aerospace		11.12	All Industries		−.75
Pharmaceuticals		7.78			

Note: *These data assume sale, at the end of 1984, of stock owned at the end of 1983. See page 5.54 for more detail on the 100 Largest U.S. Industrial Corporations.*

Source: Reprinted by permission from *Fortune;* © 1985 Time, Inc. All rights reserved.

TOTAL RETURN TO INVESTORS
1974–1984

The Ten Highest	Sales Rank	Percentage Return	The Industry Medians, cont'd.	Sales Rank	Percentage Return
Advanced Micro Devices	424	70.89	Rubber, plastic products		21.90
Prime Computer	400	66.32	Office equipment (includes computers)		21.84
Hasbro Bradley	373	63.84	Beverages		21.67
Computervision	436	58.38	Motor vehicles and parts		20.72
Wang Laboratories	165	55.92	Electronics, appliances		20.63
Tyson Foods	364	52.80	Textiles, vinyl flooring		20.42
MEI	369	52.74	Tobacco		20.27
Tracor	456	50.93	Paper, fiber, and wood products		19.56
Teledyne	113	50.31	Food		19.35
ConAgra	121	49.51	Industrial and farm equipment		18.63
The Five Lowest			Glass, concrete, abrasives, gypsum		17.09
Tosco	189	−6.99	Metal products		16.18
Manville	204	−6.57	Mining; crude-oil production		14.77
Inspiration Resources	329	−5.46	Chemicals		14.71
International Harvester	79	−4.46	Petroleum refining		14.67
Phelps Dodge	306	−3.83	Measuring, scientific, photographic equipment		14.04
The Industry Medians			Metal manufacturing		12.83
Apparel		27.70	Pharmaceuticals		8.47
Publishing; printing		27.08	Soaps, cosmetics		6.54
Aerospace		26.76	Leather		n/av.
Shipbuilding; railroad and transportation equipment		26.31	Jewelry, silverware		n/av.
Musical instruments; toys, sporting goods		25.28	Furniture		n/av.
			All Industries		18.65

Note: *The total return is an annual average, compounded, assuming the sale, at the end of 1984, of stock owned at the end of 1983. See page 5.54 for more detail on the 100 Largest U.S. Industrial Corporations.*

Source: Reprinted by permission from *Fortune;* © 1985 Time Inc. All rights reserved.

RETURN ON STOCKHOLDERS' EQUITY
1984

Stockholders' equity is the sum of capital stock, surplus, and retained earnings at the company's year-end. Redeemable preferred stock is excluded if its redemption is either mandatory or outside the control of the company, except in the case of cooperatives.

The Ten Highest	Sales Rank	Percentage Return
Weirton Steel	289	100.0
Chrysler	14	72.0
Mattel	334	56.5
Kellogg	143	51.4
Teledyne	113	49.5
Harris Graphics	475	42.3
Wilson Foods	192	38.6
Colt Industries	195	38.5
General Dynamics	44	35.9
EG&G	291	35.7

The Industry Medians	Percentages	
	1984	1983
Tobacco	23.8	n/av.
Publishing; printing	18.4	17.8
Pharmaceuticals	18.1	17.5
Soaps, cosmetics	17.4	14.7
Food	16.2	14.5
Beverages	15.7	16.9
Motor vehicles and parts	15.4	9.9
Electronics; appliances	14.5	12.0
Shipbuilding; railroad and transportation equipment	14.3	13.2

The Industry Medians, cont'd.	Percentages	
	1984	1983
Musical instruments; toys; sporting goods	14.2	.0
Measuring, scientific, photographic equipment	14.0	9.9
Aerospace	13.9	13.4
Apparel	13.9	13.0
Mining; crude-oil production	13.8	9.8
Office equipment (includes computers)	12.6	11.1
Paper, fiber, and wood products	12.4	7.1
Chemicals	12.2	9.8
Rubber, plastic products	12.1	10.0
Industrial and farm equipment	11.8	2.6
Metal products	11.7	9.5
Glass, concrete, abrasives, gypsum	9.5	8.0
Petroleum refining	9.5	9.5
Textiles, vinyl flooring	8.2	8.7
Metal manufacturing	7.1	.0
Leather	n/av.	n/av.
Furniture	n/av.	n/av.
Jewelry, silverware	n/av.	n/av.
All Industries	13.6	10.7

Note: *See page 5.54 for more detail on the 100 Largest U.S. Industrial Corporations.*

Source: Reprinted by permission from *Fortune;* © 1985 Time Inc. All rights reserved.

5.02 **Mutual Funds**

A mutual fund is a type of investment company that pools the investments of a number of individuals. The management is responsible for investing the shareholders' money according to the stated objectives of the fund. The investment company may follow one of a number of specialized policies: buying shares in a broad cross section of the economy, investing in rapidly growing companies, or buying only the shares of a particular industry, shares of foreign corporations, or bonds and preferred stocks. Many companies operate a number of funds with different objectives and allow investors to change their holdings among the various funds without charge.

An individual mutual fund investor, therefore, buys shares in the fund rather than in any one corporation. The value of these shares, the *net asset value,* is determined by dividing the total value of the fund's assets by the number of shares outstanding. Transactions in mutual funds are listed daily in the financial press and consist of: the current net asset value; the current offering price, which is the net asset value plus the maximum sales charge, if one is levied; and the change in net asset value since the previous day.

Two broad categories of mutual funds are distinguished by the sales charge or commission, known as the *load.* Share prices of load funds, which are sold through brokers, include commissions that vary with the fund. On sales of shares in no-load funds, which are made by the investment company itself directly to the public, no commission is charged. Holdings in a fund may be increased, without charge, if payments of dividends and capital gains earnings are used to buy more shares. Funds will redeem their own shares, for cash, on demand. Load funds do not usually charge a fee; no-load funds charge a fee of between 1 and 2%.

Taxation of mutual funds is fairly simple. In broad outline, the requirements are: that the mutual fund be considered "diversified" (i.e., for 50% of its holdings, no single stock may constitute more than 5% of the fund's portfolio and the fund may hold no more than 25% of the voting stock of any one issuer); that 90% of the fund's gross income be derived from interest, dividends, and stockholding profits; and that at least 90% of the income be distributed to the shareholders. Up to 100% may be distributed; any remaining income is taxable to the fund at corporate rates. Distributions to shareholders are taxable to the individuals, whether or not the money is reinvested in the fund. The details are spelled out in the Tax Code, §851 and §852, and a tax professional should be consulted for their application in specific instances.

Mutual funds offer investors several advantages:

- With a relatively small investment, the investor can create a diversified portfolio of securities.

- Systematic supervision of the fund makes it unnecessary for investors to become involved in the transactional details generally associated with stock ownership.

- Professional managers are assumed to be both astute and decisive in making the trading decisions that enable a well-balanced fund to meet specified investment goals.

- Costs can be lower than they would be if each investor were to go out and buy shares of the stocks comprising the fund.

- A well-balanced fund should perform as well as the overall market. Diversification can eliminate the unsystematic risk, that is, the variability in stock prices and returns that results from factors peculiar to an individual company. (See page 4.17 for an explanation of the risk-return relationship and the measurement of systematic or market risk.)

The following definitions of the most common investment objectives will help investors select particular goals and help clarify the information on fund rankings.

INVESTMENT OBJECTIVE DEFINITIONS

This glossary of terms used to describe the investment objectives of mutual funds has been derived from the prospectuses of the various funds and from a review of the funds' investment characteristics published in the *Lipper Equity Analysis Report on the Weighted Average Holdings of Large Investment Companies* and the *Lipper Portfolio Analysis Report on Fixed Income Funds.*

CA CAPITAL APPRECIATION FUND: A fund that aims at maximum capital appreciation, frequently by means of a portfolio turnover of 100% or more, leveraging, purchasing unregistered securities, purchasing options, etc. The fund may take large cash positions.

G GROWTH FUND: A fund that normally invests in companies whose long-term earnings are expected to grow significantly faster than the earnings of the stocks represented in the major unmanaged stock indexes.

SG SMALL COMPANY GROWTH FUND: A fund that limits its investments to companies on the basis of the size of the company.

GI GROWTH AND INCOME FUND: A fund that invests in companies whose earnings are believed to be growing and whose dividends, being steady or rising, will generate income as well.

EI EQUITY INCOME FUND: A fund that seeks relatively high current income and growth of income through investing 60% or more of its portfolio in equities.

EQUITY FUND AVERAGE: The average performance of the five categories of equity portfolios listed above.

B BALANCED FUND: A fund whose primary objective is to conserve principal by maintaining at all times a balanced portfolio of both stocks and bonds. Typically, the stock/bond ratio ranges around 60%/40%.

I INCOME FUND: A fund that normally seeks high income and has a maximum fixed income commitment of 75% of the portfolio and/or a maximum equity exposure of 60%.

NR NATURAL RESOURCES FUND: A fund that invests more than 50% of its assets in natural resources stocks.

S   **SPECIALTY FUND:** A fund that limits its investments to a specific industry, e.g., banks, utilities, etc.

GL   **GLOBAL FUND:** A fund that invests at least 25% of its portfolio in securities traded outside the United States and may own U.S. securities as well.

AU   **GOLD-ORIENTED FUND:** A fund that has at least 50% of its assets in shares of gold mines, gold-oriented mining finance houses, gold coins, or bullion.

IF   **INTERNATIONAL FUND:** A fund that invests its assets in securities primarily traded outside the United States.

OG   **OPTION GROWTH FUND:** A fund that attempts to increase its net asset value by investing at least 5% of its portfolio in options.

OI   **OPTION INCOME FUND:** A fund that writes covered options on at least 50% of its portfolio.

FI   **FIXED INCOME FUND:** A fund that normally has more than 75% of its assets in fixed income issues, e.g., money market instruments, bonds, or preferred stocks.

MUTUAL FUND INDUSTRY AVERAGE: The average of all open-end funds, excluding money market instrument funds, short-term U.S. government funds, and municipal bond funds.

MUTUAL FUND INDUSTRY MEDIAN: The midpoint in the performance range of the funds in the mutual fund industry average.

Source: Lipper Analytical Securities Corporation.

HOW MUTUAL FUNDS PERFORMED IN 1984

Type	% Change 12/31/83 to 12/27/84	% Change 12/31/82 to 12/31/83	Type	% Change 12/31/83 to 12/27/84	% Change 12/31/82 to 12/31/83
Fixed income	+10.61	+ 9.99	International	− 4.16	+32.08
Income	+ 8.59	+12.78	Global	− 4.07	+25.79
Equity income	+ 8.95	+19.69	Growth	− 3.78	+19.11
Balanced	+ 8.05	+18.75	Natural resources	− 7.11	+17.48
Specialty	+ 6.30	+18.95	Capital appreciation	− 8.87	+21.23
Option income	+ 3.45	+16.90	Small firm growth	−11.07	+26.25
Growth & income	+ 3.39	+20.46	Gold-oriented	−28.48	+ 1.55
Option growth	− 6.86	+12.29	Average, all funds	+ .61%	+17.63%

Note: *Includes reinvestment of dividends.*

Source: Lipper Analytical Services Inc.

MUTUAL FUND PERFORMANCE BY TYPE OF FUND
As of March 31, 1985

Total Reinvested Cumulative Performance (%)					
Type of Fund	No. of Current Funds	15 Years 3/31/70 to 3/31/85	10 Years 3/31/75 to 3/31/85	5 Years 3/31/80 to 3/31/85	12 Months 3/31/84 to 3/31/85
Capital Appreciation Funds	101	+364.38	+429.72	+134.46	+10.95
Growth Funds	186	+265.87	+343.21	+122.30	+13.45
Small Company Growth Funds	29	+344.74	+517.78	+145.56	+12.59
Growth and Income Funds	105	+328.68	+295.67	+125.99	+16.46
Equity Income Funds	35	+390.25	+342.76	+157.54	+19.33
Equity Funds Average	456	+309.58	+352.75	+128.93	+14.00
Balanced Funds	25	+272.51	+246.00	+124.59	+18.39
Income Funds	22	+271.86	+235.68	+121.24	+15.30
Natural Resources Funds	9	+248.87	+228.09	+ 62.09	+ 2.53
Specialty Funds	29	+235.58	+272.09	+123.09	+21.11
Global Funds	21	+376.84	+299.18	+117.23	+ 3.33
International Funds	17	+218.57	+149.54	+ 99.40	− 4.63
Gold-Oriented Funds	13	+491.40	+162.46	+ 67.20	−24.42
Option Growth Funds	4	+ 0.00	+ 0.00	+ 72.21	+10.01
Option Income Funds	12	+185.77	+222.59	+ 98.85	+12.04
Fixed Income Funds	183	+196.80	+156.79	+ 96.29	+13.71
All Funds Average	791	+297.27	+308.81	+119.60	+12.96
All Funds Median	791	+263.05	+264.14	+111.93	+14.17
Number of funds with a % change		229	384	453	690

Specialized Reinvested Indexes Cumulative Performance (%)					
Index	Value as of 3/31/85	15 Years 3/31/70 to 3/31/85	10 Years 3/31/75 to 3/31/85	5 Years 3/31/80 to 3/31/85	12 Months 3/31/84 to 3/31/85
Lipper Growth Fund Index	233.58	+185.10	+231.84	+109.94	+14.82
Lipper Growth and Income Fund Index	352.01	+302.34	+262.00	+111.91	+ 9.91
Lipper Balanced Fund Index	299.85	+238.51	+204.42	+106.51	+15.24
Cumulative Performance (%) of Unmanaged Indexes Without Dividends					
Dow Jones Industrial Average	1,266.78	+ 61.26	+ 64.91	+ 61.22	+ 8.75
Standard & Poor's 500	180.66	+101.56	+116.72	+ 76.96	+13.49

Estimated Cumulative Performance (%) of Reinvested Unmanaged Indexes					
Index	3/29/85	15 Years 3/31/70 to 3/31/85	10 Years 3/31/75 to 3/31/85	5 Years 3/31/80 to 3/31/85	12 Months 3/31/84 to 3/31/85
Dow Jones Industrial Reinvested	1,266.78	+239.20	+182.79	+112.53	+14.47
S & P 500 Reinvested	180.66	+292.60	+253.64	+127.35	+18.93

	2/28/85	15 Years 2/28/70 to 2/28/85	10 Years 2/28/75 to 2/28/85	5 Years 2/29/80 to 2/28/85	12 Months 2/29/84 to 2/28/85
Consumer Price Index	317.40	+178.67	+101.91	+34.26	+ 3.52

Note: *The method of calculating total return data on indexes uses actual dividends accumulated for the quarter and reinvested at quarter end. This calculation differs from that given in SEC release 327 of August 8, 1972, which uses the latest 12 month dividends. The latter method is used by Standard & Poor's.*

Source: Lipper Analytical Securities Corporation.

TOP 25 MUTUAL FUNDS
Selected Periods

Rank	Fund	% Rise in Return on Investment	Rank	Fund	% Rise in Return on Investment
	Fifteen Years: 3/31/70 to 3/31/85		20	Value Line Leverage Growth	669.38
1	Fidelity Magellan Fund	1442.35	21	Acorn Fund	665.94
2	International Investors	1297.84	22	Sigma Venture Shares	664.01
3	Mutual Shares Corp.	1099.69	23	Weingarten Equity	630.24
4	Templeton Growth	1026.06	24	Tudor Fund	611.50
5	Twentieth Century Select	1015.56	25	St. Paul Growth	595.57
6	Twentieth Century Growth	1005.63		**Five Years: 3/31/80 to 3/31/85**	
7	Pioneer 2	976.25	1	Fidelity Magellan Fund	389.86
8	Janus Fund	941.38	2	Lindner Fund	279.32
9	Quasar Associates	839.65	3	Lindner Dividend	273.26
10	Over-the-Counter Sec.	773.10	4	American Capital Pace	267.61
11	Weingarten Equity	717.09	5	Vanguard Qualified Dividend 1	265.51
12	Fidelity Equity–Income	713.43	6	Phoenix Stock	260.58
13	Charter Fund	674.73	7	Nicholas Fund	246.94
14	American Capital Pace	662.77	8	Lehman Capital Fund	241.93
15	Nicholas Fund	633.65	9	Sequoia Fund	240.12
16	American Capital Comstock	628.20	10	Loomis-Sayles Capital	239.40
17	Steinroe Special Fund	592.34	11	NEL Growth Fund	235.34
18	Windsor Fund	573.12	12	Pennsylvania Mutual	234.67
19	St. Paul Growth	571.25	13	Janus Fund	224.31
20	FPA Paramount	570.84	14	Phoenix Growth	222.20
21	Seligman Capital	567.74	15	Fidelity Equity–Income	217.78
22	Guardian Mutual	567.49	16	Windsor Fund	215.12
23	Security Ultra Fund	558.73	17	Tudor Fund	213.84
24	Putnam Voyager	543.18	18	Lehman Opportunity	211.73
25	American Mutal	539.87	19	Evergreen Total Return	205.11
	Ten Years: 3/31/75 to 3/31/85		20	Fidelity Destiny	205.11
1	Fidelity Magellan Fund	1588.10	21	United Vanguard Fund	204.94
2	Twentieth Century Growth	1153.55	22	FPA Paramount	204.77
3	Lindner Fund	1131.15	23	Twentieth Century Select	204.16
4	Twentieth Century Select	1035.89	24	Merrill Lynch Pacific	201.97
5	Evergreen Fund[1]	994.06	25	Ivy Growth	200.18
6	Pennsylvania Mutual	985.31		**One Year: 3/31/84 to 3/31/85**	
7	American Capital Pace	948.40	1	Pacific Horizon Aggregate Growth	54.71
8	Quasar Associates	923.68	2	Prudential-Bache Utility[2]	50.96
9	American Capital Venture	905.71	3	Fidelity Selected Utilities[1]	36.03
10	Sequoia Fund	857.57	4	Nicholas 2	35.71
11	Oppenheimer Special	778.23	5	Franklin Utilities	33.49
12	Nicholas Fund	752.20	6	Sequoia Fund	33.34
13	Mutual Shares Corp.	736.59	7	Energy & Utility Shares	33.34
14	Over-the-Counter Sec.	713.70	8	Vanguard Qualified Dividend 1	32.30
15	Fidelity Destiny	703.79	9	Franklin Equity Fund	32.26
16	American Capital Comstock	699.01	10	Guardian Park Avenue	31.91
17	Security Ultra Fund	688.47	11	Nicholas Fund	31.41
18	Pioneer 2	688.07	12	Magnacap Fund	31.06
19	Fidelity Equity–Income	670.99	13	Midamerica Mutual	31.00

(Continued)

Top 25 Mutual Funds

Rank	Fund	% Rise in Return on Investment	Rank	Fund	% Rise in Return on Investment
14	Fidelity Selected Financial[1]	30.87	7	Babson Enterprise	21.80
15	ABT Utility Income Fund	30.45	8	First Investor Discovery	21.59
16	Fidelity Qualified Dividend	30.17	9	First Investor International	20.16
17	Fidelity Selected Health[1]	30.09	10	Financial Portfolio—Gold	19.04
18	Nationwide Growth	29.68	11	Strategic Investments	19.01
19	Guardian Stock Fund	29.20	12	Westergaard Fund	18.80
20	Copley Tax-Managed	29.15	13	GIT Special Growth	18.69
21	Selected American Shares	29.03	14	United Services Gold Shares	18.50
22	Steinroe Discovery	28.74	15	ABT Emerging Growth	18.42
23	Evergreen Total Return	28.22	16	Vanguard Special—Service	18.31
24	Federated Stock Trust	28.10	17	"New Beginning" Growth	18.06
25	Clipper Fund	27.99	18	Lexington Goldfund	17.91
	First Quarter:12/31/84 to 3/31/85		19	Financial Portfolio—Leisure	17.90
1	First Investor Natural Resources	39.53	20	Vanguard Special—Health	17.77
2	Fidelity OTC	32.21	21	Franklin Gold Fund	17.73
3	Sherman, Dean Fund	31.76	22	Oppenheimer Challenger	17.31
4	Steinroe Discovery	24.26	23	Quasar Associates	16.91
5	Fidelity Selected Leisure	24.10	24	Vanguard Special—Gold	16.87
6	Fidelity Selected Health[1]	22.92	25	Fidelity Selected Precious Metals[1]	16.85

1 *Redemption fee may apply.*
2 *Performance reflects a change of 14.5% when the reversal of a reserve for taxes of $2.95 per share was distributed and reinvested at a price of $20.35 on August 24, 1984, a change necessitated when the fund became a regulated investment company under subchapter M of the IRS code.*

Source: Lipper Analytical Services, Inc.

TOP 50 MUTUAL FUNDS
1984

Assets in Millions of Dollars		Mutual Fund	Objective[1]	Closing Net Asset Value
9/30/84	9/30/83			
$95.5	$177.2	Prudential-Bache Util	EI	$11.24
76.5	49.0	*Vanguard Qualified Dividend	EI	16.51
6.2	4.9	*Copley Tax-Managed	GI	7.51
83.1	—	*American Telecommunications-Income	S	70.16
28.9	24.1	Franklin Utilities	S	6.24
9.4	9.5	*Energy & Utility Shares	S	22.42
24.7	16.4	Fidelity Select Utilities	S	17.33
188.8	133.7	*Fidelity Qualified Dividend	EI	13.16
2,287.7	1,683.4	*Windsor Fund	GI	12.65
417.1	324.8	*Sequoia Fund	G	39.26
202.0	93.8	*General Electric Long-Term Interest	FI	10.94
3.6	4.2	*Composite Income Fund	FI	9.43
21.8	15.2	Fidelity Select Financial	S	19.96
101.3	157.7	ABT Utility Income Fund	S	15.80
11.3	0.1	*Nicholas II	G	11.79
107.8	104.8	*Wellesley Income	I	13.28
33.2	—	*American Telecommunications-Growth	S	71.43
4.6	4.6	*FPA New Income	FI	8.50
43.8	22.0	*Federated Stock Trust	GI	16.04
11.9	9.6	Magnacap Fund	G	6.86
134.7	53.0	*Mutual Qualified Income	CA	16.75
19.2*	15.1	*North Star Bond Fund	FI	9.54
499.4	598.00	Eaton Vance Tx-Mgd Trust	EI	15.29
8.2	7.9	*Calvert Income	FI	15.13
35.3	37.3	Nation-Wide Securities	B	10.91
72.5	74.3	*Century Shares Trust	S	14.02
74.2	71.7	Investment Qual. Interest	FI	9.73
74.0	62.6	Franklin Income	I	2.02
51.3	48.1	American Leaders	GI	10.88
746.2	623.4	J. Hancock Bond	FI	14.36
33.2	34.1	Axe-Houghton Income	FI	4.63
21.9	23.6	Eaton Vance High Yield	I	4.84
1.9	2.0	*Ohio National-Bond	FI	9.37
13.4	1.3	*Lindner Dividend	EI	22.52
36.4	39.4	Monthly Income Shares	FI	11.08
118.1	118.2	Merrill Lynch High Quality	FI	10.44
196.1	146.5	*Federated GNMA Trust	FI	10.66
18.7	22.2	JP Income Fund	FI	8.24
81.6	80.8	*Selected American Shares	B	10.54
35.8	39.1	Eaton Vance of Boston	I	8.77
13.5	13.2	Sentinel Balanced Fund	B	9.60
289.4	281.8	Income Fund of America	EI	10.70
145.6	152.1	Putnam Income	FI	6.81
163.3	159.3	*Hutton Inv. SR-Bond	FI	10.88
56.6	43.4	Lutheran Bro. Fund	GI	14.75
436.9	238.0	*Mutual Shares Corp.	GI	50.32
3.9	0.8	*GIT Income A Rated	FI	9.75
149.0	147.3	*Federated Income Trust	I	10.38
37.6	40.5	Prudential-Bache Gov. Int.	FI	10.06
7.3	8.1	ISI Income Fund	I	3.71

Note: *Calculations include reinvestment of capital gains and dividends.*

* *Funds with no sales commission or "load."*

1 *See Investment Objective Definitions, page 5.14.*

Percentage Change Total Return					Rank		% Dividend Yield
15 yrs Dec. '69–Dec. '84	10 yrs Dec. '74–Dec. '84	5 yrs Dec. '79–Dec. '84	1 yr Dec. '83–Dec. '84	4th qtr. 1984	5 yrs Dec. '79–Dec. '84	1 yr Dec. '83–Dec. '84	12 Months
—	—	—	38.62	6.68	—	1	13.7
—	514.63	213.76	25.59	10.35	4	2	8.1
—	—	100.27	23.93	9.00	136	3	0.0
—	—	—	22.26	6.16	—	4	5.9
197.90	362.69	137.80	21.42	9.88	39	5	8.3
—	300.42	96.98	21.19	9.27	151	6	9.1
—	—	—	20.87	8.99	—	7	1.3
—	—	—	20.86	8.05	—	8	9.8
548.38	725.11	170.99	19.57	5.89	14	9	5.8
955.14	1,148.57	170.85	18.55	3.67	15	10	3.6
—	—	107.01	18.51	11.30	—	11	11.0
—	—	73.14	18.21	10.39	299	12	14.5
—	—	—	17.99	10.70	—	13	0.5
—	—	39.69	17.30	8.29	427	14	0.0
—	—	—	16.92	3.59	—	15	0.8
320.48	244.55	107.39	16.64	6.65	116	16	10.3
—	—	—	16.62	1.49	—	17	0.0
224.35	159.87	68.27	16.44	6.96	333	18	10.6
—	—	—	16.08	3.39	—	19	4.4
160.56	366.17	111.69	16.07	5.86	102	20	4.2
—	—	141.68	15.98	4.31	—	21	6.5
—	—	76.78	15.92	7.93	276	22	10.6
—	—	—	15.83	7.68	—	23	0.0
—	—	—	15.82	8.56	—	24	10.9
276.29	246.32	95.58	15.69	6.18	158	25	6.0
288.23	293.09	98.67	15.57	9.88	141	26	4.4
—	—	80.09	15.56	8.61	—	27	11.7
455.72	405.34	121.11	15.55	8.10	79	28	10.7
227.15	327.85	133.77	15.47	3.51	47	29	4.8
—	130.69	69.60	15.40	8.18	324	30	11.1
170.91	187.69	85.52	15.30	9.12	216	31	10.8
240.04	178.13	76.42	15.30	6.61	281	32	11.8
—	—	—	15.29	9.99	—	33	13.4
—	—	246.74	15.29	5.14	2	34	5.5
—	135.18	72.80	15.23	8.59	306	35	11.4
—	—	81.84	15.10	7.75	—	36	11.6
—	—	—	14.88	7.42	—	37	11.8
—	—	61.84	14.87	8.39	373	38	11.2
144.42	258.56	109.11	14.86	3.44	110	39	5.0
—	220.04	87.78	14.71	6.00	196	40	11.1
301.24	254.36	106.41	14.70	5.69	121	41	7.1
382.82	366.63	125.67	14.69	5.65	67	42	7.7
234.13	178.66	87.42	14.58	7.08	199	43	11.6
—	—	—	14.58	7.20	—	44	10.9
287.48	305.11	131.24	14.52	2.99	53	45	5.1
950.74	841.49	131.01	14.52	2.42	55	46	7.3
—	—	—	14.50	8.12	—	47	11.8
—	—	—	14.46	6.26	—	48	11.9
—	—	—	14.44	6.54	—	49	10.1
185.02	155.81	64.02	14.42	5.26	360	50	10.8

Source: Lipper Analytical Distributors.

5.03 Money Market Funds

Money market funds, like mutual funds, are offered by investment companies that pool the money of a number of shareholders to buy short-term securities such as Treasury bills, notes, certificates of deposit, repurchase agreements (repos), bankers' acceptances, and commercial paper. Interest on such funds is paid daily and is compounded. Yields are tied to the current cost of money, though there is generally a slight lag when rates shift. Activity in the money market funds is reported daily in the financial press.

The primary advantages of money market funds are their liquidity and convenience, rather than their profitability. They can be useful in combination with other investments or for temporary investments until more appropriate, long-term decisions are made. Brokers often use them to place proceeds from securities sales while deciding on new investments. An investment company might deposit new savings into a money market fund until there is enough money to invest in a specific fund. The price for such convenience is full taxation: all income, other than that from tax-exempt funds, is taxable. Advantages include the following.

- Because there are no sales commissions, or loads, on the purchase of shares in money market funds, the entire purchase price is invested.

- Interest is compounded daily.

- An account may be opened in some funds with as little as $500.

- The funds offer considerable liquidity, because shareholders may transfer their assets rapidly into whatever other types of mutual funds are offered by the same advisory firm. Most funds permit checks to be written out of the account, though such checks may take a week or more to clear.

- Such investments are generally considered safe, because the funds buy U.S. government-backed debt or that of well-rated corporations. Some money market funds are insured. Because of competition among funds, some managers may take extra risks to secure more desirable yields. For this reason, it is important to check the quality of the holdings in a fund before investing.

Because money market funds invest in short-term, fixed-income holdings, the interest rate is the key consideration. A manager who expects the cost of money to fall will try to extend maturity dates, to avoid having to invest new money for a lower yield. The success of a fund depends on the fund manager's ability to second-guess trends in the market place.

Beyond this, it is important to look for well-known, established organizations that have had many years of experience in managing fixed-income investments. It can generally be assumed that major insurance companies, brokerage firms, and mutual fund groups, to preserve their reputations, will avoid risk and take care in selecting investments.

Current yields of major money market funds may be found in the financial pages of most newspapers. More complete listings are found in *Barron's* and *The Wall Street Journal.*

SELECTED MONEY MARKET FUNDS

Fund	Year First Offered	Total Assets 4/17/85 ($000,000)	Min. $ Investment		Check Writing Minimum	Phone Exchange Priv.	Avg. Mat. (days)
			Initial	Subseq.			
Alex Brown Cash Reserve Prime	1981	595.5	1,500	500	500	no	28
Alliance Group Capital Reserves	1978	869.1	1,000	500	500	yes	47
American Capital Reserve	1974	259.2	1,000	100	500	no	34
Capital Preservation Fund	1972	1,820.9	1,000	100	500	yes	53
Capital Preservation Fund II	1980	543.2	5,000	100	100	yes	2
Cash Management Trust	1978	565.6	5,000	50	500	no	15
Columbia Daily Income	1974	467.2	1,000	500	500	yes	31
Current Interest M.M. Fund	1982	864.8	1,000	50	500	no	46
Daily Cash Accumulation	1978	1,845.2	500	100	250	no	33
DBL-Cash Fund-M.M. Portfolio[1]	1981	1,245.1	1,000	100	500	no	63
Dean Witter Active Assets[1]	1979	1,338.0	20,000	no min.	no min.	yes	n/av
Dean Witter/Sears Liquid Assets	1975	6,680.5	5,000	1,000	no min.	no	53
Delaware Cash Reserves	1978	1,476.8	1,000	25	500	yes	44
Dreyfus Liquid Assets	1974	8,489.7	2,500	100	500	yes	n/av.
Dreyfus M.M. Instruments Govt.[2]	1979	965.8	2,500	100	500	yes	n/av.
E.D. Jones Daily Passport Cash Trust	1980	640.7	1,000	1,000	500	yes	38
Fidelity Cash Reserves	1979	4,131.4	1,000	250	500	yes	32
Fidelity Daily Income	1974	2,642.8	1,000	500	no min.	yes	34
First Variable Rate (Calvert)	1976	634.2	2,000	250	250	yes	45
Franklin Money Fund	1975	1,022.7	500	25	100	no	29
Fund for Govt. Investors[2]	1975	1,941.4	2,500	100	250	yes	29
E.F. Hutton AMA Cash Fund	1982	1,996.0	10,000	no min.	no min.	no	29
E.F. Hutton Cash Reserve Management[1]	1976	4,304.0	10,000	1,000	500	no	n/av.
E.F. Hutton Govt. Fund[2]	1982	1,146.1	10,000	1,000	500	no	21
IDS Cash Management	1975	952.1	2,000	100	500	no	25
Kemper Money Market	1974	4,822.7	1,000	100	500	yes	33
Lehman Cash Management	1981	934.7	2,500	100	500	yes	26
Liquid Capital Income	1974	1,249.4	1,000	250	100	no	33
Merrill Lynch CMA Govt. Securities[1,2]	1981	1,337.0	1,000	250	100	no	n/av.
Merrill Lynch CMA Money Fund	1977	16,742.6	20,000	no min.	no min.	no	55
Merrill Lynch USA Govt. Reserves[1,2]	1977	1,434.0	5,000	1,000	500	no	n/av.
Merrill Lynch Ready Assets	1975	11,985.7	5,000	1,000	500	no	58
Merrill Lynch Retirement Reserves	1980	2,073.3	300	no min.	n/av.	no	57
NEL Cash Mgmt. Trust MM Series	1978	813.0	1,000	no min.	250	yes	35
National Liquid Reserves[1]	1974	1,463.0	1,000	100	500	no	n/av.
Oppenheimer Money Market Fund	1974	1,264.7	1,000	25	250	no	28
Prudential-Bache Command Money Fund[1]	1982	655.0	10,000	no min.	no min.	no	n/av.
Prudential-Bache Money Mart Assets[1]	1976	2,843.0	1,000	100	500	yes	n/av.
Reserve Fund-Primary	1972	1,610.0	1,000	1,000	500	no	31
T. Rowe Price Prime Reserve	1975	3,120.0	1,000	100	500	yes	34
Scudder Cash Investment Trust	1976	1,054.6	1,000	no min.	500	yes	39

Selected Money Market Funds

Fund	Year First Offered	Total Assets 4/17/85 ($000,000)	Min. $ Investment		Check Writing Minimum	Phone Exchange Priv.	Avg. Mat. (days)
			Initial	Subseq.			
Seligman Cash Management Fund-Prime Portfolio	1977	380.6	1,000	no min.	250	yes	29
Shearson/American Express Daily Dividend	1979	3,612.4	5,000	1,000	n/av.	no	47
Shearson/American Express Govt. and Agencies[2]	1980	1,434.4	5,000	1,000	n/av.	no	54
SteinRoe Cash Reserves	1976	858.4	2,500	100	50	yes	38
Summit Cash Reserves	1982	500.9	5,000	1,000	500	no	46
Value Line Cash Fund	1979	480.4	1,000	100	500	yes	33
Vanguard Money Market Prime	1981	1,700.0	1,000	100	250	yes	37
Webster Cash Reserve	1979	1,325.1	1,500	500	n/av.	no	39

Note: *Data on minimum investment, check writing, and phone exchange as of 3/21/84.*
1 *All data as of 3/21/84.*
2 *Investing in government securities; most funds of this nature are too small to have qualified for this listing.*

Source: *The Industrial Investor's Guide to No-Load Mutual Funds,* © 1984, The American Association of Individual Investors, Chicago, Illinois.

TAX-EXEMPT MONEY MARKET FUNDS

Fund	Year First Offered	Total Assets 4/17/85 ($000,000)	Min. $ Investment		Check Writing Minimum	Phone Exchange Priv.	Avg. Mat. (days)
			Initial	Subseq.			
Active Assets Tax-Free (Dean Witter)[1]	1981	309.0	20,000	1,000	no min.	yes	n/av.
D.L. Babson Tax-Free Income[1]	1981	2.8	1,000	100	1,000	yes	n/av.
Calvert Tax-Free Reserves	1981	274.0	2,000	250	250	yes	99
Carnegie Tax-Free Income	1982	128.7	5,000	500	250	no	24
Centennial Tax-Exempt Trust[1]	1981	60.0	500	no min.	n/av.	yes	n/av.
Daily Cash Tax-Exempt	1981	127.6	1,000	100	250	no	23
Daily Tax-Free Income	1982	856.2	5,000	100	250	yes	32
DBL Tax-Free	1983	275.1	1,000	100	500	no	56
Dean Witter/Sears Tax-Free Daily Income[1]	1981	296.0	5,000	100	500	no	n/av.
Delaware Tax-Free Money Fund	1981	53.6	5,000	100	500	no	96
Dreyfus Tax-Exempt Money Market	1980	2,098.4	5,000	100	500	yes	71
Eaton Vance Tax-Free Reserve[1]	1982	20.1	1,000	no min.	500	yes	n/av.
Fidelity Tax-Exempt	1980	3,203.2	10,000	500	500	yes	57
Franklin Tax-Exempt	1980	76.4	500	25	100	no	41
IDS Tax-Free Money Fund	1980	68.3	2,000	100	500	no	75
Kemper Tax-Exempt Money Market[1]	1981	250.0	1,000	100	500	yes	n/av.
Kidder, Peabody Tax-Exempt	1981	455.2	1,500	500	n/av.	no	n/av.
Lehman Tax-Exempt[1]	1982	266.6	2,500	100	500	yes	n/av.
Lexington Tax-Free Daily	1977	72.9	1,000	50	250	yes	50
Liquid Green Tax-Free Trust	1983	16.4	1,000	100	250	yes	97
Merrill Lynch CMA Tax-Exempt	1981	5,083.2	20,000	1,000	no min.	no	54
Midwest Group Tax-Free Trust[1]	1981	35.5	2,500	250	500	yes	n/av.
Municipal Cash Reserve (Hutton)	1981	1,584.1	10,000	1,000	500	no	59
New England Life Tax-Exempt[1]	1983	14.9	1,000	no min.	250	yes	n/av.
Nuveen Tax-Exempt Money	1981	2,062.2	25,000	no min.	n/av.	no	47
Nuveen Tax-Free Reserve	1982	121.4	1,000	100	500	no	41
Provident Minifund[1]	1980	1,083.0	5,000	no min.	n/av.	no	n/av.
Prudential Bache Tax-Free Money	1979	332.7	2,500	500	500	yes	56
T. Rowe Price Tax-Exempt Money	1981	961.2	1,000	100	500	yes	80
Scudder Tax-Free Money	1980	290.2	1,000	no min.	500	yes	n/av.
Shearson Daily Tax-Free	1982	429.5	5,000	1,000	n/av.	no	61
Shearson FMA Municipal	1982	497.3	25,000	no min.	n/av.	no	52
SteinRoe Tax-Exempt	1983	154.0	2,500	100	100	yes	50
Tax-Free Money Fund (Provident)	1981	452.8	5,000	100	500	no	27
Tucker Anthony Tax-Exempt	1982	87.2	2,500	250	500	no	80
Vanguard Municipal Bond Money Market Portfolio	1980	570.0	3,000	100	250	yes	74

Note: *Data on minimum investment, check writing, and phone exchange as of 3/21/84.*
1 *All data as of 3/21/84.*

Source: *The Individual Investor's Guide to No-Load Mutual Funds,* © 1984, The American Association of Individual Investors, Chicago, Illinois.

5.04 Fund Directory

The following directory provides addresses for most of the mutual funds and money market funds ranked in the previous pages. Information about each fund is published in a prospectus, which may be obtained from the sponsoring company.

Active Assets Tax-Free (Dean Witter)
Dean Witter Reynolds, Inc.
One World Trade Center
New York, NY 10048
(212) 938-4554

Aetna Income Shares
151 Farmington Avenue
Hartford, CT 06156

AGE High Income
155 Bovet Road
San Mateo, CA 94402

Alliance Group
140 Broadway
New York, NY 10005

American Capital Reserve
American Investors Corp.
88 Field Point Road
P.O. Box 255
Greenwich, CT 06836
(800) 243-5353 (203) 622-1600

American Leaders Fund
421 Seventh Avenue
Pittsburgh, PA 15219

American National Bond Fund
Two Moody Plaza
Galveston, TX 77550

Analytic Optioned Equity
222 Martin Street
Irvine, CA 92715

D. L. Babson Tax-Free Income
Jones & Babson, Inc.
3 Crown Center
2440 Pershing Road
Kansas City, MO 64108
(800) 821-5591 (816) 471-5200

Bank Stock Fund
333 North Tejon Street
Colorado Springs, CO 80903

Bond Portfolio for Endowments
P.O. Box 7650
Two Embarcadero Center
San Francisco, CA 94120

Boston Company Government Income
Boston Company Special Growth
(no-load)
The Boston Company Advisors, Inc.
One Boston Place
Boston, MA 02106
(800) 343-6324 (617) 956-9740

Calvert Tax Free Reserves
Calvert Municipal Management
Company
1700 Pennsylvania Avenue, N.W.
Washington, D.C. 20006

Capital Preservation T Note Trust
755 Page Mill Road
Palo Alto, CA 94304

Carnegie Government ITS
Carnegie Tax-Free Income
429 Euclid Avenue
Cleveland, OH 44114

Cash Management Trust
P.O. Box 60822, Terminal Annex
Los Angeles, CA 90060

Centennial Tax-Exempt Trust
One New York Plaza
New York, NY 10004
(212) 825-8196

Charter Fund
Republic National Bank Tower
Dallas, TX 75201

Colonial Fund
Colonial Tax-Managed Account
    75 Federal Street
    Boston, MA 02110

Columbia Daily Income Trust
Columbia Growth (no-load)
    621 S.W. Morrison St.
    Portland, OR 97205
    (800) 547-1037 (503) 322-3600

Composite Income Fund
    402 Spokane & Eastern Building
    Sea First Financial Center
    Spokane, WA 92201

Concord Fund
    60 State Street
    Boston, MA 02109

Copley Tax-Managed
    109 Howe Street
    Fall River, MA 02724

Corporate Leaders TR-B
    580 Sylvan Avenue
    Englewood Cliffs, NJ 07632

Country Capital Income
    1701 Towanda Avenue
    Bloomington, IL 61701

Current Interest Fund
    3 Allen Center
    Houston, TX 77002

Daily Cash Accumulation Fund
Daily Cash Tax-Exempt
    3600 S. Yosemite Street
    Denver, CO 80237
    (303) 770-2345

Daily Tax-Free Income
    100 Park Avenue
    New York, NY 10017
    (212) 370-1240

Dean Witter High Yield
Dean Witter/Sears Tax-Free
    Daily Income
    Dean Witter Reynolds, Inc.
    One World Trade Center
    New York, NY 10048
    (212) 938-4554

Decatur Income Fund
    7 Penn Center Plaza
    Philadelphia, PA 19103

Delaware Cash Reserve Fund
Delaware Tax-Free Money Fund
    Delaware Management Company
    10 Penn Center Plaza
    Philadelphia, PA 19103
    (800) 523-4640 (800) 462-1597

Dreyfus Tax-Exempt Money Market Fund
    Dreyfus Corporation
    600 Madison Avenue
    New York, NY 10022
    (800) 223-5525 (212) 223-0303

Eaton & Howard Stock
    24 Federal Street
    Boston, MA 02110

Eaton Vance Tax-Free Reserve
    24 Federal Street
    Boston, MA 02110
    (617) 482-8260

Eberstadt Energy-Resources
    61 Broadway
    New York, NY 10006

Energy Fund
    522 Fifth Ave.
    New York, NY 10036

Evergreen Fund (no-load)
    Saxon Woods Asset Management
      Corporation
    550 Mamaroneck Avenue
    Harrison, NY 10528
    (914) 698-5711 (212) 828-7700

Federated Fund
    421 Seventh Ave.
    Pittsburgh, PA 15219

Fidelity Cash Reserve
Fidelity Management Group
Fidelity Selected Energy Fund
Fidelity Tax-Exempt
    82 Devonshire Street
    Boston, MA 02109
    (800) 225-6190 (617) 523-1919

Finomic Investment
    First International Plaza
    1100 Louisiana
    Houston, TX 77002

First Investors Option Fund
First Investors 90/10
    120 Wall Street
    New York, NY 10005

First Variable Rate Fund
Government Securities Management Co.
1700 Pennsylvania Avenue NW
Washington, DC 20006
(800) 368-2748 (301) 951-4820

F.L. Income-Short-Term
Vanguard Group
Drummer's Lane, Box 1100
Valley Forge, PA 19482
(800) 523-7025
PA only: (800) 362-0539
  (215) 648-6000

44 Wall Street Fund, Inc. (no-load)
Forty-Four Management, Ltd.
150 Broadway
New York, NY 10038
(800) 221-7836 (212) 267-2820

Founders Income
Founders Special Fund (no-load)
Founders Mutual Depositor Corp.
655 Broadway, Suite 700
Denver, CO 80203
(800) 525-2440 (303) 623-1567

FPA Paramont Mutual
1888 Century Park East
Los Angeles, CA 90067

Franklin Money Fund
Franklin Option Fund
Franklin Tax-Exempt
155 Bovet Road
San Mateo, CA 94402
(415) 570-3045

Fund of America
2777 Allen Parkway
Houston, TX 77019

Fund for Government Investors
1735 K Street NW
Washington, DC 20006
(202) 861-1800 collect

Fund of the Southwest
P.O. Box 2994
Dallas, TX 75221

Golconda Investors Ltd. (no-load)
11 Hanover Square
New York, NY 10005
(212) 785-0900

Government Investors Trust
1800 North Kent Street
Arlington, VA 22209

G.T. Pacific Fund (no-load)
G. T. Capital Management, Inc.
601 Montgomery Street, Suite 1400
San Francisco, CA 94111
(415) 392-6181

Guardian Mutual Fund, Inc. (no-load)
Neuberger & Berman Management
342 Madison Avenue
New York, NY 10173
(212) 850-8300

Guardian Park Avenue Fund
201 Park Avenue South
New York, NY 10003

Hartwell Leverage Fund (no-load)
Hartwell Management Company
50 Rockefeller Plaza
New York, NY 10020
(212) 247-8740

High Yield Securities
11 Greenway Plaza
Houston, TX 77046

E. F. Hutton AMA Cash Fund
E. F. Hutton Cash Reserve Management
E. F. Hutton Government Fund
1 Battery Park
New York, NY 10004
(212) 742-5000

IDS Extra Income Fund
IDS Tax-Free Money Fund
Investors Diversified Services
1000 Roanoke Building
Minneapolis, MN 55402
(800) IDS-EDEA (800) 437-4332

Investors' Selective
1000 Roanoke Building
Minneapolis, MN 55402

ISI Trust Fund
ISI Corp., Whelpley Associates
1608 Webster Street
Oakland, CA 94623
(415) 832-1400

John Hancock
U.S. Government Securities
Hancock Place
P.O. Box 111
Boston, MA 02117

Kemper Money Market Fund
Kemper Tax-Exempt Money Market Fund
120 S. LaSalle Street
Chicago, IL 60603
(800) 621-1048 (312) 781-1121

Keystone B-4
99 High Street
Boston, MA 02104

Kidder Peabody Tax Exempt
Kidder Peabody & Company, Inc.
555 California Street
San Francisco, CA
(415) 836-0900

Legg Mason Value (no-load)
421 Seventh Avenue
Pittsburgh, PA 15219

Lehman Capital Fund (no-load)
Lehman Cash Management
Lehman Tax-Exempt
Lehman Management Company, Inc.
55 Water Street
New York, NY 10041
(212) 558-3288

Lexington Gold Fund (no-load)
Lexington Tax-Free Daily Income
Lexington Management Corporation
Box 1515, 580 Sylvan Avenue
Englewood Cliffs, NY 07632
(800) 526-4791 (800) 932-0838 (NY only)

Lindner Fund for Income (no-load)
Lindner Management Corporation
200 South Bemiston
St. Louis, MO 63105
(314) 727-5305

Liquid Capital Income
831 National City Bank Building
Cleveland, OH 44114
(216) 781-4440

Loomis-Sayles Capital Development
(no-load)
P.O. Box 449
Back Bay Annex
Boston, MA 82117
(617) 267-6601

Lord Abbott Income
63 Wall Street
New York, NY 10005

Lowry Market Timing
419 Boylston Street
Boston, MA 02116

Magnacap Fund
Magna Income Trust
185 Cross Street
Fort Lee, NJ 07024

Massachusetts Financial Bond
200 Berkeley Street
Boston, MA 02116

Merrill Lynch CMA Tax-Exempt
Merrill Lynch Government Reserve
Merrill Lynch Government Securities
Merrill Lynch Money Fund
Merrill Lynch Ready Reserves
Merrill Lynch Retirement Reserves
633 Third Avenue
New York, NY 10017
(212) 692-2929

Midwest Group Tax-Free Trust
Midwest Income Trust
Midwest Advisory Service, Inc.
522 Dixie Terminal Building
Cincinnati, OH 45202
(800) 543-8721 OH:(800) 582-7396
(513) 579-0414

Municipal Cash Reserve (Hutton)
E. F. Hutton
One Battery Park Plaza
New York, NY 10004
(212) 742-5000

Mutual Omaha Income
3102 Farnam St.
Omaha, NE 68131

Mutual Qualified Income (no-load)
Mutual Shares Corp. (no-load)
Heines Securities Corporation
26 Broadway
New York, NY 10004
(212) 908-4048

Nation-Wide Securities
One Wall Street
New York, NY 10005

National Liquid Reserves
National Income Fund
National Preferred Fund
605 Third Avenue
New York, NY 10016

NEL Series Bond Income
New England Life Cash Management
Account
New England Life Income Fund
New England Life Tax-Exempt
501 Boylston Street
Boston, MA 02117
(617) 578-2000

Newton Income Fund
733 North Van Buren Street
Milwaukee, WI 53202
(414) 347-1141

Nicholas Fund
312 E. Wisconsin Avenue
Milwaukee, WI 53202
(414) 272-6133

Nuveen Tax-Exempt Money Fund
Nuveen Tax-Exempt Reserve
Nuveen Advisory Corporation
115 S. LaSalle Street
Chicago, IL 60603
(312) 782-2655

Oppenheimer Money Market Fund
Two Broadway
New York, NY 10004
(212) 422-9103

Paine Webber Cashfund
815 Connecticut Ave. NW
Washington, DC 20006
(202) 887-6000

Pennsylvania Mutual (no-load)
1414 Avenue of the Americas
New York, NY 10019
(800) 221-4268 (215) 376-6771

Phoenix Capital
Phoenix Growth
Phoenix High Yield
535 Boylston Street
Boston, MA 02117

Pilgrim Adjustable Rate
185 Cross Street
Fort Lee, NJ 07024

Pioneer Bond Fund
60 State Street
Boston, MA 02109

Pro Income Fund
1107 Bethlehem Pike
Flourtown, PA 19031

Provident Fund for Income
Provident Muni-Fund
Suite 204
Webster Building
Concord Plaza
Washington, Delaware 19810
(800) 441-7450 (302) 478-6945

Prudential Bache Command
Money Fund
Prudential Bache Money Mart Assets
Prudential Bache Tax-Free Money
Prudential Bache Securities
100 Gold Street
New York, NY 10292
(800) 221-7984 (212) 791-4654
(NY call collect)

Quasar Associates (no-load)
Alliance Capital Management
140 Broadway
New York, NY 10005
(800) 221-7780 (212) 269-1500

Quest for Value Fund
One New York Plaza
New York, NY 10004

Rainbow Fund
60 Broad Street
New York, NY 10004

Research Equity Fund
155 Bovet Road
San Mateo, CA 94402

Reserve Fund Primary
810 Seventh Avenue
New York, NY 10019

T. Rowe Price Prime Reserve
T. Rowe Price Tax-Exempt Money
T. Rowe Price Associates, Inc.
100 E. Pratt Street
Baltimore, MD 21202
(800) 638-5660 (301) 547-2308

Safeco Special Bond
Safeco Plaza
Seattle, WA 98185

St. Paul Fiduciary
P.O. Box 43284
Minneapolis, MN 55164

Scudder Cash Investment Trust
Scudder International (no-load)
Scudder Target Government
Scudder Target USGT
Scudder Tax-Free Money
Scudder, Stevens & Clark, Investment
Counsel
175 Federal Street
Boston, MA 02110
(800) 225-2470 (617) 426-8300 (MA only)

Security Bond Fund
700 Harrison St.
Topeka, KS 66636

Selected American Shares
111 West Washington Street
Chicago, IL 60602

Seligman Cash Management Fund Prime
J.&W. Seligman & Company, Inc.
One Bankers Trust Plaza
New York, NY 10006
(800) 221-2450 (212) 432-4000

Sentinel Bond Fund
One Exchange Place
Jersey City, NJ 07302

Sequoia Fund (no-load)
540 Madison Avenue
New York, NY 10022

**Shearson/American Express Cash
Management Fund**
**Shearson/American Express Daily
Dividend**
**Shearson/American Express
Government and Agencies**
Shearson Daily Tax Free
Shearson FMA Municipal
Two World Trade Center
New York, NY 10048
(212) 577-5794

Sherman Dean Fund
120 Broadway
New York, NY 10005

Smith Barney Inc.
1345 Avenue of the Americas
New York, NY 10019

Sogen International Fund
630 Fifth Ave.
New York, NY 10020

Sovereign Investors
1401 Walnut Street
Philadelphia, PA 19102

State Farm Interim
One State Farm Plaza
Bloomington, IL 61701

Stein Roe Bond Fund
Stein Roe Cash Reserves Fund
Stein Roe Tax-Exempt Fund
Stein Roe & Farnham
150 S. Wacker Drive
Chicago, IL 60606
(800) 621-0320 (312) 368-7826

Strategic Investments Fund
10110 Crestover
Dallas, TX 75220
(214) 484-1326

Strong Investment (no-load)
Strong Total Return (no-load)
815 E. Mason Street
Milwaukee, WI
(800) 558-1030 (414) 765-0620

Tax-Free Money Fund (Provident)
Suite 204
Webster Building
Concord Plaza
Washington, DC 19810
(800) 441-7450 (302) 478-6945

Transamerica New Income
P.O. Box 2438
Los Angeles, CA 90051

Trustee Commingled, Ltd. (no-load)
Drummers Lane
Valley Forge, PA 19482

Tucker, Anthony, Tax-Exempt
2 Beacon Street
Boston, MA 02108
(617) 725-2000

Tudor Fund (no-load)
Tudor Management Company, Inc.
One New York Plaza
New York, NY 10004
(800) 223-3332 (212) 908-9582

Twentieth Century Growth (no-load)
Twentieth Century Select (no-load)
Twentieth Century US Government
Investors Research Corporation
P.O. Box 200, 605 West 47th Street
Kansas City, MO 64141
(816) 531-5575

Unified Accumulation Fund
207 Guaranty Building
Indianapolis, IN 46204

United High Income
One Crown Center
P.O. Box 1343
Kansas City, MO 64141

United Service Gold
P.O. Box 2098
Universal City, TX 78148

USAA Income Fund
98 Fredricksburg Road
San Antonio, TX 78288

US Gold Shares (no-load)
Growth Research & Management, Inc.
P.O. Box 29467
San Antonio, TX 78229
(800) 531-5777 (512) 696-1234

Valley Forge Fund
P.O. Box 262
Valley Forge, PA 19481

Value Line Cash Fund
Value Line Special Situations Fund
(no-load)
Arnold Bernhard & Company, Inc.
711 Third Avenue
New York, NY 10017
(800) 223-0818 (800) 522-5217
NY only: (212) 687-3965

Vanguard MMT Prime
Vanguard Municipal Bond Money
Market Portfolio
Vanguard Group
Drummer's Lane, Box 1100
Valley Forge, PA 19482
(800) 523-7025 PA only: (800) 362-0539
(215) 648-6000

Venture Income (+) Plus
231 Washington Avenue, Suite 2
Santa Fe, NM 87501

Webster Cash Reserve Fund
10 Hanover Square
New York, NY 10005

Weingarten Equity (no-load)
Weingarten Management Corporation
331 Madison Avenue
New York, NY 10017
(212) 557-8787

Wellesley Income Fund
Drummers Lane
Valley Forge, PA 19482

Windsor (Vanguard) (no-load)
Vanguard Group
Drummer's Lane, Box 1100
Valley Forge, PA 19482
(800) 523-7025 (800) 362-0530
PA only: (215) 648-6000

5.05 Pension Funds

Provisions of the Employee Retirement Income Security Act of 1974 (ERISA) made it possible for incorporated professionals to set up profit-sharing plans utilizing a portion of each participant's annual compensation. (See Qualified Employee Benefit Plans, page 1.77) According to this act, a qualified pension or profit-sharing plan is an employer-established program that sets aside dollars from current earnings and may also include optional employee contributions. These funds are not subject to corporate income tax, and all growth and income accumulates tax-free, provided it remains in the plan. Taxes are paid only when the employee starts receiving money from the plan, either as monthly income or in a lump sum. Generally, by the time the employee receives this income, he or she is retired and in a lower tax bracket.

As might be expected, numerous investment firms rapidly developed programs specifically designed to meet the criteria established for pension funds. Some have clearly fared better than others, but movement from year to year continues to indicate significant shifting in the ranks.

When investing pension fund assets, the most important considerations should be safety, income, and growth—in that order. The investor should look for high quality securities offered by financially strong, profitable corporations. Some of the most widely held investments include common stocks, debt issues, thrift accounts, U.S. government retirement bonds, mutual funds, real estate, guaranteed income contracts, and zero coupon bonds.

TOP 200 PENSION FUNDS' ASSET MIX
Four-Year Comparison; Years Ending 9/30

Investment	1981	1982	1983	1984
Stocks	40.6%	37.0%	44.2%	41.2%
Bonds	37.5	39.0	34.9	33.4
Cash	12.1	10.5	8.2	10.4
Real Estate	3.7	3.5*	3.3	3.3
Mortgages	—	4.0	3.5	2.2
Mortgage-backed securities	—	—	—	2.9
Guaranteed Income Certificates (GICs)	—	3.0	2.4	3.0
Annuities	—	1.0	0.3	—
Other	6.1	2.0	2.3	3.6
Total	$393.5 billion	$469.3 billion	$605.6 billion	$641.4 billion

* *Equity only.*

Source: *Pension & Investment Age*, January 21, 1985. © Crain Communications.

ASSET MIX TOP 200 PENSION FUNDS

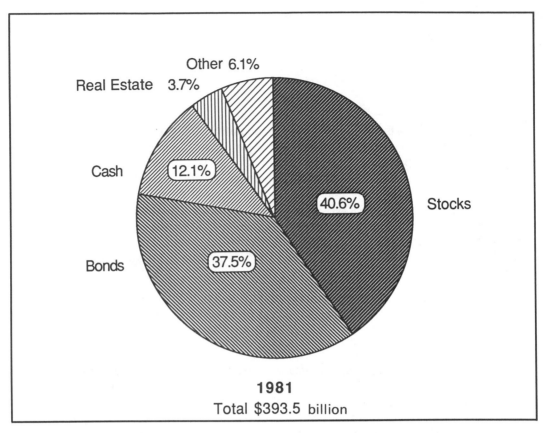

Other 6.1%

Real Estate 3.7%

Cash 12.1%

Stocks 40.6%

Bonds 37.5%

1981
Total $393.5 billion

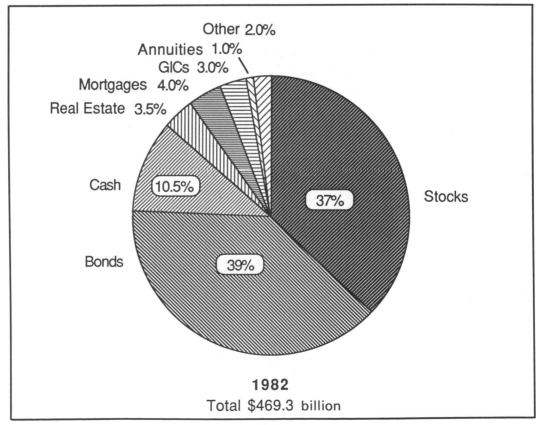

Other 2.0%

Annuities 1.0%

GICs 3.0%

Mortgages 4.0%

Real Estate 3.5%

Cash 10.5%

Stocks 37%

Bonds 39%

1982
Total $469.3 billion

Asset Mix Top 200 Pension Funds

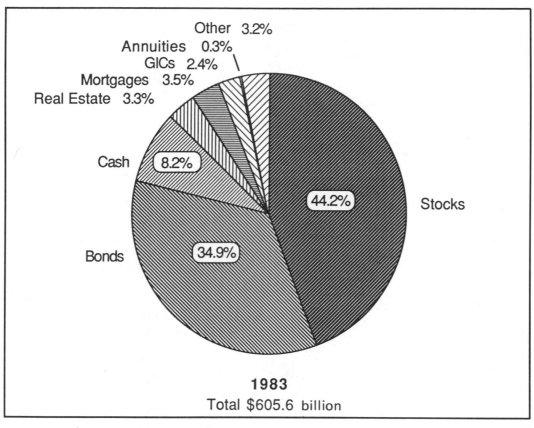

Other 3.2%
Annuities 0.3%
GICs 2.4%
Mortgages 3.5%
Real Estate 3.3%

Cash 8.2%

Stocks 44.2%

Bonds 34.9%

1983
Total $605.6 billion

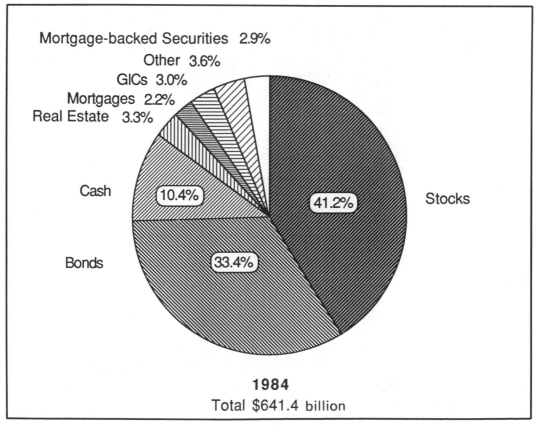

Mortgage-backed Securities 2.9%
Other 3.6%
GICs 3.0%
Mortgages 2.2%
Real Estate 3.3%

Cash 10.4%

Stocks 41.2%

Bonds 33.4%

1984
Total $641.4 billion

200 LARGEST PENSION FUNDS, 1984
Assets in Millions of Dollars

Rank	Fund	Assets	Rank	Fund	Assets
1	New York State Common, New York	22,800	48	Alabama Retirement Systems,	
2	General Motors Corp., New York	22,799		Montgomery, AL	4,095
3	California Public Employees,		49	Mobil Oil Corp., New York	4,000
	Sacramento, CA	22,717	50	Illinois Teachers, Springfield, IL	3,788
4	AT&T, New York	21,455	51	Westinghouse Electric, Pittsburgh	3,650
5	New York City Employees, New York	21,154	52	United Nations Joint Staff, New York	3,610
6	General Electric Co., Stamford, CT	13,338	53	Southwestern Bell Corp., St. Louis	3,590
7	New York State Teachers, Albany, New York	12,826	54	United Air Lines, Chicago	3,500
8	California State Teachers, Sacramento, CA	12,300	55	Tennessee Consolidated, Nashville, TN	3,400
9	IBM, Stamford, CT	10,918	56	Allied Corp., Morristown, NJ	3,200
10	Texas Teacher System, Austin, TX	9,753	57	Standard Oil Co. (Ind.), Chicago	3,144
11	Ford Motor Co., Dearborn, MI	9,300	58	Arizona State System, Phoenix	3,063
12	New Jersey Investment, Trenton, NJ	9,166	59	South Carolina Retirement, Columbia, SC	3,036
13	Michigan State Employees, Lansing, MI	8,951	60	Chevron Corp., San Francisco	3,034
14	Wisconsin Investment Board, Madison, WI	8,692	61	Connecticut Trust Funds, Hartford, CT	2,979
15	Ohio Public Employees, Columbus, OH	8,584	62	U S WEST, Englewood, CA	2,944
16	Ohio Teachers, Columbus, OH	8,507	63	Atlantic Richfield Co., Los Angeles	2,840
17	E.I. du Pont de Nemours, Wilmington, DE	8,120	64	Prudential Insurance, Newark, NJ	2,785
18	North Carolina Retirement, Raleigh, NC	7,967	65	United Mine Workers, Washington, D.C.	2,784
19	Exxon Corp., New York	7,388	66	Caterpillar Tractor Co., Peoria, IL	2,782
20	Florida State, Tallahassee, FL	7,029	67	Hughes Aircraft Co., Culver City, CA	2,722
21	Ameritech, Chicago	7,000	68	General Dynamics, Clayton, MO	2,700
22	U.S. Steel & Carnegie, New York	6,850	69	RCA Corp., New York	2,500
23	Pennsylvania School Employees,		70	Union Carbide Corp., Danbury, CT	2,500
	Harrisburgh, PA	6,597	71	Texas Employees, Austin, TX	2,459
24	Bell Atlantic Corp., Philadelphia	6,300	72	Mass. Employees & Teachers, Boston	2,400
25	Minnesota Investment Board, St. Paul, MN	5,607	73	The LTV Corp., Dallas	2,338
26	BellSouth Corp., Atlanta	5,500	74	Bethlehem Steel Corp., Bethlehem, PA	2,337
27	Washington Investment Board, Olympia, WA	5,400	75	Metropolitan Life Insurance, New York	2,325
28	Pacific Telesis Group, San Francisco	5,300	76	Gulf Oil Corp., Pittsburgh	2,238
29	Teamsters, Central States, Chicago, IL	5,169	77	Hawaii Employees, Honolulu	2,200
30	Teamsters, Western Conference, Seattle	5,129	78	Monsanto Co., St. Louis	2,200
31	Eastman Kodak, Rochester, New York	5,103	79	Chrysler Corp., Detroit	2,186
32	Boeing Co., Seattle	4,948	80	Iowa Public Employees, Des Moines	2,173
33	GTE Service Co., Stamford, CT	4,900	81	Missouri Public School, Jefferson City, MO	2,100
34	Rockwell International, Pittsburgh	4,900	82	Texaco Inc., White Plains, New York	2,086
35	Sears, Roebuck & Co., Chicago	4,808	83	Pacific Gas & Electric, San Francisco	2,068
36	Georgia State Systems, Atlanta	4,723	84	Phillips Petroleum Co., Bartlesville, OK	2,055
37	United Technologies Corp., Hartford, CT	4,631	85	Detroit Retirement Systems, Detroit	2,021
38	Shell Oil Co., Houston	4,517	86	Illinois Municipal Retirement, Chicago	1,932
39	Pennsylvania State Employees,		87	American Airlines, Dallas	1,912
	Harrisburg, PA	4,453	88	Procter & Gamble, Cincinnati	1,886
40	NYNEX Corp., New York	4,400	89	Kansas Public Employees, Topeka, KS	1,870
41	Los Angeles County, Los Angeles	4,394	90	Trans World Airlines, New York	1,857
42	University of California, Berkeley, CA	4,200	91	Goodyear Tire & Rubber, Akron, OH	1,854
43	Oregon Public Employees, Salem, OR	4,200	92	Aluminum Co. of America, Pittsburgh	1,824
44	Colorado Public Employees, Denver	4,108	93	Delta Air Lines, Atlanta	1,800
45	McDonnell Douglas, St. Louis	4,108	94	Conoco Inc., Wilmington, DE	1,800
46	Maryland State Systems, Baltimore	4,107	95	Tenneco Inc., Houston	1,800
47	Lockheed Corp., Burbank, CA	4,102	96	Utah Retirement Fund, Salt Lake City	1,793

200 Largest Pension Funds, 1984

Rank	Fund	Assets	Rank	Fund	Assets
97	Virginia Retirement, Richmond, VA	1,793	148	World Bank, Washington, D.C.	1,189
98	Mississippi Public, Jackson, MS	1,773	149	Southern California Edison, Atlanta	1,175
99	Grumman Corp., Bethpage, NY	1,726	150	Citicorp, New York	1,158
100	J.C. Penney Co., New York	1,718	151	Raytheon Co., Lexington, MA	1,150
101	Northrop Corp., Los Angeles	1,700	152	FMC Corp., Chicago	1,148
102	San Francisco City & County, San Francisco	1,700	153	Textron Inc., Providence, RI	1,147
103	ITT Corp., New York	1,683	154	Getty Oil Co., Los Angeles	1,128
104	Alaska State Systems, Juneau, Alaska	1,663	155	Continental Group Inc., Stamford, CT	1,119
105	Illinois State Board, Chicago	1,630	156	Travelers Corp., Hartford, CT	1,110
106	Xerox Corp., Stamford, CT	1,611	157	New York Life Insurance, New York	1,102
107	Deere & Co., Moline, IL	1,590	158	PPG Industries, Pittsburgh	1,070
108	R.J. Reynolds, Winston-Salem, NC	1,582	159	L.A. City Employees, Los Angeles	1,061
109	Illinois State Universities, Champaign, IL	1,581	160	National Rural Electric, Washington, D.C.	1,055
110	United Methodist, Evanston, IL	1,578	161	Oklahoma Teachers, Oklahoma City	1,045
111	Ohio Police & Firemen, Columbus, OH	1,559	162	National Hospital & Health Care, New York	1,037
112	General Foods, White Plains, NY	1,555	163	McDermott International, New Orleans	1,037
113	Minnesota Mining & Mfg., St. Paul, MN	1,542	164	Intl. Union of Oper. Eng., Washington, D.C.	1,037
114	Signal Co., La Jolla, CA	1,500	165	Philip Morris, New York	1,025
115	Eastern Air Lines, Miami	1,500	166	International Paper, New York	1,014
116	Kentucky Teachers, Frankfort, KY	1,485	167	Bakery & Confectionary, Kensington, MD	1,010
117	Ohio School Employees, Columbus, OH	1,484	168	L.A. Water & Power, Los Angeles	1,000
118	Sperry Corp., New York	1,461	169	Bechtel Power Corp, San Francisco	985
119	Martin Marietta Corp., Bethesda, MD	1,450	170	Cigna Corp., Hartford, CT	982
120	Los Angeles Fire & Police, Los Angeles	1,449	171	Hercules Inc., Wilmington, DE	965
121	Tennessee Valley Authority, Knoxville, TN	1,449	172	United Presbyterian Church, Philadelphia	965
122	Armco Inc., Middletown, OH	1,436	173	Firestone Tire & Rubber, Akron, OH	964
123	Boilermakers, Blacksmiths, Kansas City	1,420	174	Southern New England Telephone, New Haven, CT	930
124	Dow Chemical, Midland, MI	1,400			
125	Owens-Illinois Inc., Toledo, OH	1,400	175	New Mexico Educational, Santa Fe, NM	929
126	Sun Co., Radnor, PA	1,381	176	Arkansas Teacher Retirement, Little Rock, AK	924
127	Dart & Kraft, Northbrook, IL	1,373			
128	Consolidated Edison, New York	1,359	177	Motorola Inc., Schaumberg, IL	905
129	Aetna Life & Casualty, Hartford, CT	1,356	178	Eli Lilly & Co., Indianapolis	902
130	Kentucky Retirement, Frankfort, KY	1,356	179	Greyhound Corp., Phoenix	900
131	Chicago Teachers, Chicago	1,343	180	Texas Municipal Retirement, Austin, TX	900
132	Indiana Public Employees, Indianapolis	1,338	181	Chicago Municipal Employees, Chicago	896
133	TRW Inc., Cleveland, OH	1,336	182	Halliburton Co., Duncan, OK	881
134	Southern Baptist, Dallas	1,300	183	John Hancock Mutual Life, Boston	873
135	Southern Co., Atlanta	1,294	184	Florida Power & Light, Miami	869
136	Honeywell Inc., Minneapolis	1,285	185	Philadelphia Municipal, Philadelphia	860
137	National Intergroup, Pittsburgh	1,280	186	Texas Instruments, Dallas	850
138	Marathon Oil Co., Lindlay, OH	1,271	187	Teledyne Inc., Los Angeles	848
139	West Virginia Board of Inv., Charleston, WV	1,265	188	Marine Engineers Benefit, Baltimore	840
140	Louisiana State Employees, Baton Rouge, LA	1,242	189	Episcopal Ministers Church, New York	820
141	Standard Oil Co. (Ohio), Cleveland	1,240	190	City of Milwaukee, Milwaukee, WI	814
142	Nevada Public Employees, Carson City, NV	1,237	191	Eaton Corp., Cleveland	813
143	International Harvester, Chicago	1,227	192	Texas County & District, Austin, TX	803
144	Commonwealth Edison Co., Chicago	1,218	193	I.A.M. National, Washington, DC	800
145	Inland Steel Co., Chicago	1,217	194	Dresser Industries, Dallas	800
146	Unocal Corp., Los Angeles	1,194	195	Ashland Oil Inc., Russell, KY	795
147	Pan American World Airways, New York	1,193	196	K-Mart Corp., Troy, Michigan	780

(Continued)

200 Largest Pension Funds, 1984

Rank	Fund	Assets	Rank	Fund	Assets
197	Houston Retirement, Houston	774	200	Sandia National Labs, Albuquerque, NM	764
198	Indiana State Teachers, Indianapolis	773		TOTAL	641,400
199	Army & Air Force Exchange, Dallas	765			

Source: *Pension & Investment Age*, January 21, 1985. © Crain Communications.

PENSION FUNDS RANKING 201–1,000, in 1984
Assets in Millions of Dollars

Rank	Fund		Assets	Rank	Fund		Assets
201	Merck & Co.	Rahway, N.J.	749	249	Manufacturers		
202	American Can Co.	Greenwich, Conn.	754		Hanover	New York	635
203	Delaware State	Dover	746	250	United Telecom	Shawnee, Kan.	635
204	North American			251	W.R. Grace	New York	623
	Philips	New York	743	252	Niagara Power	Syracuse, N.Y.	622
205	Abbott Labs	North Chicago, Ill.	740	253	B.F. Goodrich	Akron, Ohio	620
206	Batus Inc.	Louisville, Ky.	737	254	Pfizer	New York	616
207	American Cyanamid	Wayne, N.J.	730	255	Ariz. Public Safety	Phoenix	614
208	Litton Industries	Beverly Hills, Calif.	728	256	United Parcel	Greenwich, Conn.	609
209	Kaiser Permanente	Oakland, Calif.	725	257	Burroughs Corp.	Detroit	607
210	Amer. Electric Power	Columbus, Ohio	724	258	Philadelphia Electric	Philadelphia	606
211	Chicago Policemen	Chicago	720	259	PBGC	Washington	600
212	Michigan Municipal	Lansing	720	260	McGraw-Edison	Rollings Meadows, Ill.	594
213	Colgate-Palmolive Co.	New York	711	261	Federated Stores	Cincinnati	590
214	Fireman's Fund	Larkspur, Calif.	711	262	Consumers Power	Jackson, Mich.	580
215	Hewlett Packard Co.	Palo Alto, Calif.	710	263	Manville Corp.	Denver	576
216	Warner-Lambert Co.	Morris Plains, N.J.	709	264	N.H. Retirement	Concord	576
217	Idaho PERS	Boise	708	265	SmithKline Beckman	Philadelphia	575
218	Bristol-Myers Co.	New York	707	266	Corning Glass	Corning, N.Y.	574
219	American Bar Assoc.	Chicago	705	267	Engineers, So. Calif.	Pasadena, Calif.	570
220	Dun & Bradstreet	New York	703	268	CIBA-Geigy	Ardsley, N.Y.	570
221	Montana Board	Helena	703	269	Boise Cascade	Boise, Idaho	566
222	Oklahoma PERS	Oklahoma City	699	270	S. Dakota Retirement	Pierre	565
223	Arkansas PERS	Little Rock	693	271	YMCA Retirement	New York	565
224	Pacific Lighting Corp.	Los Angeles	693	272	Borg-Warner	Chicago	564
225	ILGWU	New York	689	273	Weyerhaeuser Co.	Tacoma, Wash.	563
226	Santa Fe Southern	Chicago	688	274	Chicago Transit	Chicago	562
227	Duke Power Co.	Charlotte, N.C.	685	275	Operating Engrs. #3	San Francisco	561
228	NADA Retirement	McLean, Va.	683	276	InterNorth	Omaha, Neb.	560
229	Carpenters, So. Calif.	Los Angeles	681	277	Burlington Industries	Greensboro, N.C.	559
230	Texas Utilities	Dallas	680	278	Northwest Airlines	St. Paul, Minn.	556
231	Rohm & Haas	Philadelphia	680	279	Kaiser Aluminum	Oakland, Calif.	555
232	NCR Corp.	Dayton, Ohio	678	280	Hoffmann La Roche	Nutley, N.J.	553
233	Maine Retirement	Augusta	678	281	Times Mirror Co.	Los Angeles	552
234	Whirlpool	Benton Hbr., Mich.	675	282	Brown & Root	Houston	551
235	American Standard	New York	675	283	Wyoming Retirement	Cheyenne	550
236	Financial Institutions	White Plains, N.Y.	670	284	Dana Corp.	Toledo, Ohio	550
237	Upjohn Co.	Kalamazoo, Mich.	668	285	Middle South Utilities	New Orleans	549
238	S. Calif. Food & Com.	Cypress, Calif.	661	286	Georgia-Pacific Corp.	Atlanta	543
239	Montgomery Ward	Chicago	660	287	Consolidated Nat. Gas	New York	541
240	Colt Industries	New York	660	288	Public Serv. E&G	Newark, N.J.	535
241	Olin Corp.	Stamford, Conn.	654	289	Johnson & Johnson	New Brunswick, N.J.	535
242	GenCorp.	Akron, Ohio	650	290	Crown Zellerbach	San Francisco	533
243	Safeway Stores	Oakland, Calif.	649	291	Union Pacific Corp.	New York	532
244	Jewel Companies	Chicago	648	292	Sheet Metal Workers	Washington	527
245	Columbia Gas	Wilmington, Del.	647	293	General Public Utilities	Parsippany, N.J.	526
246	UFCW Union	Chicago	641	294	Control Data	Minneapolis	525
247	Hallmark Cards	Kansas City, Mo.	640	295	Westvaco Corp.	New York	523
248	Scott Paper Co.	Philadelphia	638	296	Carpenters, N. Calif.	San Francisco	521

(Continued)

Pension Funds Ranking 201–1,000

Rank	Fund		Assets	Rank	Fund		Assets
297	ARAMCO Serv. Co.	Houston	520	346	Avco Corp.	Greenwich, Conn.	425
298	Polaroid Corp.	Cambridge, Mass.	520	347	Emhart Corp.	Hartford, Conn.	423
299	Operating Engrs.	Seattle	517	348	Sherwin-Williams Co.	Cleveland	423
300	Wayne County			349	CBS Inc.	New York	420
	System	Detroit	518	350	Mass. Bay Trans.	Boston	420
301	Household Int'l	Prospect Heights, Ill.	516	351	Schlumberger Ltd.	New York	417
302	Ingersoll-Rand Co.	Woodcliff Lake, N.J.	512	352	Contra Costa County	Martinez, Calif.	416
303	Consolidated Rail	Philadelphia	510	353	E-Systems Inc.	Dallas	415
304	Missouri Retirement	Jefferson City	508	354	Winn-Dixie Stores	Jacksonville, Fla.	415
305	AMAX	Greenwich, Conn.	506	355	Owens Corning	Toledo, Ohio	415
306	San Diego County	San Diego, Calif.	504	356	Laborers, Texas	Dallas	412
307	Electricians, Emp.	Flushing, N.Y.	500	357	St. Regis Paper	New York	410
308	Central & Southwest	Dallas	500	358	J.P. Stevens & Co.	New York	410
309	Combustion Eng.	Stamford, Conn.	498	359	Clothing & Textile	New York	410
310	Detroit Edison	Detroit	494	360	White Consolidated	Cleveland	409
311	American Red Cross	Washington	493	361	General Mills	Minneapolis	404
312	Minneapolis Emp.	Minneapolis	485	362	Milwaukee County	Milwaukee	403
313	American Baptist	New York	478	363	San Diego City	San Diego	403
314	Budd Co.	Troy, Mich.	475	364	Baltimore Gas & Elec.	Baltimore	403
315	Cook County	Chicago	471	365	Stauffer Chemical	Westport, Conn.	400
316	City Investing	New York	469	366	Motion Picture Ind.	Studio City, Calif.	400
317	United Ch. of Christ	New York	467	367	Occidental Petroleum	Los Angeles	400
318	Campbell Soup	Camden, N.J.	467	368	U.S. Air	Washington	399
319	Kimberly-Clark Corp.	Neenah, Wis.	466	369	Norfolk Southern		
320	N. Dakota State	Bismarck	465		Corp.	Roanoke, Va.	399
321	American Brands	New York	465	370	Fluor Corp.	Irvine, Calif.	398
322	Libbey-Owens-Ford	Toledo, Ohio	463	371	Time Inc.	New York	396
323	Singer Co.	Stamford, Conn.	460	372	San Bernardino City	California	395
324	Cincinnati Retirement	Cincinnati	457	373	Great A&P Tea	Montvale, N.J.	395
325	Beatrice Companies	Chicago	457	374	El Paso Nat. Gas	El Paso, Texas	394
326	Savings Banks	New York	450	375	Teamsters, N. England	Boston	393
327	State Farm Insurance	Bloomington, Ill.	450	376	Fruehauf Corp.	Detroit	391
328	Orange County	Santa Ana, Calif.	450	377	Ralston Purina	St. Louis	390
329	Cooper Industries	Houston	450	378	Continental Telecom	Atlanta	387
330	NL Industries	New York	450	379	Pillsbury Co.	Minneapolis	387
331	Armstrong World Ind.	Lancaster, Pa.	449	380	Dayton Hudson Corp.	Minneapolis	387
332	IC Industries	Chicago	448	381	Nebraska State	Lincoln	384
333	Northeast Utilities	Berlin, Conn.	448	382	Dallas Retirement	Dallas	384
334	PepsiCo Inc.	Purchase, N.Y.	445	383	IBEW	Washington	380
335	Gulf & Western	New York	440	384	General Signal Corp.	Stamford, Conn.	380
336	Kellogg Co.	Battle Creek, Mich.	440	385	Republic Airlines	Minneapolis	380
337	Farmland Industries	Kansas City, Mo.	438	386	Southland Corp.	Dallas	379
338	Ethyl Corp.	Richmond, Va.	438	387	Deseret Mutual	Salt Lake City	378
339	Lutheran Church, Mo.	St. Louis, Mo.	434	388	Vermont Retirement	Montpelier	377
340	Alameda County	Oakland, Calif.	431	389	Champion Int'l	Stamford, Conn.	376
341	Nabisco Brands	Parsippany, N.J.	431	390	Reynolds Metals	Richmond, Va.	375
342	Denver Public School	Denver	431	391	Air Products	Allentown, Pa.	375
343	Northern States Power	Minneapolis	430	392	San Jose Retirement	San Jose, Calif.	373
344	Cummins Engine Co.	Columbus, Ind.	429	393	Sacramento County	Sacramento, Calif.	372
345	Blue Cross	Chicago	425	394	U.S. Gypsum Co.	Chicago	365

Pension Funds Ranking 201–1,000

Rank	Fund		Assets	Rank	Fund		Assets
395	Coca-Cola Co.	Atlanta	363	445	Chicago Fire	Chicago	316
396	Panhandle Eastern	Kansas City, Mo.	358	446	ENSERCH Corp.	Dallas	316
397	Cincinnati Bell	Cincinnati	357	447	Carpenters 971, 1819	Reno, Nev.	315
398	Intl. Teamsters	Washington	356	448	Consolidated Foods	Chicago	311
399	Allis-Chalmers Corp.	Milwaukee	355	449	Laborers	Chicago	311
400	Southern Pacific Co.	San Francisco	354	450	Tektronix	Beaverton, Ore.	310
401	Harris Corp.	Melbourne, Fla.	353	451	Burlington Northern	Seattle	310
402	Borden	New York	351	452	Kroger Co.	Cincinnati	310
403	Digital Equipment	Maynard, Mass.	350	453	Amer. Hosp. Supply	Evanston, Ill.	310
404	Mead Corp.	Dayton	350	454	Piedmont Aviation	Winston-Salem, N.C.	310
405	CSX Corp.	Richmond, Va.	350	455	New England Electric	Westboro, Mass.	309
406	Rhode Island	Providence	350	456	De Luxe Check	St. Paul, Minn.	308
407	Quaker Oats Co.	Chicago	349	457	Penn Central Corp.	Greenwich, Conn.	307
408	Cincinnati Milacron	Cincinnati	348	458	Interlake Inc.	Oak Brook, Ill.	306
409	Morton Thiokol	Chicago	348	459	Avon Products	New York	306
410	Teamsters #710	Chicago	344	460	Phelps Dodge	New York	305
411	Allied Stores	New York	343	461	Schering-Plough Corp.	Madison, N.J.	305
412	Marsh & McLennan	New York	342	462	Container Corp.	Chicago	304
413	Nat'l. Food Workers	Washington	340	463	Oper. Engrs. #150	Countryside, Ill.	302
414	Masters, Mates, Pilots	New York	340	464	ICI Americas	Wilmington, Del.	302
415	Peoples Energy Corp.	Chicago	340	465	Liberty Mutual	Boston	302
416	Levi Strauss	San Francisco	340	466	Nat. Distillers & Chem.	New York	301
417	Pennsylvania P&L	Allentown, Pa.	339	467	Elec. Workers #11	Los Angeles	300
418	Crane Co.	New York	339	468	Mich. Cons. Gas	Detroit	300
419	Ohio Edison	Akron, Ohio	339	469	Wis. Electric Power	Milwaukee	299
420	Carpenters, N.Y.C.	New York	337	470	A.O. Smith	Milwaukee	298
421	Ralph M. Parsons	Pasadena, Calif.	336	471	Longshoremen	New York	298
422	Arthur D. Little	Cambridge, Mass.	335	472	AMF Inc.	White Plains, N.Y.	297
423	Teamsters, Central Pa.	Reading, Pa.	335	473	Uniroyal Inc.	Middlebury, Conn.	297
424	Pitney Bowes	Stamford, Conn.	334	474	National Maritime	New York	294
425	Emerson Electric	St. Louis	333	475	Amer. Nat. Resources	Detroit	294
426	American Lutheran	Minneapolis	330	476	Clark Equipment	Buchanan, Mich.	294
427	Allegheny Power	New York	330	477	Northwest Indus.	Chicago	294
428	Montgomery County	Rockville, Md.	330	478	F.W. Woolworth	New York	293
429	R.R. Donnelley & Sons	Chicago	329	479	Teamsters #959	Anchorage, Alaska	292
430	Navy Resale	Staten Island, N.Y.	327	480	West. Union	U. Saddle River, N.J.	292
431	Graphic Arts Int'l	Washington	327	481	Plumbers #30	Los Angeles	291
432	Memphis City	Memphis, Tenn.	326	482	Pennwalt Corp.	Philadelphia	291
433	May Dept. Stores	St. Louis	325	483	Teamsters #705	Chicago	291
434	Norton Co.	Worcester, Mass.	324	484	AMP Inc.	Harrisburg, Pa.	290
435	Sundstrand Corp.	Rockford, Ill.	324	485	Fairchild Indus.	Germantown, Md.	290
436	Anheuser-Busch	St. Louis	324	486	Mars Inc.	McLean, Va.	290
437	Painters, Allied Trades	Washington	324	487	Houston Industries	Houston	288
438	Gillette Co.	Boston	321	488	Pennzoil	Houston	287
439	Battelle Institute	Columbus, Ohio	321	489	McGraw-Hill	New York	287
440	Louisiana School	Baton Rouge	320	490	Union Electric	St. Louis	287
441	Ex-Cell-O Corp.	Troy, Mich.	319	491	Longshoremen	San Francisco	287
442	Cleveland Electric	Cleveland	318	492	CPC International	Englewood Cl., N.J.	286
443	Rexnord Inc.	Milwaukee	317	493	N.Y. State E&G	Ithaca, N.Y.	285
444	Roadway	Akron, Ohio	317	494	Musicians' Federation	New York	284

(Continued)

Pension Funds Ranking 201–1,000

Rank	Fund		Assets	Rank	Fund		Assets
495	Aerospace Corp.	El Segundo, Calif.	283	543	Cincinnati G&E	Cincinnati	250
496	S. Calif. Laborers	Los Angeles	281	544	Carpenters	Chicago	248
497	Squibb Corp.	New York	280	545	Lumber, Western	Portland, Ore.	248
498	Carnation Co.	Los Angeles	280	546	Savings Bank Emp.	Boston	248
499	Allen-Bradley Co.	Milwaukee	279	547	Mercantile Stores	New York	248
500	Cleveland Carpenters	Cleveland	279	548	Ventura County	Ventura, Calif.	246
501	Amsted Industries	Chicago	279	549	Operating Eng., #18	Columbus, Ohio	246
502	Boston City	Boston	278	550	S. Calif. Rapid Transit	Los Angeles	244
503	Baltimore County	Baltimore	278	551	Building Trades	Milwaukee	242
504	Briggs & Stratton	Milwaukee	278	552	Allegheny		
505	Florida Progress Corp.	St. Petersburg, Fla.	278		International	Pittsburgh	242
506	Stone & Webster	New York	278	553	Hughes Tool Co.	Houston	240
507	Walgreen Co.	Deerfield, Ill.	277	554	Tribune Co.	Chicago	240
508	Transco Energy Co.	Houston	277	555	Wheeling-Pittsburgh	Pittsburgh	239
509	Screen Actors Guild	Hollywood, Calif.	277	556	Iron Workers,		
510	Graphic Arts	Washington	276		California	Oakland	239
511	ABC	New York	275	557	Kern County	Bakersfield, Calif.	238
512	ASARCO Inc.	New York	275	558	Va. Electric & Power	Richmond, Va.	238
513	BOC Group	Montvale, N.J.	274	559	N.Y. State Teamsters	Utica, N.Y.	238
514	H.J. Heinz	Pittsburgh	271	560	Seafarers, Great Lakes	Camp Springs, Md.	237
515	Missouri Employees	Jefferson City	270	561	Baker International	Orange, Calif.	235
516	Teamsters, W. Pa.	Pittsburgh	270	562	Esmark	Chicago	235
517	Texas Eastern	Houston	269	563	San Diego G&E	San Diego	234
518	Union Camp	Wayne, N.J.	269	564	McKesson Corp.	San Francisco	234
519	Typographical Union	Colorado Springs	268	565	Laborers, National	Washington	233
520	Miami City	Miami	268	566	AFTRA	New York	232
521	Amstar Corp.	New York	267	567	Carpenters, C.&W.		
522	Service Emp., #328	New York	266		Ind.	Indianapolis	232
523	ICMA Retirement	Washington	265	568	Rapid-American Corp.	New York	232
524	Great North. Nekoosa	Stamford, Conn.	265	569	Kerr-McGee	Oklahoma City	230
525	Inco United States	New York	264	570	California Butchers	Oakland, Calif.	230
526	Laborers	Forest Park, Ill.	264	571	Gannett Co.	Rochester, N.Y.	230
527	Marriott Corp.	Washington	262	572	Arthur Andersen &		
528	Paper Industry	Nashville, Tenn.	261		Co.	Chicago	229
529	American Motors	Southfield, Mich.	260	573	Perkin-Elmer	Norwalk, Conn.	229
530	N.J. Hospital Assoc.	Princeton, N.J.	260	574	Chicago Bridge & Iron	Oak Brook, Ill.	229
531	United Cement			575	MidCon Corp.	Lombard, Ill.	228
	Workers	Elk Grove Village, Ill.	260	576	Steelcase	Grand Rapids, Mich.	227
532	Hormel	Austin, Minn.	258	577	Fire and Police	Denver	227
533	Jacksonville			578	Fort Worth Employees	Fort Worth, Texas	227
	Employees	Jacksonville, Fla.	258	579	GrandMet USA	Montvale, N.J.	226
534	Seattle Employees	Seattle	257	580	Blue Bell	Greensboro, N.C.	226
535	Continental Air Lines	Houston	256	581	Norton Simon	New York	226
536	Sonat	Birmingham, Ala.	254	582	UAW, Dist. 65	New York	225
537	Northern Illinois Gas	Aurora, Ill.	252	583	Akzona Inc.	Asheville, N.C.	225
538	Am. Home Products	New York	252	584	Carpenter Technology	Reading, Pa.	225
539	Belk/Leggett Stores	Charlotte, N.C.	251	585	Brunswick Corp.	Skokie, Ill.	225
540	Celanese Corp.	New York	250	586	Maytag Co.	Newton, Iowa	225
541	Western Air Lines	Los Angeles	250	587	Reader's Digest	Pleasantville, N.Y.	225
542	Lever Brothers	New York	250	588	Inter-Am. Dev. Bank	Washington	224

Pension Funds Ranking 201–1,000

Rank	Fund		Assets	Rank	Fund		Assets
589	Anchor Hocking Corp.	Lancaster, Ohio	224	636	Mellon Bank	Pittsburgh	200
590	Milliken & Co.	Spartanburg, S.C.	223	637	Jim Walter Corp.	Tampa, Fla.	200
591	Joseph E. Seagram	New York	223	638	United Food Workers	Chicago	199
592	Operating Engrs.,			639	St. Louis Schools	St. Louis	199
	#324	Birmingham, Mich.	222	640	AMFAC Inc.	San Francisco	198
593	Champion Spark Plug	Toledo, Ohio	222	641	Denver Employees	Denver	198
594	Colo. Public Service	Denver	222	642	Printing Pressmen	Los Angeles	197
595	Fresno County	Fresno, Calif.	221	643	Gould	Rolling Meadows, Ill.	197
596	Carolina Power & Light	Raleigh, N.C.	220	644	Hartford Employees	Hartford, Conn.	197
597	Boston Edison	Boston	220	645	Pickands Mather	Cleveland	193
598	Minneapolis Teachers	Minneapolis	220	646	Brooklyn Union Gas	Brooklyn, N.Y.	193
599	Fairfax County	Fairfax, Va.	220	647	ONEOK Inc.	Tulsa, Okla.	192
600	Miles Laboratories	Elkhart, Ind.	219	648	Tacumseh Products	Tecumseh, Mich.	191
601	Nalco Chemical	Oak Brook, Ill.	219	649	Washington Gas Light	Washington	190
602	AMA	Chicago	219	650	Food Workers	Los Angeles	189
603	Typographical Union	Chicago	218	651	Phoenix Employees	Phoenix	188
604	Dallas Police and Fire	Dallas	217	652	Gerber Products Co.	Fremont, Mich.	188
605	Becton Dickinson	Paramus, N.J.	216	653	AMCA International	Hanover, N.H.	187
606	Boy Scouts of			654	National Steelworkers	Pittsburgh	187
	America	Irving, Texas	215	655	Mitre Corp.	Bedford, Mass.	187
607	American Stores Co.	Salt Lake City	215	656	Detroit Carpenters	Southfield, Mich.	186
608	Graybar Electric Co.	St. Louis	214	657	United Energy Res.	Houston	185
609	GAF Corp.	Wayne, N.J.	214	658	Diamond Shamrock	Dallas	185
610	Flint Employees	Flint, Mich.	213	659	Federal Mogul Corp.	Detroit	185
611	Centel Corp.	Chicago	213	660	Nestle	White Plains, N.Y.	185
612	Rohr Industries	Chula Vista, Calif.	212	661	Coastal Corp.	Houston	184
613	Teamsters	Philadelphia	212	662	Zenith	Glenview, Ill.	184
614	R.H. Macy & Co.	New York	211	663	Plumbers, #597	Chicago	184
615	S.C. Johnson & Son	Racine, Wis.	211	664	San Mateo County	Redwood City, Calif.	184
616	Food Workers, #455	Atlanta	211	665	Freeport-McMoran	New York	184
617	Diamond International	New York	210	666	Textile Workers	New York	184
618	Cleveland-Cliffs Iron	Cleveland	210	667	Baton Rouge Emp.	Baton Rouge, La.	184
619	Int'l Minerals & Chem.	Mundelein, Ill.	210	668	Agway Inc.	Syracuse, N.Y.	184
620	Ogden Corp.	New York	210	669	N. Ind. Pub. Service	Hammond, Ind.	184
621	Johnson & Higgins	New York	210	670	SCM Corp.	New York	183
622	Nat'l Auto. Sprinkler	Silver Springs, Md.	208	671	Rochester G&E	Rochester, N.Y.	183
623	Sandoz	East Hanover, N.J.	208	672	Arizona Public Service	Phoenix	182
624	Gates Corp.	Denver	207	673	Oakland Munic. Emp.	Oakland, Calif.	182
625	STA-ILA	Baltimore, Md.	205	674	Humana	Louisville, Ky.	181
626	Sterling Drug	New York	205	675	Auto Workers, #65	New York	181
627	Memphis Light	Memphis, Tenn.	203	676	Texas Gas Trans.	Owensboro, Ky.	181
628	Lear Siegler	Santa Monica, Calif.	201	677	Flying Tiger Line	Los Angeles	180
629	Northwest Pipeline	Salt Lake City	201	678	Western Metal		
630	Outboard Marine Corp.	Waukegan, Ill.	201		Industry	Seattle	180
631	National Fuel & Gas	Buffalo, N.Y.	200	679	National Can	Chicago	180
632	Johnson Controls	Milwaukee	200	680	Hershey	Hershey, Pa.	180
633	Longshoremen	Houston	200	681	Sheet Metal, #108	Los Angeles	180
634	Alexander &			682	Int'l Operating Eng.	Washington	178
	Alexander	Baltimore	200	683	Publix Super Markets	Lakeland, Fla.	177
635	Joy Manufacturing	Pittsburgh	200	684	Gleason Works	Rochester, N.Y.	176

(Continued)

Pension Funds Ranking 201–1,000

Rank	Fund		Assets	Rank	Fund		Assets
685	Sanitary Employees	Chicago	176	732	Automotive Industries	Oakland, Calif.	162
686	National Geographic	Washington	176	733	Santa Fe International	Alhambra, Calif.	162
687	Upholsterers Int'l	Philadelphia	176	734	Cameron Iron Works	Houston	162
688	Ohio Laborers	Columbus	176	735	Cone Mills Corp.	Greensboro, N.C.	162
689	Vulcan Materials Co.	Birmingham, Ala.	176	736	Sybron Corp.	Rochester, N.Y.	162
690	Sacramento Emp.	Sacramento, Calif.	175	737	Brown Group	St. Louis	162
691	Lone Star Industries	Greenwich, Conn.	175	738	Salt River Project	Tempe, Ariz.	162
692	Food Workers	Madis. Hts., Mich.	175	739	Mobay Chemical Corp.	Pittsburgh	162
693	Lukens	Coatesville, Pa.	174	740	Thyssen-Bornemisza	New York	161
694	Mass. Carpenters	Burlington, Mass.	173	741	Carpenters, W. Wash.	Seattle	161
695	EG&G Inc.	Wellesley, Mass.	172	742	Frontier Airlines	Denver	161
696	Arkla	Shreveport, La.	171	743	Square D	Palatine, Ill.	161
697	Nat'l Telephone Co-op	Washington	170	744	Tyler Corp.	Dallas	161
698	Hospital Corp. of Amer.	Nashville, Tenn.	170	745	Voluntary Hospital Lge.	New York	160
699	Potlatch Corp.	San Francisco	170	746	Daniel International	Greenville, S.C.	160
700	Springs Industries	Fort Mill, S.C.	170	747	Electrical Wrkrs. #134	Chicago	160
701	Caltex Petroleum	Dallas	170	748	Texasgulf	Stamford, Conn.	159
702	Arlington County	Arlington, Va.	170	749	Pechiney Corp.	Greenwich, Conn.	158
703	Acco Babcock	Fairfield, Conn.	169	750	Park Employees	Chicago	158
704	Moorman Mfg.	Quincy, Ill.	169	751	Norfolk Employees	Norfolk, Va.	158
705	Cessna Aircraft	Wichita, Kan.	169	752	Cargill	Minneapolis	158
706	McDonald's Corp.	Oak Brook, Ill.	168	753	Williams Companies	Tulsa, Okla.	157
707	Commerce Clearing	Chicago	168	754	TPF&C	Philadelphia	157
708	First Boston	New York	168	755	BASF Wyandotte	Parsippany, N.J.	157
709	Mo. Highway Emp.	Jefferson City, Mo.	168	756	Austin Employees	Austin, Texas	157
710	Sanders Assoc.	Nashua, N.H.	168	757	McKinsey & Co.	New York	156
711	Equifax Inc.	Atlanta	168	758	Armstrong Rubber	New Haven, Conn.	156
712	Wickes Companies	Santa Monica, Calif.	167	759	Reliance Electric	Cleveland	156
713	Potomac Electric	Washington	167	760	A.C. Nielsen Co.	Northbrook, Ill.	155
714	Alumax Inc.	San Mateo, Calif.	167	761	Stanley Works	New Britain, Conn.	155
715	Knight-Ridder	Miami	167	762	Cultural Institutions	New York	155
716	Illinois Tool Works	Chicago	167	763	Major League Players	New York	155
717	Brockway Inc.	Brockway, Pa.	167	764	Interco Inc.	St. Louis	155
718	Amerada Hess Corp.	New York	166	765	Tandy Corp.	Fort Worth	154
719	Illinois Power	Decatur, Ill.	165	766	Consolidated Papers	Wis. Rapids, Wis.	153
720	Birmingham Emp.	Birmingham, Ala.	165	767	Morrison-Knudsen	Boise, Idaho	153
721	Pacific Power & Light	Portland, Ore.	165	768	National Auto Workers	Detroit	153
722	Cyclops Corp.	Pittsburgh	165	769	NVF Co.	Miami Beach	152
723	St. Louis Employees	St. Louis	165	770	Pittston Co.	Greenwich, Conn.	152
724	Hearst Corp.	New York	165	771	Mass. Laborers	Newton, Mass.	152
725	Baxter Travenol Labs	Deerfield, Ill.	165	772	Hawaiian Electric	Honolulu	152
726	Royal Indemnity Co.	New York	164	773	Tampa Fire & Police	Tampa, Fla.	152
727	Columbus/S. Ohio Elec.	Columbus, Ohio	164	774	Acme-Cleveland Corp.	Cleveland	150
728	Machinists, #9	Bridgeton, Mo.	164	775	S'western Public Serv.	Amarillo, Texas	150
729	National Industrial	Florham Park, N.J.	163	776	Illinois Carpenters	Geneva, Ill.	150
730	Pacific Maritime Assoc.	San Francisco	163	777	Dravo Corp.	Pittsburgh	150
731	Oklahoma G&E	Oklahoma City	163	778	American Hoechst	Somerville, N.J.	150
				779	Foster Wheeler	Livingston, N.J.	150

Pension Funds Ranking 201–1,000

Rank	Fund		Assets	Rank	Fund		Assets
780	American Insurance	New York	149	829	Marine Engineers, #2	Brooklyn, N.Y.	132
781	Graphic Arts	Chicago	149	830	SKF Industries	King of Prussia, Pa.	132
782	Capital Holding Corp.	Louisville, Ky.	146	831	New York Times Co.	New York	132
783	Chubb Corp.	New York	146	832	Auto Mechanics,		
784	Hanna Mining Co.	Cleveland	146		#701	Chicago	132
785	Kansas City P&L	Kansas City, Mo.	145	833	Food Workers, #174	New York	132
786	Alaska Laborers	Seattle	144	834	Loews Corp.	New York	132
787	Marmon Group	Chicago	144	835	Peabody Holding Co.	St. Louis	131
788	Ohio Iron Workers	Charleston, W. Va.	143	836	Clevepak Corp.	Purchase, N.Y.	131
789	Greater Cleve. Hospital	Cleveland	143	837	La. Land & Exploration	New Orleans	130
790	Thomas J. Lipton	Englewood Cl., N.J.	143	838	W. Pa. Carpenters	Pittsburgh	130
791	ACF Industries	New York	143	839	Alco Standard Corp.	Valley Forge, Pa.	130
792	Harsco Corp.	Camp Hill, Pa.	142	840	Marin County Emp.	San Rafael, Calif.	130
793	Utah Power & Light	Salt Lake City	142	841	Oakland County Emp.	Pontiac, Mich.	130
794	Elec. Workers #1547	Anchorage, Alaska	142	842	Wang Laboratories	Lowell, Mass.	130
795	Allegheny Ludlum	Pittsburgh	142	843	A.B. Dick Co.	Chicago	130
796	Bricklayers Int'l.	Washington	142	844	Auto Club of S. Calif.	Los Angeles	130
797	Santa Barbara County	Santa Barbara, Calif.	141	845	N. Calif. Laborers	San Francisco	128
798	National Gypsum Co.	Dallas	141	846	Wichita Employees	Wichita, Kan.	128
799	Texas Iron Workers	Houston	140	847	Gulf States Utilities	Beaumont, Texas	127
800	Foxboro Co.	Foxboro, Mass.	140	848	Hammermill Paper	Erie, Pa.	127
801	Castle & Cooke Inc.	Honolulu	140	849	Hiram Walker & Sons	Detroit	127
802	Mid-Jersey Truck			850	Blue Cross, Michigan	Detroit	127
	#701	N. Brunswick, N.J.	140	851	No. N.J. Iron Workers	Newark, N.J.	126
803	Phil. Carpenters	Philadelphia	140	852	Cannon Mills Co.	Kannapolis, N.C.	126
804	Fresno Employees	Fresno, Calif.	139	853	N. Dakota Emp.	Bismarck	126
805	MAPCO Inc.	Tulsa, Okla.	138	854	Peat Marwick Mitchell	New York	126
806	N. Calif. Sheet Metal	Dublin Calif.	138	855	ARA Services	Philadelphia	125
807	Food Workers, #27	Baltimore	136	856	Weymouth Contrib.	E. Weymouth, Mass.	125
808	Leo Burnett Co.	Chicago	136	857	Witco Chemical Corp.	New York	125
809	Anderson, Clayton	Houston	136	858	Black & Decker	Towson, Md.	125
810	Fort Howard Paper	Green Bay, Wis.	135	859	Laborers, #472, #172	Newark, N.J.	125
811	Curtiss Wright Corp.	Woodridge, N.J.	135	860	El Paso Employees	El Paso, Texas	124
812	Burroughs Wellcome	Research Tri., N.C.	135	861	Copperweld Corp.	Pittsburgh	124
813	St. Joe Minerals Corp.	New York	134	862	Signode Industries	Glenview, Ill.	124
814	Atlanta Employees	Atlanta	134	863	Harnischfeger Corp.	Milwaukee	124
815	Dayton Power & Light	Dayton, Ohio	134	864	Grand Union Co.	Elmwood Park, N.J.	124
816	Beech Aircraft Corp.	Wichita, Kan.	134	865	Operating Eng., #825	Newark, N.J.	123
817	Duquesne Light Co.	Pittsburgh	134	866	Newmont Mining		
818	E.W. Scripps Co.	Cincinnati	134		Corp.	New York	123
819	Carter Hawley Hale	Los Angeles	133	867	W. Pa. Laborers	Pittsburgh	123
820	James River Corp.	Richmond, Va.	133	868	W.W. Grainger Inc.	Skokie, Ill.	123
821	Atlantic City Electric	Pleasantville, N.J.	133	869	Shelby County	Memphis, Tenn.	123
822	Ark. State Highway	Little Rock, Ark.	133	870	San Joaquin County	Stockton, Calif.	123
823	Delmarva P&L	Wilmington, Del.	133	871	Media General	Richmond, Va.	122
824	Associated Dry Goods	New York	133	872	Davy Inc.	Cleveland	122
825	Western Greyhound	Phoenix, Ariz.	133	873	S. Calif. Plasterers	Los Angeles	122
826	St. Paul Teachers	St. Paul, Minn.	133	874	Reserve Mining Co.	Silver Bay, Minn.	122
827	Retail Clerks	Atlanta	133	875	Lincoln Electric	Cleveland	122
828	Commercial Credit	Baltimore	132	876	Adolph Coors Co.	Golden, Colo.	121

(Continued)

Pension Funds Ranking 201–1,000

Rank	Fund		Assets	Rank	Fund		Assets
877	Puget Sound P&L	Bellevue, Wash.	121	922	Ampco Pittsburgh		
878	Arthur Young	New York	121		Corp.	Boston	108
879	U.S. Borax	Los Angeles	121	923	Ideal Basic Industries	Denver	108
880	Louisiana-Pacific	Portland, Ore.	120	924	Pennsylvania		
881	Longshoremen	New Orleans	120		Municipal	Harrisburg, Pa.	108
882	Molders', Allied			925	Kaiser Steel	Fontana, Calif.	108
	Workers	Cincinnati	120	926	Alexander & Baldwin	Honolulu	108
883	Varian Associates	Palo Alto, Calif.	120	927	Indianapolis P&L	Indianapolis	108
884	Dennison Mfg.	Waltham, Mass.	120	928	Kansas City Schools	Kansas City, Mo.	107
885	Wean United	Pittsburgh	119	929	Ernst & Whinney	Cleveland	107
886	Wis. Public Service	Green Bay, Wis.	119	930	YWCA Retirement	New York	107
887	Ohio Casualty Group	Hamilton, Ohio	118	931	Retail Clerks, 1105	Seattle	107
888	St. Louis Police	St. Louis	118	932	Machinists, #289	Seattle	107
889	Rochester Telephone	Rochester, N.Y.	118	933	Figgie International	Richmond, Va.	107
890	Richardson-Vicks	Wilton, Conn.	117	934	Nat'l. Football League	New York	107
891	Dow Jones	Princeton, N.J.	117	935	Machinists, #67	Washington	107
892	Yellow Freight	Overland Park, Kan.	117	936	Rubbermaid Inc.	Wooster, Ohio	106
893	Reliance Group	New York	117	937	Iron Workers	Seattle	106
894	Bell & Howell	Chicago	117	938	Stanislaus County	Modesto, Calif.	106
895	St. Louis Firemen	St. Louis	116	939	Grain Processing Corp.	Muscatine, Iowa	106
896	Barnes Group	Bristol, Conn.	116	940	Arvin Industries	Columbus, Ind.	106
897	Indiana Public Service	Plainfield, Ind.	116	941	Beneficial Corp.	Wilmington, Del.	106
898	N'western Steel &			942	United Brands Co.	New York	106
	Wire	Sterling, Ill.	116	943	PSA Inc.	San Diego	105
899	MCA Inc.	Universal City, Calif.	115	944	Teamsters, #83	Richmond, Va.	105
900	American Petrofina	Dallas	115	945	American International	New York	105
901	Copley Press	La Jolla, Calif.	115	946	IUE AFL-CIO	Bloomfield, N.J.	105
902	IU International	Philadelphia	115	947	Capital Cities Comm.	New York	104
903	Screen Extras, Equity	New York	114	948	United Tech. Auto	Dearborn, Mich.	104
904	PACCAR Inc.	Bellevue, Wash.	114	949	Commonwealth		
905	Revere Copper &				Energy	Cambridge, Mass.	104
	Brass	New York	114	950	Toledo Edison	Toledo, Ohio	103
906	Iron Workers, #25	Detroit	114	951	Bulova Watch Co.	Flushing, N.Y.	103
907	Stanadyne Inc.	Windsor, Conn.	113	952	Carpenters, #1310	St. Louis	102
908	S.C. Electric & Gas	Columbia, S.C.	111	953	Dillon Companies	Hutchinson, Kan.	102
909	United Services Auto	San Antonio, Texas	111	954	Houston Natural Gas	Houston	102
910	Laborers, #395	Phoenix	111	955	Tampa Employees	Tampa, Fla.	102
911	Gries Dynacast	New Rochelle, N.Y.	111	956	S. Calif. Permanente	Los Angeles	102
912	William Wrigley Jr.	Chicago	111	957	Eagle-Picher	Cincinnati	101
913	Pontiac General Emp.	Pontiac, Mich.	111	958	Operating Engr. #542	Norristown, Pa.	101
914	Wisconsin Gas	Milwaukee	110	959	Sheller-Globe Corp.	Toledo, Ohio	101
915	San Antonio Fire/			960	Scovill	Waterbury, Conn.	101
	Police	San Antonio, Texas	110	961	Combined Insurance	Northbrook, Ill.	100
916	Syntex Corp.	Palo Alto, Calif.	110	962	Lowe's Companies	N. Wilkesboro, N.C.	100
917	N.Y. Stock Exchange	New York	109	963	Long Island Lighting	Mineola, N.Y.	100
918	Minnegasco Inc.	Minneapolis	109	964	Laclede Gas Co.	St. Louis	100
919	Amer. Water Works	Haden Heights, N.J.	109	965	Houdaille Industries	Fort Lauderdale, Fla.	100
920	Tacoma Employees	Tacoma, Wash.	109	966	Masco Corp.	Taylor, Mich.	100
921	Bucyrus-Erie Co.	Milwaukee	108	967	Operating Eng., #15	New York	100

Pension Funds Ranking 201–1,000

Rank	Fund		Assets	Rank	Fund		Assets
968	Omaha Public Power	Omaha, Neb.	100	984	Greenwood Mills	Greenwood, S.C.	97
969	Wal-Mart Stores	Bentonville, Ark.	100	985	Teamsters, #330	W. Chicago, Ill.	97
970	Banco Popular	Hato Rey, P. Rico	100	986	Revlon	New York	97
971	Parker-Hannifin Corp.	Cleveland, Ohio	99	987	Teamsters, #282	Elmont, N.Y.	97
972	Federal Express Corp.	Memphis, Tenn.	99	988	Longview Fibre Co.	Longview, Wash.	97
973	Young & Rubicam Inc.	New York	99	989	Ladish Co.	Cudahy, Wis.	97
974	Southern California Food Workers	Los Angeles	99	990	Warner Comm.	New York	97
975	Iron Workers	New York	99	991	Andersen Corp.	Bayport, Minn.	97
976	Manitowoc Co.	Manitowoc, Wis.	99	992	Sonoco Products Co.	Hartsville, S.C.	96
977	Keystone Consol.	Peoria, Ill.	99	993	Laborers, #253	Jacksonville, Ill.	96
978	Jack Eckerd Corp.	Clearwater, Fla.	99	994	Tulare County Emp.	Visalia, Calif.	96
979	Amica Mutual Ins.	Providence, R.I.	99	995	Chesebrough-Ponds	Greenwich, Conn.	96
980	Allegheny County	Pittsburgh	98	996	S. Calif. Retail Clerks	Los Angeles	96
981	Knoxville Employees	Knoxville, Tenn.	98	997	WSSC	Hyattsville, Md.	96
982	Laborers, Mason	New York	98	998	Lubrizol Corp.	Wickliffe, Ohio	95
983	Plumbers, #638	New York	98	999	Woodward Governor	Rockford, Ill.	94
				1000	Consol. Freightways	Palo Alto, Calif.	94

Source: *Pension & Investment Age,* January 21, 1985. © Crain Communication.

5.06 **Profit-Sharing Plans**

Qualified profit-sharing or pension plans are established by employers to enable companies to set aside part of current earnings; some plans also include contributions from the employees. The employer's contributions and any growth in the fund are not taxable until the employee starts to receive payments from the fund, either as a lump sum or as monthly income.

25 LARGEST PROFIT-SHARING PLANS, 1984
(Millions of Dollars)

Rank	Fund	Assets	Rank	Fund	Assets
1	Sears, Roebuck & Co.	3,259	14	Philip Morris Inc.	310
2	Procter & Gamble	1,874	15	Boeing Co.	301
3	Chevron Corp.	1,461	16	Texas Instruments	300
4	Xerox Corp.	1,210	17	Caterpillar Tractor Co.	284
5	Lockheed Corp.	1,143	18	Shell Oil Co.	200
6	Bechtel Power Corp.	985	19	The LTV Corp.	183
7	J.C. Penney Co.	981	20	Dart & Kraft Inc.	173
8	Eastman Kodak	847	21	Citicorp	166
9	Halliburton Co.	842	22	John Hancock Mutual Life Insurance	117
10	Motorola Inc.	632	23	CIGNA Corp.	116
11	Northrop Corp.	590	24	Florida Power & Light Co.	116
12	Unocal	379	25	Dow Chemical Co.	100
13	Standard Oil Co. (Ohio)	334		**TOTAL**	**$16,903**

Source: *Pensions & Investment Age,* January 21, 1985. © Crain Communications.

COMPARISON OF TOTAL RETURN ON A
QUALIFIED PLAN vs. OTHER INVESTMENTS

This graph shows the results of an investment of $5,000 annually in a qualified plan (pension or profit-sharing) compared with the results of the same amounts being invested elsewhere and, therefore, fully taxable. The rate of interest is assumed to be 5%. The graph takes into account the reduction in net interest from tax on interest income.

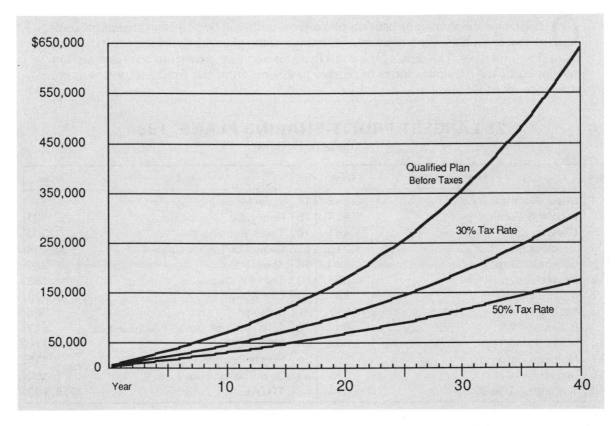

Source: Loren Dunton, *Your Book of Financial Planning,* 1983. Reprinted with permission of Reston Publishing Company, a Prentice-Hall company, 11480 Sunset Hills Road, Reston VA 22090.

5.07 The Biggest

Biggest is not necessarily best. However, size does indicate that a company has been sufficiently successful at what it does to prosper and grow. The following information is probably most useful in annual performance comparisons. Steady, if moderate, growth might be more beneficial to a company than an erratic pattern of peaks and valleys.

Some of the information about the biggest deals or biggest buyouts is interesting for its own sake, but also provides a useful sketch of the changing composition of various companies and the expansion of their products and services.

100 LARGEST U.S. INDUSTRIAL CORPORATIONS

The compilation of this listing of the 100 largest industrial corporations in the U.S. has been based on a number of assumptions:

Sales: All companies on the list must have derived more than 50% of their sales from manufacturing and/or mining. Sales include rental and other revenues, but exclude dividends, interest, and other non-operating revenues. Sales of subsidiaries are included if they are consolidated. Sales from discontinued operations are included if these figures are published. Sales that are at least 10% higher for this reason are distinguished by a superscript 11 next to the sales figure. All figures are for the year ending December 31, 1984, unless otherwise noted. Sales figures do not include excise taxes collected by the manufacturer, and so the figures for some corporations — most of which sell gasoline, liquor, or tobacco — may be lower than those published by the corporations themselves. Sales that are at least 5% lower for this reason are distinguished by a superscript 1 next to the sales figure.

Assets: Assets are those shown at the company's fiscal year-end.

Net income: Net income is shown after taxes and after extraordinary credits or charges if any are shown in the income statement. An extraordinary credit reflecting at least 10% of the net income shown is distinguished by a superscript 9; an extraordinary charge of at least 10% by a superscript 5. Figures in parentheses indicate a loss.

Stockholders' equity: Stockholders' equity is the sum of capital stock, surplus, and retained earnings at the company's year-end. Redeemable preferred stock is excluded if its redemption is either mandatory or outside the control of the company, except in the case of cooperatives. In calculating *net income as a percentage of stockholders' equity*, any dividends paid on redeemable preferred stock, if that stock's redemption is either mandatory or outside the control of the company, have been subtracted from the net income figure.

Employees: The figure shown is a year-end total except when it is followed by a superscript 2, in which case it is an average for the year.

Earnings per share: For all companies the figures shown are the primary earnings per share that appear on the company's income statement. These figures are based on a weighted average of the number of common shares and common stock equivalents outstanding during the year. Per-share earnings for 1983 and 1984 are adjusted for stock splits and stock dividends. They are not restated for mergers, acquisitions, or accounting changes made after 1974. An extraordinary credit reflecting at least 10% of the net income is indicated by a superscript 9; an extraordinary charge of at least 10% by a superscript 5. The growth rate is the average annual growth, compounded. No growth rate is given if the company has a loss in either 1974 or 1984.

Total return to investors: Total return to investors includes both price appreciation and dividend yield to an investor in the company's stock. The figures shown assume sales at the end of 1984 of stock owned at the end of 1974 and 1983. It has been assumed that any proceeds from cash dividends, the sale of rights and warrant offerings, and stock received in spinoffs were reinvested at the end of the year in which they were received. Returns are adjusted for stock splits, stock dividends, recapitalizations, and corporate reorganizations as they occur; however, no effort has been made to reflect the cost of brokerage commissions or of taxes. If companies have more than one class of shares outstanding, only the more widely held and actively traded has been considered.

Total return percentages shown are the returns received by the hypothetical investor described above. The ten-year figures are annual averages, compounded. If corporations were substantially reorganized — e.g., because of mergers — the predecessor companies used in calculating total return are the same as those cited in the footnotes to the earnings-per-share figures.

Industry code: Industry code numbers used in the directory indicate which industry represents the greatest volume of industrial sales for each company. The numbers refer to the industry groups listed below, which are based on categories established by the U.S. Office of Management and Budget and issued by the Federal Statistical Policy and Standards Office.

INDUSTRY CODE NUMBERS

Industry	Code Number	Industry	Code Number
Mining; crude-oil production	10	Electronics, appliances	36
Food	20	Shipbuilding; railroad and transportation equipment	37
Tobacco	21		
Textiles; vinyl flooring	22	Measuring, scientific, photographic equipment	38
Apparel	23		
Furniture	25	Motor vehicles and parts	40
Paper, fibre, and wood products	26	Aerospace	41
Publishing; printing	27	Pharmaceuticals	42
Chemicals	28	Soaps, cosmetics	43
Petroleum refining	29	Office equipment (includes computers)	44
Rubber, plastic products	30	Industrial and farm equipment	45
Leather	31	Jewelry, silverware	46
Glass, concrete, abrasives, gypsum	32	Musical instruments; toys; sporting goods	47
Metal manufacturing	33	Beverages	49
Metal products	34		

100 LARGEST U.S. INDUSTRIAL CORPORATIONS
Ranked by Sales

Rank		Company	Sales ($ 000)	Assets		Net Income	
1984	1983			($ 000)	Rank	($ 000)	Rank
1	1	Exxon, N.Y.	90,854,000[1]	63,278,000	1	5,528,000	2
2	2	General Motors, Detroit	83,889,900	52,114,900	2	4,516,500	3
3	3	Mobil, N.Y.[3]	56,047,000[1]	41,851,000	4	1,268,000	13
4	4	Ford Motor, Dearborn, Michigan	52,366,400	27,485,600	8	2,906,800	4
5	6	Texaco, Harrison, N.Y.[4]	47,334,000	37,744,000	6	306,000[5]	62
6	5	International Business Machines, Armonk, N.Y.	45,937,000	42,808,000	3	6,582,000	1
7	7	E.I. du Pont de Nemours, Wilmington, Delaware	35,915,000	24,098,000	11	1,431,000	11
8		American Tel. & Tel., N.Y.	33,187,500	39,826,600	5	1,369,900	12
9	10	General Electric, Fairfield, Connecticut	27,947,000	24,730,000	10	2,280,000	6
10	8	Standard Oil (Indiana), Chicago	26,949,000[1]	25,734,000	9	2,183,000	7
11	9	Chevron, San Francisco[7,8]	26,798,000	36,358,000	7	1,534,000	9
12	12	Atlantic Richfield, Los Angeles	24,686,000	22,130,000	13	567,000	30
13	13	Shell Oil, Houston	20,701,000[1]	23,729,000	12	1,772,000	8
14	21	Chrysler, Highland Park, Michigan	19,572,700	9,062,700	31	2,380,000	5
15	15	U.S. Steel, Pittsburgh	18,274,000	18,989,000	14	493,000[9]	37
16	18	United Technologies, Hartford	16,331,757	9,904,536	25	645,015	24
17	16	Phillips Petroleum, Bartlesville, Oklahoma	15,537,000	16,965,000	17	810,000	18
18	14	Occidental Petroleum, Los Angeles	15,373,000	12,273,100	20	568,700	29
19	19	Tenneco, Houston	14,779,000	18,205,000	15	631,000	25
20	17	Sun, Radnor, Pennsylvania	14,466,000	12,789,000	19	538,000	31
21	20	ITT, N.Y.	14,000,988	13,277,188	18	448,046	43
22	22	Procter & Gamble, Cincinnati[10]	12,946,000	8,898,000	32	890,000	16
23	23	R.J. Reynolds Industries, Winston-Salem, N.C.	11,902,000[1,11]	9,272,000	29	1,210,000	14
24	25	Standard Oil (Ohio), Cleveland	11,692,000	17,487,000	16	1,488,000	10
25	28	Dow Chemical, Midland, Michigan	11,418,000	11,419,000	21	585,000	27
26	29	Allied, Morris Township, N.J.	10,864,000	8,189,000	34	488,000	40
27	31	Unocal, Los Angeles	10,838,400	10,202,800	24	700,400	21
28	30	Eastman Kodak, Rochester, N.Y.	10,600,000	10,778,000	22	923,000	15
29	27	Boeing, Seattle	10,354,000	8,485,000	33	787,000	19
30	34	Westinghouse Electric, Pittsburgh	10,264,500	9,150,400	30	535,900	32
31	32	Goodyear Tire & Rubber, Akron, Ohio	10,240,800	6,194,300	42	411,000	47
32	35	Philip Morris, N.Y.	10,137,800[1]	9,339,200	28	888,500	17
33	33	Dart & Kraft, Northbrook, Illinois	9,758,700	5,284,900	55	455,800	42
34	42	McDonnell Douglas, St. Louis	9,662,600	6,191,300	43	325,300	56
35	37	Union Carbide, Danbury, Connecticut	9,508,000	10,518,000	23	323,000	57
36	36	Beatrice Foods, Chicago[13]	9,327,000	4,464,000	66	433,000	45
37	43	Rockwell International, Pittsburg[14]	9,322,100	5,869,500	47	496,500	36
38	38	Xerox, Stamford, Connecticut	8,971,300	9,537,100	27	290,500	64
39	41	General Foods, Rye Brook, N.Y.[15]	8,599,754	4,431,782	67	317,105	58
40	44	PepsiCo, Purchase, N.Y.	8,427,994	4,950,234	57	212,547	87
41	39	Amerada Hess, N.Y.	8,277,184	6,352,832	39	170,455	109
42	45	Ashland Oil, Russell, Kentucky[14]	8,252,564	4,036,941	74	(172,478)	474
43	50	Lockheed, Burbank, California	8,113,400	3,165,600	99	344,100	53
44	46	General Dynamics, St. Louis	7,839,000	3,034,800	101	381,700	51
45	47	Minnesota Mining & Manufacturing, St. Paul	7,705,000	6,094,000	44	773,000	20

100 Largest U.S. Industrial Corporations

Stockholders' Equity ($ 000)	Rank	Employees Number	Rank	Net Income as % of: Sales %	Rank	Net Income as % of: Stockholders' Equity %	Rank	Earnings per Share $ 1984	1983	1974	1974–84 Growth Rate %	Rank	Total Return to Investors 1984 %	Rank	1974–84 Average %	Rank	Ind. Code
28,851,000	1	150,000[2]	10	6.1	145	19.2	85	6.77	5.78	3.51	6.79	231	9.36	31	18.85	220	29
24,214,300	3	748,000[2]	1	5.4	186	18.7	97	14.22	11.84	3.27	15.83	77	14.36	113	17.76	233	40
13,624,000	6	178,900	8	2.3	386	9.3	342	3.11	3.70	2.57	1.93	302	2.00	202	18.93	216	29
9,837,700	13	383,700[2]	3	5.6	176	29.6	17	15.79	10.29	2.06	22.60	30	11.21	132	16.62	256	40
13,107,000	7	68,088	46	0.7	432	2.3	437	1.03[5]	4.80	5.84	(15.93)	383	3.48	190	13.34	319	29
26,489,000	2	394,930	2	14.3	8	24.9	28	10.77	9.04	3.12	13.20	113	4.28	183	15.77	274	44
12,233,000	11	157,783	9	4.0	286	11.7	290	5.93	4.70	2.73	8.05	219	0.77	217	10.73	355	28
13,762,900	5	365,000	4	4.1	276	9.1[6]	345	1.25	0.13	5.27	(13.40)	381	8.42	154	11.75	343	36
12,573,000	8	30,000[2]	5	8.2	70	18.1	107	5.03	4.45	1.67	11.66	147	0.00	226	17.64	236	36
12,524,000	9	53,581	62	8.1	77	17.4	125	7.70	6.39	3.43	8.42	214	10.10	143	14.56	295	29
14,763,000	4	37,761	101	5.7	166	10.4	319	4.48	4.65	2.87	4.55	275	(2.82)	257	17.47	240	29
9,948,000	12	39,400	94	2.3	383	5.7	403	2.21	6.03	2.09	0.56	316	8.96	151	11.36	350	29
12,512,000	10	34,699	112	8.6	53	14.2	225	5.73	5.28	2.30	9.55	191	44.06	15	21.88	174	29
3,305,900	36	100,435[2]	18	12.2	20	72.0	2	11.88	5.79[9]	(0.92)	—		18.01	89	18.65	223	40
5,722,000	19	88,753[2]	27	2.7	360	8.1[6]	362	3.52[9]	(12.07)	7.81	(7.66)	369	(10.70)	328	6.39	397	29
4,169,450	26	205,500	7	4.0	288	15.5	183	4.90	3.97	1.65	11.47	151	3.79	186	21.10	184	41
6,624,000	16	29,300	132	5.2	197	12.2	274	5.26	4.71	2.65	7.10	229	36.52	22	12.08	340	29
2,903,600	42	40,630	91	3.7	307	11.3[6]	298	3.08	2.03[9]	4.74	(4.22)	347	22.61	62	16.28	263	10
6,153,000	17	98,000	22	4.3	262	9.3[6]	344	4.01	4.75	4.08	(0.17)	323	(0.72)	234	11.69	344	29
5,272,000	21	37,000	104	3.7	304	10.2	327	4.67	3.84	3.92	1.77	303	10.69	138	15.74	275	29
6,032,662	18	252,000	6	3.2	333	7.4	374	2.97	4.50	3.63	(1.99)	334	(29.17)	417	14.88	287	36
5,080,000	22	61,700	51	6.9	116	17.5	122	5.35	5.22	1.92	10.76	164	4.62	182	7.29	390	43
4,478,000	25	97,551	23	10.2	38	25.8[6]	24	10.27	7.25	3.49	11.38	153	29.22	32	16.92	249	21
8,390,000	14	44,200	79	12.7	17	17.7	116	6.14	6.14	1.01	19.81	45	(0.22)	229	14.77	290	10
5,062,000	23	49,800	69	5.1	205	11.6	292	3.02	1.71[9]	3.01	0.02	320	(12.21)	341	4.79	411	28
3,043,000	40	114,500	15	4.5	241	13.3[6]	251	5.03	0.09	3.62	3.34	291	(2.47)	252	11.65	346	28
5,694,300	20	20,664	180	6.5	124	12.3	271	4.03	3.60	2.23	6.10	246	20.16	74	17.82	232	29
7,137,000	15	123,900	14	8.7	52	12.9	259	5.71	3.41	3.90	3.89	285	(0.92)	237	5.50	406	38
3,695,000	32	86,600[2]	30	7.6	96	21.3	49	8.09	3.67	0.76	26.68	19	32.63	26	36.85	26	41
3,740,800	31	126,849[2]	13	5.2	196	14.3	218	3.04	2.54	0.15[5]	34.66	6	(1.00)	238	24.14	136	36
3,171,300	39	133,271[2]	12	4.0	283	13.0	256	3.87	3.06[9]	2.18	5.91	248	(9.47)	316	14.15	305	30
4,092,900	28	68,000	47	8.8	50	21.7	41	7.24	7.17	1.57	16.48	71	16.93	97	16.38	259	21
2,598,000	49	72,286[2]	43	4.7	234	17.5	121	9.02	7.92	3.41[12]	10.22	172	34.17	23	15.51	276	20
2,343,800	56	88,391	28	3.4	326	13.9	237	8.10	6.91	2.77	11.33	154	24.59	53	27.24	82	41
4,924,000	24	98,366	21	3.4	325	6.6	393	4.59	1.13[5]	8.69	(6.18)	359	(36.02)	440	5.10	409	28
2,028,000	69	72,000	44	4.6	235	21.4	47	3.99	0.27	1.55	9.92	180	(6.90)	292	12.48	334	20
2,521,600	52	105,759	16	5.3	189	19.7	75	3.25	2.52	1.03	12.12	135	(5.02)	270	26.27	98	41
4,101,000	27	103,457	17	3:2	331	5.9[6]	399	2.53	4.42	4.18	(4.90)	353	(17.42)	368	1.59	432	38
2,040,180	67	55,000	59	3.7	308	15.5	181	6.10	5.73	2.40	9.78	183	13.58	117	18.22	228	20
1,853,376	76	150,000	11	2.5	370	11.5	295	2.25	3.01	1.23	6.23	242	16.44	99	16.34	261	49
2,573,218	50	8,806[2]	316	2.1	393	6.6	392	2.01	2.43	2.35	(1.56)	333	(12.16)	340	16.75	253	29
845,899	171	33,900	114	—	—			(7.40)	2.46	2.97	—		(10.18)	321	14.89	286	29
1,151,900	122	81,300	35	4.2	266	29.9	13	5.28	4.18	0.68	22.75	28	11.12	134	43.41	14	41
1,062,100	134	99,000	20	4.9	222	35.9	9	8.08	5.30	1.01	23.09	26	21.29	71	35.10	33	41
3,814,000	30	86,707	29	10.0	40	20.3	64	6.27	5.67	2.66	8.95	206	(0.58)	231	9.62	369	38

(Continued)

100 Largest U.S. Industrial Corporations

Rank 1984	Rank 1983	Company	Sales ($ 000)	Assets ($ 000)	Assets Rank	Net Income ($ 000)	Net Income Rank
46	48	Coca-Cola, Atlanta	7,363,993	5,958,069	45	628,818	26
47	51	Georgia-Pacific, Atlanta	7,128,000	4,785,000	59	119,000	144
48	78	LTV, Dallas[16]	7,046,100	6,926,000	35	(378,200)	482
49	49	Consolidated Foods, Chicago[10]	7,000,310	2,821,757	107	188,441	100
50	53	W.R. Grace, N.Y.	6,727,800	5,328,000	54	195,600	94
51	52	Monsanto, St. Louis	6,691,000	6,373,000	38	439,000	44
52	64	Caterpillar Tractor, Peoria, Illinois	6,576,000	6,223,000	41	(428,000)	483
53	55	Anheuser-Busch, St. Louis	6,501,200[1]	4,524,700	64	391,500	49
54	56	Nabisco Brands, Parsippany, N.J.	6,253,100	3,761,200	79	308,900	61
55	58	Coastal, Houston	6,225,362	3,295,733	91	101,716	164
56	60	Honeywell, Minneapolis	6,138,300	4,759,800	61	239,000	76
57	57	Johnson & Johnson, New Brunswick, N.J.	6,124,500	4,541,400	63	514,500	33
58	59	Raytheon, Lexington, Massachusetts	6,104,159	3,600,118	82	243,242	73
59	63	TRW, Cleveland	6,061,691	3,480,615	85	266,842	67
60	75	Hewlett-Packard, Palo Alto, California[17]	6,044,000	5,153,000	56	665,000	23
61	54	Signal Companies, La Jolla, California	6,005,000	5,511,000	51	285,000	65
62	65	Aluminum Co. of America, Pittsburgh	5,750,800	6,341,900	40	256,000	69
63	77	Texas Instruments, Dallas	5,741,600	3,423,400	86	316,000	59
64	62	General Mills, Minneapolis[18]	5,600,800	2,858,100	106	233,400	78
65	84	Digital Equipment, Maynard, Massachusetts[10]	5,584,426	5,593,253	50	328,779	55
66	70	Weyerhaeuser, Tacoma, Washington	5,549,738	5,957,723	46	226,187	80
67	81	Motorola, Schaumburg, Illinois	5,534,000	4,194,000	71	387,000	50
68	69	Bethlehem Steel, Bethlehem, Pennsylvania	5,392,100	4,387,300	69	(112,500)[9]	471
69	66	Sperry, N.Y.[15]	5,237,900	5,502,600	52	216,200	85
70	86	Champion International, Stamford, Connecticut[19]	5,121,089	6,815,396	37	(5,968)	454
71	76	Control Data, Minneapolis	5,026,900	9,588,900	26	31,600	348
72	71	Ralston Purina, St. Louis[14]	4,980,100	2,004,200	153	242,700	74
73	72	Colgate-Palmolive, N.Y.	4,909,957	2,568,343	122	71,550	207
74	83	Archer Daniels Midland, Decatur, Illinois[10]	4,906,962	2,592,704	120	117,717	146
75	74	Litton Industries, Beverly Hills, California[20]	4,899,526	4,379,903	70	313,380	60
76	82	Burroughs, Detroit	4,808,300	4,504,200	65	244,900	72
77	67	Gulf & Western Industries, N.Y.[20]	4,805,600[11]	4,148,600	72	259,900	68
78	73	American Home Products, N.Y.	4,804,299	3,032,583	102	682,082	22
79	104	International Harvester, Chicago[17]	4,802,347	3,248,925	92	(55,441)	466
80	80	International Paper, N.Y.	4,715,600	5,795,100	48	120,100	141
81	85	Borden, N.Y.	4,568,018	2,884,127	105	191,407	96
82	87	Armco, Middletown, Ohio	4,543,100	3,686,600	80	(295,000)[5]	480
83	89	Diamond Shamrock, Dallas	4,483,200	5,396,400	53	242,200	75
84	79	American Brands, N.Y.	4,474,977[2]	4,428,844	68	414,120	46
85	94	Martin Marietta, Bethesda, Maryland	4,416,526[11]	2,224,320	141	(191,764)	476
86	92	Deere, Moline, Illinois[17]	4,399,168	5,697,296	49	104,944	160
87	90	CPC International, Englewood Cliffs, N.J.	4,373,300	2,683,400	113	193,400	95
88	97	North American Philips, N.Y.	4,326,000	2,518,000	126	131,000	131
89	103	PPG Industries, Pittsburgh	4,242,000	3,796,700	76	302,600	63
90	96	IC Industries, Chicago	4,233,700	4,840,200	58	122,800	140

100 Largest U.S. Industrial Corporations

| Stockholders' Equity | | Employees | | Net Income as % of: | | | | Earnings per Share | | | | | Total Return to Inventors | | | | Ind. Code |
| | | | | Sales | | Stockholders' Equity | | $ | | | 1974–84 Growth Rate | | 1984 | | 1974–84 Average | | |
($ 000)	Rank	Number	Rank	%	Rank	%	Rank	1984	1983	1974	%	Rank	%	Rank	%	Rank	
2,778,066	47	40,500	92	8.5	54	22.6	32	4.76	4.10	1.64	11.24	156	21.75	67	14.08	306	49
2,035,000	68	40,000	93	1.7	409	5.2[6]	410	0.97	0.97	1.79	(5.95)	358	3.84	185	8.65	377	26
1,366,200	98	58,600	55	—	—			(5.84)	(3.64)[5]	10.32[9]	—		(45.24)	454	2.47	429	33
956,908	153	90,900	26	2.7	361	19.7	74	3.25	2.88	1.20	10.43	169	27.12	39	24.52	127	20
2,197,400	61	80,000	37	2.9	348	8.9	352	4.02	3.28	4.02	0.00	321	(5.97)	285	12.62	332	28
3,634,000	33	50,574	67	6.6	122	12.1	279	5.42	4.89	4.63	1.60	306	(12.11)	339	13.27	321	28
2,852,000	43	61,189[2]	52	—	—			(4.47)	(3.74)	2.67	—		(31.75)	427	3.22	424	45
1,951,000	73	38,461	97	6.0	149	18.7[6]	95	7.40	6.50	1.42	17.95	59	19.01	85	14.99	284	49
1,544,200	89	68,200	45	4.9	217	20.0	67	5.02	4.86	1.37	13.87	101	30.93	29	23.59	145	20
577,886	222	5,324	421	1.6	412	17.1[6]	137	4.50	4.02	2.64	5.48	256	(5.30)	276	23.06	157	29
2,380,900	55	94,274	24	3.9	295	10.0	331	5.10	5.03	1.96	10.01	178	0.23	224	23.72	140	44
2,932,000	41	74,200	40	8.4	63	17.6	120	2.75	2.57	0.93	11.41	152	(8.75)	309	5.16	408	42
1,979,203	72	73,300	42	4.0	285	12.3	272	2.88	3.55	0.96	11.58	148	(3.71)	261	23.48	149	36
1,758,328	79	93,524	25	4.4	248	15.2	193	7.14	5.53	3.05	8.88	207	(5.37)	279	22.79	163	40
3,545,000	34	82,000	34	11.0	33	18.8	91	2.59	1.69	0.38	21.00	37	(19.61)	374	16.78	252	44
2,805,000	45	54,000	61	4.8	228	10.2	329	2.50	0.90	2.55	(0.21)	324	3.23	193	25.85	107	41
3,343,600	35	41,100[2]	89	4.5	242	7.7	371	3.13	2.15	2.57	1.99	301	(14.87)	361	14.07	307	33
1,540,500	90	86,563	31	5.5	178	20.5	58	13.05	(6.09)	3.92	12.78	121	(12.35)	345	7.63	388	36
1,224,600	112	80,297	36	4.2	274	19.1	88	4.98	4.89	1.59	12.09	136	1.46	211	13.62	314	20
3,979,216	29	85,600	32	5.9	154	8.3	359	5.73	5.00	1.27	16.29	72	53.82	8	20.67	189	44
3,188,352	38	37,806	100	4.1	278	7.0[6]	382	1.52	1.36	2.17	(3.50)	343	(9.85)	318	4.02	420	26
2,278,000	59	99,900	19	7.0	113	17.0	139	3.27	2.09	0.84	14.56	95	(24.40)	398	13.66	312	36
1,157,000	121	51,400[2]	65	—	—			(2.91)[9]	(3.92)[9]	7.85	—		(36.49)	443	2.11	431	33
2,802,900	46	73,447	41	4.1	277	7.7	370	4.17	2.65	3.27	2.46	300	(7.60)	295	7.87	384	44
2,496,837	53	58,700	54	—	—			(0.36)	1.22	3.24	—		(21.56)	385	12.69	331	26
1,775,600	78	54,123	60	0.6	436	1.8	442	0.81	4.20	0.06[9]	28.69	13	(20.67)	382	21.84	175	44
997,500	144	49,300	71	4.9	221	24.3	30	2.68	2.58	0.85	12.12	134	32.14	27	15.41	277	20
1,231,991	111	42,800[2]	83	1.5	417	5.8	401	0.86	2.42	1.73	(6.75)	364	21.65	68	5.78	402	43
1,649,866	82	8,745	319	2.4	376	7.1	380	1.25	1.28	0.56	8.28	216	1.11	214	16.31	262	20
2,012,963	71	65,500	48	6.4	131	15.6	180	7.32	5.41	(1.06)	—		(5.45)	281	39.82	20	36
2,297,400	57	65,000	49	5.1	207	10.7	308	5.40	4.60	3.66	3.97	284	17.82	92	0.57	436	44
1,836,500	77	57,640	57	5.4	184	14.1[6]	227	3.57	(2.86)	1.72	7.56	226	(2.82)	258	18.85	219	23
2,088,584	64	47,298	73	14.2	9	32.7	11	4.43	4.00	1.42	12.05	139	7.08	166	9.09	372	42
(415,860)	494	31,104	123	—	—			(1.34)	(15.70)	4.46	—		(29.35)	418	(4.46)	443	40
3,298,000	37	32,300	118	2.6	368	3.6	426	1.88	4.61	5.95	(10.88)	377	(4.62)	266	9.15	371	26
1,367,944	96	32,200[2]	119	4.2	271	14.0	233	7.13	6.56	2.72	10.12	174	19.29	81	18.53	226	20
999,400	143	44,383	78	—	—			(4.55)[5]	(10.27)	4.47	—		(52.34)	460	0.30	437	33
2,708,800	48	12,738	249	5.4	185	8.9	351	1.78	(0.71)	2.89	(4.73)	350	(1.84)	247	11.46	348	29
2,167,334	62	75,968	39	9.3	46	18.5[6]	99	7.20	6.76	2.58	10.81	163	14.70	111	23.62	143	21
626,113	211	43,200	80	—	—			(5.82)	4.23	1.59	—		28.22	36	28.49	71	41
2,290,828	58	43,011	81	2.4	378	4.6	418	1.55	0.34	2.77	(5.66)	357	(20.13)	378	7.64	386	45
1,324,300	102	39,000	95	4.4	246	14.6	209	3.98	2.81	2.09[9]	6.63	236	9.61	146	14.92	285	20
987,000	147	57,404	58	3.0	342	13.3	252	4.53	3.38	1.41	12.34	129	1.67	208	24.99	115	36
2,015,100	70	37,700[2]	102	7.1	107	15.0	197	4.33	3.34	1.50	11.16	157	(1.72)	245	20.84	187	32
1,539,300	91	53,164	63	2.9	349	7.4[6]	376	2.89	2.36	1.78	4.97	264	25.61	49	25.20	113	20

(Continued)

100 Largest U.S. Industrial Corporations

Rank		Company	Sales ($ 000)	Assets		Net Income	
1984	1983			($ 000)	Rank	($ 000)	Rank
91	105	American Motors, Southfield, Michigan	4,215,191	1,830,160	164	15,469[9]	414
92	93	Bristol-Myers, N.Y.	4,189,400	3,248,580	93	472,374	41
93	111	Emerson Electric, St. Louis[14]	4,178,810	2,979,560	103	349,203	52
94	102	Pillsbury, Minneapolis[18]	4,172,300	2,608,300	118	169,800[9]	111
95	95	Firestone Tire & Rubber, Akron, Ohio[17]	4,161,000	2,571,000	121	102,000[9]	163
96	98	Agway, DeWitt, N.Y.[10]	4,101,458	1,388,354	211	n/av.[21]	
97	101	NCR, Dayton, Ohio	4,074,327	3,589,132	83	342,640	54
98	100	H.J. Heinz, Pittsburgh[22]	3,953,761	2,342,970	132	237,530	77
99	106	Borg-Warner, Chicago	3,915,600	2,782,800	109	206,100	89
100	107	American Cyanamid, Wayne, N.J.	3,856,726	3,326,900	88	215,918	86

1 *Does not include excise taxes; see the explanation of sales on page 5.54.*
2 *Average for the year; see the reference to employees on page 5.54.*
3 *Figures include Superior Oil (1983 rank: 196), acquired September 28, 1984.*
4 *Figures include Getty Oil (1983 rank: 24), acquired February 17, 1984.*
5 *Reflects an extraordinary charge of at least 10%; see the explanations of net income and earnings per share on page 5.54.*
6 *Dividends paid by the company on its mandatory redeemable preferred stock were subtracted from net income in calculating this figure.*
7 *Name changed from Standard Oil of California July 1, 1984.*
8 *Figures include Gulf Oil (1983 rank: 11), acquired June 15, 1984.*
9 *Reflects an extraordinary credit of at least 10%; see the explanations of net income and earnings per share on page 5.54.*

Source: Reprinted by permission from *Fortune;* © 1984 Time Inc. All rights reserved.

100 Largest U.S. Industrial Corporations

Stockholders' Equity ($ 000)	Rank	Employees Number	Rank	Net Income as % of: Sales %	Rank	Stockholders' Equity %	Rank	Earnings per Share $ 1984	1983	1974	1974–84 Growth Rate %	Rank	Total Return to Inventors 1984 %	Rank	1974–84 Average %	Rank	Ind. Code
278,759	340	24,400	157	0.4	443	2.1[6]	439	0.04[9]	(2.11)	0.94	(27.07)	389	(44.00)	450	1.24	433	40
2,145,901	63	36,200	107	11.3	28	22.0	39	3.45	3.00	0.94	13.89	100	27.51	37	18.89	217	42
1,869,239	75	57,800[2]	56	8.4	65	18.7	96	5.10	4.42	1.66	11.88	141	8.08	160	14.76	291	36
1,046,200	136	79,400	38	4.1	279	16.2	161	3.91	3.19	1.26	11.99	140	26.30	41	21.71	176	20
1,236,000	110	59,900	53	2.5	373	8.3	360	2.21[9]	2.26	2.71	(2.02)	335	(20.00)	375	8.00	380	30
296,859	331	18,778	194	—		—		n/av.	n/av.	n/av.	—		—		—		29
2,075,942	65	62,000	50	8.4	62	16.5	150	3.30	2.64	0.92	13.66	105	(14.41)	360	24.76	123	44
1,120,112	126	44,568	77	6.0	150	21.2[6]	51	3.40	3.01	0.95[9]	13.64	106	16.97	96	22.02	169	20
1,595,400	86	82,900[2]	33	5.3	194	12.9	261	2.28	2.03	0.66	13.11	114	(10.16)	320	26.50	95	40
1,668,065	81	38,157	98	5.6	173	12.9	258	4.41	3.41	3.24	3.13	292	3.72	187	14.71	292	28

10 *Figures are for fiscal year ended June 30, 1984.*
11 *Includes sales from discontinued operations of at least 10%; see explanation of sales on page 5.54.*
12 *Figure is for Kraftco.*
13 *Figures are for fiscal year ended February 29, 1984.*
14 *Figures are for fiscal year ended September 30, 1984.*
15 *Figures are for fiscal year ended March 31, 1984.*
16 *Figures include Republic Steel (1983 rank: 145), acquired June 29, 1984.*
17 *Figures are for fiscal year ended October 31, 1984.*
18 *Figures are for fiscal year ended May 31, 1984.*
19 *Figures include St. Regis (1983 rank: 141), acquired November 20, 1984.*
20 *Figures are for fiscal year ended July 31, 1984.*
21 *Cooperatives provide only net margin figures, which are not comparable with the net income figures in these listings.*
22 *Figures are for fiscal year ended April 30, 1984.*

50 LARGEST COMMERCIAL BANK COMPANIES
Ranked by Assets

Rank 1984	Rank 1983	Company	Assets[1] ($000)	Deposits ($000)	Rank	Loans[2] ($000)	Rank
1	1	Citicorp, New York	150,586,000	90,349,000	2	102,707,000	1
2	2	BankAmerica Corp., San Francisco	117,679,502	94,047,703	1	84,043.461	2
3	3	Chase Manhattan Corp., New York[5]	86,883,018	59,680,011	3	61,241,947	3
4	4	Manufacturers Hanover Corp., New York	75,713,707	44,025,759	4	57,580,748	4
5	5	J.P. Morgan & Co., New York	64,126,000	38,760,000	5	35,239,000	6
6	6	Chemical New York Corp.	52,236,326	33,697,684	6	36,881,590	5
7	9	Security Pacific Corp., Los Angeles	46,117,443	31,006,339	8	32,491,663	7
8	7	First Interstate Bancorp., Los Angeles	45,543,888	33,603,785	7	28,567,464	8
9	10	Bankers Trust New York Corp.	45,208,147	25,559,080	10	23,148,662	11
10	11	First Chicago Corp.	39,845,731	28,591,917	9	25,284,052	9
11	13	Mellon Bank Corp., Pittsburgh[6]	30,602,815	18,997,309	12	19,382,857	13
12	8	Continental Illinois Corp., Chicago	30,413,791	15,055,931	19	23,969,789	10
13	12	Wells Fargo & Co., San Francisco	28,184,124	20,201,237	11	22,633,556	12
14	17	First Bank System, Minneapolis	22,437,746	14,782,096	20	13,158,129	22
15	14	Crocker National Corp., San Francisco[7]	22,322,223	18,015,352	13	15,514,472	14
16	19	Bank of Boston Corp.	22,078,819	15,258,266	18	14,346,131	17
17	15	Marine Midland Banks, Buffalo[6]	22,055,697	15,690,831	16	15,042,480	16
18	16	InterFirst Corp., Dallas	21,617,000	17,211,000	14	15,064,000	15
19	21	RepublicBank Corp., Dallas	21,594,769	15,622,377	17	14,124,035	18
20	18	Norwest Corp., Minneapolis	21,345,800	14,614,900	21	13,311,800	20
21	20	Texas Commerce Bancshares, Houston	20,732,000	14,481,000	22	13,261,000	21
22	28	MCorp., Dallas[9]	20,697,000	16,585,000	15	13,656,000	19
23	22	Irving Bank Corp., New York	18,982,403	13,446,875	23	11,047,130	24
24	23	First City Bancorp. of Texas, Houston	17,318,567	13,032,828	24	11,400,103	23
25	25	NCNB Corp., Charlotte, N.C.	15,678,599	11,310,882	25	9,487,189	26
26	26	Bank of New York Co.	15,156,758	10,527,969	27	10,172,079	25
27	27	PNC Financial Corp., Pittsburgh	14,869,845	8,976,249	30	7,775,340	27
28	24	NBD Bancorp., Detroit	14,231,951	10,086,581	28	6,969,064	30
29	30	Barnett Banks of Florida, Jacksonville	12,501,130	10,966,449	26	7,522,789	28
30	29	Republic New York Corp.	12,382,370	8,236,782	32	2,738,911	76
31	48	National City Corp., Cleveland[11]	12,372,576	9,238,234	29	6,974,622	29
32	51	First National State Bancorp., Newark[12]	10,679,863	8,711,658	31	5,826,906	35
33	32	Southeast Banking Corp., Miami	9,868,844	7,640,927	35	5,978,538	33
34	34	CoreStates Financial Corp., Philadelphia	9,848,247	7,070,301	39	6,117,878	32

50 Largest Commercial Bank Companies

Employees		Net Income		Stockholders' Equity		Net Income as % of Equity		Earnings Per Share $					Total Return to Investors			
											74–84 Growth Rate		1984		74–84 Average	
Number	Rank	($000)	Rank	($000)	Rank	%	Rank	1984	1983	1974	%	Rank	%	Rank	%	Rank
71,000	2	890,000	1	6,426,000	1	13.8³	41	6.45	6.48	2.54	9.77	42	9.80	64	8.07	86
87,317	1	345,525	5	5,118,511	2	6.8	91	1.77	2.18	1.86	(0.49)	87	(5.29)	84	6.75	87
43,600	3	405,818	3	3,961,044	3	10.1³	77	9.01	10.96	5.64	4.80	78	12.97	58	13.29	76
32,335	5	352,509	4	3,287,447	5	10.7	72	7.12	8.37	4.30	5.17	77	4.70	70	10.73	80
12,939	15	537,600	2	3,734,000	4	14.4	27	6.07	5.26	2.17	10.83	35	22.45	39	9.29	82
20,126	7	340,775	6	2,544,731	6	13.4	45	6.48	6.33	2.68	9.21	50	25,49	33	18.62	53
29,803	6	291,022	8	1,962,917	9	14.8	23	3.96	3.61	0.95	15.37	10	5.67	69	24.92	3
33,476⁴	4	276,340	9	2,277,527	7	12.1	58	6.16	5.76	2.36	10.07	40	8.86	66	21.39	29
10,409	19	306,814	7	2,104,328	8	13.9³	37	9.52	8.55	3.38	10.91	34	26.76	28	21.11	36
13,913	13	86,369	31	1,924,159	10	4.5	96	1.19	3.92	2.65	(7.69)	90	(10.56)	88	8.16	85
14,532	11	158,544	13	1,499,486	12	9.9³	79	5.64	7.44	2.94	6.71	71	(3.24)	82	15.90	68
9,618	22	(1,087,732)	100	1,737,068	11	—		(26.99)	2.63	2.75	—		(69.14)	94	(1.46)	89
15,400	10	169,265	11	1,343,670	13	12.6	53	6.85	6.03	2.39	11.10	31	24.38	36	20.05	46
9,490⁴	24	131,107	16	1,112,106	20	11.8	63	4.15	4.23	1.90	8.10	62	3.65	75	10.21	81
14,100	12	(324,442)	99	1,143,892	18	—		(15.93)	(0.63)	2.40	—		6.43	68	12.72	77
16,000	8	164,054	12	1,185,444	14	13.8	38	8.35	7.40	2.95	10.98	33	3.88	73	16.28	66
11,845⁴	16	106,451	23	1,009,330	22	9.5³	80	5.01	4.85	3.20	4.58	79	21.41	41	14.00	75
10,442	18	117,900	19	1,160,000	17	10.2	75	1.76	(2.82)	1.24	3.56	81	(34.74)	93	0.93	88
8,587	27	137,341	15	1,134,195	19	12.1	59	5.15	4.60	2.08	9.47	44	(5.21)	83	15.55	70
15,900	9	69,500	39	1,160,100	16	6.0	94	1.90	4.05	2.13	(1.14)	89	(26.25)	92	8.60	84
8,129	29	183,000	10	1,168,000	15	15.7	16	5.64	5.50	1.35	15.33	11	(2.31)	81	14.04	74
11,819	17	107,700	21	1,081,000	21	10.0	78	3.56	3.98	1.10	12.42	23	(17.42)	90	14.54	72
9,500	23	98,112	27	878,429	25	11.2	70	5.11	4.86	2.19	8.84	54	28.47	24	21.23	33
8,804	26	81,038	33	978,505	23	8.3	85	1.97	1.23	1.35	3.85	80	(15.63)	89	10.87	79
9,329	25	119,225	17	804,338	28	14.8	24	4.07	3.68	1.05	14.51	15	35.32	12	22.39	25
7,457	33	107,520	22	760,262	29	14.1	31	6.40	5.70	2.84	8.46	58	14.17	53	18.90	51
7,219	34	143,172	14	926,849	24	15.5	20	6.51	5.66	2.19¹⁰	11.51	29	12.93	59	21.67	28
7,092⁴	35	94,523	29	855,501	26	11.1	71	7.90	6.75	3.75	7.72	66	18.95	46	20.46	42
12,946	14	103,436	25	668,496	32	15.5	19	5.48	4.61	1.32	15.30	12	15.78	50	25.74	8
2,400	97	96,530	28	826,440	27	11.3³	69	5.49	5.47	1.69	12.48	22	12.55	60	25.66	9
9,780	21	65,895	40	539,266	39	11.9³	61	5.45	4.26	2.49	8.16	60	29.46	21	17.01	62
8,500	28	85,673	32	607,982	34	14.1	33	7.06	7.27	3.26	8.04	63	19.82	44	19.66	47
7,087	36	64,127	43	517,481	41	12.4	55	3.30	3.01	1.70	6.85	70	10.86	63	16.34	65
6,517	40	104,480	24	567,592	36	16.9³	7	6.30	5.70	2.26	10.77	36	48.52	5	23.87	17

(Continued)

50 Largest Commercial Bank Companies

Rank 1984	Rank 1983	Company	Assets[1] ($000)	Deposits ($000)	Deposits Rank	Loans[2] ($000)	Loans Rank
35	35	Comerica, Detroit	9,630,510	7,621,089	36	5,116,349	42
36	39	Allied Bancshares, Houston	9,629,655	7,896,050	34	6,943,091	31
37	31	Sun Banks, Orlando, Florida	9,401,581	7,979,388	33	5,788,734	37
38	43	Banc One Corp., Columbus, Ohio	9,106,093	7,407,238	37	5,791,783	36
39	42	Harris Bankcorp., Chicago[13]	8,828,211	6,247,909	43	4,598,804	50
40	36	Valley National Corp., Phoenix	8,777,274	7,388,354	38	5,827,550	34
41	41	National Westminster Bank USA, New York	8,726,726	7,019,218	40	5,602,057	38
42	40	Wachovia Corp., Winston-Salem, N.C.	8,716,984	6,380,998	42	4,927,382	46
43	44	Sovran Financial Corp., Norfolk, Virginia	8,286,484	6,237,867	44	5,487,861	39
44	45	Citizens & Southern Georgia Corp., Atlanta	8,030,037	5,727,790	48	5,001,495	44
45	38	Union Bank, Los Angeles[14]	7,970,656	5,943,808	45	5,057,319	43
46	68	Norstar Bancorp., Albany, N.Y.	7,909,251	6,423,669	41	4,005,395	56
47	53	Rainier Bancorp., Seattle	7,762,145	5,471,159	50	5,146,673	41
48	33	European American Bancorp., New York[15]	7,518,548	5,621,899	49	5,452,520	40
49	49	U.S. Bancorp., Portland, Oregon	7,496,128	4,944,324	54	4,621,110	49
50	47	First Union Corp., Charlotte, N.C.	7,320,207	4,092,687	76	4,085,155	55

1 *As of December 31, 1984.*
2 *Net of unearned discount and loan loss reserve. Figure includes lease financing.*
3 *Dividends paid by company on its mandatory redeemable preferred stock were subtracted from net income in calculating this figure.*
4 *Average for the year.*
5 *Acquired Lincoln First Banks on July 1, 1984.*
6 *Name changed from Mellon National Corp., September 30, 1984.*
7 *Company is 57% owned by Midland Bank.*

50 Largest Commercial Bank Companies

Employees		Net Income		Stockholders' Equity		Net Income as % of Equity		Earnings Per Share $					Total Return to Investors				
											74–84 Growth Rate		1984		74–84 Average		
Number	Rank	($000)	Rank	($000)	Rank	%	Rank	1984	1983	1974	%	Rank	%	Rank	%	Rank
6,070	43	56,896	50	491,456	46	11.6	67	4.81	4.39	2.71	5.90	76	18.52	47	20.14	45
3,600	81	118,782	18	569,854	35	20.8	3	2.89	2.55	0.49	19.36	4	(19.00)	91	—	—
9,796	20	64,940	42	556,048	38	11.7	66	2.95	3.08	1.20	9.41	45	19.15	45	20.91	38
7,901	31	107,973	20	668,787	31	16.1	13	2.88	2.55	0.84	13.13	19	13.52	56	22.74	22
6,263	41	41,199	67	514,228	42	8.0	88	n/av.	4.71	4.51	—	—	—	—	—	
6,941	38	60,440	46	475,186	48	12.7	51	3.60	2.72	1.23	11.31	30	21.33	42	19.28	49
4,500	62	40,062	68	504,534	44	7.9	89	n/av.	n/av.	n/av.	—	—	—	—	—	
6,755	39	100,301	26	566,345	37	17.7	5	3.11	2.63	1.03	11.68	27	31.53	17	23.31	21
8,066	30	80,244	34	506,293	43	15.9	15	4.73	4.12	1.94	9.32	48	8.29	67	23.43	20
6,200	42	72,435	37	440,546	50	16.4	10	2.26	1.89	0.32	21.59	2	39.44	8	16.98	63
5,277	50	44,404	59	476,364	47	9.3	82	n/av.	n/av.	n/av.	—	—	—	—	—	
7,787	32	77,254	36	643,154	33	12.0	60	4.75	4.55	2.15	8.23	59	12.38	61	21.13	35
5,436	49	61,386	44	444,440	49	13.8	39	3.13	2.45	0.94	12.81	20	26.86	27	26.22	6
4,199	66	(132,844)	98	292,972	75	—	—	n/av.	n/av.	n/av.	—	—	—	—	—	
5,491	47	60,127	47	524,599	40	11.5	68	3.05	2.66	1.30	8.88	53	25.30	34	17.79	57
5,645	46	80,024	35	495,835	45	16.1	14	4.33	3.59	1.10	14.65	14	28.49	23	29.16	2

8 *Company is 51% owned by the Hongkong & Shanghai Banking Corp.*
9 *Formed by merger of Mercantile Texas Corp. and Southwest Bancshares on October 10, 1984.*
10 *Figure is for Pittsburgh National.*
11 *Acquired BancOhio on November 9, 1984.*
12 *Acquired Fidelity Union Bancorp. on April 4, 1984.*
13 *Company is owned by Bank of Montreal.*
14 *Company is wholly owned by Standard Chartered Bank PLC.*
15 *Company is wholly owned by six European banks.*

50 LARGEST PROPERTY-CASUALTY COMPANIES
Ranked by Net Premiums, 1982, in Thousands of Dollars

Company	Rank	Total P-C Cos. Premiums	Total P-C Prems. Less A & H	A & H Prems. of P-C Cos.	A & H Prems. of Life Cos.	Life Insurance Premiums[1]	Total Premiums Volume	Total Premiums Rank
State Farm	1	9,504,241	9,328,103	176,138	—	654,634	10,158,875	2
Allstate	2	5,850,560	5,814,354	36,206	479,380	259,732	6,589,673	6
Aetna Life & Casualty	3	4,223,887	3,920,444	303,443	2,012,553	3,226,525	9,462,964	3
CIGNA	4	3,416,713	3,331,929	84,784	2,193,051	2,513,854	8,123,618	5
Travelers	5	3,212,999	2,963,919	249,080	1,954,113	3,738,523	8,905,635	4
Farmers Insurance	6	2,874,411	2,874,411	—	61,299	183,822	3,119,532	10
Continental Insurance	7	2,869,548	2,769,011	100,537	119,650	69,263	3,058,461	11
Liberty Mutual	8	2,827,300	2,655,742	171,558	10,622	96,797	2,934,718	14
Fireman's Fund	9	2,532,359	2,492,382	39,978	266,688	102,401	2,901,449	15
Hartford Fire	10	2,516,740	2,516,740	—	385,007	341,369	3,243,116	9
Nationwide	11	2,211,858	1,961,369	250,489	37,969	787,139	3,036,965	12
USF&G	12	1,965,400	1,940,857	24,543	2,689	62,674	2,030,763	22
Kemper	13	1,806,163	1,661,843	144,321	36	482,803	2,289,002	20
Crum and Forster	14	1,704,990	1,697,014	7,976	—	—	1,704,990	26
Home Insurance	15	1,683,669	1,658,091	25,578	100,172	104,459	1,888,300	24
St. Paul	16	1,572,772	1,572,747	25	89,783	88,952	1,751,507	25
American International	17	1,564,979	1,492,699	72,279	118,718	354,435	2,038,132	21
CNA	18	1,535,676	1,372,385	163,291	630,913	497,719	2,664,309	18
Commercial Union	19	1,473,311	1,464,564	8,746	684	30,897	1,504,892	27
Royal Insurance	20	1,280,637	1,276,184	4,453	—	13,659	1,294,296	29
Chubb	21	1,227,896	1,212,329	15,566	77,849	179,672	1,485,416	28
Prudential of America	22	1,137,301	1,044,840	92,461	3,374,282	6,400,812	10,912,396	1
USAA	23	1,118,397	1,118,397	—	—	83,138	1,201,535	31
American Financial	24	1,017,014	1,014,645	2,369	4,360	249,900	1,271,274	30
Reliance	25	1,008,187	1,008,148	39	35,932	136,380	1,180,500	32
Wausau Insurance	26	911,011	911,011	—	120,257	61,489	1,092,756	35
American General	27	836,244	836,024	220	295,242	1,512,448	2,643,935	19
SAFECO	28	831,725	831,725	—	81,052	190,642	1,103,418	34
General Re.	29	827,802	827,802	—	235,735	905,300	1,968,836	23
Ohio Casualty	30	798,055	794,940	3,114	—	10,646	808,700	38

(Continued)

Fifty Leading Property-Casualty Companies

Company	Rank	Total P-C Cos. Premiums	Total P-C Prems. Less A & H	A & H Prems. of P-C Cos.	A & H Prems. of Life Cos.	Life Insurance Premiums[1]	Total Premiums Volume	Rank
GEICO	31	727,877	723,797	4,080	192	1,919	729,988	41
Sentry	32	721,987	698,262	23,726	189,248	150,396	1,061,632	36
General Accident	33	720,762	719,499	1,263	—	—	720,762	42
American Family	34	684,107	600,584	83,523	414	60,899	745,420	39
Zurich	35	671,398	644,796	26,602	2,909	15,184	689,492	43
Transamerica	36	650,391	650,381	11	591,599	3,411,969	4,653,960	8
Lincoln National	37	630,189	608,634	21,555	650,964	1,698,835	2,979,988	13
Armco Insurance	38	578,427	572,867	5,560	123	13,612	592,163	45
Auto Club of Southern California	39	572,593	572,593	—	—	—	572,593	47
Teledyne	40	557,552	557,552	—	139,937	216,523	914,012	37
Hanover Insurance	41	555,078	554,297	781	—	—	555,078	48
Ohio Med. Indemnity Mut.	42	550,031	—	550,031	—	—	550,031	49
Swiss Reinsurance	43	512,308	335,279	177,028	8,182	224,188	744,679	40
Motors Insurance	44	509,990	509,990	—	10,001	23,623	543,614	50
Winterthur Swiss	45	498,455	436,129	62,327	2,965	15,234	516,654	51
California State Auto Assn.	46	495,569	492,736	2,833	—	—	495,569	52
Metropolitan	47	473,094	414,984	58,110	1,457,309	4,071,956	6,002,359	7
ERC	48	472,027	262,057	209,970	36,496	84,586	593,110	44
Auto-Owners	49	440,736	440,655	81	295	25,530	466,562	53
Auto Club of Michigan	50	429,213	429,144	69	231	4,351	433,796	55

Note: Data reflect only premiums written by domestic companies.
1 Accrual basis, including annuity and other fund deposits.

Source: Moody's Bank and Finance Manual, 1984.

25 LARGEST LIFE INSURANCE COMPANIES
Ranked by Assets

Rank 1984	Rank 1983	Company	Assets 12/31/84 ($000)	Premium and Annuity Income[1] ($000)	Rank	Net Investment Income ($000)	Rank
1	1	*Prudential, Newark	78,924,395	15,082,208	1	4,898,424	2
2	2	*Metropolitan, New York	67,353,970	7,410,470	2	5,467,822	1
3	3	*Equitable Life Assurance, New York	44,531,655	1,913,326	10	2,665,915	4
4	4	Aetna Life, Hartford[6]	33,970,737	3,080,153	5	2,671,184	3
5	5	*New York Life	25,599,526	1,083,075	21	2,007,127	5
6	6	*John Hancock Mutual, Boston	24,671,322	2,347,658	7	1,450,041	8
7	7	Travelers, Hartford[7]	23,301,833	4,055,026	3	1,941,242	6
8	8	*Connecticut General Life, Bloomfield[8]	19,234,102	3,608,308	4	1,294,471	9
9	9	Teachers Insurance & Annuity, New York	19,204,699	1,752,423	11	1,918,035	7
10	10	*Northwestern Mutual, Milwaukee	15,895,696	2,142,824	8	1,172,318	10
11	11	*Massachusetts Mutual, Springfield	13,448,692	1,603,273	13	1,064,226	11
12	12	*Bankers Life, Des Moines	12,717,242	2,551,278	6	1,058,408	12
13	13	Mutual of New York	9,538,770	1,331,858	15	699,009	15
14	14	*New England Mutual, Boston	9,384,789	1,914,311	9	799,562	13
15	15	*Mutual Benefit, Newark	8,349,612	996,218	24	715,728	14
16	16	*Connecticut Mutual, Hartford	7,289,765	1,046,621	22	553,122	16
17	17	State Farm Life, Bloomington, Illinois	5,668,911	1,034,576	23	478,385	17
18		Southwestern Life, Dallas[9]	4,648,220	431,288	38	148,010	50
19	18	Lincoln National Life, Fort Wayne, Indiana[10]	4,622,326	1,527,331	14	324,576	21
20	21	Nationwide Life, Columbus, Ohio	4,434,642	483,975	36	248,707	27
21	19	Continental Assurance, Chicago[11]	4,414,547	1,278,866	17	171,534	46
22	25	Variable Annuity Life, Houston	4,351,130	581,443	35	381,521	19
23	27	Executive Life, Los Angeles	4,212,996	683,612	30	421,367	18
24	26	IDS Life, Minneapolis [12]	4,175,347	798,809	28	339,300	20
25	22	*Phoenix Mutual, Hartford	4,008,432	664,199	31	282,026	23

Note: *Data for all companies are on the statutory accounting basis required by state insurance regulatory authorities. Information as of December 31, 1984.*

* *Indicates a mutual company.*

1 *Includes premium income from life, accident, and health policies, annuities, and from contributions to deposit administration funds.*

2 *After dividends to policyholders and federal income taxes, excluding capital gains and losses. Figures in parentheses indicate a loss.*

3 *Face value of all life policies as of December 31, 1984.*

Source: Reprinted by permission from Fortune; © 1985 Time, Inc. All rights reserved.

25 Largest Life Insurance Companies

Net Gain from Operations[2]			Life Insurance in Force[3]		Increase in Life Insurance in Force[4]				Employees[5]	
($000)	Rank		($000)	Rank	($000)	Rank	Percent	Rank	Number	Rank
	Mutual	Stock								
219,290	2		532,990,221	1	23,026,700	2	4.5	29	58,398	1
433,151	1		464,761,946	2	13,853,061	4	3.1	34	38,000	3
75,414	5		248,211,312	3	9,785,623	8	4.1	31	21,408	4
314,469		1	204,636,320	4	5,902,221	19	3.0	35	16,838	9
209,256	3		179,184,986	5	7,134,352	13	4.2	30	19,746	5
186,899	4		158,669,592	6	5,477,860	21	3.6	32	19,562	7
136,088		5	137,206,481	7	6,941,317	15	5.0	27	43,800	2
314,179		2	110,027,340	10	5,222,996	22	5.0	28	10,609	11
159,854		4	13,659,743	43	1,115,737	33	8.9	21	2,276	41
60,860	6		107,564,490	11	14,942,109	3	16.1	9	7,450	17
58,642	7		65,416,607	14	3,842,013	24	6.2	25	10,031	12
48,882	8		59,421,395	16	7,169,621	12	13.7	11	7,781	15
5,901	23		51,362,807	19	(185,667)	44	—	—	7,680	16
22,233	14		45,979,229	24	5,062,621	23	12.4	16	9,115	14
35,716	11		53,235,890	18	1,419,004	31	2.7	39	4,689	24
24,985	12		43,876,979	25	3,625,614	25	9.0	20	6,038	21
82,652		9	82,859,829	12	9,201,881	9	12.5	15	17,667	8
17,161		18	68,257,746	13	57,617,278	1	—	—	4,445	25
128,133		6	114,225,107	9	10,711,468	7	10.4	19	4,159	28
36,689		13	16,346,695	38	440,648	38	2.8	38	6,702	19
61,868		11	46,725,324	22	11,493,734	6	32.6	2	n/av.	—
5,367		20	3,973	49	(109)	42	—	—	1,076	45
2,419		21	27,904,946	28	6,221,934	17	28.7	3	500	47
28,542		15	13,729,309	42	979,370	35	7.7	23	4,942	22
21,469	15		55,393,928	17	6,392,590	16	13.1	14	3,455	33

4 *Change between December 31, 1983, and December 31, 1984.*
5 *Includes home office, field force, and full-time agents.*
6 *Wholly owned by Aetna Life and Casualty.*
7 *Wholly owned by Travelers Corp.*
8 *Wholly owned by CIGNA.*
9 *Wholly owned by Tenneco.*
10 *Wholly owned by Lincoln National.*
11 *Wholly owned by a subsidiary of Loews.*
12 *Wholly owned by American Express.*

TOP COMMERCIAL REAL ESTATE BROKERS IN 1984

Rank	Firm/Headquarters	Annual Gross Revenues ($000,000)	Rank	Firm/Headquarters	Annual Gross Revenues ($000,000)
1	Coldwell Banker Real Estate Services Group Los Angeles, California	353.9	17	Julian J. Studley, Inc. New York, New York	15.0*
2	Grubb & Ellis Co. San Francisco, California	215.0	18	Norrig Beggs & Simpson San Francisco, California	11.5*
3	Goldman Sachs & Co. New York, New York	140.0*	19	Jackson-Cross Co. Philadelphia, Pennsylvania	11.2
4	Cushman & Wakefield Inc. New York, New York	111.0*	20	Leggat, McCall & Werner, Inc. Boston, Massachusetts	10.5
5	Rubloff Inc. Chicago, Illinois	53.0	21	Swearingen Dallas, Texas	+10.0*
6	Edward S. Gordon Co. Inc. New York, New York	45.0*	22	Strouse Greenberg & Co., Inc. Philadelphia, Pennsylvania	10.0
7	Johnstown American Cos. Atlanta, Georgia	41.6	23	The Seeley Co. Los Angeles, California	10.0*
8	Marcus & Millichap Palo Alto, California	39.5	24	Ostendorf-Morris Co. Cleveland, Ohio	10.0*
9	The Keyes Co. Realtors Miami, Florida	38.0*	25	Kenneth D. Laub & Co., Inc. New York, New York	10.0*
10	Fuller Commercial Brokerage Co. Chicago, Illinois	32.4	26	Bennett & Kahnweiler Associates Chicago, Illinois	8.8*
11	Helmsley-Spear New York, New York	25.0*	27	Charles Dunn Co. Los Angeles, California	8.5
12	Cross & Brown Co. New York, New York	22.0*	28	Del E. Webb Realty & Management Co. Phoenix, Arizona	8.4
13	Arvida Realty Sales Inc. Boca Raton, Florida	20.0[1]	29	Schneider Commercial Real Estate Los Angeles, California	8.0
14	Carter & Associates, Inc. Atlanta, Georgia	20.0	30	Oliver Realty Inc. Pittsburgh, Pennsylvania	7.5
15	The Horne Co. Houston, Texas	20.0	31	CPS Associates Sunnyvale, California	6.5*
16	Frederick Ross Co. Denver, Colorado	16.0	32	Spaulding & Slye Burlington, Massachusetts	5.0

* *Estimate.*
1 *Estimated residential and commercial; $10 million commercial.*

Source: Stephen Roulac & Company.

TOP RESIDENTIAL REAL ESTATE BROKERS IN 1984

Rank	Firm/Headquarters	Annual Gross Revenues ($000,000)	Rank	Firm/Headquarters	Annual Gross Revenues ($000,000)
1	Coldwell Banker Real Estate Services Group Los Angeles, California	353.9	12	J.I. Sopher & Co. New York, New York	25.0*
2	Merrill Lynch Realty Associates Stamford, Connecticut	323.0	13	Walker & Lee Inc. Santa Ana, California	23.3
3	Long & Foster Realtors Fairfax, Virginia	65.0	14	Mount Vernon Realty Inc. Alexandria, Virginia	20.5
4	Century 21 Real Estate Corp. Irvine, California	64.1[1]	15	F.C. Tucker Co., Inc. Indianapolis, Indiana	+18.0*
5	Fred Sands Realtors Los Angeles, California	54.9	16	Goodman, Segar & Hogan Virginia Beach, Virginia	17.5
6	Schlott Realtors Fair Lawn, New Jersey	50.0	17	ERA Shawnee Mission, Kansas	17.0[2]
7	Shannon & Luchs Co. Washington, D.C.	46.8	18	Russ Lyon Realty Co. Phoenix, Arizona	16.8*
8	O'Conor, Piper & Flynn Realtors Baltimore, Maryland	39.6	19	West Shell Inc. Cincinnati, Ohio	15.5
9	Cornish & Carey Palo Alto, California	36.0	20	Better Homes & Gardens Real Estate Service Des Moines, Iowa	15.0[3]
10	Van Schaack & Co. Denver, Colorado	31.0	21	Frank Howard Allen Realtors Greenbrae, California	14.5
11	Baird & Warner Inc. Chicago, Illinois	28.7	22	MacPherson's Inc. Realtors Seattle, Washington	12.5

* *Estimate.*
1 *Corporate revenues; $1.4 billion for franchises.*
2 *Corporate estimate; $371 million for franchises.*
3 *Corporate estimate; $329 million for franchises.*

Source: Stephen Roulac & Company.

THE BIGGEST DEALS OF 1984

Mergers and Acquisitions and Debt and Equity Offerings

Deals eligible for the list include:

1. U.S. public offerings of individual securities (except short-term securities) by domestic and foreign corporations issued under a single prospectus or offering circular.

2. Cash tender offers by domestic corporations or by foreign corporations tendering in the U.S., including those of companies buying in their own stock.

3. Mergers or acquisitions in which the buyer or seller is a U.S. company (or part of one). To be eligible, offerings must be effective in 1984 and tender offers must have expired during the year. Mergers and acquisitions are eligible if legally closed during the year or, when not legally closed, if the prospective buyer has paid a portion of the purchase price in cash during the year.

The list excludes short-term financings, government securities, and financings other than public offerings — such as bank borrowings and private placements.

When two companies merge through an exchange of stock to form a new company, the company whose stockholders received the largest share of the new company is treated as the buyer. When the buyer or seller is a subsidiary, the parent's name is given in parentheses.

Value of Deal: Amounts of cash offerings are the total amounts raised; for tenders the total amount paid. All securities issued in acquisitions or mergers are valued at the market price on the date of closing. Exception: when a new company is formed by merger, only those shares issued to stockholders of the smaller company are valued.

Percentage of Book Value: Book value calculations indicate the price paid (or amount of equity capital raised) per share as a percentage of the shareholders' equity per share of the acquired company (or issuer) at the end of the last quarter preceding the transaction.

Transaction: Dates under this heading are effective dates for offerings, expiration dates for tenders, and closing dates for acquisitions and mergers.

Financial Intermediaries: For underwritten public offerings, the co-managers are listed, and the lead manager is indicated by an asterisk. In the case of acquisitions and mergers, the intermediaries are typically investment banking firms that assisted in the transaction.

Fee: The figures represent the amounts charged by the financial intermediaries assisting in the deals. In underwritings, part of the fee is paid to other members of the underwriting syndicate or to dealers other than the co-managers.

Biggest Deals of 1984

1 CHEVRON (formerly Standard Oil of California) acquired GULF OIL

Acquisition for cash, June 15

Value of Deal ($000)	% of Book Value	Companies	Financial Intermediaries	Fee ($000)	Fee as % of Deal
13,231,253		Chevron	Morgan Stanley	16,900	.13
	129.7	Gulf	Salomon Bros., Merrill Lynch	28,235[1]	.21
				18,765	.14

1 *Estimate by* Fortune *magazine.*

2 TEXACO acquires GETTY OIL

Acquisition for cash, February 17

Value of Deal ($000)	% of Book Value	Companies	Financial Intermediaries	Fee ($000)	Fee as % of Deal
10,129,245		Texaco	First Boston	10,750	.11
	102.2	Getty	Goldman Sachs, Kidder Peabody, Salomon Bros.	18,500	.19
				15,500	.15
				n/av.	—

3 MOBIL acquires SUPERIOR OIL

Acquisition for cash and debentures, September 28

Value of Deal ($000)	% of Book Value	Companies	Financial Intermediaries	Fee ($000)	Fee as % of Deal
5,696,704		Mobil	Goldman Sachs	1,742	.03
	227	Superior	Morgan Stanley	12,688	.22

(Continued)

Biggest Deals of 1984

4 BEATRICE COS. (food and consumer products) acquired ESMARK (food and consumer products)[1]
Acquisition of 99% for cash, August 7

Value of Deal ($000)	% of Book Value	Companies	Financial Intermediaries	Fee ($000)	Fee as % of Deal
2,699,891	208.3	Beatrice	Lazard Frères	4,500	.17
		Esmark	Oppenheimer, Salomon Bros.	8,000	.30
				7,500	.28

1 *Beatrice previously owned 1%.*

5 KIEWIT-MURDOCK INVESTMENT CORP.[1] acquired CONTINENTAL GROUP (paper, forest products, insurance, and energy)
Acquisition for cash and stock, November 1

Value of Deal ($000)	% of Book Value	Companies	Financial Intermediaries	Fee ($000)	Fee as % of Deal
2,686,051	167.8	Peter Kiewit Sons'	None	—	—
		Pacific Holding Corp.	None	—	—
		Continental Group	Morgan Stanley, Goldman Sachs	5,400	.20
				5,400	.20

1 *Acquiring firm 80% held by Peter Kiewit Sons', a construction, mining, and finance concern, and 20% by Pacific Holding, owned by David Murdock.*

6 GENERAL MOTORS acquired ELECTRONIC DATA SYSTEMS
Acquisition for cash, stock, and notes, October 19

Value of Deal ($000)	% of Book Value	Companies	Financial Intermediaries	Fee ($000)	Fee as % of Deal
2,555,336	777.8	General Motors	Salomon Bros.	n/av.	—
		Electronic Data Systems	Lazard Frères	4,000	.16

(Continued)

THE FINANCIAL DESK BOOK

Biggest Deals of 1984

7 BROKEN HILL PROPRIETARY (natural resources) acquired UTAH INTERNATIONAL (natural resources) from General Electric
Acquisition for cash, April 2

Value of Deal ($000)	% of Book Value	Companies	Financial Intermediaries	Fee ($000)	Fee as % of Deal
2,400,000	n/av.	Broken Hill Proprietary	First Boston	n/av.	—
		General Electric	Morgan Stanley	n/av.	—

8 CHAMPION INTERNATIONAL (paper and forest products) acquired ST. REGIS (forest products)
Acquisition for cash and stock, November 20

Value of Deal ($000)	% of Book Value	Companies	Financial Intermediaries	Fee ($000)	Fee as % of Deal
1,827,958	138	Champion International	Goldman Sachs	5,000	.27
		St. Regis	Morgan Stanley	6,400	.35

9 TELEDYNE (manufacturing and insurance) repurchased its common stock
Cash tender for common stock, May 25

Value of Deal ($000)	% of Book Value	Companies	Financial Intermediaries	Fee ($000)	Fee as % of Deal
1,732,211	151.7	Teledyne	None	—	—

10 MANUFACTURERS HANOVER (financial services) acquired CIT FINANCIAL from RCA
Acquisition for cash, stock, and notes, April 30

Value of Deal ($000)	% of Book Value	Companies	Financial Intermediaries	Fee ($000)	Fee as % of Deal
1,510,000	106.5	Manufacturers Hanover	Goldman Sachs	n/av.	—
		RCA	Lazard Frères, Lehman Bros.	4,000	.26
				n/av.	—

(Continued)

5.75

Biggest Deals of 1984

11 | FEDERAL NATIONAL MORTGAGE ASSOCIATION (mortgage holder) sold bonds

Offering of 12.25% debentures due 1987, April 10

Value of Deal ($000)	% of Book Value	Companies	Financial Intermediaries	Fee ($000)	Fee as % of Deal
1,500,000		Federal National Mortgage Association	Various dealers	2,198	.15

12 | PHILLIPS PETROLEUM acquired AMINOIL and GEYSERS GEOTHERMAL (energy) from R.J. Reynolds

Acquisition for cash, October 26

Value of Deal ($000)	% of Book Value	Companies	Financial Intermediaries	Fee ($000)	Fee as % of Deal
1,300,000	246.2	Phillips Petroleum	Morgan Stanley	n/av.	—
		R.J. Reynolds	Dillon Read	n/av.	—

13 | DUN & BRADSTREET (communications and publishing) acquired A.C. NIELSEN (research services)

Acquisition for stock, August 29

Value of Deal ($000)	% of Book Value	Companies	Financial Intermediaries	Fee ($000)	Fee as % of Deal
1,282,005	106.4	Dun & Bradstreet	Goldman Sachs	n/av.	.27
		A.C. Nielsen	Lehman Bros.	n/av.	.05

14 | INTERNATIONAL BUSINESS MACHINES acquired ROLM (telecommunications products)[1]

Acquisition 77% for 7.875% debentures due 2004, November 21

Value of Deal ($000)	% of Book Value	Companies	Financial Intermediaries	Fee ($000)	Fee as % of Deal
1,279,745	231.3	IBM	Salomon Bros.	n/av.	.27
		Rolm	Goldman Sachs	n/av.	.38

1 *IBM previously owned 23%.*

(Continued)

Biggest Deals of 1984

15 PACE INDUSTRIES (new company)[1] acquired three subsidiaries[2] of CITY INVESTING
Leveraged buyout for cash, December 13

Value of Deal ($000)	% of Book Value	Companies	Financial Intermediaries	Fee ($000)	Fee as % of Deal
1,251,000	n/av.	Pace Industries	Merrill Lynch	14,200[3]	1.13
		City Investing	First Boston	6,000	.48

1 New corporation formed by Kohlberg Kravis Roberts and Merrill Lynch Capital Markets.
2 Rheem Manufacturing (water heaters), World Color Press, and Uarco (printing).
3 Includes fees for other services to City Investing prior to deal.

16 AMERICAN GENERAL (insurance) acquired the insurance units of GULF UNITED
Acquisition for stock, warrants, and cash, January 5

Value of Deal ($000)	% of Book Value	Companies	Financial Intermediaries	Fee ($000)	Fee as % of Deal
1,225,482	141.6	American General	First Boston	1,200	.10
		Gulf United	Lehman Bros., Smith Barney	2,450	.20
				900	.07

17 FEDERAL NATIONAL MORTGAGE ASSOCIATION sold bonds
Offering of 11.55% debentures due 1987, November 7

Value of Deal ($000)	% of Book Value	Companies	Financial Intermediaries	Fee ($000)	Fee as % of Deal
1,200,000		Federal National Mortgage Association	Various dealers	1,800	.15

(Continued)

Biggest Deals of 1984

18 AMERICAN STORES (food and drug retailer) acquired JEWEL COS. (food and drug retailer)

Acquisition for stock and cash, November 16

Value of Deal ($000)	% of Book Value	Companies	Financial Intermediaries	Fee ($000)	Fee as % of Deal
1,184,961	187	American Stores	Lehman Bros.	4,000	.34
		Jewel Cos.	Morgan Stanley	4,300	.36

19 OCCIDENTAL PETROLEUM sold stock and notes

Offering of 9.65% notes due 1994 and stock, October 23

Value of Deal ($000)	% of Book Value	Companies	Financial Intermediaries	Fee ($000)	Fee as % of Deal
1,171,500		Occidental Petroleum	Drexel Burnham Lambert, First Boston, Donaldson Lufkin & Jenrette, Kidder Peabody, Dean Witter	28,500	2.43

20 GENERAL ELECTRIC FINANCIAL SERVICES (General Electric) acquired EMPLOYERS REINSURANCE from Texaco[1]

Acquisition for cash, July 2

Value of Deal ($000)	% of Book Value	Companies	Financial Intermediaries	Fee ($000)	Fee as % of Deal
1,075,000	141.3	General Electric	None	—	—
		Texaco	Goldman Sachs	n/av.	—

1 Texaco had acquired Employers Reinsurance as part of Getty Oil.

(Continued)

Biggest Deals of 1984

21 | TEXAS EASTERN (oil and gas) acquired PETROLANE (oil and gas)[1]
Acquisition of 98.1% for cash, September 26

Value of Deal ($000)	% of Book Value	Companies	Financial Intermediaries	Fee ($000)	Fee as % of Deal
1,025,600	235.8	Texas Eastern	First Boston	5,500[2]	.54
		Petrolane	First Boston	—	—

1 Texas Eastern previously owned 1.9%.
2 First Boston advised both companies.

22 | FEDERAL NATIONAL MORTGAGE ASSOCIATION sold bonds
Offering of 11.55% debentures due 1988, January 10

Value of Deal ($000)	% of Book Value	Companies	Financial Intermediaries	Fee ($000)	Fee as % of Deal
1,000,000		Federal National Mortgage Association	Various dealers	1,680	.17

23 | FEDERAL NATIONAL MORTGAGE ASSOCIATION sold bonds
Offering of 11.05% debentures due 1987, February 3

Value of Deal ($000)	% of Book Value	Companies	Financial Intermediaries	Fee ($000)	Fee as % of Deal
1,000,000		Federal National Mortgage Association	Various dealers	1,410	.14

24 | FEDERAL NATIONAL MORTGAGE ASSOCIATION sold bonds
Offering of 12.10% debentures due 1989, March 12

Value of Deal ($000)	% of Book Value	Companies	Financial Intermediaries	Fee ($000)	Fee as % of Deal
1,000,000		Federal National Mortgage Association	Various dealers	1,950	.20

(Continued)

Biggest Deals of 1984

25 FEDERAL NATIONAL MORTGAGE ASSOCIATION sold bonds

Offering of 13.05% debentures due 1986, June 11

Value of Deal ($000)	% of Book Value	Companies	Financial Intermediaries	Fee ($000)	Fee as % of Deal
1,000,000		Federal National Mortgage Association	Various dealers	1,143	.11

26 FEDERAL NATIONAL MORTGAGE ASSOCIATION sold bonds

Offering of 13.65% debentures due 1987, July 10

Value of Deal ($000)	% of Book Value	Companies	Financial Intermediaries	Fee ($000)	Fee as % of Deal
1,000,000		Federal National Mortgage Association	Various dealers	1,440	.14

27 FEDERAL NATIONAL MORTGAGE ASSOCIATION sold bonds

Offering of 12.90% debentures due 1986, September 10

Value of Deal ($000)	% of Book Value	Companies	Financial Intermediaries	Fee ($000)	Fee as % of Deal
1,000,000		Federal National Mortgage Association	Various dealers	1,175	.12

28 FEDERAL NATIONAL MORTGAGE ASSOCIATION sold bonds

Offering of 13.20% debentures due 1988, September 10

Value of Deal ($000)	% of Book Value	Companies	Financial Intermediaries	Fee ($000)	Fee as % of Deal
1,000,000		Federal National Mortgage Association	Various dealers	1,645	.17

(Continued)

Biggest Deals of 1984

29

FEDERAL NATIONAL MORTGAGE ASSOCIATION sold bonds
Offering of 11.25% debentures due 1988, December 10

Value of Deal ($000)	% of Book Value	Companies	Financial Intermediaries	Fee ($000)	Fee as % of Deal
1,000,000		Federal National Mortgage Association	Various dealers	1,638	.16

30

CHEVRON sold notes
Offering of 12.75% notes due 1987, August 4

Value of Deal ($000)	% of Book Value	Companies	Financial Intermediaries	Fee ($000)	Fee as % of Deal
992,770		Chevron	Salomon Bros., Dillon Read	1,000[1]	.10
				1,000	.10

1 *Estimate by Fortune magazine.*

31

SCHLUMBERGER (oil services and electronics) acquired SEDCO (oil services)
Acquisition for cash and stock, December 24

Value of Deal ($000)	% of Book Value	Companies	Financial Intermediaries	Fee ($000)	Fee as % of Deal
970,142	171.2	Schlumberger	Lazard Frères	n/av.	—
		Sedco	Goldman Sachs	1,500	.15

32

JWK ACQUISITION CORP. (private investors) acquired METROMEDIA (communications)
Leveraged buyout for cash, warrants, and debentures, June 21

Value of Deal ($000)	% of Book Value	Companies	Financial Intermediaries	Fee ($000)	Fee as % of Deal
962,536	485.6	JWK Acquisition Corp.	Boston Ventures Management	4,000	.42
		Metromedia	Lehman Bros., Bear Stearns	4,685	.49
				2,500	.26

(Continued)

Biggest Deals of 1984

33 ARA ACQUIRING CORP. (private investors) acquired ARA SERVICES (food, transportation, and health care)

Leveraged buyout for cash, December 19

Value of Deal ($000)	% of Book Value	Companies	Financial Intermediaries	Fee ($000)	Fee as % of Deal
883,287	150.5	ARA Acquiring Corp.	Goldman Sachs	10,000	1.13
		ARA Services	Salomon Bros.	1,250	.14

34 AMERICAN MEDICAL INTERNATIONAL (health care services) acquired LIFEMARK (health care services)

Acquisition for stock, January 19

Value of Deal ($000)	% of Book Value	Companies	Financial Intermediaries	Fee ($000)	Fee as % of Deal
863,449	346.1	American Medical International	Goldman Sachs	2,787	.32
		Lifemark	First Boston	3,588	.42

35 WOMETCO ENTERPRISES ACQUISITION CORP. (private investors)[1] acquired WOMETCO ENTERPRISES (communications and bottling)

Leveraged buyout for cash, April 12

Value of Deal ($000)	% of Book Value	Companies	Financial Intermediaries	Fee ($000)	Fee as % of Deal
820,016	373.5	Wometco Enterprises Acquisition	None	—	—
		Wometco	Kohlberg Kravis Roberts, Drexel Burnham Lambert, Merrill Lynch	10,000	1.2
				3,900	.48
				200	.02

1 *Group led by Kohlberg Kravis Roberts.*

(Continued)

Biggest Deals of 1984

36 TEXACO acquired some European marketing and manufacturing operations of CHEVRON
Acquisition for cash, April 1

Value of Deal ($000)	% of Book Value	Companies	Financial Intermediaries	Fee ($000)	Fee as % of Deal
800,000[1]	n/av.	Texaco	None	—	—
		Chevron	None	—	—

1 *Estimate by Fortune magazine.*

37 FEDERAL NATIONAL MORTGAGE ASSOCIATION sold bonds
Offering of 13.125% debentures due 1989, August 6

Value of Deal ($000)	% of Book Value	Companies	Financial Intermediaries	Fee ($000)	Fee as % of Deal
750,000		Federal National Mortgage Association	Various dealers	1,500	.20

38 AMERICAN EXPRESS (financial services) acquired INVESTORS DIVERSIFIED SERVICES (financial services) from Alleghany
Acquisition for stock, cash, and a promissory note, January 12

Value of Deal ($000)	% of Book Value	Companies	Financial Intermediaries	Fee ($000)	Fee as % of Deal
743,875	188.1	American Express	Morgan Stanley, S. B. Lewis	n/av.	—
				3,500	.47
		Alleghany	First Boston	n/av.	—

39 R.J. REYNOLDS repurchased its common stock
Cash tender for common stock, November 21

Value of Deal ($000)	% of Book Value	Companies	Financial Intermediaries	Fee ($000)	Fee as % of Deal
735,000	174.4	R.J. Reynolds	Dillon Read	1,500	2.0

(Continued)

Biggest Deals of 1984

40 EQUITABLE LIFE ASSURANCE acquired shopping centers from GENERAL GROWTH PROPERTIES
Acquisition for cash and assumption of mortgages, November 30

Value of Deal ($000)	% of Book Value	Companies	Financial Intermediaries	Fee ($000)	Fee as % of Deal
707,795	n/av.	Equitable Life Assurance	None	—	—
		General Growth Properties	None	—	—

41 GULF & WESTERN acquired PRENTICE-HALL (publishing)
Acquisition for cash, December 21

Value of Deal ($000)	% of Book Value	Companies	Financial Intermediaries	Fee ($000)	Fee as % of Deal
705,322	319	Gulf & Western	Kidder Peabody	3,500	.50
		Prentice-Hall	Dillon Read	875	.12

42 FEDERAL NATIONAL MORTGAGE ASSOCIATION sold bonds
Offering of 11.60% debentures due 1989, February 3

Value of Deal ($000)	% of Book Value	Companies	Financial Intermediaries	Fee ($000)	Fee as % of Deal
700,000		Federal National Mortgage Association	Various dealers	1,320	.19

43 OCCIDENTAL PETROLEUM sold stock, warrants, and notes
Offering of 8.95% notes due 1994, warrants, and stock, April 17

Value of Deal ($000)	% of Book Value	Companies	Financial Intermediaries	Fee ($000)	Fee as % of Deal
682,500		Occidental Petroleum	Drexel Burnham Lambert, First Boston, Donaldson Lufkin & Jenrette, Goldman Sachs, Kidder Peabody, Dean Witter	17,500	2.56

(Continued)

Biggest Deals of 1984

44 A.H. BELO (publishing and broadcasting) acquired six television stations from DUN & BRADSTREET
Acquisition for cash, February 29

Value of Deal ($000)	% of Book Value	Companies	Financial Intermediaries	Fee ($000)	Fee as % of Deal
606,000	n/av.	A.H. Belo	None	—	—
		Dun & Bradstreet	Goldman Sachs	n/av.	

45 COASTAL CORP. (oil and gas) sold notes
Offering of 14.60% notes due 1994, August 9

Value of Deal ($000)	% of Book Value	Companies	Financial Intermediaries	Fee ($000)	Fee as % of Deal
585,000		Coastal	Drexel Burnham Lambert	15,000	2.56

46 HH ACQUIRING CORP. (private investors) acquired HARTE-HANKS COMMUNICATIONS
Leveraged buyout for cash and debentures, September 11

Value of Deal ($000)	% of Book Value	Companies	Financial Intermediaries	Fee ($000)	Fee as % of Deal
575,932	225	HH Acquiring Corp.	Salomon Bros.	1,000	.17
		Harte-Hanks Communications	Goldman Sachs	9,000	1.56

47 PHILADELPHIA SAVING FUND SOCIETY acquired FAMILY FINANCIAL SERVICES from General Electric Credit Corp.
Acquisition for cash, January 24

Value of Deal ($000)	% of Book Value	Companies	Financial Intermediaries	Fee ($000)	Fee as % of Deal
568,000	n/av.	Philadelphia Saving Fund Society	Salomon Bros.	n/av.	—
		General Electric Credit Corp.	Goldman Sachs	n/av.	—

(Continued)

Biggest Deals of 1984

48 IC INDUSTRIES (consumer and commercial products, transportation) acquired PNEUMO (aerospace, food and drug retailing)

Acqusition for cash and stock, October 18

Value of Deal ($000)	% of Book Value	Companies	Financial Intermediaries	Fee ($000)	Fee as % of Deal
562,300	268.4	IC Industries	Salomon Bros.	2,475	.44
		Pneumo	Merrill Lynch	3,674	.65

49 PITTCO ACQUISITION CORP. (private investors)[1] acquired MALONE & HYDE (food and retailing)

Leveraged buyout for cash, August 29

Value of Deal ($000)	% of Book Value	Companies	Financial Intermediaries	Fee ($000)	Fee as % of Deal
550,146	273.5	Pittco Acquisition	Kohlberg Kravis Roberts	6,750	1.22
				3,500	.60
		Malone & Hyde	Lehman Bros., Kidder Peabody	750	.13

1 *Group led by Kohlberg Kravis Roberts.*

50 BANK OF MONTREAL acquired HARRIS BANKCORP

Acquisition for cash, September 4

Value of Deal ($000)	% of Book Value	Companies	Financial Intermediaries	Fee ($000)	Fee as % of Deal
546,734	132.6	Bank of Montreal	Morgan Stanley	n/av.	—
		Harris Bankcorp	First Boston	1,516[2]	.28

1 *Estimate by Fortune magazine.*

5.08 Publicly Registered Investment Programs

For a description of the workings of the publicly registered and private investment programs known as limited partnerships, see Chapter 3, page 3.139. That section also includes, under the heading Due Diligence, some guidelines for the prospective investor on evaluating the sponsors of such programs.

TOP FUNDRAISERS OF 1984
IN PUBLICLY REGISTERED LIMITED PARTNERSHIPS
(In Millions of Dollars)

Sponsor	Sales			Percentage Change 1983–1984	Percentage Share of 1984 Market
	1982	1983	1984		
Balcor/American Express	251.7	581.5	630.2	8.4	7.6
JMB Realty Corp.	188.0	551.0	521.5	−5.4	6.3
Merrill Lynch	216.0	347.8	441.0	26.8	5.3
Integrated Resources	196.4	288.4	407.0	41.1	4.9
Consolidated Capital	275.8	272.9	341.4	25.1	4.1
Equitec Financial Group	52.8	194.0	282.9	45.8	3.4
E.F. Hutton	169.0	341.1	282.4	−17.2	3.4
Damson Oil Corp.	329.1	536.0	280.8	−47.6	3.4
Prudential-Bache	0.0	126.2	279.6	121.6	3.4

Source: *The Stanger Review.*

REAL ESTATE PROGRAMS
Sponsors' Market Share (in Millions of Dollars)

Rank	Sponsor/Dealer Manager(s)	Sales		Percentage Change 1983–1984	Percentage Share of 1984 Market
		1983	1984		
1	Balcor/American Express Balcor/American Express	581.5	630.2	8.4	11.1
2	JMB Realty Corp. Carlyle Securities Corp.	551.0	521.5	−5.4	9.2
3	Merrill Lynch Merrill Lynch	261.2	400.0	53.1	7.0
4	Consolidated Capital Companies Consolidated Capital Securities Corp.	272.9	341.9	25.3	6.0
5	Integrated Resources Integrated Resources	150.7	315.8	109.6	5.6

Real Estate Programs

Rank	Sponsor/Dealer Manager(s)	Sales		Percentage Change 1983–1984	Percentage Share of 1984 Market
		1983	1984		
6	CRI Inc. Merrill Lynch	110.0	255.5	132.3	4.5
7	Equitec Financial Group Inc. Equitec Securities	175.4	250.8	43.0	4.4
8	Public Storage Inc. Dean Witter	113.4	207.8	83.2	3.7
9	American First Capital Associates Ltd. E.F. Hutton		200.0		3.5
10	Franchise Finance Corporation of America E.F. Hutton	150.0	170.0	13.3	3.0
11	E.F. Hutton E.F. Hutton	120.0	167.4	39.5	2.9
12	Fox and Carskadon Fox and Carskadon Securities Corp.	201.4	120.9	−40.0	2.1
13	Paine Webber Properties Paine Webber Jackson and Curtis	87.4	107.4	22.9	1.9
14	First Capital Properties Corp. First Capital Investment Corp.	167.4	92.9	−44.5	1.6
15	Dean Witter Dean Witter		92.8		1.6
16	Landsing Corp. Landsing Capital Corp.	77.4	76.0	−1.8	1.3
17	Angeles Realty Corp. Angeles/Quinoco Securities	80.1	73.3	−8.5	1.3
18	Prudential Bache/VMS Realty Inc. Prudential-Bache	85.6	65.4	−23.6	1.2
19	Wespac Financial Corp. Wespac Securities		61.0		1.1
20	I.R.E. Advisors Corp. U.S. Securities Inc.	63.7	59.7	−6.3	1.1
21	August Financial Partners August Securities	35.4	59.3	67.5	1.0
22	USAA Financial Services USAA Investment Management	25.0	57.5	130.0	1.0
23	Southmark Corporation Southmark Capital	81.1	57.9	−28.6	1.1
24	Centennial Beneficial Corp. None	40.0	53.1	32.8	0.9
25	Shelter Realty Corp. E.F. Hutton	53.4	46.3	−13.3	0.8
26	Shearson/American Express Shearson/American Express	54.0	45.1	−16.5	0.8
27	Realty Income Corp. Cameron, Murphy and Spangler	46.2	43.5	−5.8	0.8

Real Estate Programs

Rank	Sponsor/Dealer Manager(s)	Sales		Percentage Change 1983–1984	Percentage Share of 1984 Market
		1983	1984		
28	NTS Corp. NTS-Securities	19.8	42.9	116.7	0.8
29	Koger Properties Inc. Koger Securities		41.3		0.7
30	Montgomery Realty Company Merrill Lynch		40.2		0.7
31	Liberty Real Estate Corp. Torchmark Securities Corp.	36.5	39.0	6.8	0.7
32	McNeil Realty Investors Corp. McNeil Security Corp.	14.8	37.0	150.0	0.7
33	New England Life NEL Equity Service Corp.	32.6	36.9	13.2	0.6
34	Krupp Corp. Smith Barney	65.0	35.3	−45.7	0.6
35	DeAnza Corp. DeAnza Securities		35.0		0.6
36	Kidder Peabody Kidder Peabody	0.0	33.6	100.0	0.6
37	Sierra Real Estate Advisors Inc. Capital Alliance Investments		31.6		0.6
38	Winthrop Corp. Winthrop Securities Co.	165.7	31.1	−81.2	0.5
39	Shurgard Inc. Shurgard Securities	19.9	28.9	45.2	0.5
40	Connecticut General CIGNA Securities	24.6	28.3	15.0	0.5
41	Nooney Advisors Ltd. Nooney Advisors	16.8	25.8	53.6	0.5
42	W.P. Carey & Co. E.F. Hutton	69.0	25.3	−63.3	0.4
43	Travelers Corporation Keystone/Shearson/American Express	21.5	31.4	46.0	0.5
44	Dain Bosworth Dain Bosworth/Rauscher Pierce Ref.	18.0	22.9	27.2	0.4
45	McCombs Corp. McCombs Securities	29.4	22.2	−24.5	0.4
46	Sierra Pacific Capital Co. Sierra Pacific Securities	8.6	22.0	155.8	0.4
47	Realty Southwest Investment Corp. Rotan Mosle	4.0	20.0	400.0	0.4
48	Rancho Consultants Inc. Rancho Consultants Securities		18.8		0.3
49	DBL Properties Corp. Drexel Burnham Lambert	11.5	18.7	62.6	0.3

(Continued)

Real Estate Programs

Rank	Sponsor/Dealer Manager(s)	Sales		Percentage Change 1983–1984	Percentage Share of 1984 Market
		1983	1984		
50	John Hancock Realty Equities Merrill Lynch	6.7	16.9	152.2	0.3
51	National Housing Partnership Dean Witter		16.0		0.3
52	Freeman Diversified Properties Inc. Freeman Investments	2.8	15.4	450.0	0.3
53	Jacques Miller Realty JM Investment Co.	7.2	14.9	106.9	0.3
54	Diversified Historic Advisors Delaware Securities		14.6		0.3
55	J.M. Jayson and Company Westmoreland Capital Corp.	9.0	14.0	55.6	0.2
56	Griffin Real Estate Griffin Securities Corp.	13.7	13.2	−3.6	0.2
57	National Partnership Investment Corp. E.F. Hutton/Shearson Amex	53.7	51.9	−3.4	0.2
58	Occidental Land Research None	1.0	12.8	1,180.0	0.2
59	Property Resources Inc. PRI Securities	10.3	12.1	17.5	0.2
60	MB Mortgage Inc. Mutual Benefit Financial Services Corp.		11.9		0.2
61	Penn Mutual Life Insurance Janney Montgomery Scott	18.3	11.7	−36.1	0.2
62	Southwest Realty Ltd. Dean Witter/Eppler/Rauscher Pierce		10.9		0.2
63	DSI Properties Inc. Diversified Securities	11.3	10.8	−4.4	0.2
64	Brauvin Realty Inc. A.G. Edwards/Brauvin Sec. Inc.	7.8	9.5	21.8	0.2
65	National Development and Investment, Inc. NDII Securities	11.3	8.9	−21.2	0.2
66	Lang, Wayne F., & Tyler, Daniel S. Houston Investment Group		8.8		0.2
67	TCC Center Development Piper Jaffery	0.6	8.2	1,266.7	0.1
68	Capital Sunbelt Investments, Inc. None		7.8		0.1
69	Windsor Corp. Windsor Securities	0.2	7.6	3,700.0	0.1
70	Damson Properties Inc. Damson Securities		7.5		0.1
71	Boyle, Stephen B. Berry & Boyle Securities		7.2		0.1

Real Estate Programs

Rank	Sponsor/Dealer Manager(s)	Sales		Percentage Change 1983–1984	Percentage Share of 1984 Market
		1983	1984		
72	Bellevue Corporation Bellevue Mortgage Investors	4.0	7.1	77.5	0.1
73	American Republic Realty Corp. ASI/Blunt Ellis & Loewi	9.0	7.0	−22.2	0.1
74	Calmark Realty Calmark Securities Inc.		7.0		0.1
75	Gulledge Corp., The Gulledge Securities		6.7		0.1
76	Continental Wingate Company Inc. Continental Wingate Securities Corp.	6.9	6.5	−5.8	0.1
77	Del Taco Inc. Private Ledger Financial Services	5.2	6.4	23.1	0.1
78	Brichard Properties Inc. Brichard & Company Inc.	5.4	5.6	3.7	0.1
79	AEI Incorporated AEI Incorporated		5.0		0.1
80	Comart, Martin None		5.0		0.1
81	Mariner Capital Management Inc. McDonald Securities		5.0		0.1
82	Security Spring Security Spring and Boe Investment Corp.	8.1	4.6	−43.2	0.1
83	Titan Realty Corp. Titan Capital Corp.	n/av.[1]	4.2	100.0	0.1
84	Keller, Brian R. None		4.0		0.1
85	Murray Realty Investors Murray Securities	5.4	4.0	−25.9	0.1
86	Western Entertainment Venture University Securities Corp.	2.7	4.0	48.1	0.1
87	Kecor Financial Butterfield Securities Corp.	3.0	4.8	60.0	0.1
88	Financial Service Realty Corp. FSC Securities Corp.	2.0	3.5	75.0	0.1
89	Amshel Properties, Inc. Amshel Sec.	3.5	3.4	−2.9	0.1
90	Sasak, Timothy L. None		3.4		0.1
91	AIF Corporation First Equity Securities		3.3		0.1
92	Super 8 Motels Brown and Broche	8.2	3.2	−61.0	0.1
93	B.F. Saul-Avenel, Ltd. B.F. Saul Securities Inc.		2.9		0.1

(Continued)

Real Estate Programs

Rank	Sponsor/Dealer Manager(s)	Sales		Percentage Change 1983–1984	Percentage Share of 1984 Market
		1983	1984		
94	Boettcher and Company Boettcher & Company	28.2	2.7	−90.4	*
95	Tree Top Inc. None		2.7		*
96	Brown, Dennis None		2.4		*
97	Sungrowth Equities Corp. Sungrowth Securities		2.3		*
98	Tessier Properties H.J. Tessier		2.3		*
99	Trion Ltd. Trion Securities Corp.		2.3		*
100	Hanover Bank & Trust Company None		2.2		*
101	Secured Investments Resources Hoyt Securities		2.2		*
102	American Development Team, Inc. Tucker Anthony	3.0	2.0	−33.3	*
103	H-L Properties Inc. None		2.0		*
104	CFS Real Estate CFS Securities Corp.	1.4	1.9	35.7	*
105	Oliver Realty Inc. O.R. Securities	2.7	2.4	−11.1	*
106	S-B-F Partners None		1.4		*
107	Albin, Jerry R. Albin Securities Corp.		1.3		*
108	Decade Securities Inc. Decade Investment Corp.		1.3		*
109	Deines, John M. K&D Securities		1.3		*
110	Pacific Partners Joint Venture Norwestern Securities		1.3		*
111	Reilly Equities Inc. Reilly Securities	1.3	1.3	0.0	*
112	RWB Realty Corp. RWB Financial Svcs.		1.2		*
113	Wells, Leo F., III Wells Investment Securities		1.2		*
114	HCW Pension Real Estate Inc. None		1.1		*
115	Wheaton Properties IRE Securities Inc.		1.1		*

Real Estate Programs

Rank	Sponsor/Dealer Manager(s)	Sales 1983	Sales 1984	Percentage Change 1983–1984	Percentage Share of 1984 Market
116	Denco International Equity Corp. None		1.0		*
117	Trademark Real Properties, Inc. None		1.0		*
118	Naples Fund Management Heritage Investment Securities Inc.	1.2	0.9	−25.0	*
119	Marion Bass Capital Mgt. Corp. Marion Bass Securities		0.8		*
120	Kanter Keyes Corp. Keyes Investment Group Inc.	8.3	0.5	−94.0	*
121	Aetna Life & Casualty Company Federated Securities		0.4		*
122	American Property Equities Diverse Financial Corp.		0.3		*
123	Your Attic Properties Inc. Your Attic Securities	0.0	0.3		*
124	Jason-Northco Properties Inc. Northwest Capital Investment	1.2	0.2	−83.3	*
125	Kenman Corp. Kenman Securities Corp.		0.2		*
126	Admiralty General Corp. Warner Beck, Inc.	n/a.[1]	n/av.[1]	0.0	*
127	Kemper/Cymrot Partners, LP None		0.0	0.0	*
128	McCracken Intervest MPI Securities		n/av.[1]	0.0	*
129	Oxford Residential Properties I Corp. Merrill Lynch		0.0	0.0	*
130	Rocky Mountain Investment Fund Inc. None		n/av.[1]	0.0	*
131	Silber, Walter B., Griffith, Samuel D. Brentwood Financial Corp.		0.0	0.0	*
132	T. Rowe Price Real Estate Fund Mgt. Inc. None		0.0	0.0	*
133	Western Capital Venture Corporation W.R.S. Securities		0.0	0.0	*
	TOTAL	$4,406.5	$5,685.9	29.0%	100.0%

* *Less than .1%.*
1 *Information not available from sponsor.*

Source: *The Stanger Review,* 1985.

OIL AND GAS DRILLING PROGRAMS
Sponsors' Market Share (in Millions of Dollars)

Rank	Sponsor/Dealer Manager(s)	Sales		Percentage Change 1983–1984	Percentage Share of 1984 Market
		1983	1984		
1	Woods Petroleum Corporation Woods Securities Corp.	82.0	41.0	−50.0	10.1
2	Dyco Petroleum Corporation Dain Bosworth	66.8	40.5	−39.4	10.0
3	Belden & Blake Oil Production, Inc. None	12.8	23.3	82.0	5.7
4	May Petroleum Inc. May Securities	40.4	20.6	−49.0	5.1
5	Stone Petroleum Corp. Stone Programs Corp.	36.0	20.0	−44.4	4.9
6	Red Eagle Exploration None	22.7	19.5	−14.1	4.8
7	Parker & Parsley Petroleum Company Shearson/Amex	42.8	19.4	−54.7	4.8
8	Samson Properties, Inc. Samson Securities	24.1	18.8	−22.0	4.6
9	HCW Oil & Gas Inc. None	28.3	18.1	−36.0	4.5
10	Callon Petroleum Co. Callon Securities Co.	28.6	17.1	−40.2	4.2
11	Sterling Drilling and Production Smith Barney	26.7	15.7	−41.2	3.9
12	Natural Resource Management NRM Corporation		11.6		2.9
13	Hawkins Exploration Chase Franklin Corp.	9.9	10.0	1.0	2.5
14	Kimbark Oil & Gas Company Kidder Peabody	10.3	8.3	−19.4	2.0
15	Coastal Corporation Paine Webber		8.0		2.0
16	Apache Corp. Apache Programs	17.9	7.5	−58.1	1.8
17	Tenneco Oil Company None		7.0		1.7
18	Clinton Oil Company Ohio Company/Baker, Watts	6.9	6.7	−2.9	1.6
19	Brock Exploration Corp. Brock Securities	7.7	6.4	−16.9	1.6
20	Columbian Energy Corporation The Columbian Sec. Corp.	15.8	6.4	−59.5	1.6
21	GeoVest Energy Inc. None	8.0	6.0	−25.0	1.5

Oil and Gas Drilling Programs

Rank	Sponsor/Dealer Manager(s)	Sales		Percentage Change 1983–1984	Percentage Share of 1984 Market
		1983	1984		
22	Pominex Inc. Gradison/R.G. Dickinson/Moore & Schley	4.0	4.6	15.0	1.1
23	Snyder Partners Rotan Mosle	5.4	4.5	−16.7	1.1
24	Merrico Resources Merrico Investment Corp.	21.0	4.4	−79.0	1.1
25	Bogert Oil Company Bogert Funds		4.3		1.1
26	Resources Partners Mission Securities	2.6	3.6	38.5	0.9
27	LGS Energy Edward D. Jones	7.1	3.3	−53.5	0.8
28	North Coast Energy NCE Securities	2.5	3.3	32.0	0.8
29	Pioneer Western Energy Corp. PW Securities	3.5	3.3	−5.7	0.8
30	Walker Exploration Inc. Walker Securities		3.3		0.8
31	Stratigraphic Petroleum Company Stratigraphic Resources	8.0	3.0	−62.5	0.7
32	Basic Energy None		2.6		0.6
33	Castle Energy Corp./JMS Resources Janney Montgomery Scott	7.3	2.5	−65.8	0.6
34	Integrated Resources Integrated Resources	5.4	2.5	−53.7	0.6
35	Texland Petroleum Inc. McDonald & Company	5.7	2.5	−56.1	0.6
36	Kidder Peabody Kidder Peabody		2.3		0.6
37	Cotton Petroleum Corp. None	2.5	2.2	−12.0	0.5
38	Pan Exploration and Development Inc. Burch & Company Inc./Financial Planners Equity Corp.	1.9	2.2	15.8	0.5
39	Faith Hydrocarbons First Albany Corp.		2.1		0.5
40	Smith Oil & Gas Exploration Co. H.B. Shaine & Co. Inc.	2.5	2.1	−16.0	0.5
41	Unit Drilling and Exploration Co. Unit Securities	3.0	1.9	−36.7	0.5

(Continued)

Oil and Gas Drilling Programs

Rank	Sponsor/Dealer Manager(s)	Sales		Percentage Change 1983–1984	Percentage Share of 1984 Market
		1983	1984		
42	Mid-America Petroleum Inc. None	8.0	1.7	−78.8	0.4
43	USENCO Assets Planning & Development Inc.		1.6		0.4
44	ConVest Energy Corporation ConVest Securities	7.1	1.4	−80.3	0.3
45	Midcontinent Oil & Gas Associates Midcontinent Capital Corporation		1.4		0.3
46	AWM Energy Corp. Empire Securities Corp.	0.7	1.2	71.4	0.3
47	Carr, Richard R. None		1.1		0.3
48	ECC Resources ECC Financial Corp.	0.8	1.1	37.5	0.3
49	Energy Funds Inc. AEI Incorporated	1.8	1.1	−38.9	0.3
50	Delta Western Oil Company None	0.5	1.0	100.0	0.2
51	Wells Development Company Inc. L.J. Wells Investments Inc.	0.0	1.0	100.0	0.2
52	Energy Productions Inc. Source Securities		0.7		0.2
53	Royal Petroleum Properties Inc. White, William B.		0.5		0.1
54	Deep Wilcox Deep Wilcox Securities		0.4		0.1
55	Dohler-Walsh None		0.1		*
56	Petroleum Resources Company Midland Management Corp.	3.8	0.0	−100.0	*
	TOTAL	754.3	406.7	−46.1	100.0

* *Less than .1%.*

Source: *The Stanger Review*, 1985.

OIL AND GAS INCOME PROGRAMS
Sponsors' Market Share (in Millions of Dollars)

Rank	Sponsor/Dealer Manager(s)	Sales		Percentage Change 1983–1984	Percentage Share of 1984 Market
		1983	1984		
1	Damson Oil Corp. Damson Securities	536.0	273.3	−49.0	27.7
2	Natural Resource Management NRM Corp.	240.1	141.6	−41.0	14.4
3	Quinoco Oil and Gas, Inc. Quinoco Sec. Inc.	122.0	128.0	4.9	13.0
4	Prudential-Bache Energy Production Inc. Prudential-Bache	81.7	86.7	6.1	8.8
5	E.F. Hutton E.F. Hutton	76.9	64.5	−16.1	6.5
6	HCW Oil and Gas Inc. None	30.0	60.8	102.7	6.2
7	Enex Resources Corp. Enex Securities	51.9	58.3	12.3	5.9
8	EMCOR Petroleum Inc. Energy Methods Securities Co. Inc.	59.1	40.5	−31.5	4.1
9	Callon Petroleum Company Callon Securities Co.	22.1	23.8	7.7	2.4
10	ConVest Energy Inc. ConVest Securities	30.3	21.8	−28.1	2.2
11	Morgan Energy Morgan Securities	7.5	18.9	152.0	1.9
12	Snyder Oil Company E.F. Hutton/Butcher & Singer		11.2		1.1
13	Kidder Energy Inc. Kidder, Peabody & Co.	24.4	9.3	−61.9	0.9
14	Western Energy Development Company Inc. Western Securities	1.0	7.2	620.0	0.7
15	Paine Webber/Geodyne Properties Inc. Paine Webber		6.2		0.6
16	Merrico Resources Merrico Investment Corp.		4.7		0.5
17	Mid-America Petroleum Inc. Mid-American Securities	2.5	4.1	64.0	0.4
18	Resources Partners Mission Securities	5.8	4.1	−29.3	0.4
19	DE-TEX II Energy Company Source Securities Inc.	0.9	3.9	333.3	0.4
20	Pioneer Western Energy Corp. PW Securities	3.9	3.9	0.0	0.4
21	Energysearch Inc. Butcher and Singer	9.8	3.8	−61.2	0.4

(Continued)

Oil and Gas Income Programs

Rank	Sponsor/Dealer Manager(s)	Sales		Percentage Change 1983–1984	Percentage Share of 1984 Market
		1983	1984		
22	Pan Exploration and Development Inc. Burch & Company Inc./Financial Planners Equity Corporation	1.5	2.7	80.0	0.3
23	ECC Resources ECC Financial Corp.	0.8	1.8	125.0	0.2
24	Entex Petroleum Inc. Merrill Lynch		1.5		0.2
25	Samson Properties Inc. Samson Securities Company	5.1	1.5	−70.6	0.2
26	Coastal Company Coastal Securities	0.3	1.0	233.3	0.1
27	Noarko Resources Inc. None	0.7	0.4	−42.9	*
	TOTAL	2,010.4	985.5	−51.0	100.0

* *Less than .1%.*

Source: *The Stanger Review*, 1985.

OIL AND GAS ROYALTY AND COMPLETION PROGRAMS
Sponsors' Market Share (in Millions of Dollars)

Rank	Sponsor/Dealer Manager(s)	Sales		Percentage Change 1983–1984	Percentage Share of 1984 Market
		1983	1984		
1	E.F. Hutton/Energy Assets E.F. Hutton	14.8	42.0	183.8	65.8
2	Integrated Resources, Inc. Integrated Resources Marketing, Inc.	1.2	18.1	1,408.3	28.4
3	American Completion and Development Corp. American Completion Securities	19.4	3.7	−80.9	5.8
	TOTAL	101.8	63.8	−37.3	100.0

Source: *The Stanger Review*, 1985.

OIL AND GAS COMBINATION PROGRAMS
Sponsors' Market Share (in Millions of Dollars)

Rank	Sponsor/Dealer Manager(s)	Sales		Percentage Change 1983–1984	Percentage Share of 1984 Market
		1983	1984		
1	Apache Petroleum Company E.F. Hutton/Dean Witter/Smith Barney/Piper Jaffray	45.8	61.5	34.3	75.0
2	Thomson McKinnon Energy Management Thomson McKinnon		5.5		6.7
3	Swift Energy Company V.J. McGuiness Co.		4.4		5.4
4	Wedco Oil & Gas None		4.0		4.9
5	Energysearch, Inc. Butcher and Singer	4.5	3.7	−17.8	4.5
6	Baytide Petroleum Inc. Baytide Securities	1.0	1.6	60.0	2.0
7	EMCOR Petroleum Inc. Energy Methods Sec.		1.3		1.6
	TOTAL	114.6	82.0	−28.4	100.0

Source: *The Stanger Review*, 1985.

5.09 Quality of Life

Where one lives, one's occupation, and one's income are a few of the key factors affecting the quality of one's life. The information presented here concerns such topics as trends in the job market, how well localities serve the needs of the retired population, quality of life in metropolitan areas (personal income, unemployment, the cost of a home, crime rate, and weather conditions), and localities with the highest income and fastest growth.

QUALITY OF LIFE IN U.S. METROPOLITAN AREAS

Location	Per Capita Personal Income 1982	% Jobless April 1984	Projected Ann. % Growth 1979-1993		Avg. Home Price 7/83 ($000)	Crime Rate Per 100,000 1982[1]	Mean No. of Days[2] clr.–cldy./pt.cldy.	Mean No. of Days Temp. Below 32°F	Normal Daily Max. Temp. °F Aug.
			Jobs	Income					
Anaheim-Santa Ana-Garden Gr., Calif.	$13,927	4.3	3.1	3.5	$132.9	6,092.3	n/av.	n/av.	n/av.
Atlanta, Ga.	11,590	4.8	2.6	3.4	95.7	6,946.2	108–149	58	86.4
Baltimore, Md.	11,560	5.9	1.0	2.2	72.9	6,867.9	107–149	99	85.1
Birmingham, Ala.	9,941	10.1	1.0	1.6	n/av.	6,222.7	99–155	60	89.7
Boston-Lowell-Brockton-Lawrence-Haverhill, Mass.	13,087	4.3[3]	1.7	2.7	91.5	6,031.3	100–160	99	79.3
Bridgeport-Stamford-Norwalk-Danbury, Conn.	16,878	4.8[4]	1.6	2.5	n/av.	5,842.1	103–160	135	80.4
Buffalo, N.Y.	11,160	8.5	—	1.0	n/av.	4,970.4	55–208	132	77.6
Chicago	13,069	8.7	0.6	1.6	95.2	5,283.3	86–173	99	82.3
Greater Cincinnati	11,224	n/av.	0.6	1.6	n/av.	5,450.4	n/av.	125	85.8
Cleveland	12,757	9.3	0.2	1.1	71.7	5,345.9	68–199	121	80.4
Columbus	10,629	7.8	1.5	2.3	88.4	6,634.1	73–186	121	83.7
Dallas-Ft.Worth	13,846	3.9	2.7	3.6	101.7	8,047.6	138–132	41	96.1
Dayton	11,579	8.4	3.8	1.4	n/av.	6,488.0	80–184	118	83.4
Denver-Boulder	13,964	4.1	2.5	3.2	119.7	7,961.0	117–120	157	85.8
Detroit	12,092	n/av.	0.2	1.1	76.2	8,175.4	80–177	139	81.8
Ft. Lauderdale-Hollywood, Fla.	13,091	4.6	2.9	4.1	81.2	8,122.4	n/av.	n/av.	n/av.
Hartford-New Britain-Bristol, Conn.	13,416	3.9[5]	1.6	2.5	n/av.	6,176.0	81–175	136	81.9
Honolulu	12,130	4.7	1.8	2.4	103.8	6,444.4	86–100	0	87.4
Houston	14,128	7.3	2.3	3.2	105.3	7,612.8	97–157	24	94.3
Indianapolis	11,236	7.9	1.7	1.8	66.5	5,579.5	90–177	121	84.0
Kansas City	10,994	6.1	0.7	1.9	78.9	6,897.0	120–154	109	88.7
Los Angeles - Long Beach	13,080	7.3	1.4	2.6	132.9	8,172.2	185–74	0	79.9
Louisville	10,579	n/av.	3.6	1.4	60.4	5,671.3	93–169	92	86.8
Greater Memphis	9,968	7.5	0.9	2.1	n/av.	6,822.7	120–149	58	90.6
Miami	11,717	6.7	2.2	3.4	81.2	10,289.4	74–117	0	89.9
Milwaukee	12,597	6.6	0.7	1.6	84.0	5,429.7	94–172	144	79.7
Minneapolis-St. Paul	12,811	4.7	1.5	2.5	91.2	5,897.3	99–165	156	80.8
Nashville-Davidson, Tenn.	10,229	5.7	1.6	2.6	n/av.	5,511.7	103–157	78	89.2
Newark	13,671	6.1	0.9	1.8	114.7	5,977.8	96–158	87	83.7
New Orleans	11,680	7.8	1.3	2.8	n/av.	7,557.9	108–139	13	90.6
New York	12,874	7.1	1.1	2.1	114.7	8,496.6	107–133	81	82.5
Philadelphia	11,946	6.7	0.9	1.9	80.3	4,937.2	93–161	99	84.8
Phoenix	11,086	3.9	2.9	3.6	102.4	7,819.4	213–71	10	102.2
Pittsburgh	11,762	11.3	—	1.4	71.1	3,226.5	50–203	124	80.9
Portland	11,793	8.3	0.9	2.5	89.1	5,608.8	69–227	44	78.1
Providence-Warwick-Pawtucket, R.I.	10,748	6.8	0.9	1.9	n/av.	5,251.8	101–161	121	79.8
Riverside-San Bernardino-Ontario, Calif.	10,092	8.7	2.9	4.0	n/av.	7,918.2	n/av.	n/av.	n/av.
Rochester, N.Y.	12,463	5.9	0.7	1.7	65.7	5,479.3	61–196	135	80.1
Sacramento	11,176	8.4	2.4	3.2	n/av.	8,356.4	191–101	17	91.3
St. Louis	12,338	8.8	0.8	1.8	79.2	5,988.0	105–160	105	87.2
Salt Lake City - Ogden	9,670	6.1	1.7	2.6	133.2	6,406.7	127–135	128	90.2
San Antonio	10,131	5.1	3.1	3.8	n/av.	6,739.6	107–141	23	95.9
San Diego	11,638	6.0	3.2	3.5	134.5	6,080.8	147–100	0	77.3
San Francisco - Oakland	17,131	6.2	1.4	2.3	139.3	7,775.3	162–104	0	68.2
San Jose, Calif.	14,998	5.0	3.0	3.6	139.3	6,768.2	n/av.	n/av.	n/av.
Seattle-Everett, Wash.	13,239	8.4	1.5	3.0	103.8	7,241.9	71–201	16	74
Tampa-St. Petersburg, Fla.	10,675	5.1	3.2	3.9	72.8	7,153.4	97–126	4	90.4
Washington, DC	14,960	4.0	1.5	2.2	160.8	6,324.5	101–161	117	86

1 *Includes all crime.*
2 *Daylight only; clear denotes zero to 0.3 sky cover; cloudy denotes 0.8 to complete sky cover.*
3 *Boston only.*
4 *Bridgeport only.*
5 *Hartford only.*

Source: *The World Almanac & Book of Facts,* 1985 edition, copyright © Newspaper Enterprise Association, Inc., New York, N.Y. 10166.

ZIP CODE MARKETING

Truth or Consequences lives again. No, not the old TV show, but the three-digit Zip Code area (879) in New Mexico that is number six among the ten Zips with the fastest growth in personal income between 1969 and 1979. So the Internal Revenue Service reports as a result of an analysis of income by Zip Code area.

Eight of the ten Zips with the fastest growth in adjusted gross income (AGI) are associated with energy resource development projects: three in Kentucky, three in Texas, and one each in Oklahoma and Wyoming. In contrast, half of the ten Zips with the highest AGI are in the industrial belt: two in Illinois, one each in New York, New Jersey, and Michigan. The Zip with the highest AGI, 220-221, is in northern Virginia, well populated by federal civil servants. The runner-up, Zip 079, in New Jersey, boasts an unusually high ratio (12%) of taxpayers in the $50,000-and-over bracket. Many of them live in Summit but work in New York City. Wyoming's Rock Springs, Zip 829, enjoys the unique distinction of being the only Zip that is in both the high-income and fastest-growing categories.

Zips with the highest income ...			... and the fastest growth		
Zip Code Area	3-digit Code	Median AGI[1] ($)	Zip Code Area	3-digit Code	% Gain[2] 1969-79
Northern Virginia	220-221	17,934	LaGrange, Tex.	789	59.1
Summit, N.J.	079	17,883	Bellaire, Tex.	774	57.0
Shawnee Mission, Kans.	662	17,625	Corbin eastern suburbs, Ky.	408	53.4
Denver southern suburbs	801	17,437	Hazard western area, Ky.	417	51.8
Rock Springs eastern area, Wyo.	829	17,389	Woodward, Okla.	738	51.7
Hicksville, N.Y.	118	17,159	Truth or Consequences, N.Mex.	879	51.1
Seattle suburbs	980	16,926	Conroe, Tex.	773	50.7
Chicago southern suburbs (west)	605	16,913	Sheldon, Iowa	512	49.7
Peoria suburbs, Ill.	615	16,771	Ashland southern suburbs, Ky.	412	49.0
Flint, Mich.	484	16,731	Rock Springs eastern area, Wyo.	829	47.4

1 *Adjusted gross income.*
2 *Calculated in constant dollars.*

Source: Internal Revenue Service, *Statistics of Income Bulletin,* Spring 1983.

CITIES AND COUNTIES
The Most, The Highest, The Largest

CRIME RATES

Cities with the most crimes per 100,000 residents:

Atlantic City, N.J.	32,232
Hartford, Connecticut	17,930
W. Palm Beach, Florida	17,131
Daytona Beach, Florida	15,937
Muskegon, Michigan	15,743
Camden, N.J.	15,715
Paramus, N.J.	15,418
Orange, N.J.	15,114
Flint, Michigan	14,864
Miami, Florida	14,864

POVERTY LEVEL

Counties with highest percentage of persons living below poverty level:

Tunica, Mississippi	52.9
Starr, Texas	50.6
Owsley, Kentucky	48.3
Holmes, Mississippi	46.9
Greene, Alabama	45.7
Wilcox, Alabama	45.3
Lowndes, Alabama	45.0
Humphreys, Mississippi	44.7
Shannon, South Dakota	44.7
Lee, Arkansas	44.3

ELDERLY RESIDENTS

Cities with highest percentage of residents 65 and over:

Miami Beach, Florida	51.8
Hallandale, Florida	49.8
Tamarac, Florida	44.7
Deerfield Beach, Florida	41.3
Lauderdale Lakes, Florida	37.6
Boynton Beach, Florida	36.1
Dunedin, Florida	35.9
Seal Beach, California	35.1
Lake Worth, Florida	32.6
Delray Beach, Florida	29.9

HOME VALUES

Counties with the highest median value of owner occupied dwellings:

Pitkin, Colorado	$200,000
Marin, California	151,000
Honolulu, Hawaii	130,400
San Mateo, California	124,400
Maui, Hawaii	113,600
Santa Clara, California	109,400
Orange, California	108,100
Mono, California	106,000
San Francisco, California	104,600
Santa Barbara, California	104,000

Cities and Counties

HIGHEST INCOMES

Cities with the largest median household incomes:

Rancho Palos Verdes, California	$41,973
Saratoga, California	41,143
Northbrook, Illinois	39,926
Highland Park, Illinois	38,542
Wilmette, Illinois	36,980
Los Altos, California	36,525
Ridgewood, N.J.	34,464
Naperville, Illinois	34,147
Glenview, Illinois	33,078
Bowie, Maryland	32,373

BANK DEPOSITS

Counties with highest annual bank deposits per capita:

New York, N.Y.	$63,682
San Francisco, California	34,449
Lipscomb, Texas	20,818
Suffolk, Massachusetts	19,905
Midland, Texas	17,081
Irion, Texas	15,303
Russell, Kansas	15,246
Bedford, Virginia	15,192
Sheridan, Kansas	15,182
Galax, Virginia	15,054

MOST EDUCATED

Cities with highest percentage of residents over 25 with 16 or more years of education:

Chapel Hill, N.C.	68.7
East Lansing, Michigan	65.4
Davis, California	60.9
State College, Pennsylvania	59.5
Ann Arbor, Michigan	56.2
Blacksburg, Virginia	56.1
Wilmette Village, Illinois	54.0
Palo Alto, California	54.0
College Station, Texas	53.9
Berkeley, California	52.3

HIGHEST DENSITY

Counties with the largest population per square mile:

New York, N.Y.	64,395
Kings, N.Y.	31,762
Bronx, N.Y.	28,006
Queens, N.Y.	17,411
San Francisco, California	14,636
Philadelphia, Pennsylvania	12,413
Hudson, N.J.	11,993
Suffolk, Massachusetts	11,472
Baltimore, Maryland	9,793
St. Louis, Missouri	7,379

Source: Census Bureau.

THE BEST AND WORST U.S. CITIES

Rand McNally recently compiled statistics, by city, for climate and terrain, housing, health care, transportation, education, the arts, recreation, and economic outlook. Based on these data, Rand McNally ranked 329 U.S. cities according to an index of desirability.

The Top 10	**The Bottom 10**
1 Pittsburgh, Pennsylvania	320 Andersen, Indiana
2 Boston, Massachusetts	321 Rockford, Illinois
3 Raleigh-Durham, North Carolina	322 Casper, Wyoming
4 San Francisco, California	323 Gadsden, Alabama
5 Philadelphia, Pennsylvania	324 Benton Harbor, Michigan
6 Nassau-Suffolk counties, New York	325 Albany, Georgia
7 St. Louis, Missouri	326 Dothan, Alabama
8 Louisville, Kentucky	327 Modesto, California
9 Norwalk, Connecticut	328 Pine Bluff, Arkansas
10 Seattle, Washington	329 Yuba City, California

Source: *Places Rated Almanac,* Richard Boyer and David Savageaux; © 1985 Rand McNally.

CHAPTER 6

Professional Development

CONTENTS

The financial planning profession offers a wide variety of rewarding career opportunities and fields of specialization. This chapter presents information on six topics of concern to practitioners and those considering careers in financial planning:

- Credentials, certification, and continuing education
- NASD licenses and professional designations
- Professional organizations
- Professional ethics and malpractice
- Computer applications and databases
- Finance publications (periodicals and books)

6.01 Credentials, Certification, and Continuing Education

No specific educational requirements or professional credentials and certification have been formalized for the financial planning field. Most financial planners, however, have at least a four-year college degree. Courses that provide the best preparation for financial planning practitioners include: accounting, finance, economics, marketing, general business, business law, small business management, mathematics, public speaking, English, human behavior, and counseling. Specific coursework could also include classes in investments, taxes, financial planning, estate planning, and introductory courses in computer science that emphasize microcomputers.

Many colleges and universities offer programs directed toward the financial planning field, and curriculums are rapidly being established. But few individuals become financial planners directly after completing college. Most instead seek employment as stockbrokers, insurance agents, bank officers, accountants, or lawyers. Currently, the greatest increases in entry-level hiring are occurring in sales, particularly in the sales divisions of stockbrokerage firms and insurance companies.

Source: International Association for Financial Planning, "Financial Planning as a Career" (brochure), 1984.

EDUCATIONAL INSTITUTIONS

A number of colleges and universities offer instruction in financial planning. The list below gives the names and addresses of the institutions and the degree, certificate, or courses offered.

Institution	Offering
The College for Financial Planning 9725 Hampden Avenue, Suite 200 Denver, CO 80231 (303) 755-7101	Certificate: Certified Financial Planner (CFP)
The American College 270 Bryn Mawr Avenue Bryn Mawr, PA 19010 (215) 896-4500	Certificates: Chartered Life Underwriter (CLU) Chartered Financial Consultant (ChFC) Degree: M.S. in Financial Services
Adelphi University Garden City, NY 11530	Certificates: Certificate in Financial Planning Degree: B.S. in Management and Communication (four major courses in Financial Planning)
Boston University/Metropolitan College 755 Commonwealth Avenue Boston, MA 02215 (617) 353-4496	Certificates: Certificate in Investment Planning
Brigham Young University 395JKB Provo, UT 84601 (801) 378-1211	Degree: B.S. in Business Management with concentration in Finance, emphasis in Financial and Estate Planning B.S. in Family Science with concentration in Family Financial Planning and Counseling
California State University, Long Beach School of Business Department of Finance Long Beach, CA 90840 (213) 498-4569	Proposed course and college major in Personal Financial Planning (write for status or details)
Drake University Cole Hall, Room 204 Des Moines, IA 50311 (515) 271-3921	Degree: B.S. and B.A. in Finance with concentration in Personal Financial Planning
Georgia State University College of Business Department of Insurance University Plaza Atlanta, GA 30303 (404) 658-3840	Degrees: M.B.A. with major in Insurance and concentration in Financial Planning Ph.D. with major in Insurance and concentration in Financial Planning
Golden Gate University 536 Mission Street San Francisco, CA 94105 (415) 442-7272	Certificates: Certified Financial Planner (CFP) (in cooperation with the College for Financial Planning)

Educational Institutions

Institution	Offering
Golden Gate University 818 West 7th Street Suite 1001 Los Angeles, CA 90017 (213) 623-6000	Certificates and Degrees: Same as Golden Gate University, San Francisco
Kirkwood Community College 6301 Kirkwood Blvd., S.W. P.O. Box 2068 Cedar Rapids, IA 52406 (319) 398-5411	Certificate: Money Management Adviser

San Diego State University
3092 Lloyd Street
San Diego, CA 92119
(714) 265-5200
	Degrees:
	B.B.A. with major in Finance and a
	    concentration in Financial Services
	M.S. in Business Administration with a
	    concentration in Financial Services

University of California Berkeley Extension 2223 Fulton Street Berkeley, CA 94720 (415) 642-4111	Certificate: Professional designation in Personal Financial Planning
University of California Davis Extension Davis, CA 95616 (916) 752-0880	Certificate: Professional designation in Personal Financial Planning
UCLA Extension Department of Management & Business Post Office Box 24901 Los Angeles, CA 90024 (213) 825-7031	Certificate: Professional designation in Personal Financial Planning

University of Sarasota
2080 Ringling Boulevard
Sarasota, FL 33577
(813) 955-4228
	Degrees:
	B.B.A. with Financial Planning major
	M.B.A. with Financial Planning major
	Note: Learning credits are available for
	    students with work experience in Financial
	    Planning

Accredited Institutions

In addition to taking the home-study Certified Financial Planner Professional Education Program directly from the College for Financial Planning, candidates may take the program through one of the major colleges and universities offering it under a licensing arrangement with the College for Financial Planning. These institutions are:

Bentley College
Center for Continuing Education
Waltham, MA 02554

Brookhaven College
Farmers Branch, TX 75234

Broward Community College
Pompano Beach, FL 33063

California Lutheran College
Thousand Oaks, CA 91360

Charles Stewart Mott Community College
Flint, MI 48503

Cleveland State University
Cleveland, OH 44115

College of Mount Saint Vincent
Riverdale, NY 10471

Eastern Washington University
Cheney, WA 99004

Franklin University
Division of Continuing Education
Columbus, OH 43215

Fox Valley Technical Institute
Appleton, WI 54913-2277

George Washington University
Washington, DC 20052

George Washington University, Virginia
Tidewater Center
Hampton, VA 23666

Golden Gate University, Los Angeles
Los Angeles, CA 90017

Golden Gate University, San Francisco
San Francisco, CA 94105

Wm. Rainey Harper College
Palatine, IL 60067

Indiana University
Division of Continuing Studies
Indianapolis, IN 46202

Jersey City State College
Jersey City, NJ 07305

Metropolitan State College
Denver, CO 80204

Monmouth College
West Long Branch, NJ 07764

Roosevelt University
Chicago, IL 60605

St. John Fisher College
Rochester, NY 14618

St. Vincent College
Latrobe, PA 15650

San Diego State University
San Diego, CA 92182

Scott Community College
Bettendorf, IA 52722

University of Detroit
Detroit, MI 48226

University of Houston
Central Campus
Houston, TX 77002

University of Houston
Downtown College
Houston, TX 77002

University of Miami
Miami, FL 33124

University of Missouri, Kansas City
Kansas City, MO 64110

University of Southern California
Los Angeles, CA 90007

University of Southern California, Valley
Camarillo Valley, CA 93010

University of Tampa, Metro College
Tampa, FL 33606

University of Virginia
Roanoke Regional Center
Roanoke, VA 24018

6.02 Professional Licenses and Designations

NASD LICENSES

The National Association of Securities Dealers (NASD) administers qualifications examinations for the securities industry. Over 4,000 securities firms belong to the NASD, and over 250,000 individuals are registered NASD representatives (securities salespeople) and principals (officers of securities firms).

The three most-broadly held licenses are:

- NASD Series 6, designed for the individual who will be marketing a broad range of mutual fund products, including money market fund investments. This registration also qualifies a person to sell variable annuities, variable life insurance, and other securities-based products.

- NASD Series 22, designed for individuals who will be marketing tax-shelter programs (limited partnership programs in oil and gas, real estate, agriculture, and equipment leasing).

- NASD Series 7, the general securities registration, which qualifies individuals to market a broad spectrum of investment products.

Other examinations administered by the NASD include:

Series	Examination
2	SEC/NASD Non-Member General Securities Examination
3	National Commodity Futures Examination
4	Registered Options Principal Examination
5	Interest Rate Options Examination
8	General Securities Sales Supervisor Examination
9	General Securities Sales Supervisor Options Module Re-Examination
15	Foreign Currency Options Qualifications Examination
20	New York Futures Exchange/Chicago Mercantile Exchange Index and Options Examination
24	General Securities Principal Examination
26	Investment Company Products/Variable Contracts Principal Examination
39	Direct Participation Programs Principal Examination
52	Municipal Securities Representative Examination
53	Municipal Securities Principal Examination
63	Uniform Securities Agent State Law Examination

EXAMINATION REQUIREMENTS

Individuals not previously registered or qualified with the NASD must pass certain examinations and meet other requirements in order to be able to participate in the securities industry.

General Securities Firms

EXAMINATION REQUIREMENTS:

Principals—Series 7 prerequisite representative examination and the Series 24 general securities principal examination Financial and operations principal—Series 27 examination (unless exempt from requirement)

Representatives — Series 7 general securities representative examination

Minimum net capital requirement: $25,000

Direct Participation Firms

EXAMINATION REQUIREMENTS:

Principals—Series 22 prerequisite limited representative examination and Series 39 direct participation programs examination (unless qualified by Series 24)

Representatives—Series 22 limited representative examination (unless qualified by Series 7)

Minimum net capital requirement: $5,000

Investment Company/Variable Contract (IC/VC) Firms

EXAMINATION REQUIREMENTS:

Principals—Series 6 prerequisite limited representative examination and Series 26 investment company/variable contract principal examination (unless qualified by Series 24)

Representatives—Series 6 limited representative examination (unless qualified by Series 7)

Minimum net capital requirement: $2,500

Real Estate Securities Firms

EXAMINATION REQUIREMENTS:

Principals—Series 53 municipal securities principal examination (if the principal also functions as a municipal securities representative, Series 52 municipal securities representative examination is required)

Financial and operations principal—Series 54 municipal financial principal examination (unless qualified by Series 27)

Representatives—Series 52 municipal securities representative examination (unless qualified by Series 27)

Minimum net capital requirement: $25,000

Municipal Fund Brokerage Firms

EXAMINATION REQUIREMENTS:

Principals—Series 6 prerequisite limited representative examination and Series 26 IC/VC examination (unless qualified as general securities principals)

Representatives—Series 6 limited representative examination (unless qualified as general securities representatives)

DATE AND PLACE OF EXAMINATIONS

Examinations are given once a month, on the first Saturday. The examinations are taken on the NASD's computerized PLATO system at Control Data Learning Centers in the cities and locations listed below. Appointments are necessary for all candidates for the examination and may be made by telephoning the Examination Section of the NASD Membership Department in Washington, D.C., (202) 728-8800. The caller must specify the candidate's name, social security number, the name of the firm, the series number of the examination, and the test center location desired. Such appointments must be made eight full business days before the examination.

Control Data Corporation Learning Centers

ALABAMA
Birmingham Learning Center
  2112 Eleventh Avenue South,
  Suite 418
  Birmingham, AL 35205
  (205) 322-1708

ARIZONA
Phoenix Learning Center
  914 East Camelback Road, Suite 3
  Phoenix, AZ 85014
  (602) 266-9808

CALIFORNIA
Irvine Learning Center
  18831 Von Karman Avenue
  Irvine, CA 92715
  (714) 851-5622

Los Angeles Learning Center
  5630 Arbor Vitae Boulevard
  Los Angeles, CA 90045
  (213) 642-2568

San Francisco Learning Center
  1930 Market Street
  San Francisco, CA 94102
  (415) 393-6997

San Jose Learning Center
  911 Bern Court
  San Jose, CA 94050
  (408) 744-5794

COLORADO
Denver Learning Center
  720 South Colorado Blvd.
  Denver, CO 80222
  (303) 692-8745

CONNECTICUT
Farmington Learning Center
  312 Farmington Avenue
  Farmington, CT 06032
  (203) 677-4040

DISTRICT OF COLUMBIA
Washington Learning Center
  2201 Wisconsin Ave., N.W.
  Washington, DC 20007
  (202) 789-6430

FLORIDA
Miami Learning Center
  2550 Douglas Road, Suite 107
  Coral Gables, FL 33134
  (305) 446-3613

Orlando Learning Center
  3711 East Colonial Drive
  Orlando, FL 32803
  (305) 896-0543

GEORGIA
Atlanta Learning Center
  3379 Peachtree Rd., N.E.
  Atlanta, GA 30326
  (404) 261-7700

ILLINOIS
Chicago Learning Center
  214 N. Michigan Avenue,
  2nd Floor
  Chicago, IL 60601
  (312) 454-8481

O'Hare Learning Center
  1072 Tower Lane
  Bensonville, IL 60106
  (312) 350-1455

INDIANA
Indianapolis Learning Center
  8900 Keystone Crossing, Suite 310
  Indianapolis, IN 46240
  (317) 846-8287

KANSAS

Kansas City Learning Center
   Gateway Centre Tower II,
   Suite 800
   4th and State Streets
   Kansas City, KS 66101
   (913) 321-3400

KENTUCKY

Louisville Learning Center
   Triad East, Suite 150
   10200 Linn Station Road
   Louisville, KY 40223
   (502) 423-1660

LOUISIANA

New Orleans Learning Center
   6600 Plaza Drive, Suite 105
   New Orleans, LA 70127
   (504) 245-1604

MARYLAND

Baltimore Learning Center
   307 N. Charles St.
   Baltimore, MD 21201
   (301) 332-3492

MASSACHUSETTS

Cambridge Learning Center
   1 Alewife Place
   Cambridge, MA 02140
   (617) 876-1155

MICHIGAN

Southfield Learning Center
   20300 Civic Center Drive
   Southfield, MI 48076
   (313) 552-6772

MINNESOTA

Edina Learning Center
   6811 York Avenue South
   Edina, MN 55435
   (612) 830-8383

Energy Park Learning Center
   1450 Energy Park Drive
   St. Paul, MN 55108
   (612) 642-3170

Minneapolis Learning Center
   1001 Washington Avenue, North
   Minneapolis, MN 55401
   (612) 375-4799

MINNESOTA (continued)

St. Paul Learning Center
   245 East Sixth Street
   St. Paul, MN 55101
   (612) 292-2699

MISSOURI

St. Louis Learning Center
   8515 Delmar Boulevard
   University City, MO 63124
   (314) 993-6015

NEBRASKA

Lincoln Learning Center
   4700 S. 19th Street
   South Industrial Park
   Lincoln, NE 68512
   (402) 423-1001

Omaha Learning Center
   11615 I Street
   Omaha, NE 68137
   (402) 333-0850 ext. 410

NEW JERSEY

West Orange Learning Center
   347 Mt. Pleasant Avenue
   West Orange, NJ 07052
   (201) 325-2288

NEW MEXICO

Albuquerque Learning Center
   300 San Mateo Blvd., N.E.,
   Suite 900
   Albuquerque, NM 87108
   (505) 262-5040

NEW YORK

Buffalo Learning Center
   4242 Ridge Lea Rd., Suite 2
   Buffalo, NY 14226
   (716) 835-1477

Garden City Learning Center
   1325 Franklin Avenue, Suite 100
   Garden City, NY 11530
   (516) 741-3720

New York Learning Center
   201 East 42nd Street,
   at 3rd Avenue
   27th Floor
   New York, NY 10017
   (212) 697-9350

NEW YORK (continued)
Rochester Learning Center
  2522 Monroe Avenue
  Rochester, NY 14618
  (716) 473-3030

NORTH CAROLINA
Charlotte Learning Center
  3726 Latrobe Drive, Suite 101
  Charlotte, NC 28211
  (704) 366-9337

OHIO
Cincinnati Learning Center
  360 McLean Drive
  Cincinnati, OH 45222
  (513) 761-3800

Cleveland Learning Center
  6701 Rockside Road
  Independence, OH 44131
  (216) 447-1095 ext. 2001

Columbus Learning Center
  555 Metro Place, North,
  Suite 100
  Dublin, OH 43017
  (614) 766-3054

Toledo BTC Learning Center
  1946 N. 13th, Suite 301
  Toledo, Ohio 43624
  (419) 255-6700

OKLAHOMA
Oklahoma City Learning Center
  3613 N.W. 56th, Suite 100
  3 Corporate Plaza
  Oklahoma City, OK 73112
  (405) 949-7673

OREGON
Portland Learning Center
  10200 S.W. Eastridge Ave.
  Portland, OR 97225
  (503) 297-4841

PENNSYLVANIA
Philadelphia Learning Center
  4 Penn Center Plaza, Suite 600
  16th & J.F. Kennedy Blvd.
  Philadelphia, PA 19103
  (215) 854-3936

PENNSYLVANIA (continued)
Pittsburgh Learning Center
  One Allegheny Center Mall
  Pittsburgh, PA 15212
  (412) 321-1224

SOUTH CAROLINA
Charleston Learning Center
  701 East Bay Street
  Charleston, SC 29403
  (803) 722-1219

TENNESSEE
Memphis Learning Center
  Penn Marc Building, Suite 110
  6401 Poplar Avenue
  Memphis, TN 38119
  (901) 767-1180

Nashville Learning Center
  1101 Kermit Drive, Suite 305
  Nashville, TN 37217
  (615) 367-0871

TEXAS
Dallas Learning Center
  14801 Quorum Drive, Suite 500
  Dallas, TX 75240
  (214) 385-5778

Houston Learning Center
  2990 Richmond Avenue, 6th Floor
  Houston, TX 77098
  (713) 522-6000

UTAH
Salt Lake City Learning Center
  4424 South, 700 East, Suite 150
  Salt Lake City, UT 84107
  (801) 263-9646 or 9645

VIRGINIA
Richmond Learning Center
  2809 Emerywood Parkway,
  Suite 175
  Richmond, VA 23229
  (804) 285-8706

WASHINGTON
Seattle Learning Center
  2308 Sixth Avenue
  Seattle, WA 98121
  (206) 467-8168

WEST VIRGINIA
Charleston Learning Center
512 West Washington Street
Charleston, WV 25302
(304) 344-5025

WISCONSIN
Milwaukee Learning Center
804 N. Milwaukee St.
Milwaukee, WI 53202
(414) 223-0226

The NASD does offer a written examination. The appointment procedure is slightly different and the examinations can only be taken in the locations listed below.

ALASKA
University of Alaska
Anchorage

ARKANSAS
University of Arkansas at Little Rock

HAWAII
The Westin Ilikai
Honolulu

IOWA
Drake University
Des Moines

MONTANA
College of Great Falls
Great Falls

NEVADA
University of Nevada at Las Vegas

NEW YORK
Siena College
Loudonville

NORTH DAKOTA
Bismarck Junior College
Bismarck

PUERTO RICO
University of Puerto Rico
Rio Piedras

SOUTH DAKOTA
Augustana College
Sioux Falls

TEXAS
Amarillo College
Amarillo

WASHINGTON
Kinman Business University
Spokane

WYOMING
Casper College
Casper

The written examinations may also be taken abroad. The appointment request form must be submitted a month before the examination, which is offered, on the third Saturday of the month on a varying monthly schedule, at each location:

England
London

France
Paris

Germany
Heidelberg

Japan
Tokyo

Switzerland
Geneva

For all the examinations, schedules and locations are subject to change. The NASD membership kit contains all the forms necessary for filing an application for membership. For application information, write to:

National Association of Securities Dealers, Inc.
1735 K Street, N.W.
Washington, D.C. 20006

PROFESSIONAL DESIGNATIONS

CLU

The Chartered Life Underwriter (CLU) professional designation is offered by the American College, headquartered in Bryn Mawr, Pennsylvania. This designation has been awarded to people who are active in life and health insurance and allied vocations and is considered to be a standard of professional excellence. In addition to maintaining high ethical standards and meeting experience requirements, CLUs must demonstrate their academic achievements by successfully completing a ten-part series of comprehensive examinations.

ChFC

The Chartered Financial Consultant (ChFC) program of professional study was also developed by the American College in Bryn Mawr, Pennsylvania. This program offers educational opportunities for financial professionals who wish to expand their ability to provide comprehensive financial counseling and planning services.

CFP

The Certified Financial Planner is an individual who has successfully completed the established educational requirements and has met the experience standards established by the College for Financial Planning in Denver, Colorado. The six-part curriculum includes Introduction to Financial Planning, Risk Management, Investments, Tax Planning and Management, Employer Benefits and Retirement Planning, and Estate Planning. The candidate must pass a test on each section.

CPCU

The Chartered Property/Casualty Underwriter (CPCU) professional designation is granted by the American Institute for Property and Liability Underwriters in Malvern, Pennsylvania. The CPCU designation is recognized by property and casualty insurers as the standard of professional excellence and high academic achievement in the insurance industry. This course of study is recommended for experienced insurance industry personnel who have a strong knowledge of insurance practices and some formal study of the insurance principles that underlie these practices. The CPCU curriculum provides courses in management, economics, accounting, and finance. The candidate must successfully complete each of the ten nationally administered examinations.

SEC REGISTRATION:
REGISTERED INVESTMENT ADVISER (RIA)

A financial professional who accepts payment *other than commissions* for advice about securities *may* be required by law to register as an investment adviser with the Securities and Exchange Commission (SEC). The Investment Advisers Act of 1940 defines *investment adviser* as someone who engages in the business of "advising others, either directly or through publications or writings, as to the value of securities or as to the advisability of investing in, purchasing, or selling securities," or who "for compensation and as part of a regular business, issue[s] or promulgate[s] analyses or reports concerning securities."

In less technical language, federal law may require financial professionals to register with the SEC if they represent themselves to be financial planners and charge a fee for their services—whether they provide investment advice on specific securities or investment advice in general. (For more detailed information, consult a qualified securities attorney.) Among those who need *not* register are properly licensed brokers who accept no payment for their services other than commissions on products, and attorneys, accountants, or other professionals whose investment advising is incidental to their principal professional functions.

Professionals who decide to register must pay a $150 registration fee and file Form ADV—a magazine-sized questionnaire.

Some financial professionals are also required to register in each state in which they do business. State laws vary: Some states, for example, permit investment advisers to sell products, other states do not. (For detailed information, consult an attorney familar with your state's security laws.)

To request a copy of Form ADV, write or call:

Securities Exchange Commission
500 N. Capitol Street, NW
Washington, D.C., 20549
(202) 655-4000

Source: Andrew M. Rich, "RIA—How to Register," *Digest of Financial Planning Ideas*, January 1985; © Consolidated Capital Communications Group, Inc.

6.03 **Professional Organizations**

INTERNATIONAL ASSOCIATION FOR
FINANCIAL PLANNING (IAFP)

The IAFP, headquartered in Atlanta, Georgia, is a professional organization for those who work in the financial planning industry, both those who advise individual and corporate clients and those who provide planners with products and services. Over 21,000 members belong to 117 local chapters in all 50 states, 15 foreign countries, and U.S. possessions. Members represent a cross section of the financial services industry, coming from all disciplines related to financial planning: accounting, law, banking, securities, insurance, real estate, and financial product and service supply.

The four main objectives of the IAFP are: to provide members with opportunities for continuing education; to build awareness for a unified approach to problem solving; to establish a forum for ongoing dialogue with other financial industry professionals; and to maintain high ethical standards.

Among the programs sponsored by the IAFP are:

- The annual IAFP Convention, which features lectures, seminars, and workshops conducted by industry leaders and experts. A concurrent exhibition gives corporate suppliers an opportunity to present products and services designed to enhance financial planners' professional abilities.

- An annual Practice Management Conference, which emphasizes specific problems encountered by financial planners.

- The annual IAFP World Congress, which offers planners the chance to exchange ideas, techniques, and methods with their foreign counterparts.

- Regularly scheduled seminars and workshops throughout the year, which address changes in laws, taxation, and industry trends.

- The Registry of Financial Planning Practitioners ®, which serves the public and the financial services industry by identifying practitioners who meet high professional standards.

Publications of the IAFP include *Financial Planning*, a monthly magazine for members and nonmembers that provides practical information and reports on issues, trends, problems, and opportunities within the industry. For members only, the IAFP edits *IAFP Financial Planning Update, IAFP News*, and *Regulatory Alert Service* (all published monthly).

For more information, call or write:

> International Association for Financial Planning
> Suite 120-C
> 5775 Peachtree-Dunwoody Road
> Atlanta, Georgia 30342
> (404) 252-9600

Source: International Association for Financial Planning, "IAFP: A Profile," 1985.

INSTITUTE OF CERTIFIED FINANCIAL PLANNERS (ICFP)

The ICFP is the national professional association of individuals who have received the CFP (Certified Financial Planner) designation from the College for Financial Planning in Denver, Colorado. Over 18,000 CFPs across the country are members.

The goals and purposes of the ICFP are to promote public knowledge of financial planning as a profession; to promote recognition of the CFP designation as representing a high level of professional educational achievement; to promote and enforce high standards of ethical conduct for financial planners; and to promote excellence by supporting financial planning education and training. Members are required to fulfill 30 hours of continuing education credit a year.

Among the programs and services sponsored by the ICFP are:

- The ICFP Annual Conference and Annual Retreat, both of which give members the opportunity to keep current with the most recent changes in the profession.

- The ICFP Annual International Retreat, which enables members to explore global investment opportunities.

- Regional seminars and specialized practice management programs, which are held throughout the year.

- A referral service, which provides members of the general public with information and referrals to CFPs.

The ICFP also publishes a number of newsletters and quarterly reports for its members:

- *Newsworthy*, a monthly publication that provides timely information on professional topics and events.

- *Journal of the ICFP*, a scholarly quarterly that presents articles of both practical and academic interest, written by CFPs, academicians, and leading authorities in the financial services industry.

- *Institute Communiqué*, a newsletter for the timely dissemination of fast-breaking news.

For more information, call or write:

Institute of Certified Financial Planners
3443 South Galena, Suite 190
Denver, CO 80231-5093
(303) 751-7600

Source: Institute of Certified Financial Planners, "Fact Sheet," 1984.

6.04 **Professional Ethics and Conduct**

IAFP CODE OF ETHICS

The basic objective of the International Association for Financial Planning (IAFP) Code of Ethics is to set forth particulars of the minimum ethical conduct expected of members as professionals and to facilitate voluntary compliance with standards higher than the minimum.

The code prescribes three kinds of standards:

- *Canons* are maxims that express model standards of exemplary professional conduct.

- *Rules* are specific standards derived from the general concepts and principles set forth by the canons.

- *Guidelines* are explanatory statements that help members interpret, understand, and apply the canons and rules. (For a copy of the IAFP guidelines, write the IAFP, Suite 120-C, 5775 Peachtree Dunwoody Rd., Atlanta, GA 30342.)

CANON 1

Members should endeavor as professionals to place the public interest above their own.

R1.1 A member has a duty to understand and abide by all *Rules* of Professional Conduct which are prescribed in the Code of Professional Ethics of the Association.

R1.2 A member shall not directly or indirectly condone any act which the member is prohibited from performing by the Rules of this Code.

CANON 2

Members should seek continually to maintain and improve their professional knowledge, skills, and competence.

R2.1 A member shall keep informed on all matters that are essential to the maintenance of the member's professional competence in the area in which he/she specializes and/or claims expertise.

CANON 3

Members should obey all laws and regulations, and should avoid any conduct or activity which would cause unjust harm to others.

R3.1 A member will be subject to disciplinary action for the violation of any law or regulation, to the extent that such violation suggests the likelihood of professional misconduct.

R3.2 A member shall not allow the pursuit of financial gain or other personal benefit to interfere with the exercise of sound professional judgment and skills.

R3.3 In the conduct of business or professional activities, a member shall not engage in any act or omission of a dishonest, deceitful, or fraudulent nature.

CANON 4

Members should be diligent in the performance of their occupational duties.

R4.1 A member shall competently and consistently discharge the member's occupational duties, to every employer, client,* purchaser, or user of the member's services, so long as those duties are consistent with what is in the client's best interests.

As used throughout this Code, the term client refers broadly to any individual, business firm, governmental body, educational institution, or other entity that engages the professional advice or services of a member, as an independent professional and not as a common law employee of the client.

CANON 5

Members should establish and maintain honorable relationships with other professionals, with those whom the members serve in a professional capacity, and with all those who rely upon the members' professional judgments and skills.

R5.1 A member has a duty to know and abide by the legal limitations imposed upon the scope of the member's professional activities.

R5.2 In rendering or proposing to render a professional service for another individual or an organization, a member shall not knowingly misrepresent or conceal any material limitation on the member's ability to provide the quantity or quality of service that will adequately meet the financial planning needs of the individual or organization in question.

R5.3 In marketing or attempting to market a product to another individual or an organization, a member shall not knowingly misrepresent or conceal any material limitations on the product's ability to meet the financial planning needs of the individual or organization in question.

R5.4 A member shall not disclose to another person any confidential information entrusted to or obtained by the member in the course of the member's business or professional activities, unless a disclosure of such information is required by law or is made to a person who necessarily must have the information in order to discharge legitimate occupational or professional duties.

R5.5 In the making of oral or written recommendations to clients, a member shall (a) distinguish clearly between fact and opinion, (b) base the recommendations on sound professional evaluations of the client's present and future needs, (c) place the needs and best interests of the client above the interests of the member or the member's employer or business associates, (d) support the recommendations with appropriate research and adequate documentation of facts, and (e) scrupulously avoid any statements which are likely to mislead the client regarding the projected future results of any recommendation.

R5.6 Before rendering any professional service, a member has a duty to disclose, to a prospective client, any actual or potential conflict of interest that is or should be known by the member and is likely to impair the member's objectivity as an adviser or provider of professional services to the prospective client in question.

R5.7 In the rendering of a professional service to a client, a member has the duty to maintain the type and degree of professional independence that (a) is required of practitioners in the member's occupation or (b) is otherwise in the public interest, given the specific nature of the service being rendered.

CANON 6

Members should assist in improving the public understanding of financial planning.

R6.1 A member shall support efforts to provide laypersons with objective information concerning their financial planning needs, as well as the resources which are available to meet their needs.

R6.2 A member shall not misrepresent the benefits, costs, or limitations of any financial planning service or product, whether the product or service is offered by the member or by another individual or firm.

CANON 7

Members should use the fact of membership in a manner consistent with the Association's Rules of Professional Conduct.

R7.1 A member shall not misrepresent the criteria for admission to Association membership, which criteria are: (1) a professional interest in financial planning; and (2) a written commitment to abide by the Bylaws and the Code of Professional Ethics of the Association.

R7.2 A member shall not misstate his/her authority to represent the Association. Specifically, a member shall not write, speak, or act in such a way as to lead another to believe that the member is officially representing the Association, unless the member has been duly authorized to do so by the officers, directors, or Bylaws of the national Association.

R7.3 A member shall not use the fact of membership in the Association for commercial purposes but may use the fact of membership for the following noncommercial purposes: in resumes, prospectuses, and in introductions if the speaker clearly states that the opinions and ideas presented are his/her own and not necessarily those of the IAFP.

R7.4 A member or prospective member applying for Association membership shall not misrepresent any credentials or affiliations with other organizations.

CANON 8

Members should assist in maintaining the integrity of the Code of Professional Ethics of the Association.

R8.1 A member shall not sponsor as a candidate for Association membership any person who is known by the member to engage in business or professional practices which violate the Rules of this Code.

R8.2 A member possessing unprivileged information concerning an alleged violation of this Code shall, upon request, reveal such information to the body or other authority empowered by the Association to investigate or act upon the alleged violation.

Source: International Association for Financial Planning, "The Code of Professional Ethics," 1985.

THE BEST SAFEGUARDS AGAINST MALPRACTICE SUITS

Insurance and legal experts who review malpractice claims against financial professionals are convinced that many suits could have been avoided — if only all professionals observed a few fundamental rules. Here are the ten most important guidelines to follow in order to minimize chances of being sued if you are a financial professional. Clients will find these guidelines helpful in determining standards of conduct to expect from their financial and investment advisers.

1. **Maintain good relations with every client.** There is no better preventive measure than the maintenance of harmonious relations with all your clients. Keep them informed, answer their questions, and treat them with the appropriate degree of respect. Always view each client as an individual, someone with highly individualized goals, aspirations, and needs. In virtually every case of alleged malpractice, the client is not just disappointed, but angry — angry about something (or a series of things) that the financial professional did or said quite apart from the alleged negligent conduct. The malpractice suit is often merely the final stage of a deteriorating relationship between adviser and client. Communicate with every client regularly. Be sure to ask each client, at least once a year (making it clear that you ask these questions of all your clients), "How is our service to you? Is there anything we've done that has not been satisfactory to you? Any suggestions for improving our service?"

2. **Keep accurate and detailed records.** Up-to-date and detailed records may be your principal ally in court:

   • Document with a memo every initial client interview in as much detail as possible, including date, participants, and topics covered.

   • Record personal information that highlights the client's financial objectives and personal feelings about home, family, job, education, retirement, and the like.

   • Document every follow-up interview and every telephone conversation with a brief memo. In particular, lay down a "paper trail" with respect to discussion of a recommended investment and its suitability for the client. Use an Investment Disclosure Checklist (see page 6.26).

3. **Disclose all material investment information.** Do not take shortcuts in disclosing the essential details of recommended investments. The investor is entitled to the fullest possible disclosure of all material facts as a matter of law. The U.S. Supreme Court has ruled that a fact is "material" when there is "a substantial likelihood that the disclosure of the omitted fact would have been viewed by the reasonable investor as having significantly altered the total mix of information made available." Your duty to disclose all material facts is particularly pertinent when you are in a situation involving a potential conflict of interest with your client.

   • Always disclose the risks of any investment you discuss with a client.

   • Always make sure that your client fully understands the risks.

   • Always provide a prospectus for every recommended investment that has an offering prospectus.

   • Keep a record of the date such literature is mailed or given to the client and make sure the client gives you a signed receipt.

4. **Never guarantee anything.** One's enthusiasm for a particular investment can sometimes lead one to an unintentional overemphasis of the investment's potential benefits. Make a pact with yourself never to use the word *guaranteed* when discussing investments with clients. Even better, use the word *guaranteed* only to point out that *no investment yield or return is ever guaranteed*. Always document the fact that you brought this issue to your client's attention. You can use the Investment Disclosure Checklist for this purpose.

5. **Don't exceed your limitations.** The law does not expect you, as a financial professional, to be an expert in every aspect of the profession. That would be unreasonable. However, the law does expect you to recognize your need to consult with an expert and to seek necessary professional help on matters clearly beyond your capabilities:

   - Consult an estate attorney on the drafting of wills and trusts, as well as on estate-transfer matters in general.

   - Consult a certified public accountant on matters calling for specialized knowledge of federal or state tax laws, valuation and basis problems, stock options and buy-out agreements, and the like.

   - Consult a chartered property-casualty underwriter on matters calling for specialized knowledge of coverage and costs for home, automobile, business, and liability insurance.

   - Consult a qualified securities analyst in evaluating a client's securities portfolio. If you have any doubt about a technical issue, seek other professionals who can provide comprehensive and authoritative advice. This is a case in which the concept of "safety in numbers" takes on practical importance as one of your best safeguards against being sued.

6. **Make sure the investment is suitable for a client.** Both by law and by regulation you have a continuing responsibility to ascertain your client's risk threshold when you are recommending a particular security. Thus, before making a recommendation you must elicit facts about your client as well as information about the investment. Remember: No investment is suitable for every investor, some are unsuitable for almost all investors. Failure to adhere to the letter and intent of the suitability doctrine may well be the single most likely source of litigation against financial advisers.

7. **Follow up on every case.** The key is organization. Don't let back-office problems get out of hand. Never assume that everything is all right just because no one has yet complained. Use checklists to guide you through the long list of follow-up actions that may slip your mind. Pay particular attention to:

   - Transmittals to investment sponsors at or near investment-closing deadlines

   - IRA/Keogh rollover deadlines

   - Tax filing or extension deadlines

   - Other transactions for which timing is critical

   Remember, the simplest oversight on your part can cause your biggest lawsuit.

8. **Diligently supervise subordinates.** You are legally responsible for any negligent conduct by those to whom you delegate responsibilities. Your failure to exercise careful supervision over administrative or paraprofessional staff leaves you wide open to suit. So, take pains to hire capable staff assistants, and give

(continued on page 6.27)

INVESTMENT DISCLOSURE CHECKLIST

Use this checklist to record your disclosure discussions with clients. Fill out a checklist for each product you recommend to a client. (Note: Not every item will apply to every investment nor to every client; for example, you will need to outline general risk factors to novice investors but not necessarily to experienced investors or long-term clients.)

Client's name: _____

Investment vehicle: _____

Date: _____

☐ Client has received prospectus and signed prospectus receipt.

_____

    (date)

Risk Factors

☐ General risks of investing (e.g., general investment outlook; stock market performance; interest rates; inflation)

☐ Investment-specific risks (e.g., industry trends, competition, obsolescence, regulation; interest rate fluctuations; demographic trends)

☐ Differences between fixed-dollar debt instruments and equity instruments

☐ Bond ratings; relationship of bond value and interest rates

☐ Risks of leveraged investment

☐ Illiquidity, limitations on transferability

☐ Tax benefits:

- No guarantee that intended benefits will be allowed by the IRS

- Phantom income may be generated

- Alternative minimum tax may reduce tax benefits

☐ *No* guarantees regarding:

- Investment yield, profit, appreciation

- Anticipated cash distributions

- Inflation hedges

☐ Other:

_____

Sponsor's Track Record

☐ Sponsor's background and experience

☐ Sponsor's performance in prior programs

☐ Due diligence reports

☐ Possible conflicts of interest

☐ Other:

_____

Commissions, Fees, Costs

☐ Broker-dealer commissions

☐ Sales charges (as percentage of investment)

☐ Administrative, set-up, transfer fees

☐ Limited partnership fees:

- Total front-end costs

- Percentage of investment "in ground"

- Liquidation fees

☐ Other:

Investor-Investment Suitability

☐ Client meets investment's financial suitability standards

☐ Compatible overall financial objectives

☐ Client's risk threshold (comfort level)

☐ Client's investment sophistication

☐ Client's willingness to assume risks

☐ Other:

---

them the necessary training, both formal and informal. Make certain they know exactly what is expected of them and that they understand the limits of their responsibilities. Finally, do some periodic spot-checking by asking trusted clients if they have experienced any particular problems with office procedures or personnel. Correct these problems immediately.

9. **Maintain client confidentiality.** Nothing can more irrevocably destroy a client's trust and faith than a professional's indiscriminate disclosure of a client's personal financial data. While the law has not yet established formal safeguards of confidentiality in relationships between financial advisers and clients, all financial professional organizations have established strict ethical standards for professional conduct. The rule is simple: *Never* — except in response to a legal subpoena — reveal confidential information about a client to any outside party without the client's express permission.

10. **Keep current in your field.** By representing yourself as a financial professional, you are legally subject to the standards of care applicable to the profession as a whole. Such standards require that you keep reasonably abreast of current practices and the state of knowledge in the field. Do so eagerly. Take all the continuing education courses you can. Attend local, regional, and national seminars and conferences where you can learn from others about the latest developments in the field. The knowledge you gain will make you a better professional, and that is one of your best safeguards against being sued.

RISK MANAGEMENT CHECKLISTS

Checklists can help you structure your own professional liability risk management plan — a plan that may save you thousands of dollars and endless aggravation.

Client Relations

1. Devote ample time during the first interview to get to know your client.

2. Make sure your staff understands the importance of maintaining good client relations. Reward staff members for outstanding instances of good client relations.

3. Maintain regular contact with your clients — through periodic phone calls, mailers, seminars, or newsletters.

4. Respond to clients' problems immediately — before they turn into complaints.

5. Whenever you receive information that has negative consequences for a particular investment, call the affected clients immediately. Tell them what you know and its implications, *before* they hear the bad news from another source.

6. Consider terminating your relationship with any client who is unreasonable, uncooperative, or excessively demanding.

Securities Transactions

1. Observe the letter of the law. Discuss all potential risks as well as possible rewards.

2. Make detailed inquiries about the client's suitability for each investment recommended.

3. Obtain a receipt from your client when you provide a prospectus (see sample included in the Investment Disclosure Checklist, page 6.26).

4. Make sure your client fully understands that no guarantees accompany any investment; record that understanding in the file.

5. Never display "broker-dealer information only" material to a client, and never leave such information with him.

6. Establish office procedures to assure that all orders are processed promptly and accurately.

Record Keeping

1. Keep detailed up-to-date records on all clients.

2. Always complete an investment disclosure checklist when introducing a client to a new investment.

3. Get signed prospectus receipts and file them.

4. Document all telephone discussions with clients while the details are still fresh in your memory.

5. Carefully document any incidents that reflect a client's dissatisfaction, antagonism, or threats to sue.

Office Procedures

1. Make sure all office procedures for processing securities transactions are rigorously followed. Do occasional spot checks.

2. Establish clear guidelines for prompt handling of incoming telephone calls.

3. Hire competent staff and supervise them carefully. Make sure they are properly trained and do not exceed their authority.

4. Initiate back-up procedures for processing paperwork — a safeguard against papers that get lost or go astray.

General

1. Keep current with the professional literature and the latest practices in your field.

2. Establish personal contacts with outside experts on law, accounting, taxation, pension plan development, and the like. Consult these experts as circumstances require.

3. Know your personal limitations and do not hesitate to call on experts for advice and guidance.

4. Make client relations a top priority as long as you remain in practice.

LIABILITY INSURANCE

All practitioners should obtain professional liability insurance and maintain adequate coverage for their client load and the nature of their financial advisory services. Rates are relatively low, and the peace of mind is well worth the price.

Financial planners who are members of the International Association for Financial Planning (IAFP) can apply for coverage of up to $5 million per claim. For an application or information, contact:

Robin Chamberlain
    Alexander & Alexander   (800) 527-5751, except:
    717 N. Harwood, 19th Floor   in Texas, (800) 442-1499
    Dallas, Texas 75201   in Alaska or Hawaii, (214) 573-6124

Source: Eli P. Bernzweig, J.D., "The Ten Best Safeguards Against Malpractice Suits," *Digest of Financial Planning Ideas,* October 1984; © Consolidated Capital Communications Group, Inc.

6.05 **Computers: Software and Databases**

For a comprehensive introduction to computers, one might consult the books listed on page 6.55. For timely discussion of new hardware and software, one must rely on periodicals—many aspects of the computer industry are changing too fast for most book publishers to keep pace.

The following primer touches on selected broad issues: feasibility, needs assessment, software for specific financial applications (property management, real estate, appraisal and investment analysis, taxes), selected on-line databases, and selected database vendors. A glossary of computer-related terms will help the novice converse intelligently with computer consultants and other experts.

FEASIBILITY

The proliferation of computer hardware and software and the extremely dynamic nature of the field make it difficult to determine the best equipment for each particular user. To assure the most appropriate equipment for a specific application, it is advisable to consult an expert in the field who is familiar with the latest technology.

Duane C. Abbey, a consultant, suggests the following computer feasibility and cost-benefit guidelines:

The cardinal rule is to determine exactly what you are going to do with the computer before you get it. . . . There are several types of feasibility considerations. The four that would be of the greatest interest to a financial planner are:

1. Economic feasibility: Will the systems make money?
2. Financial feasibility: Can I afford it?
3. Technical feasibility: Can the computer do what I want it to do?
4. Operational feasibility: Am I or my firm ready and willing to accept such technology?

Cost-benefit analysis forces one to quantify and calculate all of the costs (general for a period of years) and then to assess the benefits that the system will provide. Answering the feasibility questions and performing a cost-benefit analysis are musts for financial planners who intend to use the computer in their practice.

Source: *The Financial Planner,* February 1983.

Computer Utilization

The following table summarizes computer utilization options for small- to medium-sized financial planning applications.

TIME-SHARE

Batch, send-in mode.
Interactive via terminal devices.

Examples:	COAP, Tymshare's FINPLAN, ExecuPlan.
Costs:	Variable depending upon sophistication of plan.
	Repetitive costs for each run.
Comments:	Highly viable mode of operation in certain situations.
	High-quality output is available.

PRIMITIVE MICROCOMPUTER SYSTEM

Small individual systems and programs.
Generally written in BASIC.
Can be run on almost any computer system.

Examples:	See microcomputer journals.
Costs:	$50–$250 per system or program.

VISICALC-BASED MICROCOMPUTER SYSTEMS

Extensive modular systems.
Generally written in VisiCalc or SuperCalc.
Fairly wide applicability to various computer systems.

Examples:	Moneytree, Universal Modelers.
Costs:	$500–$2500.
Comments:	Offers considerable flexibility.
	User must integrate word processing, database, client tracking, transaction logs.

COMPREHENSIVE MICROCOMPUTER SYSTEMS

Comprehensive integrated systems.
Limited applicability—written specifically for selected computer systems.

Examples:	IFDS, Leonard System.
Costs:	$10,000–$35,000.
Comments:	Complete package of software and hardware.
	Word processing, database, client tracking, and transaction logs integrated.

CUSTOM-DESIGNED MICRO- OR MINICOMPUTER SYSTEMS

Custom-designed programs and systems.

Examples:	See local programmers and systems analysts.
Costs:	$50–$100/hour for design and development.
Comments:	Provides financial planner with exact requirements.
	Can be extremely expensive.

Source: *The Financial Planner,* February 1983.

COMPUTER RESOURCES FOR FINANCIAL PLANNING

This list consists of the names of software producers who provide financially oriented computer services. No attempt was made to evaluate either the software or the services. For each company is given the name, address, and telephone number, a listing of the software programs available or services offered, and a note on the applicable hardware and operating services.

A.F. Software Services Inc.
1106 Greenfield Circle
Geneva, IL 60134
(312) 232-0790
Trust Accounting
Government and School Fund Accounting
Government and School Payroll
Most microcomputers

AMIFI Limited
P.O. Box 1138
Concord, MA 01742
(617) 369-2738
Options analysis
Portfolio analyzer
Real Estate Analyzer
Personal Accountant
Hewlett Packard 110, 150
IBM PC with 62K of available memory and optional printer

ARA Incorporated
2319 South Ridgewood Avenue
P.O. Box 486
Edgewater, FL 32032
(904) 428-8421
A broad line of financial software from elementary to sophisticated electronic spread sheet and business analysis programs.
Apple
Texas Instruments
Hewlett Packard
IBM
Many other major mainframe computers

Aardvark/McGraw-Hill
1020 North Broadway
Milwaukee, WI 53202
(414) 225-7500
Fixed Asset Accounting
Professional Tax Planner
Estate Tax Planner
Tax Shelter-Investment Planner
IBM PC
Apple CP/M

Abacus Data Systems Inc.
722 Genevieve Street, Suite C
Solano Beach, CA 92075
(619) 755-0505
FastPlan II — A database investment tracking, tax analysis, capital needs analysis, financial planning system
IBM PC and compatibles

Actuarial Micro Software
3915 A Valley Court
Winston-Salem, NC 27106
(919) 765-5588
Monte Carlo Simulations
GASS
Valuations
Programs for financial planning and retirement.
IBM PC
Apple

Agency Automation Computers
10834 Old Mill Road, Suite 4
Omaha, NE 68154
(402) 333-0378
AGENT Computer Tools — Annuity illustrations, business valuation, comprehensive capital needs analysis, estate tax analysis, loan analysis, and retirement needs analysis
Sharp
Hewlett Packard
Wang
IBM and compatibles

Alpine Data
635 Main Street
Montrose, CO 81401
(303) 249-1400
TAX/PACK
Apple II
Compaq
Osborne
IBM PC
Epson QX-10
Xerox
Northstar
Kaypro
Radio Shack

American College
270 Bryn Mawr Avenue
Bryn Mawr, PA 19010
(800) 441-9466
Money Manager — Tool for comprehensive financial planning
Franklin Ace
Wang PC
IBM PC and compatibles
Apple II

Computer Resources for Financial Planning

Ampersand Corporation
128 South George Street
P.O. Box M-84
York, PA 17405
(717) 845-5602
BRANCHBANKER — A
program designed to sell and
cross-sell retail financial
services
IBM XT

Anidata Incorporated
7200 Westfield Avenue
Pennsauken, NJ 08110
(609) 663-8123
MARKET ANALYST —
Technical analysis and portfolio
management
Apple II, II+, IIe
IBM PC, XT

Aplitec Incorporated
5206 FM 1960 West,
Suite 200
Houston, TX 77069
(713) 893-2611
*Financial and tax planning
system*
*Universal life insurance proposal
system*
*Term and deposit term
insurance proposal system*
TRS-80
IBM XT
Apple II

Applied Systems
P.O Box 400
Monee, IL 60449
(312) 534 5575
The Agency Manager
Wang PC
IBM XT
Apple CP/M

Automated Analysis
232 North Avenue 54
Los Angeles, CA 90042
(213) 257-5077
Investment Analysis — Break,
depreciation, loan, and return
Hewlett Packard 125, 3000
North Star Advantage
IBM PC

**Bankers Systems Financial
Services Incorporated**
P.O. Box 97
St. Cloud, MN 56302
(612) 251-3060
*Personal financial planning
system and support*
*Discount brokerage services
and support*

Benefit Analysis Incorporated
996 Old Eagle School Road
#1105
Wayne, PA 19087
(215) 293-0808
Investment Plan
Family asset distribution plan
Family financial plan
IBM PC, XT, AT and
compatibles
Apple
Kaypro

Blankenship and Company
5620 FM 1960 West, # 219
Houston, TX 77069
(713) 370-0006
The Professional Plan — Client
net worth, tax planning, immediate needs, future needs,
estate planning, investments,
budget cash flow
IBM PC and compatibles

Brock Computer Services
2729 East Grand River
Howell, MI 48843
(517) 546-1075
Amortization Program
TRS-80 I, III, IV

**Buck Pension Fund Services
Incorporated**
Two Pennsylvania Plaza
New York, NY 10121
(212) 279-4400
Optamix — A portfolio
allocation and optimization
system that runs on a personal
computer.

CALI Computer Systems Inc.
One Plaza Road
Greenvale, NY 11548
(516) 484-1920
TAXMASTER ALERT — Tax
strategy program
CALI Tuition Aid Program —
Tuition management program
IBM PC and compatibles

Calcugram Company, The
P.O. Box 3037
Walnut Creek, CA 94598
(415) 933-3708
Stock Option Analysis
IBM PC
TRS-80 I, III, IV

Citation Systems
683 Cumberland Road N. E.
Atlanta, GA 30306
(404) 874-3282
*Real estate property
management*
TRS-80 I, III, IV

**College Planning Systems
Inc.**
740 Veterans Highway,
Suite 205
Hauppauge, NY 11788
(800) 742-4826
*Comprehensive college financial
planning software program*
IBM PC, XT, and compatibles
Sharp 1500, Hand Held 1261

**Commercial Software
Systems**
7689 West Frost Drive
Littleton, CO 80123
(303) 761-8062
*Real Estate Models for the
Eighties*
Apple II, II+, IIe, III
Hewlett Packard 125
IBM PC, XT

Computer Resources for Financial Planning

Compu Trac
P.O. Box 15951
New Orleans, LA 70115
(800) 535-7990
Technical analysis software for position and day traders of stocks and futures
IBM PC, XT and compatibles
Apple II+, IIe

Compu-Risk Software
1326 Wilder Street
Thousand Oaks, CA 91362
(805) 497-6200
Workers Compensation Retention Program
Retrospective Rating Program
Self-Insurance Program
Paid Loss Retro Program
Premium Allocation Program
Apple II, II+, IIe, IIc, III
IBM PC, XT

Computer Merchant Limited
571 Main Street
South Weymouth, MA 02190
(617) 331-7160
Easy — Estate administration system
BFS — Comprehensive small business system
Altos
Wang PC
Eagle
Stearns
Xerox
IBM PC

Computer Services International
3410 East McDowell Road
Mesa, AZ 85203
(602) 832-8230
Life Insurance
Pension and Profitsharing
Time Management
Mortgage Amortization and Interval Rates of Return
IBM XT
ASCII, terminal for timesharing

Computone Systems Incorporated
One Dunwoody Park
Atlanta, GA 30338
(404) 393-3010
Variety of financial planning and insurance oriented software programs
IBM PC, XT
Panasonic PC and hand held computers

Comtronic Systems
31620 121st Avenue, S. E.
Auburn, WA 98002
(206) 735-2916
Property Management
Collection System
IBM PC, XT
Eagle
Columbia
Compaq
Corona

Confidential Financial Services
3014 Washington Street
P.O. Box 1671
Midland, MI 48641-1671
(517) 839-0197
TSA Exclusion Allowance Annuities
Radio Shack Model III
Commodore PET and 64
Apple and compatibles
IBM PC and compatibles

Confidential Planning Services
2507 North Verity Parkway
Middletown, OH 45042
(513) 424-1656
ProPlan — Comprehensive financial planning system
IBM PC and compatibles
Micromation Mariner

Continuum Company Incorporated
3429 Executive Center Drive
Austin, TX 78731
(512) 345-5700
Financial Security Analysis
Estate Analysis
Business Valuation
Universal Life Porposals
Client Information System
IBM PC, XT

Corporate Data Systems
3700 Science Center
Philadelphia, PA 19104
(215) 243-1906
FERM — Foreign exchange risk management
IBM PC, XT, AT

Data Workers Incorporated
4000 Birch Street, # 114
Newport Beach, CA 92660
(714) 553-0344
Property Management
Real Estate Investment Analysis
IBM PC, XT
Alpha Micro

Decision Resource Corporation
2101 East Broadway, #31
Tempe, AZ 85282
(602) 968-4568
Ultra Library of Real Estate Computer Programs
IBM PC, XT with 10 MB storage

Delphi Information Sciences
1520 Cloverfield Boulevard
Santa Monica, CA 90404
(213) 828-5541
Mortgage Processing, Closing, and Tracking
Credit Reporting
Regulation Z Disclosure
Bond Trading
IBM PC, XT, and compatibles

Computer Resources for Financial Planning

Delta Computers
1470 MacArthur
Alexandria, LA 71301
(318) 442-0217
Accounts Receivable
Accounts Payable
General Ledger
Payroll
Retail Accounts Receivable
Alpha Micro

Diamond Business Systems Inc.
P.O. Box 2995
Joplin, MO 64803
(417) 782-6886
Charitable Analysis Transaction Simulation
IBM PC and compatibles

Diamond Head Software
841 Bishop Street,
Suite 1618
Honolulu, HI 96813
(808) 537-4972
Stock Market
IBM PC
Compaq
Columbia

Dimensional Business Systems Incorporated
250 N.W. Fourth Diagonal
Boca Raton, FL 33432
(305) 368-0276
Total automation package for insurance agencies and brokers
IBM XT
CP/M Micros

Distributed Planning Systems Corporation
23632 Calabassas Road,
Suite 107
Calabassas, CA 91302
(818) 992-4447
Bankreporter 1
Gapmanager 1
Callreporter 1
S and L Reporter 1
Profitability 1
IBM PC, XT

Dominion Financial Projection
2551 Almeda Avenue
Norfolk, VA 23513
(804) 855-2398
Real estate investment analysis
IBM PC and compatibles

Dynacomp Incorporated
P.O. Box 18129
Rochester, NY 14618
(716) 442-8960
Financial Planning Investments
Taxation
Net Worth
Payroll Record Keeping
Commodore
Kaypro
Osborne
TRS-80
Morrow
IBM PC
Apple

E.B.G. and Associates Inc.
320 N. Michigan Avenue,
#1100
Chicago, IL 60601
(312) 580-2261
PensionMaker — Defined benefit for 401K plans
IBM PC and XT

Eagle Software Publishing
993 Old Eagle School Road,
#405
Wayne, PA 19087
(215) 964-8660
Tax Decisions — Tax planning for the professional
Money Decisions — Business and financial planner
Portfolio Decisions — Portfolio management
Wang Professional
IBM PC and compatibles
Apple II, IIe
Victor 9000
DEC Rainbow 100

Executive Data Systems Inc.
1845 The Exchange,
Suite 140
Atlanta, GA 30339
(800) 272-3374
THE PROSPECTOR — Client data base, depreciation schedules, general ledger for service businesses
IBM PC and compatibles
Most CP/Ms

Executive Software Inc.
Bay Street
Shanty Bay, Ontario LOL 2LO
(705) 722-3373
PLAN80 — A financial modeling language with financial planning, budgeting, and forecasting.
IBM PC and compatibles

FIPSCO Incorporated
15 South Fairview
Park Ridge, IL 60068
(312) 823-8455
Life insurance proposal and marketing systems
Osborne
IBM PC
Apple
TRS-80
Xerox

Ferox Microsystems Inc.
1701 N. Ft. Myer Drive,
Suite 611
Arlington, VA 22209
(703) 841-0800
Financial planning
Strategic planning
Cash flow forecasting
Corporate consolidations
Financial reporting and projecting
Budgetary planning and control
Investment analysis
Merger acquisition analysis
Sensitivity analysis
IBM PC and compatibles

Computer Resources for Financial Planning

Financial Data Planning Corp.
2675 South Bayshore Drive
Miami, FL 33133
(395) 858-8200
Financial planning
Estate taxation
Mortgage amortization
Income tax calculations
Compound interest
Life insurance proposals
Agency database
Universal life proposals
Pension proposals
Pension administration
IBM PC and compatibles

Financial Planning Consultants
2507 N. Verity Parkway
Middletown, OH 45042-0429
(513) 424-1656
Comprehensive financial planning
IBM PC and compatibles
Micromation

Financial Planning Systems Incorporated
525 East 300 South
Salt Lake City, UT 84102
(801) 322-0527
Financial planning
Retirement needs analysis
Estate planning
Income tax planning
Cash flow planning
Household budget
IBM PC and compatibles
Wang PC

Financial Profiles Inc.
5900 Wilshire Boulevard
Los Angeles, CA 90036
(213) 937-8400
Financial profiles
Life and disability insurance
Services investment products
Estate planning
IBM PC and compatibles

Financial Software Inc.
11401 Westridge Circle
Chardon, OH 44024
(800) 392-2669
*Investment — Product Name
Market Maverick*
Apple II, II+, III, IIe, IIc and compatibles
IBM PC and compatibles

Financier Incorporated
2000 W. Park Drive
P.O. Box 670
Westboro, MA 01581
(617) 366-0950
FINANCIER II — Personal, small business financial record keeping
FINANCIER TAX SERIES — Tax planning, forecasting
IBM PC
DEC Rainbow 100 and 100+
Wang PC
Texas Instruments Professional

Financiometrics Incorporated
P.O. Box 1788
Lafayette, CA 94549
(415) 376-9455
Investment matrix
Assorted financial programs
IBM PC and compatibles

First New England Consortium Incorporated
Admiral's Hill
90 Commandant's Way
Chelsea, MA 02150
(617) 889-4823
Office automation and computer services
Personal computers used in timesharing network

Futuresoft, Inc.
3809 Eubank Boulevard, N.E.
Albuquerque, NM 87111
(505) 292-8844
Financial planning software
Database client and practice management software
IBM PC
AT&T PC
Apple Macintosh

Gifford Fong Associates
3730 Mt. Diablo Boulevard, Suite 350
Lafayette, CA 94549
(415) 283-8363
Investments
IBM PC

Good Software Corporation
12900 Preston Road, Suite 600
Dallas, TX 75230
(214) 239-6085
AMORTIZER 3
INVESTOR 3
IBM PC and compatibles
Compaq
Texas Instruments
Corona
Columbia

Group Benefits Shoppers
1420 N. Claremont Boulevard, #105D
Claremont, CA 91711
(714) 625-3911
Group health insurance
IBM PC and compatibles

H and H Scientific
13507 Pendleton Street
Ft. Washington, MD 20744
(301) 292-2958
Stock Option Analysis Program (SOAP) — Investments, financial planning
Stock Option Scanner (SOS) — Investments, financial planning
Apple II, II+, IIe
IBM PC

Computer Resources for Financial Planning

HowardSoft
8008 Girard Avenue, # 310
La Jolla, CA 92037
(619) 454-0121
Real Estate Analyzer
IBM PC
Compaq, Compaq Plus
Apple II Series

IAFP Data Communications Network
5775 Peachtree Dunwoody
Road, Suite 120-C
Atlanta, GA 30342
(800) 241-2148
A nationwide computer
network featuring financial
news, securities quotations,
electronic mail, etc.
Most personal computers with
300/1200 baud modem

IFDS Incorporated
P.O. Box 888870
Atlanta,GA 30356
(800) 554-8004
Professional Series/4
Professional Series/3
Professional Series/2
Professional Series/1
Professional Series/E1
Client database management
software
Color graphics software
Presentation system
IBM PC, XT, and compatibles
Wang PC, Televideo 1603,
1605

Industry Software Sales Inc.
1755 Lynnfield, Suite 173
Memphis, TN 38119
(901) 767-3759
Commercial loan
Safe deposit
IBM PC
Altos
Televideo
Texas Instruments
Monroe

Informatics General Corp.
9441 LBJ Freeway
Dallas, TX 75243
(214) 231-1400
FNA-II — Financial needs
analysis software
iFile — Client file software
MultiMate — Word Processing;
links to *FNA II* and *iFile*
IBM PC
Wang PC

Insurance Micro Software
1611 W. Harry
P.O. Box 13318
Wichita, KS 67213
(316) 265-5695
Life insurance
Financial planning
Taxation
IBM PC
Apple II

InteleCom Incorporated
1101 North Bluemound Drive
Appleton, WI 54915
(800)-558-3483
TC talking computer
telecommunications

Interactive Data Communications Systems
5150 West El Camino
Los Altos, CA 94022
(415) 961-0666
Computer services in franchise
sales, individual purchasers, and
ancillary product/service sales.

Interactive Planning Systems
1800 Century Blvd.,
Suite 890
Atlanta, GA 30305
(404) 241-3246
General ledger, plus accounts
payable
Asset, liability management
CD accounting
Bond accounting
Fixed asset accounting
Payroll accounting
Shareholder accounting
TELLERGRAPH
Safe-deposit box accounting
IBM PC and compatibles

Investors Heritage Life Insurance
P.O. Box 717, 200 Capital
Frankfort, KY 40601
(502) 223-2361
Financial management analysis
— Comprehensive financial
planning package
Asset accumulator program
Hand held Panasonic

Investors Life Insurance Company of North America
1600 Arch Street, 21 Tower
Philadelphia, PA 19101
(215) 241-5125
Financial security analysis:
Death benefits, planning,
retirement planning, choice of
capital conservation, capital
utilization or a special
intermediate method.
IBM PC, XT, AT, and
compatibles
TRS-80 II/12/16

James Baker and Company
Suite 1050, City Center Bldg.
Oklahoma City, OK 73102
(405) 236-2663
Asset, liability management
Software sales and
development

John Wiley and Sons Inc.
605 Third Avenue
New York, NY 10158
(212) 850-6540
Investment Tax Analyst — A
tax planner that lets an
individual or financial
professional determine tax
benefits of investment before
investing
The Personal Financial Advisor
— A personal financial planning
program that analyzes a range
of *what if* options
IBM PC
Apple

Computer Resources for Financial Planning

K-Waye Financial Services
P.O. Box 1675
Sausalito, CA 94965
(415) 388-9474
Advisor — Portfolio
management
Analyst — Technical stock and
commodity analysis
IBM PC
DEC Rainbow
CPM-80 computers

Kingstone Reed
Bay Street
Shanty Bay, Ont. LOL 2LO
(705) 722-3373
Decision Analyst — decision
making package
CPM-80, CPM-86 computers

Kinnaird SoftPlans
2953 N.E. Brogden Street
Hillsboro, OR 97124
(503) 640-2875
L.I.F.E. GOALS — Financial
planning software
IBM PC and compatibles

LFP Systems Incorporated
4600 Marriott Drive
Box 30365
Raleigh, NC 27622
(800) 632-3044
Advanced Planning System
Mini System
Tax Investment Planning
Module
Client Manager
Color graphics (*Mini System*
only)
Compu-Loan
IBM PC
Columbia
Televideo
Wang

Larry Rosen Company
7008 Springdale Road
Louisville, KY 40222
(502) 228-4343
Investment analysis: After-tax
IRR for stocks, bonds and real
estate
Apple (not Apple III)
IBM PC

Lawson Group Incorporated,
The
4520 B West Village Drive
Tampa, FL 33624
(813) 962-2554
The Human Resource
Customized plans (e.g., 401(k),
Pension calculation system)
IBM PC and compatibles

Leonard Financial Planning
Systems Incorporated
P.O. Box 30365
Raleigh, NC 27622
(800) 632-3044
Leonard Advanced Planning
System
Leonard Mini Plan
Leonard Client Manager
IBM PC and compatibles

Life Insurance Rx Corporation
180 Harbor Drive
P.O. Box O
Sausalito, CA 94965
(415) 332-2266
RX ASSET — Life insurance,
comparison and replacement
Life insurance, proposal
illustrations
IBM PC
Radio Shack
Apple II, II+, IIe

Life-Work Planning
Corporation
1267 Cook Avenue
Lakewood, OH 44107
(216) 228-1890
LIFEPLAN — Financial planning
proposal system
Database management
software for client tracking
IBM PC and compatibles

LifePlan Incorporated
200 Market Place, Suite 240
Roswell, GA 30075
(404) 993-6803
Personal Financial Planner
Personal Financial Manager
Personal Financial Planner,
Professional Edition

Lincoln National Sales Corp.
1300 S. Clinton Street
P.O. Box 1110
Fort Wayne, IN 46801
(219) 427-3206
PRO ESTATE ANALYSIS —
Estate and state tax calculations
Liquidity
Survivor income need
projections
Project asset growth
Will and trust selections
Apple II+, IIe
Radio Shack
IBM PC

Lord and Ware Incorporated
P.O. Box 404
Westfield, IN 46074
(317) 896-2643
Programs for microcomputers
and Panasonic hand held
computers for insurance
companies
Microcomputers
Hand held Panasonic

Lumen Systems Inc.
4300 Stevens Creek Blvd.,
Suite 270
San Jose, CA 94129
(408) 984-8134
LIFEPLAN — Comprehensive
integrated financial planning
software based on the *Touche*
Ross Guide to Personal Financial
Management
IBM PC
IBM XT
COMPAQ

Lytron Systems Incorporated
385 East 800 South
Orem, UT 84058
(801) 227-2300
LOIS/Financial Planner —
Comprehensive integrated
financial planning software
LOIS/Report Manager —
System report generation
software
IBM PC and compatibles

Computer Resources for Financial Planning

MDCR Incorporated
760 Highway 18
East Brunswick, NJ 08816
(201) 257-5700
IMPACT — Corporate financial planning, business modeling, reporting, analysis
IBM PC
Wang PC
DEC
Data General
Radio Shack

McBride Accounting Service
P.O. Box 423
Star, NC 27356
(919) 428-4814
Federal income tax
Cash flow
Depreciation
TRS-80, I, III, IV

McGraw-Hill Training Systems
1221 Avenue of the Americas
New York, NY 10020
(212) 512-2590
Taxation, investments, real estate income properties, sales forecasting, etc.
Numerous financial planning software programs available that are compatible with various hardware and operating systems. Free catalogue available upon request.

Merlin Information Systems Incorporated
P.O. Box 178510
San Diego, CA 92117
(619) 483-6485
Profit planning for business
IRA prospector
Fixed asset management
Shareholder accounting
Bond accounting
Sales call reporting
Personnel
Forms/supply inventory
Asset/liability/management
IBM PC and compatibles
Apple II, III

Michael D. Weinberg Consultants
4025 S. Oneida Street
Denver, CO 80237
(303) 759-4004
Mike Weinberg's Estate Projector
IBM PC
Apple II, IIe, III

Micro Futures
P.O. Box 2765
Livonia, MI 48154
(313) 422-0914
Investment Software — Commodity futures, stocks, options, and mutual funds
Comdata
MJK Access
Warner Access
Chartpac
IBM PC
Apple II
TRS-80 I, III, IV
TRS-80 II/12/16

Micro Lab
2699 Skokie Valley Road
Highland Park, IL 60035
(312) 433-7550
Tax Manager
Personal Banker
Asset Manager
Apple II
IBM PC

Micro Planning Systems Inc.
1499 Bayshore Highway, #214
Burlingame, CA 94010
(415) 692-0407
Professional financial planning system

MicroComputing Research
29-A Estancia Drive
Marana, AZ 85238
(602) 682-4444
THE COMPUTING INVESTOR Series — Stock market portfolios and stock market analysis
Apple II+, IIe, IIc

Mimics Incorporated
6427 Hillcroft # 331
Houston, TX 77081
(713) 663-7083
Investments accounting
Safekeeping
Pay agent/shareholder accounting
Syndicate management
Bond bidding/debt service
Alpha Micro
IBM PC and compatibles

Money Tree Software
P.O. Box 54
Corvallis, OR 97339
(800) 533-3914
MoneyCalc — Spread sheet analysis for Lotus, VisiCalc, Symphony
MoneyPlan — Total practice management, client data control, word processing
Effective integrated plan preparation
Apple
IBM PC and compatibles

Moneycare Incorporated
253 Martens Avenue
Mt. View, CA 94040
(415) 962-0333
Financial Navigator — A personal financial management system based on the personal computer

Multiple Funding Services
280 Park Avenue
New York, NY 10017
(212) 370-0060
Family income needs valuation
Estate tax and liquidity valuation
Comprehensive business valuation
Dial-Our-Computer
Universal life microfile
IBM PC and compatibles

Computer Resources for Financial Planning

Murnane and Associates
1056 Metro Circle
Palo Alto, CA 94303
(415) 856-0619
Personal Banking —
Retirement, IRA, college, life
insurance, savings, mortgage
amortization
IBM PC

N-Squared Computing
5318 Forest Ridge Road
Silverton, OR 97381
(503) 873-5906
N-Squared Market Analyzer
N-Squared Market Illustrator
N-Squared Stock Analyzer
N-Squared Interface
Apple
IBM PC

Network Microdesigns Corp.
200 Fifth Avenue, S.E.
Cedar Rapids, IA 52401
(319) 398-1870
Individual retirement account
planning program
Personal insurance needs
analysis program
IBM PC and compatibles
Apple II, II+, IIe

New England Management Services
345 Whitney Avenue
New Haven, CT 06511
(203) 787-3452
INVESTWARE
IBM PC and compatibles
DEC Rainbow
Wang PC
Altos 986 Multi-user

Newport-West Data Services Incorporated
301 Saratoga Avenue
Los Gatos, CA 95030
(408) 395-1778
Commercial Applications —
Accounts payable, accounts
receivable, payroll, general
ledger, inventory control
Non-profit organizations and
scout councils — Fund
development, registrations,
cookie sales
Data General, Nova and Eclipse
Bluebird (IBM compatible)

Options-80
Box 471-FP
Concord, MA 01742
(617) 369-1589
Stock Option Analyzer
IBM PC and compatibles
Wang PC
Tandy 2000
Apple II family
TRS-80 family

Original Software Creations Incorporated
231-A Raritan Avenue
Highland Park, NJ 08904
(201) 246-4507
Life insurance
Split dollars
Estate planning
Business needs
Family needs
Client file
IBM PC
TRS 80
Apple II, IIe, II+
Kaypro

Owens Financial Planning Inc.
5400 California Avenue,
S.W., Suite A
Seattle, WA 98136
(206) 932-2111
Income tax
Real estate planning
Tax shelter
Capital needs
Retirement needs
IRA-HR-10
Savings
IBM PC

PCP Systems Incorporated
11960 Westline Industrial
Drive, Suite 322
St. Louis, MO 63146
(314) 878-0380
Home Attorney — Wills, power
of attorney, promissory notes
IBM PC

PENTABS
829 De La Vina Street
Santa Barbara, CA 93101-
3284
(805) 963-8881
ERISA/TEFRA System
Data Management System
401-K System
The Pension Selector
Financial Calculations
Trust Accounting
Word Management
Time and Charges
IBM XT
Vector Graphic 3032, 3005,
V430, V440

Pennvest Corporation
320 King of Prussia Road,
Suite 120
Radnor, PA 19087
(800) 523-4590
Investment planning software

Computer Resources for Financial Planning

Philanthrotec Incorporated
23201 Mill Creek Drive, #200
Laguna Hills, CA 92653
(714) 859-7350
Analysis of charitable tax
planning techniques relating
individual financial, estate, and
insurance planning
IBM PC and compatibles

Pictorial Publishers Inc.
8081 Zionsville Road
Indianapolis, IN 46268
(317) 872-7220
*Financial Planning — Estates
(FP-E)*
*Capital Management Analysis
(CMA)*
*Business Valuation Service
(BVS)*
*RomPower-Universal Life IRA
Program*
Time Deposit Analysis
V-MARC 88
Panasonic Hand Held

**Pro Data Systems
Incorporated**
2418 Casa Bona Avenue
Belmont, CA 94002
(415) 592-6460
Personal Property Inventory
IBM PC and compatibles

Programmed Press
2301 Baylis Avenue
Elmont, NY 11003
(516) 775-0933
Investment Software — Bonds
and interest rate annuities
program
Stock market software
Options and arbitrage
Commodities and futures
Foreign exchange
Statistical forecasting
IBM PC
Radio Shack
Apple
Sanyo
Commodore 64

Quadram Corporation
4350-E International
Boulevard
Norcross, GA 30093
(404) 564-1975
The Tax Strategist — Tax
planning program
The Investment Strategist —
Tax shelter investment analysis
program
IBM PC and compatibles
IBM PC Jr.
Corona
Columbia
Zenith 150 - PC AT

R and R Newkirk
6213 Las Pas Trail
Indianapolis, IN 46268
(800) 428-3846
ProPlan/Ezy Plan — Performs
calculations and projections of
financial reports
Cash flow
Income statements and tax
planning endowment
development system
Charitable financial planning
IBM PC and compatibles

**R. R. James and Associates
Limited**
920 Davis Road, Suite 305
Elgin, IL 60120
(312) 742-4703
Group policy analysis — Single
company system
Group policy analysis — Multi-
company system
IBM PC and compatibles

REMS Software
526 N.W. 2nd Street
Corvallis, OR 97330
(503) 757-8887
Real estate investment analysis
Loan analysis
IBM PC and compatibles
Apple Series

Realty Software
1926 S. Pacific Coast High-
way, # 229
Redondo Beach, CA 90277
(213) 372-9419
Property management
Property listings, comparables
Real estate analysis program
modules
IBM PC and compatibles
Apple
TRS-80
Kaypro
Osborne
Columbia
Wang
NCR
Altos
Eagle - PC
Morrow Micro

Regal Computer Systems
910 Taywood Road
Englewood, CO 45322
(513)832-0111
TELESUN — Financial planning
(comprehensive)
Portfolio analyzer
Life insurance analysis
410-K benefit illustration
Selective executive incentive
plan
Budget
Investment triangle
IBM PC and compatibles

Reston Publishing Company
11480 Sunset Hills Road
Reston, VA 22090
(703) 437-8900
Personal Money Dynamics by
Venita VanCaspel —
Presentation tool to sell
financial planning products and
services; gives clients an
overview of the concepts of
financial planning
IBM PC

Computer Resources for Financial Planning

Richard Lorance and Associates Limited
P.O. Box 5278
Phoenix, AZ 85010-5278
(602) 954-0767
Summary responses for:
  College fund planning
  Retirement fund planning
Six loan calculations
Thirteen options for investment planning
Twelve options for diversifying by lump sum or by periodic accumulations
Deflation calculations
Apple II+

S. Tracy Rodgers
1125 Wall Street
La Jolla, CA 92037
(619) 454-4261
Investments — accounting for trust departments, portfolio managers, etc.
Digital Equipment Corporation
DecMate II

Savant Corporation
P.O. Box 440278
Houston, TX 77244-0278
(800) 231-9900
Technical analysis
Fundamental analysis
Black-Sholes option evaluation
IBM PC

Sawhney Software
888 Seventh Avenue
New York, NY 10106
(212) 541-8020
ExecPlan II — comprehensive planning software
Planmode — Federal and state tax planning software
Taxmode — Federal tax planning software

Sigma Software
248 Columbia Turnpike
Florham Park, NJ 07932
(201) 966-1633
Life support
Interest-sensitive proposals
Spread sheet and graphics
Word processing
Client management system
Tom Wolff's *FNA I* and *FNA II*
Estate planning
Multi-life deferred compensation
Wang 2200 Series
IBM PC, IBM Series I

Softbridge Microsystems Corp.
186 Alewife Brook Parkway, Suite 206
Cambridge, MA 02138
(800) 325-6060
Comprehensive financial planning — Plan generation
Practice management
Analysis of financial condition
Tax planning
Estate planning business valuation
Risk management
IBM PC and compatibles

Specialists in Financial Planning
160 Washington, S.E., Suite 48
Albuquerque, NM 87108
(505) 265-8308
Universal life and financial planning programming for insurance companies
Client database and word processor
Financial needs analysis program
Policy comparison program
IBM PC and compatibles
Apple II+, Ile,
TRS-80 II, 12, 16
Epson QX-10

Synaptic Software Incorporated
5628 Linden Circle
Des Moines, IA 50325
(515) 276-4885
Estate planning
Capital needs analysis
Business valuation
Group insurance proposal
Auto policy rating
Income tax planning
IBM PC and compatibles

Synergistic Financial Services Incorporated
1780 North Main Street
Walnut Creek, CA 94596
(415) 932-6092
Computerized financial planning

Syntax Corporation
4500 West 72nd Terrace
Prairie Village, KS 66208
(913) 362-9667
Tax planning
IBM PC and compatibles
Radio Shack II/12/16
Apple II, Ile

Systems Plus Incorporated
1120 San Antonio Road
Palo Alto, CA 94303
(415) 969-7047
"Books"
The Electric Ledger
Client Manager
General Ledger
CPA Client-Writing
IBM PC and compatibles
DEC CP/M 80 + 86
MP/M 80 + 86
Apple

Computer Resources for Financial Planning

Systems Strategy Incorporated
P.O. Box 333
Brielle, NJ 08730
(201) 223-5575
Qualified plan illustration system
EBP valuation system
Wang PC
Wang 2200
IBM PC and compatibles
IBM 370/xx, 30xx, 43xx

T.B.S.(Todd Blackley Software)
P.O. Box 11368
Provo, UT 84603
(801) 375-7596
Insurance rating programs —
Personal Lines, Auto/home
Multi-comprehensive
Form filling programs —
Insurance, invoice, etc.
Bank escrow program (Apple only)
Bank IRA, Keogh program (Apple only)
IBM PC and compatibles
Apple

TaxCalc Software Incorporated
4210 West Vickery Boulevard
Fort Worth, TX 76107
(817) 738-3122
TaxCalc Tax Planner
Real Estate Tax Planner
Estate Tax Planner
Stock Option Planner
IBM PC and compatibles
Columbia
Corona
Apple IIe, II+, III
Macintosh
Tandy
DEC

Technical Data Corporation
45 Milk Street, 4th Floor
Boston, MA 02109
(800) 343-7745
Fixed Income Analysis and Management
The Yield Calculator
The Fixed Income Portfolio Manager
The Rate of Return Analyzer
The Mortgage Calculator
The Bond Swap Analyzer
The IDC Data Link
IBM PC and compatibles

Trax Softworks Incorporated
10801 National Boulevard
Los Angeles, CA 90064
(213) 475-8729
ESS — Electronic spread sheet
Tieline
IBM - 370 mainframe or equivalent

Unified Management Corporation
Guaranty Building
20 North Meridian Street
Indianapolis, IN 46204
(800) 862-7283
UNISAVE — Central Asset Account
On-line computer services
Research
Financial planning system
COMPLAN — Mutual funds
Money market funds

Valentino Sabuco and Company
333 Mendocino Ave., Suite 110
Santa Rosa, CA 95401
(707) 578-1048
The Valentino Sabuco Comprehensive Financial Planning System — Turnkey comprehensive financial planning systems for accountants, attorneys, trust departments and other professionals interested in financial planning

Valuation Systems Company
Kensington Galleria Tower One
7130 South Lewis, Suite 235
Tulsa, OK 74136-5401
(918) 496-7655
THE FINANCIAL ANALYSIS SYSTEM (FAS) — Investment management
Mortgage routines
Equity routines
Present value
Valuation analysis
After-tax analysis
Statistical routines
Special analysis
Wang 2200
Microcomputers

Wall Street Graphics Inc.
P.O. Box 562, Wall Street Station
New York, NY 10268
(212) 495-4488
Market EAS-Alyzer — Stock market timing software
IBM PC and compatibles
Apple IIe, II+

Western Planning Corporation
1240 E. Missouri
Phoenix, AZ 85014
(602) 274-6805
Group Comp II — Group health insurance
Trustflo — Financial needs analysis
IBM PC and compatibles
Apple II, IIe, III
TRS-80 I/II/III, 12/16

Yousoufian Software Inc.
20 Old City Hall
625 Commerce Street
Tacoma, WA 98402
(206) 383-9940
Real estate investment analysis and syndication software
IBM PC and compatibles
Apple

Sources: *The International Association of Financial Planning Directory of Products and Services,* 1985; and other sources.

Real Estate Software

The following listings offer guidelines for various real estate software applications. The sales packages are oriented toward the needs of real estate brokers; property-management packages are designed for landlords or property managers; and investment-analysis packages are useful for investors, portfolio managers, consultants, appraisal firms, and acquisitions staff.

REAL ESTATE SALES PACKAGES: DESIRABLE FEATURES

Property Listings:

- Maintains information on agency listings

- Maintains or ties into MLS listings

- Analyzes listings by agency, broker, geographic region, or other criteria defined by the user

- Stores sales information for comparisons

Client Listings:

- Maintains information on current, past, and prospective clients

- Matches interests of clients with available properties

Word Processing:

- Maintains library of standard forms

- Permits personalized mailings about general issues or specific properties, according to customers' interests

Financial Features:

- Qualifies buyers

- Calculates mortgage payments, including those on new loans, assumptions, federal and veterans' mortgages, and so on

- Analyzes mortgages, breaking out amortization and interest portions

- Performs rent-versus-buy analyses

- Analyzes cash-flow and other investment criteria for income properties

- Ties into banks (via telephone and modem) for current interest rates

Accounting:

- Performs standard accounting functions

- Builds and maintains budgets

- Allows budget-versus-actual comparisons

- Produces comparative financial statements on schedule or on demand

- Tracks and ages pending closings

- Forecasts agency cash flow

Functions for Board of Realtors:

- Maintains membership roster

- Bills dues

- Produces mailing labels, either for entire membership or special lists

PROPERTY MANAGEMENT SOFTWARE: DESIRABLE FEATURES

Tenant Accounting (Receivables):

- Prepares rent rolls

- Keeps accounts and historical data for current, past, and future tenants

- Bills recurrent charges

- Computes subsidies and expenditures that must be reported for federal programs

- Produces vacancy and lease-expiration reports on schedule or on demand

- Produces delinquency reports automatically or on demand

- Flags or adjusts nonrecurrent items and escalators in leases

- Permits tenant files to interact with general ledger and other accounting functions

- Permits separate charts of accounts for each property

- Permits specialized rent-due or other dated transactions

- Uses cash- or accrual-based accounting

Other Accounting Features:

- Produces operating reports and financial statements automatically or on demand

- Permits automatic check writing

- Builds and maintains budgets

- Allows budget-versus-actual comparisons

- Performs cash-flow analyses

- Maintains vendor files and analyzes vendor payments

- Permits financial modeling

Miscellaneous Features:

- Analyzes energy use

- Produces charts and graphs

- Does accounting and profit distribution for trusts and limited partnerships

- Does job costing

- Maintains and analyzes files on prospective lessees

APPRAISAL AND INVESTMENT-ANALYSIS PACKAGES: DESIRABLE FEATURES

Information Storage and Retrieval:

- Stores information on individual properties (descriptive, historical, financial)

- Stores information on individual leases (dates of inception and expiration, escalators, options, special notices, nonrecurrent and recurrent charges, and so on)

- Stores information on portfolios (number and types of properties, geographic distribution, value, history)

- Updates financial information for both properties and leases, according to lease schedules or changes in taxes, operating expenses, and so on

- Tracks depreciable assets and calculates depreciation schedules by various methods

- Produces directories, reports, and summaries by portfolio, property, tenant, or criteria specified by the user

Financial Analysis:

- Analyzes individual properties to report current and estimated future cash flows, operating performance, capital investment, debt service, gross revenue, internal rate of return, financial-management rate of return, and so forth

- Analyzes portfolios to report current and estimated future performance by a variety of criteria

- Provides ready-to-use programs for specific analyses such as multiple-regression, stepped-up income, accelerated cost recovery

- Provides flexible spreadsheet or other programs for functions specified by the user, including lease-by-lease analysis

---

Source: Copyright 1983 by Cahners Publishing Company, Division of Reed Holdings Inc. Reprinted with permission from *Business Computer Systems*, May 1983.

SELECTED ON-LINE BUSINESS AND FINANCIAL DATABASES

On-line databases are collections of computer-stored data that are retrievable by remote terminals. The databases are collected and organized by a producer, who provides the database to a vendor, who then distributes the data by a telecommunication network to the user. Often a vendor will offer a large number of different databases. In some instances the producer and vendor are the same.

Using an on-line database requires: a terminal (a typewriter-like device usually equipped with a video display) to receive data and send commands to the vendor's computers, and a modem for coupling the terminal to a telephone line. Printouts (hard copy) of the desired information can be obtained from electronic printers located at the user's terminal or ordered from the vendor. The user accesses the database by dialing a telephone number and then typing (on the terminal keyboard) a password provided by the vendor. Searching the database is done with special commands and procedures peculiar to each base.

The contents of databases vary. Some provide statistical data only—usually in the form of time series. Other bases provide bibliographic references and, in some instances, abstracts or the full text of articles. Specifics about database contents, instructions, and prices are available from vendors. Listed here are some major business databases and vendors (see page 6.51), from whom more complete information should be requested.

Databases

ABI Inform
Provides references on all areas of business management with emphasis on how-to information
Producer: Data Courier, Inc. (Louisville, Kentucky)
Vendors: BRS, DIALOG, SDC

Accountants Index
Contains reference information on accounting, auditing taxation, management, and securities
Producer: American Institute of Certified Public Accountants (New York)
Vendor: SDC

Advertising and Marketing Intelligence
Covers consumer trends, new products, media planning, sales promotion
Producer: New York Times Information Service and J. Walter Thompson Co. (Parsippany, New Jersey)
Vendor: New York Times Information Service

American Profile
Provides statistical information on U.S. households, including population, income, and dependents; also provides data on types of businesses in an area
Producer: Donnelly Marketing (Stamford, Connecticut)
Vendor: Business Information Service

BI Data
Maintains international statistical data, including national accounts, labor, foreign trade, consumption, prices, production
Producer: Business International Corp. (New York)
Vendors: General Electric Information Service, I.P. Sharp, DIALOG

Business Credit Service
Provides business credit and financial information
Producer: TRW, Inc. (Orange, California)
Vendor: TRW

Canadian Business Periodicals Index
Provides references to a wide variety of topics from Canadian business publications
Producer: Micromedia Limited (Toronto, Canada)
Vendor: SDC

CIS Index

Contains references and abstracts from nearly every publication resulting from Senate and House Committee meetings since 1970
Producer: Congressional Information Services, Inc. (Washington, D.C.)
Vendors: DIALOG, SDC

Commodities Market Data Bank

Provides statistical data on all traded commodities
Producer: Data Resources, Inc. (Lexington, Massachusetts)
Vendor: Data Resources, Inc.

CompuServe, Inc.

Provides reference, statistical, and full text retrieval of information of personal interest, including health, recipes, gardening, financial and investment data, including the Compustat and Value Line databases
Producer: CompuServe, Inc. (Columbus, Ohio)
Vendor: CompuServe

Compustat

Provides extensive financial data on companies
Producer: Standard and Poor's Compustat Service, Inc. (Englewood, Colorado)
Vendors: ADP, Business Information Services, CompuServe, Data Resources, Chase Econometrics/Interactive Data Corp.

Computerized Engineering Index

Provides a broad coverage of the international literature on engineering and technology
Producer: Engineering Index (New York)
Vendors: BRS, DIALOG, SDC

Disclosure II

Provides extracts of 10K and other reports filed with the Securities and Exchange Commission
Producer: Disclosure, Inc. (Bethesda, Maryland)
Vendors: Business Information Services (Control Data), DIALOG, Dow Jones, New York Times Information Services, Mead Data Central

Dow Jones News/Retrieval Service and Stock Quote Reporters

Contains text of articles appearing in major financial publications, including *The Wall Street Journal* and *Barrons*. Quote service provides quotes on stocks, bonds, mutual funds
Producer: Dow Jones & Company (New York)
Vendors: BRS, Dow Jones & Company

DRI Capsule/EEI Capsule

Provides over 3,700 U.S. social and economic statistical time series such as population, income, and money supply data
Producers: Data Resources, Inc. (Lexington, Massachusetts) and Evans Economics Inc. (Washington, D.C.)
Vendors: Business Information Services, United Telecom Group, I.P. Sharp

EIS Industrial Plants

Offers statistical data on industrial establishments with annual sales of more than $500,000 and with more than 20 employees. Data include location of each plant, shipment values, market share
Producer: Economic Information Systems (New York)
Vendors: Business Information Services (Control Data), DIALOG

Federal Register Abstracts

Provides coverage of federal regulatory agencies as published in the *Federal Register*
Producer: Capitol Services (Washington, D.C.)
Vendor: DIALOG, SDC

GTE Financial System One Quotation Service

Provides current U.S. and Canadian quotations and statistical data on stocks, bonds, options, commodities, and other market data
Producer: GTE Information Systems (Mount Laurel, New Jersey)
Vendor: GTE Information Systems, Inc.

The Information Bank

Provides an extensive current affairs data source consisting of abstracts from numerous English-language publications
Producer: The New York Times Information Service
Vendor: The New York Times Information Service

LEXIS

Contains full text references to a wide range of legal information, including court decisions, regulations, government statutes
Producer: Mead Data Central (New York)
Vendor: Mead Data Central

NEXIS

Provides full text business and general news, including management, technology, finance, science, politics, religion
Producer: Mead Data Central (New York)
Vendor: Mead Data Central

Quick Quote

Provides current quotations, volume, high-low data for securities of U.S. public corporations
Producer: CompuServe, Inc.
Vendor: CompuServe

Quotron 800

Provides up-to-the-minute quotations and statistics on a broad range of securities such as stocks, bonds, options, commodities
Producer: Quotron Systems Inc. (Los Angeles)
Vendor: Quotron Systems Inc.

The Source

Covers a broad variety of consumer services, business and financial information, including travel information, reservations, restaurant reviews, etc.
Producer: Source Telecomputing (McLean, Virginia)
Vendor: Source Telecomputing Corp.

Value Line II

Provides extensive financial data from the *Value Line Investment Survey* covering over 1,600 major companies
Producer: Arnold Bernhard & Co. (New York)
Vendors: ADP Service, Chase Econometrics/Interactive Data Corp., CompuServe Data Resources, Inc.

Sources: A.T. Kruzas and J. Schmittroth, *Encyclopedia of Information Systems*, Gale Research (Detroit), revised periodically; *Information Industry Market Place*, R. R. Bowker (New York), annual; V. Maynos and D.M. Werner, *Data Bases for Business*, Chilton Book Co. (Radnor, Pa.) 1982.

Database Vendors

ADP Network Services, Inc.
175 Jackson Plaza
Ann Arbor, MI 48106
(313) 769-6800

BRS, Inc.
1200 Route 7
Latham, NY 12110
(518) 783-1161
(800) 833-4707

Business Information Services
Control Data Corporation
500 West Putnam Avenue
Greenwich, CT 06830
(203) 622-2000

Chase Econometrics/Interactive Data Corporation
486 Totten Pond Road
Waltham, MA 02154
(617) 890-1234

CompuServe, Inc.
5000 Arlington Centre Blvd.
Columbus, OH 43220
(614) 457-8600

Data Resources, Inc. (DRI)
29 Hartwell Avenue
Lexington, MA 02173
(617) 861-0165

DIALOG Information Services, Inc.
3460 Hillview Avenue
Palo Alto, CA 94304
(415) 858-3810
(800) 227-1960

Dow Jones & Company, Inc.
P.O. Box 300
Princeton, NJ 08540
(609) 452-2000
(800) 257-5114

General Electric Information Services Co.
401 North Washington Street
Rockville, MD 20850
(301) 340-4000

GTE Information Systems, Inc.
East Park Drive
Mount Laurel, NJ 08054
(609) 235-7300

Mead Data Control
200 Park Avenue
New York, NY 10017
(212) 883-8560

The New York Times Information Services, Inc.
1719-A Route 10
Parsippany, NJ 07054
(201) 539-5850

Quotron Systems, Inc.
5454 Beethoven Street
Los Angeles, CA 90066
(213) 398-2761

SDC Search Service
2500 Colorado Avenue
Santa Monica, CA 90406
(213) 820-4111
(800) 421-7229

I.P. Sharp Associates
145 King Street West
Toronto, Ontario
Canada M5H 1J8
(416) 364-5361

Source Telecomputing Corporation
1515 Anderson Road
McLean, VA 22102
(703) 734-7500 x546
(800) 336-3366

TRW Information Services Division
1 City Boulevard
Orange, CA 92668
(714) 937-2700

United Telecom Computer Group
5454 West 110 Street
Overland Park, KA 66211
(913) 341-9161

GLOSSARY

The following glossary of key words should help consumers as they are shopping for personal computers.

Acoustic coupler. A device that allows other electronic devices to communicate by making, and also listening to sounds made over an ordinary telephone. *See* **Modem**.

Address. Designates the location of an item of information stored in the computer's memory. Without this, finding stored information would be an insurmountable task.

ALU (Arithmetic Logic Unit). The part of a CPU where binary data is acted upon.

ASCII (American Standard Code for Information Interchange). A 7-bit code used to represent alphanumeric characters.

Assembly language. A machine-oriented language in which mnemonics are used to represent each machine-language instruction. Each CPU has its own specific assembly language.

BASIC (Beginner's All-purpose Symbolic Instruction Code). A popular computer language used by many small and personal computer systems.

Baud rate. Serial-data transmission speed. Originally a telegraph term, 300 baud is approximately equal to a transmission speed of 30 bits per second.

Binary. Refers to the base-2 number system in which the only allowable digits are 0 and 1.

Bit. Short for binary digit, the smallest unit of information stored in a computer. It always has the binary value of "0" or "1."

Boot, booting, or bootstrap. The program, or set of commands, that gets the computer to move into action.

Bubble memory. A relatively new type of computer memory, it uses tiny magnetic "pockets" or "bubbles" to store data.

Bug. A mistake that occurs in a program within a computer or in the unit's electrical system. (When a mistake is found and corrected, it's called "debugging.")

Byte. An 8-bit sequence of binary digits. Each byte corresponds to one character of data, representing a single letter, number, or symbol. Bytes are the most common unit for measuring computer and disk storage capacity.

Cassette. Unit used to store information for mini- and microcomputers; similar in size and shape to an audio recording cassette.

Chip. An integrated circuit and its package, which contains coded signals.

Compiler. A program that translates a high-level language, such as **Basic**, into machine language.

CPU (Central Processing Unit). The part of the computer that executes the instructions that the user gives the system.

Crunch. To make a certain amount of information fit into a smaller amount of space than normally required.

Cursor. The symbol on the computer **monitor** that marks the place where the operator is working.

Database. A large amount of data stored in a well-organized format. A *database management system* is a program that allows access to the information.

Density. The amount of data that can be stored on one sector of one track of a disk.

Disk. A revolving plate on which information and programs are stored. *See also* **Floppy Disk**.

Disk drive. A peripheral machine that stores information on disks.

Documentation. User or operator instructions that come with some hardware and software that tells how to use the material.

DOS (Disk Operating System). A collection of programs designed to facilitate the use of a **disk drive** and **floppy disk**.

Error message. A statement by the computer indicating that the user has done something incorrectly.

File. A logical group of pieces of information labeled by a specific name, considered a single unit by the computer. It is used commonly on microcomputers and word processors.

Floppy disk. A small, inexpensive disk used to record and store information. It must be used in conjunction with a **disk drive**.

Format. The arrangement by which information is stored.

Graphics. The pictures or illustrations in the computer program.

Hardware. The physical apparatus or "nuts and bolts" that make up a computer: silicon chips, transformers, boards and wires, etc. Also used to describe various pieces of equipment, including the computer, **printer**, **modem**, etc.

Hexadecimal. Refers to the base-16 number system. Machine language programs are often written in hexadecimal notation.

Interface. The hardware or software necessary to connect one device or system to another.

K (kilo-byte). Denotes 1,024 units of stored matter.

Language. Any set of compiled, unified, or related commands or instructions that are acceptable to a computer.

Load. The actual operation of putting information and data into the computer or memory.

Memory. The internal storage of information.

Microcomputer. A small, complete computer system. Most personal computers now in use are microcomputers.

Minicomputer. An intermediate computer system sized between the very small microcomputer and the large computer.

Modem (modulating-demodulating). An acoustic or nonacoustic coupler, used either with a telephone or on a direct line, for transmitting information from one computer to another.

Monitor. The screen on which the material from the computer appears and can be read. Looks like a small TV screen but produces more vivid characters than a home TV.

Port. A channel through which data is transferred to and from the CPU. An 8-bit CPU can address 256 ports.

Printer. A computer output device that, when attached to a computer, will produce printed copy on paper.

Program. Coded instructions telling a computer how to perform a specific function.

RAM (random-access memory). A type of microchip whose patterns can be changed by the user; the information it generates can be stored on tape, disk, or in printed form.

ROM (read-only memory). A type of microchip that cannot be altered by the user.

Software. The programs, or sets of instructions, procedural rules, and, in some cases, documentation that make the computer function.

Source code. A nonexecutable **program** written in a high-level language. A **compiler** or assembler must translate the source code into an object code (machine language) that the computer can understand.

Terminal. A work station away from the main computer that allows several people to have access to a single main computer.

User friendly. Hardware or software designed to help people become familiar with their computer. Usually includes simple and easy-to-follow instructions.

Word. Number of bits treated as a single unit by the CPU. In an 8-bit machine, the word length is 8 bits; in a 16-bit machine, it is 16 bits.

Word processor. A text-editing program or system that allows electronic writing and correcting of articles, books, etc.

Source: *The World Almanac and Book of Facts*, 1984 edition, copyright © Newspaper Enterprise Association, Inc., 1984, New York, NY 10166.

6.06   Finance Publications

BOOKS ON FINANCE

Historical Perspectives

The American Business Cycle: Continuity & Change
by Robert J. Gordon
National Bureau of Economic Research, 1984

Why Stocks Go Up (and Down): A Guide to Solid Investing
by William H. Pike
Dow-Jones Irwin, 1983

A Year of Insider Trades
prepared by the staff of *The Insider's Chronicle*
Capital Publications, 1984

Taxation

U.S. Master Tax Guide
Commerce Clearing House
(published annually) 1985

Before You Give Another Dime
by Robert F. Sharpe
Thomas Nelson Publishers, 1978

Income Tax Benefits for Older Taxpayers
Commerce Clearing House, 1983

Julian Block's Guide to Year-Round Tax Savings
by Julian Block
Dow-Jones Irwin, 1984

Personal Financial Planning

Trends in Employee Benefit Plans
by Isidor Goodman
Commerce Clearing House, 1983

Tactical Investing: Strategies for Getting the Most Out of Your Money
by Daniel A. Blumberg
Consolidated Capital/Simon & Schuster, 1985

Pension Reform Handbook
by Martin E. Holbrook
Prentice-Hall, 1984

Commerce Clearing House Estate Planning Guide Including Financial Planning
by Sidney Kess and Bertil Westlin
Commerce Clearing House, 1983

The Dow-Jones Irwin Guide to Personal Financial Planning
by Frederick Amling and William G. Droms
Dow-Jones Irwin, 1982

Estate Planning after the Reagan Tax Cut
by Peter E. Lippett
Reston Publishing Co., 1982

The Power of Money Dynamics
by Venita VanCaspel
Reston Publishing Co., 1983

The Dow-Jones Irwin Guide to Estate Planning
by William C. Clay, Jr.
Dow-Jones Irwin, 1982

Everyone's Guide to Financial Planning W.I.N.N. (When If Not Now)
by Helen P. Rogers
Wellington Publications, 1984

Family Financial Planning for the 1980s
by Tom Klein, 1983
Ernst & Whinney, (212) 888-9100

The Financial Planner's Tax Almanac
by Robert W. Richards, Robert J. Nagoda, and Patrick R. Smith
Liberty Publishing, 1984

Financial Planning
Prentice-Hall, 1984

Your Book of Financial Planning: The Consumer's Guide to a Better Financial Future
edited by Loren Dunton
Reston Publishing Co., 1983

Investment and Financial Planning: The Complete Picture
by Ronald C. Gable
Reston Publishing Co., 1983

Guide to Social Security
William M. Mercer-Meidinger, Inc.
(published annually)

*The Money-Go-Round: A Guide to Managing Your Money
and Achieving Financial Peace of Mind*
by Lawrence A. Krause
Consolidated Capital/Simon & Schuster, 1985

Measures, Calculations, and Formulas

The Time Value of Money
by Gary E. Clayton and Christopher B. Spivey
W. B. Saunders Co., 1978

Rankings

The Dow-Jones Irwin Guide to Using The Wall Street Journal
by Michael B. Lehman
Dow-Jones Irwin, 1984

How to Buy Stocks
by Louis Engel and Brendan Boyd
Bantam Books, 1983

The Real Estate Investment Pocket Guide: Key Concepts for Understanding Real Estate Programs
by Alan Parisse and Richard G. Wollack with Joyce G. Harold
Consolidated Capital Communications Group, 1983

William E. Donoghue's No-Load Mutual Fund Guide
by William E. Donoghue with Thomas Tilling
Harper and Row, 1983

Stanger's Drilling Fund Yearbook
Robert A. Stanger & Company
(published annually)

Stanger's 1984 Partnership Sponsor Directory
Robert A. Stanger & Company
(published annually)

Professional Development

Securities Essentials Program
Consolidated Capital Communications Group
(Self-study system for passing the National Association of Securities Dealers Series 7 exam)

Creative Marketing Strategies for the Financial Planner
by Craig Donoff
Farnsworth Publishing Company

Tax-Advantaged Investments
by Alan Parisse and Richard G. Wollack
Consolidated Capital Communications Group, 1982
(Self-study program explaining tax-advantaged investments)

How to Survive and Succeed in a Small Financial Planning Practice
by Andrew M. Rich
Reston Publishing Co., 1984

Computers

Automating Your Financial Portfolio: An Investor's Guide to Personal Computers
by Donald R. Woodwell
Dow-Jones Irwin, 1983

Computer Guide for Financial Planners
College of Financial Planning (Denver, Colorado) 1985

The Individual Investor's Microcomputer Resource Guide
by Norm Nicholson
American Association of Individual Investors (Chicago, Illinois), 1984

Stock Trading Software Guide
by Rod E. Packer
Prentice-Hall, 1984

FINANCE PERIODICALS

Barron's
(\$55/year)
22 Cortlandt Street
New York, NY 10007
(212) 285-5000

Business Week
(\$34.95/year)
1221 Avenue of the Americas
New York, NY 10020
(212) 997-1221

Digest of Financial Planning Ideas
(\$197/year)
2000 Powell Street
Emeryville, CA 94608
(415) 652-7171 ext. 9009

Dow Theory Letters
(\$185/year)
P.O. Box 1759
La Jolla, CA 92038
(714) 454-0481

Financial Planning Magazine
(\$30/year)
5775 Peachtree-Dunwoody Road
Suite 120-C
Atlanta, GA 30342
(404) 252-9600

Forbes
(\$36/year)
60 Fifth Avenue
New York, NY 10011
(212) 620-2200

Fortune Magazine
(\$36/year)
1271 Avenue of the Americas
New York, NY 10020
(212) 586-1212

The Insiders
(\$100/year)
3471 North Federal Highway
Fort Lauderdale, FL 33306
(305) 563-9000

Insiders' Chronicle
(\$325/year)
Suite 1660
1300 N. 17th Street
Arlington, VA 22209
(703) 276-7100

Money
(\$25.95/year)
P.O. Box 2519
Boulder, CO 80322
(303) 447-9330

OTC Review
(\$36/year)
110 Pennsylvania Avenue
Oreland, PA 19075
(215) 887-9000

Professional Tape Reader
(\$245/year)
P.O. Box 2407
Hollywood, FL 33022
(305) 981-5963

SEC Today
(\$115/year)
c/o Washington Service Bureau
1225 Connecticut Avenue, N.W.
Washington, DC 20036
(202) 833-9200

Speculator
(\$157.50/year)
108 Christopher Columbus Drive
Jersey City, NJ 07302
(201) 432-8900

Standard & Poor's
P.O. Box 11370
New York, NY 10249
(212) 248-2525

Street Smart Investing
(\$195/year)
P.O. Box 173
Katonah, NY 10536
(914) 232-5084

Value Line
711 Third Avenue
New York, NY 10017
(212) 687-3965

The Wall Street Journal
(\$94/year)
22 Cortlandt Street
New York, NY 10007
(212) 285-5000

Weekly Insider Report
(\$85/year)
19 Rector Street
New York, NY 10006
(212) 482-8300

CHAPTER 7

Government and Financial Industry Directory

CONTENTS

This chapter consists of a compilation of useful names and addresses—all of which are available elsewhere, but are so scattered as to be inconvenient. The listing of associations in the financial services industry covers the field from actuaries through underwriters, by way of management accounting and real estate—to name a few. In addition to their addresses and telephone numbers, most associations have supplied a brief outline of their goals and purposes.

The listing for the federal government gives telephone numbers for cabinet members and addresses of the various departments of the three branches of government: executive, legislative, and judicial, in addition to those for selected congressional committees likely to be of interest to the financial professional.

Finally, in acknowledgement of the tentacles of government, there is included a list of all the federal information centers organized by state.

7.01 Associations in the Financial Services Industry

American Academy of Actuaries

1835 K Street, N.W., Suite 515, Washington, DC 20006   (202) 223-8196
Executive Director: Stephen G. Kellison
Purpose: To provide a liaison with state and federal government and with other professions; to provide public information about the actuarial profession and issues affecting it; to develop standards of professional conduct and practice.

American Bankers Association

1120 Connecticut Avenue, N.W., Washington, DC 20036   (202) 467-4000
Executive Vice President: Willis W. Alexander
Purpose: To enhance the ability of America's banks and bankers to serve the needs and desires of the American public; to determine commercial banking's position on proposed federal regulations and on national legislation; to set goals for the association's communications program, and to decide on issues relating to educational activities. Their ultimate goal is to promote community banks as the key provider of financial services to the local community.

American Bar Association

1155 E. 60th Street, Chicago, IL 60637   (312) 947-4000

American Business Association

1025 Connecticut Avenue N.W., Washington, DC 20036   (202) 293-5890

American Business Women's Association

9100 Ward Parkway, Kansas City, MO 64114   (816) 316-6621

American Conference of Real Estate Investment

608 13th Street, N.W., Washington, DC 20005   (202) 347-9464
Secretary: Joseph A. Baldinger
Purpose: Education organization to provide a forum dealing with real estate investments and trusts.

American Council of Life Insurance

1850 K Street, N.W., Washington, DC 20006   (202) 862-4000
Purpose: To represent the life insurance business before state and federal government, business and consumer groups, and the public; to provide information to the business on developments in public opinion and government activities.

American Economic Association

1313 21st Avenue S., Nashville, TN 37212   (615) 322-2595

American Federation of Small Businesses

407 S. Dearborn Street, Chicago, IL 60605   (312) 427-0206

American Institute of Certified Public Accountants

1620 Eye Street N.W., Washington, DC 20006   (202) 872-8190
1211 Avenue of the Americas, New York, NY 10036   (212) 575-6200
Purpose: To provide services to members, participate in the profession's self-regulatory process and formulate auditing standards.

American Law Institute

4025 Chestnut Street, Philadelphia, PA 19104   (215) 243-1600
Purpose: To promote clarification and simplification of the law and its adaptation to social needs; to secure the better administration of justice; and to encourage scholarly and scientific legal work.

American Society of Certified Life Underwriters (CLU)

270 Bryn Mawr Avenue, Bryn Mawr, PA 19010   (215) 896-4300
Director: John R. Driskill, CLU
Purpose: To assure the highest standards of competence and service in financial planning for economic security; to promote the common interest, and thereby serve the public interest by providing continuing education, ethical guidance, and public recognition for its members; to encourage and assist others in the attainment of the CLU designation.

American Society of Real Estate Counselors

430 N. Michigan Avenue, Chicago, IL 60611   (312) 329-8431
Purpose: To provide competent, disinterested and unbiased advice and guidance to people, institutions and businesses in the broad field of real estate.

American Stock Exchange

86 Trinity Place, New York, NY 10006   (212) 938-6000

American Women's Society of Certified Public Accountants

500 N. Michigan Avenue, Chicago, IL 60611   (312) 661-1700
Director: Karen Wojdyla
Purpose: To advance the professional interests of women certified public accountants.

Association for Advanced Life Underwriting

1922 F Street, Washington, DC 20006   (202) 331-6081
Director: Madelyn Guilian
Purpose: To present to Congress and government agencies the position of the advanced life underwriter and his clients on estate and gift taxes, taxation of small business, retirement plans, employee benefit plans and other subjects related to the formation of capital for security; to provide a forum in which advanced life underwriters may develop and exchange ideas and meet together in the pursuit of their common goals; to encourage the study and creation of new and constructive approaches, methods, and ideas involving the use of life insurance for the benefit of American families and businesses; to inform the public, Congress, and government agencies of the greater financial security inherent in the use of life insurance in its more advanced forms; to promote the continuing education of the advanced life underwriter.

Financial Women's Association of New York

One Bankers Trust Plaza, Level A, New York, NY 10006   (212) 764-6476
Executive Director: Ellen Davidow
Purpose: To advance and maintain high professional standards for women pursuing careers in the financial community; to attain higher recognition for women's achievements in business; and to encourage women to seek careers in the financial industry.

Health Insurance Association of America

332 So. Michigan Avenue, Chicago, IL 60604   (312) 322-0800
919 Third Avenue, New York, NY 10022   (212) 486-5520
1750 K Street, N.W., Washington, DC 20006   (202) 331-1336
President: James Moorefield
Purpose: To assist its member companies in the promotion and development of private health insurance; to promote higher standards of professionalism in the business; to broaden public recognition of the social and economic importance of health insurance and increase public understanding of the business's policies, practices, and services.

Independent Bankers Association of America

1625 Massachusetts Avenue, N.W., Suite 202, Washington, DC 20036   (202) 332-8980
Director: Kenneth A. Guenther
Purpose: To represent over 7,000 small and medium-sized banks.

Independent Insurance Agents of America, Inc.

100 Church Street, 19th Floor, New York, NY 10007   (212) 285-4250
Executive Vice President: Jeffrey M. Yates
Purpose: To provide a wide range of services to the entire IIAA membership, including legislative activities, education and research; to assist the independent agent in maintaining and strengthening his position in the marketplace.

Institute of Certified Financial Planners

3443 S. Galena, Suite 190, Denver, CO 80231   (303) 751-7600
Purpose: To develop and maintain a rigid code of ethics and standards of professional conduct; to assist members in keeping abreast of the latest financial planning techniques and to share ideas and experiences on a high professional level; to sponsor local continuing education groups throughout the country.

Institute of Chartered Financial Analysts

University of Virginia, P.O. Box 3668, Charlottesville, VA 22903   (804) 977-6600
Executive Director: O. Whitfield Broome, Jr.
Purpose: To foster high standards of education, professional development, and professional conduct in investment management, analysis and counseling. The ICFA offers a three-level study and examination program leading to the registered professional designation of Chartered Financial Analyst (CFA). It provides continuing professional education for its members and others and administers a self-regulation program.

Institute of Financial Education

111 East Wacker Drive, Chicago, IL 60601   (312) 644-3100
President: Dale C. Bottom
Purpose: To provide multilevel professional education and training programs to

savings institutions and financial services personnel; to develop educational programs to address the universal training needs of all financial service industries.

Institute of Internal Auditors

249 Maitland Avenue, Altamonte Springs, FL 32701   (305) 830-7600
Purpose: To provide comprehensive professional development activities and standards for the professional practice of internal auditing; to research and provide knowledge and information concerning auditing, including internal control and related subjects.

Institute of Management Accounting

215 City Center Building, Ann Arbor, MI 48104   (313) 662-1986
Managing Director: James Bulloch
Purpose: To enhance the professional recognition of the management accountant; to establish management accounting as a recognized profession by identifying the role of the management accountant and financial manager and the underlying body of knowledge, and by outlining a course of study by which such knowledge can be acquired; to foster higher educational standards in the field of management accounting; to establish an objective measure of an individual's knowledge and competence in the field of management accounting.

Institute of Real Estate Management

430 N. Michigan Avenue, Chicago, IL 60611   (312) 661-1930
Executive Vice President: Ronald Vukas
Purpose: To establish high standards of practice and identify for the public those firms and managers who have met stringent requirements in the areas of education, experience, and ethics; to prepare property managers to perform optimally in today's real estate industry through ongoing development of educational programs.

Insurance Institute of America and American Institute for Property & Liability Underwriters, Inc.

Providence & Sugartown Rds., Malvern, PA 19355   (215) 644-2100
President: Dr. Edwin S. Overman, CPCU
Purpose: To identify and meet educational needs of people in all segments of property liability insurance, developing programs to meet these needs.

International Association for Financial Planning, Inc.

5775 Peachtree Dunwoody Road, Suite 120-C, Atlanta, GA 30342   (404) 252-9600
Executive Director: Hubert L. Harris
Purpose: To enable the individual IAFP member to further his or her professional development through a wide variety of membership services; to promote the concept of financial planning to the public and to the members of the financial services industry.

The International College of Real Estate Consulting Professionals

1908 First Bank Place West, Minneapolis, MN 55402   (612) 665-6280
President: William A. Russell
Purpose: To develop new sources of information for professional real estate consultants; to recognize experienced consultants, and provide continuing education for members through seminars, journals and research projects. The college also serves as a referral service for its members.

Investment Company Institute

1775 K Street N.W., Washington, DC 20006   (202) 293-7700
President: David Silver
Purpose: To represent its members in matters of federal and state legislation, regulation, taxation, and the effective operation of fund companies; to provide educational seminars on new funds and new packages for existing fund products, for example, how money market funds are coping with lower interest rates and new competition, the small corporate plan market, how the shareholder can be better served, and how the products will be sold.

The Life Insurance Marketing and Research Association

P.O. Box 208, Hartford, CT 06141   (203) 677-0033
President: George G. Joseph
Purpose: To support and enhance the marketing function of its member companies through industry-sponsored research and services.

Life Office Management Association

100 Colony Square, Atlanta, GA 30361   (404) 892-7272
President: Lynn G. Merritt
Purpose: To improve the management of insurance company operations in home and field offices through cooperative research and information exchange.

The Life Underwriter Training Council

1922 F Street, N.W., Washington, DC 20006   (202) 393-5240
Purpose: To contribute to the constant improvement of the quality of life underwriting by engaging in educational and training activities for field life insurance underwriters; by cooperating in the educational and training activities of associations of life underwriters, training departments of companies, the American College, the American Society, other institutional groups, recognized educational institutions and others interested in the education and training of those who sell and service life insurance; and by serving as a clearinghouse for information on life underwriter education and training.

Million Dollar Round Table

2340 River Road, Suite 300, Des Plaines, IL 60018   (312) 298-1120
Executive Vice President: Roderick L. Geer
Purpose: To foster a highly ethical approach to life insurance sales and services.

Mortgage Bankers Association of America

1125 15th Street, N.W., Washington, DC 20005   (202) 861-6500
Executive Vice President: Dr. Mark J. Riedy
Purpose: Nationwide trade association devoted exclusively to the field of real estate finance.

National Association of Accountants

919 Third Avenue, New York, NY 10022   (212) 754-9700
Executive Director: Robert L. Shultis
Purpose: To develop the individual management accountant professionally; to provide business management with the most advanced techniques and procedures. The NAA is a nonprofit educational organization.

National Association of Bank Women, Inc.

500 N. Michigan Avenue, Suite 1400, Chicago, IL 60611   (312) 661-1700
Executive Vice President: Phyllis M. Haeger
Purpose: To advance the careers of women bankers; to encourage continued professional excellence and promote banking as a career for women; to develop and administer training and career planning programs for bankers.

National Association of Business Economists

28349 Chagrin Blvd., Cleveland, OH 44122   (216) 464-7986
President: Don R. Conlan
Purpose: Professional society of persons with an active interest in business economics who are employed by private, institutional, or governmental concerns in the area of business-related economic analysis.

National Association of Enrolled Federal Tax Accountants

6108 N. Harding Avenue, Chicago, IL 60569   (312) 473-5577
Executive Director: Seymour A. Rish

National Association of Estate Planning Councils

2017 Walnut Street, Philadelphia, PA 19103   (215) 569-3650
Purpose: To develop estate planning so that it is of paramount benefit to the community as a whole; to enable life underwriters, trust officers, attorneys, and accountants to become better acquainted; to develop mutual trust and understanding; to foster cooperation among disciplines.

National Association of Health Underwriters

45 North Avenue, P.O. Box 278, Hartland, WI 53029   (414) 367-3248
Executive Vice President: John K. Pardee
Purpose: A professional society composed of licensed agents, general agents, managers, brokers, and others engaged in the marketing and servicing of health and disability income insurance; to further develop the professionalism and education of its members.

National Association of Insurance Women

1847 E. 15th, Tulsa, OK 74104   (918) 744-5195
Executive Director: Mary Lynn Clairborne
Purpose: To promote insurance education and support professional advancement.

National Association of Investment Clubs

1515 E. 11 Mile Rd., Royal Oak, MI 48067   (313) 543-0612

National Association of Life Companies

3340 Peachtree Road, Suite 1060, Atlanta, GA 30026   (404) 262-3737
Executive Vice President: S. Roy Woodall, Jr.
Purpose: To provide a forum for younger progressive companies for the discussion, study, and solution of common problems; to keep members informed of pertinent legislative matters.

National Association of Life Underwriters

1922 F Street, N.W., Washington, DC 20006   (202) 331-6000
Executive Vice President: Jack E. Bobo
Purpose: To protect and advance the interests of those who own and sell private life

and health insurance and the American Agency System of distributing insurance products; to enhance the professionalism of those engaged in life underwriting.

National Association of Real Estate Investment Trusts

1101 17th Street, N.W., Washington, DC 20036   (202) 785-8717

National Association of Realtors

777 14th Street, N.W., Washington, DC 20005   (202) 383-1000
430 N. Michigan Avenue, Chicago, IL 60611   (312) 329-8200
Executive Vice President: Dr. Jack Carlson
Purpose: To create unity in the real estate profession; to encourage the compilation of relevant information concerning real estate; to protect and promote private owner-ship of real property; to establish professional standards of practice.

The National Association of Securities Dealers

1735 K Street N.W., Washington, DC 20006   (202) 833-7200

National Center for Financial Education

2107 Van Ness Avenue, Suite 301, San Francisco, CA 94102   (415) 474-8496
President and Executive Director: Loren Dunton
Purpose: A nonprofit corporation for public education, dedicated to helping consum-ers do a better job of saving, investing, insuring, and planning their financial futures.

The National Savings and Loan League

1101 15th St, N.W., Suite 400, Washington, DC 20005   (202) 331-0270
Executive Director: William L. Reynolds
Purpose: To represent the nation's progressive thrift institutions, including savings and loan associations and savings banks. It is primarily a lobbying and information organization.

National Security Traders' Association

One World Trade Center, Suite 4511, New York, NY 10048   (212) 524-0484
*Purpose: To foster the highest standards of business conduct and ethics in the over-the-counter (**OTC**) market.*

National Society of Accountants for Cooperatives

6320 Augusta Drive, Springfield, VA 22150   (703) 569-3088
Executive Director: Nelda Griffin
Purpose: To provide educational services to accountants, auditors, and financial management.

National Society of Public Accountants

1010 North Fairfax Street, Alexandria, VA 22314   (703) 549-6400
Executive Director: Stanley H. Stearman, CAE
Purpose: To improve the accounting profession and the status of the individual practitioner.

No-Load Mutual Fund Association, Inc.

11 Penn Plaza, Suite 2204, New York, NY 10001   (212) 563-4540
Executive Director: Laura J. Berger
Purpose: A nonprofit organization founded for the purpose of broadening public awareness and understanding of no-load mutual funds.

Professional Insurance Agents

400 N. Washington St., Alexandria, VA 22314   (703) 836-9340
Executive Vice President: Trevor A. White
Purpose: To promote the welfare and protect the future of its members and the American Agency System so that both may better serve the insurance buying public.

Real Estate Securities and Syndication Institute

430 N. Michigan Avenue, Chicago, IL 60611   (312) 670-6760
Executive Vice President: William A. Collis
Purpose: To raise standards and improve skills of licensed realtors and broker/dealers actively engaged in real estate syndication.

Realtors National Marketing Institute

430 N. Michigan Avenue, Chicago, IL 60611   (312) 670-3780
Purpose: To enhance the professional competence of its designees, candidates, other realtors, and realtor associates in the marketing of real estate; to provide special recognition and service for designees.

Risk and Insurance Management Society

205 East 42nd Street, New York, NY 10017   (212) 286-9292
Executive Director: Ron Judd
Purpose: To foster recognition of the contribution of the risk management function within the corporate environment; to encourage professionalism on the part of risk management practitioners.

Securities Industry Association

120 Broadway, New York, NY 10271   (212) 608-1500
490 L'Enfant Plaza East, S.W., Washington, DC 20024   (202) 488-4664
President: Edward I. O'Brien
Purpose: To provide investors and issuers with a wide spectrum of securities and investment banking services; to speak with a unified voice in representing the business interests of its members, both on federal and state levels; to provide a broad range of management services, enabling members to operate more efficiently and effectively; and to serve as a medium through which ideas, experiences, and information may be exchanged for the mutual benefit of the membership.

Society of Actuaries

500 Park Blvd., Itasca, IL 50143   (312) 773-3010
Executive Director: John E. O'Connor, Jr.
Purpose: An educational research association for the actuarial profession.

Society of Chartered Property and Casualty Underwriters

Kahler Hall, Providence Road, CB No. 9, Malvern, PA 19355   (215) 648-0440
Executive Vice President: James W. Hamilton
Purpose: To maintain an effective, participative, and progressive organization; to promote visibility and acceptance of the CPCU designation as a highly respected certification in an essential profession; to foster professionalism in insurance, risk management, and related services; to encourage responsible participation in industry matters affecting the public interest.

U.S. Chamber of Commerce, National Headquarters

1650 H Street, N.W., Washington, DC 20062   (202) 463-5391
President: Richard Lesher

The United States League of Savings Institutions

1709 New York Avenue, N.W., Suite 801, Washington, DC 20006   (202) 637-8900
111 East Wacker Drive, Chicago, IL 60601   (312) 644-3100
President: William B. O'Connell
Purpose: To further the concepts of thrift and home ownership by serving savings institutions today and helping them prepare for the future.

Women's Council of Realtors

430 N. Michigan Avenue, Chicago, IL 60611   (312) 329-8483
Executive Vice President: Catherine Collins
Purpose: To provide a support system dedicated to preparing women for leadership roles in business and community services through its network of state and local chapters.

7.02 **Government Directory**

THE PRESIDENTIAL ADMINISTRATION

President of the United States: Ronald Reagan	(202) 456-1414
Vice President of the United States: George Bush	(202) 456-2326

The Cabinet

Secretary of State: George P. Shultz	(202) 632-4910
Secretary of the Treasury: James Baker	(202) 566-2533
Secretary of Defense: Caspar W. Weinberger	(202) 695-5261
Attorney General: Edwin Meese, III	(202) 633-2001
Secretary of the Interior: Donald Hodel	(202) 343-7351
Secretary of Agriculture: John R. Block	(202) 447-3631
Secretary of Commerce: Malcolm Baldridge	(202) 377-2112
Secretary of Labor: William E. Brock	(202) 523-8271
Secretary of Health & Human Services: Margaret Heckler	(202) 245-7000
Secretary of Housing & Urban Development: Samuel R. Pierce, Jr.	(202) 755-6417
Secretary of Transportation: Elizabeth Dole	(202) 426-1111
Secretary of Energy: John Herrington	(202) 252-2610
Secretary of Education: William Bennett	(202) 426-6420

Cabinet Rank Members

Director of the CIA: William J. Casey	(202) 351-1100
Director of Office of Management & Budget: David A. Stockman	(202) 395-4840

FEDERAL GOVERNMENT

Executive Branch

The White House

1600 Pennsylvania Avenue N.W., Washington, DC 20500   (202) 456-1414

Council of Economic Advisors

Old Executive Office Building, Washington, DC 20506   (202) 395-5108

Office of Management & Budget

Old Executive Office Building, Washington, DC 20500   (202) 395-3080

Office of Policy Development

Old Executive Office Building, Washington, DC 20500   (202) 456-2562

Regulatory Information Service Center

2100 M Street N.W., Washington, DC 20037   (202) 653-7246

Department of Agriculture

14th Street & Independence Ave. S.W., Washington, DC 20250   (202) 447-2791

Department of Commerce

14th & E Streets S.W., Washington, DC 20230   (202) 377-4901

Bureau of the Census/Data User Services Div.

Silver Hill & Suitland Rds., Suitland, MD 20233   (301) 568-1200

Bureau of Economic Analysis

1401 K Street N.W., Washington, DC 20230   (202) 523-0793

Economic Development Administration

Commerce Building, Washington, DC 20230   (202) 377-5113

Fraud Hot Line (Economic Development)

Commerce Building, Washington, DC 20230   (800) 424-5197

Social Security Research

1875 Connecticut Avenue N.W., Washington, DC 20530   (202) 673-5602

Department of Housing & Urban Development

451 Seventh St. S.W., Washington, DC 20410   (202) 755-6420

Fraud Hot Line (Housing)

451 Seventh St. S.W., Washington, DC 20410   (800) 424-8590

Department of the Interior

C & 19th Streets N.W., Washington, DC 20240   (202) 343-3171

Department of Justice

    Tenth Street & Constitution Avenue N.W., Washington, DC 20530   (202) 633-2007

Antitrust Division

    Tenth Street & Constitution Avenue N.W., Washington, DC 20530   (202) 633-2481

Community Relations Service

    5550 Friendship Boulevard, Chevy Chase, MD 20815   (301) 492-5939

Department of Labor

    200 Constitution Avenue N.W., Washington, DC 20210   (202) 523-7316

Department of State

    2201 C Street N.W., Washington, DC 20520   (202) 632-6575

Department of Transportation

    400 Seventh Street S.W., Washington, DC 20590   (202) 426-4321

Department of the Treasury

    15th Street & Pennsylvania Avenue N.W., Washington, DC 20220   (202) 566-2041

Internal Revenue Service

    1111 Constitution Avenue N.W., Washington, DC 20224   (202) 566-4743

    • Central Region

        555 Main Street, Cincinnati, OH 45202   (513) 684-3613

    • Mid-Atlantic Region

        2 Penn Center Plaza, Philadelphia, PA 19102   (215) 597-2040

    • Midwestern Region

        1 N. Wacker Drive, Chicago, IL 60606   (312) 886-5600

    • North Atlantic Region

        90 Church Street, New York, NY 10007   (212) 264-7061

    • Southeastern Region

        1365 Peachtree St. N.E., Atlanta, GA 30303   (404) 221-6048

    • Southwestern Region

        7839 Churchill Way, Dallas, TX 75251   (214) 729-5855

    • Western Region

        525 Market Street, San Francisco, CA 94105   (415) 974-9492

IRS Business & Pension Statistics

    1111 Constitution Avenue N.W., Washington, DC 20224   (202) 376-0151

Legislative Branch

The Senate

Capitol Building, Washington, DC 20510 · (202) 224-3121

The House of Representatives

Capitol Building, Washington, DC 20515 · (202) 224-3121

Congressional Budget Office

300 D Street S.W., Washington, DC 20515 · (202) 226-2921

General Accounting Office

441 G Street N.W., Washington, DC 20548 · (202) 275-2812

Library of Congress

10 First Street S.E., Washington, DC 20540 · (202) 287-5108

Selected Congressional Committees

Senate Committees:

Banking, Housing & Urban Affairs

5300 Dirksen Building, Washington, DC 20510 · (202) 224-7391

Budget

204 Carroll Arms Annex, Washington, DC 20510 · (202) 224-0642

Finance

2227 Dirksen Building, Washington, DC 20510 · (202) 224-4515

Small Business

424 Russell Building, Washington, DC 20510 · (202) 224-5175

Select Committee on Ethics

113 Carroll Arms Annex, Washington, DC 20510 · (202) 224-2981

House Committees:

Budget

214 House Annex I, Washington, DC 20515 · (202) 225-7200

Education & Labor

2181 Rayburn Building, Washington, DC 20515 · (202) 225-4527

Energy & Commerce

2125 Rayburn Building, Washington, DC 20515 · (202) 225-2927

Science & Technology

2321 Rayburn Building, Washington, DC 20515 · (202) 225-6371

Small Business

    2361 Rayburn Building, Washington, DC 20515   (202) 225-5821

Ways & Means

    1102 Longworth Building, Washington, DC 20515   (202) 225-3625

Joint Committees:

Joint Economic Committee

    G133 Dirksen Building, Washington, DC 20510   (202) 224-5171

Joint Committee on Taxation

    1015 Longworth Building, Washington, DC 20515   (202) 225-3621

Judicial Branch

Administrative Office of the U.S. Courts

    Washington, DC 20544   (202) 633-6097

Federal Judicial Center

    1520 H Street N.W., Washington, DC 20005   (202) 633-6011

Supreme Court of the U.S.

    One First Street N.E., Washington, DC 20453   (202) 252-3000

U.S. Court of Claims

    717 Madison Place N.W., Washington, DC 20005   (202) 633-7257

U.S. Tax Court

    400 Second Street N.W., Washington, DC 20217   (202) 376-2754

Independent Agencies & Commissions

Board of Governors of the Federal Reserve System

    Federal Reserve Building, Washington, DC 20551   (202) 452-3000

Chamber of Commerce of the U.S.

    1615 H Street N.W., Washington, DC 20062   (202) 659-6000

Commodity Futures Trading Commission

    2033 K Street N.W., Washington, DC 20581   (202) 254-8630

Federal Financing Bank

    15th Street & Pennsylvania Avenue N.W., Washington, DC 20220   (202) 566-2045

Federal Home Loan Bank Board

    1700 G Street N.W., Washington, DC 20552   (202) 577-6000

Federal Home Loan Mortgage Corp.

    1776 G Street N.W., Washington, DC 20552   (202) 789-4448

Federal Reserve System

Federal Reserve Building, Washington, DC 20551   (202) 452-3204

Federal Trade Commission

Pennsylvania & Sixth Street N.W., Washington, DC 20580   (202) 523-3598

Federal Trade Commission Consumer Protection Bureau

Pennsylvania & Sixth Street N.W., Washington, DC 20580   (202) 724-1870

Interstate Commerce Commission

12th Street & Constitution Avenue N.W., Washington, DC 20423   (202) 275-7252

Legal Services Corp.

733 15th Street N.W., Washington, DC 20005   (202) 272-4000

Securities & Exchange Commission

500 N. Capitol Street, Washington, DC 20549   (202) 272-2650

     Region 1: 26 Federal Plaza, New York, NY 10278   (212) 264-1636

     Region 2: 150 Causeway Street, Boston, MA 02114   (617) 223-2721

     Region 3: 1375 Peachtree Street N.E., Atlanta, GA 30367   (404) 881-4768

     Region 4: 219 S. Dearborn Street, Chicago, IL 60604   (312) 353-7390

     Region 5: 411 W. Seventh Street, Ft. Worth, TX 76102   (817) 334-3821

     Region 6: 410 17th Street, Denver, CO 80202   (303) 837-2071

     Region 7: 10960 Wilshire Blvd., Los Angeles, CA 90024   (213) 473-4511

     Region 8: 915 Second Avenue, Seattle, WA 98174   (206) 442-7990

     Region 9: Ballston Center Tower 3, Arlington, VA 22203   (202) 724-0424

7.03 **Federal Information Centers**

For information about government agencies and programs or for help on any question about the federal government, contact the nearest federal information center.

Alaska	Federal Building and U.S. Courthouse 701 C Street, Anchorage AK 99513 (907) 271-3650
Arizona	Federal Building 230 N. First Avenue, Phoenix AZ 85025 (602) 261-3313
California	Federal Building 300 N. Los Angeles Street, Los Angeles CA 90012 (213) 668-3800
	Federal Building 650 Capitol Mall, Sacramento CA 95814 (916) 440-3344
	Federal Building and U.S. Courthouse 450 Golden Gate Avenue, San Francisco CA 94102 (415) 556-6600
Colorado	Federal Center Building 41 Denver CO 80225 (303) 234-7181
Florida	Federal Building 144 First Avenue S., St. Petersburg FL 33701 (813) 893-3495
Georgia	Federal Building and U.S. Courthouse 75 Spring Street, N.W., Atlanta GA 30303 (404) 221-6891
Hawaii	Federal Building 300 Ala Moana Boulevard, Honolulu HI 96850 (808) 546-8620
Illinois	E. M. Dirksen Building 219 S. Dearborn Street, Chicago IL 60604 (312) 353-4242
Indiana	Federal Building 575 N. Pennsylvania, Indianapolis IN 46204 (317) 269-7373
Iowa	Federal Building 210 Walnut Street, Des Moines IA 50309 (515) 284-4448

Kansas	Federal Building and U.S. Courthouse 444 S.E. Quincy, Topeka KS 66683 (913) 295-2866
Louisiana	U.S Custom House 423 Canal Street, New Orleans LA 70130 (504) 589-6696
Maryland	Federal Building 31 Hopkins Plaza, Baltimore MD 21201 (301) 962-4980
Massachusetts	J. W. McCormack Post Office and U.S. Courthouse Boston MA 02109 (617) 223-7121
Michigan	Federal Building 477 Michigan Avenue, Detroit MI 48226 (313) 226-7016
Minnesota	Federal Building and U.S. Courthouse 110 S. Fourth Street, Minneapolis MN 55401 (612) 349-5333
Missouri	Federal Building 601 E. Twelfth Street, Kansas City MO 64106 (816) 374-2466 Federal Building 1520 Market Street, St. Louis MO 63103 (314) 425-4106
Nebraska	U.S. Courthouse and Post Office 215 N. 17th Street, Omaha NE 68102 (402) 221-3353
New Jersey	Federal Building 970 Broad Street, Newark NJ 07102 (201) 645-3600
New Mexico	Federal Building and U.S. Courthouse 500 Gold Avenue S.W., Albuquerque NM 87102 (505) 766-3091
New York	Federal Building 111 W. Huron, Buffalo NY 14202 (716) 846-4010 Federal Building 26 Federal Plaza, New York NY 10278 (212) 264-4464
Ohio	Federal Building 550 Main Street, Cincinnati OH 45202 (513) 684-2801 Federal Building 1240 E. Ninth Street, Cleveland OH 44199 (216) 522-4040

Oklahoma U.S. Courthouse and Post Office
201 N.W. Third Street, Oklahoma City OK 73102
(405) 231-4868

Oregon Federal Building
1220 S.W. Third Avenue, Portland OR 97204
(503) 221-2222

Pennsylvania Federal Building
600 Arch Street, Philadelphia PA 19106
(215) 597-7042

Federal Building
1000 Liberty Avenue, Pittsburgh PA 15222
(412) 644-3456

Texas Lanham Federal Building
819 Taylor Street, Fort Worth TX 76102
(817) 334-3624

Federal Building and U.S. Courthouse
515 Rusk Avenue, Houston TX 77002
(713) 229-2552

Utah Federal Building
125 S. State Street, Salt Lake City UT 84138
(801) 524-5353

Virginia Federal Building
200 Granby Mall, Norfolk VA 23510
(804) 441-3101

Washington Federal Building
915 Second Avenue, Seattle WA 98174
(206) 442-0570

CHAPTER 8

Quick Reference Data

CONTENTS

Every day we refer to most of the miscellaneous information contained within this section, but we often have to check several sources to get it. To eliminate all this tiresome paper shuffling, we've placed this information in one convenient location. The contents include:

U.S. and International Area Codes

Instructions for Making International Calls

International Time Differences

Metric Conversion Charts

Population of the U.S. (1970 to 1980)

A Three-Year Calendar for Long-Term Planning

8.01 Long Distance Area Codes of Major Cities

ALABAMA		Bell	213	Coachella	619
All locations	205	Bellflower	213	Colton	714
ALASKA		Berkeley	415	Colusa	916
All locations	907	Beverly Hills	213	Compton	213
ARIZONA		Big Bear Lake	714	Concord	415
All locations	602	Big Pine	619	Corona	714
ARKANSAS		Bishop	619	Corona del Mar	714
All locations	501	Blythe	619	Coronado	619
		Boron	619	Costa Mesa	714
CALIFORNIA		Borrego	619	Covina	818
Alameda	415	Borrego Springs	619	Crowley Lake	619
Albany	415	Brawley	619	Cucamonga	714
Alhambra	818	Brea	714	Culver City	213
Alpine		Bridgeport	619	Cupertino	408
(Alpine Co.)	916	Buena Park	714	Cypress	714
Alpine		Burbank (LA Co.)	818	Daggett	619
(San Diego Co.)	619	Burbank		Daly City	415
Altadena	818	(Santa Clara Co.)	408	Dana Point	714
Alviso	408	Burlingame	415	Davis	916
Anaheim	714	Calexico	619	Death Valley	619
Angels Camp	209	California City	619	Delano	805
Antioch	415	Callpatria	619	Del Mar	619
Apple Valley	619	Camarillo	805	Descanso	619
Arcadia	213	Cambria	805	Desert Hot Springs	619
Arlington	714	Campbell	408	Dinuba	209
Arrowhead	714	Campo	619	Downey	213
Arroyo Grande	805	Canoga Park	818	Duarte	818
Artesia	213	Capistrano Beach	714	Dulzura	619
Atascadero	805	Cardiff	619	Dunsmuir	916
Atherton	415	Carlsbad	619	Earlimart	805
Auburn	916	Carmel	408	Earp	714
Avila	805	Carmichael	916	East Los Angeles	213
Azusa	213	Carpinteria	805	El Cajon	619
Baker	619	Castro Valley	415	El Centro	619
Bakersfield	805	Castroville	408	El Cerrito	415
Balboa	714	Cathedral City	619	El Monte	818
Baldwin Park	213	Chatsworth	818	El Segundo	213
Banning	714	Chico	916	Elsinore	714
Barstow	619	China Lake	619	Emeryville	415
Bass Lake	209	Chowchilla	209	Encinitas	619
Beaumont	714	Chula Vista	619	Encino	818
		Claremont	714	Escondido	619
		Clovis	209	Etiwanda	714

(Continued)

Long Distance Area Codes of Major Cities

City	Code	City	Code	City	Code
Eureka	707	La Verne	714	Pasadena	818
Exeter	209	Lemon Grove	619	Paso Robles	805
Fairfax	415	Livermore	415	Pebble Beach	408
Fairfield	707	Lodi	209	Perris	714
Fallbrook	619	Lomita	213	Petaluma	707
Fillmore	805	Lompoc	805	Pico Rivera	213
Folsom	916	Lone Pine	619	Piedmont	415
Fontana	714	Long Beach	213	Pismo Beach	805
Fort Bragg	707	Los Angeles	213	Pittsburg	415
Frazier Park	805	Lynwood	213	Placerville	916
Fresno	209	Madera	209	Point Mugu	805
Fullerton	714	Manhattan Beach	213	Pomona	714
Furnace Creek	619	Marysville	916	Port Hueneme	805
Gardena	213	Maywood	213	Porterville	209
Garden Grove	714	Merced	209	Poway	619
Gilman Hot Springs	714	Mill Valley	415	Ramona	619
Gilroy	408	Millbrae	415	Rancho Santa Fe	619
Glendale	818	Modesto	209	Red Bluff	916
Glendora	818	Mojave	805	Redding	916
Grass Valley	916	Monrovia	818	Redlands	714
Hanford	209	Montebello	213	Redondo	213
Hawthorne	213	Monterey	408	Redwood City	415
Hayward	415	Montrose	818	Reedley	209
Hemet	714	Moorpark	805	Reseda	818
Hermosa Beach	213	Morro Bay	805	Rialto	714
Hollister	408	Mountain View	415	Richmond	415
Holtville	619	Mulberry	408	Riverside	714
Hueneme	805	Napa	707	Rosamond	805
Huntington Beach	213	National City	619	Rosemead	818
Huntington Park	818	Needles	619	Sacramento	916
Idyllwild	714	Newhall	805	Salinas	408
Imperial Beach	619	Newport Beach	714	San Anselmo	415
Indio	619	Norco	714	San Bernardino	714
Inglewood	213	North Hollywood	818	San Bruno	415
Inyokern	619	Northridge	818	San Clemente	714
Jacumba	619	Norwalk	213	San Diego	619
Jamul	619	Oakland	415	San Fernando	818
Joshua Tree	619	Oceanside	619	San Francisco	415
Julian	619	Ojai	805	San Gabriel	818
June Lake	619	Ontario	714	Sanger	209
Kernville	619	Orange	714	San Jacinto	714
Kingsburg	209	Orinda	415	San Jose	408
La Canada	818	Oxnard	805	San Juan Capistrano	714
La Crescenta	818	Pacific Beach	619	San Leandro	415
Laguna Beach	714	Pacoima	818	San Luis Obispo	805
La Habra	213	Pala	619	San Mateo	415
La Jolla	619	Palm Desert	619	San Pedro	213
Lake Arrowhead	714	Palm Springs	619	San Rafael	415
Lakewood	213	Palmdale	805	San Simeon	805
La Mesa	619	Palo Alto	415	Santa Ana	714
Lancaster	805	Paradise	916	Santa Barbara	805
La Puente	818	Paramount	213	Santa Clara	408

Long Distance Area Codes of Major Cities

Santa Cruz	408	Westmorland	619	Tallahassee	904
Santa Fe Springs	213	Whittier	213	Tampa	813
Santa Maria	805	Willows	916	West Palm Beach	305
Santa Monica	213	Wilmington	213	**GEORGIA**	
Santa Paula	805	Woodland	916	Athens	404
Santa Rosa	707	Woodland Hills	818	Atlanta	404
San Ysidro	619	Woodside	415	Augusta	404
Saticoy	805	Yreka	916	Columbus	404
Saugus	805	Yuba City	916	Decatur	404
Sausalito	415	Yucaipa	714	La Grange	404
Seal Beach	213	**COLORADO**		Macon	912
Selma	209	All locations	303	Norcross	404
Sequoia	209	**CONNECTICUT**		Rome	404
Sherman Oaks	818	All locations	203	Savannah	912
Shoshone	619			Stockbridge	404
Sierra Madre	818	**DELAWARE**		Valdosta	912
Simi Valley	805	All locations	302	**HAWAII**	
Soledad	408	**DISTRICT OF COLUMBIA**		All locations	808
Sonoma	707	Washington	202	**IDAHO**	
Sonora	209			All locations	208
South Gate	213	**FLORIDA**		**ILLINOIS**	
Stockton	209	Apalachicola	904	Arlington Heights	312
Suisun	707	Atlantic Beach	904	Bloomington	309
Sunnymead	714	Bowling Green	813	Broadview	312
Sunnyvale	408	Cape Canaveral	305	Calumet City	312
Taft	805	Cape Kennedy	305	Calumet Park	312
Tahoe City	916	Cocoa Beach	305	Centralia	618
Tecate	619	Coral Gables	305	Champaign	217
Tehachapi	805	Daytona Beach	904	Chicago	312
Temecula	714	De Land	904	Chillicothe	309
Temple City	818	Edgewater	904	Columbia	618
Thousand Oaks	805	Everglades	813	Decatur	217
Thousand Palms	619	Fort Lauderdale	305	Des Plaines	312
Torrance	213	Fort Pierce	305	East St. Louis	618
Tracy	209	Gulf Port	813	Elmwood Park	312
Trona	619	Hialeah	305	Evanston	312
Truckee	916	Hollywood	305	Glen Carbon	618
Tulare	209	Inverness	904	Harrisburg	618
Turlock	209	Jacksonville	904	Havana	309
Tustin	714	Key Largo	305	Highland Park	312
Twentynine Palms	619	Key West	305	Joliet	815
Ukiah	707	Miami	305	Lake Forest	312
Upland	714	Miami Beach	305	Lansing	312
Vallejo	707	Orlando	305	La Salle	815
Van Nuys	818	Palm Beach	305	Madison	618
Venice	213	Pensacola	904	Morris	815
Ventura	805	St. Augustine	904	North Chicago	312
Victorville	619	St. Cloud	305	Oak Park	312
Visalia	209	St. Petersburg	813	Park Forest	312
Walnut Creek	415	Sarasota	813	Park Ridge	312
Warner Springs	619	South Miami	305		
Watsonville	408				

(Continued)

Long Distance Area Codes of Major Cities

Peoria	309	Lexington	606	Stoneham	617
Plainfield	815	Louisville	502	Stoughton	617
Quincy	217	Paducah	502	Taunton	617
Rock Falls	815	Shelbyville	502	Wakefield	617
Rock Island	309	Winchester	606	Waltham	617
Rockford	815			Warren	413
Seneca	815	**LOUISIANA**		Wellesley	617
Springfield	217	Baton Rouge	504	Westfield	413
Sterling	815	Lake Charles	318	Westminster	617
Troy	618	Metairie	504	Whitman	617
Waukegan	312	New Orleans	504	Wilmington	617
Winnetka	312	Shreveport	318	Winchester	617
				Worcester	617
INDIANA		**MAINE**			
Evansville	812	All locations	207	**MICHIGAN**	
Fort Wayne	219			Ann Arbor	313
Gary	219	**MARYLAND**		Battle Creek	616
Hammond	219	All locations	301	Bay City	517
Indianapolis	317			Benton Harbor	616
Kokomo	317	**MASSACHUSETTS**		Cheboygan	616
Michigan City	219	Arlington	617	Dearborn	313
South Bend	219	Boston	617	Detroit	313
Warsaw	219	Brockton	617	East Lansing	517
		Brookline	617	Escanaba	906
IOWA		Cambridge	617	Flint	313
Cedar Rapids	319	Chicopee	413	Grand Rapids	616
Council Bluffs	712	Concord	617	Jackson	517
Davenport	319	Dorchester	617	Kalamazoo	616
Des Moines	515	Dover	617	Lansing	517
Dubuque	319	East Boston	617	Lincoln Park	313
Mason City	515	Fall River	617	Livonia	313
		Falmouth	617	Marquette	906
KANSAS		Holyoke	413	Milford	313
Abilene	913	Hyannis	617	Muskegon	616
Arkansas City	316	Hyde Park	617	New Haven	313
Atchison	913	Ipswich	617	Oak Park	313
Augusta	316	Jamaica Plain	617	Sterling Heights	313
Bloomington	913	Lawrence	617	Warren	313
Chanute	316	Lexington	617		
Coffeyville	316	Lowell	617	**MINNESOTA**	
Dodge City	316	Milford	617	Duluth	218
El Dorado	316	Milton	617	Minneapolis	612
Garden City	316	New Bedford	617	New Prague	612
Hutchinson	316	Newton	617	Northfield	507
Kansas City	913	Northhampton	413	Plainview	507
Lawrence	913	Peabody	617	Proctor	218
Leavenworth	913	Plymouth	617	Red Wing	612
Manhattan	913	Quincy	617	Rochester	507
Salina	913	Randolph	617	St. Cloud	612
Topeka	913	Reading	617	St. Louis Park	612
Wichita	316	Rockland	617	St. Paul	612
		Salem	617	Sauk Rapids	612
KENTUCKY		Southwick	413	Warren	218
Ashland	606	Springfield	413		

Long Distance Area Codes of Major Cities

MISSISSIPPI		Jersey City	201	Hicksville	516
All locations	601	Kenilworth	201	Hudson	518
		Lakewood	201	Hyde Park	914
MISSOURI		Linwood	609	Ithaca	607
Bolivar	417	Long Branch	201	Kingston	914
Branson	417	Lyndhurst	201	Lackawanna	716
Chillicothe	816	Medford	609	Lake George	518
Columbia	314	Middletown	201	Lake Success	516
Fort Leonard Wood	314	Montclair	201	Long Beach	516
Grandview	816	Mount Holly	609	Manhattan	212
Independence	816	Newark	201	Mount Vernon	914
Joplin	417	New Brunswick	201	New Rochelle	914
Kansas City	816	Northfield	609	Niagara Falls	716
Oran	314	Oakhurst	201	Ossining	914
Poplar Bluff	314	Orange	201	Oswego	315
St. Joseph	816	Paterson	201	Pelham	914
St. Louis	314	Perth Amboy	201	Potsdam	315
Springfield	417	Plainfield	201	Poughkeepsie	914
University City	314	Princeton	609	Queens	718
Warren	413	Ridgewood	201	Rochester	716
Westfield	413	Salem	609	Rockville Centre	516
		Springfield	201	Roosevelt	516
MONTANA		Trenton	609	Rye	914
All locations	406	Union	201	Schenectady	518
		Vineland	609	Staten Island	718
NEBRASKA		Wayne	201	Syracuse	315
Grand Island	308	Westfield	201	Ticonderoga	518
Hastings	402	West New York	201	Troy	518
Lincoln	402	Wharton	201	Utica	315
North Platte	308	Wyckoff	201	West Point	914
Omaha	402			White Plains	914
		NEW MEXICO		Yonkers	914
NEVADA		All locations	505		
All locations	702			**NORTH CAROLINA**	
		NEW YORK		Asheboro	919
NEW HAMPSHIRE		Albany	518	Asheville	704
All locations	603	Amsterdam	518	Burlington	919
		Apalachin	607	Carthage	919
NEW JERSEY		Babylon	516	Charlotte	704
Allentown	609	Binghampton	607	Durham	919
Asbury Park	201	Bronx	212	Fayetteville	919
Atlantic City	609	Brooklyn	718	Goldsboro	919
Bayonne	201	Buffalo	716	Greensboro	919
Caldwell	201	Carthage	315	Havelock	919
Camden	609	Corning	607	Kannapolis	704
Delaware	201	Elmira	607	Newton	704
Dover	201	Far Rockaway	212	Raleigh	919
East Orange	201	Flanders	516	Rocky Mount	919
Elizabeth	201	Fulton	315	Sparta	919
Englewood	201	Garden City	516	Valdese	704
Garfield	201	Goshen	914	Wendell	919
Glen Ridge	201	Grand Island	716	Wilson	919
Hanover	201	Greenwich	518		
Hoboken	201				

(Continued)

Long Distance Area Codes of Major Cities

Winston-Salem	919	Shawnee	405	Gainesville	901
		Stillwater	405	Knoxville	615
NORTH DAKOTA		Tulsa	918	Madison	615
All locations	701	Wynona	918	Memphis	901
				Nashville	615
OHIO		**OREGON**		Oak Ridge	615
Akron	216	All locations	503		
Amherst	216			**TEXAS**	
Ashtabula	216	**PENNSYLVANIA**		Abilene	915
Brunswick	216	Allegheny	412	Alamo	512
Camden	513	Allentown	215	Amarillo	806
Canton	216	Bellevue	412	Arlington	817
Cincinatti	513	Bethlehem	215	Austin	512
Cleveland	216	Bristol	215	Beaumont	409
Columbus	614	Brook Haven	215	Bonham	214
Dayton	513	Chester	215	Bowie	817
East Cleveland	216	Clarion	814	Brownsville	512
Euclid	216	Duquesne	412	Carthage	214
Garfield Heights	216	Easton	215	Corpus Christi	512
Germantown	513	Erie	814	Crockett	713
Hamilton	513	Germantown	215	Dallas	214
Hudson	216	Gettysburg	717	Denison	214
Lakewood	216	Harrisburg	717	Denton	817
Lancaster	614	Hershey	717	Eldorado	915
Mansfield	419	Lebanon	717	El Paso	915
Marion	614	Levittown	215	Fort Bliss	915
Massillon	216	McKeesport	412	Fort Worth	817
McArthur	614	Media	215	Galveston	409
Middleton	216	Milton	717	Garland	214
Newtown	513	Penn Hills	412	Grand Prairie	214
Niles	216	Philadelphia	215	Granger	512
Plymouth	419	Pittsburgh	412	Hereford	806
Reading	513	Pottstown	215	Houston	713
Salem	216	Reading	215	Irving	214
Sandusky	419	St. Marys	814	Kingsville	512
Solon	216	Scranton	717	Kyle	512
South Euclid	216	Sharon	412	Laredo	512
Springfield	513	Strasburg	717	Liberty	409
Steubenville	614			Longview	214
Toledo	419	**RHODE ISLAND**		Lubbock	806
Warren	216	All locations	401	McAllen	512
Youngstown	216			Mesquite	214
Zanesville	614	**SOUTH CAROLINA**		Mineola	214
		All locations	803	Nixon	512
OKLAHOMA				Odessa	915
Ardmore	405	**SOUTH DAKOTA**		Pecos	915
Bartlesville	918	All locations	605	Plainview	806
Claremore	918			Port Arthur	409
El Reno	405	**TENNESSEE**		Ranger	817
Guthrie	405	Athens	615	Rio Hondo	512
Muskogee	918	Bethesda	615	San Antonio	512
Norman	405	Carthage	615	Sanger	817
Oklahoma City	405	Chattanooga	615		
		Covington	901		

Long Distance Area Codes of Major Cities

Sulphur Springs	214		Montreal, Quebec	514
Sweetwater	915		North Bay, Ontario	705
Texarkana	214		Ottawa, Ontario	613
Texas City	409		Prince Edward Island	902
Tyler	214		Quebec, Quebec	418
Waco	817		Sault Ste. Marie	705
Wichita Falls	817		Toronto, Ontario	416
			Windsor, Ontario	519

UTAH

All locations	801

VERMONT

All locations	802

VIRGINIA

Alexandria	703
Arlington	703
Charlottesville	804
Chesapeake	804
Fredericksburg	703
Hampton	804
Newport News	804
Norfolk	804
Portsmouth	804
Richmond	804
Roanoke	703
Virginia Beach	804
Winchester	703

WASHINGTON

Pullman	509
Seattle	206
Spokane	509
Vancouver	206
Walla Walla	509

WEST VIRGINIA

All locations	304

WISCONSIN

Beloit	608
Eau Claire	715
Green Bay	414
Madison	608
Milwaukee	414
Racine	414
Superior	715
Wausau	715

WYOMING

All locations	307

CANADA

London, Ontario	519

MEXICO

Mexico City
  90 + 5 + seven digits
Northwest Mexico
  70 + 6 + seven digits

PUERTO RICO

All locations	809

VIRGIN ISLANDS

All locations	809

WIDE AREA

Telecommunications
  Service (Inward WATS)

All locations	800

NUMERICAL LISTING OF LONG DISTANCE AREA CODES

201

NEW JERSEY

	Asbury Park
	Bayonne
	Caldwell
	Cedar Groves
	Delaware
	Dover
	East Orange
	Elizabeth
	Englewood
	Garfield
	Glen Ridge
	Hanover
	Hoboken
	Jersey City
	Kenilworth
	Lakewood
	Long Branch
	Lyndhurst
	Middletown
	Montclair
	Newark
	New Brunswick
	Oakhurst
	Orange
	Paterson
	Perth Amboy
	Plainfield
	Ridgewood
	Springfield
	Union
	Wayne
	Westfield
	West New York
	Wharton
	Wyckoff

202

DISTRICT OF COLUMBIA   Washington

203

CONNECTICUT   All points

204

MANITOBA   All points

205

ALABAMA   All points

206

WASHINGTON   Seattle
                             Tacoma
                             Vancouver

207

MAINE   All points

208

IDAHO   All points

209

CALIFORNIA

	Angels Camp
	Bass Lake
	Chowchilla
	Clovis
	Dinuba
	Exter
	Fresno
	Hanford
	Kingsburg
	Lodi
	Madera
	Merced
	Modesto
	Porterville
	Reedley
	Sanger
	Selma
	Sequoia
	Sonora
	Stockton
	Tracy
	Tulare
	Turlock
	Visalia

212

NEW YORK   Bronx
                       Far Rockaway
                       Manhattan

8. 14

Numerical Listing of Long Distance Area Codes

213

CALIFORNIA

Alhambra
Altadena
Arcadia
Artesia
Azusa
Baldwin Park
Bell
Bellflower
Beverly Hills
Burbank
Canoga Park
Chatsworth
Compton
Covina
Crescenta
Culver City
Downey
Duarte
East Los Angeles
El Monte
El Segundo
Encino
Gardena
Glendale
Glendora
Hawthorne
Hermosa Beach
Huntington Park
Inglewood
La Canada
La Crescenta
La Habra
Lakewood
LaPuente
Lomita
Long Beach
Los Angeles
Lynwood
Manhattan Beach
Maywood
Monrovia
Montebello

213

CALIFORNIA (continued)

Montrose
North Hollywood
Northridge
Norwalk
Pacoima
Paramount
Pasadena
Pico Rivera
Redondo
Reseda
Rosemead
San Fernando
San Gabriel
San Pedro
Santa Fe Springs
Santa Monica
Seal Beach
Sherman Oaks
Sierra Madre
South Gate
Temple City
Torrance
Van Nuys
Venice
Whittier
Wilmington
Woodlands

214

TEXAS

Bonham
Carthage
Dallas
Denison
Garland
Grand Prairie
Irving
Longview
Mesquite
Mineola
Sulphur Springs
Texarkana
Tyler

(Continued)

Numerical Listing of Long Distance Area Codes

215
PENNSYLVANIA — Allentown, Bethlehem, Bristol, Brook Haven, Chester, Easton, Germantown, Levittown, Media, Philadelphia, Pottstown, Reading

216
OHIO — Akron, Amherst, Ashtabula, Brunswick, Canton, Cleveland, East Cleveland, Euclid, Garfield Heights, Hudson, Lakewood, Massillon, Middletown, Niles, Salem, Solon, South Euclid, Warren, Youngstown

217
ILLINOIS — Champaign, Decatur, Quincy, Springfield

218
MINNESOTA — Duluth, Proctor, Warren

219
INDIANA — Fort Wayne, Gary, Hammond, Michigan City, South Bend, Warsaw

301
MARYLAND — All points

302
DELAWARE — All points

303
COLORADO — All points

304
WEST VIRGINIA — All points

305
FLORIDA — Cape Canaveral, Cape Kennedy, Cocoa Beach, Coral Gables, Fort Lauderdale, Fort Pierce, Hialeah, Hollywood, Key Largo, Key West, Miami, Miami Beach, Orlando, Palm Beach, St. Cloud, South Miami, West Palm Beach

306
SASKATCHEWAN — All points

307
WYOMING — All points

308
NEBRASKA — Grand Island, North Platte

Numerical Listing of Long Distance Area Codes

309
ILLINOIS

Bloomington
Chillicothe
Havana
Peoria
Rock Island

312
ILLINOIS

Arlington Heights
Broadview
Calumet City
Calumet Park
Chicago
Des Plaines
Elmwood Park
Evanston
Highland Park
Lake Forest
Lansing
North Chicago
Oak Park
Park Forest
Park Ridge
Waukegan
Winnetka

313
MICHIGAN

Ann Arbor
Dearborn
Detroit
Flint
Lincoln Park
Livonia
Milford
New Haven
Oak Park
Sterling Heights
Warren

314
MISSOURI

Columbia
Fort Leonard Wood
Oran
Poplar Bluff
St. Louis
University City

315
NEW YORK

Carthage
Fulton
Oswego
Potsdam
Syracuse
Utica

316
KANSAS

Arkansas City
Augusta
Chanute
Coffeyville
Dodge City
El Dorado
Garden City
Hutchinson
Wichita

317
INDIANA

Indianapolis
Kokomo

318
LOUISIANA

Lake Charles
Shreveport

319
IOWA

Cedar Rapids
Davenport
Dubuque

401
RHODE ISLAND

All points

402
NEBRASKA

Hastings
Lincoln
Omaha

403
ALBERTA

All points

404
GEORGIA

Athens
Atlanta
Augusta

(Continued)

Numerical Listing of Long Distance Area Codes

404

GEORGIA (continued)

Columbus
Decatur
La Grange
Norcross
Rome
Stockbridge

405

OKLAHOMA

Ardmore
El Reno
Guthrie
Norman
Oklahoma City
Shawnee
Stillwater

406

MONTANA

All points

408

CALIFORNIA

Alviso
Burbank (Santa Clara Co.)
Campbell
Carmel
Castroville
Cupertino
Gilroy
Hollister
Monterey
Mulberry
Pebble Beach
Salinas
San Jose
Santa Clara
Santa Cruz
Soledad
Sunnyvale
Watsonville

409

TEXAS

Beaumont
Crocket
Galveston
Liberty
Port Arthur
Texas City

412

PENNSYLVANIA

Allegheny
Bellevue
Duquesne
McKeesport
Penn Hills
Pittsburgh
Sharon

413

MASSACHUSETTS

Chicopee
Holyoke
North Hampton
Southwick
Springfield
Warren
Westfield

414

WISCONSIN

Green Bay
Milwaukee
Racine

415

CALIFORNIA

Alameda
Albany
Antioch
Atherton
Berkeley
Burlingame
Castro Valley
Concord
Daly City
El Cerrito
Emeryville
Fairfax
Fremont
Hayward
Livermore
Mill Valley
Millbrae
Mountain View
Oakland
Orinda
Palo Alto
Piedmont

Numerical Listing of Long Distance Area Codes

415

CALIFORNIA (continued)

Pittsburg
Redwood City
Richmond
San Anselmo
San Bruno
San Francisco
San Leandro
San Mateo
San Rafael
Sausalito
Walnut Creek
Woodside

416

ONTARIO — Toronto

417

MISSOURI

Bolivar
Branson
Joplin
Springfield

418

QUEBEC — Quebec

419

OHIO

Mansfield
Plymouth
Sandusky
Toledo

501

ARKANSAS — All points

502

KENTUCKY

Louisville
Paducah
Shelbyville

503

OREGON — All points

504

LOUISIANA

Baton Rouge
Metairie
New Orleans

505

NEW MEXICO — All points

506

NEW BRUNSWICK — All points

507

MINNESOTA

Northfield
Plainview
Rochester

509

WASHINGTON

Pullman
Spokane
Walla Walla

512

TEXAS

Alamo
Austin
Brownsville
Corpus Christi
Granger
Kingsville
Kyle
Laredo
McAllen
Nixon
Rio Hondo
San Antonio

513

OHIO

Camden
Cincinnati
Dayton
Germantown
Hamilton
Newtown
Reading
Springfield

514

QUEBEC — Montreal

515

IOWA

Des Moines
Mason City

(Continued)

Numerical Listing of Long Distance Area Codes

516
NEW YORK
Babylon
Flanders
Garden City
Hicksville
Lake Success
Levittown
Long Beach
Rockville Centre
Roosevelt

517
MICHIGAN
Bay City
East Lansing
Jackson
Lansing

518
NEW YORK
Albany
Amsterdam
Greenwich
Hudson
Lake George
Schenectady
Ticonderoga
Troy

519
ONTARIO
London
Windsor

601
MISSISSIPPI
All points

602
ARIZONA
All points

603
NEW HAMPSHIRE
All points

605
SOUTH DAKOTA
All points

606
KENTUCKY
Ashland
Lexington
Winchester

607
NEW YORK
Apalachin

607
NEW YORK (continued)
Binghamton
Corning
Elmira
Ithaca

608
WISCONSIN
Beloit
Madison

609
NEW JERSEY
Allentown
Atlantic City
Camden
Linwood
Medford
Mount Holly
Northfield
Princeton
Salem
Trenton
Vineland

612
MINNESOTA
Minneapolis
New Prague
Red Wing
St. Cloud
St. Louis Park
St. Paul
Sauk Rapids

613
ONTARIO
Ottawa

614
OHIO
Columbus
Lancaster
Marion
McArthur
Steubenville
Zanesville

615
TENNESSEE
Athens
Bethesda
Carthage
Chattanooga
Knoxville

Numerical Listing of Long Distance Area Codes

615
TENNESSEE (continued)

Madison
Nashville
Oak Ridge

616
MICHIGAN

Battle Creek
Benton Harbor
Cheboygan
Grand Rapids
Kalamazoo
Muskegon

617
MASSACHUSETTS

Arlington
Boston
Brockton
Brookline
Cambridge
Concord
Dorchester
Dover
East Boston
Fall River
Falmouth
Hyannis
Hyde Park
Ipswich
Jamaica Plain
Lawrence
Lexington
Lowell
Milford
Milton
New Bedford
Newton
Peabody
Plymouth
Quincy
Randolph
Reading
Rockland
Salem
Stoneham
Stoughton

617
MASSACHUSETTS (continued)

Taunton
Wakefield
Waltham
Wellesley
Westminster
Whitman
Wilmington
Winchester
Worcester

618
ILLINOIS

Centralia
East St. Louis
Glen Carbon
Harrisburg
Madison
Troy

619
CALIFORNIA

Alpine (San Diego Co.)
Apple Valley
Baker
Barstow
Big Pine
Bishop
Blythe
Boron
Borrego Springs
Brawley
Bridgeport
Calexico
California City
Callpatria
Campo
Cardiff
Carlsbad
Cathedral City
China Lake
Chula Vista
Coachella
Coronado
Crowley Lake
Daggett
Death Valley

(Continued)

Numerical Listing of Long Distance Area Codes

619		619	
CALIFORNIA (continued)	Del Mar	CALIFORNIA (continued)	Warner Springs
	Descanso		Westmorland
	Desert Hot Springs	**701**	
	Dulzura	NORTH DAKOTA	All points
	El Cajon	**702**	
	El Centro	NEVADA	All points
	Encinitas	**703**	
	Escondido	VIRGINIA	Alexandria
	Fallbrook		Arlington
	Furnace Creek		Fredericksburg
	Holtville		Roanoke
	Imperial Beach		Winchester
	Indio		
	Inyokern	**704**	
	Jacumba	NORTH CAROLINA	Asheville
	Jamul		Charlotte
	Joshua Tree		Kannapolis
	Julian		Newton
	June Lake		Valdese
	Kernville		
	La Jolla	**705**	
	La Mesa	ONTARIO	North Bay
	Lemon Grove		Sault Ste. Marie
	Lone Pine	**706** + seven-digit number	
	National City	MEXICO	Northwest Mexico
	Needles	**707**	
	Oceanside	CALIFORNIA	Eureka
	Pacific Beach		Fairfield
	Pala		Fort Bragg
	Palm Desert		Napa
	Palm Springs		Petaluma
	Poway		Santa Rosa
	Ramona		Sonoma
	Rancho Sante Fe		Suisun
	San Diego		Ukiah
	San Ysidro		Vallejo
	Shoshone		
	Tecate	**709**	
	Thousand Palms	NEWFOUNDLAND	All points
	Trona	**712**	
	Twentynine Palms	IOWA	Council Bluffs
	Victorville		

Numerical Listing of Long Distance Area Codes

713

TEXAS — Houston

714

CALIFORNIA

Anaheim
Arlington
Arrowhead
Balboa
Banning
Beaumont
Big Bear Lake
Brea
Buena Park
Capistrano Beach
Claremont
Colton
Corona
Corona Del Mar
Costa Mesa
Cucamonga
Cypress
Dana Point
Earp
Elsinore
Etiwanda
Fontana
Fullerton
Garden Grove
Gilman Hot Springs
Hemet
Huntington Beach
Idyllwild
Laguna Beach
Lake Arrowhead
La Verne
Newport Beach
Norco
Ontario
Orange
Perris
Pomona
Redlands
Rialto
Riverside
San Bernardino
San Clemente

714

CALIFORNIA (continued)

San Jacinto
San Juan Capistrano
Santa Ana
Sunnymead
Temecula
Tustin
Upland
Yucaipa

715

WISCONSIN

Eau Claire
Superior
Wausau

716

NEW YORK

Allegany
Buffalo
Grand Island
Lackawanna
Niagara Falls
Rochester

717

PENNSYLVANIA

Gettysburg
Harrisburg
Hershey
Lebanon
Milton
Scranton

718

NEW YORK

Brooklyn
Queens
Staten Island

800

INWARD WATS (Wide Area Telecommunications Service) — All states

801

UTAH — All points

802

VERMONT — All points

803

SOUTH CAROLINA — All points

(Continued)

Numerical Listing of Long Distance Area Codes

804

VIRGINIA

Chesapeake
Charlottesville
Hampton
Newport News
Norfolk
Portsmouth
Richmond
Virginia Beach

805

CALIFORNIA

Arroyo Grande
Atascadero
Avila
Bakersfield
Camarillo
Cambria
Carpinteria
Delano
Earlimart
Fillmore
Frazier Park
Hueneme
Lancaster
Lompoc
Mojave
Moorpark
Morro Bay
Newhall
Ojai
Oxnard
Palmdale
Paso Robles
Pismo Beach
Point Mugo
Port Hueneme
Rosamond
San Luis Obispo
San Simeon
Santa Barbara
Santa Maria
Santa Paula
Saticoy
Saugus
Simi

805

CALIFORNIA (continued)

Taft
Tehachapi
Thousand Oaks
Ventura

806

TEXAS

Amarillo
Hereford
Lubbock
Plainview

808

HAWAII

All points

809

PUERTO RICO

All points

812

INDIANA

Evansville

813

FLORIDA

Bowling Green
Everglades
Gulf Port
St. Petersburg
Sarasota
Tampa

814

PENNSYLVANIA

Clarion
Erie

815

ILLINOIS

Joliet
La Salle
Morris
Plainfield
Rock Falls
Rockford
Seneca
Sterling

816

MISSOURI

Chillicothe
Grandview
Independence
Kansas City
St. Joseph

Numerical Listing of Long Distance Area Codes

817

TEXAS	Arlington
	Bowie
	Denton
	Fort Worth
	Ranger
	Sanger
	Waco
	Wichita Falls

819

| QUEBEC | Trois-Rivières |

901

TENNESSEE	Covington
	Gainesville
	Memphis

902

| NOVA SCOTIA | All points |
| PRINCE EDWARD ISLAND | All points |

904

FLORIDA	Apalachicola
	Atlantic Beach
	Daytona Beach
	De Land
	Edgewater
	Inverness
	Jacksonville
	Pensacola
	St. Augustine
	Tallahassee

905 + seven-digit number

| MEXICO | Mexico City |

906

| MICHIGAN | Escanaba |
| | Marquette |

907

| ALASKA | All points |

912

GEORGIA	Macon
	Savannah
	Valdosta

913

KANSAS	Abilene
	Atchison
	Bloomington
	Lawrence
	Leavenworth
	Manhattan
	Salina
	Topeka

914

NEW YORK	Goshen
	Hyde Park
	Kingston
	Mount Vernon
	New Rochelle
	Ossining
	Pelham
	Poughkeepsie
	Rye
	West Point
	White Plains
	Yonkers

915

TEXAS	Abilene
	Eldorado
	El Paso
	Fort Bliss
	Odessa
	Pecos
	Sweetwater

916

CALIFORNIA	Alpine (Alpine Co.)
	Auburn
	Carmichael
	Chico
	Colusa
	Davis
	Dunsmuir
	Folsom
	Grass Valley
	Marysville
	Paradise
	Placerville

(Continued)

Numerical Listing of Long Distance Area Codes

916

CALIFORNIA (continued)

Red Bluff
Redding
Sacramento
Tahoe City
Truckee
Willows
Woodland

8.02 **International Dialing Codes and Instructions**

Dialing instructions

Station-to-station calls

To dial international calls, dial in sequence:

1. The International Access Code: 011

2. The Country Code

3. The City Code

4. The local telephone number

5. The "#" button—where telephone is equipped with touch-tone dialing

For example:

To place a call you would dial:

International Access Code		Country Code	City Code	
011	+	49	+ 611	+

the local telephone number +
button if touch-tone dialing

Numbers beside countries are Country Codes; numbers beside cities are City Codes.

For all other international points not listed, dial "0" and tell the Operator the country you are calling.

ALGERIA	213	**AUSTRIA**	43	**BRAZIL**	55
AMERICAN SAMOA	684	Graz	316	Belo Horizonte	31
		Vienna	222	Brasilia	61
ANDORRA	33	**BAHRAIN**	973	Porto Alegre	512
All points	078				
		BELGIUM	32	**Recife**	81
ARGENTINA	54	Antwerp	3	Rio de Janeiro	21
Buenos Aires	1	Brussels	2	Salvador	71
Cordoba	51	Ghent (Gand)	91	Sao Paulo	11
La Plata	21	Liege (Luik)	41	**CAMEROON**	237
Rosario	41	Malines (Mechelen)	15		
AUSTRALIA	61			**CHILE**	56
Adelaide	8	**BELIZE**	501	Santiago	2
Brisbane	7	**BOLIVIA**	591	Valparaiso	31
Melbourne	3	La Paz	2	**COLOMBIA**	57
Perth	9	**BRAZIL**	55	Barranquilla	5
Sydney	2	Belem	91	Bogota	—

(Continued)

International Dialing Codes and Instructions

COLOMBIA	57	**FRENCH POLYNESIA**	689	**HAITI**	509	
Bucaramanga	71	(Tahiti)		Port-au-Prince	1	
Cali	3	**GABON**	241	**HONDURAS**	504	
Cartagena	59	**GERMANY DEMOCRATIC**		**HONG KONG**	852	
Medellin	4	**REPUBLIC**	37	Castle Peak	0	
COSTA RICA	506	Berlin	2	Hong Kong	5	
CYPRUS	357	**GERMANY, FEDERAL**		Kowloon	3	
Nicosia	21	**REPUBLIC OF**	49	Kwai Chung	0	
DENMARK	45	Berlin	30	Lantau	5	
Aarhus	6	Bonn	228	Ma Wan	5	
Copenhagen	1 or 2	Bremen	421	Peng Chau	5	
Odense	9	Cologne (Koln)	221	Sha Tin	0	
ECUADOR	593	Dortmund	231	Tai Po	0	
Cuenca	4	Duisburg	203	Tsun Wan	0	
Guayaquil	4	Dusseldorf	211	**INDONESIA**	62	
Quito	2	Essen	201	Jakarta	21	
EGYPT	20	Frankfurt	611	**IRAN**	98	
Cairo	2	Gelsenkirchen	209	Abadan	631	
EL SALVADOR	503	Hamburg	40	Esfahan	31	
ETHIOPIA	251	Hannover	511	Mashad	51	
Addis Ababa	1	Munich	89	Tabriz	41	
FIJI	679	Nuremberg	911	Teheran	21	
FINLAND	358	Stuttgart	711	**IRAQ**	964	
Helsinki	0	Wuppertal	202	Baghdad	1	
Tampere	31	**GREECE**	30	**IRELAND, REPUBLIC OF**	353	
FRANCE	33	Athens	1	Cork	21	
Bordeaux	56	Drama	521	Dublin	1	
Brest	98	Ioannina	651	Limerick	61	
Grenoble	76	Iraklion (Crete)	81	Waterford	51	
Le Havre	35	Kalamata	721	**ISRAEL**	972	
Lille	20	Kavala	51	Bene Brak (Berak)	3	
Lyon	7	Larissa	41	Bet Shean	65	
Marseille	91	Patrai	61	Haifa	4	
Montpellier	67	Piraeus	1	Jerusalem	2	
Nice	93	Serrai	321	Petah Tikva	3	
Paris	1	Thessaloniki	31	Ramat Gan	3	
Reims	26	Volos	421	Tel Aviv	3	
Rennes	99	**GUAM**	671	**ITALY**	39	
Rouen	35	**GUATEMALA**	502	Bari	80	
St. Etienne	77	Amatitlan	–	Bologna	51	
Strasbourg	88	Antigua	–	Catania	95	
Toulon	94	Guatemala City	2	Florence	55	
Toulouse	61	Quetzaltenango	–	Genoa	10	
FRENCH ANTILLES	596	Villa Nueva	–	Messina	90	
		GUYANA	592			
		Georgetown	2			

International Dialing Codes and Instructions

ITALY	39	**MALAYSIA**	60	**NIGERIA**	234
Milan	2	Ipoh	5	Ibadan	22
Naples	81	Kuala Lumpur	3	Kano	64
Palermo	91	**MEXICO**	52	Lagos	1
Rome	6	Cabo San Lucas	684	**NORWAY**	47
Taranto	99	Culiacan	671	Bergen	5
Trieste	40	Ciudad Obregon	641	Oslo	2
Turin	11	Ensenada	667	Trondheim	75
Venice	41	Hermosillo	621	**OMAN**	968
Verona	45	La Paz	682	**PAKISTAN**	92
IVORY COAST	225	Los Mochis	681	Karachi	21
JAPAN	81	Mazatlan	678	**PANAMA**	507
Amagaski	6	Mexicali	656	**PAPUA NEW GUINEA**	675
Fukuoka	92	Mexico City	5	**PARAGUAY**	595
Hiroshima	82	Nogales	631	Asuncion	21
Kawasaki (Kanagawa)	44	Tijuana	66	**PERU**	51
Kitakyushu	93	**MONACO**	33	Arequipa	54
Kobe	78	All points	93	Callao	14
Kyoto	75	**MOROCCO**	212	Lima	14
Nagoya	52	Rabat	7	**PHILIPPINES**	63
Osaka	6	**NETHERLANDS**	31	Bacolod	34
Sakai (Osaka)	722	Amsterdam	20	Cebu	32
Sapporo	11	Arnhem	85	Davao	35
Tokyo	3	Breda	76	Iloilo City	33
Yokohama	45	Eindhoven	40	Manila	2
KENYA	254	Rotterdam	10	Tarlac	47
Nairobi	2	The Hague	70	**PORTUGAL**	351
KOREA, REPUBLIC OF	82	Tilburg	13	Lisbon	1
Incheon	32	Utrecht	30	Porto	2
Kwangju	62	**NETHERLANDS**		**ROMANIA**	40
Pusan	51	**ANTILLES**	599	Bucuresti	0
Seoul	2	Aruba	8	**SAN MARINO**	39
Taegu	53	Bonaire	7	All points	541
KUWAIT	965	Curacao	9	**SAUDI ARABIA**	966
LIBERIA	231	Saba	4	Jeddah	
LIECHTENSTEIN	41	St. Eustatius	3	Makkah Road	2
All points	75	St. Maarten	5	Riyadh	1
LUXEMBOURG	352	**NEW CALEDONIA**	687	**SINGAPORE**	65
LIBYAN ARAB		**NEW ZEALAND**	64	**SOUTH AFRICA**	27
PEOPLE'S SOCIALIST		Auckland	9	Bloemfontein	51
JAMAHIRIYA	218	Christchurch	3	Cape Town	21
(Libyan A.P.S.J.)		Wellington	4	Durban	31
Benghazi	61	**NICARAGUA**	505	Johannesburg	11
Misuratha	51	Leon	31		
Tripoli	21	Managua	2		
MALAWI	265				
Makwasa	474				

(Continued)

International Dialing Codes and Instructions

SPAIN	34	**UNITED ARAB**		**VENEZUELA**	58
Barcelona	3	**EMIRATES**	971	Barcelona	81
Bilbao	4	Abu Dhabi	2	Barquisimeto	51
Granada	58	Ajman	6	Caracas	2
Las Palmas		Al Ain	3	Ciudad Bolivar	85
(Canary Is.)	28	Aweir	48	Cumana	93
Madrid	1	Dubai	4	Maracaibo	61
Palma de Mallorca	71	Fujairah	70	Maracay	43
Pamplona	48	Jebel Dhana	52	Maturin	91
Seville	54	Khawanij	48	San Cristobal	76
Valencia	6	Ras-Al-Khaimah	7	Valencia	41
Zaragoza	76	Sharjah	6		
		Umm-Al-Quwain	6	**YUGOSLAVIA**	38
SRI LANKA	94			Belgrade	11
Colombo	1	**UNITED KINGDOM**	44	Zagreb	41
Kandy	8	Belfast, N. Ire.	232		
		Birmingham, Eng.	21		
SURINAME	597	Bradford, Eng.	274		
		Bristol, Eng.	272		
SWEDEN	46	Cardiff, Wales	222		
Goteborg	31	Coventry, Eng.	203		
Malmo	40	Edinburgh, Scot.	31		
Stockholm	8	Glasgow, Scot.	41		
Uppsala	18	Hillington, Eng.	485		
Vasteras	21	Huddersfield, Eng.	484		
		Leeds, Eng.	532		
SWITZERLAND	41	Leicester, Eng.	533		
Basel	61	Liverpool, Eng.	51		
Berne	31	London, Eng.	1		
Biel (Valais)	28	Manchester, Eng.	61		
Geneva	22	Newcastle-on-			
Lausanne	21	Tyne, Eng.	682		
Lucerne	41	Nottingham, Eng.	602		
Winterthur	52	Plymouth, Eng.	752		
Zurich	1	Sheffield, Eng.	742		
		Stoke-on-Trent, Eng.	782		
TAHITI	689	Wolverhampton, Eng.	902		
(French Polynesia)					
		VATICAN CITY	39		
TAIWAN	886	All points	6		
Kaohsiung	7				
Tainan	62				
Taipei	2				
THAILAND	66				
Bangkok	2				
TUNISIA	216				
Msel Bourguiba	2				
Tunis	1				
TURKEY	90				
Istanbul	11				

8.03 International Time Differences

The following table indicates the time in various principal cities of the world when it is 12 o'clock noon in Boston and New York (eastern standard time).

Country	City	Time
Algeria	Algiers	5 P.M.
Argentina	Buenos Aires	2 P.M.*
Australia	Melbourne	3 A.M.**
	Sydney	3 A.M.**
Austria	Vienna	6 P.M.
Bahamas	Nassau	12 noon
Belgium	Brussels	6 P.M.*
Bermuda	Hamilton	1 P.M.
Bolivia	La Paz	1 P.M.
Brazil	Rio de Janeiro	2 P.M.
	Sao Paulo	2 P.M.
Canada	Montreal	12 noon
	Ottawa	12 noon
	Toronto	12 noon
Ceylon	Colombo	10:30 P.M.
Chile	Santiago	1 P.M.
Colombia	Bogota	12 noon
Denmark	Copenhagen	6 P.M.
Ecuador	Quito	12 noon
France	Paris	6 P.M.*
Germany	Frankfurt	6 P.M.
Greece	Athens	7 P.M.
Haiti	Port-au-Prince	12 noon
Iceland	Reykjavik	4 P.M.
India	New Dehli	10:30 P.M.
Ireland	Dublin	5 P.M.
Israel	Tel Aviv	7 P.M.

* *Permanent daylight time*   ** *Morning of the following day.*

Country	City	Time
Italy	Rome	6 P.M.
Jamaica	Kingston	12 noon
Japan	Tokyo	2 A.M.**
Korea	Seoul	2 A.M.**
Lebanon	Beirut	7 P.M.
Luxembourg	Luxembourg City	5 P.M.
Mexico	Mexico City	11 A.M.
Morocco	Rabat	5 P.M.
Netherlands	Amsterdam	6 P.M.*
New Zealand	Wellington	5 A.M.**
Nicaragua	Managua	11 A.M.
Norway	Oslo	6 P.M.
Pakistan	Karachi	10 P.M.
Peru	Lima	12 noon
Philippines	Manila	1 A.M.**
Portugal	Lisbon	6 P.M.*
Spain	Madrid	6 P.M.*
Sweden	Stockholm	6 P.M.
Switzerland	Berne	6 P.M.
Trinidad	Port of Spain	1 P.M.
Uruguay	Montevideo	2 P.M.*
United Kingdom	London	5 P.M.
U.S.S.R.	Moscow	7 P.M.
Venezuela	Caracas	1 P.M.

* *Permanent daylight time*   ** *Morning of the following day.*

8.04 Metric Conversion Chart—Approximations

CONVERSION CHART

(Continued)

Symbol	When You Know	Multiply By	To Find
Length			
mm	millimeters	0.04	inches
cm	centimeters	0.4	inches
m	meters	3.3	feet
m	meters	1.1	yards
km	kilometers	0.6	miles
Area			
cm²	square centimeters	0.16	square inches
m²	square meters	1.2	square yards
km²	square kilometers	0.4	square miles
ha	hectares (10,000m²)	2.5	acres
Mass (weight)			
g	grams	0.035	ounces
kg	kilograms	2.2	pounds
t	tonnes (1000 kg)	1.1	short tons
Volume			
ml	milliliters	0.03	fluid ounces
—	liters	2.1	pints
—	liters	1.06	quarts
—	liters	0.26	quarts (US)
—	liters	0.22	gallons (Imp.)
m³	cubic meters	35	cubic feet
m³	cubic meters	1.3	cubic yards

Symbol	When You Know	Multiply By	To Find
Length			
in	inches	*2.5	centimeters
in	inches	30	centimeters
ft	feet	0.9	meters
yd	yards	1.6	kilometers
mi	miles		
Area			
in²	square inches	6.5	sq. centimeters
ft²	square feet	0.09	square meters
yd²	square yards	0.8	square meters
mi²	square miles	2.6	sq. kilometers
	acres	0.4	hectares
Mass (weight)			
oz	ounces	28	grams
lb	pounds	0.45	kilograms
	short tons (2000 lb.)	0.9	tonnes
Volume			
tsp	teaspoons	5	milliliters
tbsp	tablespoons	15	milliliters
fl oz	fluid ounces	30	milliliters
c	cups	0.24	liters
pt	pints	0.47	liters
qt	quarts	0.95	liters
gal	gallons (US)	3.8	liters
gal	gallons (Imp.)	4.5	liters
ft³	cubic feet	0.03	cubic meters
yd³	cubic yards	0.76	cubic meters

Conversion Chart

Symbol	When You Know	Multiply By	To Find	Symbol	Symbol	When You Know	Multiply By	To Find
	Temperature (exact)							
°C	Celsius temp.	9/5 (+32)	Fahrenheit temp.	°F				
	Temperature (exact) to Metric							
°F	Fahrenheit temp.	(-32) 5/9 of remainder	Celsius temp.	°C				

* *1 in. = 2.54 cm (exactly)*

Source: *The World Almanac & Book of Facts*, 1984 edition, copyright © Newspaper Enterprise Association, Inc., New York, NY 10166.

8.05 Population of the U.S. 1970–1980

POPULATION OF THE U.S. 1970–1980

Region, Division, and State	1980 Census	1970 Census	% Change	1980 Urban	1980 Rural	% Urban	Rank 1980	Rank 1970
United States	226,545,805	203,302,031	11.4	167,050,992	59,494,813	73.7		
Regions:								
Northeast	49,135,283	49,060,514	0.2	38,905,545	10,229,738	79.2		
Midwest	58,865,670	56,590,294	4.0	41,519,746	17,345,924	70.5		
South	75,372,362	62,812,980	20.0	50,414,258	24,958,104	66.9		
West	43,172,490	34,838,243	23.9	36,211,443	6,961,047	83.9		
New England	12,348,493	11,847,245	4.2	9,269,249	3,079,244	75.1		
Maine	1,124,660	993,722	13.2	534,072	590,588	47.5	38	38
New Hampshire	920,610	737,681	24.8	480,325	440,285	52.2	42	41
Vermont	511,456	444,732	15.0	172,735	338,721	33.8	48	48
Massachusetts	5,737,037	5,689,170	0.8	4,808,339	926,698	83.8	11	10
Rhode Island	947,154	949,723	−0.3	824,004	123,150	87.0	40	39
Connecticut	3,107,576	3,032,217	2.5	2,449,774	657,802	78.8	25	24
Middle Atlantic	36,786,790	37,213,269	−1.1	29,636,296	7,150,494	80.6		
New York	17,558,072	18,241,391	−3.7	14,858,068	2,700,004	84.6	2	2
New Jersey	7,364,823	7,171,112	2.7	6,557,377	807,446	89.0	9	8
Pennsylvania	11,863,895	11,800,766	0.5	8,220,851	3,643,044	69.3	4	3
East North Central	41,682,217	40,262,747	3.5	30,533,879	11,148,338	73.3		
Ohio	10,797,630	10,657,423	1.3	7,918,259	2,879,371	73.3	6	6
Indiana	5,490,224	5,195,392	5.7	3,525,298	1,964,926	64.2	12	11
Illinois	11,426,518	11,110,285	2.8	9,518,039	1,908,479	83.3	5	5
Michigan	9,262,078	8,881,826	4.3	6,551,551	2,710,527	70.7	8	7
Wisconsin	4,705,767	4,417,821	6.5	3,020,732	1,685,035	64.2	16	16
West North Central	17,183,453	16,327,547	5.2	10,985,867	6,197,586	63.9		
Minnesota	4,075,970	3,806,103	7.1	2,725,202	1,350,768	66.9	21	19
Iowa	2,913,808	2,825,368	3.1	1,708,232	1,205,576	58.6	27	25
Missouri	4,916,686	4,677,623	5.1	3,349,588	1,567,098	68.1	15	13
North Dakota	652,717	617,792	5.7	318,310	334,407	48.8	46	45
South Dakota	690,768	666,257	3.7	320,777	369,991	46.4	45	44

(Continued)

Population of the U.S. 1970–1980

Region, Division, and State	1980 Census	1970 Census	% Change	1980 Urban	1980 Rural	% Urban	Rank 1980	Rank 1970
West North Central								
Nebraska	1,569,825	1,485,333	5.7	987,859	581,966	62.9	35	35
Kansas	2,363,679	2,249,071	5.1	1,575,899	787,780	66.7	32	28
South Atlantic	**36,959,123**	**30,678,826**	**20.5**	**24,813,020**	**12,146,103**	**67.1**		
Delaware	594,338	548,104	8.4	419,819	174,519	70.6	47	46
Maryland	4,216,975	3,923,897	7.5	3,386,555	830,420	80.3	18	18
District of Columbia	638,333	756,668	−15.6	638,333		100.0		
Virginia	5,346,818	4,651,448	14.9	3,529,423	1,817,395	66.0	14	14
West Virginia	1,949,644	1,744,237	11.8	705,319	1,244,325	36.2	34	34
North Carolina	5,881,766	5,084,411	15.7	2,822,852	3,058,914	48.0	10	12
South Carolina	3,121,820	2,590,713	20.5	1,689,253	1,432,567	54.1	24	26
Georgia	5,463,105	4,587,930	19.1	3,409,081	2,054,024	62.4	13	15
Florida	9,746,324	6,791,418	43.5	8,212,385	1,533,939	84.3	7	9
East South Central	**14,666,423**	**12,808,077**	**14.5**	**8,166,274**	**6,500,149**	**55.7**		
Kentucky	3,660,777	3,320,711	13.7	1,862,183	1,798,594	50.9	23	23
Tennessee	4,591,120	3,926,018	16.9	2,773,573	1,817,547	60.4	17	17
Alabama	3,893,888	3,444,354	13.1	2,337,713	1,556,175	60.0	22	21
Mississippi	2,520,638	2,216,994	13.7	1,192,805	1,327,833	47.3	31	29
West South Central	**23,746,816**	**19,326,077**	**22.9**	**17,434,964**	**6,311,852**	**73.4**		
Arkansas	2,286,435	1,923,322	18.9	1,179,556	1,106,879	51.6	33	32
Louisiana	4,205,900	3,644,637	15.4	2,887,309	1,318,591	68.6	19	20
Oklahoma	3,025,290	2,559,463	18.2	2,035,082	990,208	67.3	26	27
Texas	14,229,191	11,198,655	27.1	11,333,017	2,896,174	79.6	3	4
Mountain	**11,372,785**	**8,289,901**	**37.2**	**8,685,310**	**2,687,475**	**76.4**		
Montana	786,690	694,409	13.3	416,402	370,288	52.9	44	43
Idaho	943,935	713,015	32.4	509,702	434,233	54.0	41	42
Wyoming	469,557	332,416	41.3	294,639	174,918	62.7	49	49
Colorado	2,889,964	2,209,596	30.8	2,329,869	560,095	80.6	28	30
New Mexico	1,302,894	1,017,055	28.1	939,963	362,931	72.1	37	37
Arizona	2,718,215	1,775,399	53.1	2,278,728	439,487	83.8	29	33

(Continued)

Population of the U.S. 1970–1980

Region, Division, and State	1980 Census	1970 Census	% Change	1980 Urban	1980 Rural	% Urban	Rank 1980	Rank 1970
Mountain								
Utah	1,461,037	1,059,273	37.9	1,233,060	227,977	84.4	36	36
Nevada	800,493	488,738	63.8	682,947	117,546	85.3	43	47
Pacific	**31,799,705**	**26,548,342**	**19.8**	**27,526,133**	**4,273,572**	**86.6**		
Washington	4,132,156	3,413,244	21.1	3,037,014	1,095,142	73.5	20	22
Oregon	2,633,105	2,091,533	25.9	1,788,354	844,751	67.9	30	31
California	23,667,902	19,971,069	18.5	21,607,606	2,060,296	91.3	1	1
Alaska	401,851	302,583	32.8	258,567	143,284	64.3	50	50
Hawaii	964,691	769,913	25.3	834,592	130,099	86.5	39	40
Puerto Rico	3,196,520	2,712,033	17.9	2,134,365	1,062,155	66.8		

Source: U.S. Bureau of the Census.

8.06 A Three-Year Calendar for Long-Term Planning

1986

	January							February							March				
Mon	•	6	13	20	29	•	•	3	10	17	24	•	•	•	3	10	17	24	31
Tues	•	7	14	21	30	•	•	4	11	18	25	•	•	•	4	11	18	25	•
Wed	1	8	15	22	31	•	•	5	12	19	26	•	•	•	5	12	19	26	•
Thu	2	9	16	23	•	•	•	6	13	20	27	•	•	•	6	13	20	27	•
Fri	3	10	17	24	•	•	•	7	14	21	28	•	•	•	7	14	21	28	•
Sat	4	11	18	25	•	•	1	8	15	22	•	•	•	1	8	15	22	29	•
Sun	5	12	19	26	•	•	2	9	16	23	•	•	•	2	9	16	23	30	•

	April							May							June				
Mon	•	7	14	21	28	•	•	5	12	19	26	•	•	•	2	9	16	23	30
Tues	1	8	15	22	29	•	•	6	13	20	27	•	•	•	3	10	17	24	•
Wed	2	9	16	23	30	•	•	7	14	21	28	•	•	•	4	11	18	25	•
Thu	3	10	17	24	•	•	1	8	15	22	29	•	•	•	5	12	19	26	•
Fri	4	11	18	25	•	•	2	9	16	23	30	•	•	•	6	13	20	27	•
Sat	5	12	19	26	•	•	3	10	17	24	31	•	•	•	7	14	21	28	•
Sun	6	13	20	27	•	•	4	11	18	25	•	•	•	1	8	15	22	29	•

	July							August							September				
Mon	•	7	14	21	28	•	•	4	11	18	25	•	1	8	15	22	29	•	
Tues	1	8	15	22	29	•	•	5	12	19	26	•	2	9	16	23	30	•	
Wed	2	9	16	23	30	•	•	6	13	20	27	•	3	10	17	24	•	•	
Thu	3	10	17	24	31	•	•	7	14	21	28	•	4	11	18	25	•	•	
Fri	4	11	18	25	•	•	1	8	15	22	29	•	5	12	19	26	•	•	
Sat	5	12	19	26	•	•	2	9	16	23	30	•	6	13	20	27	•	•	
Sun	6	13	20	27	•	•	3	10	17	24	31	•	7	14	21	28	•	•	

	October							November							December				
Mon	•	6	13	20	27	•	•	3	10	17	24	•	1	8	15	22	29	•	
Tues	•	7	14	21	28	•	•	4	11	18	25	•	2	9	16	23	30	•	
Wed	1	8	15	22	29	•	•	5	12	19	26	•	3	10	17	24	31	•	
Thu	2	9	16	23	30	•	•	6	13	20	27	•	4	11	18	25	•	•	
Fri	3	10	17	24	31	•	•	7	14	21	28	•	5	12	19	26	•	•	
Sat	4	11	18	25	•	•	1	8	15	22	29	•	6	13	20	27	•	•	
Sun	5	12	19	26	•	•	2	9	16	23	30	•	7	14	21	28	•	•	

Note: *Easter weekend for 1986: March 28 — March 30.*

1987

	January						
Mon	•	5	12	19	26	•
Tues	•	6	13	20	27	•
Wed	•	7	14	21	28	•
Thu	1	8	15	22	29	•
Fri	2	9	16	23	30	•
Sat	3	10	17	24	31	•
Sun	4	11	18	25	•	•

	February					
Mon	•	2	9	16	23	•
Tues	•	3	10	17	24	•
Wed	•	4	11	18	25	•
Thu	•	5	12	19	26	•
Fri	•	6	13	20	27	•
Sat	•	7	14	21	28	•
Sun	1	8	15	22	•	•

	March					
Mon	•	2	9	16	23	30
Tues	•	3	10	17	24	31
Wed	•	4	11	18	25	•
Thu	•	5	12	19	26	•
Fri	•	6	13	20	27	•
Sat	•	7	14	21	28	•
Sun	1	8	15	22	29	•

	April					
Mon	•	6	13	20	27	•
Tues	•	7	14	21	28	•
Wed	1	8	15	22	29	•
Thu	2	9	16	23	30	•
Fri	3	10	17	24	•	•
Sat	4	11	18	25	•	•
Sun	5	12	19	26	•	•

	May					
Mon	•	4	11	18	25	•
Tues	•	5	12	19	26	•
Wed	•	6	13	20	27	•
Thu	•	7	14	21	28	•
Fri	1	8	15	22	29	•
Sat	2	9	16	23	30	•
Sun	3	10	17	24	31	•

	June					
Mon	1	8	15	22	29	•
Tues	2	9	16	23	30	•
Wed	3	10	17	24	•	•
Thu	4	11	18	25	•	•
Fri	5	12	19	26	•	•
Sat	6	13	20	27	•	•
Sun	7	14	21	28	•	•

	July					
Mon	•	6	13	20	27	•
Tues	•	7	14	21	28	•
Wed	1	8	15	22	29	•
Thu	2	9	16	23	30	•
Fri	3	10	17	24	31	•
Sat	4	11	18	25	•	•
Sun	5	12	19	26	•	•

	August					
Mon	•	3	10	17	24	31
Tues	•	4	11	18	25	•
Wed	•	5	12	19	26	•
Thu	•	6	13	20	27	•
Fri	•	7	14	21	28	•
Sat	1	8	15	22	29	•
Sun	2	9	16	23	30	•

	September					
Mon	•	7	14	21	28	•
Tues	1	8	15	22	29	•
Wed	2	9	16	23	30	•
Thu	3	10	17	24	•	•
Fri	4	11	18	25	•	•
Sat	5	12	19	26	•	•
Sun	6	13	20	27	•	•

	October					
Mon	•	5	12	19	26	•
Tues	•	6	13	20	27	•
Wed	•	7	14	21	28	•
Thu	1	8	15	22	29	•
Fri	2	9	16	23	30	•
Sat	3	10	17	24	31	•
Sun	4	11	18	25	•	•

	November					
Mon	•	2	9	16	23	30
Tues	•	3	10	17	24	•
Wed	•	4	11	18	25	•
Thu	•	5	12	19	26	•
Fri	•	6	13	20	27	•
Sat	•	7	14	21	28	•
Sun	1	8	15	22	29	•

	December					
Mon	•	7	14	21	28	•
Tues	1	8	15	22	29	•
Wed	2	9	16	23	30	•
Thu	3	10	17	24	31	•
Fri	4	11	18	25	•	•
Sat	5	12	19	26	•	•
Sun	6	13	20	27	•	•

Note: *Easter weekend for 1987: April 17 — April 19.*

1988

	January				
Mon	•	4	11	18	25	•
Tues	•	5	12	19	26	•
Wed	•	6	13	20	27	•
Thu	•	7	14	21	28	•
Fri	1	8	15	22	29	•
Sat	2	9	16	23	30	•
Sun	3	10	17	24	31	•

	February				
Mon	1	8	15	22	29	•
Tues	2	9	16	23	•	•
Wed	3	10	17	24	•	•
Thu	4	11	18	25	•	•
Fri	5	12	19	26	•	•
Sat	6	13	20	27	•	•
Sun	7	14	21	28	•	•

	March				
Mon	•	7	14	21	28	•
Tues	1	8	15	22	29	•
Wed	2	9	16	23	30	•
Thu	3	10	17	24	31	•
Fri	4	11	18	25	•	•
Sat	5	12	19	26	•	•
Sun	6	13	20	27	•	•

	April				
Mon	•	4	11	18	25	•
Tues	•	5	12	19	26	•
Wed	•	6	13	20	27	•
Thu	•	7	14	21	28	•
Fri	1	8	15	22	29	•
Sat	2	9	16	23	30	•
Sun	3	10	17	24	•	•

	May				
Mon	•	2	9	16	23	30
Tues	•	3	10	17	24	31
Wed	•	4	11	18	25	•
Thu	•	5	12	19	26	•
Fri	•	6	13	20	27	•
Sat	•	7	14	21	28	•
Sun	1	8	15	22	29	•

	June				
Mon	•	6	13	20	27	•
Tues	•	7	14	21	28	•
Wed	1	8	15	22	29	•
Thu	2	9	16	23	30	•
Fri	3	10	17	24	•	•
Sat	4	11	18	25	•	•
Sun	5	12	19	26	•	•

	July				
Mon	•	4	11	18	25	•
Tues	•	5	12	19	26	•
Wed	•	6	13	20	27	•
Thu	•	7	14	21	28	•
Fri	1	8	15	22	29	•
Sat	2	9	16	23	30	•
Sun	3	10	17	24	31	•

	August				
Mon	1	8	15	22	29	•
Tues	2	9	16	23	30	•
Wed	3	10	17	24	31	•
Thu	4	11	18	25	•	•
Fri	5	12	19	26	•	•
Sat	6	13	20	27	•	•
Sun	7	14	21	28	•	•

	September				
Mon	•	5	12	19	26	•
Tues	•	6	13	20	27	•
Wed	•	7	14	21	28	•
Thu	1	8	15	22	29	•
Fri	2	9	16	23	30	•
Sat	3	10	17	24	•	•
Sun	4	11	18	25	•	•

	October				
Mon	•	3	10	17	24	31
Tues	•	4	11	18	25	•
Wed	•	5	12	19	26	•
Thu	•	6	13	20	27	•
Fri	•	7	14	21	28	•
Sat	1	8	15	22	29	•
Sun	2	9	16	23	30	•

	November				
Mon	•	7	14	21	28	•
Tues	1	8	15	22	29	•
Wed	2	9	16	23	30	•
Thu	3	10	17	24	•	•
Fri	4	11	18	25	•	•
Sat	5	12	19	26	•	•
Sun	6	13	20	27	•	•

	December				
Mon	•	5	12	19	26	•
Tues	•	6	13	20	27	•
Wed	•	7	14	21	28	•
Thu	1	8	15	22	29	•
Fri	2	9	16	23	30	•
Sat	3	10	17	24	31	•
Sun	4	11	18	25	•	•

Note: *Easter weekend for 1988: April 1 — April 3.*

Glossary

ACRS	Accelerated cost recovery system
ADR	American depository receipt
ADRS	Asset depreciation range system
AGI	Adjusted gross income
AMEX	American Stock Exchange
AMT	Alternative minimum tax
APM	Appreciation participation mortgage
APR	Annual percentage rate
ARM	Adjustable rate mortgage
CBT	Chicago Board of Trade
CCH	Commerce Clearing House
CD	Certificate of deposit
CEO	Chief Executive Officer
CFC	Chartered Financial Counselor
CFP	Certified Financial Planner
ChFC	Chartered Financial Consultant
CLU	Chartered Life Underwriter
CME	Chicago Mercantile Exchange
COLA	Cost-of-living adjustment
COMEX	New York Commodity Exchange
CPA	Certified Public Accountant
CPCU	Chartered Property-Casualty Underwriter
CPI	Consumer price index
CPI-U	Consumer price index for all urban consumers
CPI-W	Consumer price index for urban wage earners and clerical workers
DBA	Doing business as
DJIA	Dow Jones Industrial Average
DJTA	Dow Jones Transportation Average
DJUA	Dow Jones Utility Average
ERISA	Employee Retirement Income Security Act of 1974
ERTA	Economic Recovery Tax Act of 1981
ESOP	Employee stock ownership plan
FASB	Financial Accounting Standards Board
FDIC	Federal Deposit Insurance Corporation
FHA	Federal Housing Administration
FHLBB	Federal Home Loan Bank Board
FHLMC	Federal Home Loan Mortgage Association (Freddie Mac)
FICA	Federal Insurance Contributions Act
FNMA	Federal National Mortgage Association (Fannie Mae)
FREIT	Finite-life real estate investment trust
FSLIC	Federal Savings and Loan Insurance Corporation
FTC	Federal Trade Commission
FY	Fiscal year
GAAP	Generally accepted accounting principles
GAO	General Accounting Office
GNMA	Government National Mortgage Association (Ginnie Mae)
GNP	Gross national product
IAFP	International Association for Financial Planning
ICFP	Institute of Certified Financial Planners

IDB	Industrial development bond
IMF	International Monetary Fund
IRA	Individual retirement account
IRC	Internal Revenue Code
IRR	Internal rate of return
IRS	Internal Revenue Service
ITC	Investment tax credit
KCBT	Kansas City Board of Trade
MBA	Master of Business Administration
MMDA	Money market deposit account
NASD	National Association of Securities Dealers
NASDAQ	National Association of Securities Dealers Automated Quotations
NAV	Net asset value
NOW	Negotiable order of withdrawal
NPV	Net present value
NYSE	New York Stock Exchange
OASDI	Old-Age, Survivors, and Disability Insurance
OASDHI	Old-Age, Survivors, Disability, and Hospital Insurance
OID	Original issue discount
OMB	Office of Management and Budget
OTC	Over-the-counter
PE	Price-earnings ratio
Q-TIP	Qualified terminal interest property trust
REIT	Real estate investment trust
S&L	Savings and loan
S&P	Standard & Poor's
SBA	Small Business Administration
SEC	Securities and Exchange Commission
SEP	Simplified employee pension
SLMA	Student Loan Marketing Association (Sallie Mae)
SPDA	Single premium deferred annuity
SSA	Social Security Administration
T	Treasury (T-bill, T-note)
TEFRA	Tax Equity and Fiscal Responsibility Act of 1982
TRA	Tax Reform Act of 1984
UGMA	Uniform Gift to Minors Act
VA	Veterans Administration
ZBA	Zero-bracket amount

Abstract. In real estate, a document that lists the history of a parcel of land, from the original grant through each transfer of title to the present title holder. It also lists all mortgages outstanding on the property and any defects that could cloud the transfer of title.

Accelerated cost recovery system (ACRS). A system provided under the Economic Recovery Tax Act of 1981 to determine annual deductions on capital assets such as equipment, land, furniture; allows for larger deductions in the earlier years of ownership and smaller deductions in later years. ACRS also allows for faster amortization and depreciation than the Asset Depreciation Range System (ADRS) it replaced.

Acceleration clause. A clause in a deed of trust, mortgage, or similar contract that stipulates that the entire balance owing shall become due and immediately payable in the event of a breach of certain conditions of the contract, e.g., insolvency or the debtor's failure to pay taxes on mortgaged property.

Acceptance liability. The liability assumed by a bank in accepting negotiable instruments drawn upon it by its customers or by beneficiaries of letter of credit.

Accomodation endorsement. The signature of a third party on a note or draft solely for the purpose of inducing a bank to lend money to a borrower whose credit is not substantial enough to warrant a loan. The endorser, though liable to repay the amount in full, ordinarily does not expect to do so. He derives no benefit from the transaction, but acts as a guarantor or surety for the borrower.

Account. A record of all the financial transactions, and the date of each, affecting a particular phase of a business, expressed in debits and credits and showing the current balance, if any (the excess of debits over credits, or the excess of credits over debits).

Account executive. *See Registered representative.*

Accountant's opinion. The statement made by an independent accountant who has examined or audited an organization's financial records.

Accredited investor. Defined by the Securities and Exchange Commission, *Regulation D*, as an investor in a private limited partnership who has a net worth of at least $1 million, or an annual income of at least $200,000, or a net worth that is at least five times as much as his interest in the partnership and said interest is at least $150,000.

Accretion account. An account that records the increase between the acquisition value and the face value of bonds purchased at a discount. Under the accrual method of financial accounting, the discount would be accreted monthly in equal portions over the period from acquisition until maturity.

Accrual basis. In accounting, a method of recording and apportioning expense and income as they are incurred or earned, regardless of the date of payment or collection. (*Compare Cash basis.*)

Accrued dividend. A regular dividend considered earned but not declared or payable on legally issued stock or other instruments of ownership of a legally organized business or financial institution.

Accrued interest. Interest that has accumulated on a bond since the last interest payment was made; the buyer of the bond pays the market price plus accrued interest.

Accumulation plan. A plan for systematically purchasing mutual fund shares through periodic investments and reinvestments of income dividends and capital gains distributions.

Accumulation trust. A trust in which the income may in whole or in part be retained in trust instead of being distributed to the beneficiaries.

Acid-test ratio. A measure of corporate liquidity used by lending institutions to indicate the ability of a business enterprise to meet its current obligations. The calculation is:

Cash + Receivables + Marketable securities : Current liabilities

Frequently, a 1:1 ratio is considered satisfactory. Also called *quick ratio.*

Acquisition fees. The total of all fees and commissions paid to affiliates or nonaffiliates in connection with the purchase of a property for a real estate investment program. Acquisition fees include real estate commissions, development fees, selection fees, and nonrecurring management fees, but do not include loan fees (***points***) paid for mortgage brokerage services.

Acquittance. A document giving written evidence of the discharge of, or release from, a debt or financial obligation.

Actuary. A statistical mathematician who calculates premiums, dividends, reserves, and pension insurance, and annuity rates for an insurance company or other program involving fiscal risk.

Adjustable rate mortgage (ARM). Mortgage whose terms state that the interest rate will be periodically adjusted (e.g., every year, every three years) to reflect changes in a specified interest index (e.g., U.S. Treasury bills). At the outset, the interest rate for an ARM is lower than that for a conventional mortgage; but monthly payments will increase if the interest rate rises; also called a *variable rate mortgage*.

Adjusted basis. Price upon which capital gains or losses are calculated when an asset is sold. For example, the sales price of stock is adjusted to account for splits, and the cost of commissions is deducted from the sales price; the sales price of property is adjusted for depreciation.

Adjusted gross income (AGI). Interim calculation in the computation of income tax liability. From the taxpayer's gross income the following seven adjustments are made: moving expense, employee business expense, payments to an individual retirement account (IRA), payments to a Keogh account, penalty on early withdrawal of savings, alimony paid, and marital deduction for a couple both of whom work. Itemized deductions (Schedule A) or the standard deduction, allowed charitable contributions (for those who do not itemize), and personal exemptions are then subtracted from the AGI to calculate taxable income.

Adjuster. A person who investigates and determines the settlement of insurance claims. Staff, company, or independent adjusters represent insurers; public adjusters represent the policyholder for a fee.

Administration. The period of time after a decedent's death when the estate is settled under court supervision; synonymous with *probate*.

Administrator. The person or bank appointed by a court to carry out the distribution of a decedent's estate when the deceased has left no will or has left a will that fails to name an executor who is able to perform these duties.

Affidavit. A written statement sworn to or affirmed before an officer who has authority to administer an oath or affirmation.

Affiliate. A person or entity directly or indirectly controlled by another person or entity, including any officer, director, or partner of the entity. If such person is an officer, director, or partner, the company for which the person acts in such capacity is also considered an affiliate.

After-tax. The effective cost of, or return from, an investment, after the liability or credit has been taken into account.

Aggressive growth fund. A mutual fund whose primary investment objective is substantial capital gains, as opposed to current dividend income.

Alternative minimum tax (AMT). Federal income tax intended to ensure that individuals, trusts, and estates that benefit from *tax preferences* do not escape all federal income tax liability. Such taxpayers must calculate their income taxes by the regular method and by the AMT method—which disallows certain deductions, credits, and exclusions—and pay the greater of the two.

American depository receipt (ADR). Receipt held in a U.S. bank for the purchase of stock in a foreign corporation. American investors may purchase ADRs rather than buy shares directly on a foreign exchange in order to eliminate delays, fluctuations due to currency exchange rates, and related obstacles to purchase, transfer, and resale of shares.

Amortization. In banking, the gradual reduction of a debt by means of equal periodic payments sufficient to meet current interest and liquidate the debt at maturity. When the debt involves real property, the payments often include tax impounds and hazard insurance on the property.

In tax accounting, the procedure by which the acquisition cost of an intangible asset (e.g., copyright, patent, trademark, goodwill) is gradually reduced to reflect its declining resale value; similar to *depreciation* of tangible assets and *depletion* for natural resources.

Annual percentage rate (APR). Cost of a consumer loan, expressed as a simple annual percentage.

Annual renewable term insurance. A type of *term life insurance* that guarantees renewable coverage each year without evidence of insurability (e.g., a physical examination).

Annuity. An investment contract, usually purchased from an insurance company, that provides for future payments at regular intervals. Payments may be for a fixed period of time or until the annuitant's death, and their amount may be fixed or may vary with the value of the securities underlying the annuitant's account.

Annuity trust. *See Charitable remainder trust.*

Appraisal. An opinion of value (market, investment, or other) made by an expert based on facts and professional judgment.

Appraisal by comparison. In real estate, an estimate of a property's value based on a comparison with similar properties; sometimes referred to as *market approach*.

Appraisal by income. In real estate, an estimate of a property's value based on the net return it will bring.

Appraisal by summation. In real estate, an estimate of a property's value based on its *replacement cost;* sometimes known as *cost approach*.

Appreciate. To grow or increase in value.

Appreciation participation mortgage (APM). A mortgage in which the lender participates in the appreciation of the property by exchanging a reduction in the mortgage interest rate for a percentage of equity in the property. The lender shares in the appreciation at the time the loan is paid off.

Arbitrage. The simultaneous purchase and sale of foreign exchange, stocks, bonds, silver, gold, or other commodities in two markets to take advantage of price differentials between those markets.

Ascertainable standard. A beneficiary's power to consume trust principal in amounts limited to his health, education, maintenance, or support.

Asked price. The lowest price at which a seller is willing to sell a security or asset; as opposed to *bid price*, the price at which a buyer is willing to buy.

Assessed valuation. Value assigned to real property by municipal tax assessor.

Assessment. An amount of capital above his initial investment that an investor in a limited partnership may be required to contribute at a later date. The partnership prospectus indicates whether the program is assessable or nonassessable.

Asset. Any item that has commercial or exchange value and is owned by an individual or business entity. *See **Capital asset, Current asset, Fixed asset, Intangible asset.***

Asset depreciation range system (ADRS). A method for calculating the depreciation of business assets; for assets acquired after 1980, faster appreciation is accorded by the ***accelerated cost recovery system (ACRS).***

Assumption of mortgage. The taking of title to property whereby the buyer assumes liability for payment of an existing note secured by a mortgage or deed of trust against the property; the seller remains liable for the note unless explicitly released by the original lender.

Assured. The insured party or policyholder.

At-risk rules. Provisions of the Internal Revenue Code that limit a taxpayer's deductions for business losses to the amount of his liability (exposure to possible loss), which is defined to exclude borrowed amounts (1) for which an investor has no personal liability; (2) from related persons or those with an interest in the activity; and (3) protected against loss by guarantees, stop-loss agreements, and similar arrangements. At-risk rules also apply to investors' deductions for limited partnerships other than real estate; real estate partnerships are exempt from at-risk provisions.

Attestation. To bear witness to or give authenticity to a document by signing as a witness to the signature of another.

Auction. Procedure by which an item is sold at a price established by competitive bidding. In a conventional auction there is one auctioneer and many prospective buyers. In a *double-auction system* (or *two-sided market*) such as a stock exchange, many sellers and many buyers compete. In a *dutch auction* the seller ranks the bids received from highest to lowest, and accepts bids in order until the issue is sold. The lowest accepted price is then used as the price for the entire offering; Treasury bill auctions are conducted in that way.

Audit. Examination of accounting and financial documents by a professional who determines their accuracy, consistency, and conformity to legal and accounting principles.

Baby bond. Bond whose face value is $1,000 or less.

Balance sheet. An itemized statement that lists the total assets and the total liabilities of a given business to express its net worth at a given time.

Balanced mutual fund. A mutual fund that purchases common stock, preferred stock, and bonds. Such funds tend to be less volatile than all-equity funds, outperforming them in a declining market, but underperforming them in a rising market.

Balloon payment. A final installment payment on a note that is greater than the preceding payments and pays the note in full.

Bankruptcy. Insolvency (inability to pay debts when due) of an individual or an organization, judged by a federal court on the basis of a petition from the debtor (*voluntary bankruptcy*) or a creditor (*involuntary bankruptcy*). See **Chapter 7 proceeding, Chapter 11 proceeding, Chapter 13 proceeding.**

Basis. The cost and out-of-pocket expenses (e.g., commission) of acquiring an investment asset. When the investor sells the asset, the basis is subtracted from the sales price to determine the short- or long-term **capital gain (or loss).**

Basis point. One-hundredth of a percentage point (0.01%) of yield on a bond or note.

Bear. Someone who believes the stock market will decline.

Bear market. A declining stock market.

Bearer bond. A bond that does not have the owner's name registered on the books of the issuing company and that is payable to the holder.

Below-market rate loan. Any loan on which the interest rate is below prevailing rates in the marketplace. In particular, a loan between family members. (*See* **Gift loan.**)

Beneficiary. Person named in a will, trust agreement, insurance policy, annuity contract, or similar document to receive financial benefits.

Bequest. A gift of personal property made by a decedent in his will; the recipient is called the *legatee.*

Beta coefficient. A measure of a stock's volatility as compared to the Standard & Poor's 500 Index; stocks with a beta above 1 rise and fall faster than the S&P 500 Index; those with a beta below 1, more slowly than the index.

Bid price. The highest price a prospective buyer is prepared to pay to acquire a security or asset.

Big board. Colloquial term for the New York Stock Exchange.

Big eight. Colloquial term for the largest accounting firms in the U.S. In 1985 these were: Arthur Andersen & Co.; Coopers and Lybrand; Deloitte Haskins & Sells; Ernst & Whinney; Peat, Marwick Mitchell & Co.; Price Waterhouse & Co.; Touche Ross & Co.; and Arthur Young & Co.

Bill of exchange. *See* **Draft.**

Blind pool program. An investment program that at the time of inception does not have the proceeds of the offering allocated to specific projects or properties.

Block. A large holding or transaction of stock (usually 10,000 shares or more) or bonds (usually $200,000 or more).

Blue chip. The common stock of a company with a reputation for the quality and wide acceptance of its products or services, as well as a strong history of profitability and dividend payment.

Blue-sky laws. A popular name for laws enacted by various states to protect the public against securities frauds. The term is believed to have originated when a judge ruled that a particular stock had about the same value as a patch of blue sky.

Bond. Basically an IOU or promissory note of a corporation, usually issued in multiples of $1,000. A bond is evidence of a debt on which the issuing company promises to pay the bondholders a specified amount of interest and to repay the principal at maturity. A *secured bond* is backed by collateral; an unsecured bond (*debenture*), by the full faith and credit of the issuer.

Bond rating. Estimate of the financial strength of a bond issuer made to advise investors of the risk of default. The ratings—issued by Standard & Poor's, Moody's Investors Service, and Fitch's Investors Service—range from AAA down to D (in default); bonds rated B or lower are considered speculative. *See **Investment grade.***

Book value. In accounting, the cost of an asset minus its accumulated depreciation.

In securities, the net asset value of a company's stock, calculated as follows: Deduct from the company's total assets the combined value of its current liabilities, intangible assets, and the liquidation price of its preferred issues. The net asset value (or book value) divided by the number of common shares outstanding equals the *book value per common share*, which may be higher or lower than the stock's market value.

Bracket creep. The movement of taxpayers into higher tax brackets as their income rises to keep pace with inflation. Indexing, inaugurated in 1985, eliminates bracket creep by raising the brackets, personal exemptions, and standard deduction each year to reflect the rising cost of living.

Broker. In securities, a person who serves as the intermediary between a buyer and a seller, usually receiving a commission for each completed transaction.

In insurance, a person who sells policies to clients.

In real estate, a person who represents the seller and receives a commission when the property is sold.

Budget. Estimate of income and expenses for a given period (e.g., a quarter, a year).

Bull. One who believes the stock market will rise.

Bull market. An advancing stock market.

Business cycle. A period of economic expansion followed by a period of contraction, measured by the rise and decline of the gross national product. Recent business cycles have lasted an average of 30 months.

Buyer's market. *See **Soft market.***

Buy-sell agreement. An agreement among co-owners of a business promising to buy out one of their number upon death or other eventualities.

By-pass trust. An irrevocable trust whereby, upon the death of the trustor, the principal passes to the beneficiaries without being assessed estate taxes.

Call. An **option** to buy 100 shares of a certain security at a specified price (*strike price*) within a given period of time (*maturity* or *expiration date*).

Callable bond. A bond that may be redeemed by the issuer before the maturity date.

Call protection. The period of time during which a callable bond cannot be redeemed by the issuer.

Capital account. An account maintained in the name of the owner or owners of a business that indicates his or their equity in that business, usually at the close of the last accounting period.

Capital asset. In business, an asset with a life of more than one year, including all fixed assets (furniture and fixtures, land, building, machinery, etc.).

In investments, a security held for longer than six months.

Capital gain (or loss). The difference between the sales price of a capital asset and the *basis* at which it was acquired. The gain (or loss) may be short-term or long-term. Under the Tax Reform Act of 1984, the holding period for a long-term capital gain (or loss) was shortened from a year and a day to six months and a day for assets acquired after June 22, 1984. (*Capital gain* is often used as shorthand for "long-term capital gain.")

Capital gains tax. Federal tax that must be paid in the year that a capital gain is incurred. Short-term capital gains are taxed as ordinary income; long-term capital gains receive special treatment: 60% of the long-term net gain is excluded from taxable income. (*Capital gains tax* is often used as shorthand for "long-term capital gains tax.")

Capital improvement. Improvement or replacement of a capital asset that is expected to produce benefits beyond one year.

Capitalization. The total value of a company's securities, capital surplus, and accumulated retained earnings.

Capitalization rate (cap rate). An approach to evaluating the sales price of income property based on its current net income.

Carryover. Individual taxpayers may carry forward capital losses that exceed the annual allowed deduction ($3,000 against income) to subsequent tax years.

Corporations may carry back losses against profits of the preceding three years, and may then carry forward capital losses for five years and net operating losses for up to fifteen years.

Cash basis. In accounting, a method of recording income when received and expenses when they are paid out. (*Compare* **accrual basis**.)

Cash flow. An analysis of the changes in a cash account during a given period (e.g., a quarter, a year). If cash income exceeds cash expenses, the cash flow is *positive*; in the opposite case, the cash flow is *negative*.

Cash surrender value. The amount that an insurance policyholder is entitled to receive should he discontinue the coverage. Policyholders are usually able to borrow from the insurance company against the surrender value of a policy that is in force.

Cash value insurance. An insurance policy that accumulates a nonforfeitable *cash surrender value*.

Certificate of deposit (CD). A receipt issued by a bank for a cash deposit for a specified period of time (a week to several years) at a fixed rate of interest (determined by the marketplace). Upon maturity, the bank pays the depositor the principal plus all accumulated interest. *Negotiable CDs* may be transferred before maturity; *nonnegotiable CDs* are not readily transferrable and early withdrawals are subject to interest penalties.

Certified Financial Planner (CFP). A designation granted by the College of Financial Planning (Denver, Colorado) to individuals who complete a six-part curriculum in financial planning (including risk management, investments, tax planning, employee benefits, and estate planning).

Certified Public Accountant (CPA). A professional license granted by a state board of accountancy to an individual who has passed the Uniform CPA Examination (administered by the American Institute of Certified Public Accountants) and has fulfilled that state's educational and professional experience requirements for certification.

Chapter 7 proceeding. A bankruptcy proceeding whereby the court appoints a trustee to oversee the liquidation of an insolvent individual's assets and distribute the proceeds to creditors. The debtor is entitled to retain a limited interest in certain necessary items (homestead, automobile, personal effects, and tools of his trade).

Chapter 11 proceeding. A bankruptcy proceeding whereby an insolvent corporation, partnership, or unincorporated business is allowed to retain possession and control of its assets under court supervision and regulation in order to reorganize the business and return it to solvency. Under a plan that must be confirmed by the debtor, the creditors, and the court, payment schedules are renegotiated and debt restructured. Individuals may also, but rarely do, file for bankruptcy under Chapter 11 of the Bankruptcy Code.

Chapter 13 proceeding. A bankruptcy proceeding whereby, under a court-supervised plan, the debtor retains control of all his assets and reschedules the repayment of debts over a period of up to three years.

Charitable lead trust. A trust established for a set number of years (*term*) and for the benefit of a charitable institution. The trustor-donor places income-producing assets in the trust fund, and during the term of the trust the charitable institution receives all income from the trust principal. After the termination of the trust, the property reverts to the trustor-donor or to his named beneficiaries.

Charitable remainder trust. A trust established for the benefit of a charitable institution from which the trustor-donor receives annual income for life. Upon the death of the trustor (or upon the death of a named individual beneficiary), the trust is terminated and the principal reverts to the charity. The trustor receives a charitable contribution deduction in the year in which the trust is established, and he is exempt from capital gains tax on securities placed in the trust. In a charitable remainder *annuity trust,* the annual income paid to the trustor is a fixed-dollar amount or a fixed-percentage amount of the initial value of the trust principal. In a charitable remainder *unitrust,* the annual sum may be a fixed percentage of the principal's value as redetermined each year.

Chartered Financial Consultant (ChFC). A designation granted by the American College (Bryn Mawr, Pennsylvania) to individuals who pass a series of ten written examinations on topics related to financial services, taxation, economics, and estate planning.

Chartered Life Underwriter (CLU). A designation granted by the American College (Bryn Mawr, Pennsylvania) to individuals who pass a series of ten written examinations on topics related to insurance, taxation, economics, and estate planning.

Clifford trust. An inter vivos trust lasting at least ten years and a day during which income from the trust principal is paid to the beneficiary and after which the principal reverts to the trustor.

Close corporation. *See* **Privately held corporation.**

Closed mortgage. A mortgage that cannot be paid off before maturity.

Closely held corporation. A corporation whose common stock is owned and controlled by relatively few shareholders, although some shares are publicly traded. (*Compare Privately held corporation.*)

Closing costs. The expenses involved in transferring the title of real property, including the costs of title search, title insurance, and filing fees.

Codicil. An amendment or supplement to a will.

Coincident economic indicator. A measure of economic performance or activity that tends to move simultaneously and proportionally to changes in the gross national product.

Collateral. Specific property pledged by a borrower as security for the repayment of a loan. The borrower agrees that the lender shall have the right to sell the collateral to liquidate the debt if the borrower fails to repay the loan at maturity or otherwise defaults under the terms of the loan agreement.

Collectibles. Generic term for works of art, stamps, coins, antiques, and other such objects that attract investment (as opposed to hobbyist) interest.

Commercial loan. A short-term loan made by a bank to a business enterprise for the production, manufacture, or distribution of goods or to finance related services.

Commercial paper. Short-term unsecured notes issued by banks and corporations, usually backed by bank lines of credit.

Commission. Fee charged by a broker for executing the purchase or sale of securities (or the sale of property).

Commodities. Generic term for goods such as grains, foodstuffs, livestock, oils, and metals traded on national exchanges.

Common stock. Unit of ownership in the assets of a corporation. Common stockholders participate in the corporation's profits (or loss) through the payment of dividends and changes in the stock's market value, and participate in corporate management and policy through their voting rights.

Community property. Property owned jointly by a husband and wife by reason of their marriage; state laws vary. In Arizona, California, Idaho, Louisiana, Nevada, New Mexico, Texas, and Washington, all property acquired during a marriage—excluding property acquired by one partner by will, inheritance, or gift—is considered community property, and each partner is entitled to half.

Compensating balance. A stipulation in a loan agreement made by a commercial bank requiring the borrower to keep on deposit a fixed percentage of the outstanding loan balance.

Compound interest. Interest that is computed on the principal and on the interest accrued during the preceding period. Interest may be computed daily, monthly, quarterly, semiannually, or annually for compounding purposes.

Condominium. An apartment or housing complex in which individual owners hold deed and title to their living unit and pay a monthly carrying charge to management for maintenance of common areas.

Conservator. An individual appointed by a court to guard and protect the property of someone incompetent to manage his own interests.

Constant dollars. Measure of purchasing power in which actual dollar costs over a period of years are expressed in terms of the dollar's purchasing power in a given base year. By comparing constant dollar costs, one can determine if the costs of certain goods or services have shown *real* (after-inflation) increases or if the nominal changes in price simply reflect the prevailing rate of inflation.

Constructive receipt. In taxation, the treatment of a taxpayer's right to claim income as of a given date as receipt of that income, whether or not he chooses actually to receive it. Thus, a stockholder must declare end-of-year dividend income in the year in which the dividend is distributed, even if he chooses not to actually receive the monies until the following tax year.

Consumer price index (CPI). Measure of changes in the cost of consumer goods (housing, food, transportation, medical care, entertainment, and the like). The U.S. Department of Labor calculates the index each month from the cost of some 400 items in urban areas across the nation. The current CPI uses 1967=100 as a base. In 1978, the Bureau of Labor began separately calculating the CPI-U (all urban consumers) and the CPI-W (urban wage earners and clerical workers).

Continuing guaranty. A pledge given to a bank by a third party to guarantee a borrower's repayment of a loan. The guarantor promises payment should the borrower default.

Conventional mortgage. A residential mortgage loan with a fixed interest rate and term (usually 30 years) that is to be repaid in equal monthly payments.

Conversion. In securities, the exchange of one type of security for another (e.g., the exchange of bonds for common stock. Similarly, the exchange of personal or real property of one nature for that of another nature.

Regarding trusts, the illegal appropriation or use of entrusted property without right or consent.

Convertible security. A corporate bond or preferred share that may be exchanged for a stated number of shares of the corporation's common stock.

Convertible term insurance. A *term life insurance* policy that allows the insured to convert the policy to *whole-life insurance* at some future date.

Conveyance. The transfer by mortgage, deed, bill of sale, or similar instrument, of the title of a property from one party to another.

Cooperative (co-op). A membership corporation that owns real property. Shareholders receive a proprietary lease to occupy an apartment or house owned by the co-op, and they pay a monthly carrying charge to cover the co-op's mortgage, property taxes, maintenance, and payroll. In *market-resale co-ops,* shares are bought and sold at free market prices; in *par-resale co-ops,* the share price is fixed by the co-op's board of directors. Prices of shares in *controlled-resale co-ops* are indexed to the consumer price index or other measure of inflation.

Corporate bond. A debt security issued by a corporation at a given rate of interest for a specified term, usually in units with a par value of $1,000.

Corporation. A legal entity chartered by state or federal government to conduct business. The rights and liabilities of a corporation are independent of the individuals who own it; a corporation is an independent legal person.

Corpus. The property placed in a trust; synonymous with *principal,* as distinguished from income or interest.

Cost approach. *See **Appraisal by summation.***

Cost-of-living adjustment (COLA). Adjustment, usually made annually, of wages, pensions, Social Security benefits, and the like based on changes in the consumer price index or other measure of inflation.

Counter check. A non-negotiable check that may be used only to draw funds from one's own checking account.

Coupon bond. A bearer bond carrying detachable certificates that the bondholder presents to receive periodic (usually semi-annual) interest payments.

Coupon rate. The rate of interest on a bond.

Court trust. A trust that is subject to the ongoing jurisdiction of the probate court.

Covenant. A contractual promise or agreement that is legally valid and enforceable and pledges the maker to perform or refrain from performing specified acts.

Credit rating. A statement prepared by a credit bureau that lists an individual or a company's credit history (loans, charge accounts, repayment record).

Credit union. A cooperative nonprofit financial institution organized by a labor union, religious group, or similar association and chartered by state or federal law. The members are the sole owners, and all profits are returned to them in the form of dividends, rebates, or improved services.

Crown loan. A demand loan between two family members that in effect shifts the income on the loaned funds to the member in the lower tax bracket. Under the Tax Reform Act of 1984, loans of more than $10,000 must be made at market interest rates; the donor of a *gift loan* that exceeds $10,000 must declare the foregone interest as income or as a gift and is liable for the income or gift tax.

Current asset. Cash and business assets that will be converted into cash within one year, such as accounts receivable, inventory, and marketable securities. *See also **Current liability.***

Current liability. Business liabilities that will become due within one year, such as accounts payable, accrued expenses, current portion of long-term debt, and income taxes payable. (*Compare **Current asset; Fixed liability.***)

Current yield. Annual return on a bond, computed by dividing the annual **coupon rate** by the market price. Current yield equals the coupon rate for bonds purchased at par, and exceeds it for bonds purchased at discount.

Custodian. A person or institution that holds the assets of another; a bank that serves as a depository for the assets of a mutual fund, corporation, or individual. Also, an adult who assumes responsibility for the financial transactions of a minor.

Customer's broker. *See **Registered representative.***

Cyclical industries. Industries that are most dependent on the health of the national economy—for example, housing, airlines, automobiles—and whose stocks therefore tend to rise and fall quickly in response to growth and decline in the gross national product. Noncyclical industries include food, utilities, insurance, and pharmaceuticals.

Date of record. *See* ***Record date.***

Days of grace. *See* ***Grace period.***

Dealer. In business, an individual who purchases goods or services for resale to customers.

In securities, an individual or company trading for its own account.

Debenture. A promissory note backed by the general credit of a company and not secured by collateral; an unsecured bond.

Debt-to-equity ratio. A measure of a corporation's use of financial leverage. Most often calculated:

Long-term debt + par value of preferred stock : common stockholders' equity

Decreasing term. A type of ***term life insurance*** in which the premiums remain the same and face value of coverage decreases over the life of the policy.

Deductible. In insurance, the amount per claim (or per year) that the policyholder must pay out of pocket before the insurer will provide benefits.

Deductions. Item that may be subtracted from taxable income, a taxable estate or gift, thereby lowering the amount on which the tax is assessed.

Deed. Written instrument that, when properly executed and delivered, conveys title to property.

Deed of trust. Written instrument by which the title to property is transferred to a trustee as collateral for a debt or other obligation.

Defalcation. The misappropriation of money or property by one to whom it has been entrusted by reason of his employment; embezzlement.

Default. The failure to do that which is required by law or to perform on an obligation previously undertaken. Most often used to refer to a borrower's failure to meet interest or principal payments on a loan.

Deferral of taxes. *See* ***Tax deferred.***

Deferred annuity. An annuity in which income payments to the annuitant (or named beneficiary) are to begin either when the annuitant reaches a specified age or a stated number of years in the future. During the accumulation period, earnings on the annuity investment compound tax-free.

Deficit. (1) The excess of liabilities over assets. (2) An obligation or expenditure that exceeds the amount allotted for the item in a budget. (3) The excess of obligations and expenditures as a whole over a given fiscal period.

Deficit financing. Government borrowing to meet expenses that exceed revenues.

Defined-benefit plan. A ***qualified retirement plan*** under which a retiring employee will receive a specified amount of money, either in a lump sum or in installments. Annual contributions are made to the plan, by the employer or employee, at the level needed to fund the benefit. Under the Tax Equity and Fiscal Responsibility Act of 1982, annual contributions are limited to the amount needed to fund a benefit equal to $90,000 or the employee's annual salary, whichever is less.

Defined-contribution plan. A *qualified retirement plan* under which the annual contribution, made by the employer or the employee, is limited to $30,000.

Deflation. Decline in the price of goods and services.

Delivery. Formal transfer, without the right to recall, of a deed to a new owner.

Demand loan. A loan that can be called for repayment whenever the lender chooses. (*Compare* **Term loan.**)

Depletion. In tax accounting, the method by which an allowance is made and charged against taxable income for the cost of exhausting oil, gas, and other natural resources. (*Compare* **Amortization**, **Depreciation**.)

Depreciation. In tax accounting, the deduction for the amortization of the cost of fixed assets over their useful life, even though the assets may be appreciating in value. Land is not depreciable, but improvements, plant, and equipment are.

Straight-line depreciation is the recognition of depreciation in equal annual amounts over the asset's useful life.

Accelerated depreciation recognizes amounts in excess of straight-line depreciation during the early years of the asset's useful life. Upon sale or disposition of the asset, the excess of the amounts depreciated over the allowable straight-line depreciation must be declared as taxable income.

Accumulated depreciation is the sum of all deductions for depreciation that have been taken to date on an asset.

Deregulation. The reduction of government regulation of an industry.

Devaluation. Government decision to lower the value of its currency in relation to another country's currency.

Development loan. A mortgage loan to finance all or part of the cost of acquiring and developing land, including the installation of utilities, roads, drainage and sewage systems, and similar improvements before construction.

Direct reduction mortgage. A mortgage that is liquidated (*amortized*) in equal monthly payments that represent interest, principal, and, in some cases, taxes, and insurance. The interest is computed on the monthly outstanding principal balance. Over the course of repayment, the principal balance declines and, therefore, the amount of interest declines and a larger portion of the monthly payment is applied to the reduction of principal. (*Compare* **Negative amortization.**)

Disclosure. Requirement that all information relevant to an investment decision be revealed to a prospective investor.

Discount. (1) Reduction in price of merchandise or invoice in exchange for prompt payment. (2) The difference between a bond's par value and its current market price.

Discount rate. Interest rate that the Federal Reserve charges member banks for loans.

Discount yield. Measurement of the return on U.S. Treasury bills based on the bill's par value, calculated:

$$\frac{\text{Par value} - \text{market price}}{\text{Market pice}} \times \frac{360 \text{ days}}{\text{Days to maturity}}$$

Discretionary account. An account in which a client gives his broker either complete or limited powers for the purchase and sale of securities or commodities, including selection, timing, amount, and price to be paid or received.

Discretionary income. The amount of an individual's income remaining after essential expenses (taxes, housing, food, etc.) have been paid.

Discretionary trust. A trust that allows the trustee to distribute the annual trust income among such specified persons as he sees fit.

Disinflation. A slowing in the rate of inflation.

Disposable income. An individual's after-tax income. (*Compare **Discretionary income**.*)

Diversification. In investments, the placement of funds among different companies, in different fields, or different categories (equities, bonds, precious metals, etc.). Also, the participation of a large corporation in a wide range of business activities.

Dividend. The portion of a corporation's net profits that its board of directors assigns for distribution to stockholders. A dividend is declared at a certain amount per share to be paid in cash (*cash dividend*) or in additional shares of stock (*stock dividend*). Dividends are usually declared quarterly; *extra cash dividends* are one-time distributions of excess profits over and above the regular dividend. A board may also vote a *scrip dividend* to be paid out at a future date once a specified event has taken place.

Dividend exclusion. Amount of dividend income that is exempt from income tax. The federal exclusion is $100 for individuals and $200 for couples filing jointly. Most domestic corporations can exclude 85% of dividends received from another domestic corporation.

Dollar-cost averaging. A system of buying a fixed-dollar amount of securities at regular intervals. The investor thus buys more shares when the price is low and fewer shares when it rises, and the average price per share is thus lower than had he periodically bought a fixed number of shares.

Domicile. The state which a decedent's estate will be probated and taxed, based on where he intended his permanent home to be and not necessarily the state of his residence.

Double indemnity. In accident insurance, provision for doubling the principal sum benefits for an accident due to certain perils. In life insurance, provision for doubling the face amount if death results from accidental (rather than natural) causes.

Double taxation. Refers to tax treatment of corporate profits, which are first taxed as corporate income and then, when distributed as dividends, taxed as income to the stockholder.

Dow Jones averages. A set of four stock indicators calculated each trading day by Dow Jones & Co. and published in most daily newspapers. The *Dow Jones Industrial Average* (DJIA, or "the Dow") tracks the market value of 30 leading industrial stocks; the *Dow Jones Transportation Average* (DJTA) monitors 20 airline, railroad, and trucking stocks; the *Dow Jones Utility Average* (DJUA) follows 15 gas and electric utility stocks. The *Dow Jones Composite* (or "Dow 65") combines the three subaverages.

Draft. A negotiable written order that tranfers a specified sum of money from the account of the payer to that of the payee; unlike a check, a draft is not posted as a debit until it is presented for payment. A *sight draft* is payable on demand; a *time draft* is payable either on a specified date or at a fixed period after demand. In foreign transactions, a draft is called a *bill of exchange*.

Due diligence. The research conducted by broker-dealers and other financial advisors on legal and economic soundness of an investment.

Dun & Bradstreet. Business information and publishing company best known for its reports and ratings of the creditworthiness of commercial entities. Also, the parent company of *Moody's Investors Service.*

Earned income. An individual's wages, salary, and other compensation derived from the sale of goods and services; distinguished from *unearned income* such as dividends and interest.

Earnest money. A sum of money given to bind an agreement or offer.

Earnings per share. A corporation's net income (after taxes and payments to preferred shareholders and bondholders) divided by the number of outstanding shares of common stock. A key indicator in the analysis of corporate performance.

Economic indicators. Measures of national business and economic activity calculated monthly and quarterly by the U.S. Department of Commerce. Based on recent business cycles, measures are classified as *leading indicators, coincident indicators,* and *lagging indicators.*

Election. A choice or option to select among alternatives.

Employee stock ownership plan (ESOP). A profit-sharing *qualified retirement plan* in which the employer's or employees' annual contributions are used to buy shares of company stock. Also called a *Kelso plan*, after Louis Kelso, who originated the concept.

Endorsement. In insurance, a written addition to a policy, the provisions of which supersede the original policy; also called a *rider.*

In banking and securities, the signature by the holder of a negotiable instrument (check, draft, promissory note) that effects its valid transfer.

Endowment. In insurance, a policy that pays the face amount to the insured if living on the maturity date, or to a beneficiary if the insured dies before that date.

Equity. An owner's interest in a property or business: the market value of the property or business, less all claims and liens upon it.

Equity build. An increase in the owner's equity in a property due to reduction (*amortization*) of existing loans by payments of principal. Equity build is not realized in cash until the sale and collection of sales proceeds of a property for a price of at least its original cost, or until the property is financed for an amount at least equal to the original mortgage.

Equity dollars. The actual cash outlay to the seller when a property is sold, including cash deposits paid to the seller before close of escrow that are attributable to the purchase price.

Equity kicker. Provision for a lender's equity participation in a real property as an inducement to lend funds.

Equity REIT. A *real estate investment trust (REIT)* that acquires income-producing properties, as contrasted with a mortgage REIT, which makes or purchases loans on real estate.

Equivalent taxable yield. Method for comparing the aftertax returns on taxable and tax-exempt investments:

(Tax-exempt yield) ÷ (1 − t) = Equivalent taxable yield

where t = the investor's tax bracket expressed as a two-place decimal (42% bracket = 0.42).

Escalation clause. A provision in a lease that allows increases in rent when the landlord's actual costs rise or in the event of other economic factors, such as changes in the consumer price index.

Escheat. The right of a state to take possession of all property that has been abandoned or unclaimed after a lengthy period and of which there is no one qualified to claim ownership.

Escrow. The deposit of instruments and funds with a third, neutral party until the provisions of an agreement or contract are carried out.

ESOP. *See Employee stock ownership plan.*

Estate. All assets owned by an individual at the time of his death: funds, personal effects, interests in business enterprises, titles to property, and evidences of ownership, such as stocks, bonds, mortgages owned, and notes receivable.

Estate planning. Coordinated activities intended to provide for the orderly disposition of an individual's assets upon his death; includes writing a will, establishing trusts, etc.

Estate tax. The tax imposed by the federal government and some states on the estate of a decedent, taxing the decedent's privilege of leaving his property to others at his death.

Estate trust. *See Marital deduction trust.*

Excise tax. State or federal tax on the manufacture or sale of specified items, e.g., tobacco and alcohol.

Estimated tax. Quarterly income tax payments required of self-employed individuals, employed individuals whose withholding is inadequate, and individuals liable for the alternative minimum tax.

Excess reserves. The amount of funds a bank holds in reserve that exceed the legal minimum reserve requirements. These funds may be held on deposit in a federal reserve bank, in a bank approved as a depository, or carried in cash reserve within a bank's own vaults.

Ex-dividend. Said of stock traded after the record date for dividends, when the price quoted excludes the payment of any declared dividend to the buyer, and the dividend reverts to the seller.

Executor. The person named in a will to carry out the decedent's wishes for the distribution of his assets; the executor fulfills his duties under court supervision.

Exercise price. The price at which the stock or commodity underlying an option can be purchased (call option) or sold (put option); also called *strike price.*

Ex-rights. Said of common stock traded after the closing date for the corporation's offer of rights (the option to purchase new or additional shares at a discount from the prevailing market price). The buyer of shares selling ex-rights is not entitled to the rights.

Extended term insurance. A nonforfeiture option that provides the face amount of insurance for a limited time without further payment of premiums.

Face value. The principal value of an instrument; the individual or other legal entity who issues a note, bond, or other obligation, contracts to repay the face value of the obligation at maturity. The yield on interest-bearing obligations is based on face value.

Fair market value. What a willing buyer would pay a willing seller if neither were under any compulsion. The standard at which property is valued for estate tax purposes.

Family allowance. The amount allowed by a probate court for the monthly support of a surviving spouse and often, also, minor children. Takes precedence over claims of most creditors.

Family income policy. A combination of *whole life* and *decreasing term insurance.* If the insured dies before the end of a specified period, the beneficiary receives income payments through the end of the period in addition to the face amount.

Family trust. A type of trust that provides income to a spouse and, upon the spouse's death, is automatically disbursed to children.

Fannie Mae. *See Federal National Mortgage Association.*

Federal Deposit Insurance Corporation (FDIC). A corporation established by federal authority to provide insurance on demand and time deposits in participating banks, up to a maximum of $100,000 for each account.

Federal funds rate. Interest rate charged by banks for overnight loans to other banks whose reserves are below minimum requirements. The rate is negotiated among the banks and changes throughout the day.

Federal Home Loan Mortgage Corporation (FHLMC, Freddie Mac). A government-sponsored corporation whose stockholders are savings institutions across the country. The corporation buys residential mortgages from member lenders, repackages them as mortgage-backed securities, and sells these securities on the open market.

Federal Housing Administration (FHA). Federal government agency that insures loans on residential property.

Federal National Mortgage Association (FNMA, Fannie Mae). A publicly owned, government-sponsored corporation that purchases mortgages insured by the Federal Housing Administration and the Veterans Administration, repackages them as mortgage-backed securities, and sells these securities on the open market.

Federal Reserve System. Established by the Federal Reserve Act of 1913, the system acts as a central bank and fiscal agent of the U.S. Its functions include regulating the money supply, setting reserve requirements, and acting as a clearinghouse for the transfer of funds. The system is governed by the Federal Reserve Board, whose seven members are appointed by the President of the U.S. The system includes 12 regional Federal Reserve Banks, their branches, and national and state member banks.

Federal Savings and Loan Insurance Corporation (FSLIC). A federal agency that insures deposits in member institutions for up to $100,000 per account.

Fee simple absolute. In real estate, a property over which the titleholder has full ownership without limitations or end. He may dispose of it by sale, trade, or will, as he chooses.

Fiduciary. An agent who acts on behalf of another in a financial transaction: executors of wills, court-appointed conservators, receivers-in-bankruptcy, administrators of estates, trustees, and custodians.

Fiduciary income tax return. The tax return that must be filed by an estate, a trust, or other entity managed by a fiduciary.

Financial Accounting Standards Board (FASB). A seven-person national board, including four certified public accountants, that establishes standards of, and issues policies on, financial accounting and reporting.

Financial statement. A summary of numerical facts, such as a balance sheet or an income statement, that shows some aspect of the financial condition of a business.

First mortgage. A mortgage that usually takes priority over other liens on a piece of real property and which must be satisfied before any other claims on the proceeds of a property sale.

First-mortgage loan. A loan for which a first mortgage is used as security or collateral.

Fiscal year (FY). A 365-day period used for accounting and tax purposes; does not necessarily coincide with the calendar year.

Five-by-five power. The annual power to take from the principal of a trust an amount not exceeding $5,000 or 5% of the principal, whichever is greater.

Fixed annuity. An *annuity* that guarantees a set payment, to be made in a lump sum or in periodic installments for life or for a specified term. *Compare* **Variable annuity.**

Fixed asset. Tangible business property that is neither consumed nor converted into cash during the course of ordinary operations: plant, equipment, furniture, machinery, and the like.

Fixed-income investment. A security that pays a set rate of interest over the duration of the investment term, for example, a bond.

Fixed liability. Any liability that will not mature within the ensuing fiscal year; distinguished from a *current liability.*

Float. The period between the deposit of a check and the payment. Long floats are to the advantage of the bank in which the deposit is made, since it need not pay interest until the check clears. Long floats also benefit the checkwriter, while short floats benefit the depositor.

Floater. Property insurance that covers transportable items—jewelry, art objects, equipment, financial instruments, etc.—outside the policyholder's residence or place of business.

Flower bonds. U.S. Treasury obligations—last issued in 1971, with 1998 maturity—sold at discount and redeemable at par for the payment of federal estate taxes.

Foreclosure. A legal process whereby the mortgagee takes possession of the property when the mortgagor defaults on payments. The property is usually sold at a court-administered auction, with the proceeds assigned to the mortgagee to pay off the balance due; any remaining proceeds go to the former owner.

Foreign exchange. The trading in or exchange of foreign currencies, with rates of exchange based on supply, demand, and the stability of the currencies.

Fortune 500. The 500 largest U.S. manufacturing and industrial corporations, ranked annually by *Fortune* magazine according to sales. The *Fortune Service 500* are the 500 largest nonmanufacturing companies (service, financial, insurance, transportation, utilities, retail, etc.) ranked by sales or revenue.

401(k) plan. A deferred compensation plan that allows employees to place a portion (up to 25%) of their salaries into a company-established profit-sharing fund whose earnings compound tax-free until withdrawal. The employee's annual contributions are excluded from federal income tax (state laws vary) but are subject to social security tax. Optional employer-matching contributions and the cost of maintaining the plan are deductible to the corporation as a current business expense. Withdrawals are permitted only after age 59½, upon leaving the company, or for hardship, disability, or death.

Franchise. A legal right or privilege granted to an individual or business entity by a government agency. Also, the privilege given by a manufacturer to a dealer permitting him to sell the manufacturer's products.

Freddie Mac. *See **Federal Home Loan Mortgage Corporation.***

Front-end load. A sales charge incurred on the purchase of an investment (annuity, insurance policy, mutual fund shares, limited partnership units). Sales charges incurred upon sale of the investment are called *back-end load.*

Frozen asset. An asset that cannot be used nor disposed of by its owner pending the outcome of a legal action.

Full faith and credit. Said of a municipal, state, or federal security backed by the reputation and taxing power of its issuer.

Fully managed fund. A mutual fund whose investment policy gives its management complete flexibility as to the types of investments made and the proportions of each, subject only to federal and state securities laws.

Funded trust. A living trust that has had property transferred to it.

General obligation bond. A municipal bond backed by the general taxing power of its issuer.

General partner. An individual who is personally responsible for the activities and management of a partnership and has full personal liability for its debts and obligations. (*See also **Limited partnership.***)

Generally accepted accounting principles (GAAP). Procedures and rules established for the accounting profession by the Financial Accounting Standards Board, an independent self-regulatory organization.

Gift loan. Defined by the Tax Reform Act of 1984 as any loan made at below-market interest rates when the foregone interest constitutes a gift from the lender to the borrower. Foregone interest is imputed to the lender as income *except* if (1) the loan is for $10,000 or less to an individual whose total indebtedness to the lender is $10,000 or less, and the borrower does not invest the loan monies in income-producing assets; or (2) the loan is for $100,000 or less, the primary purpose of the loan is not tax avoidance, and the borrower's net investment income does not exceed $1,000.

Gift tax. A federal tax levied on the transfer of property as a gift; the tax is paid by the donor. The first $10,000 a year to each recipient is exempt from the tax ($20,000 if the donor or donee is a married couple), and gifts between spouses are exempt. Most states also impose a gift tax.

Gifts to Minors Acts. *See Uniform Gifts to Minors Act.*

Ginnie Mae. *See Government National Mortgage Association.*

Goodwill. An intangible asset that enables a business to earn a profit in excess of the usual profit earned by other similar businesses; for example, a particularly favorable location, reputation in the trade, the quality of the employer-employee relationships, monopolistic privilege, or a combination of these and other favorable conditions.

Government National Mortgage Association (GNMA, Ginnie Mae). A government-owned corporation that purchases mortgages from private lenders, repackages them as mortgage-backed certificates, and sells the certificates (*Ginnie Maes*) on the open market. Certificate holders receive payments of principal and interest each month, with timely payment guaranteed by the GNMA.

Government obligations. Debt instruments issued by the federal government and directly backed by its full faith and credit; for example, Treasury notes, bills, and bonds, and U.S. savings bonds.

Government securities. Bonds and other debt instruments issued by federal agencies. Although government securities have high credit ratings, they are not backed by the full faith and credit of the federal government.

Grace period. Length of time allowed for late payment without payee's incurring penalty or loss.

Graduated-payment mortgage. A fixed-rate mortgage in which the first few years' payments are lower, and payments gradually increase at a predetermined rate as the borrower's earning power increases, or is expected to.

Grandfather clause. A provision in a new regulation, rule, or law that allows persons or companies already following old rules to continue to do so.

Grantor. The creator of a trust; synonymous with *settlor* and *trustor.*

Gross lease. A lease in which the landlord (*lessor*) pays all property taxes, operating expenses, insurance, and improvements.

Gross multiplier. In real estate, a method of evaluating property using an analysis of the property's income compared to that of similar properties in the same or comparable market area.

Gross national product (GNP). Value of the goods and services produced in the U.S. The Department of Commerce computes the GNP quarterly and also issues figures for the *real GNP* (inflation-adjusted).

Growth fund. A mutual fund with an investment objective of long-term capital growth and capital gains, rather than of current income.

Growth investments. Investments that allow for capital growth but are not highly speculative; for example, mutual funds, managed equities, and stocks, among others. Growth investments are riskier than conservative fixed-interest investments (certificates of deposit, government securities) but less risky than speculative investments such as collectibles, penny stocks, or commodity trading.

Growth stock. A stock whose recent earnings record shows above-average growth in profitability. Growth stocks tend to have higher price-earnings ratios and lower dividend rates.

Guaranteed letter of credit. A traveler's letter of credit or commercial letter of credit for which the applicant does not pay the bank in cash upon the letter's issuance but guarantees later reimbursement to the bank; for this accommodation, the applicant is often required to pledge collateral security.

Guaranteed renewable policy. An insurance policy renewable at the option of the insured to a stated age, usually 60 or 65. The policyholder's premiums may be changed only if they are changed for an entire class of insured persons.

Guaranty. A written and legally enforceable promise by one person (the *guarantor*) to be liable for the debt of another person upon being notified by the creditor that the debtor has failed to perform his obligation.

Guardian. An individual or corporation appointed by a court to manage the legal and financial affairs or person of a minor or of an adult judged incompetent by reason of mental or physical condition.

Hard asset. *See* ***Tangible asset.***

Hedge. An investment undertaken to offset the risk entailed by another investment. For example, dealers in commodities and securities—to prevent loss due to price fluctuations—may counterbalance one transaction with another purchase or sale of a similar commodity. Individual stockholders may hedge their portfolio by buying ***puts*** or selling ***calls.***

Heir. Anyone acquiring property upon the death of another, either under terms of the decedent's will or by intestacy.

Holder in due course. An individual who assumes possession of a negotiable instrument under the following conditions: (1) that the instrument is complete and regular upon its face; (2) that he became the holder before the instrument was overdue and received no notice that it had been dishonored; (3) that he took it in good faith and for value; and (4) that he had no notice of any infirmity in the instrument or any defect in the title or capacity of the person negotiating it.

Holding company. In general, a corporation that owns enough stock in another corporation to control management and policies. In relation to public utility companies, any business entity that owns or controls at least 10% of the utility's voting shares.

Holding period. The length of time that an investor has owned a capital asset. The Tax Reform Act of 1984 shortened the capital gains holding period from a year and a day to six months and a day.

Holographic will. A will entirely in the handwriting of the testator. Holographic wills are valid and enforceable only in some states.

Homestead. A probate provision that allows a surviving spouse to continue to live in the family residence for a specified period of time.

Hypothecated account. A savings or trust account that is pledged or assigned as collateral for a loan.

Hypothecation. An agreement that permits a creditor to transfer the rights to collateral pledged to secure a loan should the loan be unpaid at maturity. A *hypothecation loan* is secured or collateralized by an existing mortgage loan, but without the retirement, reconveyance, or sale of the existing loan.

Illiquid. A security that does not have an active secondary market and is therefore difficult to convert to cash before maturity. Similarly, a tangible asset that cannot be readily converted into cash.

Impound account. In a securities offering, a fund set up by the sponsors to hold the subscription monies of investors, at a prescribed interest rate, until the offering is fully subscribed. When the impound amount is reached, the financial institution holding the funds releases them to the sponsor for use as described in the prospectus of the program.

Incentive stock option. A bonus given to executives who meet specified performance goals that allows them to purchase their company's stock at below-market prices.

Incidents of ownership. In life insurance, the totality of rights held by a policyowner (e.g., to cash in the policy, to borrow against it).

Income averaging. Method of computing income tax whereby an individual taxpayer whose income rises sharply in a given year can reduce his tax liability for that year by averaging current income and taxable income for several immediately preceding years. The Tax Reform Act of 1984 shortened the averaging period to three years and raised the threshold for current income to 140% of averageable income.

Income fund. A mutual fund whose investment objective is current income rather than capital growth. Income funds often invest in bonds and other fixed-income securities.

Indenture. A written agreement that sets forth the maturity date, interest rate, and other terms under which new bonds and debentures are to be issued.

Index. A statistical measure of change in value or quantity as compared to a standard or base. The base is usually expressed numerically as 100 (or 10), and the current value or quantity is expressed relative to the base. For example, the consumer price index (CPI) uses 1967 as a base (1967 prices = 100); when the CPI reached 300, prices had tripled from their 1967 levels.

Indexing. The use of an index of economic activity as a trigger for changes in another activity. For example, cost-of-living adjustments or income tax brackets may be indexed to the consumer price index or another measure of inflation.

Individual retirement account (IRA). A personal investment account that may be established by any individual who has earned income. Annual contributions to an IRA are deductible from gross income in the calculation of federal and state income taxes (though state laws vary), and earnings on the account accumulate tax-free until withdrawal, when they are taxed as ordinary income. Annual contributions are limited to $2,000 a year ($4,000 for a couple both of whom work, $2,250 for a couple only one of whom works). Monies withdrawn prior to age 59½ are subject to a 10% penalty in addition to being taxed as ordinary income. IRAs may be used to purchase stocks, bonds, mutual funds, limited partnership units, annuities, etc.; life insurance, collectibles, and any investments made on margin are prohibited.

Infirmity. Any known act or omission in the creation or transfer of an instrument that would invalidate it. Common examples are a missing endorsement, signature, or amount, or a discrepancy in the written and numerical figure for the amount.

Inflation. Condition in which the overall prices of goods and services continue to rise, usually caused by an undue expansion in paper money and credit relative to the supply of goods. In the U.S. the rate of inflation is measured by the ***consumer price index.***

Inheritance tax. An excise tax imposed by many states on the recipient of inherited property. (In contrast, an estate tax is imposed on the decedent's assets.)

Installment sale. A transaction in which the buyer makes periodic payments to the seller. In certain cases, the seller's tax liability for gains on the sale may be prorated over the payment period.

Instrument. A written document in which some right is conferred or some contractual relationship expressed.

Intangible Asset. An asset with no substance or physical body, for example, trademarks, licenses, *goodwill,* and patent rights.

Interest. Payment made by a borrower to a lender for the use of his money.

Interest-free loan. *See Gift loan.*

Internal rate of return (IRR). *See Net present value.*

Interstate offering. An offering of securities in more than one state. Interstate offerings are regulated both by federal securities laws and by the securities laws of each state where offered.

Inter vivos trust. (Latin: "during life.") A trust established during the trustor's lifetime; *compare Testamentary trust.*

Intestate. Legal status of a decedent who did not leave a valid will bequeathing his property; state law then determines who inherits the property.

Intrastate offering. An offering of securities within only one state, restricted to residents of that state, and regulated by the securities laws of that state.

Inventory. In business, the dollar value of all raw materials, supplies, goods, and finished products owned by a company. Also, a list of all property owned by an individual, company, or estate, including the cost or market value of each item.

Invested capital. Capital contributions of investors in a limited partnership, less the sum of cumulative surplus funds distributed to investors.

Investment company. *See Management company.*

Investment grade. Bond rate BBB or better by Standard & Poor's or another investment rating service. Issues below this level are speculative and are sometimes called *junk bonds.*

Irrevocable trust. A trust that may not be revoked or amended by its creator, except in jurisdictions that allow revocation if the trust's intentions have been fulfilled and the beneficiary agrees to the revocation.

Issue. Stocks, bonds, or securities sold by a corporation or government entity.

All persons directly descended from an individual (children, grandchildren, great-grandchildren, etc.)

Joint account. Bank or brokerage account owned by two or more individuals. May allow any one individual to make transactions or may require the consent of all co-owners.

Joint and mutual will. A single will signed by a husband and wife that disposes of their property at each death.

Joint and survivor annuity. A guaranteed periodic (usually monthly) sum payable first to one person for his lifetime and then to his designated survivor for his or her lifetime.

Joint and two-thirds survivor annuity. An annuity under which joint annuitants receive payments during their lifetimes. After the death of one annuitant, the survivor receives two-thirds of the joint annuity payments.

Joint life insurance. A policy that insures two or more lives.

Joint tenancy. Co-ownership of property by two or more people in which the survivor(s) automatically assume ownership of a decedent's interest.

Joint venture. A form of business organized by two or more persons or companies to carry out an enterprise for profit. Joint venturers share in the project's management, profits and losses, and liabilities.

Jointly and severally. Said of an obligation for which each individual obligor as well as the group of obligors may be held liable.

Jumbo certificate of deposit. A certificate of deposit whose denomination is $100,000 or more.

Junk bond. A bond rated BB or lower by Standard & Poor's or another investment rating service. Junk bonds are riskier than investment grade bonds (rated BBB or higher) and pay higher yields.

Kelso plan. *See Employee stock option plan.*

Keogh plan. A retirement plan for self-employed persons, owners of unincorporated businesses, and their employees. Annual contributions—up to the lesser of 25% of earned income or $30,000—are tax deductible and earnings on the account accumulate tax-free until withdrawal, when they are taxed as ordinary income. Withdrawals before age 59½ are subject to penalties, but withdrawals must begin by age 70½.

Kiting. Illegal scheme for taking advantage of the several days' lapse between the deposit of a check and collection from the bank on which it was drawn (*float*). The check kiter thus draws new checks against an uncollected balance.

Lagging indicator. A measurement of an economic or business activity that has historically tended to increase (or decrease) after movement in the rest of the business cycle.

Land contract. In real estate, a sale of property whereby the seller retains legal title and pays the existing mortgage until the buyer makes an agreed-upon number of payments to the seller; usually, the tax deductions accrue to the buyer. Most often used when there is a legally enforceable due-on-sale clause in the seller's mortgage.

Leading indicator. A measurement of an economic or business activity that has historically tended to increase in advance of an increase in gross national product, and to decline in advance of a decline in the gross national product. The U.S. Department of Commerce publishes a monthly composite index of 12 leading indicators: average workweek in manufacturing, average weekly claims for state unemployment insurance, new orders for consumer goods and materials, vendor performance, net business formation, contracts and orders for plant and equipment, new building permits issued, change in inventories, change in sensitive materials prices, index of stock prices, money supply (M-2), change in business and consumer credit.

Lease. A contract between a property owner (*lessor*) and tenant (*lessee*) setting forth conditions upon which tenant may occupy and use the property.

Lease option. In real estate, a contract that permits a tenant to purchase a home he has been leasing. Usually a portion of the monthly payments is applied to the purchase price.

Leaseback. In real estate, the practice of a new buyer's leasing property back to the seller for a definite time period. If extended over a long period of time, a leaseback is similar to a loan for which the seller pledges the property as collateral. Short-term lease-backs are often used to obtain a seller's guarantee of cash flow during the start-up operations of a newly developed property.

Legacy. A gift of property, usually cash, made in a will.

Legal entity. Any individual, proprietorship, partnership, corporation, association, or other organization that has the legal capacity to make a contract or an agreement and the ability to assume an obligation and discharge an indebtedness.

Legal liability insurance. Insurance policy that provides coverage for the legal liability incurred by a policyholder, e.g., damage caused by fire to another party due to insured's negligence.

Legal list. A list of investments selected by a state to restrict the types of investments that may be made by institutions and *fiduciaries,* such as insurance companies, pension funds, and banks. Legal lists are usually restricted to high-quality debt and equity securities. (Other states use the *prudent man rule* to regulate fiduciary conduct.)

Legal rate of interest. The maximum rate of interest that is permitted by the laws of the state having jurisdiction over the legality of a transaction; to charge interest in excess of this legal rate constitutes *usury.*

Lessee. A person or entity who enters into a contractual relationship to use property owned by another. In real estate, a lessee is commonly called a *tenant.*

Lessor. A property owner who enters into a contractual relationship in order to allow another person or entity to make use of that property. In real estate, a lessor is commonly called a *landlord.*

Letter of credit. An instrument issued by a bank guaranteeing the credit of an individual or corporation up to the amount stated and for the period stated.

Letters testamentary. In many states, the will or other document that evidences the authority of an executor to act for the decedent's estate.

Level term. A form of *term life insurance* in which the face value and the premiums remain level for the life of the policy.

Leverage. In investments, the investor's use of borrowed money, such as the purchase of stocks on margin or the securing of a mortgage to finance the purchase of income-producing real estate.

In business, *financial leverage* is the relation of a company's debt to its equity; shareholders benefit if the return on the borrowed funds exceeds the interest cost and as long as earnings are sufficient to retire the debt.

Liability. Any claim against the assets of a corporation: accounts payable, wages and salaries payable, dividends declared payable, accrued taxes payable, and fixed or long-term obligations such as mortgage bonds, debentures, and bank loans. *See also* **Current liability; Fixed liability.**

Lien. A claim against property that has been pledged or mortgaged to secure the performance of an obligation. A bond may be secured by a lien against specified property of a company.

Life annuity. An annuity that carries no death benefit; all benefits end when the annuitant dies, even if there is a surviving spouse.

Life estate. The right to use and enjoy property for the duration of one's life. The individual in possession of a life estate or life interest in a trust is called a *life tenant.*

Limit order. An order to buy or sell a stated amount of a security at a specified maximum or minimum price or better.

Limited partnership. A business entity formed by one or more general partners (individuals or corporations) and one or more limited partners. *General partners* are personally responsible for management of the business and are personally liable for its debts and obligations. *Limited partners* contribute cash or property to finance the business but are not responsible for management nor personally liable for the partnership's debts and obligations. The limited partnership agreement describes all the rights, powers, and duties of the partners, including fees the general partners will receive, the distribution of profits, income, and tax advantages, the transferability of interest in the partnership, and the like.

Limited payment life insurance. A type of **whole life insurance**, the premiums for which are paid over a limited number of years and are therefore higher than premiums paid over the entire term of a policy. Limited payment policies are sometimes referred to by the length of the payment period: 20-year paid-up, paid-up at 65.

Liquid asset. Cash or a marketable security easily converted into cash.

Liquidation. In general, the process of converting securities or other property into cash. Similarly, the dissolution of a business entity by the sale of its assets and payment of all indebtedness, with the proceeds distributed to the shareholders.

Liquidity. The ability of the market in a particular security or commodity to absorb a reasonable amount of buying or selling at reasonable price changes.

The ability of an individual or company to convert assets into cash without a significant loss of value.

Listed security. The stock or bond of a company traded on a securities exchange and for which a listing application and a registration statement, giving detailed information about the company and its operations, have been filed with the Securities and Exchange Commission and the exchange itself. Unlisted securities are traded over the counter.

Living trust. A trust created during the trustor's life; also called an *inter vivos trust.*

Load. *See* **Front-end load.**

Locked in. Jargon referring to an investor who is unwilling or unable to realize a paper profit.

Lock-in clause. A provision in a note that prohibits prepayment.

Long-term debt. In securities, a bond or other debt instrument with a maturity of 10 years or longer.

In finance, a debt that will not come due for at least one year.

Long-term gain (or loss). Profit (or loss) on the sale of an asset or security that has been held for longer than six months. Long-term gains receive the favorable capital gains treatment (60% of the gain is excluded from taxation, the remaining 40% is taxed as ordinary income); half of a long-term loss is tax-deductible.

Lump-sum distribution. The disbursement of the entire value of a profit-sharing plan, pension plan, annuity, or similar account to the account holder or beneficiary. Lump-sum distributions from individual retirement accounts (IRAs) may be rolled over into another tax-deferred account; sums actually received are taxed as ordinary income. Lump-sum distributions from qualified retirement plans usually receive favorable 10-year forward averaging treatment.

M-1. *See **Money supply**.*

M.A.I. appraisal. In real estate, an appraisal by a member of the American Institute of Appraisers.

Maker. Any individual, corporation, or other legal entity who signs a check, draft, note, or similar negotiable instrument as a primary responsible party.

Management. Individuals who make and administer policy for a business. In a large corporation, senior management includes the chief executive officer, chief financial officer, chairman of the board, president, and executives of comparable rank.

Management company. An investment company that, for a fee, invests the pooled funds of individual investors. Open-end management companies (*mutual funds*) issue new shares, sold at ***net asset value***, to meet investor demand; closed-end companies (*investment trusts*) have a fixed number of shares outstanding, which are traded like stock, often on the major exchanges. Annual fees for both types of companies are between 0.5% and 1.0% of net assets. In addition, some mutual funds assess a sales charge upon the purchase (*front-end load*) or redemption (*back-end load*) of shares; loads usually range from 3% to 8%. *No-load funds* do not impose any sales charge.

Margin. A client's equity in a securities account against which he can borrow money or stock from the broker. Initial and maintenance margin requirements are set by the National Association of Securities Dealers, the New York Stock Exchange, and individual brokerage houses. The securities in the account serve as collateral for the loan, the interest rate of which is detailed in the margin agreement.

In futures trading, the client's good-faith deposit on the purchase or sale of a futures contract; if futures prices move against the client, an additional deposit is required.

In business, the gross profit on the sale of goods, the difference between the sales price and the cost of producing the goods.

Margin call. A brokerage firm's demand that a client add money or securities to his margin account in order to cover a purchase or meet minimum margin requirements.

Marginal tax rate. The rate at which the next dollar of an individual's income will be taxed; often called a *tax bracket*. An individual in the 30% tax bracket, for example, does not pay 30% of his entire income in taxes; only the dollars he earns over the minimum threshold for that bracket are taxed at the 30% rate.

Marital deduction. Provision of the Economic Recovery Tax Act of 1981 that allows all the assets of a decedent spouse to pass to the surviving spouse without any estate tax liability.

Marital deduction trust. A trust created to minimize estate taxes by taking advantage of the tax-free transfer of assets from a decedent spouse to a surviving spouse without actually leaving the assets outright to the spouse. The surviving spouse must be the sole income beneficiary of the trust, but upon his or her death the principal may either remain in his or her estate or be distributed to others. *See also* **Qualified terminable interest property trust (Q-TIP).**

Marital property. Property acquired by married persons after their marriage, exclusive of property that either partner acquired by gift or inheritance.

Market. Public place where goods and services are traded, purchased, and sold.

Market approach. *See* ***Appraisal by comparison.***

Market maker. A dealer willing to quote prices and transact orders at any time for the purchase or sale of the securities of a given publicly traded company. Market makers for stocks traded on the exchanges are called *specialists.*

Market order. An order to buy or sell a stated amount of a security at the most advantageous price obtainable.

Market price. The last reported price at which a stock or bond was sold.

Market timing. Strategy, based on various economic or stock market indicators, for deciding when to buy or sell securities.

Market value. In general, the price at which a willing seller would sell and a willing buyer would buy, neither being under any compulsion.

In securities, the price at which the most recent trade was executed.

In real estate, an estimate of the highest bid a property would elicit on the open market from an intelligent and informed buyer.

Marriage penalty. The excess income tax that two working individuals pay because they are married rather than single. The penalty is lessened by a 10% deduction, up to $3,000, from the wages of the lower-paid spouse.

Maturity. The date on which a debt instrument (loan, bond, draft) becomes fully payable.

Mil. One-thousandth of a dollar ($0.001).

Money market deposit account. A bank account whose rate of interest varies with money market rates (interest rates on commercial paper, banker's acceptances, repurchase agreements, certificates of deposit, etc.). Accounts are liquid but may allow only a set number of checks to be drawn against the balance each month.

Money market fund. A mutual fund that invests in various short-term debt instruments (commercial paper, negotiable certificates of deposit, banker's acceptances, Treasury bills, and the like). Shares always maintain a net asset value of $1, but the interest rate changes daily. Annual management fees are typically less than 1% of assets.

Money purchase pension plan. A *qualified retirement plan* to which the employer makes an annual contribution for each eligible employee that represents a fixed percentage (between 3% and 25%, up to a maximum of $30,000) of the employee's total annual compensation.

Money supply. The total amount of money in the U.S. economy, measured weekly by the Federal Reserve.

M-1 represents currency in circulation, demand deposits at commercial banks and mutual savings banks, negotiable order of withdrawal (NOW) accounts at commercial banks and thrift institutions, credit union share drafts, and travelers' checks.

M-2 represents M-1 plus overnight repurchase agreements at commercial banks, overnight Eurodollar deposits, savings accounts, time deposits under $100,000, and money market mutual fund shares.

M-3 represents M-2 plus time deposits over $100,000 and term repurchase agreements.

To increase the money supply, the Federal Reserve can expand the amount of credit available in the banking system, lower bank reserve requirements, or cut the discount rate (the rate at which banks can borrow funds from the Federal Reserve). To prevent or slow increases in the money supply, the Federal Reserve can take the opposite actions or enforce selective credit controls.

Moody's Investors Service. A subsidiary of Dun & Bradstreet and one of the nation's largest financial publishers and investment rating services. Moody's rates commercial paper, preferred and common stocks, short-term municipal issues, corporate and municipal bonds, and many Treasury and government agency issues.

Moral obligation bond. A bond issued by a municipality or state agency that is backed by the moral obligation—but not the legal obligation—of the state in which issued. The absence of legal obligation results from a state legislature's legal inability to require future legislatures to assume the debt should the issuing body default.

Mortgage. An instrument by which a borrower (*mortgagor*) gives a lender (*mortgagee*) a legally valid and enforceable claim (*lien*) against property pledged as security for a loan. The mortgagor continues to have use of the property; when the loan is repaid, the lien is removed. If the mortgagor defaults on his payments, the mortgagee may petition the court to seize and auction the property (*foreclosure*) and allocate the proceeds to pay off the loan.

Mortgage bond. A long-term bond secured by a mortgage on the issuer's real property, with the lien conveyed by a deed of trust.

Mortgage REIT. A *real-estate investment trust* (REIT) that specializes in either making or buying permanent mortgage loans or providing interim or long-term financing for construction and development projects.

Mortgagee. One who holds a note secured by a mortgage on property.

Mortgagor. One who owes an obligation evidenced by a note that is secured by a mortgage on property.

Multiple. *See Price-earnings ratio.*

Multiple listing. A listing, usually an exclusive right to sell, taken by a member of an organization composed of real estate brokers, with the provisions that all member brokers will have the opportunity to find an interested client; a cooperative listing.

Municipal bond. A bond issued by a state, state agency or authority, or a political subdivision (county, city, town, or village). In general, interest paid on municipal bonds is exempt from federal income taxes and from state and local income taxes within the state of issue.

Mutual fund. A fund established by an investment management company to invest the pooled monies of individual shareholders in a diversified portfolio of securities selected to meet stated goals (e.g., current income, capital growth). New shares are sold and outstanding shares redeemed on demand; all transactions are made at the fund's ***net asset value,*** which fluctuates daily. Shareholders are assessed a management fee, usually 0.5% to 1.0% of the fund's assets, and some funds assess a sales charge (3% to 8%) upon purchase (*front-end load*) or sale (*back-end load*) of shares. Mutual funds offer their shareholders diversification, liquidity, and professional management.

Mutual fund family. A group of mutual funds established by one investment company among which shareholders can easily switch or exchange shares, often by a telephone call, as their investment strategy or needs change. A typical family includes several current income and capital growth funds of varying volatilities, precious metal, international, and specialty (industry-specific) funds.

National Association of Securities Dealers (NASD). A nonprofit self-regulatory association of brokers and dealers in the over-the-counter securities business, under the supervision of the Securities and Exchange Commission. The NASD maintains and enforces professional and ethical standards and procedures for securities trading and licenses securities professionals. NASDAQ is the association's automated quotation system for providing brokers and dealers with price quotations.

Negative amortization. Growth in the principal of a loan when payments are insufficient to meet current interest costs; the unpaid interest is added to the outstanding principal.

Negotiable instrument. An easily transferable order or promise to pay a specified sum of money, for example, a check, promissory note, or draft. The instrument must be signed by the maker or drawer, and must be payable to the bearer.

Negotiable order of withdrawal (NOW account). An interest-bearing checking account.

Negotiable security. A security (stock, bond, etc.) whose title is transferable by delivery.

Net asset value (NAV). The price at which a mutual fund sells or redeems its shares, calculated each trading day by dividing the net market value of the fund's assets (the market price of all securities owned minus liabilities) by the number of shares outstanding.

Net change. The change in the price of a security from the closing price on one trading day to the closing price on the following trading day.

Net lease. A lease in which the tenant (*lessee*) pays the real property taxes and operating expenses, and the landlord (*lessor*) pays for major improvements and debt service.

Net, net lease. A lease in which the tenant (*lessee*) pays the real property taxes, operating expenses, and insurance, and the landlord (*lessor*) pays for major improvements and for debt service.

Net, net, net lease. A lease in which the tenant (*lessee*) pays all of the costs of ownership, including debt service, and the responsibilities of the landlord (*lessor*) are limited to major improvements to the property; also called a *triple net lease.*

Net operating income. In real estate, the income from improved real property, including the land, the buildings, and other improvements, after expenses (taxes, insurance, utilities, maintenance, etc.).

Net present value (NPV). A method for evaluating the current value of a future series of payments. The future cash flow is discounted by a chosen rate of interest (*discount rate*) that represents the foregone earning power (*opportunity cost*) to the recipient.

$$\text{NPV} = C_0 + \frac{C_1}{(1 + i)} + \frac{C_2}{(1 + i)^2} + \cdots + \frac{C_n}{(1 + i)^n}$$

where C_0 is the initial cash outflow (cost of the investment), C_1 the cash flow during the first period (month or year), C_n the cash flow during the final period (month or year), and i the selected discount rate (monthly or annual). If NPV is greater than zero, then the present value of the cash flows exceeds the opportunity cost; if NPV is less than zero, the cash flows do not. The value of i for which NPV$=0$ is called the *internal rate of return* (IRR) on the investment.

Net worth. For an individual, the difference between the total value of all his assets and possessions and the total sum of all his liabilities and debts. Similarly, for a corporation, the excess of assets over liabilities, often called *net assets.*

New issue. The initial offering of a stock or bond by a corporation. Public offerings must be registered with the Securities and Exchange Commission.

No-contest clause. A clause in a will intended to disinherit any person who attacks the will's legal validity.

No-load fund. A *mutual fund* that does not assess a sales charge (*load*) on the purchase or redemption of shares.

Nominee. A bank official, broker, or other appointed agent into whose name securities are transferred by a customer in order to facilitate the paperwork entailed by the sale of securities.

Noncallable. A security that cannot be redeemed by the issuer before the maturity date.

Noncancellable. An insurance policy that may not be cancelled by the insurer during a specified term.

Non-court trust. A trust that is not subject to the ongoing jurisdiction of a probate court.

Noncumulative. A preferred stock on which omitted dividends need not be paid at a later date.

Nonforfeiture value. In insurance, the benefits due a policyholder on the termination or lapse of a policy, including cash surrender value and rights to extended term insurance or reduced paid-up insurance.

Non-recourse debt. A loan that in the event of default limits the remedies of the creditor to recovery of stated collateral; no personal judgment or other recourse may be taken against the borrower.

Nuncupative will. An oral will; valid only in some states and only for a small amount of personal property, if made a limited number of days before death.

NYSE Composite Index. A closing weighted index that reflects the price movements of all common stocks traded on the New York Stock Exchange. The base of the index sets closing market prices on December 31, 1965, equal to $50.00.

Occupancy rate. In real estate, the percentage of an income property that is leased on a given date. For multifamily housing, the number of rent-paying units divided by the number of rentable units; for commercial and industrial properties, the number of square feet leased divided by the number of leasable square feet.

Odd lot. In stock trading, a purchase or sale of fewer than 100 shares (*round lot*). Odd-lot traders pay higher commissions than round-lot traders.

Offer. The price at which a person who owns an asset or security is ready to sell; compared to *bid*, the price at which a purchaser is ready to buy.

Oil and gas limited partnership. A *limited partnership* organized to finance the drilling, completion, or operation of oil and gas wells. *Income partnerships* are designed to realize current income, while *tax-advantaged partnerships* offer tax-shelter to limited partners, principally from deductions for intangible drilling costs, depreciation, and depletion allowance.

Omitted dividend. A scheduled dividend that is not voted for distribution by the board of directors.

Open-end investment company. *See* **Management company.**

Open-end mortgage. A mortgage that provides for additional funds to be advanced by the lender to the mortgagor under certain specified conditions.

Operating profit (or loss). The difference between a business's revenues and expenses before deductions are taken for income taxes and various one-time costs (e.g., losses from sale of property or plant, bonuses and profit-sharing distributions, adjustments for changes in accounting or inventory methods, losses from flood and fire).

Opportunity cost. The return foregone on one investment when an alternative investment is chosen. For an individual investor, the difference between the known return on a relatively safe investment and the minimum projected return on a riskier investment that offers the possibility of larger rewards.

Option. In general, the purchase or acquisition of the right to buy or sell an asset at a specific price within a specified period of time. If the option holder does not exercise the option within that time period, the option expires and is valueless.

In securities trading, a *call option* is the right to buy 100 shares of a security at a fixed price (*strike price*) before a given expiration date (*maturity*). The price of the option (*premium*) is determined on the open market and varies with changes in the price of the underlying security, the nearness of the expiration date, and the volatility of the underlying security. Similarly, a *put option* is the right to sell 100 shares at a fixed price before a given expiration date.

Ordinary income. Any income that does not qualify for special tax treatment (capital gains, special averaging) and is taxed at the prevailing rates.

Original issue discount (OID). The difference between a bond's par value and the price at which it is bought. Under the Tax Reform Act of 1984, for corporate and government bonds (but not municipal or U.S. savings bonds) purchased at discount after July 18, 1984, the amount of the discount must be accreted as ordinary income and declared annually or on sale of the bond. The discount on municipal and U.S. savings bonds continues to qualify for capital gains treatment upon sale of the bond.

Over the counter (OTC) market. Market for trading securities that are not listed on the organized stock exchanges. Transactions are conducted through a telephone and computer network, administered by the National Association of Securities Dealers (NASD).

Overbought. An opinion that a stock that has recently risen sharply in price is vulnerable to a price decline. Also said of the market as a whole after a period of vigorous buying.

Oversold. An opinion that a stock that has recently declined sharply is due to increase now that all sellers are out of the market. Also said of the market as a whole after a period of vigorous selling with declining prices.

Paper profit (or loss). An unrealized profit (or loss) on a security still held. Paper profits are realized only when the security is sold.

Par. The face value or denomination of a bond. For common stock, par value per share is assigned by the company's charter for accounting purposes but has no relation to market value.

Partition. A court proceeding allowing any co-owner of property to force a separation of the co-ownership interests, usually be a court-ordered auction sale whose proceeds are divided among the owners.

Partnership. A contract of two or more persons to unite their property, labor, skill, or some combination of them, in prosecution of some joint or lawful business, and to share the profits and liabilities in certain proportions.

Passbook loan. A loan secured by the borrower's savings account balance.

Penny stock. A low-priced issue, often highly speculative, selling at less than $1 a share. Frequently used as a term of disparagement, although a few penny stocks have developed into investment-caliber issues.

Pension fund. Fund established by a corporation, labor union, or other public- or private-sector organization to invest employer and employee contributions and administer retirement benefits.

Percentage lease. A commercial lease in which the tenant (*lessee*) pays the landlord (*lessor*) a percentage of his sales, receipts, or income, usually in addition to a guaranteed minimum rent.

Performance bond. A surety bond supplied by one party to another protecting the latter against loss in the event of improper performance of the terms of a contract.

Personal property. Any property that is not real property.

Personal representative. A person who handles an estate during the period of administration, whether an executor or an administrator.

Per stirpes. (Latin: "by stock" or "by lineage.") Same as ***right of representation***.

Phantom income. Taxable income in excess of cash income received; arises in an investment program, for example, when the actual cash distributions to investors are less than the program's reportable income as proportionally assigned to each investor.

Plant. A business entity's land, buildings, machinery, equipment, furniture, fixtures, natural resources, and similar fixed assets. Sometimes used to refer only to land and buildings or to buildings alone.

Point. In commercial lending, amount paid to a lender as a loan fee, representing 1% of the total principal.

In bonds, a 1% change relative to the face value of the bond. Also, *point* is sometimes used to mean *basis point*, one-hundredth of a percentage point of yield.

In stocks, a change of $1 in market price.

Policy loan. Loan from an insurance company that is secured by the cash value of a life insurance policy.

Pooled income fund. A type of *annuity* that pools the assets of a number of investors, each of whom proportionally shares the income.

Portfolio. Holding of diverse securities and financial assets by an individual or institution. A portfolio may contain bonds, preferred and common stocks, commodities, tangible assets, etc.

Pour-over trust. A testamentary trust that leaves property to an established living trust.

Power of appointment. The power to designate who shall be the owner of property.

Power of attorney. A document by which one person grants to another the legal right to perform on his behalf. A power of attorney may be *limited* to certain activities or may give *full power.*

Preferred stock. A class of stock with claim over the company's earnings before payment may be made on the common stock, and usually entitled to priority over common stock if the company liquidates. Generally, preferred stockholders are entitled to dividends at a specified rate, declared by the board of directors. Most preferred issues are *cumulative:* omitted dividends must be paid at a later date.

Preliminary distribution. A distribution of some of the property in a probate estate before the estate is ready to be closed.

Premium. For a preferred stock or bond, the part of the market price that is above par value.

For new issues of bonds or stocks, the amount by which the market price rises over the original offering price.

For options, the price a buyer of a put or call must pay for the option contract.

In insurance, the fee paid by the insured to purchase coverage.

Premium waiver feature. An optional feature of some insurance policies that waives the continued payment of premiums if the insured is disabled and unable to pay them.

Prepaid interest. The payment of advance interest on a loan.

Prepayment privilege. A provision in a note that gives the borrower the privilege of paying all or part of the unpaid balance of the note at any time without penalty; usually expressed by stating that the mortgagor shall make payments of X dollars "or more." If the note does not have a prepayment privilege, the borrower will be assessed a *prepayment penalty* upon accelerating repayment of the note.

Present value. The discounted value of a certain sum due and payable on a specified future date; the discount reflects the recipient's present foregone earnings on the future payment.

Pretermitted child. A child unintentionally omitted from the will of his parents, often entitled to a statutory share of their estate.

Price-earnings ratio (p/e). The market price of a share of stock divided by its annual earnings per share; also called the *price-earnings multiple* or simply *multiple.*

Prime rate. The interest rate a bank charges its most creditworthy commercial customers.

Prime tenant. *See* ***Principal tenant.***

Principal. (1) A dealer buying or selling for his own account or the person for whom a broker executes an order; (2) investment capital, exclusive of earnings; (3) the face amount of a debt instrument; (4) the property comprising a trust, as distinguished from income or interest; synonymous with *corpus* and *res.*

Principal tenant. A corporation, person, or group of related persons who is the largest single occupant of a piece of real property and who generally occupies more than 25% of the aggregate square footage; also called a *prime tenant.*

Private annuity. A noncommercial contract in which one person sells property to another in exchange for a promise of lifetime income.

Private corporation. *See* ***Privately held corporation.***

Private limited partnership. A ***limited partnership*** whose offering is not registered with the Securities and Exchange Commission, under an exemption granted in the Securities Act of 1933. Shares or units in the partnership are sold by investment advisors, financial planners, and brokerage firms to investors who meet financial suitability requirements for income and net worth. Private limited partnerships may be established to provide income or tax shelter; typical enterprises include real estate, gas and oil, equipment leasing, research and development, and venture capital projects.

Private placement. The sale of securities or private limited partnership units directly to a limited number of investors. Such offerings need not be registered with the Securities and Exchange Commission.

Privately held corporation. A corporation whose shares are held by a few people and are not for sale to the public; also called *close corporation, private corporation.*

Probate. The period of time when a decedent's affairs are handled under court supervision; synonymous with *administration.*

Profit-sharing plan. An agreement under which employees share in the profits of the company that employs them. The company makes annual contributions to each eligible employee's account, with the amount of such contributions reflecting the company's profits for the year. Funds are invested in stocks, bonds, and other securities, and they usually accumulate tax-free until the employee retires or leaves the company.

Profit taking. Selling of stock after a sharp rise upward by short-term traders. Profit taking causes the stock's price to fall temporarily before resuming an upward trend.

Pro forma. (Latin: "according to form.") In financial planning, an analysis that incorporates hypothetical assumptions and data to tax or other financial obligations.

Pro forma projection. Statement of a business's expected operating income and expenses based on assumptions about various financial factors.

Pro forma rents. Estimate of rental income for an income-producing property based on assumptions regarding rental prices, market levels, and similar relevant variables.

Promissory note. A negotiable instrument that is evidence of a debt contracted by a borrower from a creditor. The note states the sum of money borrowed, the repayment date (or an indication that repayment is due on demand), and the interest rate, if any.

Property and casualty insurance. Insurance coverage to provide for the replacement of or compensation for property lost, stolen, damaged, or destroyed.

Prospectus. The document that offers a new issue of securities to the public; mutual funds and limited partnerships also issue offering prospectuses. The prospectus provides all the information an investor needs to make an educated decision about the offering.

Proxy. Written authorization given by a shareholder that allows someone else to represent him and vote his shares at a shareholders meeting.

Proxy statement. Information that must be given to stockholders before the solicitation of proxies, as required by the Securities and Exchange Commission.

Prudent man rule. An investment standard for **fiduciaries** and institutions in states that do not compile a **legal list.** The fiduciary is permitted to invest in a security if it is one that a prudent person of discretion and intelligence, who is seeking a reasonable income and preservation of capital, would buy.

Public limited partnership. A **limited partnership** that is registered with the Securities and Exchange Commission and distributed in a public offering by broker-dealers or employees of the sponsor. Partnerships may be organized to provide income or tax shelter; typical enterprises include real estate, oil and gas, and equipment leasing.

Purchase-money mortgage. A mortgage used in lieu of cash for the purchase of real property.

Purchasing power. The value of the dollar in terms of the goods and services it can buy. As the consumer price index rises, purchasing power declines.

Put. An **option** to sell 100 shares of stock at a definite price (*strike price*) within a specified period of time. For this right, the buyer pays a *premium*; if he does not exercise the option before it expires, he forfeits the premium and the option is worthless.

Qualified retirement plan. A pension, profit-sharing, or deferred-income plan established by an employer for his employees in conformity with IRS rules such that: employees pay no current income tax on employer's contributions on their behalf, contributions accumulate tax-free until withdrawal, and contributions are deductible to the employer as a current business expense.

Qualified terminable interest property trust (Q-TIP). A trust, whose sole beneficiary is the trustor's spouse, whereby the trust qualifies for the marital deduction. The trustor may also direct the disposition of the trust upon the beneficiary's death.

Quick asset. An asset that in the ordinary course of business will be converted into cash within a reasonably short time or can be readily converted into cash without substantial loss.

Quick ratio. *See **Acid-test ratio.***

Quotation. The highest bid to buy and the lowest offer to sell a security in a given market at a given time; often shortened to *quote.*

Quoted price. The last price at which the sale and purchase of a security or commodity was made.

Rally. A brisk rise following a decline in the general price level of the stock market or an individual stock.

Rate of return. For a stock, the annual dividend divided by the purchase price. For a bond, the **coupon rate** divided by the purchase price.

Rating. A formal opinion by Standard & Poor's, Moody's Investors Service, or a similar company on the credit reputation of an issuer and the investment quality of its securities, expressed on a scale from AAA (highest quality) to D (in default).

Real estate. Land, all improvements on it (buildings, landscaping), and the rights to the air above and earth beneath it; also called *real property*.

Real estate investment trust (REIT). A company that invests in equity (equity REIT) or mortgages (mortgage REIT) on all types of properties and offers shares that are publicly traded.

Real interest. The nominal interest rate adjusted for inflation.

Real return. The nominal rate of return adjusted for inflation.

Realization. The act of converting an asset, or the total assets, of an individual or business into cash.

Realtor. A real estate broker holding active membership in a real estate board affiliated with the National Association of Real Estate Boards.

Recapture of depreciation. Upon the sale or certain other disposition of property, the portion of gain that represents the excess of accelerated depreciation over straight-line depreciation with respect to real property, and of all depreciation deductions taken with respect to personal property, must be declared as ordinary income.

Receiver. Individual appointed by the court to supervise a bankruptcy by effecting the liquidation of the bankrupt's assets or overseeing a reorganization of them.

Recession. Contraction in the national economy, often defined as two or more consecutive quarters of decline in the gross national product.

Record date. The date on which a sharcholder must be registered on the stock book of a company in order to receive a declared dividend or to vote on company affairs.

Recourse. The rights of a ***holder in due course*** of a negotiable instrument to force endorsers on the instrument to meet their legal obligations.

Recourse loan. A loan for which a guarantor or endorser may be held liable should the borrower default.

Redemption. Repayment of a bond, bill, or note on or before maturity. Redemption prices are stated in the initial offering. Bonds called for redemption that are not surrendered cease to accrue interest.

Red herring. Jargon for a preliminary prospectus used to obtain indications of interest from prospective buyers of a new issue. The sobriquet stems from the statement printed in red ink across each page that the contents are subject to change.

Registered bond. A bond that is recorded in the name of the owner on the books of the issuing company. It can be transferred only when endorsed by the registered owner.

Registered representative. An employee of a member firm of an exchange or of a broker-dealer who has met the requirements of an exchange as to background and knowledge of the securities business, acts as a customer's broker, and is compensated on a commission basis. Also known as an *account executive* or *customer's broker*.

Registrar. A trust company, bank, or other agent charged with the responsibility of maintaining files of current stockholders or bondholders and preventing the issuance of more stock than authorized by a company.

Registration. Procedure whereby a planned public offering of new securities by a company is reviewed by the Securities and Exchange Commission. The issuer's registration statement must disclose pertinent information relating to the company's operations, securities, management, and the purpose of the public offering.

Regulator principal payments. Periodic payments required to amortize a note or contract payable, exclusive of special or balloon payments.

Regulation D. The Securities and Exchange Commission regulation that defines an *accredited investor* in a private limited partnership.

Regulation Q. The Federal Reserve Board regulation that places a limit on the rates of interest that can be paid by banks on time deposits; to be phased out by 1986.

Regulation T. The Federal Reserve Board regulation governing the amount of credit that may be advanced by brokers and dealers to customers for the purchase of securities.

Regulation U. The Federal Reserve Board regulation governing the amount of credit that may be advanced by a bank to its customers for the purchase of securities.

Remainder. The property interest passing to a new owner (remainder man) after a life estate or other interim interest has terminated.

Renewable term insurance. Insurance policy that is renewable at the end of its term at the insured's option and without evidence of insurability, but at a higher premium.

Reorganization. A change in the financial structure of a company after it has entered a *Chapter 11 proceeding.* During the reorganization, the company is protected from its creditors and a plan to return the company to solvency is arranged.

Replacement cost. In real estate, an estimate of the cost of constructing a new building of equivalent operating or productive capability as a present building. The estimate generally does not reflect the property's current market value and is sometimes calculated on a square-footage basis with reference to published indexes.

Reproduction cost. In real estate, the cost of reproducing a like property in the same location.

Repudiation. The intentional and willful refusal to pay a debt in whole or in part.

Repurchase agreement (repo). An agreement between a seller and a buyer that the seller will buy back a note, security, or other property at the expiration of a period of time, on the completion of certain conditions, or both.

Res. (Latin: "thing.") The property comprising a trust; synonymous with *principal* and *corpus.*

Reserve. In banking, the deposit level that must be maintained by a commercial bank to meet the Federal Reserve Board's requirements for liquidity.

In business, a segregated fund allocated to a specific purpose, such as improvements, contingencies, or retirement of debt.

Residue. All the property left to be disposed of by will after specific items have been distributed or bequeathed to specific persons. The will's *residuary clause* directs the disposition.

Return. The pretax profit on an investment, expressed as an annual percentage of the investor's original capital: the sum of the net change in the investment's market value and any dividends or interest paid is divided by the purchase price.

Return of capital. A distribution to an investor from a source other than net income as determined for tax or accounting purposes; a return of capital is not taxable.

Revenue bond. A municipal bond to be repaid from revenues produced from a particular project, such as a toll road, hospital, or sports stadium.

Reverse-annuity mortgage. A mortgage whereby a homeowner who has no outstanding liens on his property pledges a share of his equity in exchange for a lifetime monthly annuity. Upon the homeowner's death, the mortgagee takes title to the property, with the decedent's remaining equity passing into his estate.

Reversion. The possibility or certainty that after a donor has given property away, it may or will come back into the donor's ownership.

Revive. To reinstate to legal effectiveness a previously revoked will.

Revocable trust. A trust that may at any time be revoked or amended by its creator, as distinguished from an *irrevocable trust.*

Rider. *See **Endorsement.***

Right. The opportunity given by a company to its stockholders to buy newly issued securities at a price below a prospective public offering. Rights are transferable and are often actively traded. Most rights expire within two to six weeks.

Right of representation. The disposition of willed property such that the share bequeathed to a predeceased person passes to his heir.

Right of survivorship. Right of a co-owner in a ***joint tenancy*** to assume automatically the share owned by a deceased joint tenant.

Risk. The possibility that an investor, owner, or business entity will see his capital, inventory, and the like fail to increase in value or decline in value. Certain risks may be mitigated by insurance or defensive investment strategies.

Rollover. Reinvestment of funds from a maturing security (e.g., certificate of deposit, bond, Treasury bill) into another similar security. Similarly, reinvestment of a lump-sum distribution from a qualified retirement plan, individual retirement account, or other tax-deferred account into another tax-deferred account.

Round lot. The standard unit of trading, or a multiple thereof, on an exchange; usually 100 shares for stocks and $1,000 *par* value for bonds.

Rule against perpetuities. A rule prescribing the maximum period during which an owner may dictate who shall own or use his property, and thus determining how long a trust may exist.

Rule of 72. A simple method for approximating the number of years it takes an investment to double at a given compound interest rate: Divide the interest rate into 72.

Safe harbor. Provision in a law, rule, or regulation that excuses a business entity from liability for noncompliance under certain stated conditions.

Savings bond. A nontransferable U.S. government bond issued in denominations from $50 to $10,000. They are sold at discount with their effective interest rate pegged to

Treasury securities. Income from savings bonds is exempt from state and local income taxes, and federal income tax is deferred until redemption.

Scheduled rent. In real estate, the amount of rental income due from an income property at current rent levels for occupied units and at new rent levels for vacant units should they be rented.

Scrip. A document that entitles the holder or bearer to receive stock or a fractional share of stock in a corporation, cash, or some other article of value upon demand or at some specified future date. *Scrip dividends* may be issued by a company that is short of cash.

Seasonal adjustment. Statistical adjustment of raw data to account for regular variations that follow an annual cycle (weather, holidays, etc.).

Seasoned security. A high-quality issue that has demonstrated liquidity in the ***secondary market.***

Second mortgage. A loan that is secured by real estate already encumbered by a first mortgage. In the case of default, the first mortgage has priority of claim.

Secondary distribution. The public sale of a large block of stock by an institution or corporation that is not the issuing company. The sale is handled off the exchange by an investment banking firm or group of firms, and the shares are usually offered at a fixed price.

Secondary market. Market in which securities are bought and sold subsequent to their original issue; the original issuer does not participate in the trading or its proceeds. Stock exchanges and over-the-counter (OTC) markets are secondary markets.

Secondary mortgage market. The market in which original lenders sell their mortgage loans to investment bankers or federal agencies (Federal National Mortgage Association, Government National Mortgage Association), which then sell mortgage-backed securities on the open market. The secondary mortgage market offers lenders a degree of liquidity, which allows new lending, and enables small investors to participate in the market.

Secured loan. A loan for which the borrower pledges marketable assets as ***collateral.***

Securities and Exchange Commission (SEC). A federal regulatory and enforcement agency that oversees public investment trading activities by facilitating fair and orderly securities markets, enforcing statutory corporate disclosure requirements, and regulating investment companies, investment advisors, and public utility holding companies.

Security. Evidence of direct ownership (stock) or creditorship (bond) or indirect ownership (rights, warrants, options). Also, a synonym for ***collateral.***

Self-directed IRA. An ***individual retirement account*** (IRA) that is actively managed by the account holder through instructions to the account's custodian.

Self-liquidating loan. A short-term commercial loan, usually supported by a lien on a given product or commodity, which is liquidated from the proceeds of the sale of the product.

Self-liquidating program. An investment vehicle that from its inception provides for liquidation and distribution of assets at a future date; for example, the organizational documents of some limited partnerships provide for a limited life.

Seller financing. In real estate, the participation of the seller in financing the buyer's purchase by offering a note that covers all or part of the difference between the buyer's down payment and the purchase price. Usually seller financing takes the form of a short-term (5 to 10 years) loan with a ***balloon payment.***

Selling short. The sale by an investor of stock or a commodity futures contract that he does not own but has borrowed from his broker in expectation of a drop in the stock's value. If the stock does decline, the investor can purchase it at the lower price to cover his short position; if the stock price rises, the investor suffers a loss.

Separate property. Property owned by a spouse before marriage or acquired during marriage by gift or inheritance.

Sequestered account. An account that has been impounded under due process of law, with disbursements subject to court order.

Serial bond. Typically, a municipal bond issue that is segmented into a series of maturities, scheduled at regular intervals.

Settlor. The person who creates a living (inter vivos) trust; synonymous with *trustor* and *grantor.*

Severance. The conversion of a ***joint tenancy*** into a ***tenancy in common.***

Share. Unit of equity ownership in a corporation, mutual fund, or limited partnership. Shareholders' rights are detailed in the bylaws of the corporation or in the partnership agreement.

Share loan. A simple interest loan secured by funds on deposit at a credit union or savings and loan institution.

Short-term debt. Debt obligation that will come due within the ensuing year.

Short-term gain (or loss). Profit (or loss) on the sale of an asset or security that has been held for under six months. Short-term gains are taxed as ordinary income to the extent they are offset by short-term losses.

Simplified employee pension plan (SEP). A pension plan that establishes for each participant an ***individual retirement account*** (IRA) to which the employee and employer may contribute. The employee may contribute up to $2,000 a year; employer contributions are limited to the lesser of $15,000 or 15% of the employee's annual salary.

Single-payment loan. A loan whose entire principal is due on one maturity date.

Single-premium deferred annuity (SPDA). An ***annuity*** that is purchased by a lump-sum payment (single premium). Proceeds are taxed only upon distribution to the annuitant.

Sinking fund. Money regularly set aside in a custodial account by a company to redeem its bonds, debentures, or preferred stock.

Soft market. Market in which supply exceeds demand; also called a *buyer's market.*

Special assessment bond. Municipal bond that is to be repaid from taxes, levies, or user fees on residents who will benefit from the project to be funded. If an issue is also backed by the issuer's ***full faith and credit,*** it is called a *general obligation special assignment bond.*

Specialist. A member of a stock exchange who is approved by the exchange to maintain an orderly market in a security by buying or selling for his own account when there is a temporary disparity between supply and demand. The specialist also acts as a brokers' broker, executing floor brokers' ***limit orders.***

Specialty fund. A mutual fund that invests only in one industry or industrial sector (e.g., energy, financial services, health care, precious metals, technology, utilities).

Speculation. Participation in a transaction that involves a high level of risk in expectation of high return.

Spendthrift clause. Protective trust clause stating that the beneficiary's interest may not be attached by his creditors or taken in bankruptcy.

Split. The division of the outstanding shares of a corporation into a larger number of shares at a proportionally smaller value per share. A 3-for-1 split by a company with 1 million shares outstanding results in 3 million shares outstanding, each worth one-third of an old share.

Sponsor. Any person instrumental in organizing and managing a limited partnership; a *general partner.*

Sprinkling trust. A trust that authorizes the trustee to distribute ("sprinkle") the income among various beneficiaries; synonymous with *discretionary trust.*

Standard & Poor's. Investors services and financial publishing corporation, a subsidiary of McGraw-Hill, best known for its bond ratings, stock reports, and stock indexes.

The *Standard & Poor's 500 (S & P 500)* is a weighted index of 500 widely held stocks: 400 industrials, 40 financial company stocks, 40 public utilities, and 20 transportation stocks.

The S & P credit rating system assigns a letter grade to stocks and bonds based on the creditworthiness of their issuer. The four highest ratings (AAA, AA, A, BBB) indicate *investment grade* issues; ratings of BB or lower (down through D) indicate increasingly speculative issues.

Standard deduction. The deduction for certain expenses (e.g., medical costs, state and local taxes, interest paid, and charitable contributions) that an individual may claim in calculating his income tax without itemizing their cost.

Statement of changes in financial position. A financial statement designed to show, for a specified period of time, the sources of funds acquired by a business entity and the distribution and general effect of such funds upon the assets, liabilities, and capital of that business.

Stepped-up basis. Provision whereby an heir's *basis* in inherited property is equal to the property's value at the date of the testator's death.

Step-up interest. Change in the interest rate on a variable-interest note prescribed to occur at specified intervals over the course of the loan.

Stock. Ownership shares of a corporation. *See also **Common stock; Preferred stock.***

Stock certificate. A document that evidences stock ownership, indicating the number of shares, class (common or preferred), and voting rights. Endorsed stock certificates are negotiable.

Stock dividend. A *dividend* paid in securities rather than cash—either additional shares of the issuing company or shares of another company (usually a subsidiary) held by the issuing company. These dividend shares are not taxable until sold.

Stock exchange. An organization registered under the Securities Exchange Act of 1934 that offers physical facilities for member brokers and dealers to buy and sell securities in a two-way auction. The two largest exchanges are the New York Stock Exchange (NYSE) and the American Stock Exchange (Amex), both located in New York City. Smaller regional exchanges are located in Boston, Chicago, Philadelphia, and other cities around the country.

Stock power. An assignment and power of attorney form authorizing transfer of a stock certificate to another party.

Stockholder of record. A stockholder whose name is registered on the books of the issuing corporation. Dividends and distributions are made only to such shareholders.

Stop order. An order to a securities broker to buy at a price above or to sell below the current market price. *Stop buy orders* are generally used to limit loss or protect unrealized profits on a short sale. *Stop sell orders* are generally used to protect unrealized profits or limit loss on a holding.

Straddle. The purchase of an equal number of call options and put options at the same strike price and maturity date. (*See* **Option.**)

Straight life annuity. An *annuity* that guarantees payments to the annuitant for life, but provides no benefits to survivors after his death.

Straight-line depreciation. *See* **Depreciation.**

Straight loan. A loan granted an individual or other legal entity on the basis of the borrower's general creditworthiness, unsupported by any form of collateral security.

Street name. Said of securities held in the name of a broker instead of the customer's to facilitate the transfer of shares.

Strike price. Price per share at which an *option* may be exercised.

Student Loan Marketing Association (SLMA, Sallie Mae). Government-sponsored, privately owned corporation that purchases, services, and sells student loans made by primary lenders (banks). Bonds issued by the SLMA, called *Sallie Maes,* are backed by the full faith and credit of the federal government. The SLMA thus provides liquidity for lenders, enabling them to make new loans, and allows individual investors to participate in the market.

Subchapter S corporation. A corporation electing to be taxed as a partnership, allowing the flow-through of tax consequences to the owners as partners; also known as an *S corporation.*

Subject-to provision. A provision in a property's purchase agreement that conditions the close of escrow, such as one giving the purchaser the right to verify rental income and expenses, structural soundness, or a waiver of due-on-sale clause before the transaction is finally consummated.

Subordinated incentive fee. Compensation to the general partners of a limited partnership as an added incentive for profitable operations. The partnership agreement specifies performance standards to be achieved in order for the fee to be earned.

Subordination agreement. An agreement by which all legal entities who have an interest or claim upon the assets of a prospective borrower grant a bank a priority claim or preference to the assets of the borrower ahead of any claim that they may have. Such an agreement may be required by a bank before it extends new credit to the borrower.

Subscriber. One who agrees in writing to purchase a certain offering, such as a certain number of shares of designated stock of a given corporation or a certain number of bonds of a given face value. The agreement is called a *subscription.*

Subscription. *See **Subscriber.***

Subscription right. *See **Right.***

Suitability rules. Rules of professional practice that require brokers and dealers to have reasonable grounds for believing that a customer's financial means are adequate to assume the risks involved in speculative investments. Such rules are developed and enforced by brokerage firms and organizations like the National Association of Securities Dealers.

Surety. An individual who agrees, usually in writing, to be responsible for the performance of another on a contract, or for a certain debt of another individual. An insurance, bond, guaranty, or other security that protects a person, corporation, or other legal entity in case of another's default in the payment of a given obligation or proper performance of a given contract.

Surrender value. The amount due a policyholder should he elect to terminate his policy; the cash surrender value also determines how much the policyholder may borrow against his policy.

Surrogate court. What some states call their probate court.

Takeout commitment. A commitment by a lending institution to assume or liquidate a short-term construction loan and issue a permanent mortgage.

Tangible asset. An asset of a physical and material nature (e.g., cash, property) as distinguished from an *intangible asset* (trademark, license). Also called *hard asset.*

Tax basis. The original cost of an asset if purchased, or the fair market value of that asset if inherited, less accumulated depreciation.

Tax bracket. Range of taxable income that is taxed at a certain rate. Brackets are expressed by their *marginal tax rate.*

Tax credit. A direct dollar-for-dollar reduction in tax liability allowed for various expenses such as child and dependent care, residential energy improvements, and foreign taxes.

Tax deductible. An expense that is deducted from a taxpayer's *adjusted gross income* to determine taxable income; for example, medical expenses, state and local taxes, interest paid, and charitable contributions that are itemized on Schedule A.

Tax deferred. Said of an investment whose earnings are not taxed until they are distributed to the investor; for example, funds placed in an individual retirement account (IRA) or Keogh plan are not taxed until withdrawn; similarly, the earnings from an annuity are not taxed until the annuitant begins receiving payments. Insurance policies, U.S. Savings bonds, and reinvested dividends are also tax-deferred vehicles.

Tax-exempt security. A security whose interest income is exempt from federal income tax; a municipal bond.

Tax loss carryback (carryforward). *See **Carryover.***

Tax loss pass-through. In a limited partnership, the tax loss proportionally allocated to the limited partners, which they use to offset (shelter) income from other sources.

Tax preference. Type of income or deduction against income that qualifies for special tax treatment; for example, long-term capital gains, accelerated depreciation, costs of research and development, depletion, and intangible drilling costs. Such preference items are disallowed in the computation of the ***alternative minimum tax (AMT)***.

Tax shelter. An investment that lowers a taxpayer's current tax liability by providing deductions against taxable income. Contributions to individual retirement accounts (IRAs) and Keogh plans, for example, are deductible in the year in which made, and income on funds in those accounts accrues ***tax deferred. Limited partnerships*** in real estate, oil and gas, equipment leasing, and similar ventures provide limited partners with deductions for depreciation, depletion, and interest payments (in leveraged partnerships) and investment credits for the purchase of equipment.

Tenancy by the entirety. A ***joint tenancy*** between spouses, with the right of survivorship.

Tenancy in common. Co-ownership by two or more people in which each owns a defined percentage of the whole.

Tender. To submit a bid for a security, e.g., a Treasury offering. To submit a security in response to an offer to buy at a fixed price.

Ten-year trust. *See **Clifford trust.***

Term bond. An issue of long-term bonds that have a single maturity, as compared to a ***serial bond*** issue.

Term certificate. *See **Certificate of deposit.***

Term life insurance. A life insurance policy written to cover a specified period of time, as compared to a ***whole life insurance policy***.

Term loan. A loan made for a specified period of time, as compared to a *demand loan,* which must be repaid at the lender's request.

Testamentary capacity. The legal capacity to make a will.

Testamentary trust. A trust created in a will that does not come into existence until after the testator's death.

Testate. Leaving a valid will, as opposed to dying *intestate*.

Testator. A person who writes a will.

Throwback rule. If accumulated trust income is distributed in a tax year after the one in which it is earned, it is generally then taxed at the bracket of the beneficiary for the year in which is was earned.

Time deposit account. A deposit on which a bank guarantees a fixed rate of interest for a fixed period of time and can refuse or impose a penalty on early withdrawals.

Timing. *See **Market timing***.

Title. Legal document or evidence of a claim of a right in or to, or full ownership of, a specific piece of property.

Totten trust. Not really a trust, but a special banking arrangement whereby the depositor holds the account "in trust" for another and retains sole ownership of the funds for the rest of the depositor's life.

Transfer agent. An agent appointed by a corporation to keep a record of the name of each registered shareowner, his or her address, and the number of shares owned, and to see that certificates presented to his office for transfer are properly cancelled and that new certificates are issued in the name of the transferee.

Treasuries. General term for all negotiable securities of the U.S. government.

Treasury bills (T-bills) are short-term obligations (three- and six-month maturities) that do not pay interest but are sold at a discount from their face value.

Treasury bonds are issured in $1,000 units with maturity of 10 years or longer, and are traded on the market like other bonds.

Treasury notes are medium-term obligations (1 to 10 years) sold by subscription.

Treasury stock. The title to previously issued stock of a corporation that it has reacquired by purchase, gift, or bequest.

Triple net lease. *See **net, net, net lease.***

Triple tax-exempt security. A municipal bond whose interest is exempt for federal, state, and local income tax. Usually only bonds issued within the bondholder's state of residence are triple tax-exempt.

Trust. A legal entity created by an individual (*trustor*) in which one person or institution (*trustee*) holds and manages property for the benefit of someone else (*beneficiary*). The *trust indenture* describes the properties to be placed in the trust, the duties of the trustee in administering the property, the rights of the beneficiaries named and their proportionate share in the trust, the duration of the trusteeship, the distribution of income from the trust principal, and the distribution of the **remainder** at the termination of the trust.

Trustee. A person who holds trust property for the benefit of another.

Trustor. A person who creates a trust; synonymous with *settlor* and *grantor*.

Two-sided. *See **Auction.***

Umbrella liability. Insurance coverage in excess of underlying liability policies, which may also provide coverage for situations excluded by underlying policies.

Underwriter. In securities, an investment banker who buys an entire issue of securities from the issuer and then sells them to individual and institutional investors.

In insurance, the company that assumes the cost of policyholders' claims in exchange for their payments (*premiums*).

Undivided interest. The percentage of ownership held by an individual in a **tenancy in common**.

Unearned income. In accounting, income that has been collected in advance of the performance of a contract, or consideration to be met in order to earn the income.

In taxation, personal income from sources other than wages, salary, or compensation for goods and services; for example, dividends, interest, and rent.

Unencumbered. An owned asset that is free of any claims by or rights granted to another.

Unfunded trust. A living trust that has not had any property actually transferred to it.

Unified credit. A once-in-a-lifetime credit that may be applied against an individual's gift or estate taxes. For decedents who die in 1985, the credit in effect exempts the first $600,000 of an estate from estate taxes.

Uniform Commercial Code. Statute adopted in most states that regulates the sales of goods, commercial paper (including checks and bank collections), and secured transactions in personal property.

Uniform Gifts to Minors Act. Statute adopted in most states that governs the administration of assets assigned to a minor until the minor comes of age by an adult *custodian*, often a parent.

Uniform Probate Code. Statute adopted in several states that reduces the court's involvement in the probate process, thus reducing the time and cost of the proceeding.

Universal life insurance. A *term life insurance* policy that accumulates a cash *surrender value*. The policyholder may choose to raise or lower both the amount of coverage and amount to be accumulated.

Unlimited marital deduction. Allows the transfer of any amount of property between spouses free of gift or estate taxes.

Unsecured loan. A loan made by a bank, based on the creditworthiness of the borrower and without the pledge of collateral.

Usury. The practice of charging a rate of interest for the use of money or for credit extended that exceeds the legal limit allowed for that type of transaction by the state whose laws govern the legality of the transaction.

Variable annuity. An *annuity* whose principal is invested in stocks or other equities, at the annuitant's election, so that the eventual payout depends on the performance of the underlying securities.

Variable life insurance. A form of *whole life insurance* in which the policyholder's cash accumulation is invested in stocks, bonds, or money market instruments, at the policyholder's election. The policy's death benefit is guaranteed but the cash value depends on the performance of the underlying securities.

Variable rate mortgage. *See Adjustable rate mortgage.*

Vest. To bestow upon, such as a title to property.

Vested benefits. Those benefits of a retirement, pension, or profit-sharing plan that belong to the employee outright. In some plans the employee is immediately fully vested; in others, a vesting schedule determines the employee's percentage of ownership based on years of participation in the program (e.g., 10% a year). If an employee leaves the program, he or she forfeits any nonvested benefits.

Veterans Administration (VA) mortgage. Residential mortgage loan granted by a lender and guaranteed by the Veterans Administration. Interest rates are set by the VA, and the lender may require *points* if the rate is substantially below market rates.

Volatile. Said of a market price that displays rapid and extreme fluctuations.

Voting right. A stockholder's right to vote or assign his right to vote (*proxy*) on corporate affairs. Most common shares have one vote each. Preferred stock usually gains the right to vote when preferred dividends are in default for a specified period.

Waiver. The voluntary relinquishment of a legal right or legally enforceable claim against another.

Warrant. A certificate, usually issued with a bond or with shares of preferred stock, that gives the holder the right to purchase a number of shares of common stock at a stipulated price (usually higher than the current market price) within a period of years or in perpetuity. Warrants are transferable and are traded on the major exchanges.

Wash sale. The sale and purchase of a security within a short period of time. Wash sales conducted to create the impression of active trading in a security constitute a criminal and civil offense. For tax purposes, an individual investor may not deduct any loss on the sale of a security that he has also purchased within 30 days before or after the date of sale (*30-day wash rule*).

Watch list. List of securities placed under surveillance to detect any illegal or unethical practices or other irregularities. The lists are compiled by brokerage firms, investment rating services, stock exchanges, and self-regulatory organizations that monitor erratic swings in price, sudden heavy trading, and new issues.

When issued. Shorthand for "when, as, and if issued" to indicate a transaction conditional on a security that has been authorized for issue but not yet actually issued. "When issued" transactions may be settled only after the date of issue.

Whole life insurance. A life insurance policy that remains in force for the insured's lifetime, unless the policy lapses or is canceled for cause. Whole life policies accumulate a cash value, and the fixed annual premiums do not rise over the course of the policy. Earnings on the cash value accumulate tax-deferred until they are distributed, and the policyholder can borrow against them (*policy loan*). Also called *ordinary, permanent*, or *straight life insurance*.

Will. A document wherein an individual (*testator*) provides for the distribution of his property and wealth after his death, names a guardian for his minor children, and names an **executor**. A *holographic will* is written entirely by hand and is dated and signed. A *formal will* is a witnessed document. A *nuncupative will* is an oral statement witnessed at a time of probable death. The validity of a will and distribution of assets of a decedent who dies **intestate** are determined by state law.

Will contest. Litigation to overturn a decedent's will for lack of testamentary capacity or lack of due execution.

Withdrawal plan. An agreement with mutual fund that permits the shareholder to receive monthly or quarterly withdrawals of specified dollar amounts, usually involving the invasion of principal. Alternately, a plan may permit varying withdrawals based on the liquidation of a fixed number of shares monthly or quarterly.

Withholding. Requirement that an employer deduct a portion of employees' gross wages as payment toward their income and Social Security taxes; these funds must be deposited in a Treasury tax and loan account. Similarly, in certain cases disbursing agents are required to withhold a portion of dividend and interest income, pension and annuity distribution, or large cash prizes.

Workers' compensation. State programs that provide cash benefits and medical care to workers injured or disabled by work-related accidents or illnesses; survivors' benefits are paid to the families of workers killed in such accidents. Coverage and benefits vary.

Working capital. The portion of the capital of a business enterprise that is kept liquid to provide for day-to-day working needs.

In accounting, the excess of current assets over current liabilities.

Working control. Effective control of a corporation by shareholders who own less than 51% of the company's voting stock.

Wraparound mortgage. A mortgage that packages an existing assumable mortgage on a property and the additional amount the buyer-borrower needs to purchase the property. The borrower makes one monthly payment, from which the lender makes the payment on the assumed loan.

Yield. In general, the amount of profit on an investment of capital.

For stocks or bonds, *current yield* is the rate of annual dividends or interest expressed as a percentage of the current market price.

Yield curve. A graph that shows the interest rates for bonds of comparable quality and different maturities. If short-term rates are higher, the graph shows a *positive yield curve;* if long-term rates are higher, a *negative yield curve.* When short- and long-term rates are roughly equal, the yield curve is *flat.*

Yield to call. The *yield* of a bond were it to be redeemed by the issuer at the earliest call date allowed.

Yield to maturity. The *yield* of a bond were it held to maturity, taking into account purchase price, coupon rate, and present value (see ***Net present value***).

Zero-bracket amount (ZBA). Synonymous with ***standard deduction***.

Zero-coupon bond. A bond that is sold at a deep discount from par value, and therefore appreciates substantially, but makes no payments of interest. The bondholder, therefore, does not receive any payments until maturity, although the annual accrued appreciation is taxable unless the bond is a municipal zero, which is tax-exempt.

Index

INDEX

Italicized page numbers indicate tables; daggers (†) indicate charts. Definitions of technical terms are found in the Glossary (pages 9.1–53) and are not indexed here.

A

M

N

R

W

Y

Z

THE MONEY·GO·ROUND

A Guide to Managing Your Money and Achieving Financial Peace of Mind

by Lawrence A. Krause

This book simplifies money. Cited by *The New York Times* as "one of the nation's leading financial planners," Larry Krause offers easy-to-understand guidelines that can substantially change your life. He shows how to

- manage money anxiety by understanding personal goals and their relationship to money,

- ensure financial peace of mind by creating custom-made financial plans that minimize risk and maximize security, and

- eliminate guesswork by applying solid financial principles to individual circumstances

224 pages
hardbound, $14.95

Tactical Investing
Strategies for Getting the Most Out of Your Money

by Daniel A. Blumberg

By the author of *Tactical Economics*, who has twenty years experience as a highly successful entrepreneur in the financial services industry, this book offers straight-shooting, hard-hitting advice on making sound investment and tax-planning decisions. Blumberg applies his financial savvy to making use of economic predictions; maximizing real estate investments; new opportunities in American businesses; stock market strategies; when to invest in mutual funds, unit trusts, or bonds; investment taxation; using contrarian techniques profitably; predicting interest rates; and more.

Tables ■ Graphs ■ Glossary ■ Index

288 pages
hardbound, $16.95

The Real Estate Investment Pocket Guide

by Alan J. Parisse and Richard G. Wollack

Brief and clear descriptions of key points about real estate investing are offered in this abundantly illustrated, easy-to-understand layman's guide. Depreciation, recapture, deductibility, amortization, and numerous other concepts are covered in a Q & A format.

- Illustrations ▪ Graphs ▪ Charts
- Indexed glossary ▪ Evaluation checklist

96 pages
paper, $7.95

The Oil and Gas Investment Pocket Guide

by the editors of Consolidated Capital Communications Group, Inc.

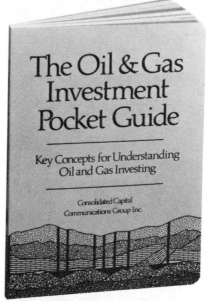

- Illustrations
- Graphs
- Charts
- Indexed glossary
- Evaluation checklist

An outstanding introduction to the basics of oil and gas investing, this easy-to-read book explains key concepts of oil and gas by means of simple examples, numerous illustrations, and clear and concise discussion in a Q & A format of risk factors, taxation and a variety of oil and gas investment alternatives.

96 pages
paper, $7.95

YOUR IDEAS ARE IMPORTANT TO US!

The goal of *The Financial Desk Book* is to meet the needs of all individuals who must make financial decisions. We'd like to have *your* suggestions about anything we could do to make this unique publication even more useful to you. Please use the attached card to let us know about any suggestions you may have about content, format, or any other aspects of our publication. If the card has already been removed, you may mail your suggestions to:

> *The Financial Desk Book*
> Consolidated Capital Communications Group
> 2000 Powell Street
> Emeryville, CA 94608

THE FINANCIAL DESK BOOK
Reader Services Card — We Need Your Input

Consolidated Capital Communications Group prides itself on its high-quality publications *by* financial professionals, *for* financial professionals and investors. Please take a moment to complete this card — we need your comments and suggestions to help us better meet your needs.

1. Overall I found *The Financial Desk Book*
   ☐ excellent ☐ very useful ☐ good ☐ fair ☐ poor

2. Comments: _____
   _____
   _____

3. In upcoming editions I'd like to see: _____
   _____
   _____

☐ Send me a copy of the special prepublication announcement of the next edition of *The Financial Desk Book*.

☐ Send me a free copy of CCCG's catalog of financial and investor publications and professional marketing and training materials.

Name: _____ Firm: _____
Street: _____
City: _____ State: _____ Zip: _____
Business Telephone: ( )_____ FDB 0985

I am a ☐ financial planner ☐ stockbroker ☐ insurance agent
☐ accountant ☐ private investor ☐ attorney
☐ other: _____

To order additional copies of *The Financial Desk Book*,
Call Toll-Free 800-227-1870, extension 9009

BUSINESS REPLY MAIL
FIRST CLASS PERMIT NO. 5593 OAKLAND, CA

POSTAGE WILL BE PAID BY ADDRESSEE

**Consolidated Capital
Communications Group, Inc.**
2000 Powell Street
Emeryville, CA 94608

**NO POSTAGE
NECESSARY
IF MAILED
IN THE
UNITED STATES**

BUSINESS REPLY MAIL
FIRST CLASS PERMIT NO. 5593 OAKLAND, CA

POSTAGE WILL BE PAID BY ADDRESSEE

**Consolidated Capital
Communications Group, Inc.**

2000 Powell Street
Emeryville, CA 94608

**NO POSTAGE
NECESSARY
IF MAILED
IN THE
UNITED STATES**

BUSINESS REPLY MAIL
FIRST CLASS PERMIT NO. 5593 OAKLAND, CA

POSTAGE WILL BE PAID BY ADDRESSEE

**Consolidated Capital
Communications Group, Inc.**

2000 Powell Street
Emeryville, CA 94608